SCENE 56 /// House of Villainy, I'm Home

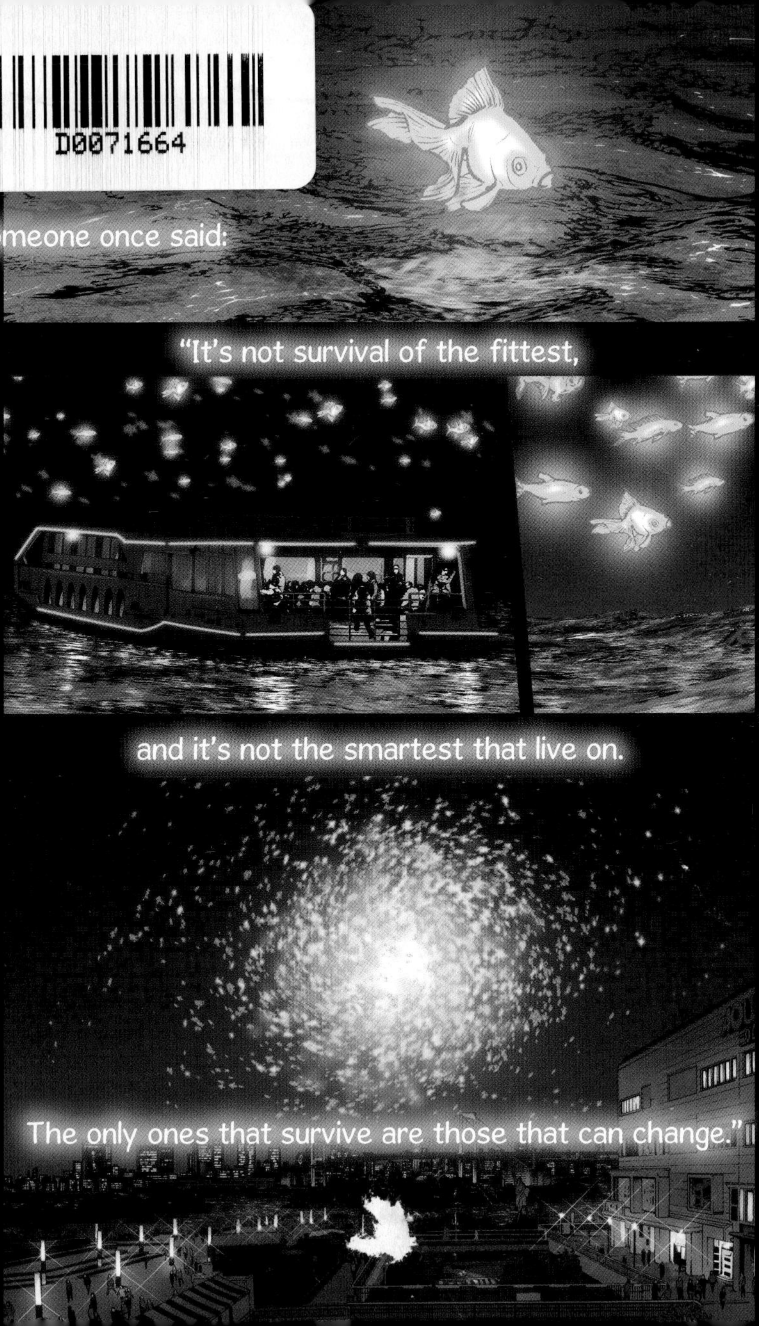
Someone once said:
"It's not survival of the fittest,
and it's not the smartest that live on.
The only ones that survive are those that can change."

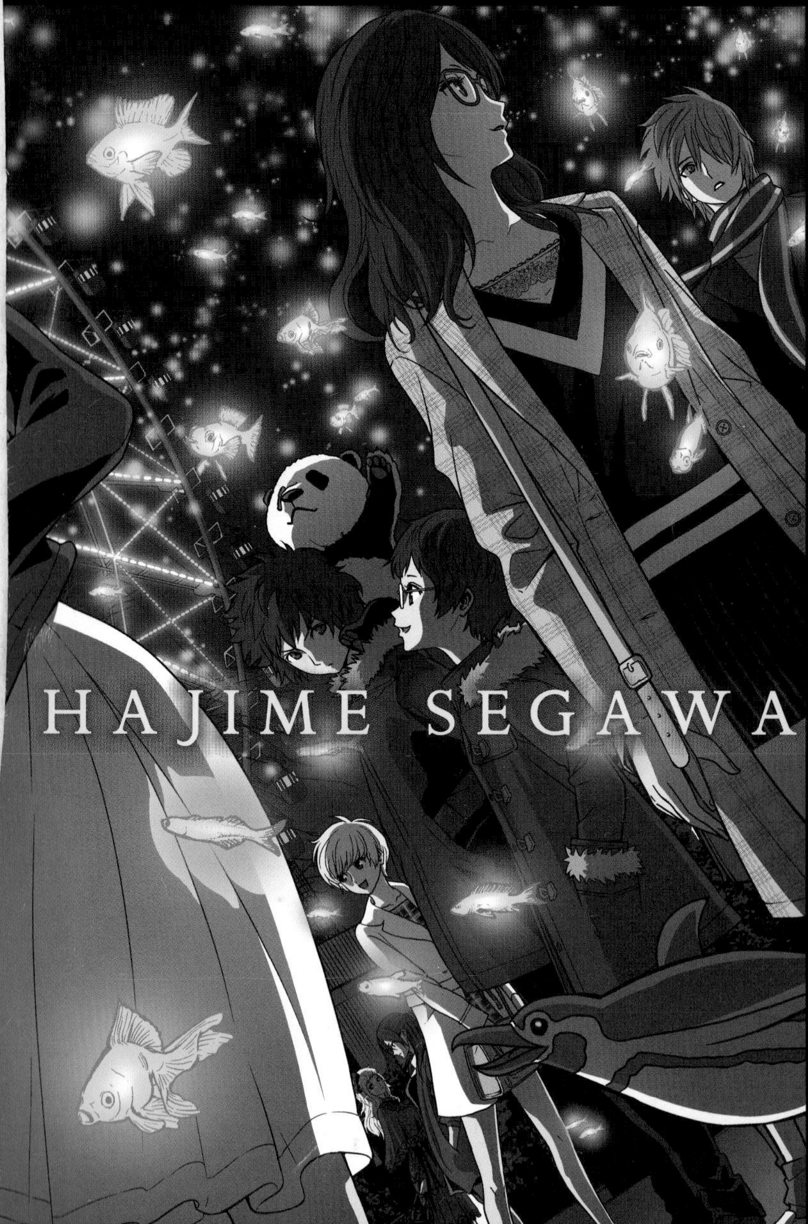
HAJIME SEGAWA

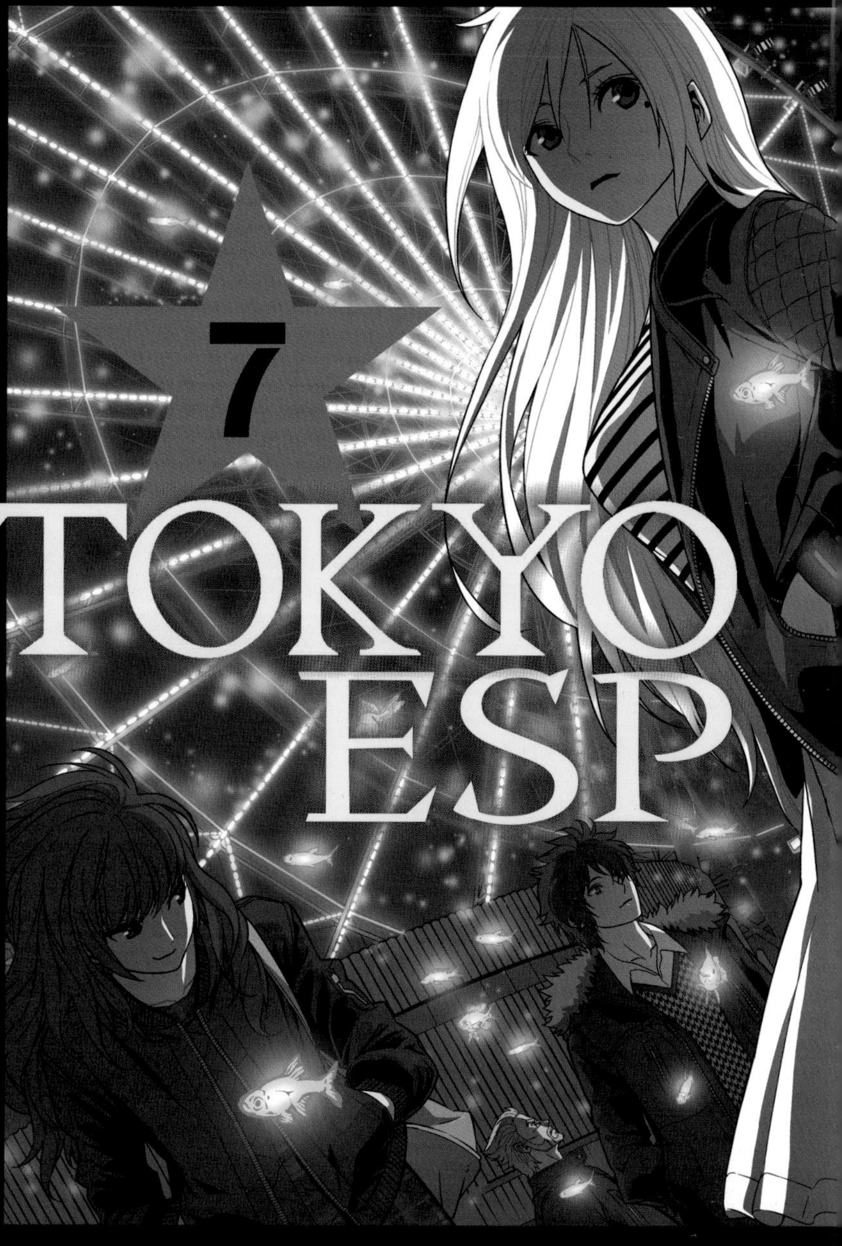
7
TOKYO
ESP

CONTENTS 7

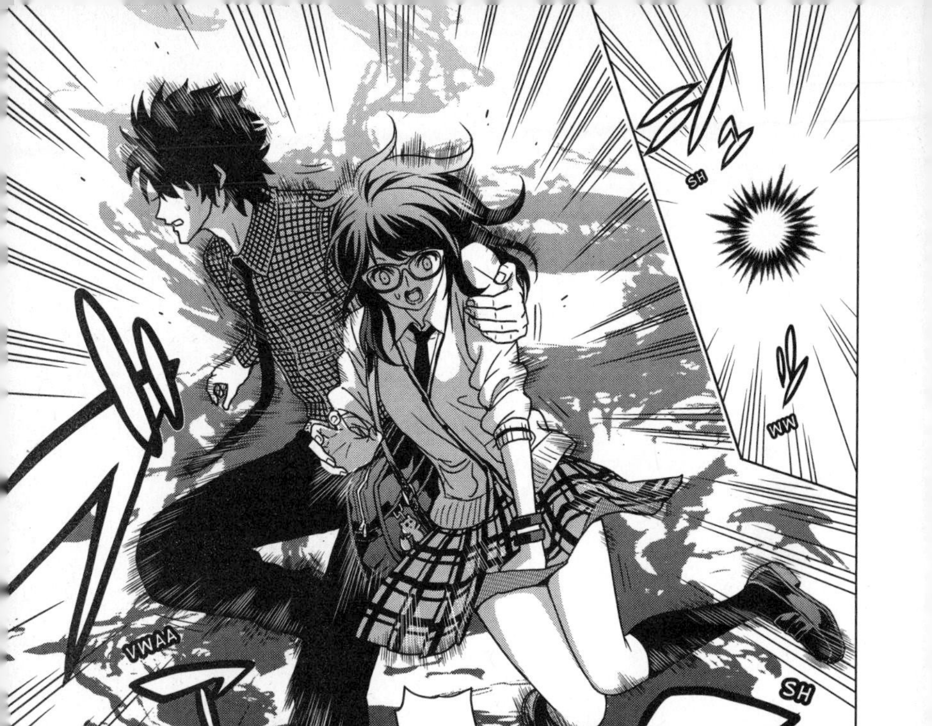
SH
WW
SH
WAH!
VWAA

SCENE 56 /// House of Villainy, I'm Home

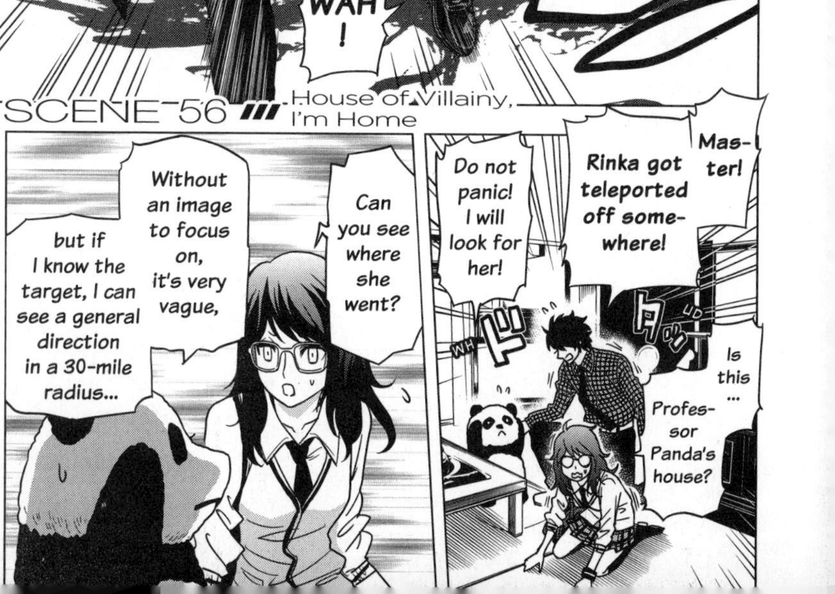
Mas-ter!
Rinka got teleported off some-where!
Do not panic! I will look for her!
UD
WH
Is this... Profes-sor Panda's house?
Can you see where she went?
Without an image to focus on, it's very vague,
but if I know the target, I can see a general direction in a 30-mile radius...

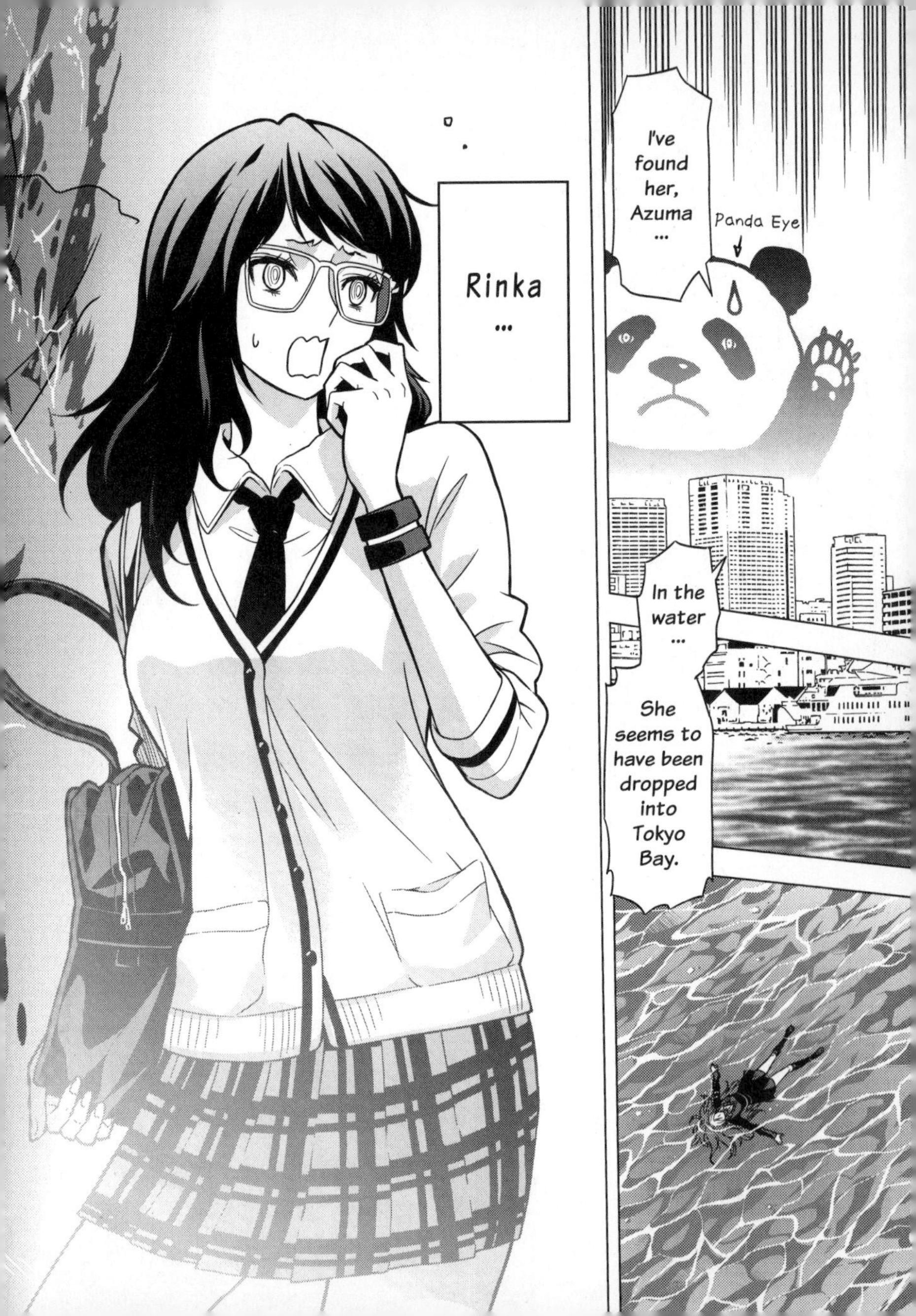
I've found her, Azuma ...
Panda Eye
In the water ...
She seems to have been dropped into Tokyo Bay.
Rinka ...

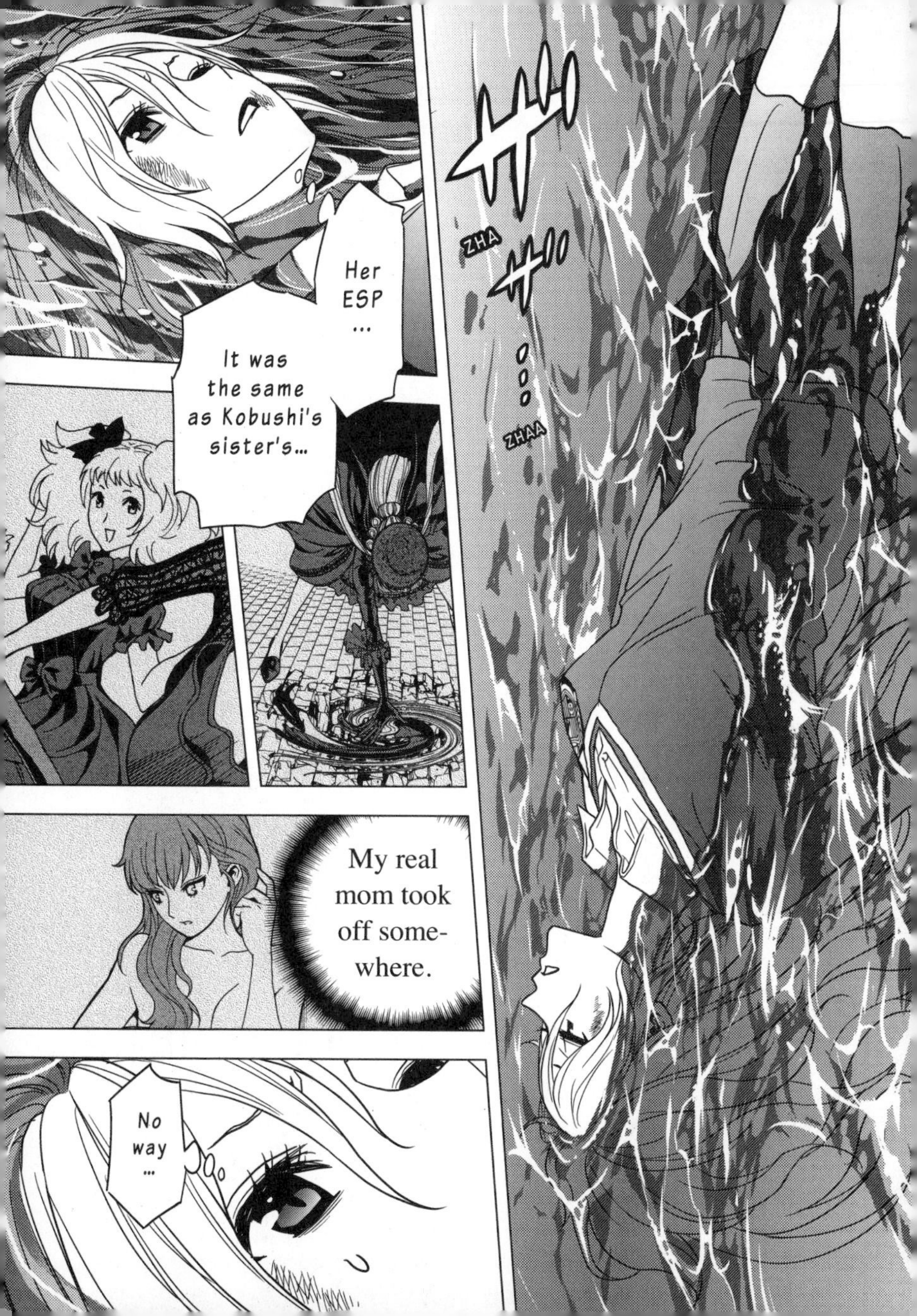
ZHA
ZHAA
Her ESP ...
It was the same as Kobushi's sister's...
My real mom took off some-where.
No way ...

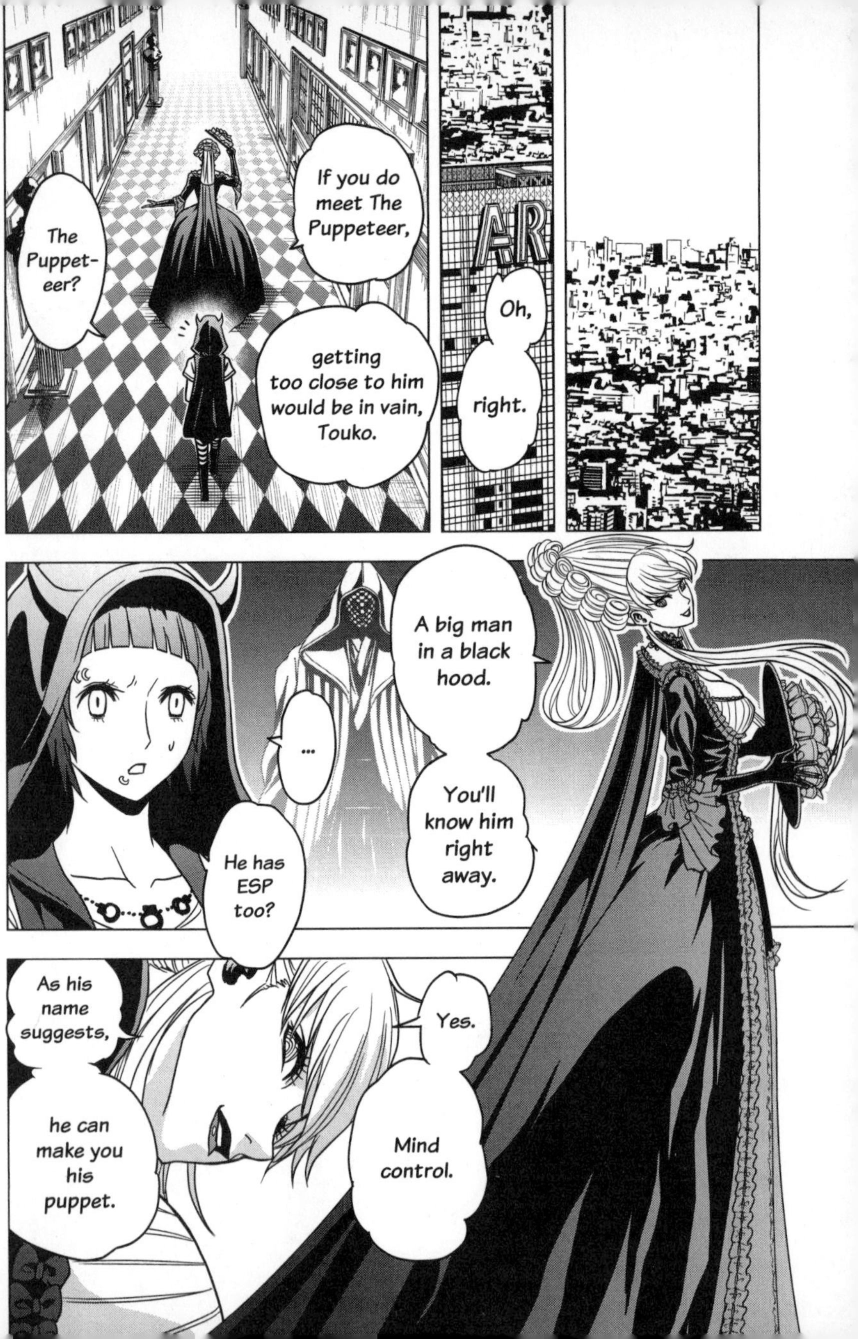
Oh,
right.
If you do meet The Puppeteer,
getting too close to him would be in vain, Touko.
The Puppet-eer?
A big man in a black hood.
You'll know him right away.
...
He has ESP too?
Yes.
Mind control.
As his name suggests,
he can make you his puppet.

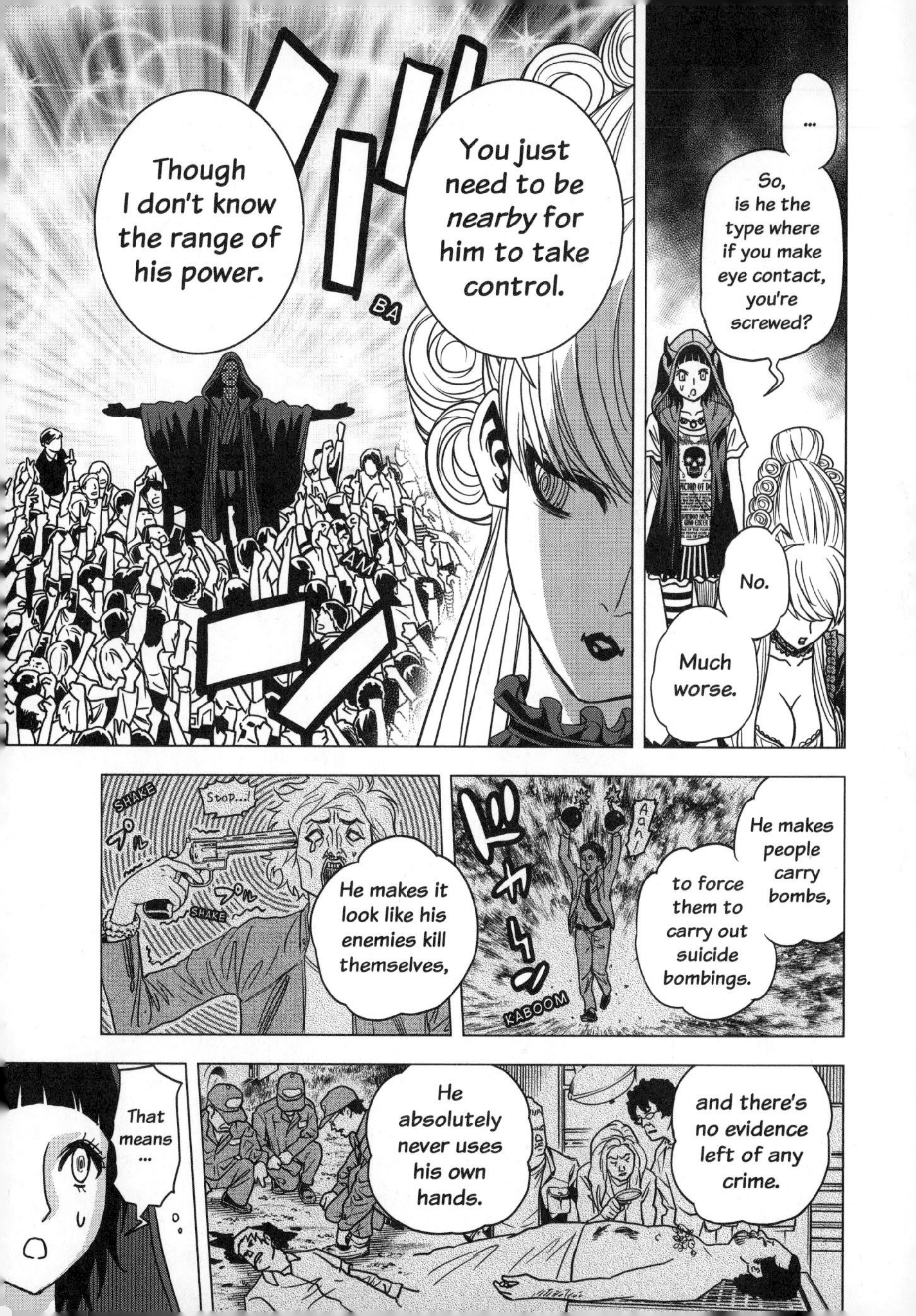
...
So, is he the type where if you make eye contact, you're screwed?
No.
Much worse.
You just need to be nearby for him to take control.
Though I don't know the range of his power.
BA
AM
He makes people carry bombs,
to force them to carry out suicide bombings.
Aah!
KABOOM
He makes it look like his enemies kill themselves,
Stop...!
SHAKE
SHAKE
and there's no evidence left of any crime.
He absolutely never uses his own hands.
That means ...

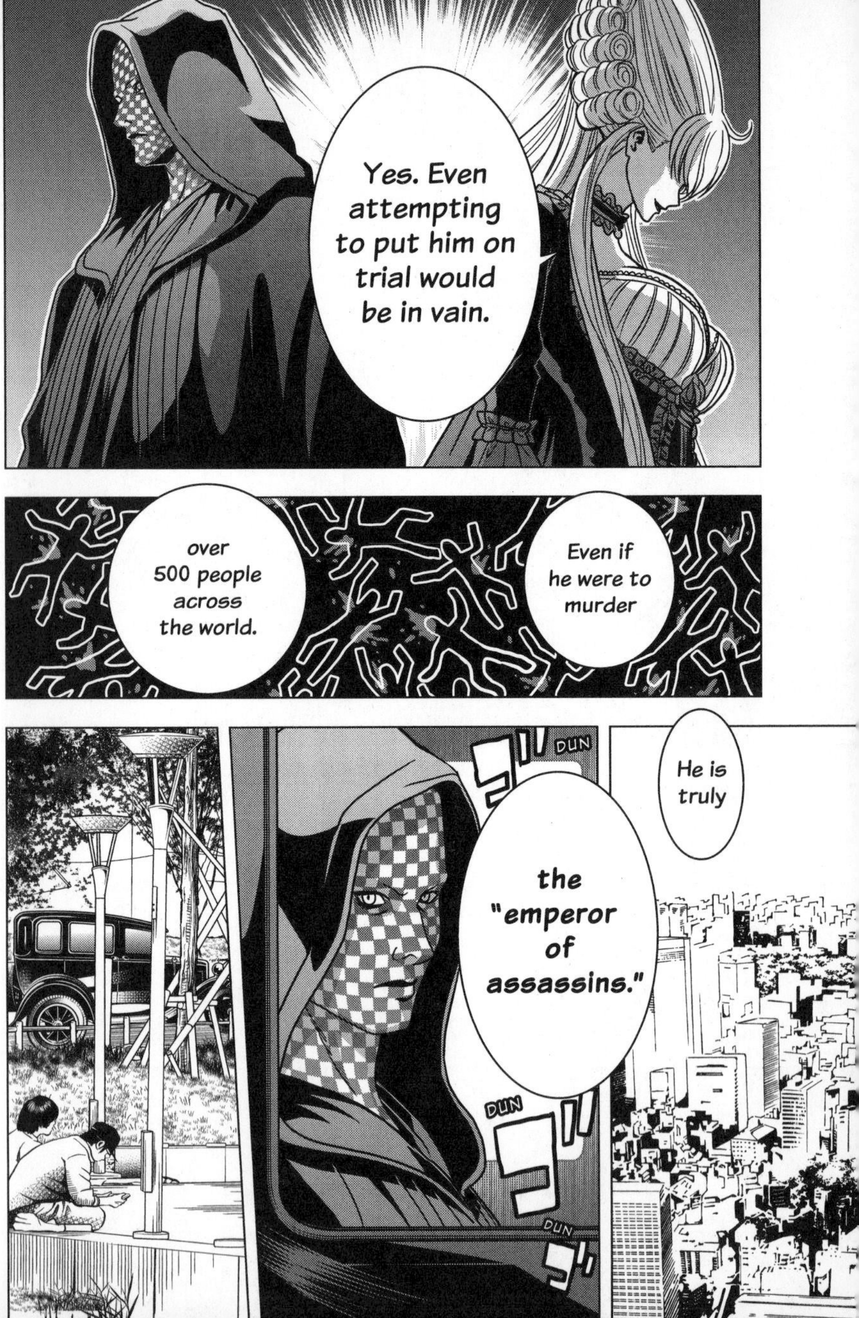
Yes. Even attempting to put him on trial would be in vain.
Even if he were to murder
over 500 people across the world.
He is truly
the "emperor of assassins."
DUN
DUN
DUN

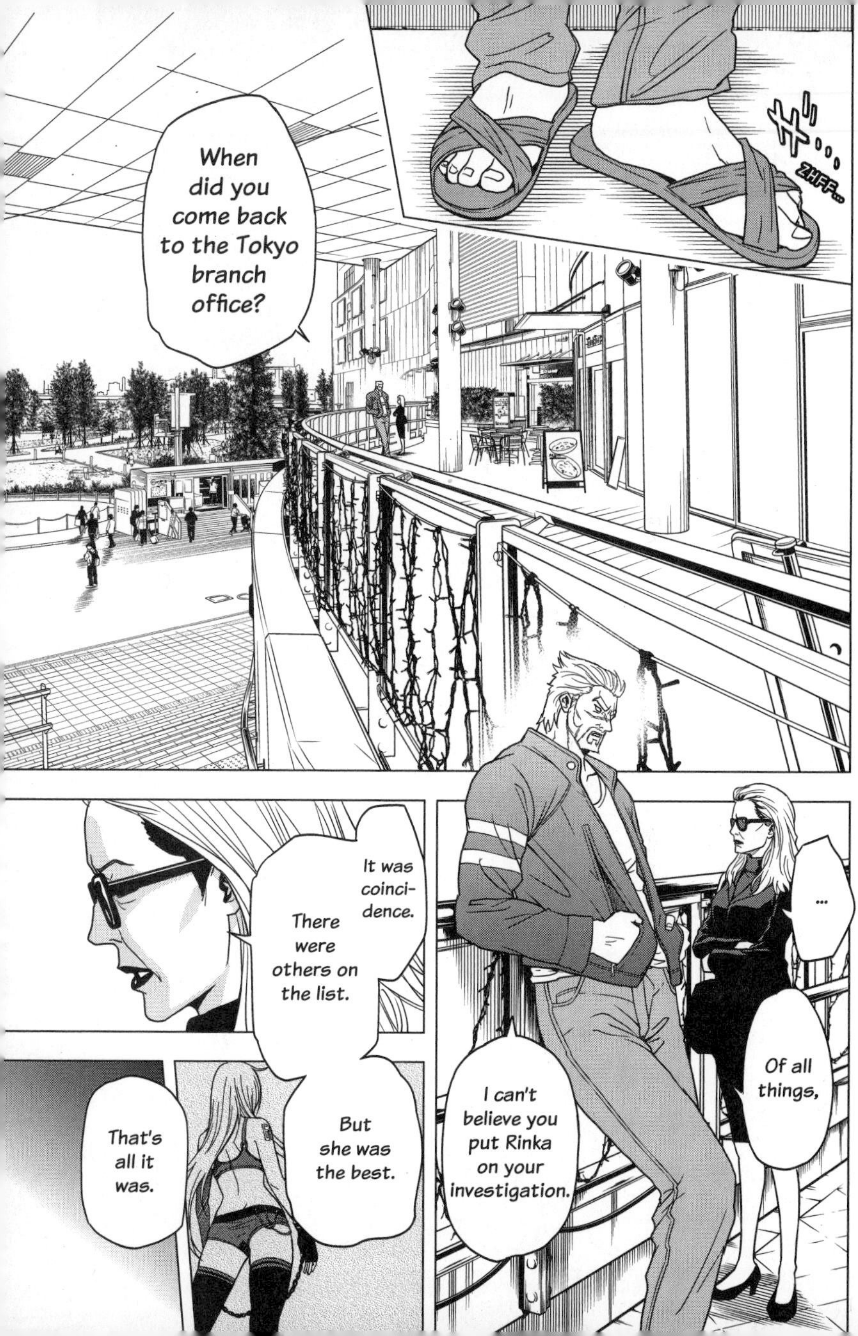
ZHFF...
When did you come back to the Tokyo branch office?
...
Of all things,
I can't believe you put Rinka on your investigation.
It was coincidence.
There were others on the list.
But she was the best.
That's all it was.

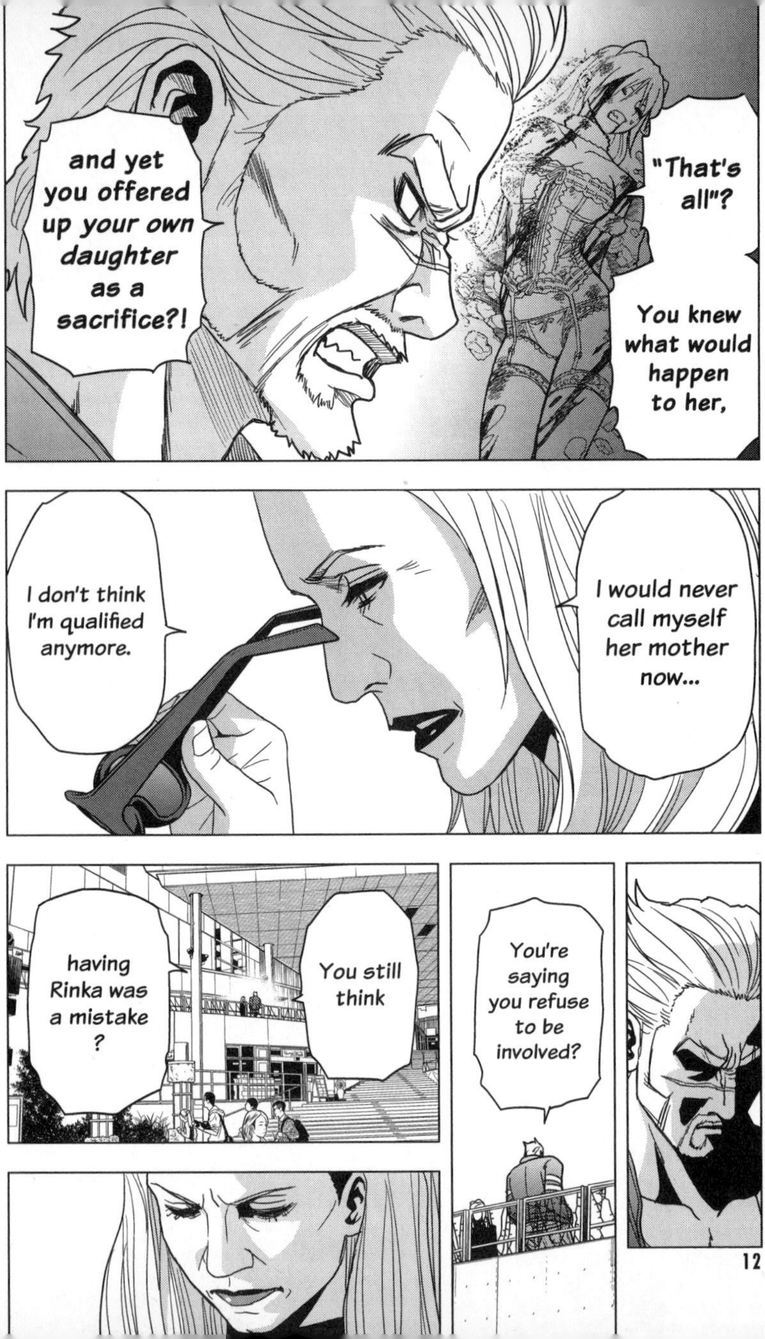
"That's all"?
You knew what would happen to her,
and yet you offered up your own daughter as a sacrifice?!
I would never call myself her mother now...
I don't think I'm qualified anymore.
You're saying you refuse to be involved?
You still think
having Rinka was a mistake ?

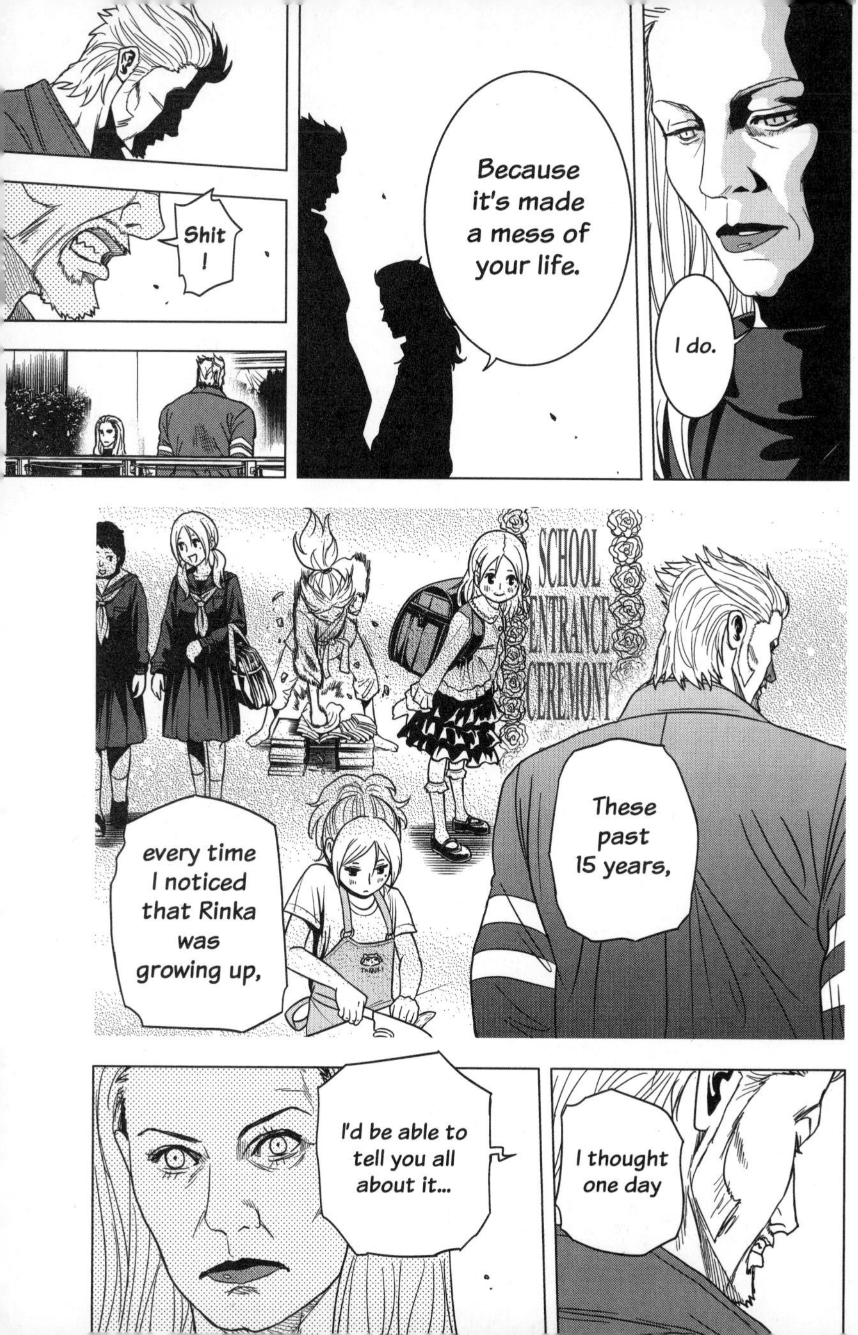
I do.
Because it's made a mess of your life.
Shit!
SCHOOL ENTRANCE CEREMONY
These past 15 years,
every time I noticed that Rinka was growing up,
I thought one day
I'd be able to tell you all about it...

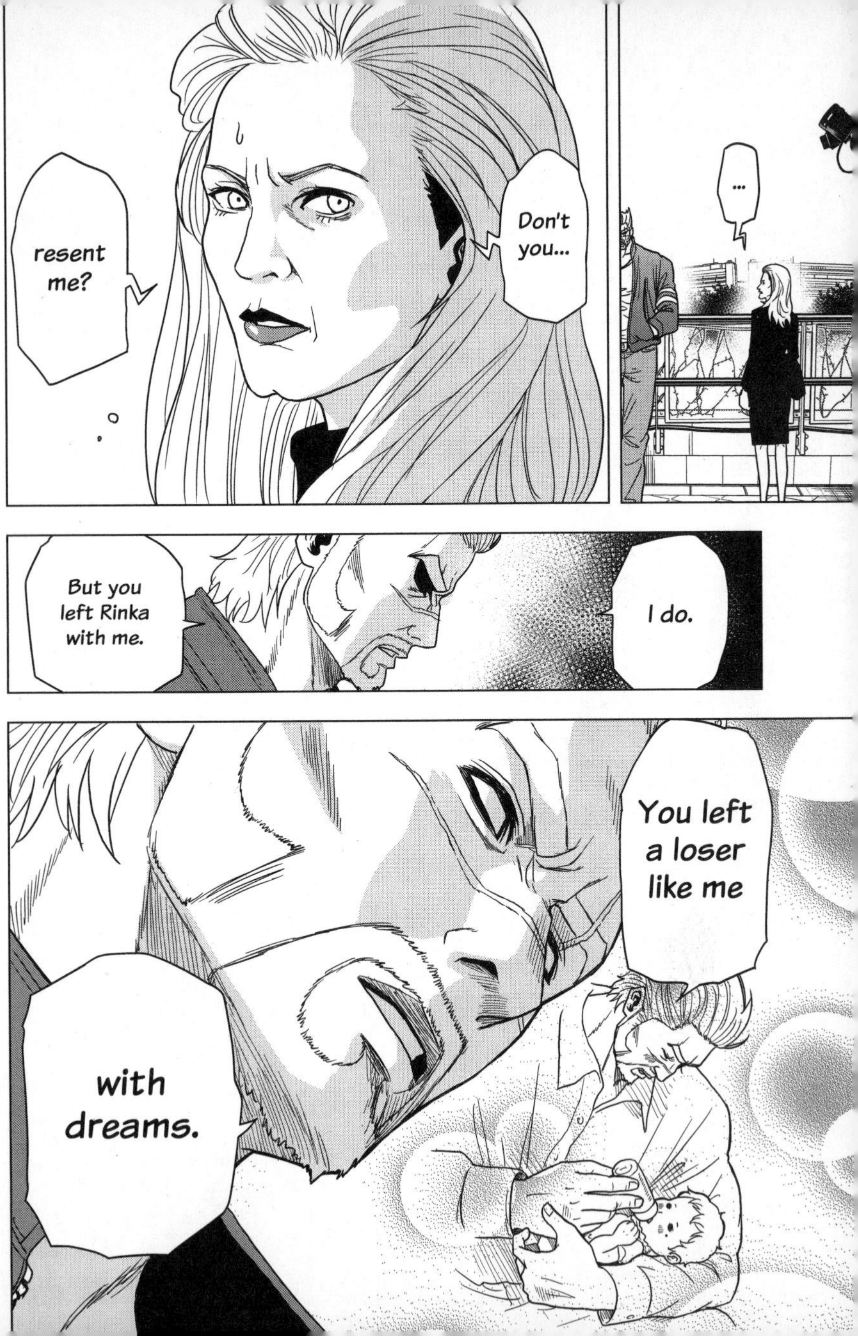
...
Don't you...
resent me?
I do.
But you left Rinka with me.
You left a loser like me
with dreams.

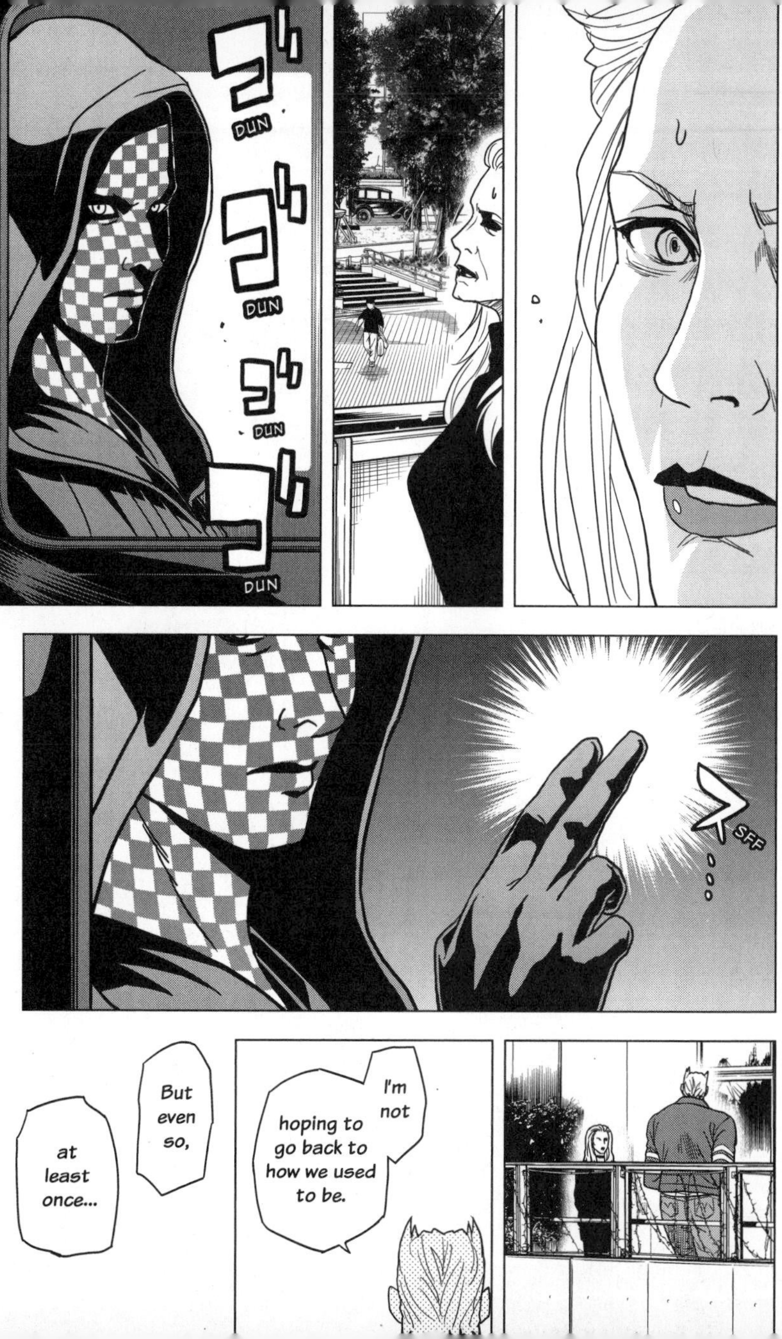
DUN
DUN
DUN
DUN
SFF
I'm not hoping to go back to how we used to be.
But even so,
at least once...

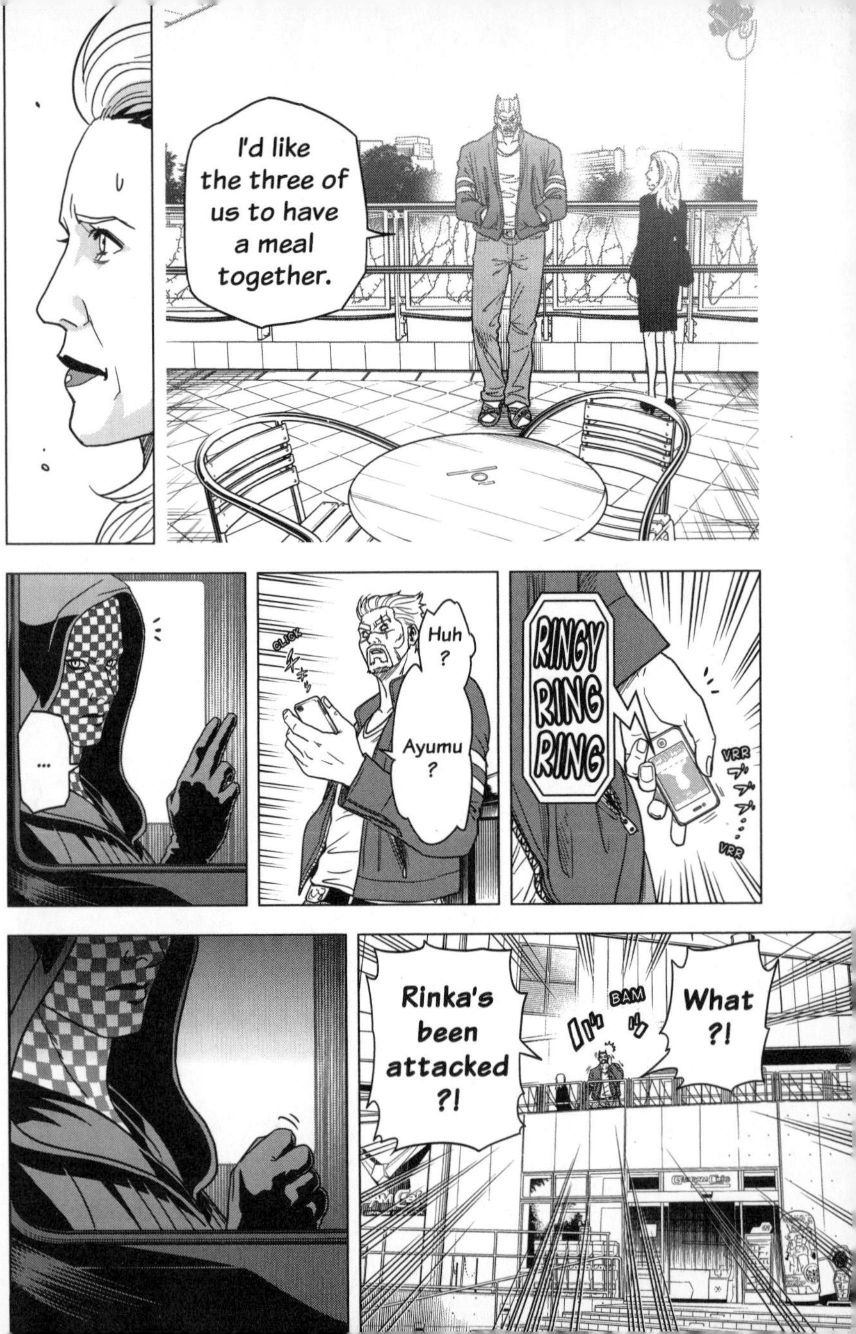
I'd like the three of us to have a meal together.
RINGY RING RING
VRR
VRR
CLICK
Huh?
Ayumu?
...
What?!
BAM
Rinka's been attacked?!

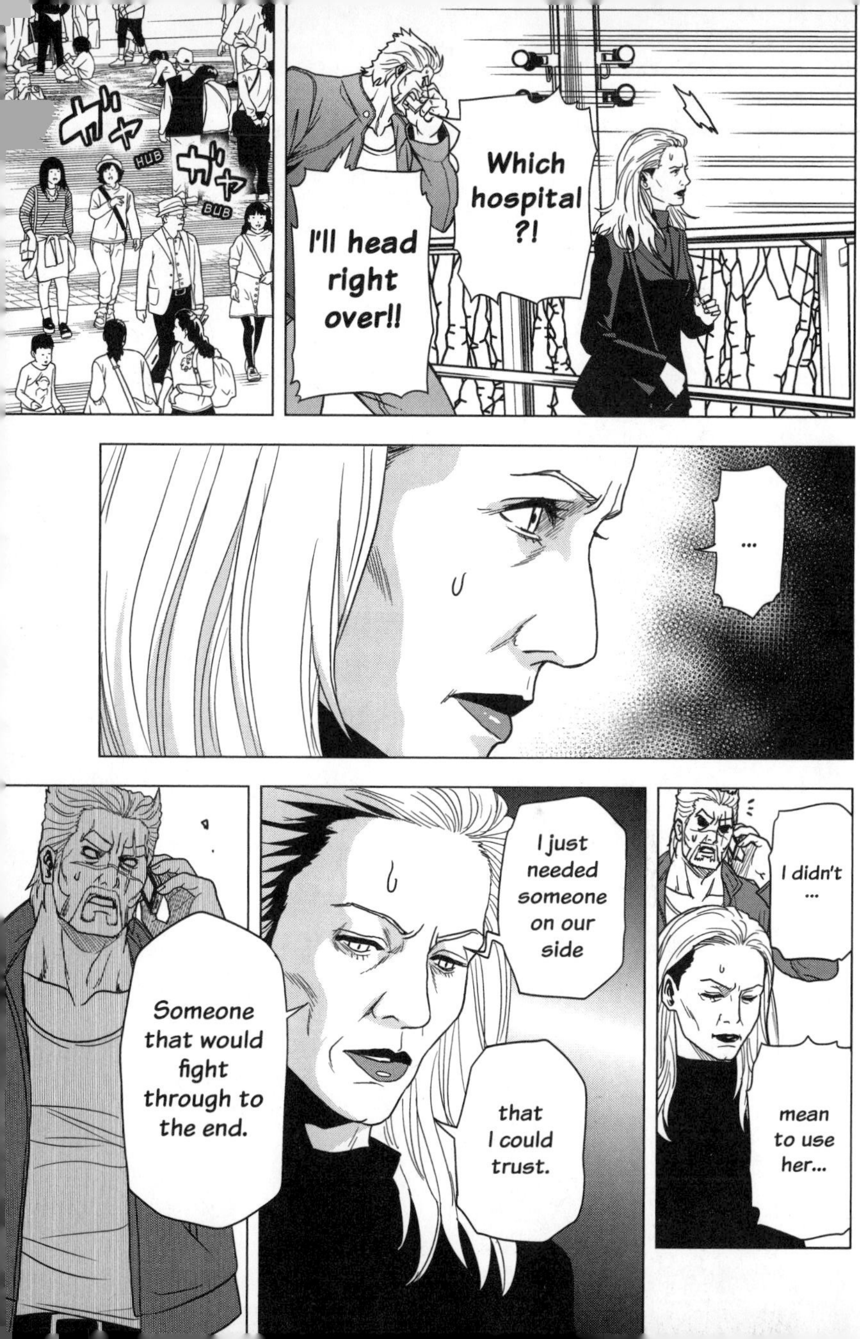
Which hospital ?!
I'll head right over!!
ガヤ
HUB
ガヤ
BUB
...
I didn't ...
mean to use her...
I just needed someone on our side
that I could trust.
Someone that would fight through to the end.

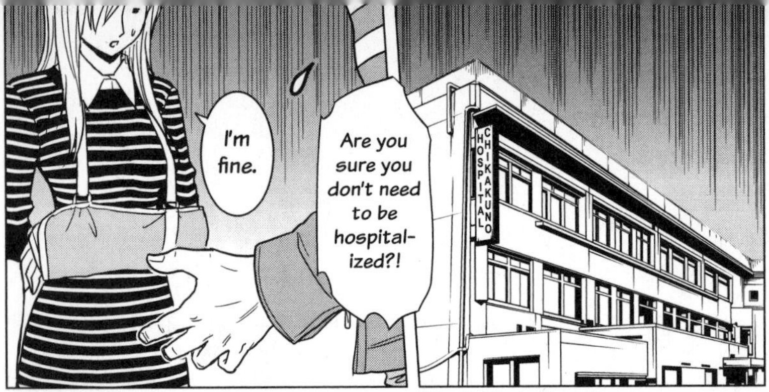
CHIKAKUNO HOSPITAL
Are you sure you don't need to be hospital-ized?!
I'm fine.

*Literally, "Nearby Hospital"

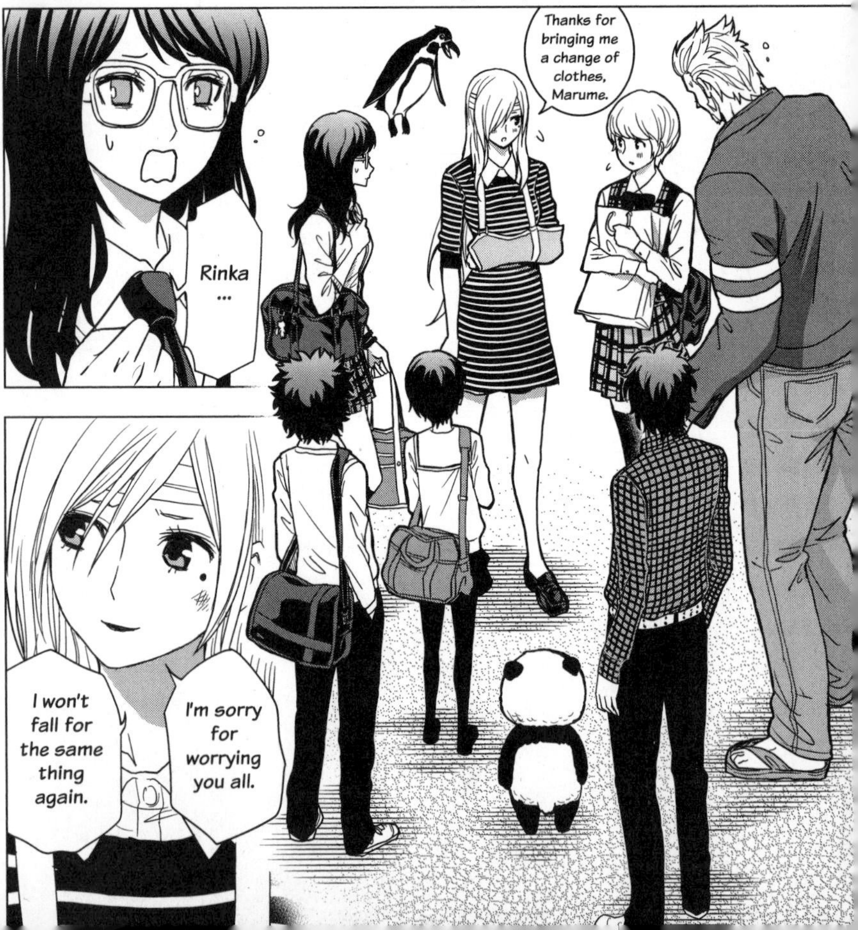
Thanks for bringing me a change of clothes, Marume.
Rinka ...
I'm sorry for worrying you all.
I won't fall for the same thing again.

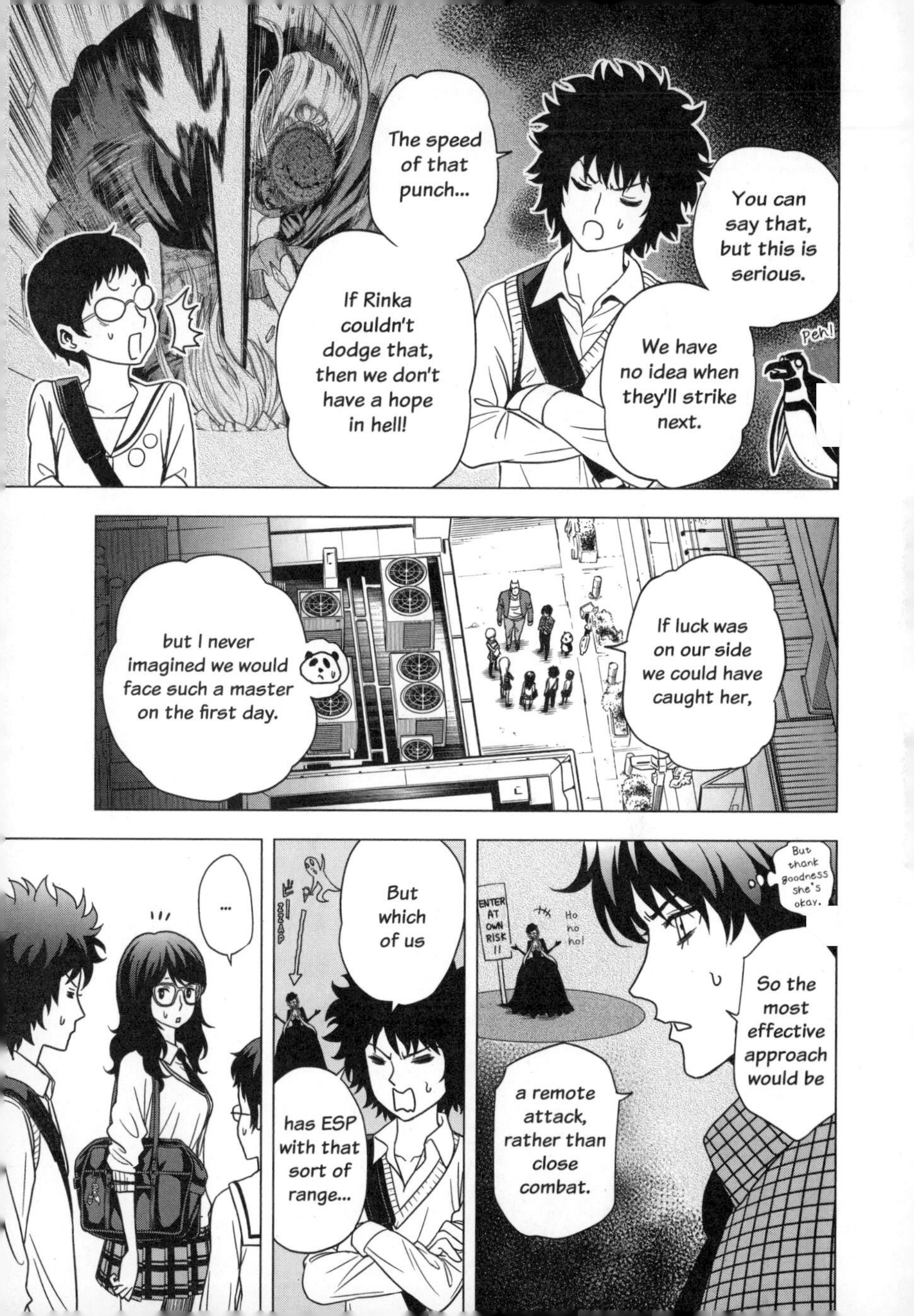
The speed of that punch...
If Rinka couldn't dodge that, then we don't have a hope in hell!
You can say that, but this is serious.
We have no idea when they'll strike next.
Peh!
If luck was on our side we could have caught her,
but I never imagined we would face such a master on the first day.
But thank goodness she's okay.
So the most effective approach would be
a remote attack, rather than close combat.
ENTER AT OWN RISK !!
Ho ho ho!
But which of us
has ESP with that sort of range...
...

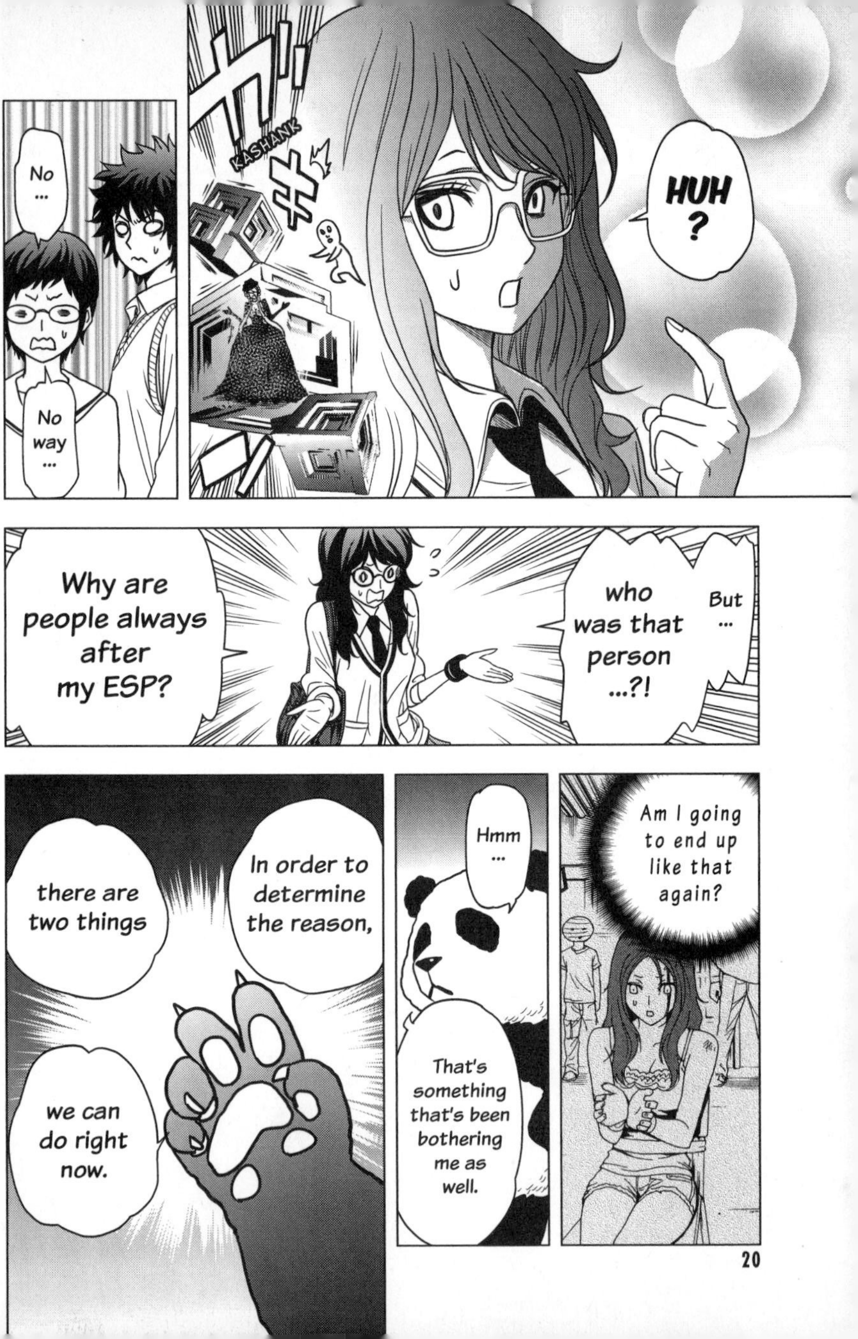
HUH?
KASHANK
No ...
No way ...
But ...
who was that person ...?!
Why are people always after my ESP?
Am I going to end up like that again?
Hmm ...
That's something that's been bothering me as well.
In order to determine the reason,
there are two things
we can do right now.

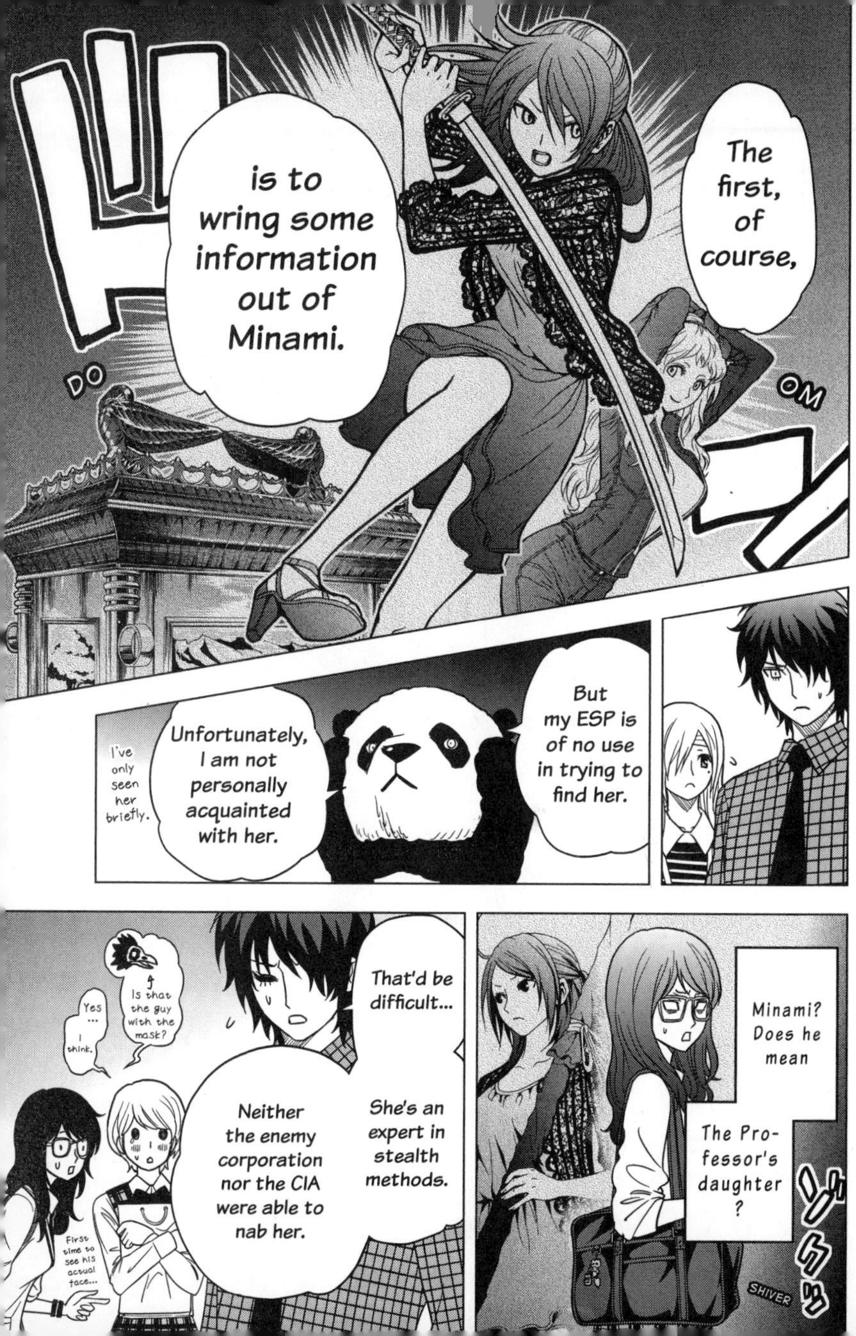

The first, of course,
is to wring some information out of Minami.
DO
OM
But my ESP is of no use in trying to find her.
Unfortunately, I am not personally acquainted with her.
I've only seen her briefly.
Minami? Does he mean
The Professor's daughter?
SHIVER
That'd be difficult...
She's an expert in stealth methods.
Neither the enemy corporation nor the CIA were able to nab her.
Is that the guy with the mask?
Yes ... I think.
First time to see his actual face...

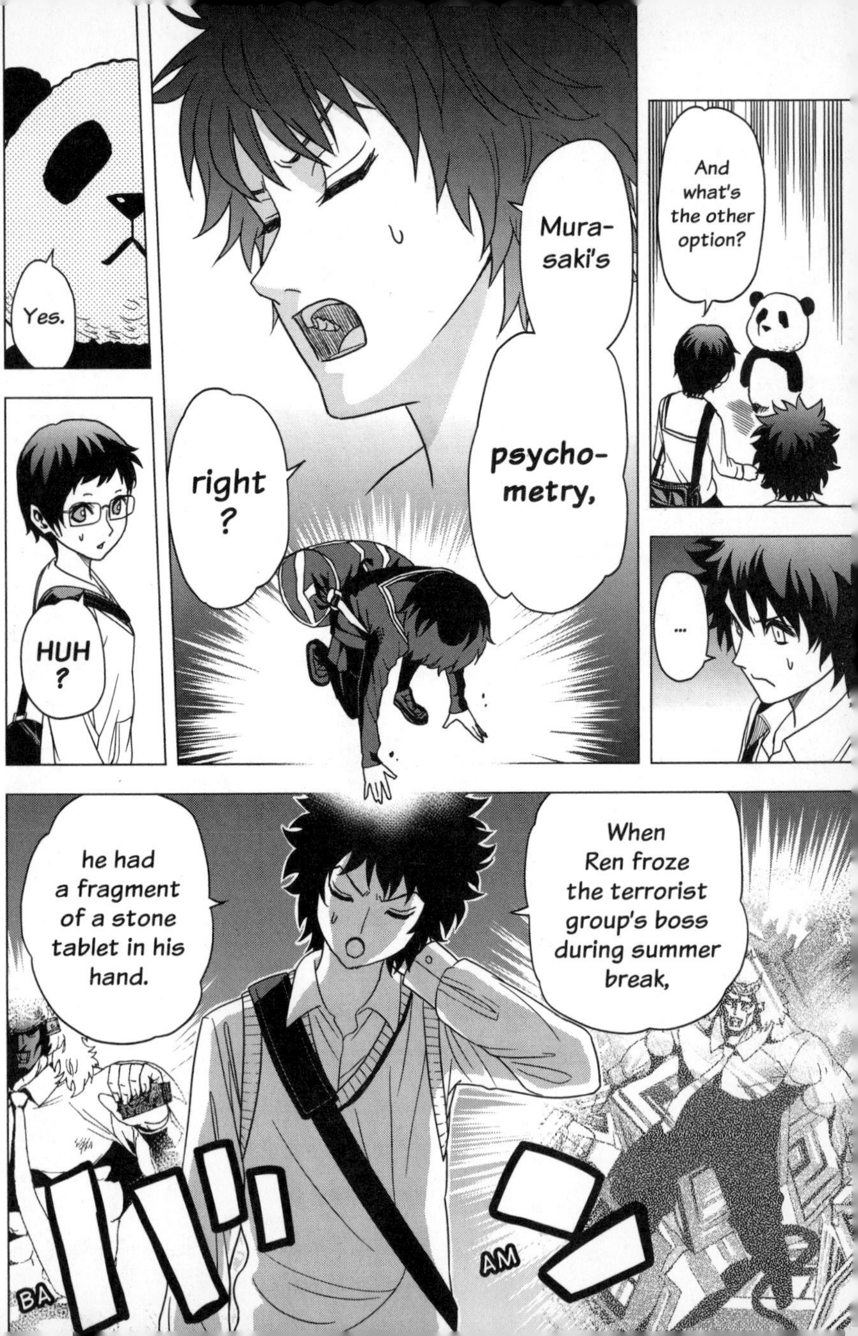
And what's the other option?
...
Mura-saki's
psycho-metry,
right?
Yes.
HUH?
When Ren froze the terrorist group's boss during summer break,
he had a fragment of a stone tablet in his hand.
BA
AM

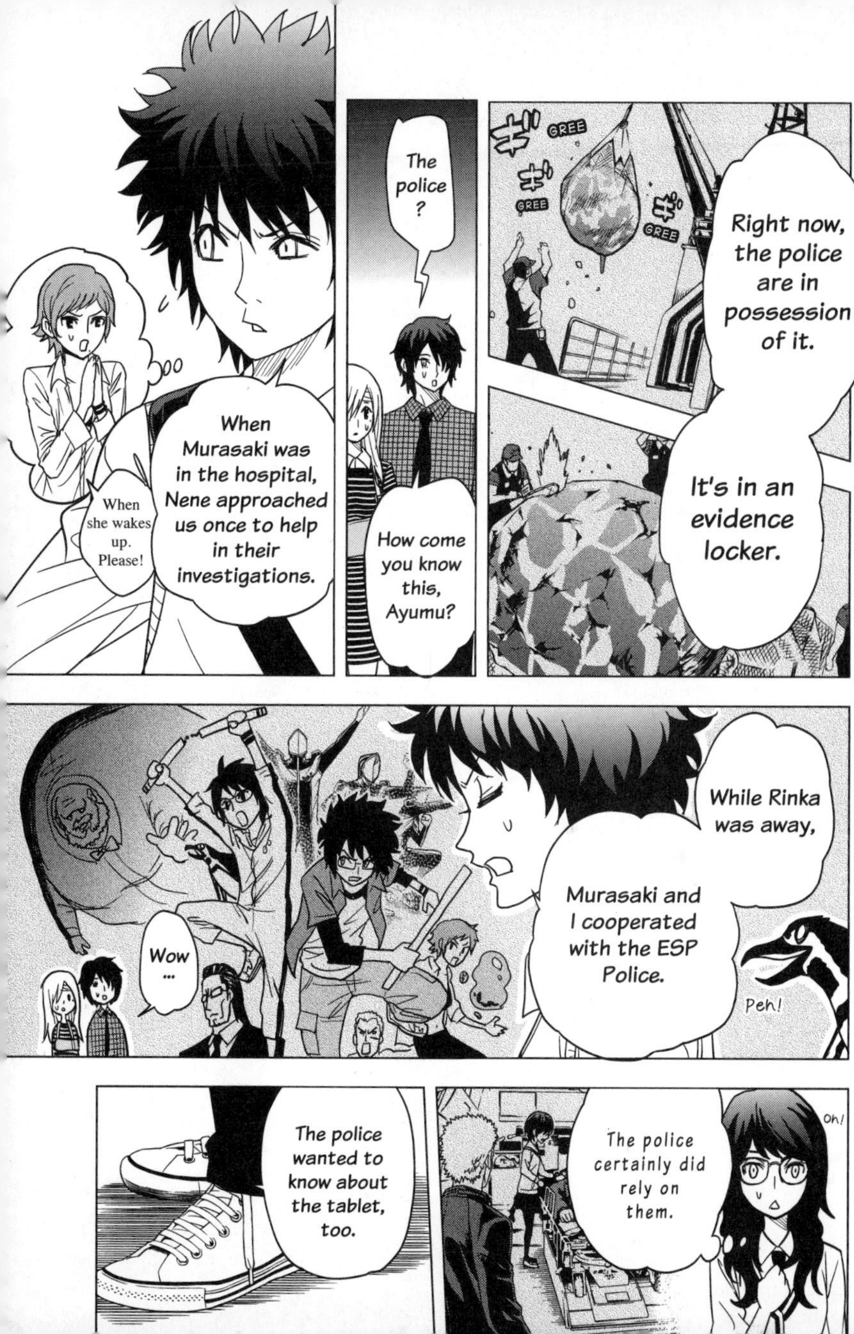
GREE
GREE
GREE
Right now, the police are in possession of it.
It's in an evidence locker.
The police?
How come you know this, Ayumu?
When Murasaki was in the hospital, Nene approached us once to help in their investigations.
When she wakes up. Please!
While Rinka was away,
Murasaki and I cooperated with the ESP Police.
Peh!
Wow ...
Oh!
The police certainly did rely on them.
The police wanted to know about the tablet, too.

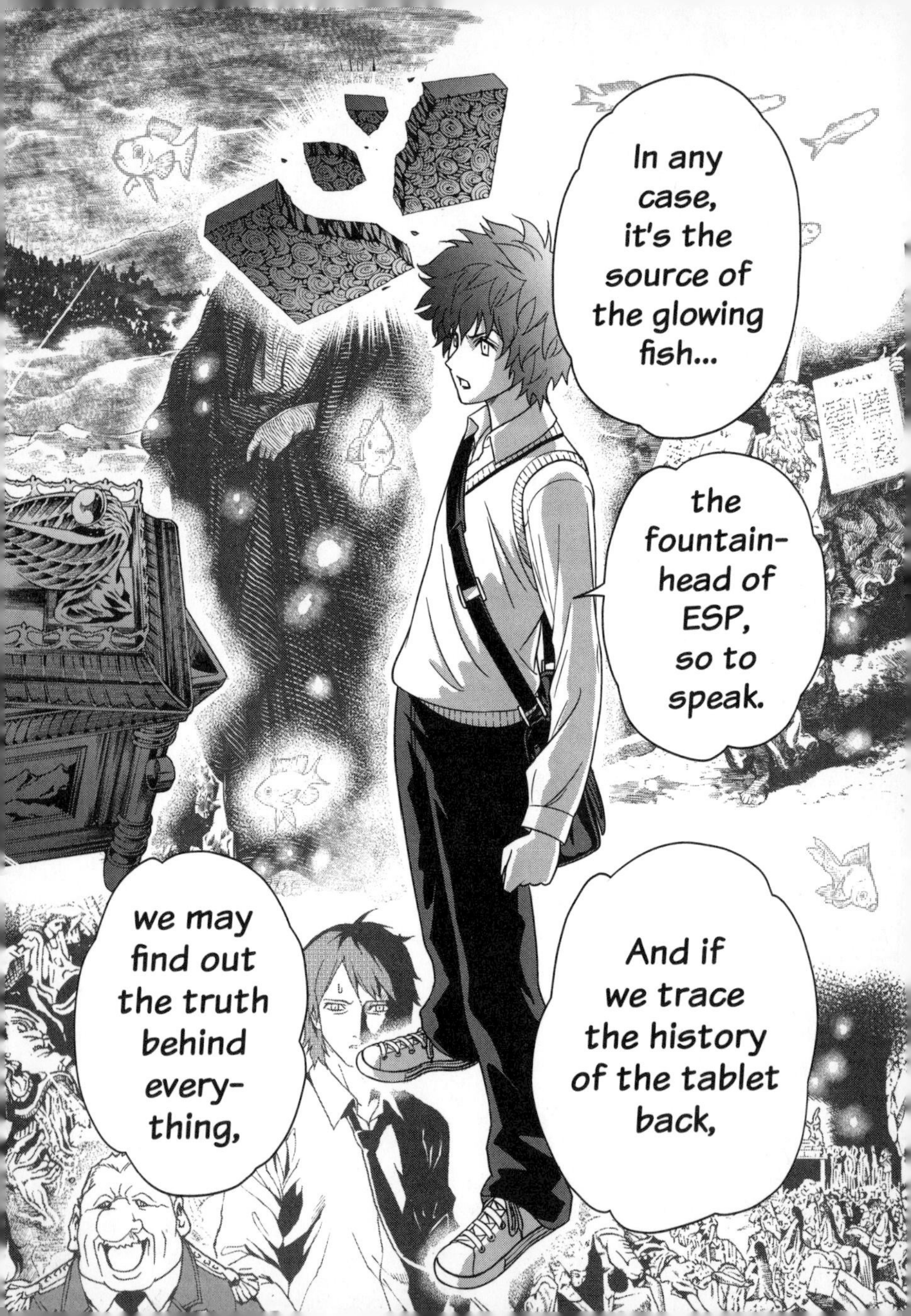
In any case, it's the source of the glowing fish...
the fountain-head of ESP, so to speak.
And if we trace the history of the tablet back,
we may find out the truth behind every-thing,

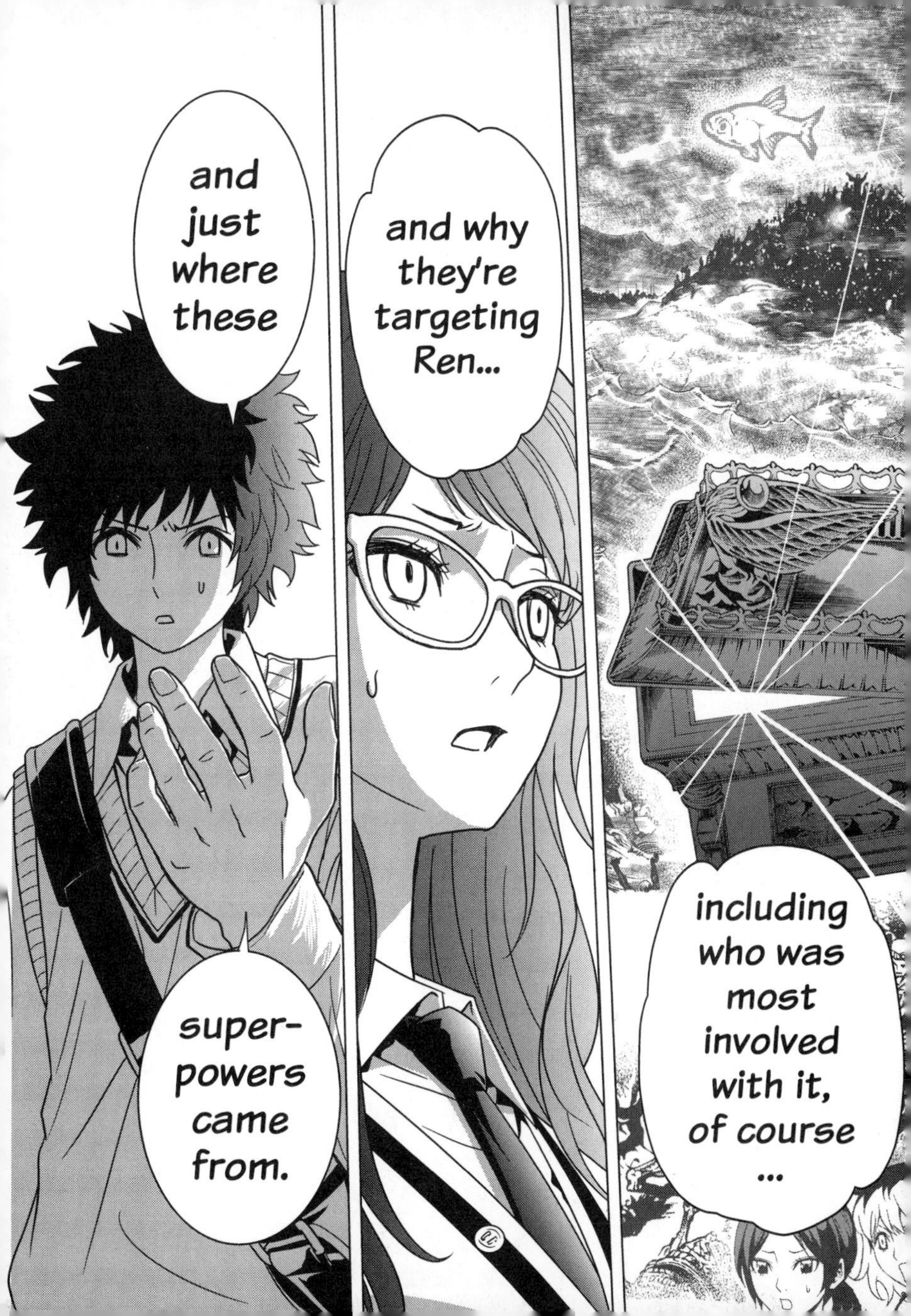
including who was most involved with it, of course ...
and why they're targeting Ren...
and just where these
super-powers came from.

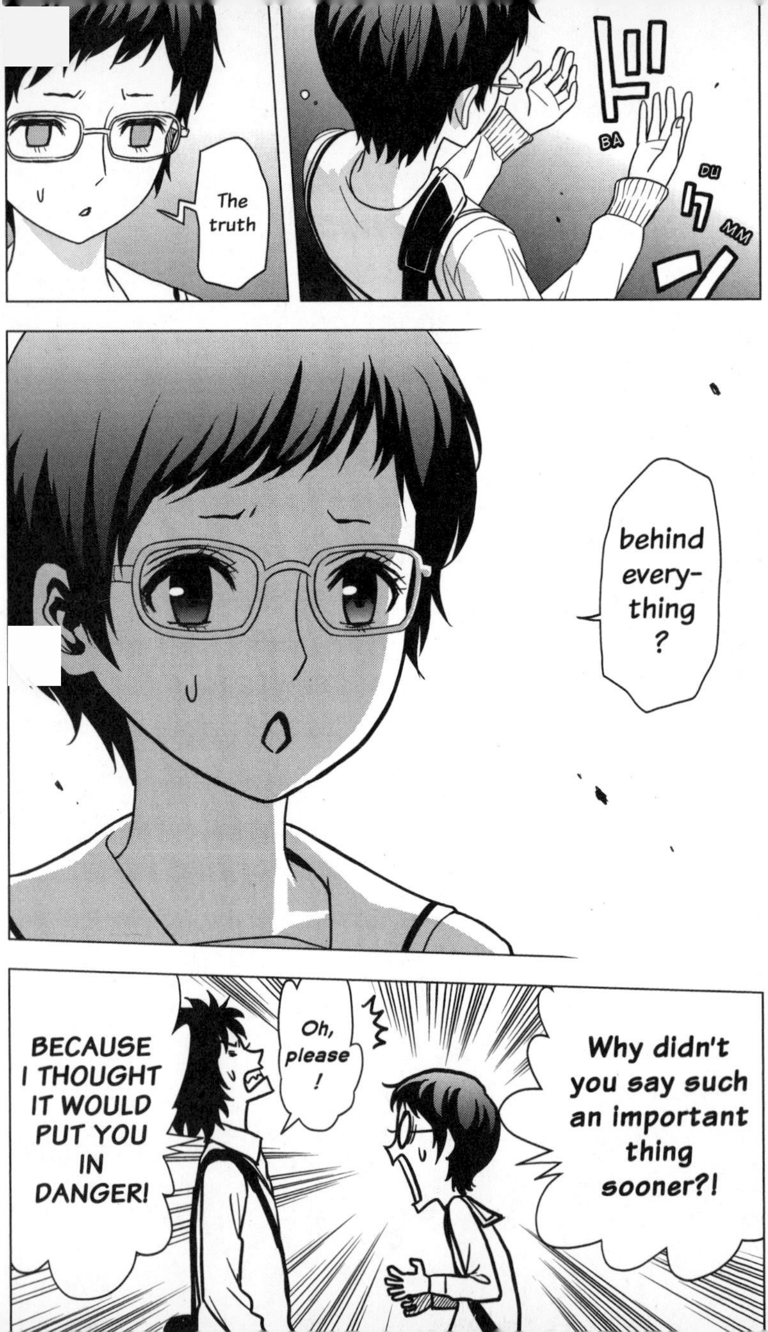
BA
DU
MM
The truth
behind every-thing?
Why didn't you say such an important thing sooner?!
Oh, please!
BECAUSE I THOUGHT IT WOULD PUT YOU IN DANGER!

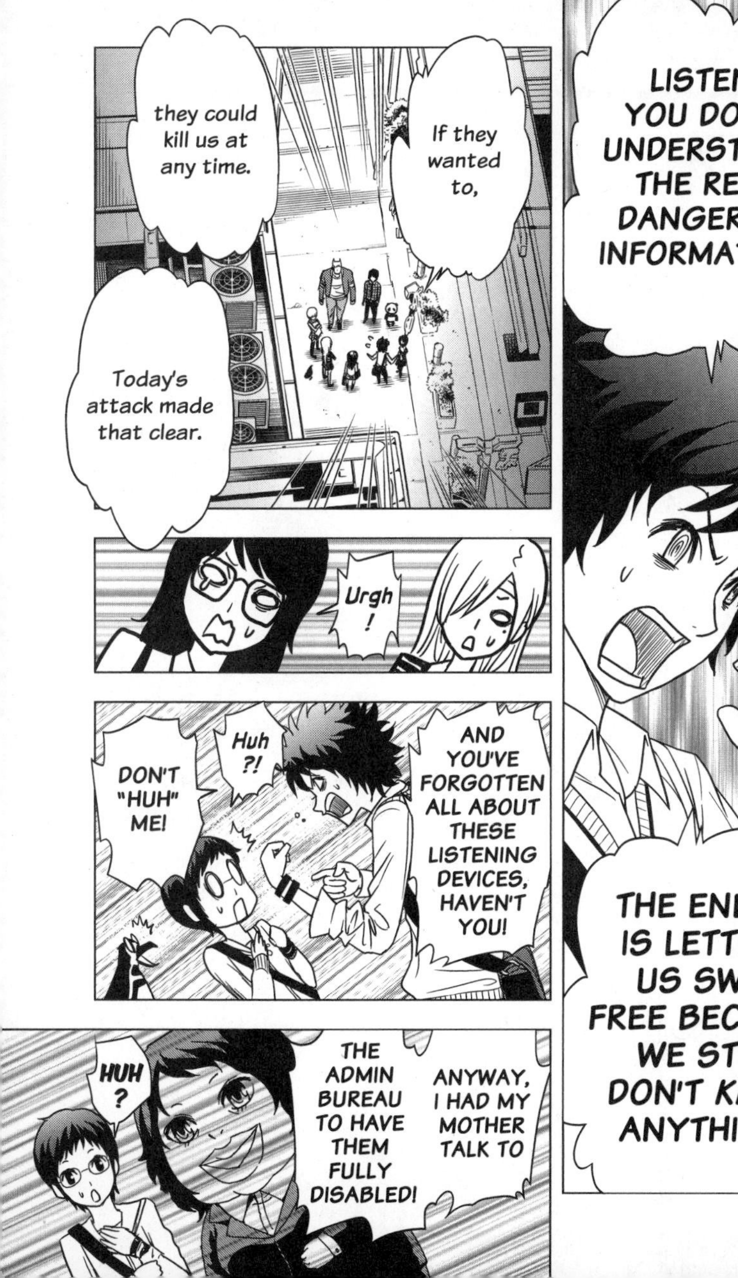
LISTEN! YOU DON'T UNDERSTAND THE REAL DANGER OF INFORMATION!
THE ENEMY IS LETTING US SWIM FREE BECAUSE WE STILL DON'T KNOW ANYTHING!
If they wanted to,
they could kill us at any time.
Today's attack made that clear.
Urgh!
AND YOU'VE FORGOTTEN ALL ABOUT THESE LISTENING DEVICES, HAVEN'T YOU!
Huh?!
DON'T "HUH" ME!
ANYWAY, I HAD MY MOTHER TALK TO
THE ADMIN BUREAU TO HAVE THEM FULLY DISABLED!
HUH?

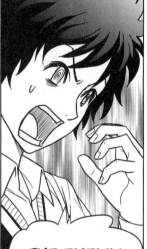

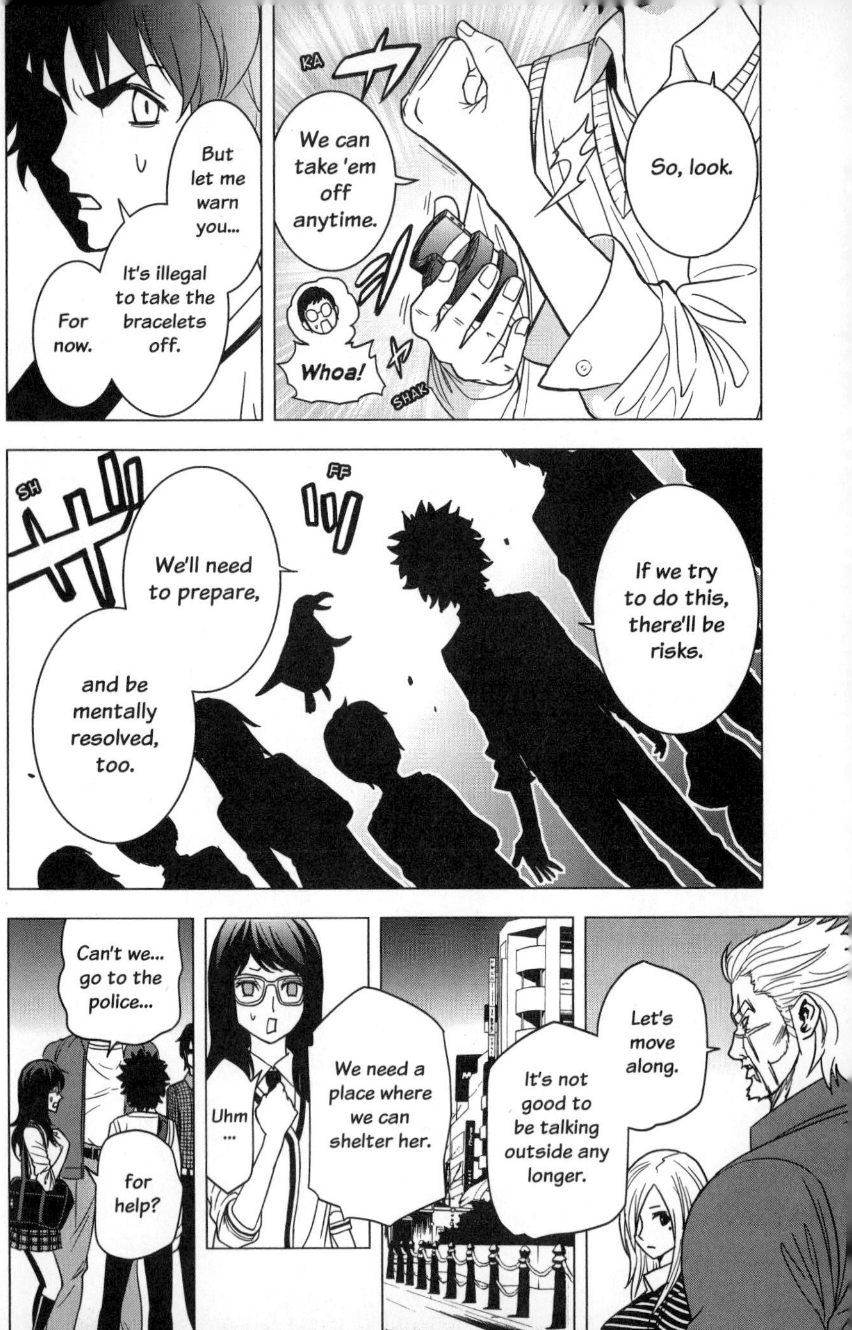
So, look.
KA
We can take 'em off anytime.
Whoa!
SHAK
But let me warn you...
It's illegal to take the bracelets off.
For now.
If we try to do this, there'll be risks.
FF
SH
We'll need to prepare,
and be mentally resolved, too.
Let's move along.
It's not good to be talking outside any longer.
We need a place where we can shelter her.
Uhm ...
Can't we... go to the police...
for help?

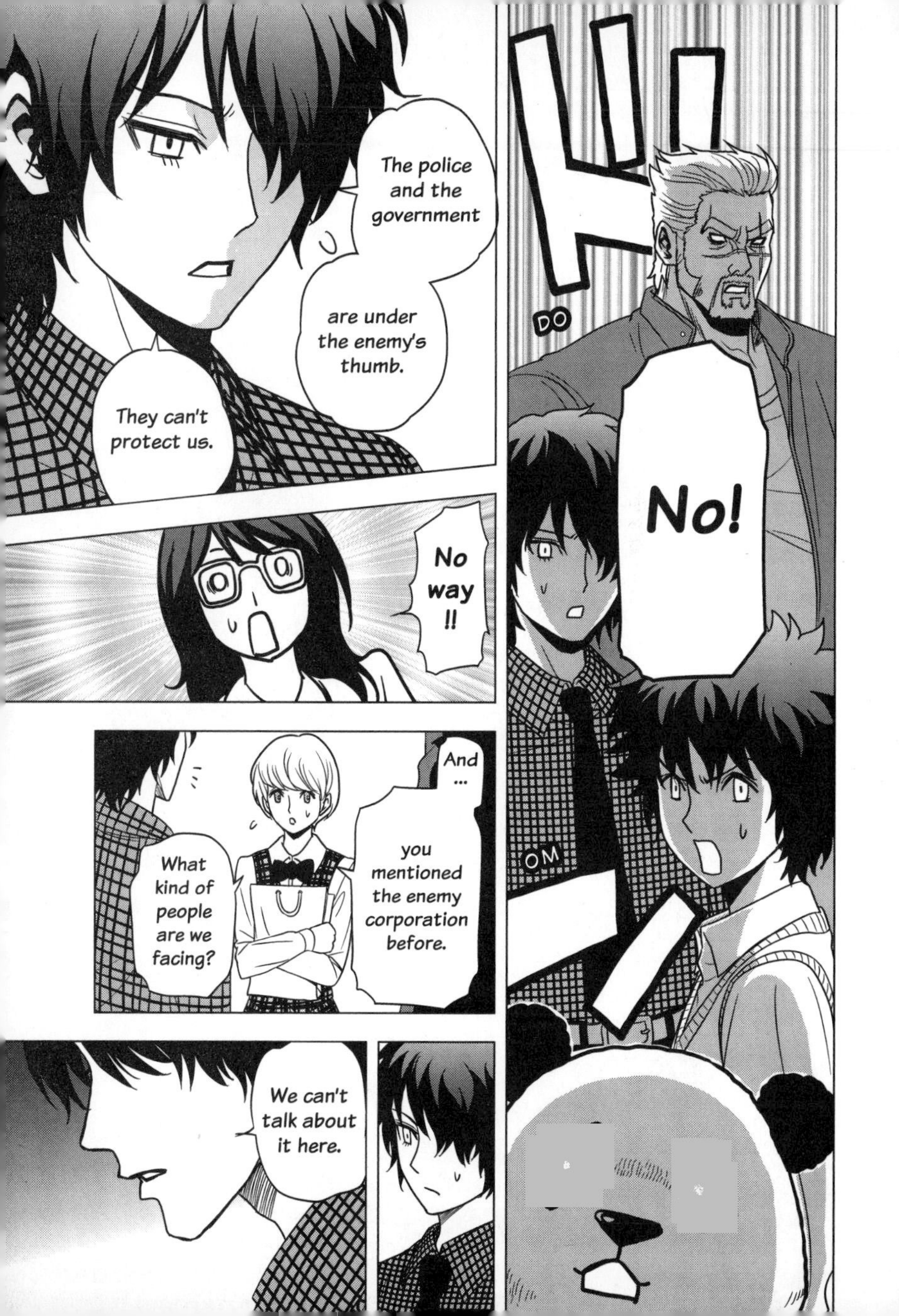
DO
No!
OM
The police and the government
are under the enemy's thumb.
They can't protect us.
No way !!
And ...
you mentioned the enemy corporation before.
What kind of people are we facing?
We can't talk about it here.

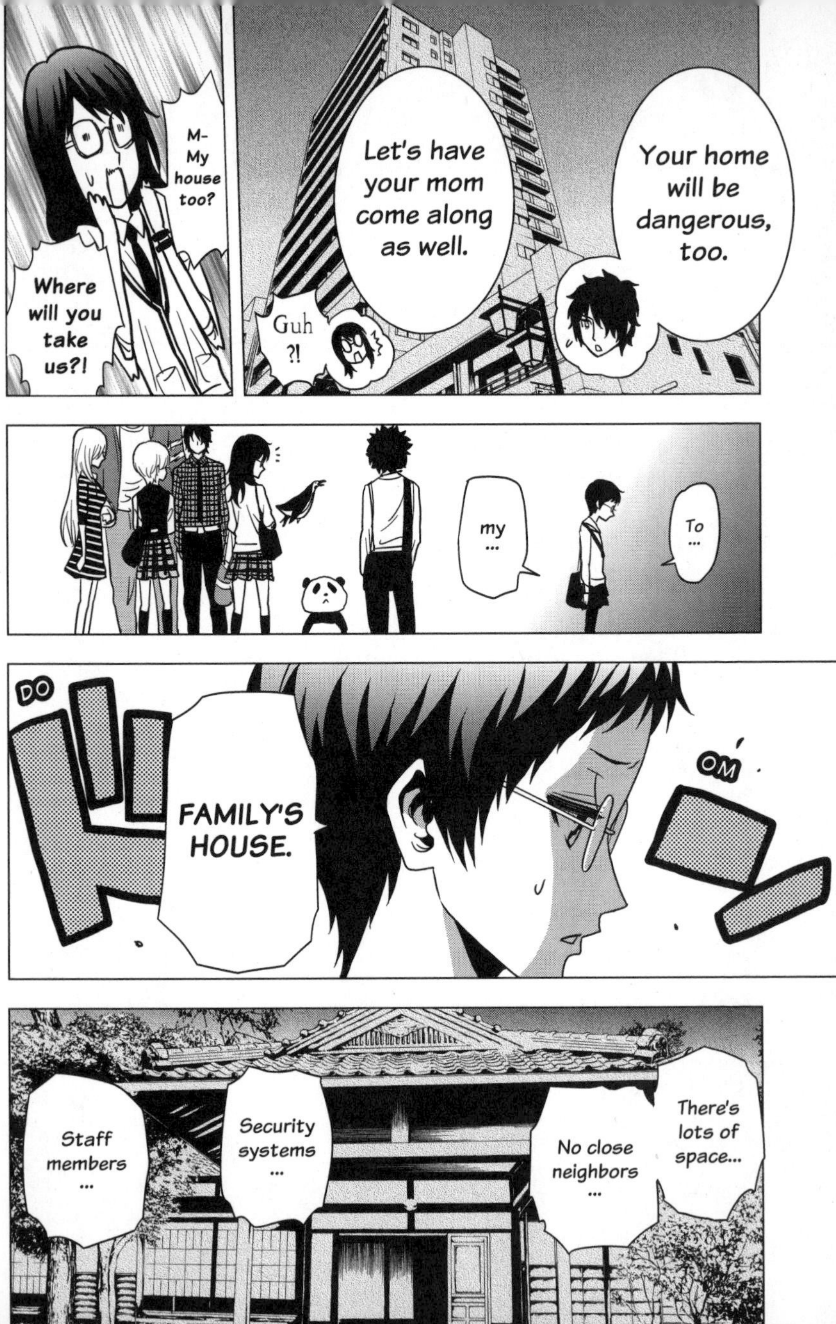
Your home will be dangerous, too.
Let's have your mom come along as well.
Guh ?!
M- My house too?
Where will you take us?!
To ...
my ...
FAMILY'S HOUSE.
DO
OM
There's lots of space...
No close neighbors ...
Security systems ...
Staff members ...

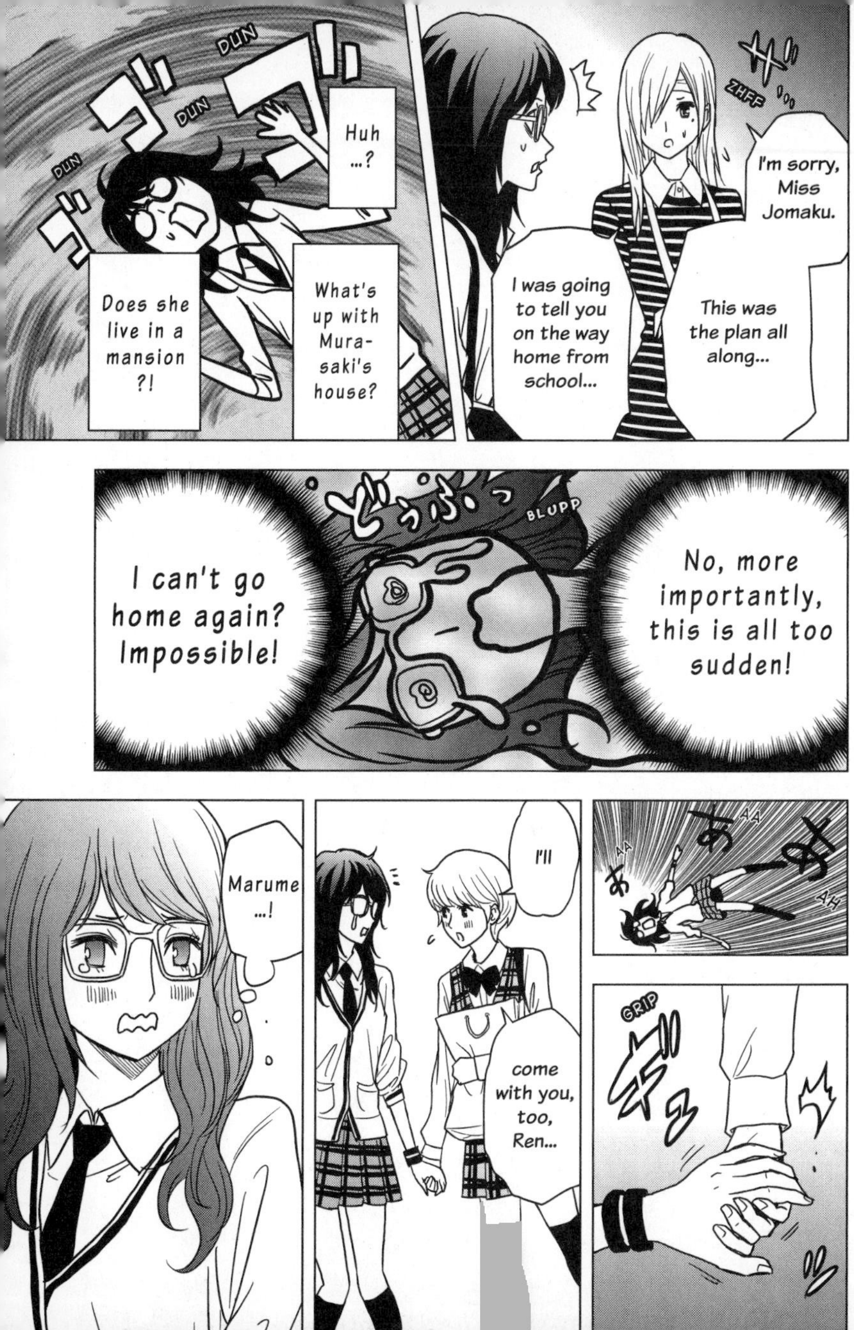
ZHFF
I'm sorry, Miss Jomaku.
This was the plan all along...
I was going to tell you on the way home from school...
DUN
DUN
DUN
Huh ...?
What's up with Murasaki's house?
Does she live in a mansion ?!
BLUPP
No, more importantly, this is all too sudden!
I can't go home again? Impossible!
AA
AA
AH
GRIP
I'll
come with you, too, Ren...
Marume ...!

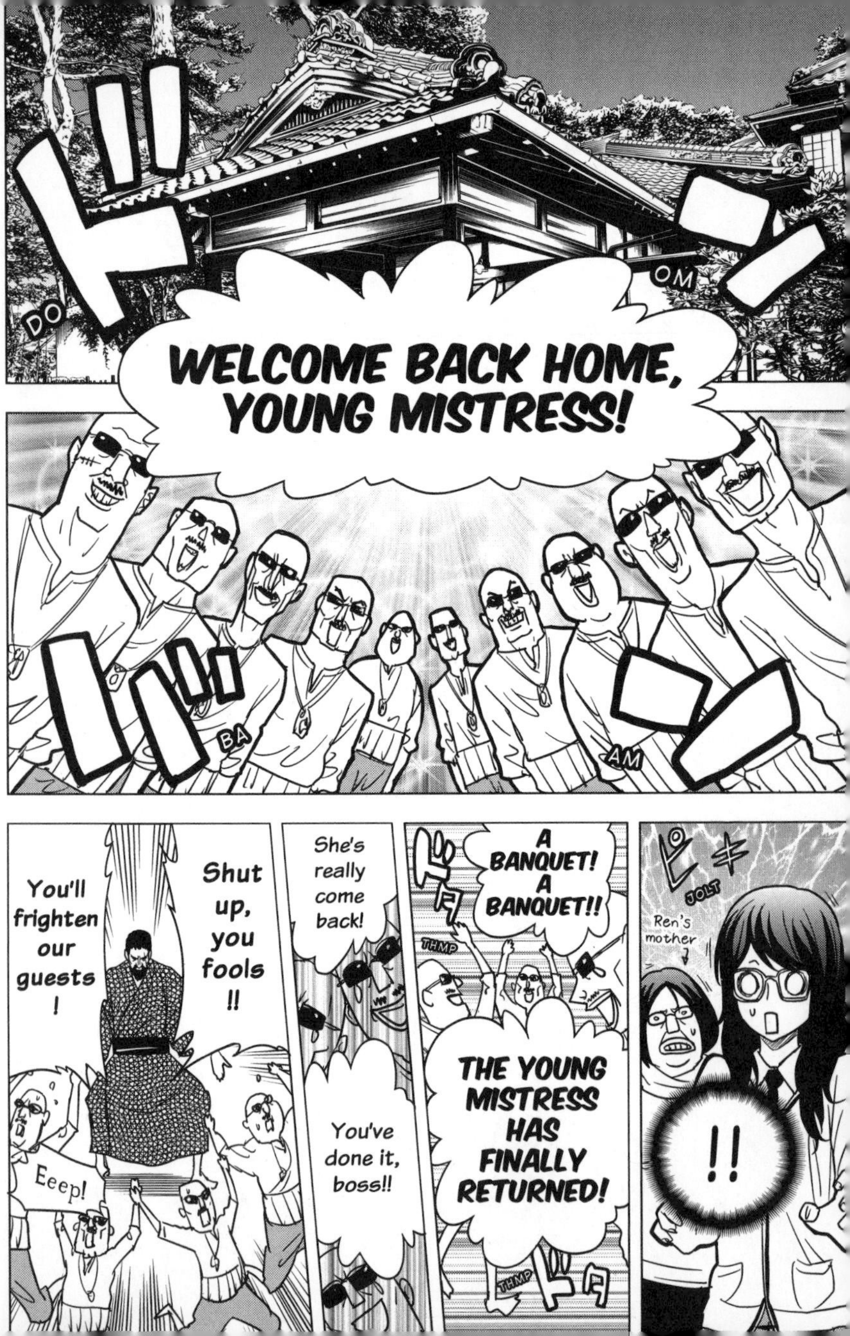
DO
OM
WELCOME BACK HOME, YOUNG MISTRESS!
BA
AM
JOLT
Ren's mother
!!
A BANQUET! A BANQUET!!
THMP
THE YOUNG MISTRESS HAS FINALLY RETURNED!
THMP
She's really come back!
You've done it, boss!!
Shut up, you fools!!
You'll frighten our guests!
Eeep!

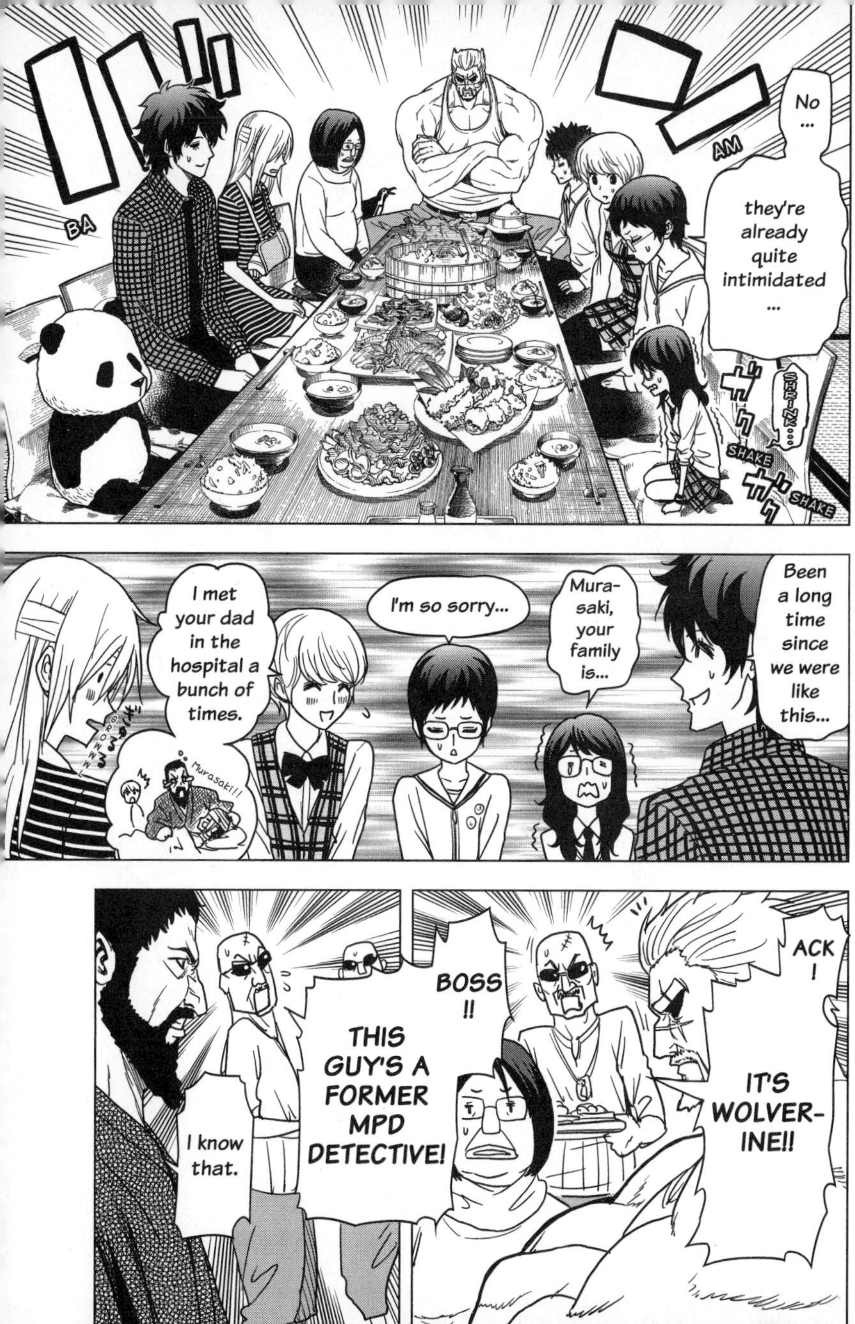
No ...
they're already quite intimidated ...
AM
SHRINK...
SHAKE
SHAKE
BA
Been a long time since we were like this...
Mura-saki, your family is...
I'm so sorry...
I met your dad in the hospital a bunch of times.
GROWWWL
Murasaki!!
ACK!
IT'S WOLVER-INE!!
BOSS!!
THIS GUY'S A FORMER MPD DETECTIVE!
I know that.

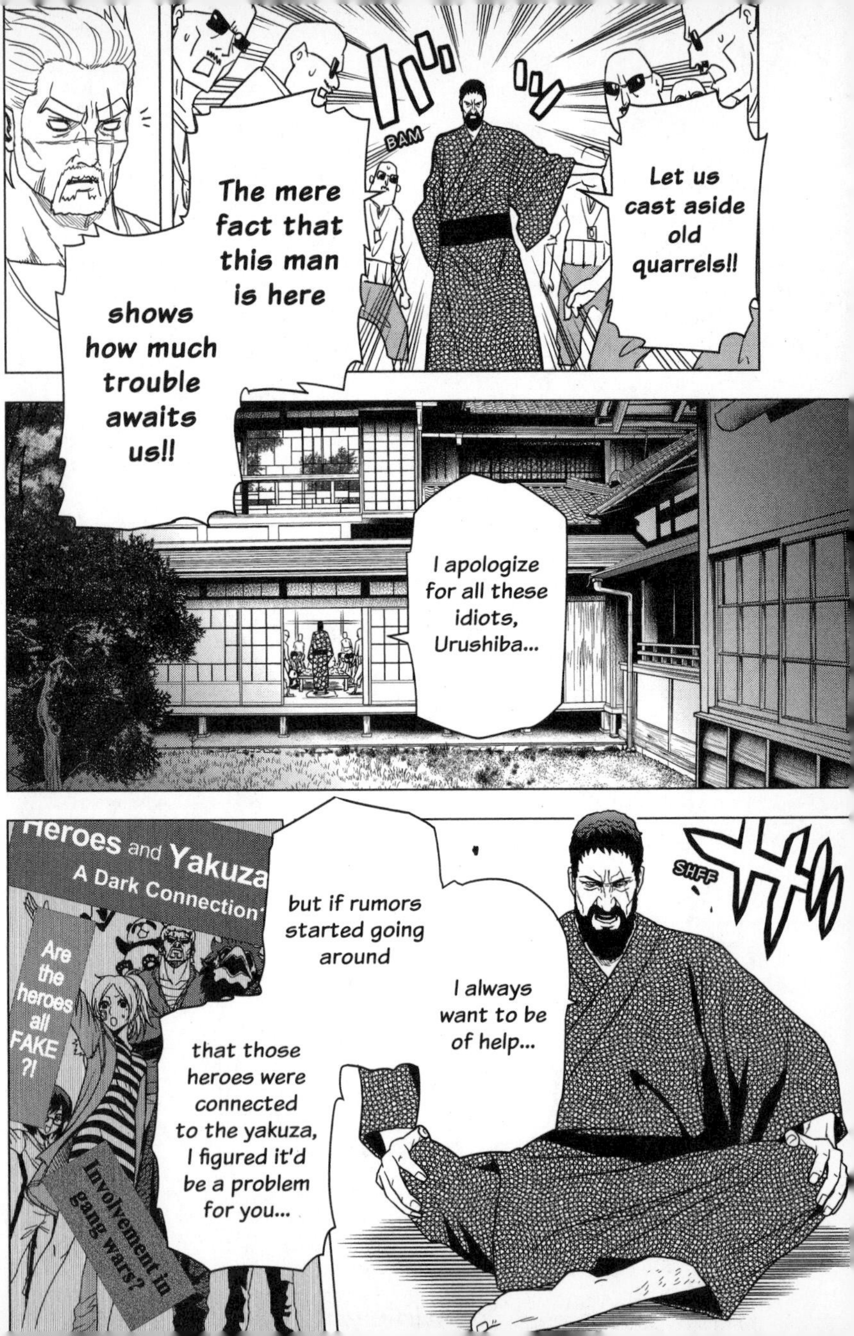
Let us cast aside old quarrels!!
BAM
The mere fact that this man is here
shows how much trouble awaits us!!
I apologize for all these idiots, Urushiba...
SHFF
I always want to be of help...
but if rumors started going around
that those heroes were connected to the yakuza, I figured it'd be a problem for you...
Heroes and Yakuza A Dark Connection
Are the heroes all FAKE?!
Involvement in gang wars?

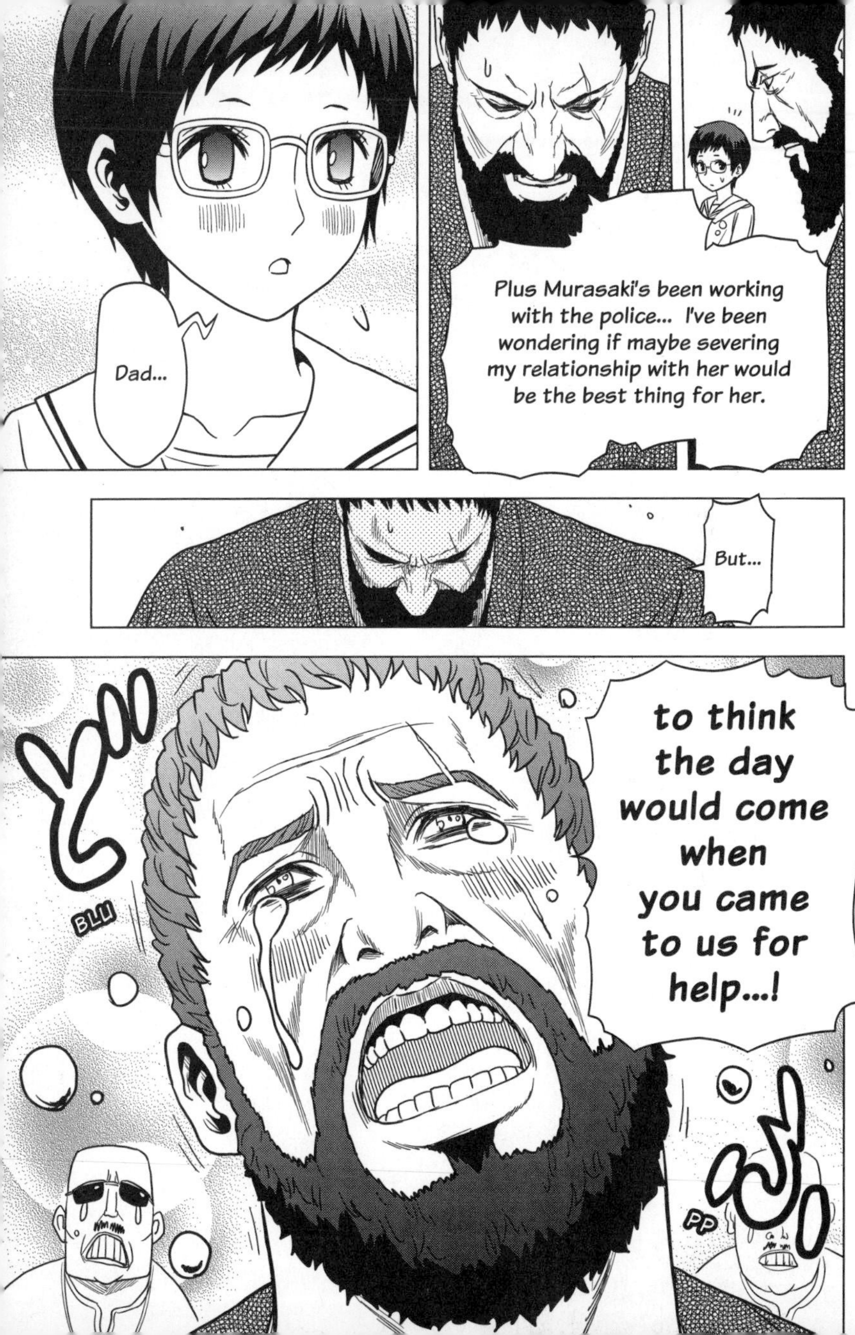
Plus Murasaki's been working with the police... I've been wondering if maybe severing my relationship with her would be the best thing for her.
Dad...
But...
to think the day would come when you came to us for help...!
PP
BLU

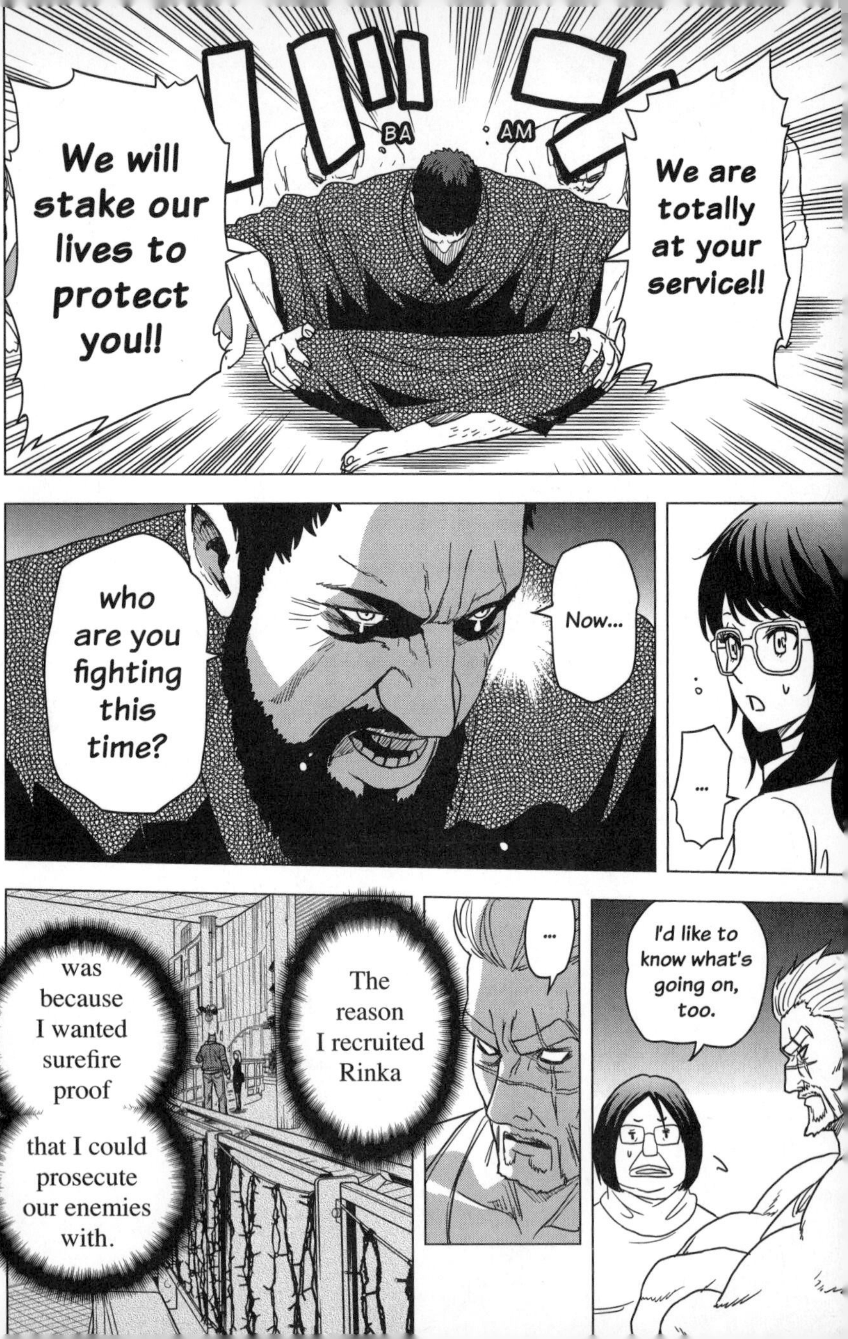
BA AM
We are totally at your service!!
We will stake our lives to protect you!!
...
Now...
who are you fighting this time?
I'd like to know what's going on, too.
...
The reason I recruited Rinka
was because I wanted surefire proof
that I could prosecute our enemies with.

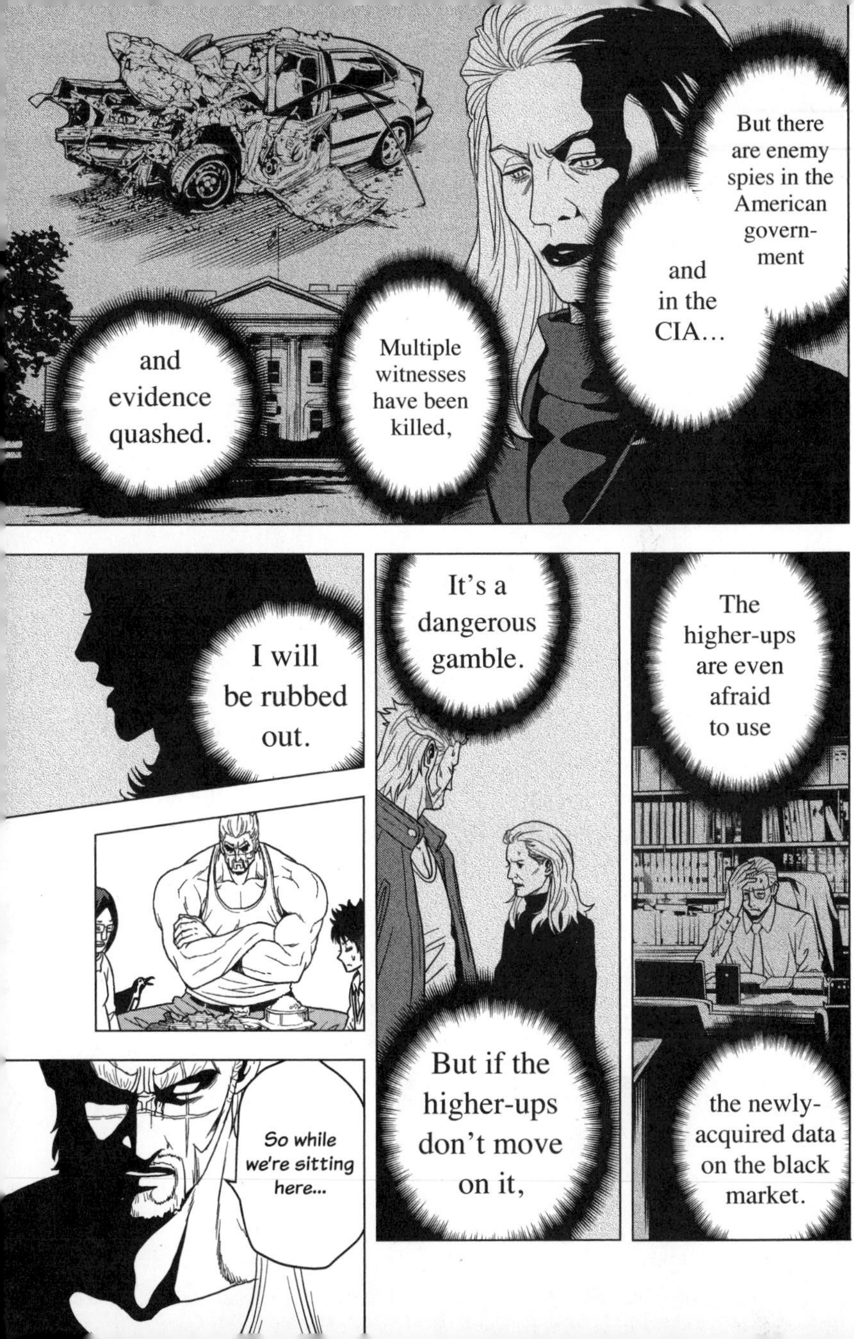
But there are enemy spies in the American govern-ment
and in the CIA…
Multiple witnesses have been killed,
and evidence quashed.
The higher-ups are even afraid to use
the newly-acquired data on the black market.
It's a dangerous gamble.
But if the higher-ups don't move on it,
I will be rubbed out.
So while we're sitting here…

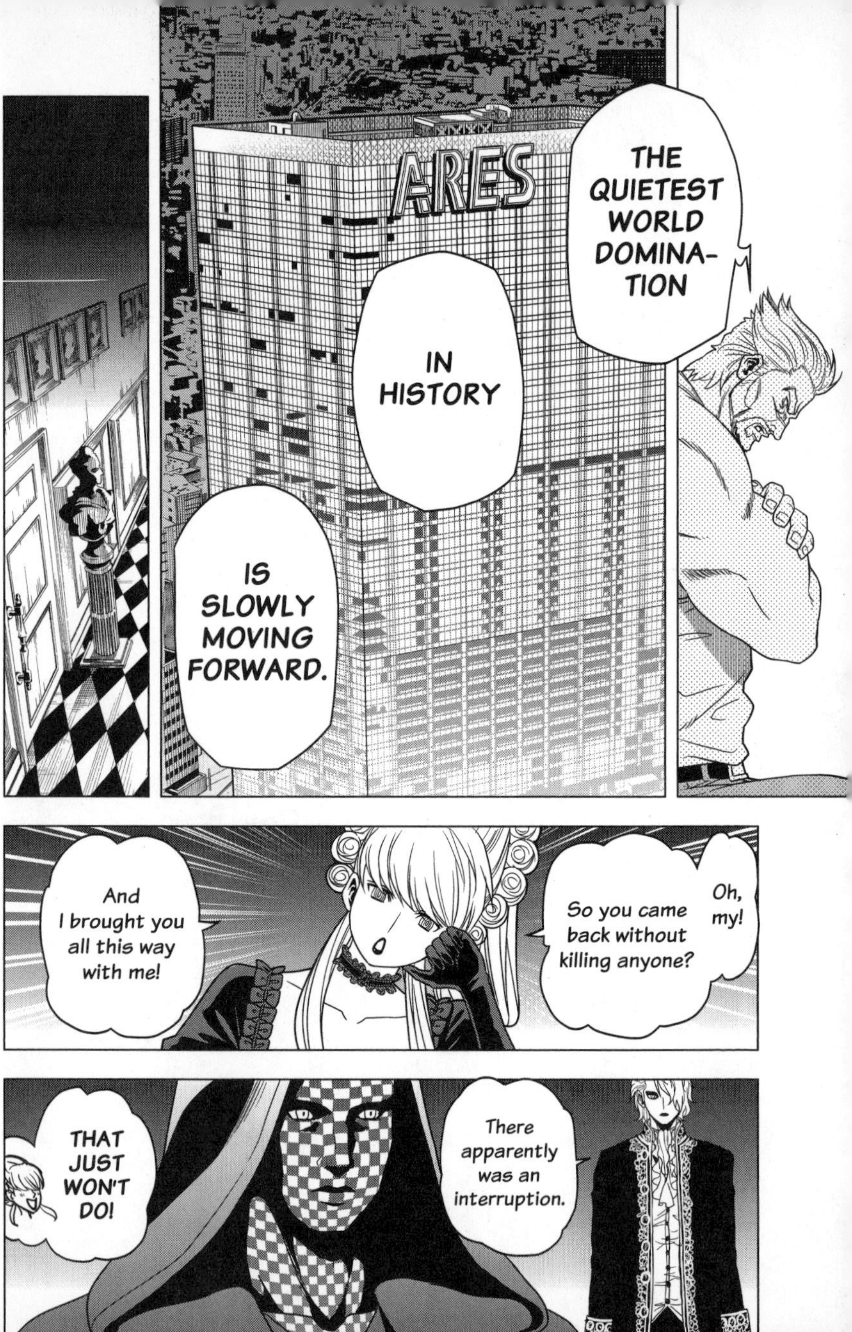
THE QUIETEST WORLD DOMINA-TION
ARES
IN HISTORY
IS SLOWLY MOVING FORWARD.
Oh, my!
So you came back without killing anyone?
And I brought you all this way with me!
There apparently was an interruption.
THAT JUST WON'T DO!

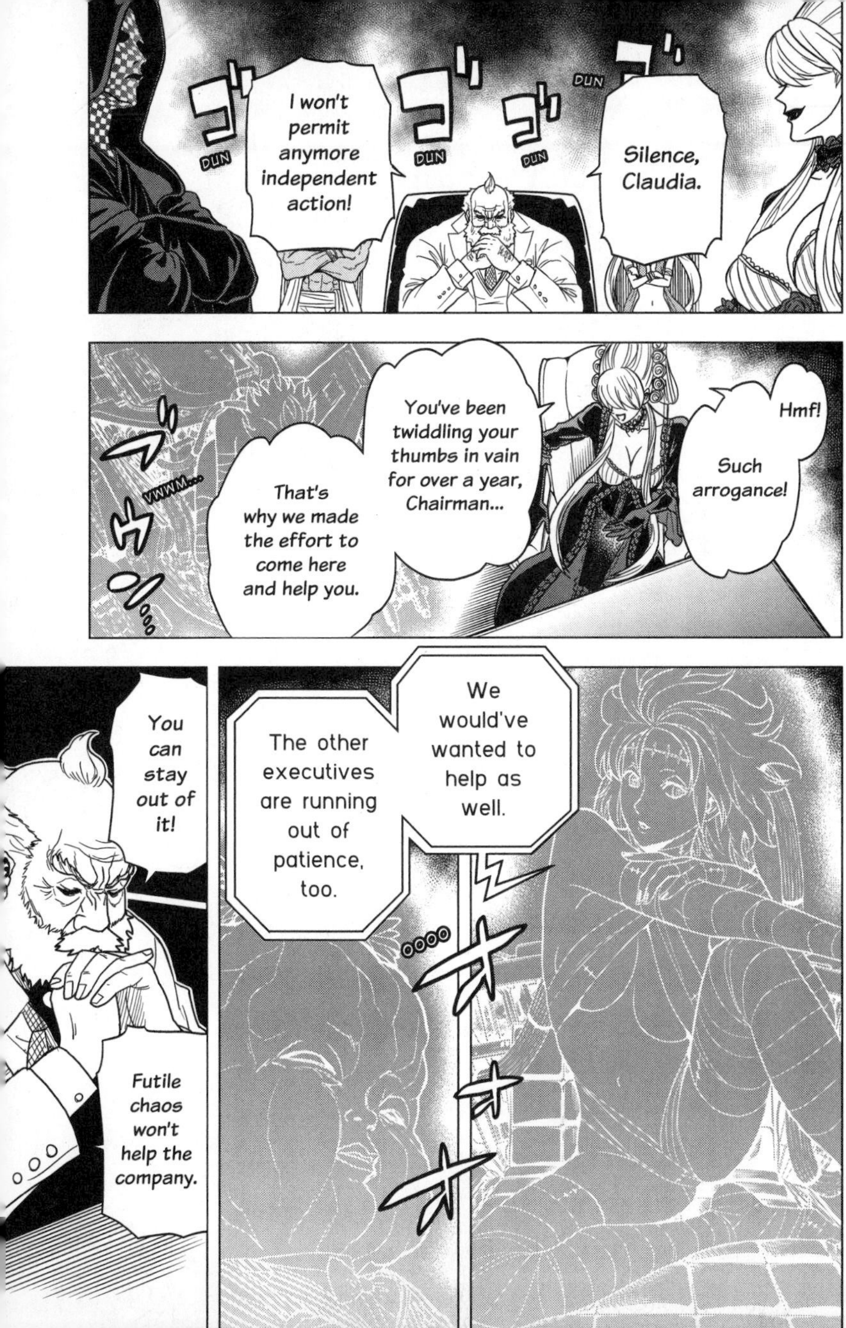
DUN
Silence, Claudia.
DUN
DUN
I won't permit anymore independent action!
DUN
Hmf!
Such arrogance!
You've been twiddling your thumbs in vain for over a year, Chairman...
That's why we made the effort to come here and help you.
VWWM...
We would've wanted to help as well.
The other executives are running out of patience, too.
You can stay out of it!
Futile chaos won't help the company.

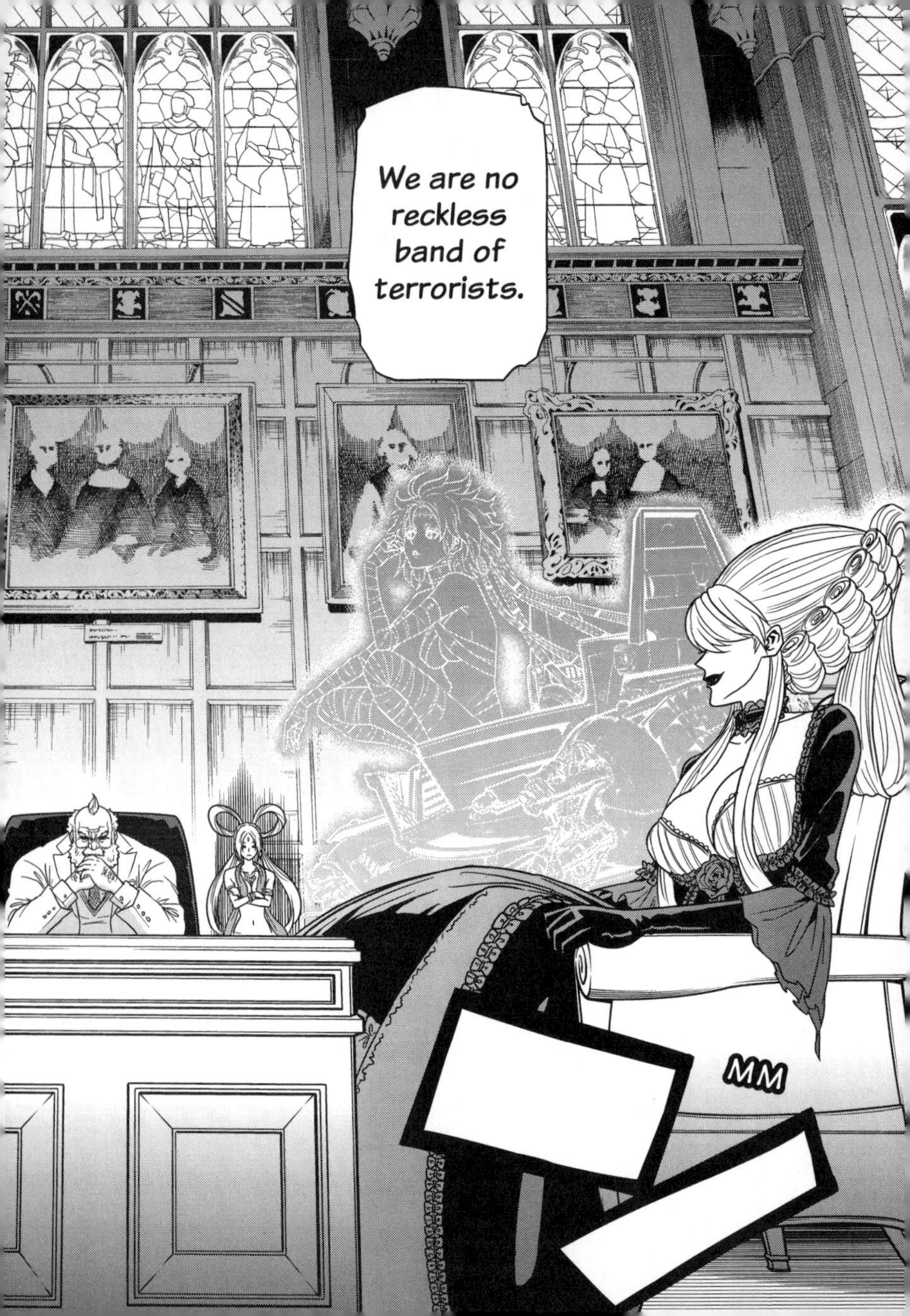
We are no reckless band of terrorists.
MM

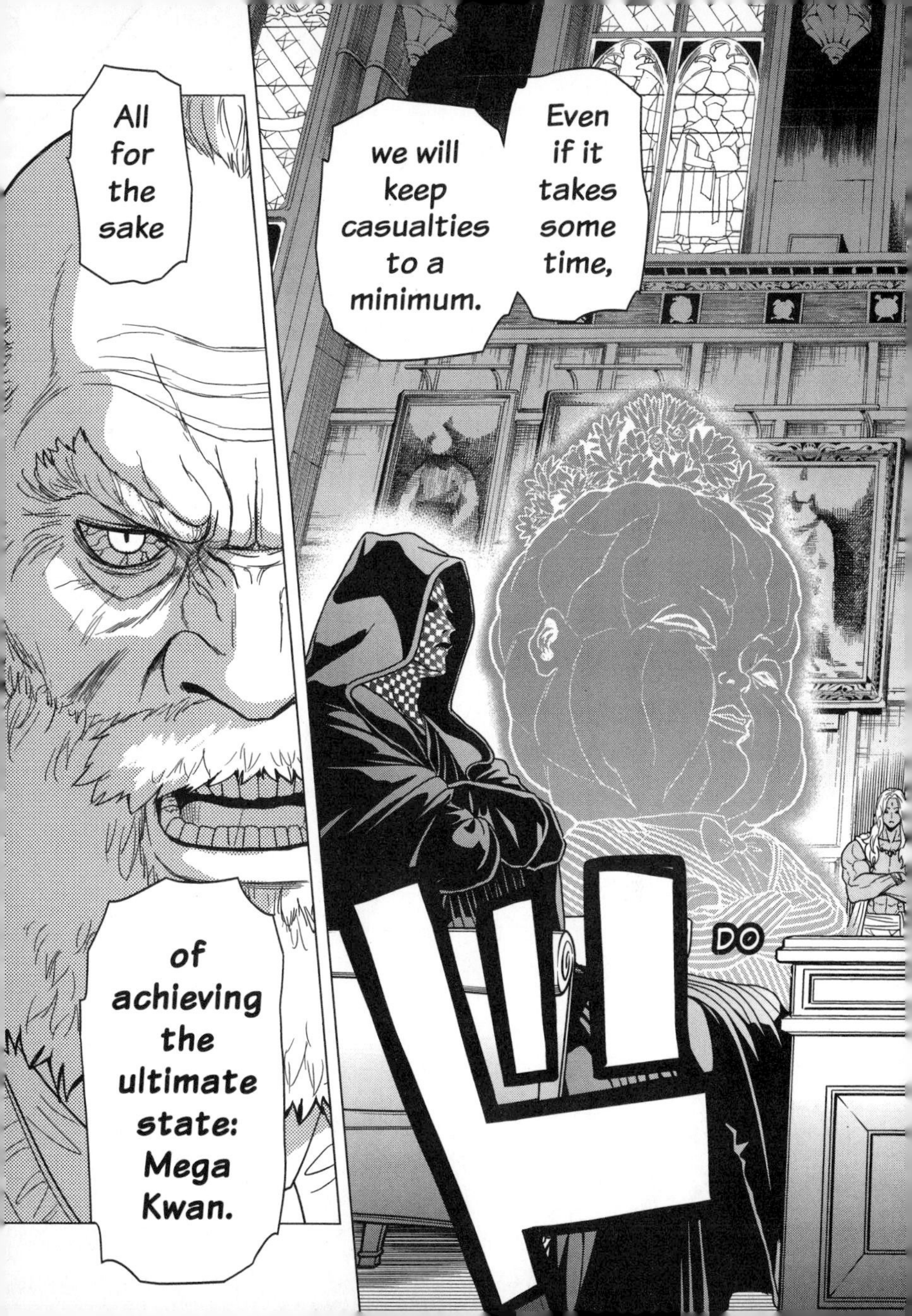
Even if it takes some time,
we will keep casualties to a minimum.
ド
DO
All for the sake
of achieving the ultimate state: Mega Kwan.

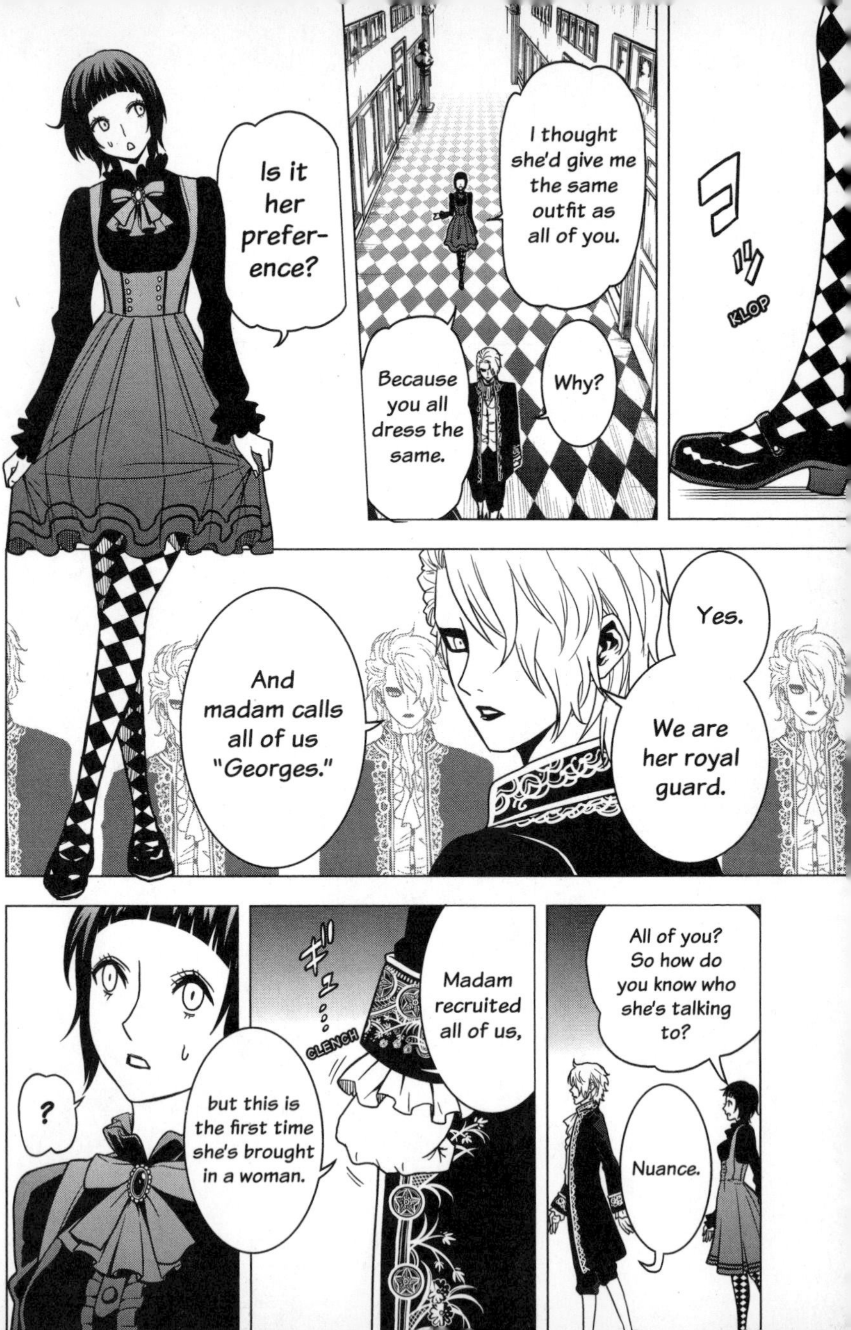
KLOP
I thought she'd give me the same outfit as all of you.
Why?
Because you all dress the same.
Is it her preference?
Yes.
We are her royal guard.
And madam calls all of us "Georges."
All of you? So how do you know who she's talking to?
Nuance.
Madam recruited all of us,
CLENCH
but this is the first time she's brought in a woman.
?

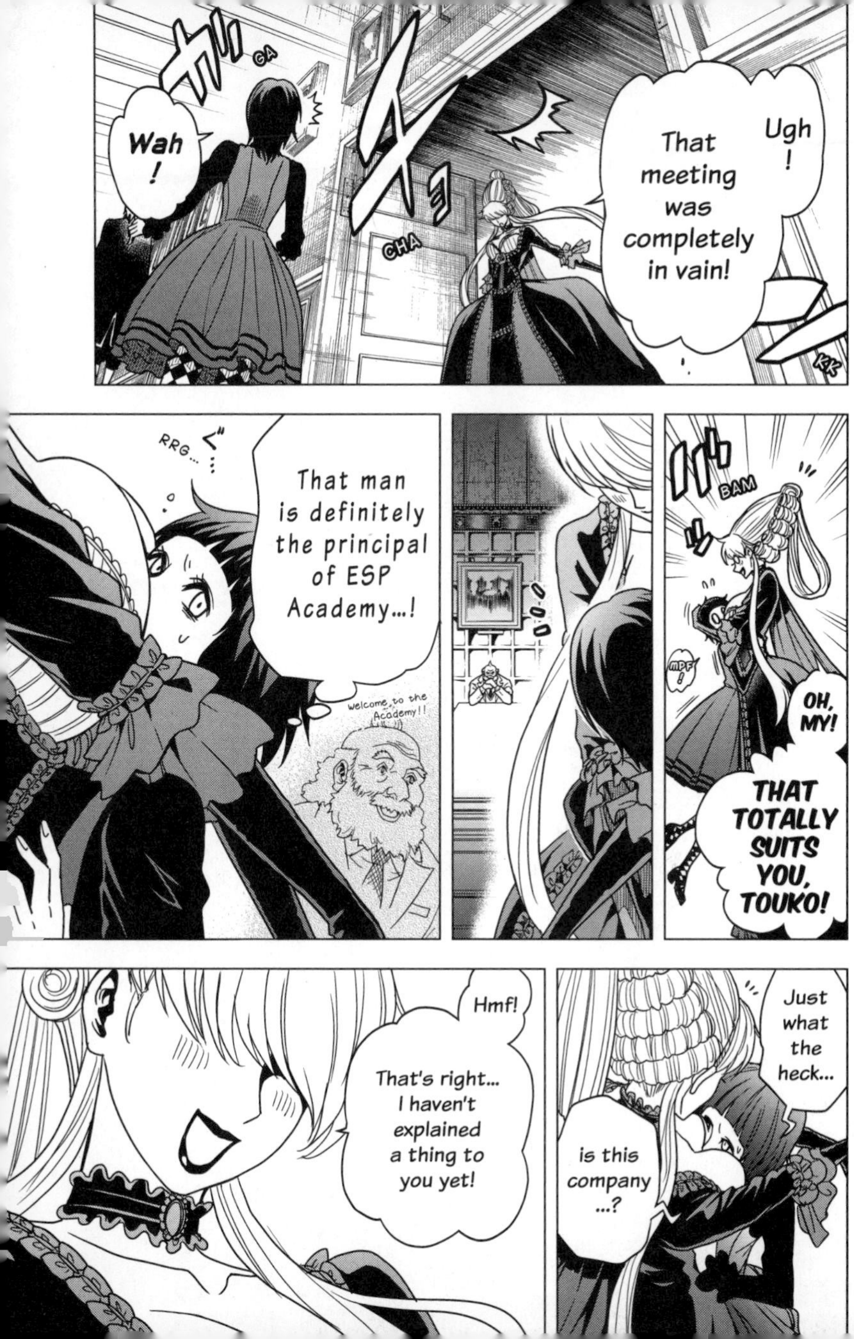
Ugh!
That meeting was completely in vain!
GA
Wah!
CHA
KK
BAM
MPF!
OH, MY!
THAT TOTALLY SUITS YOU, TOUKO!
RRG...
That man is definitely the principal of ESP Academy...!
Welcome to the Academy!!
Just what the heck...
is this company...?
Hmf!
That's right... I haven't explained a thing to you yet!

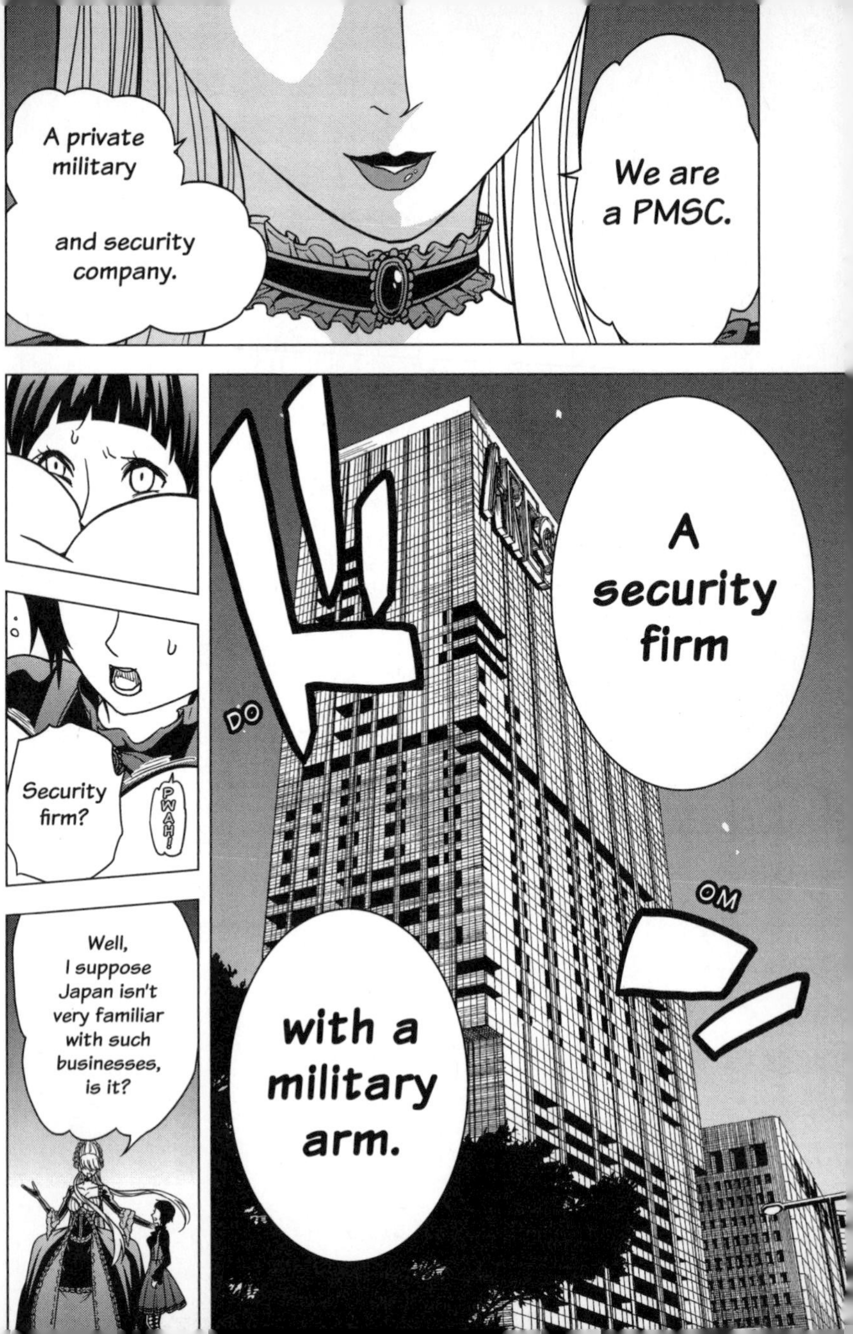
We are a PMSC.
A private military
and security company.
A security firm
DO
OM
with a military arm.
PWAH!
Security firm?
Well, I suppose Japan isn't very familiar with such businesses, is it?

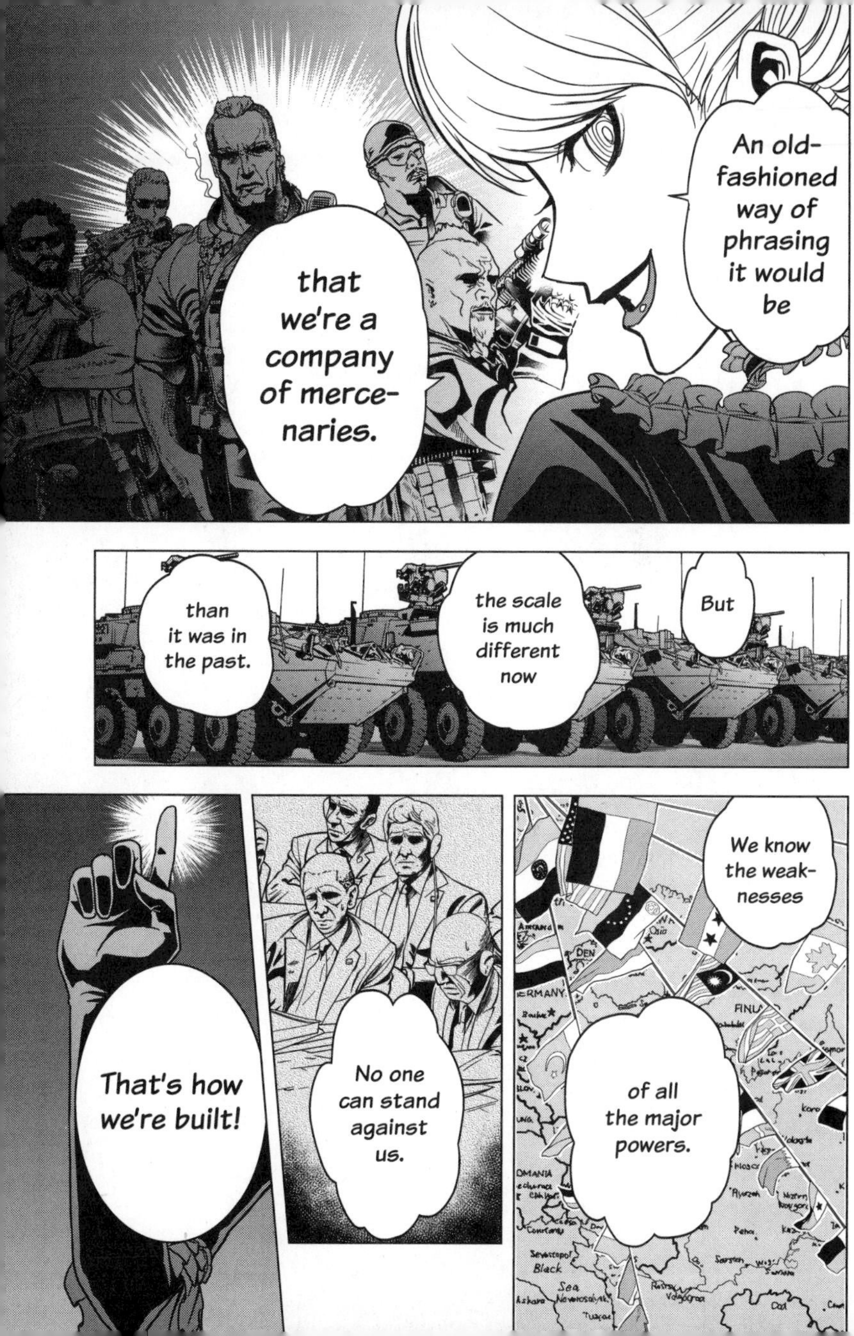
An old-fashioned way of phrasing it would be
that we're a company of mercenaries.
But
the scale is much different now
than it was in the past.
We know the weaknesses
of all the major powers.
No one can stand against us.
That's how we're built!

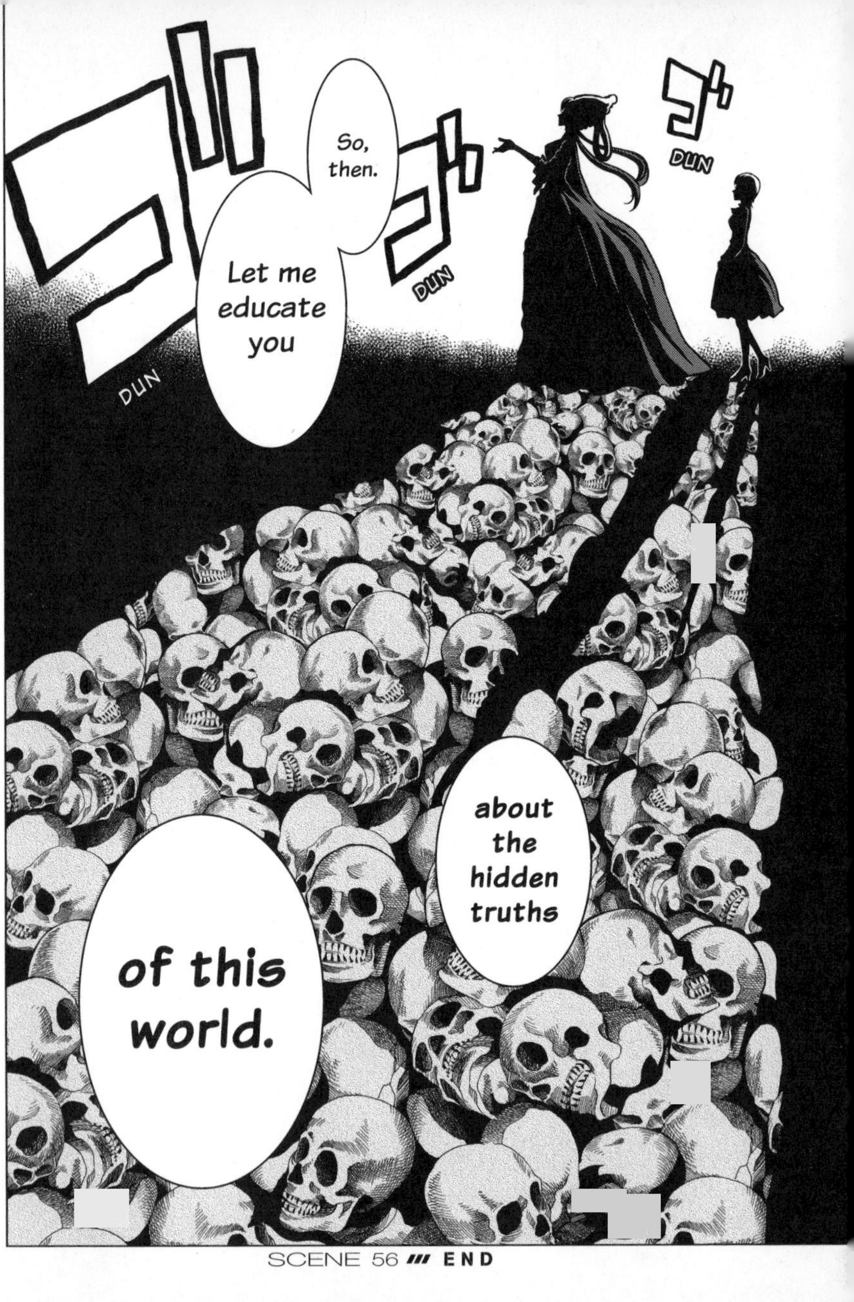
DUN
So, then.
DUN
Let me educate you
DUN
about the hidden truths
of this world.

SCENE 56 /// END

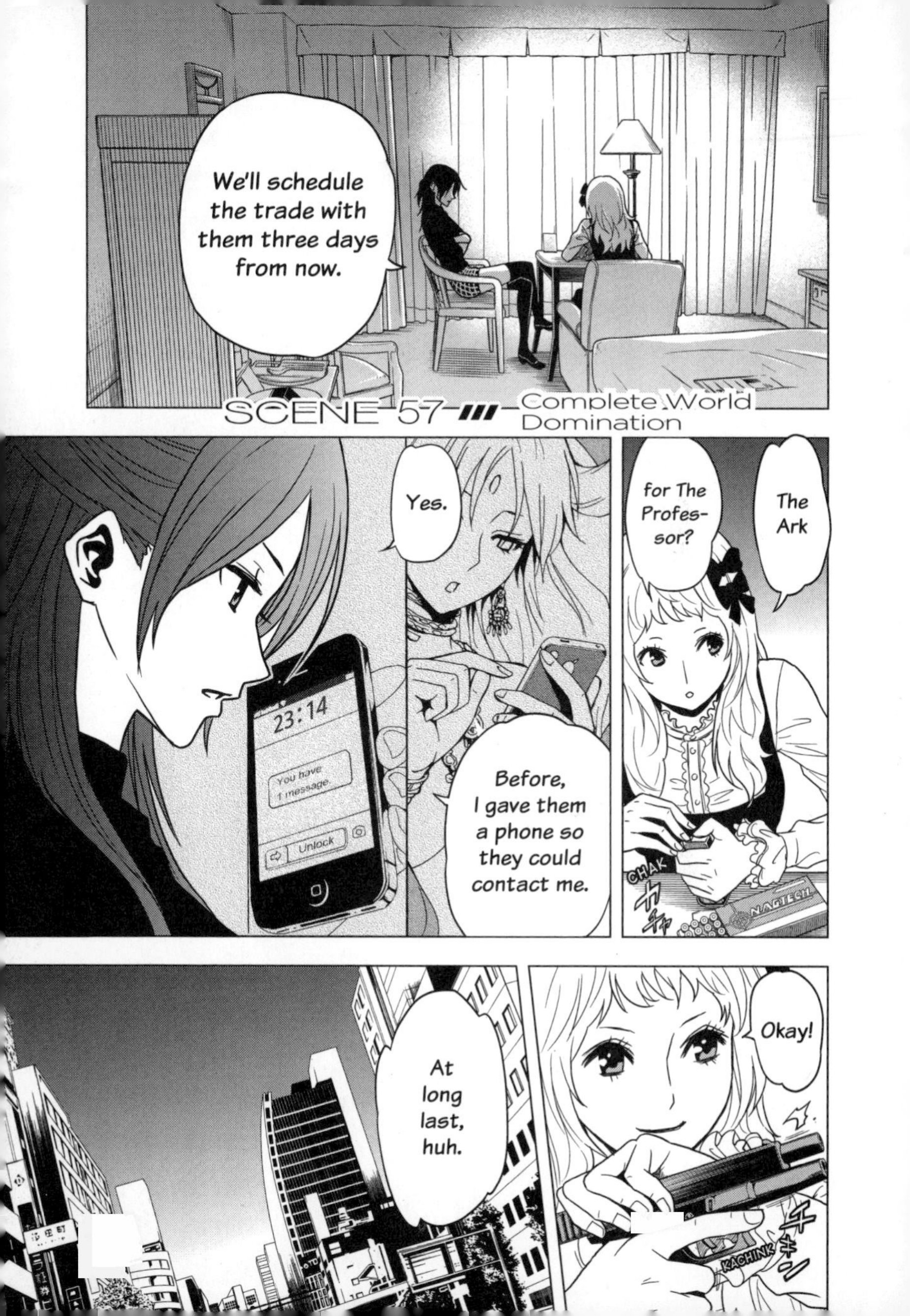
We'll schedule the trade with them three days from now.
SCENE 57 /// Complete World Domination
The Ark
for The Profes-sor?
CHAK
Yes.
Before, I gave them a phone so they could contact me.
23:14
You have 1 message.
Unlock
Okay!
KACHINK
At long last, huh.

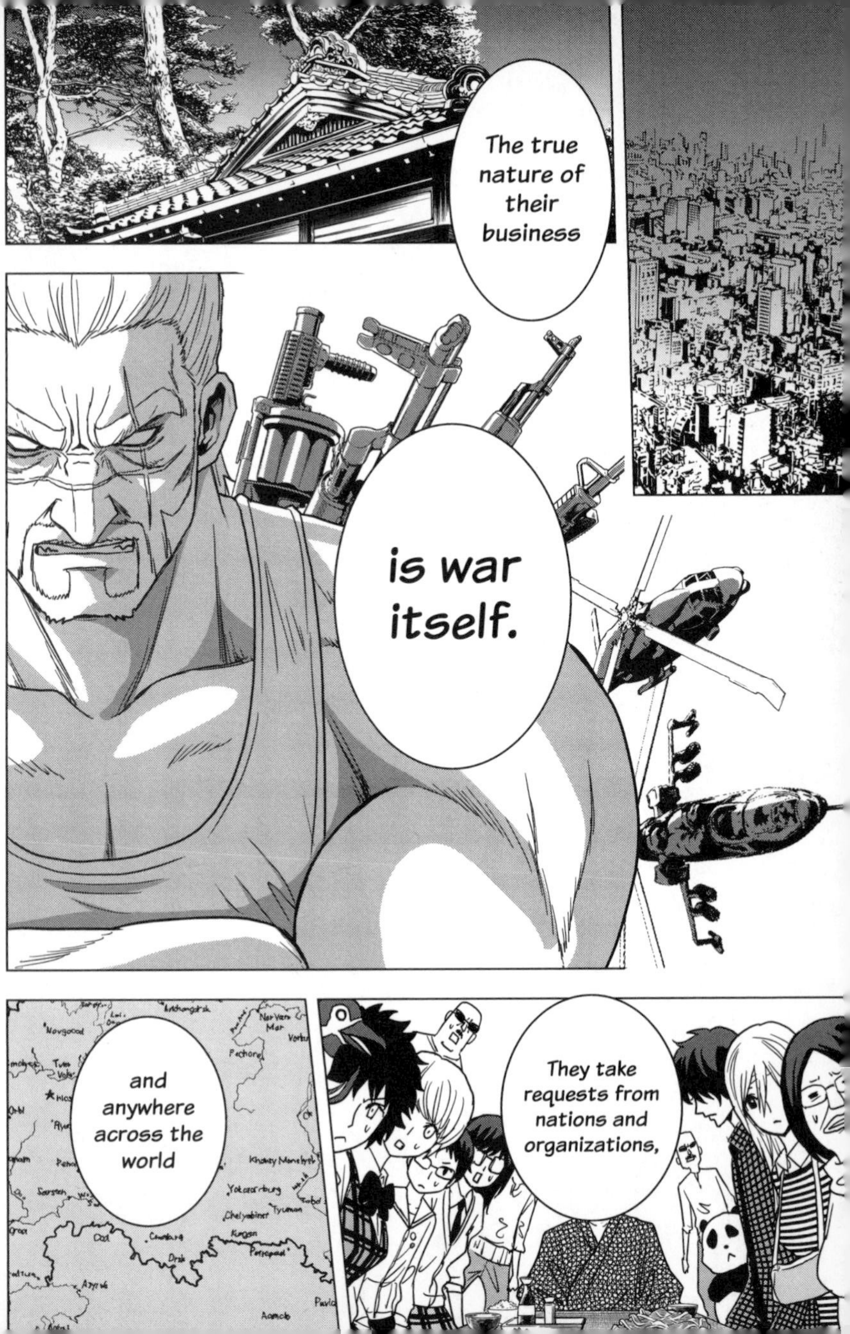
The true nature of their business
is war itself.
They take requests from nations and organizations,
and anywhere across the world

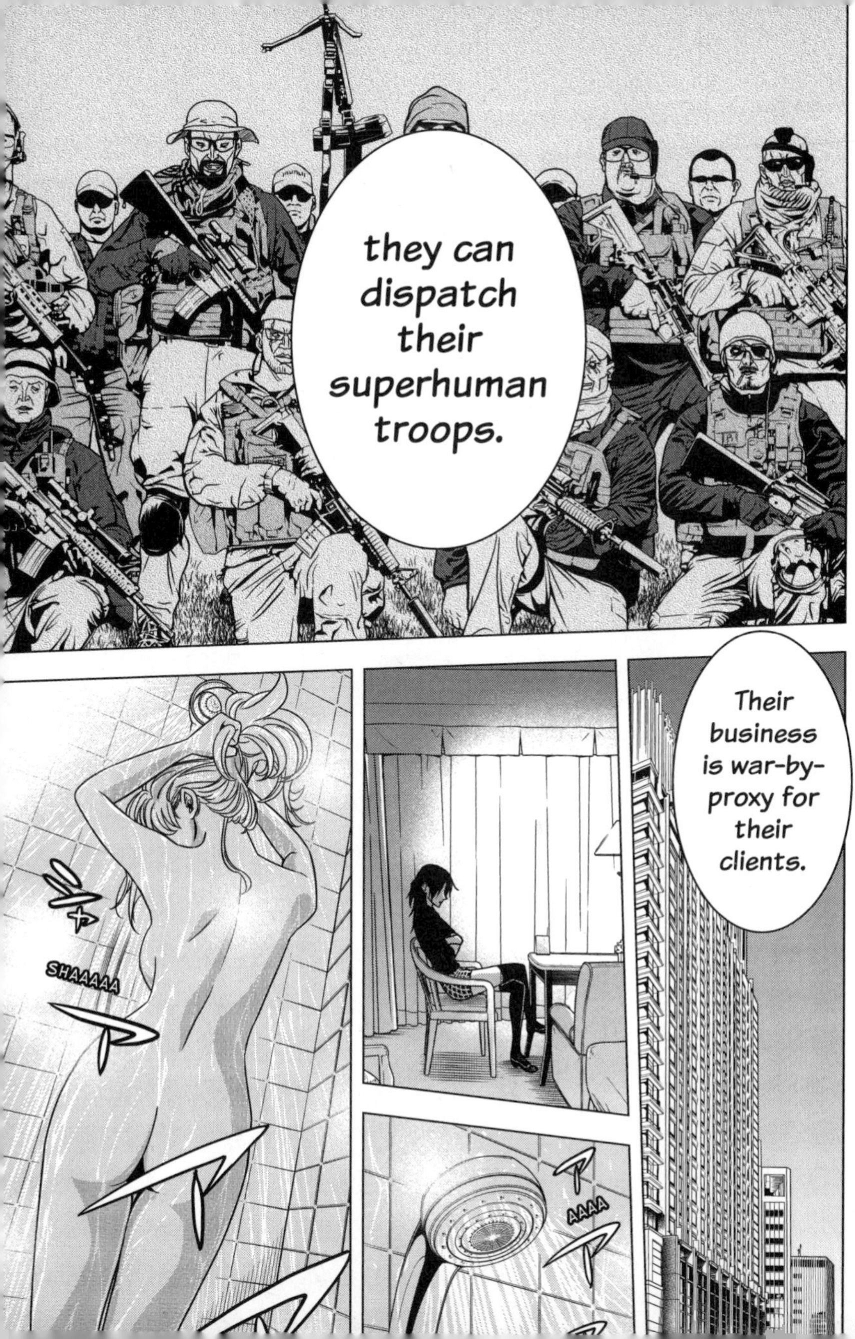
they can dispatch their superhuman troops.
Their business is war-by-proxy for their clients.
AAAA
SHAAAAA

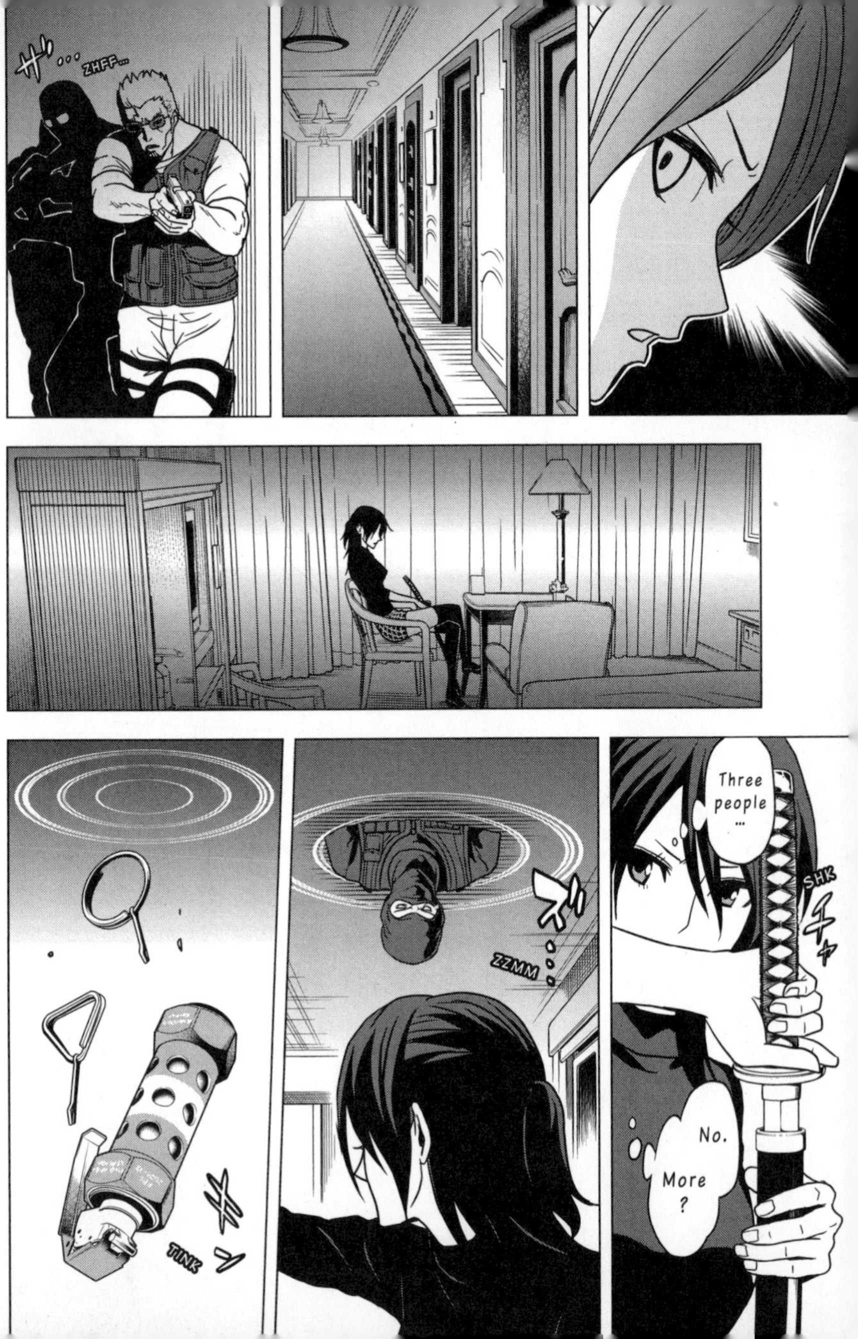
ZHFF...
Three people ...
SHK
No. More ?
ZZMM
TINK

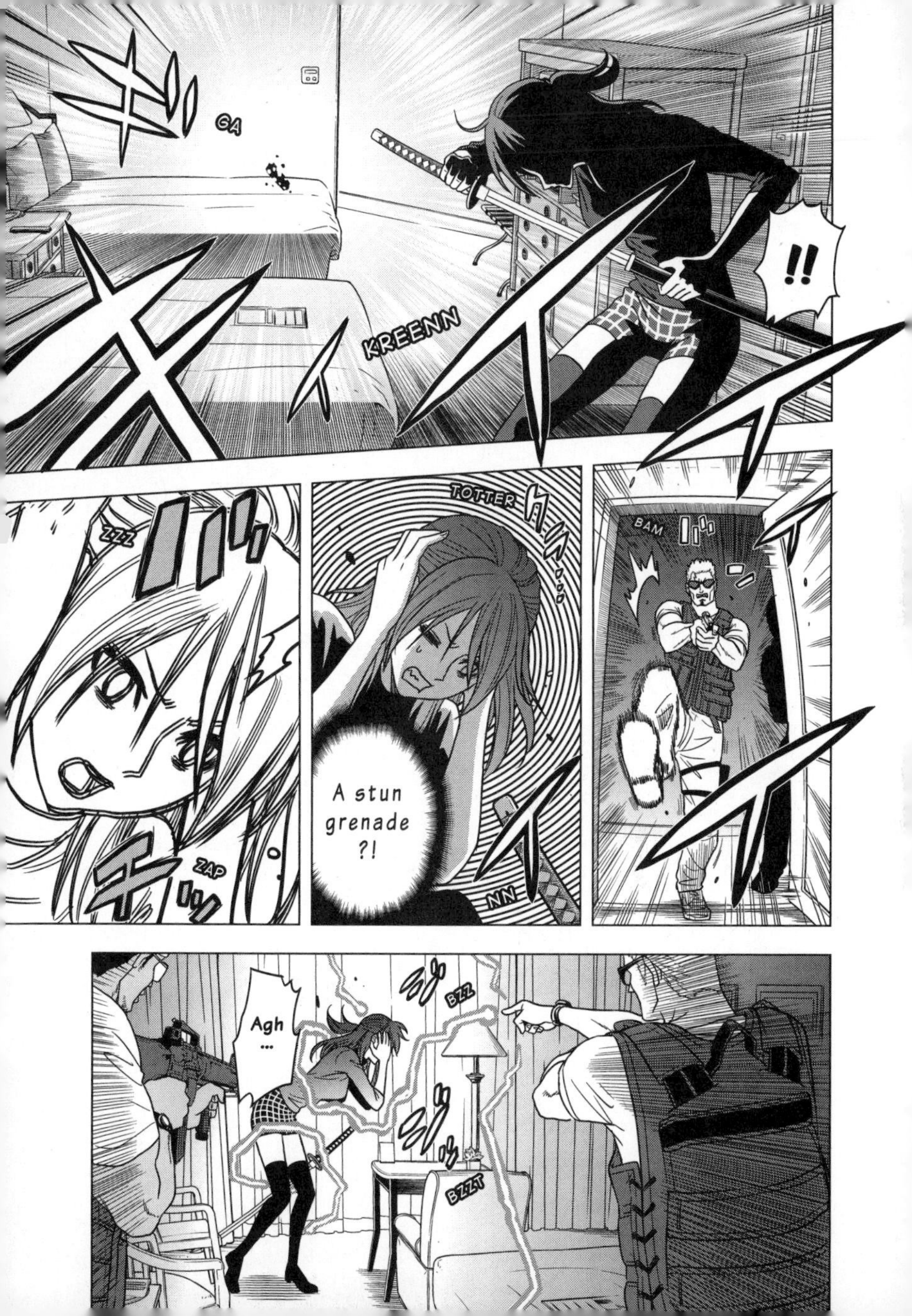
!!
GA
KREENN
BAM
TOTTER
A stun grenade ?!
NN
ZZZ
ZAP
BZZ
Agh ...
BZZT

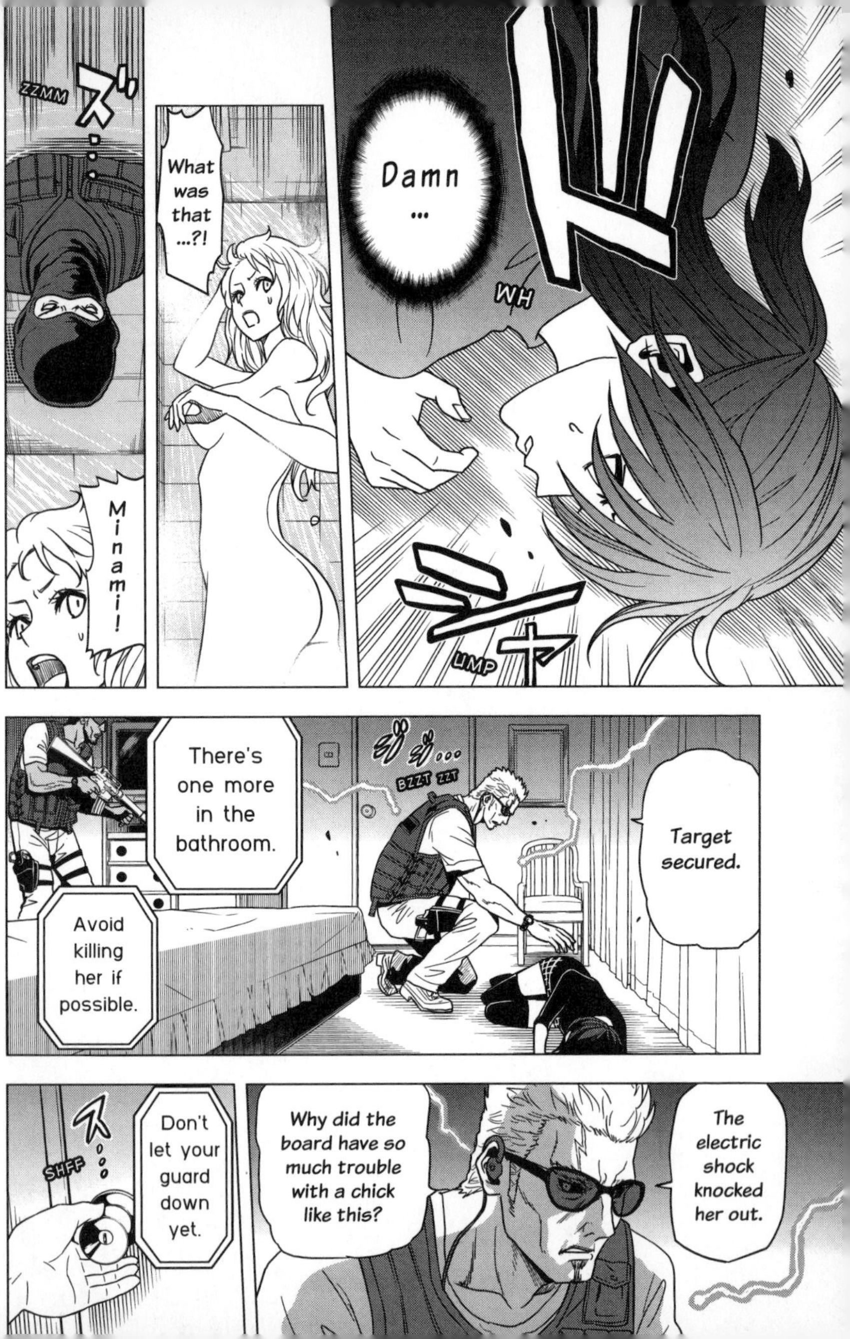
Damn ...
WH
UMP
What was that ...?!
ZZMM
Minami!
Target secured.
BZZT ZZT
There's one more in the bathroom.
Avoid killing her if possible.
The electric shock knocked her out.
Why did the board have so much trouble with a chick like this?
Don't let your guard down yet.
SHFF

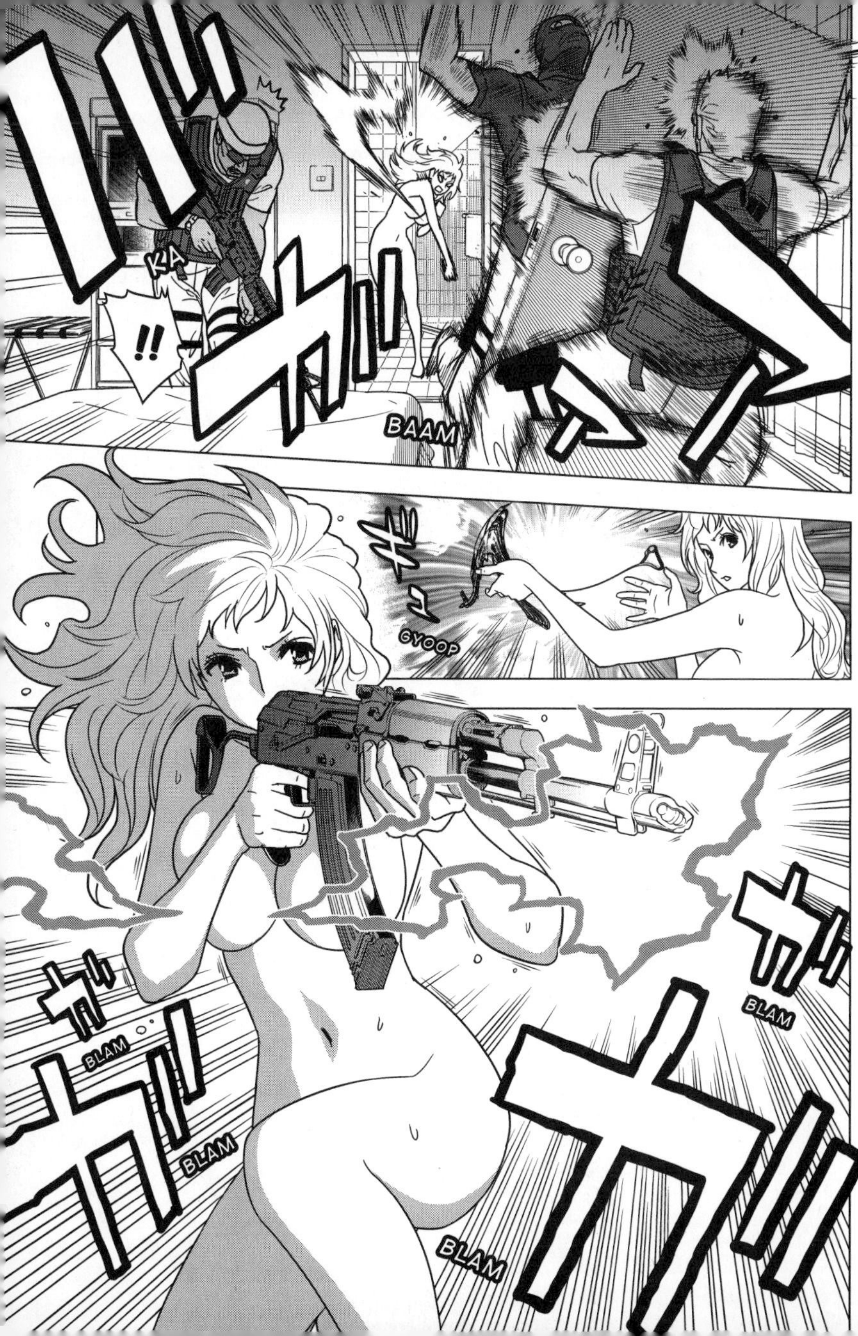
KA
!!
BAAM
GYOOP
BLAM
BLAM
BLAM
BLAM

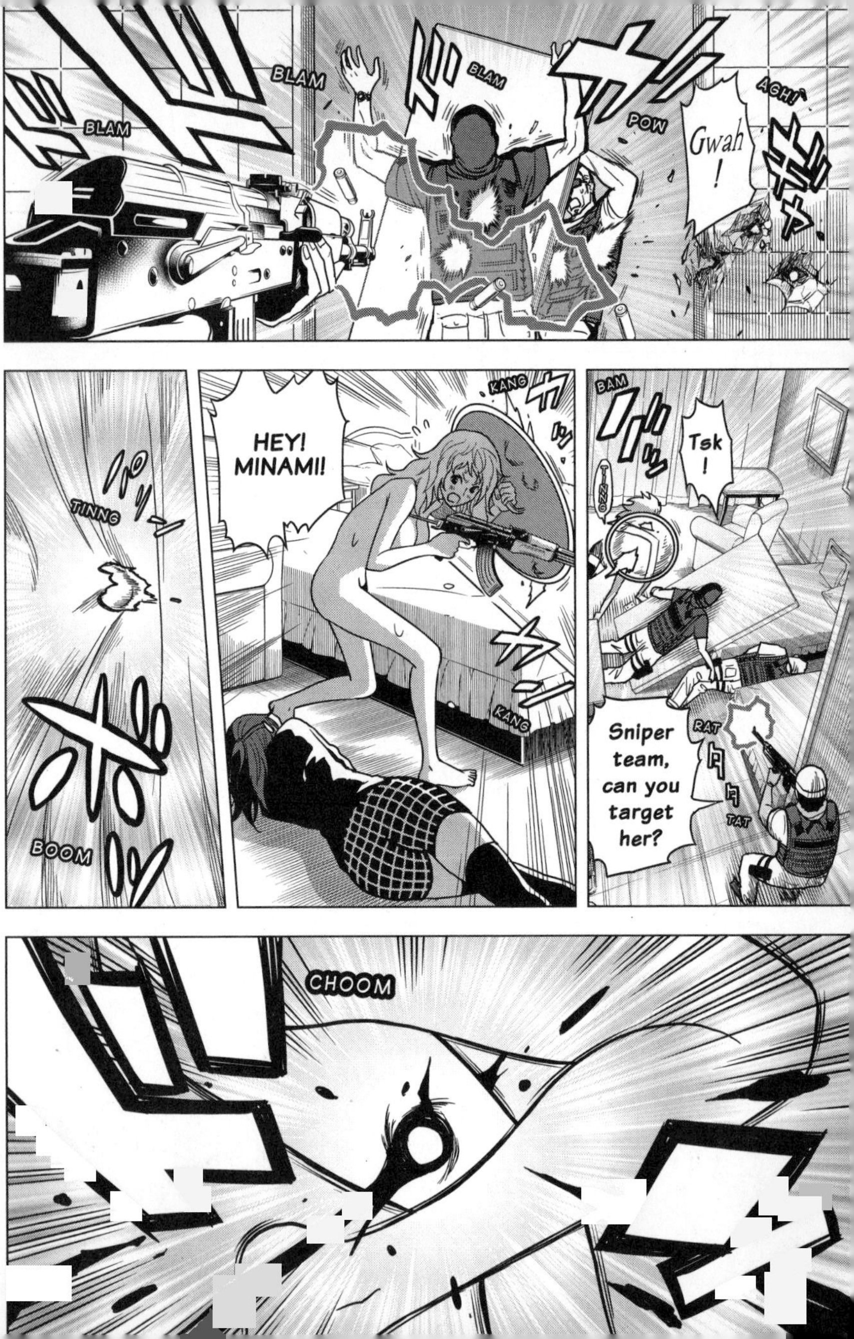
AGH!
Gwah!
POW
BLAM
BLAM
BLAM
BAM
Tsk!
TINNG
Sniper team, can you target her?
RAT
TAT
KANG
HEY! MINAMI!
KANG
TINNG
BOOM
CHOOM

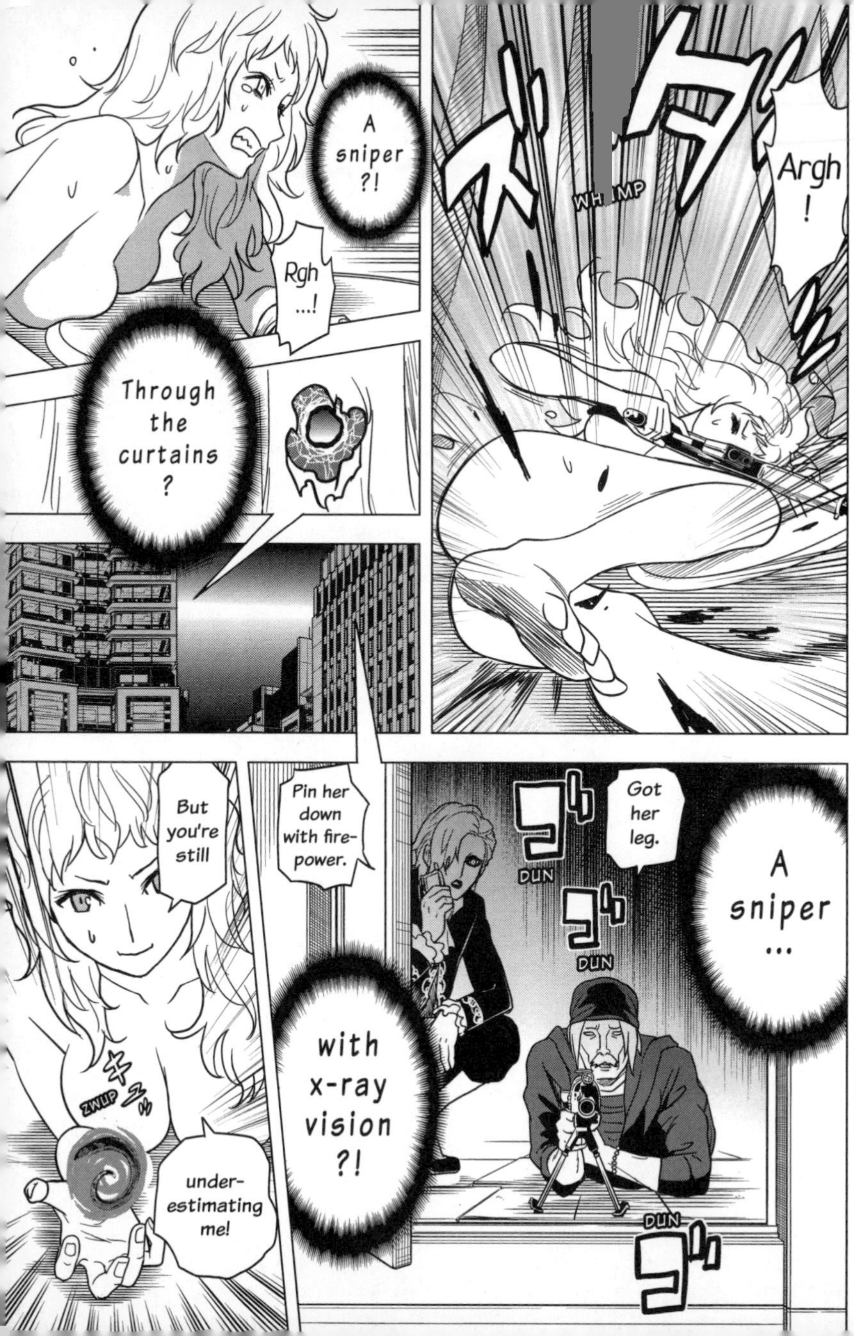
Argh!
WHUMP
A sniper?!
Rgh...!
Through the curtains?
A sniper...
Got her leg.
DUN
DUN
Pin her down with fire-power.
with x-ray vision?!
DUN
But you're still
ZWUP
under-estimating me!

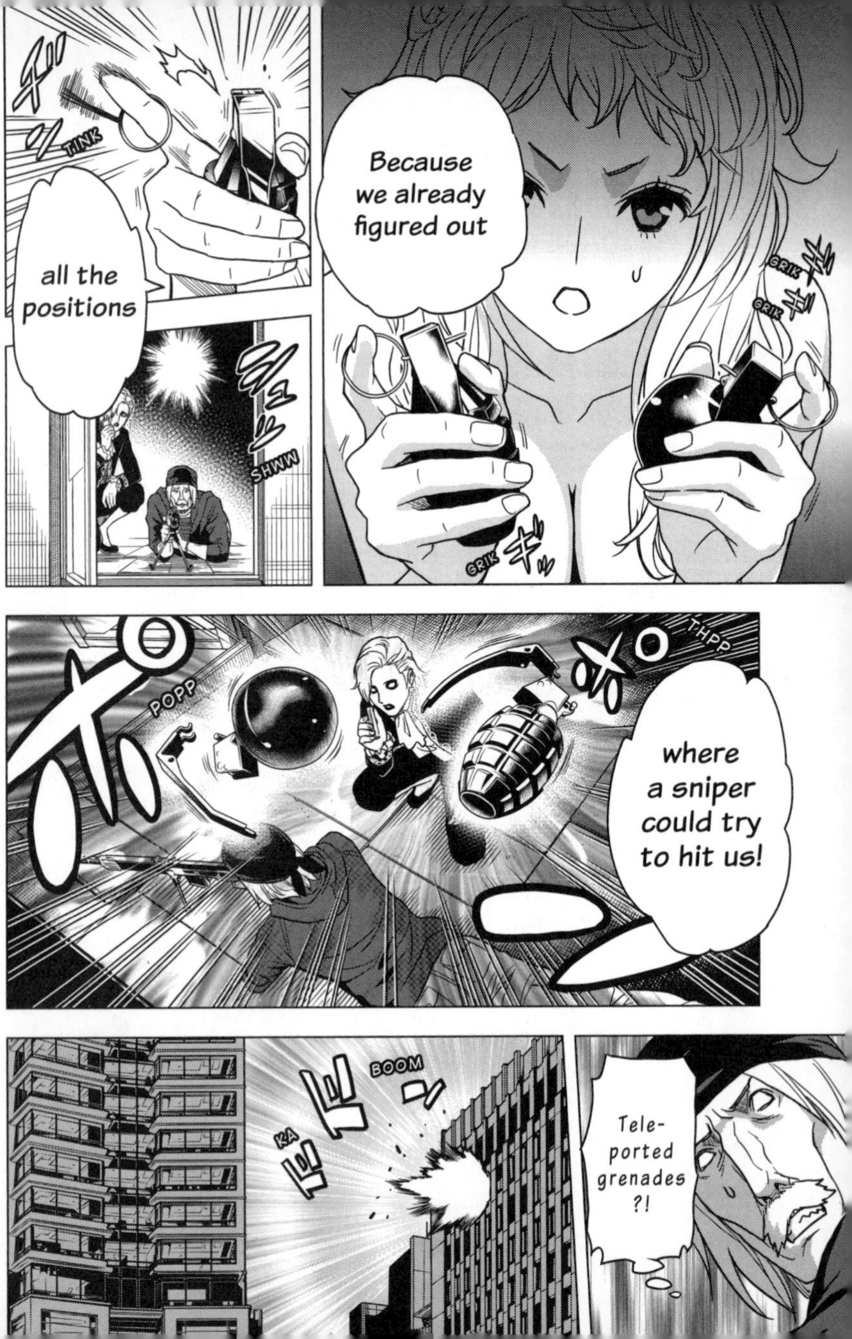
Because we already figured out
GRIK
GRIK
GRIK
TINK
all the positions
SHWW
THPP
POPP
where a sniper could try to hit us!
Tele-ported grenades ?!
BOOM
KA

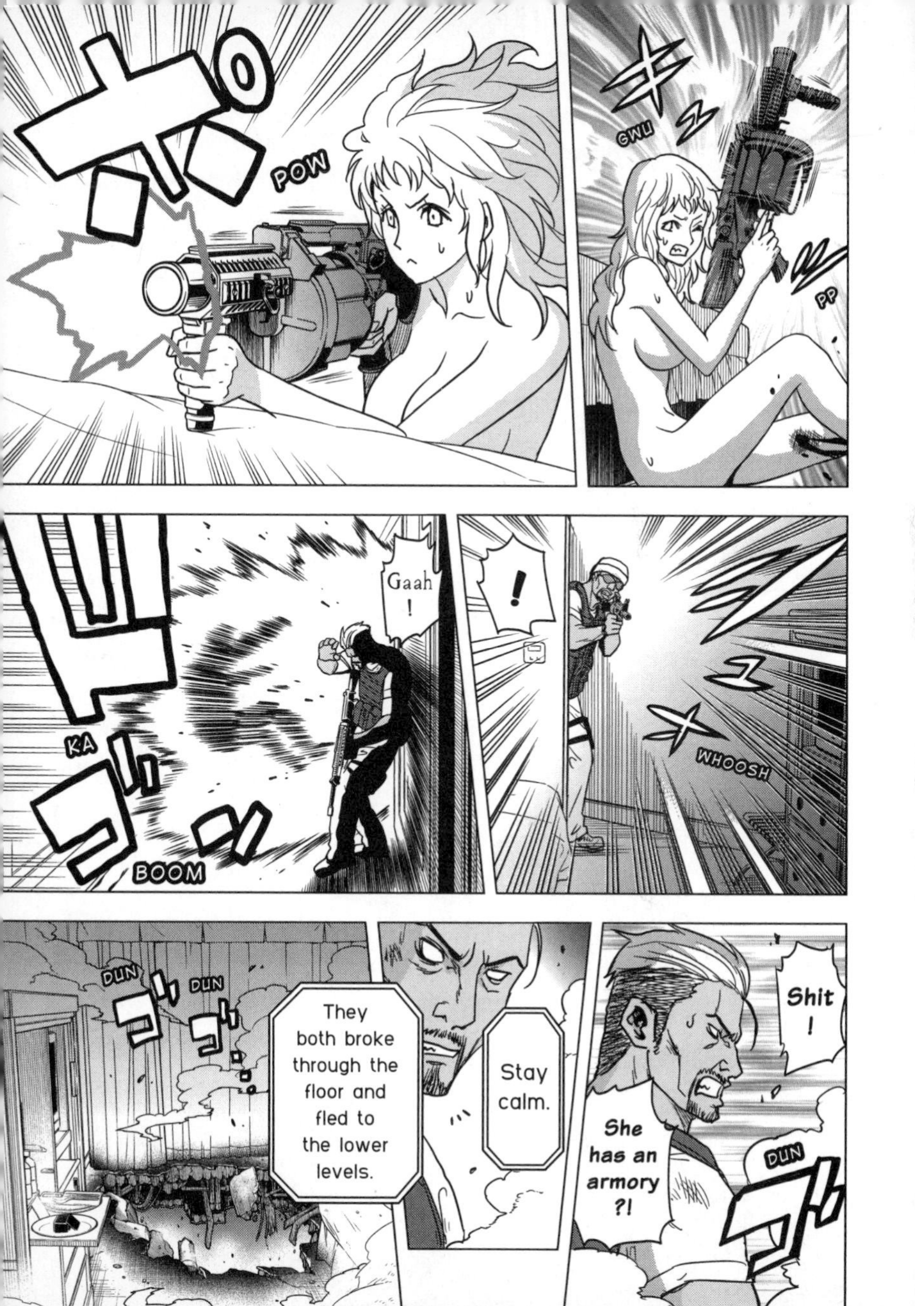
GWU
PP
POW
!
WHOOSH
Gaah!
KA
BOOM
Shit!
She has an armory?!
DUN
Stay calm.
They both broke through the floor and fled to the lower levels.
DUN
DUN

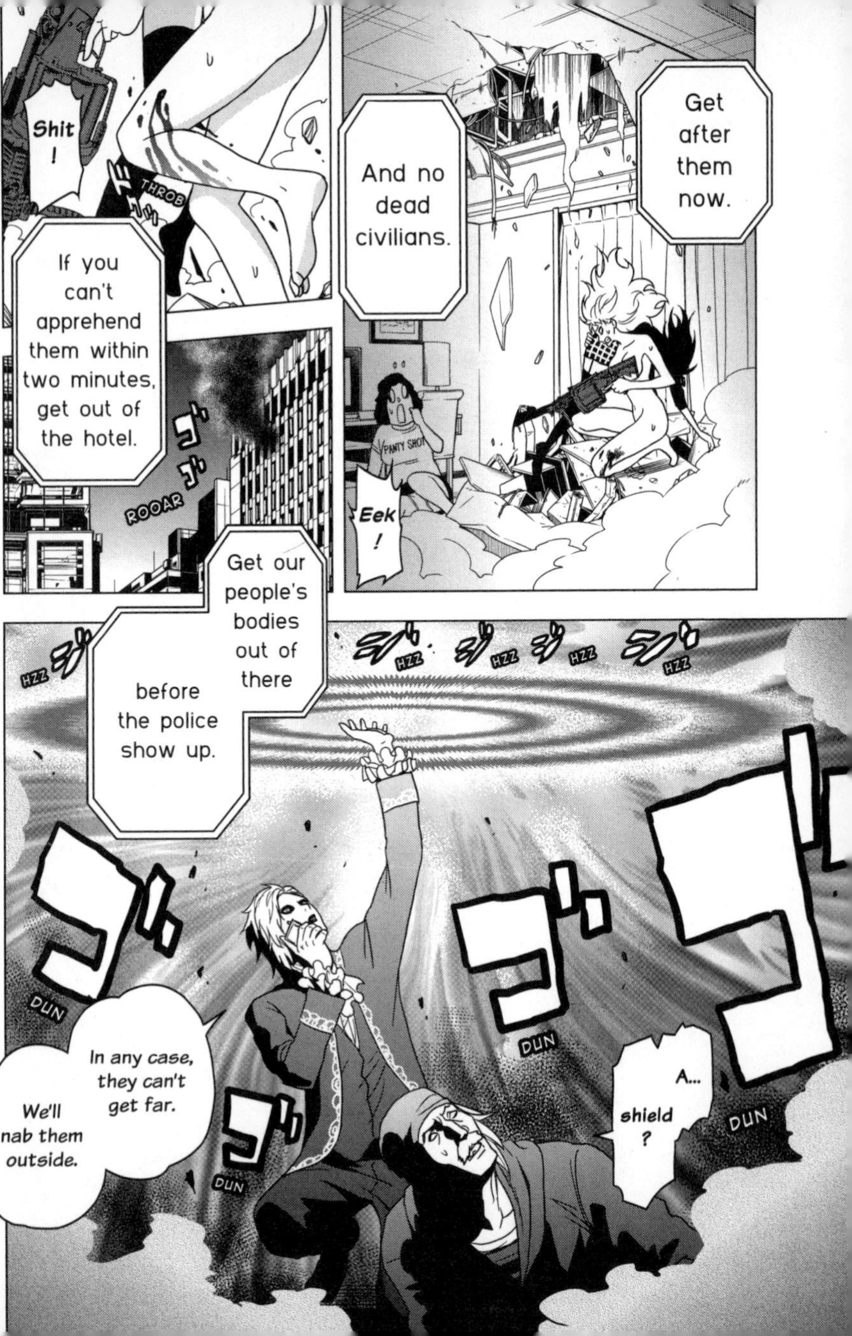
Get after them now.
And no dead civilians.
Eek!
Shit!
THROB
If you can't apprehend them within two minutes, get out of the hotel.
ROOAR
Get our people's bodies out of there before the police show up.
HZZ
HZZ
HZZ
HZZ
HZZ
DUN
DUN
A... shield?
DUN
In any case, they can't get far.
We'll nab them outside.
DUN

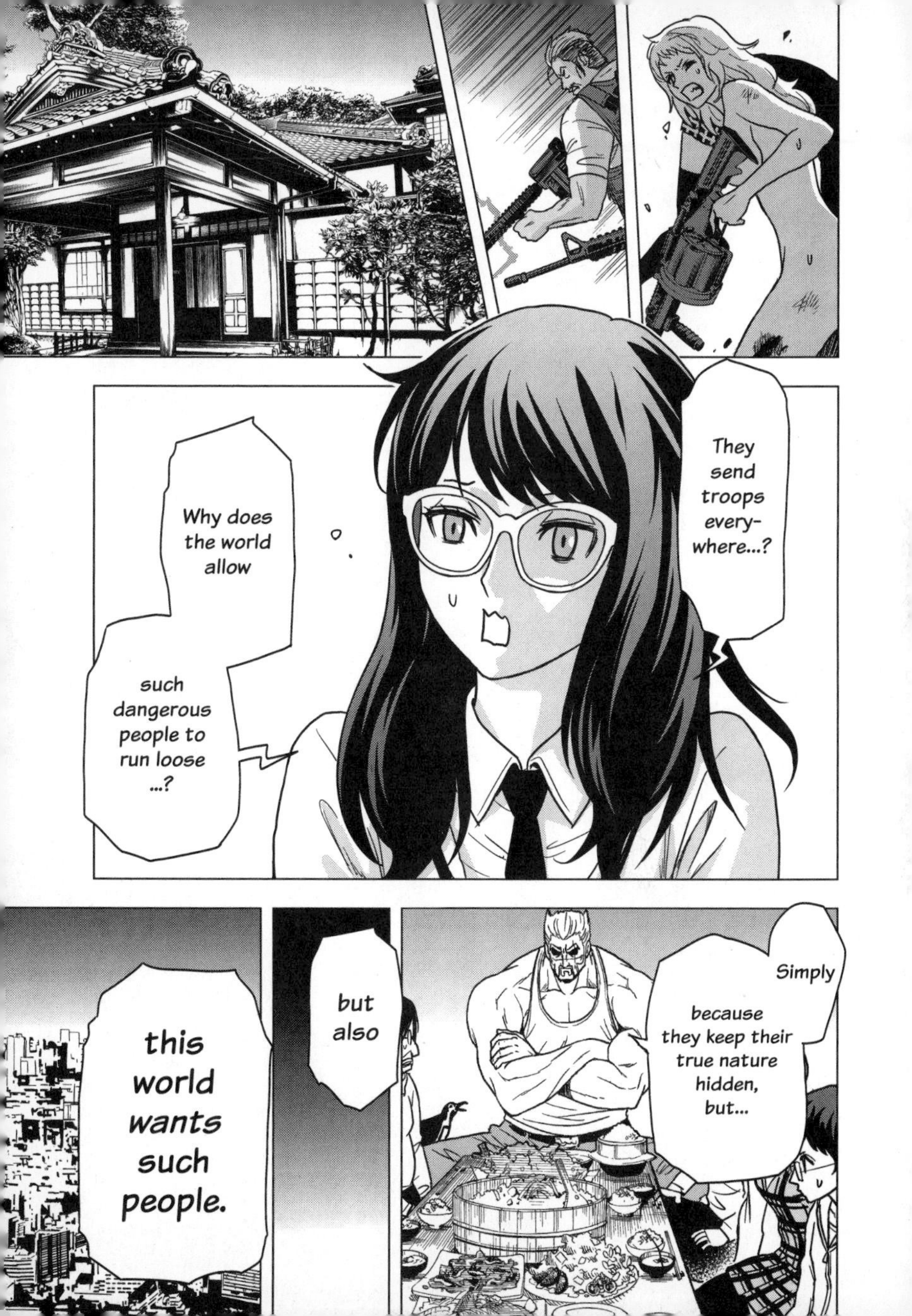
They send troops every-where...?
Why does the world allow
such dangerous people to run loose ...?
Simply
because they keep their true nature hidden, but...
but also
this world wants such people.

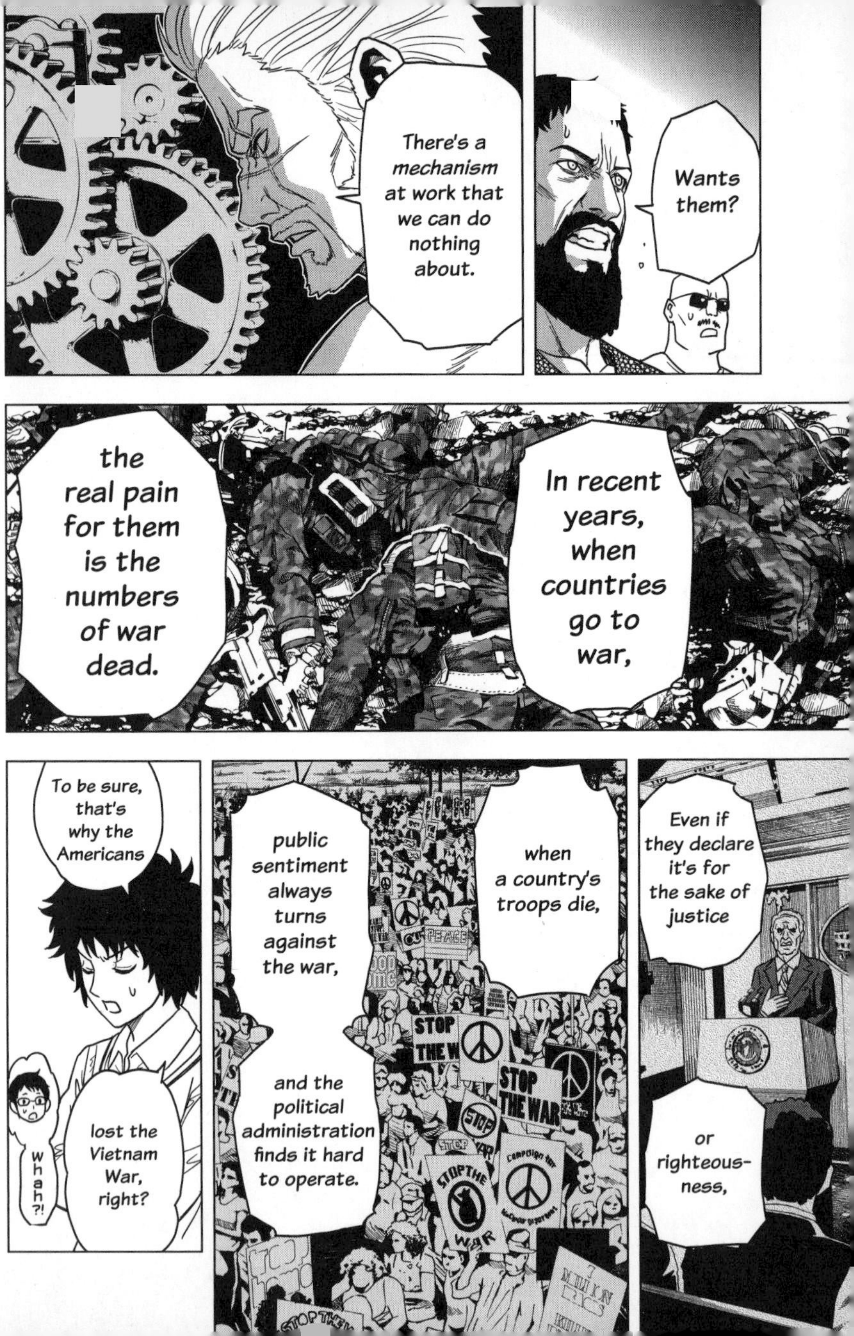
Wants them?
There's a mechanism at work that we can do nothing about.
In recent years, when countries go to war,
the real pain for them is the numbers of war dead.
Even if they declare it's for the sake of justice
or righteous-ness,
when a country's troops die,
public sentiment always turns against the war,
PEACE
STOP THE W
STOP THE WAR
and the political administration finds it hard to operate.
To be sure, that's why the Americans
lost the Vietnam War, right?
Whah?!

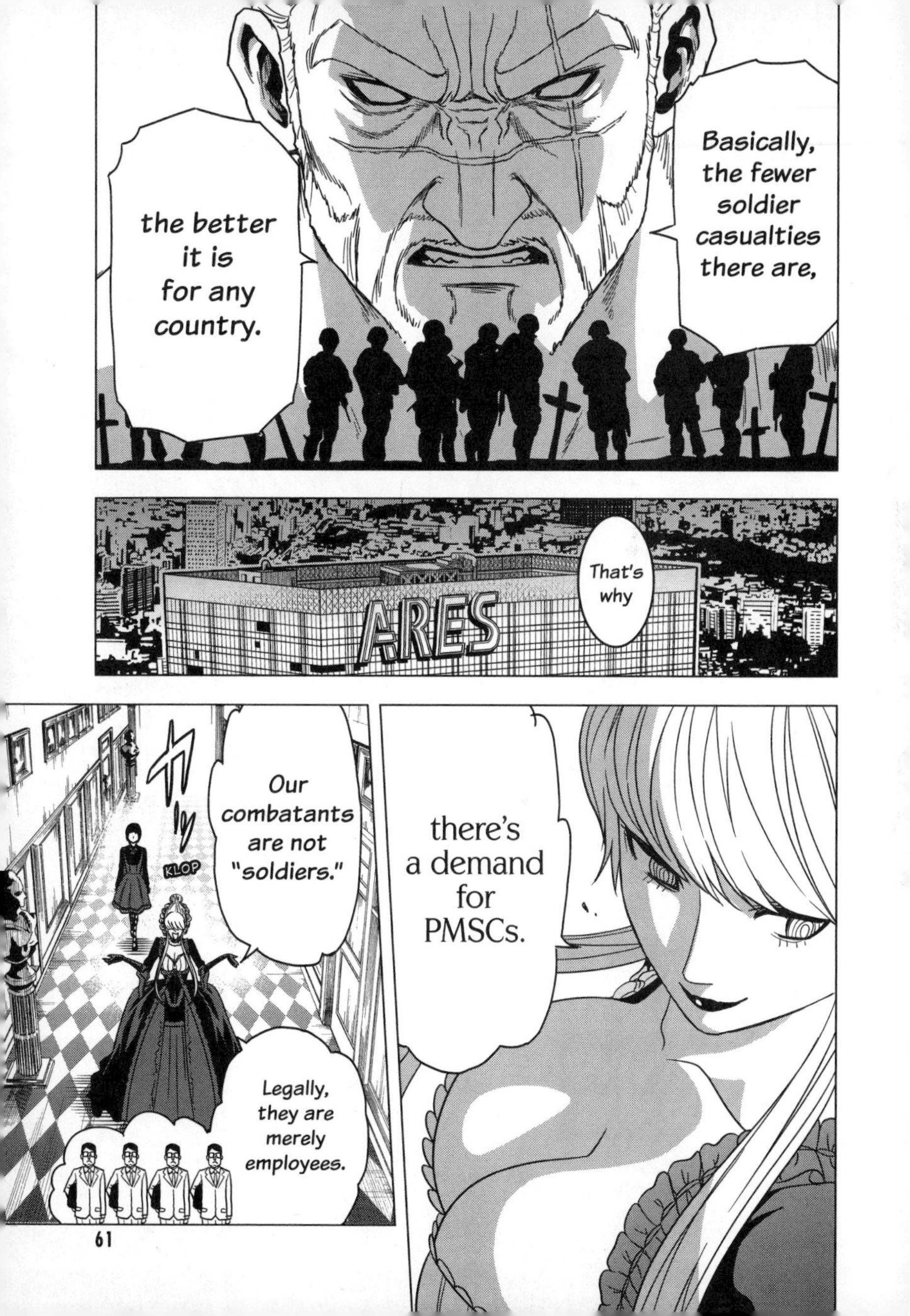
Basically, the fewer soldier casualties there are,
the better it is for any country.
ARES
That's why
there's a demand for PMSCs.
Our combatants are not "soldiers."
KLOP
Legally, they are merely employees.

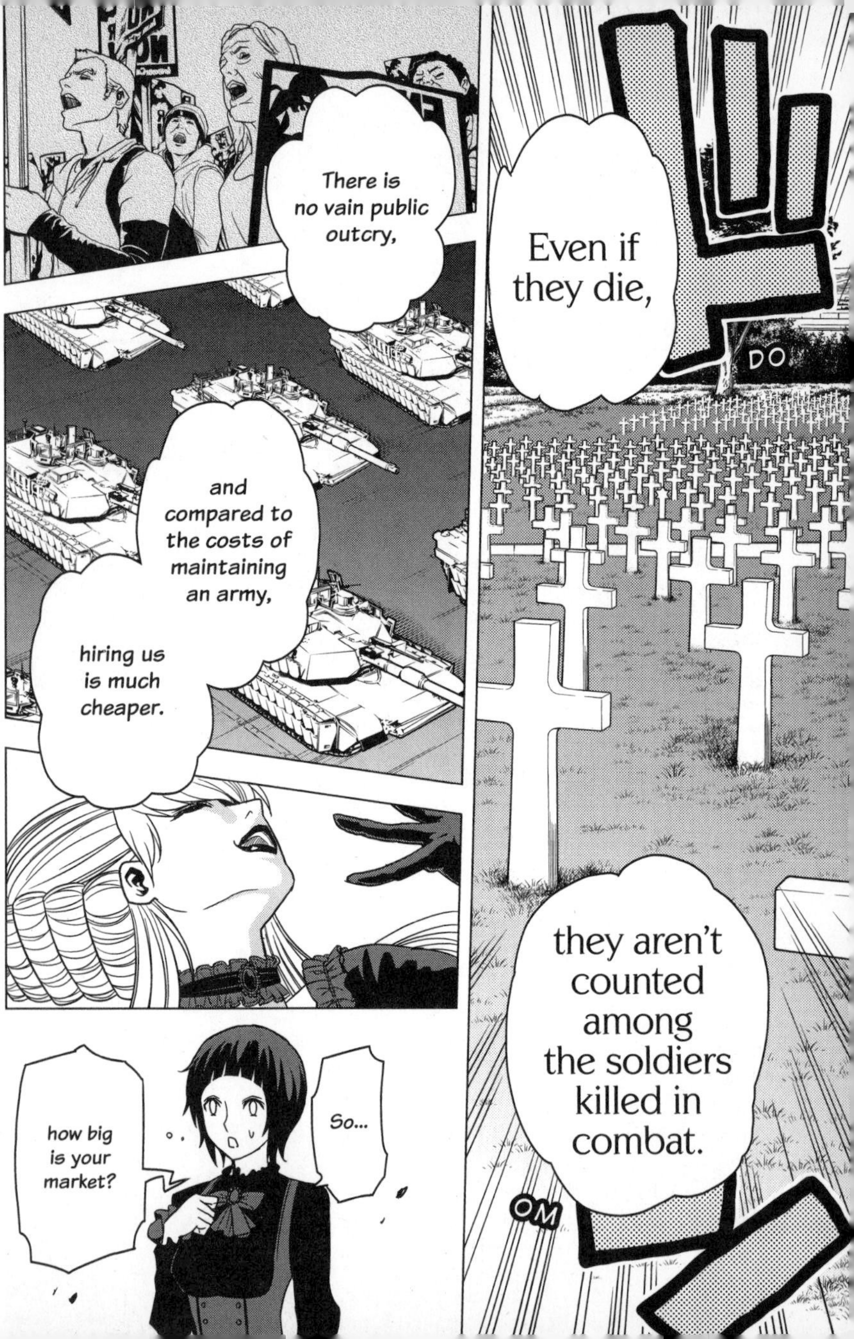
Even if they die,
DO
they aren't counted among the soldiers killed in combat.
OM
There is no vain public outcry,
and compared to the costs of maintaining an army,
hiring us is much cheaper.
So...
how big is your market?

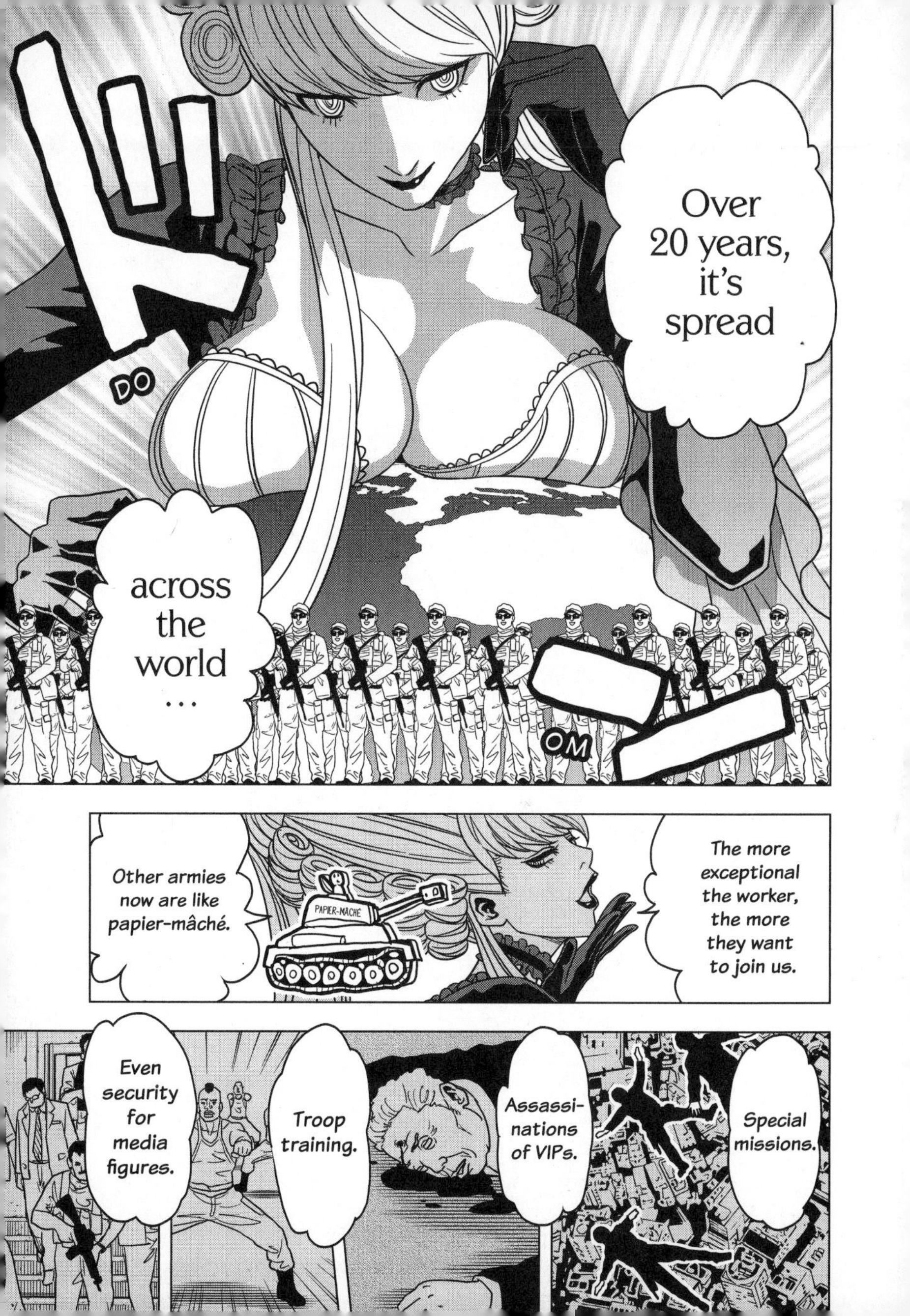
Over 20 years, it's spread
across the world …
DO
OM
The more exceptional the worker, the more they want to join us.
Other armies now are like papier-mâché.
PAPIER-MÂCHÉ
Special missions.
Assassi-nations of VIPs.
Troop training.
Even security for media figures.

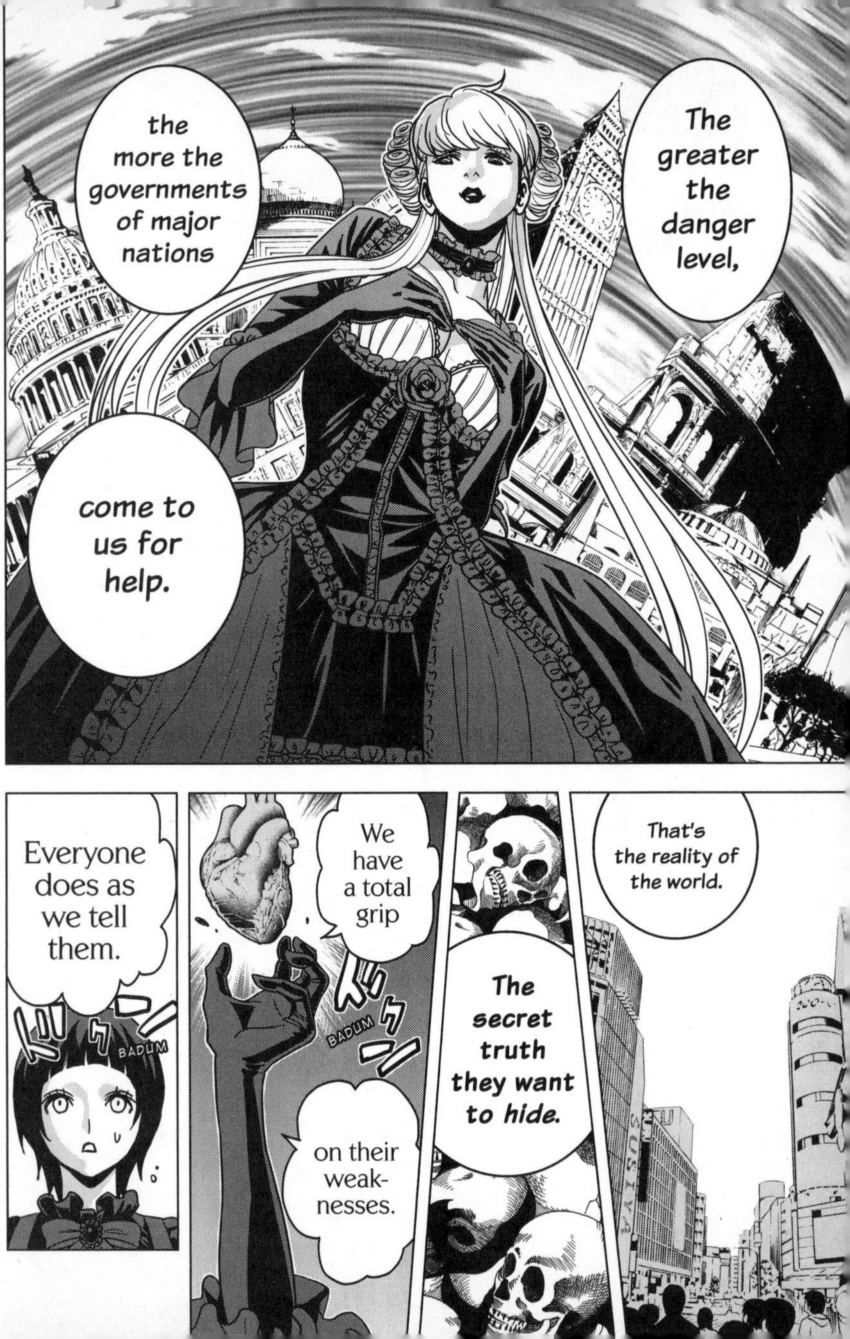
The greater the danger level,
the more the governments of major nations
come to us for help.
That's the reality of the world.
The secret truth they want to hide.
We have a total grip
BADUM
on their weaknesses.
Everyone does as we tell them.
BADUM

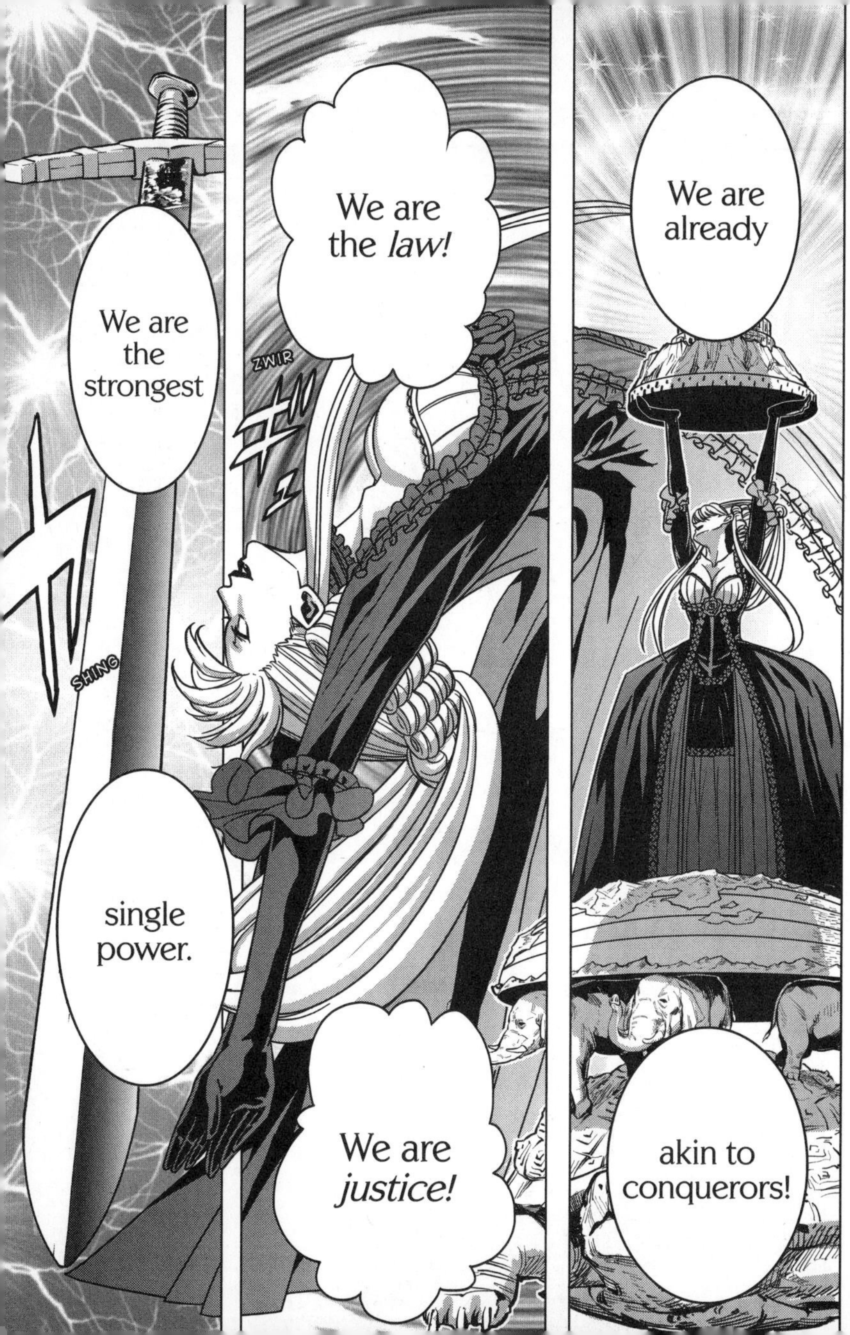
We are already
akin to conquerors!
We are the *law!*
ZWIR
We are *justice!*
We are the strongest
single power.
SHING

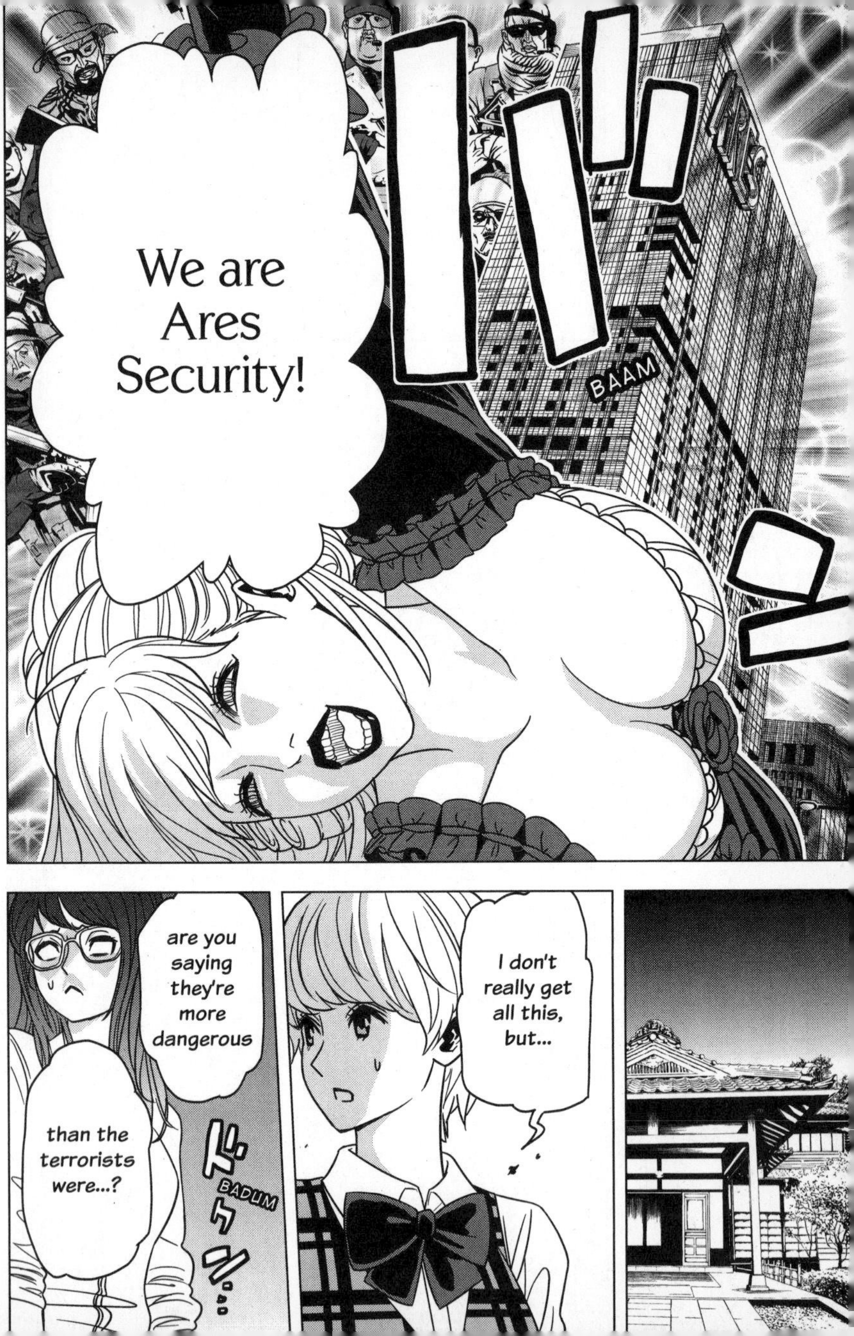
We are Ares Security!
BAAM
I don't really get all this, but...
are you saying they're more dangerous
than the terrorists were...?
BADUM

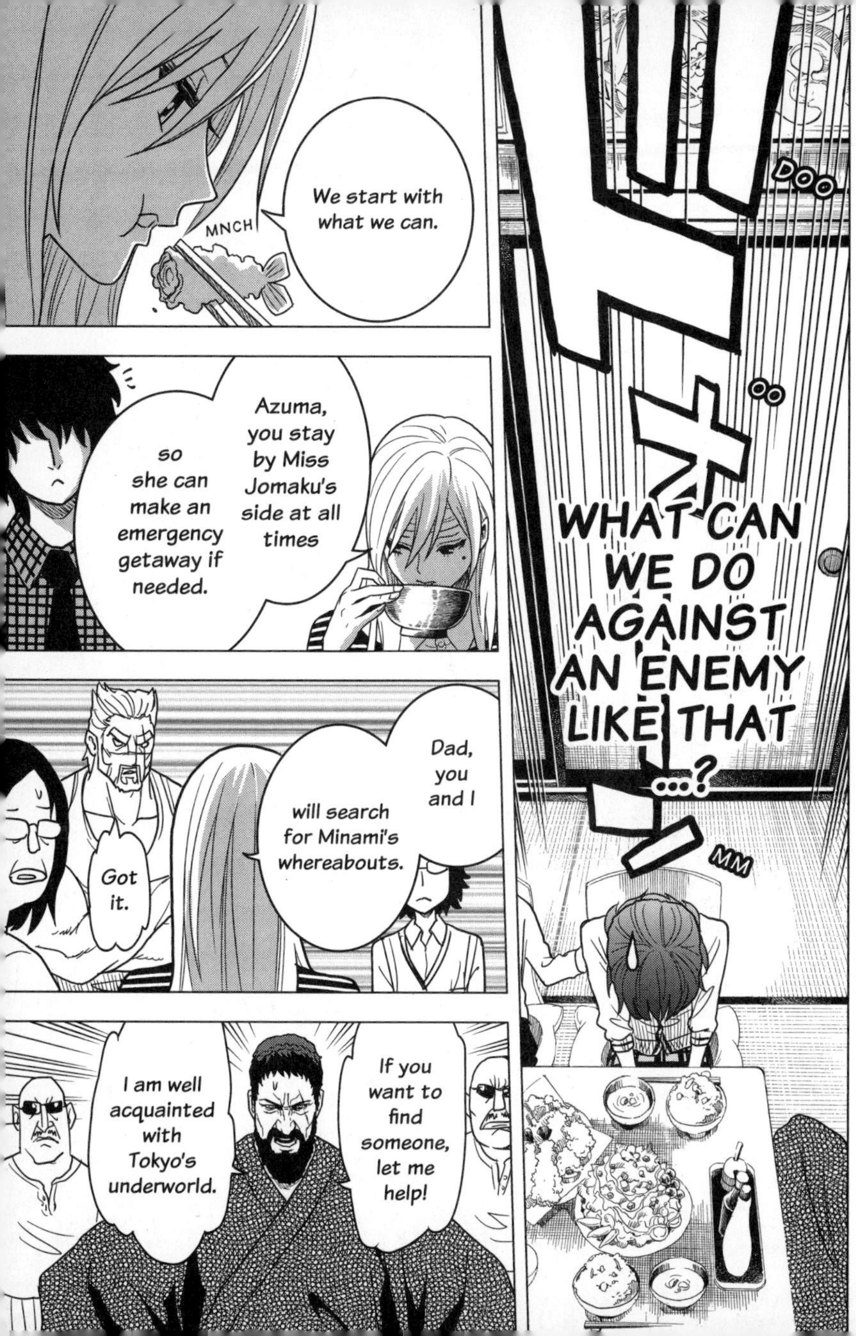
DOO
WHAT CAN WE DO AGAINST AN ENEMY LIKE THAT ...?
MM
We start with what we can.
MNCH
Azuma, you stay by Miss Jomaku's side at all times
so she can make an emergency getaway if needed.
Dad, you and I
will search for Minami's whereabouts.
Got it.
If you want to find someone, let me help!
I am well acquainted with Tokyo's underworld.

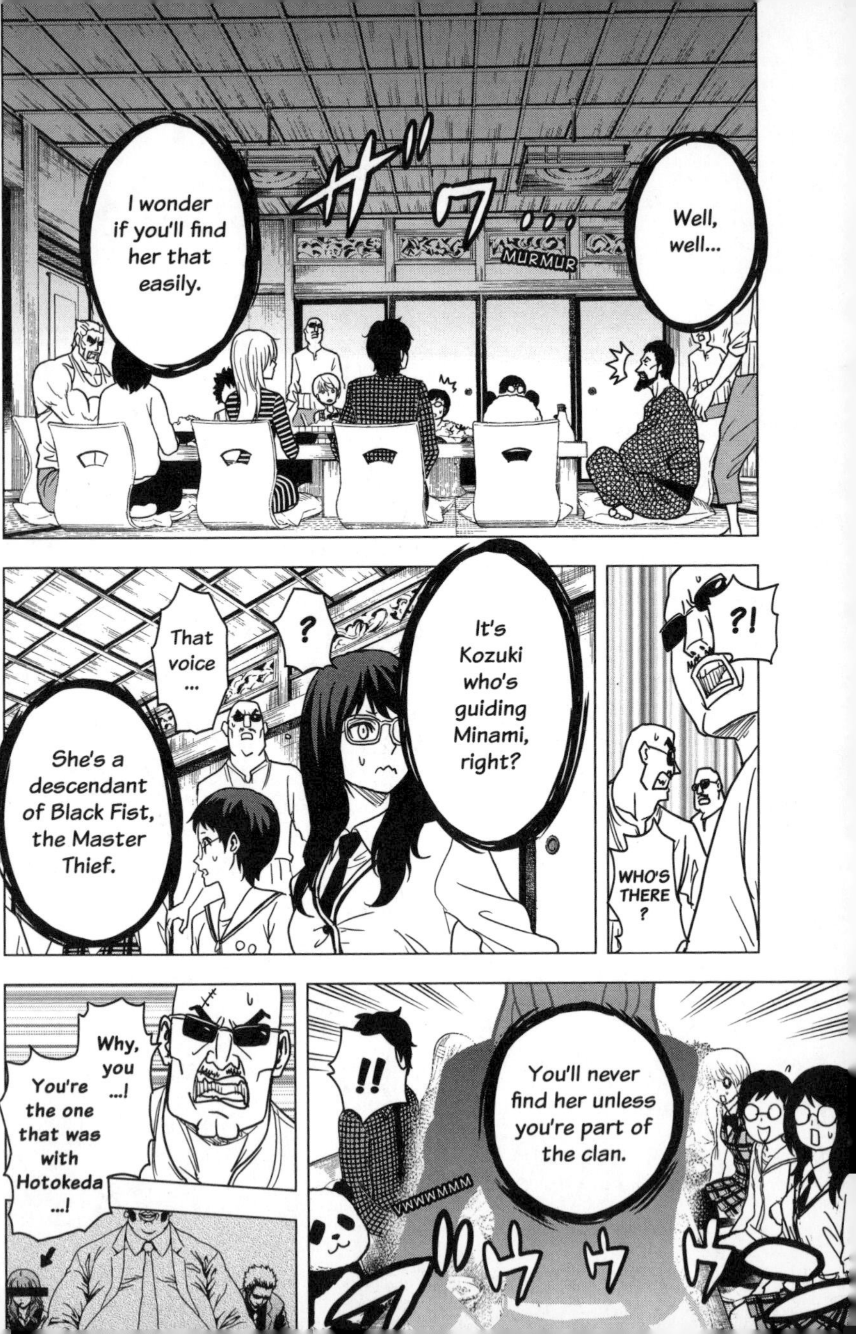
Well, well...
MURMUR
I wonder if you'll find her that easily.
?!
WHO'S THERE ?
It's Kozuki who's guiding Minami, right?
?
That voice ...
She's a descendant of Black Fist, the Master Thief.
You'll never find her unless you're part of the clan.
!!
VWWWMMM
Why, you ...!
You're the one that was with Hotokeda ...!

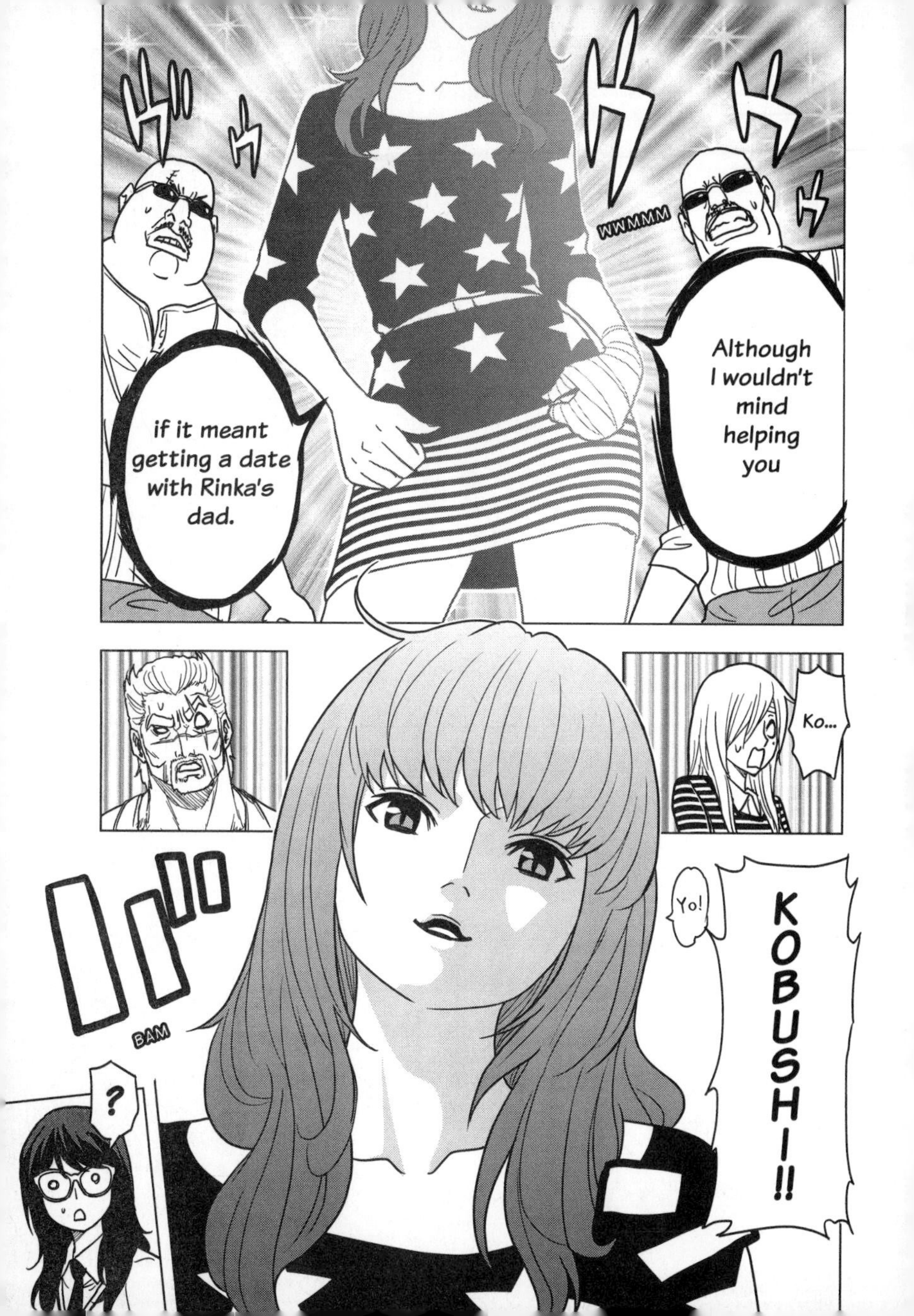
Although I wouldn't mind helping you
WWMMM
if it meant getting a date with Rinka's dad.
Ko...
Yo!
KOBUSHI!!
BAM
?

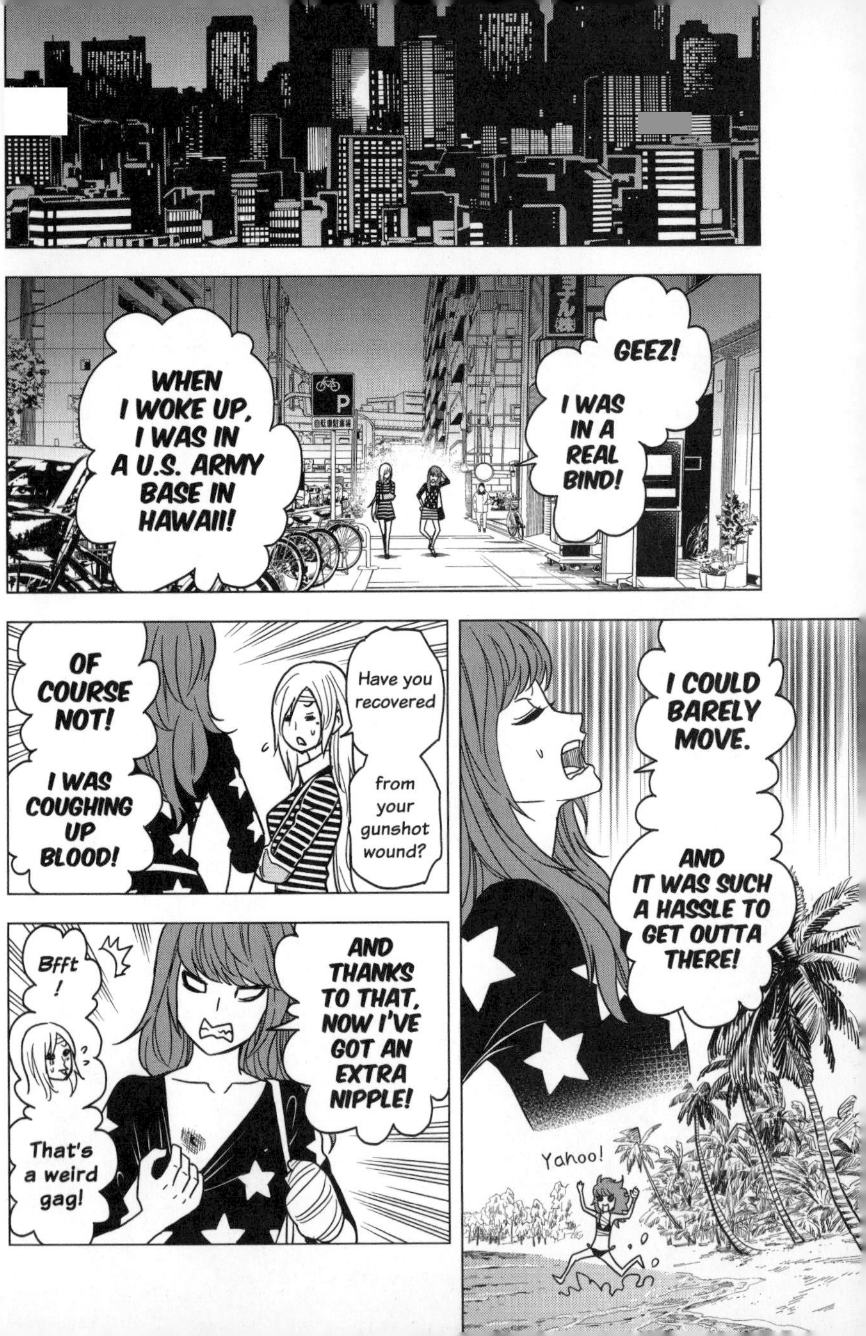
GEEZ!
I WAS IN A REAL BIND!
WHEN I WOKE UP, I WAS IN A U.S. ARMY BASE IN HAWAII!
I COULD BARELY MOVE.
AND IT WAS SUCH A HASSLE TO GET OUTTA THERE!
Yahoo!
Have you recovered from your gunshot wound?
OF COURSE NOT! I WAS COUGHING UP BLOOD!
AND THANKS TO THAT, NOW I'VE GOT AN EXTRA NIPPLE!
Bfft!
That's a weird gag!

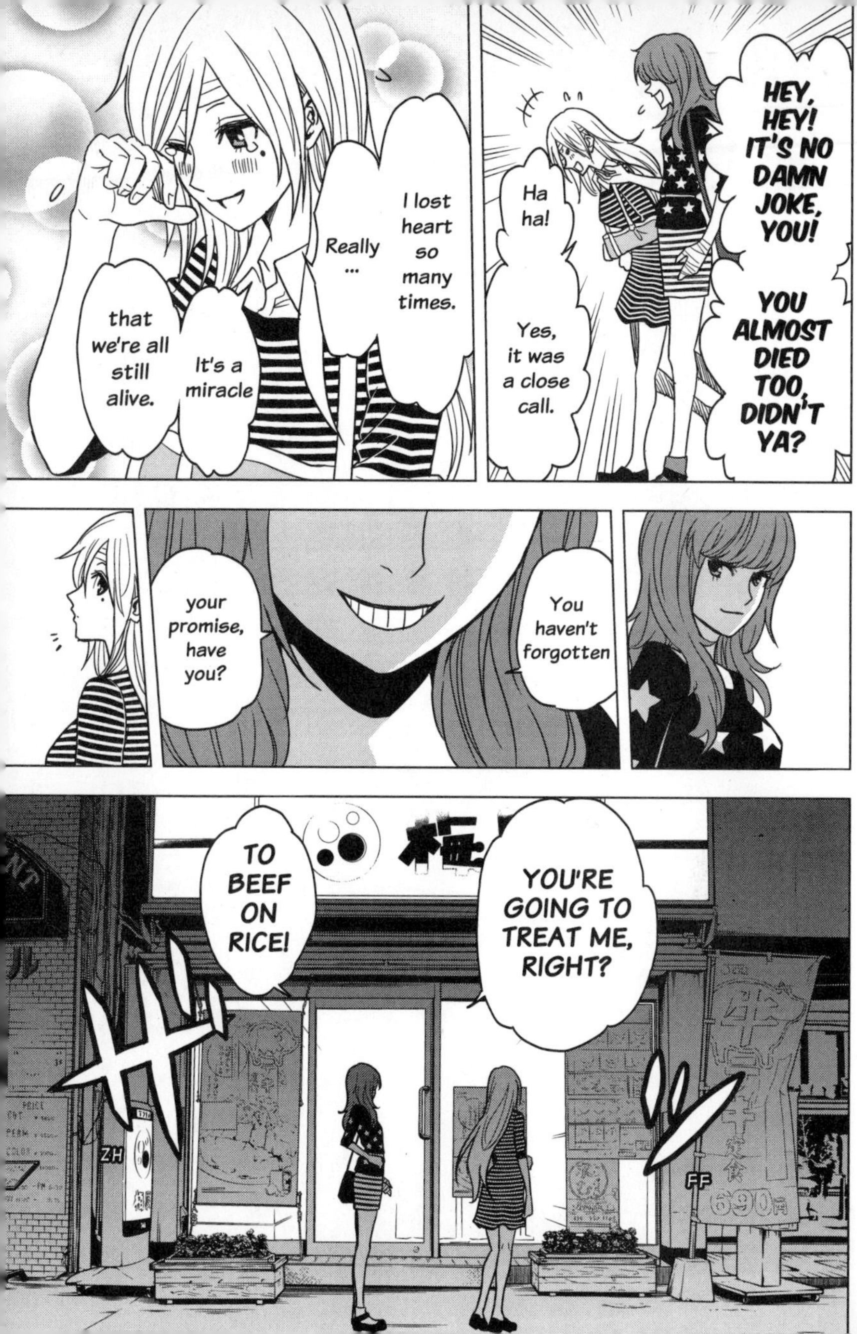
HEY, HEY! IT'S NO DAMN JOKE, YOU!
YOU ALMOST DIED TOO, DIDN'T YA?
Ha ha!
Yes, it was a close call.
Really ...
I lost heart so many times.
It's a miracle
that we're all still alive.
You haven't forgotten
your promise, have you?
YOU'RE GOING TO TREAT ME, RIGHT?
TO BEEF ON RICE!

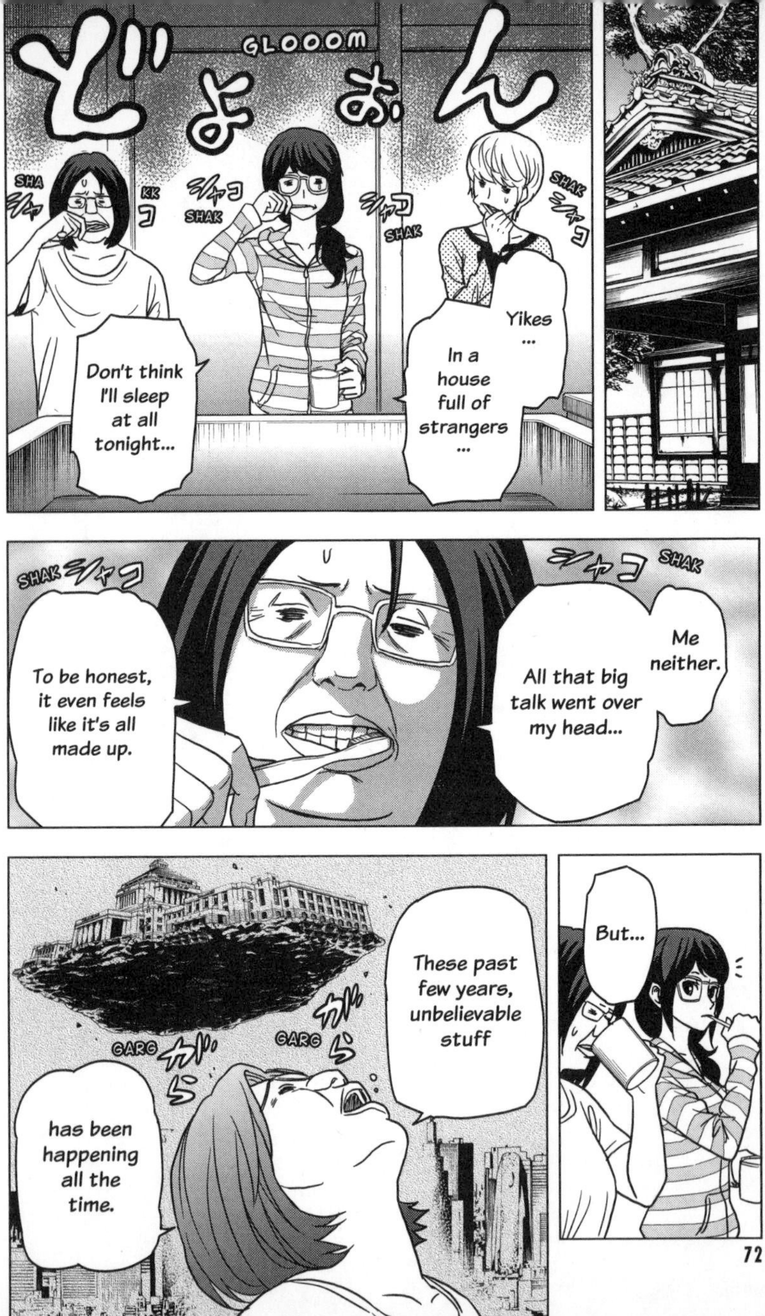
どよぉん
GLOOOM
SHAK シャコ
Yikes... In a house full of strangers...
SHAK シャコ
SHAK
SHA シャ KK コ
Don't think I'll sleep at all tonight...
SHAK シャコ
Me neither.
All that big talk went over my head...
To be honest, it even feels like it's all made up.
SHAK シャコ
But...
These past few years, unbelievable stuff
GARG ガら
GARG ガら
has been happening all the time.

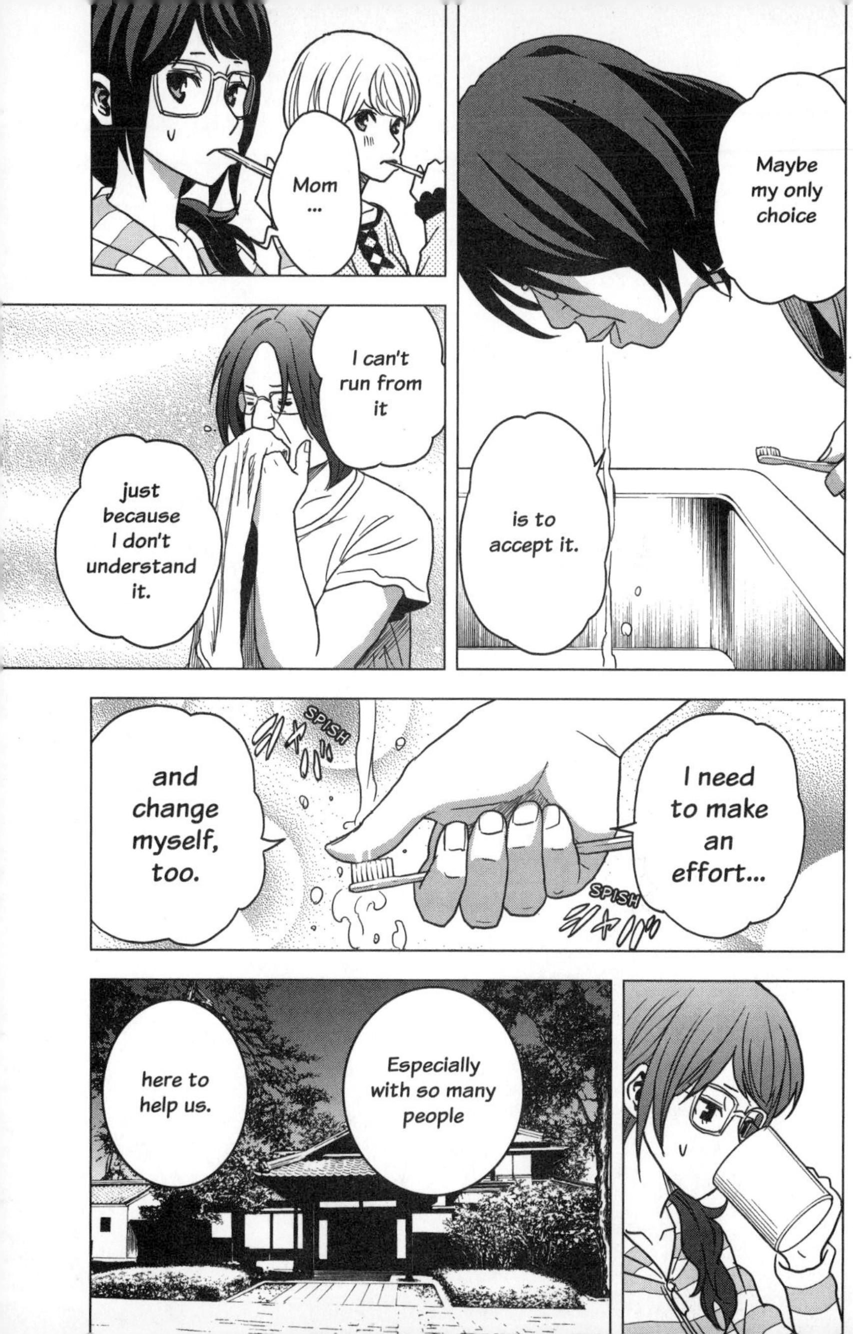
Maybe my only choice
is to accept it.
Mom ...
I can't run from it
just because I don't understand it.
SPISH
I need to make an effort...
SPISH
and change myself, too.
Especially with so many people
here to help us.

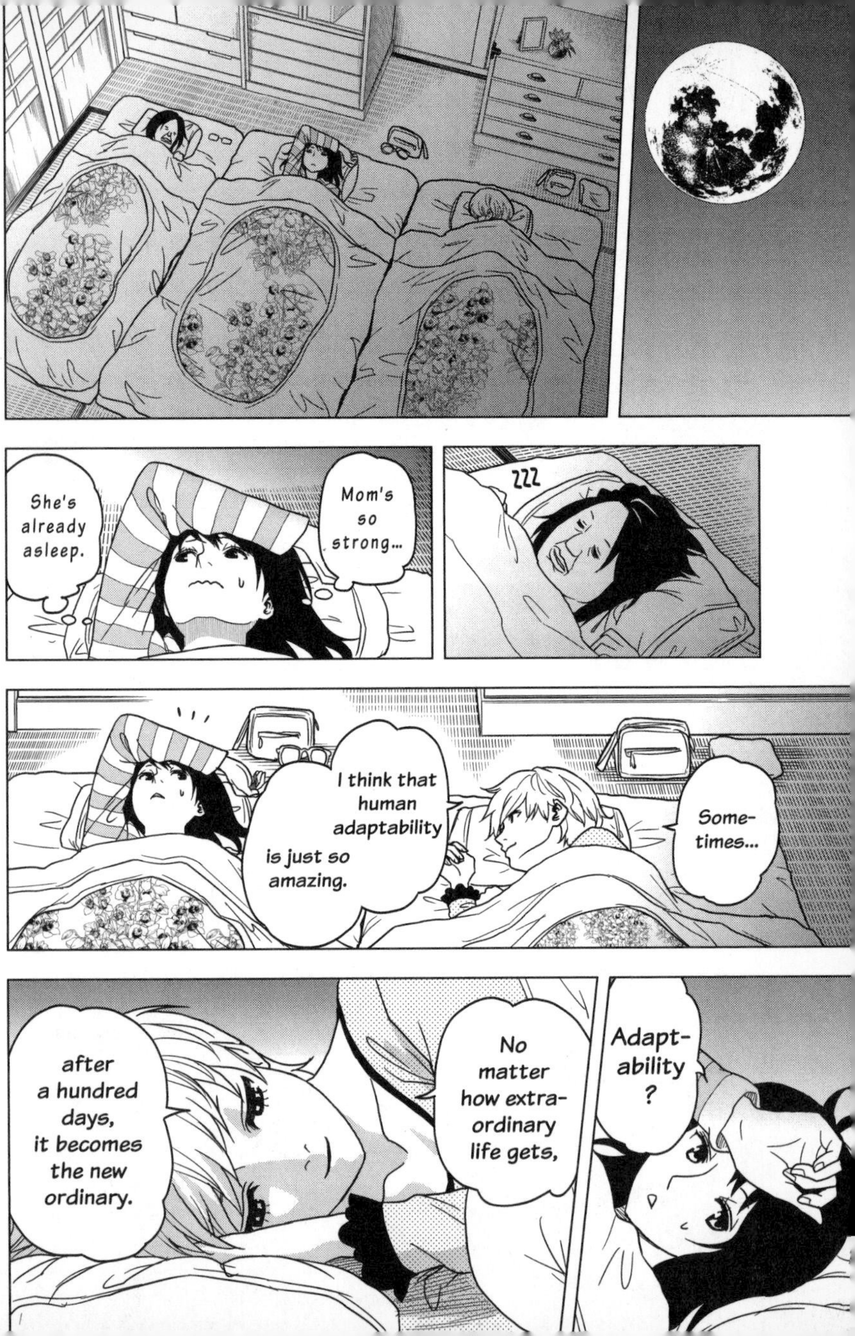
ZZZ
Mom's so strong...
She's already asleep.
Some-times...
I think that human adaptability is just so amazing.
Adapt-ability?
No matter how extra-ordinary life gets,
after a hundred days, it becomes the new ordinary.

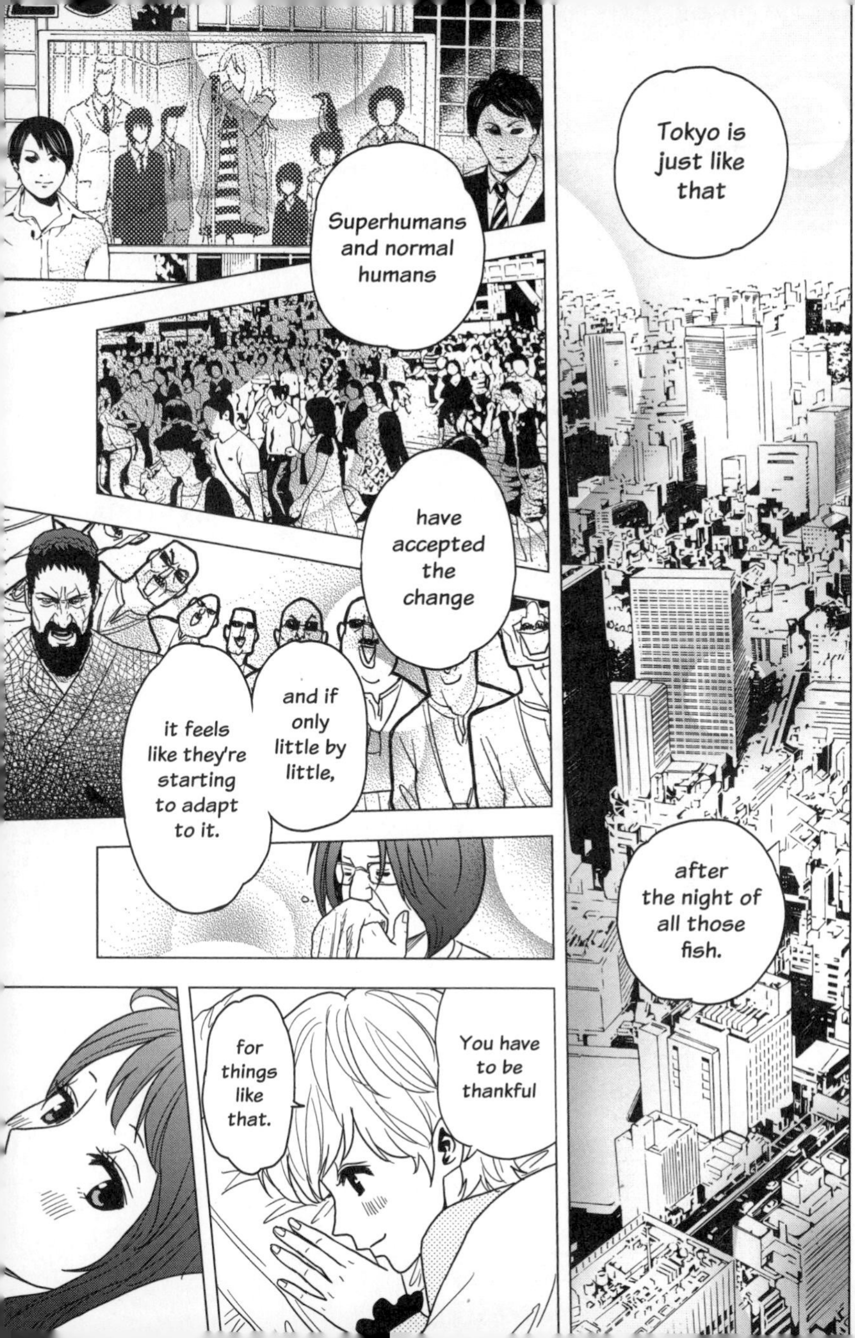
Tokyo is just like that
after the night of all those fish.
Superhumans and normal humans
have accepted the change
and if only little by little,
it feels like they're starting to adapt to it.
You have to be thankful
for things like that.

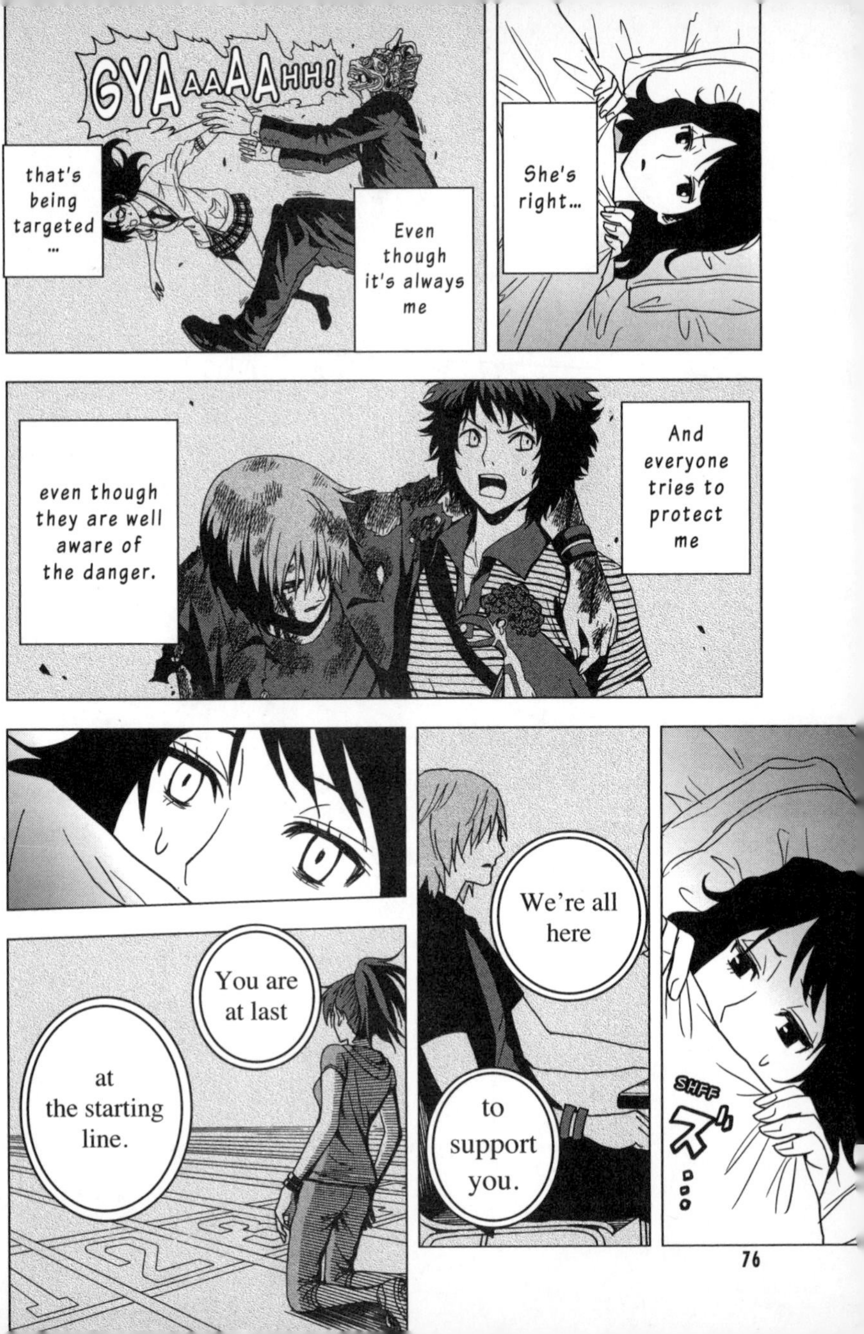
She's right…
GYAAAAAHH!
Even though it's always me
that's being targeted …
And everyone tries to protect me
even though they are well aware of the danger.
SHFF
…
We're all here
to support you.
You are at last
at the starting line.

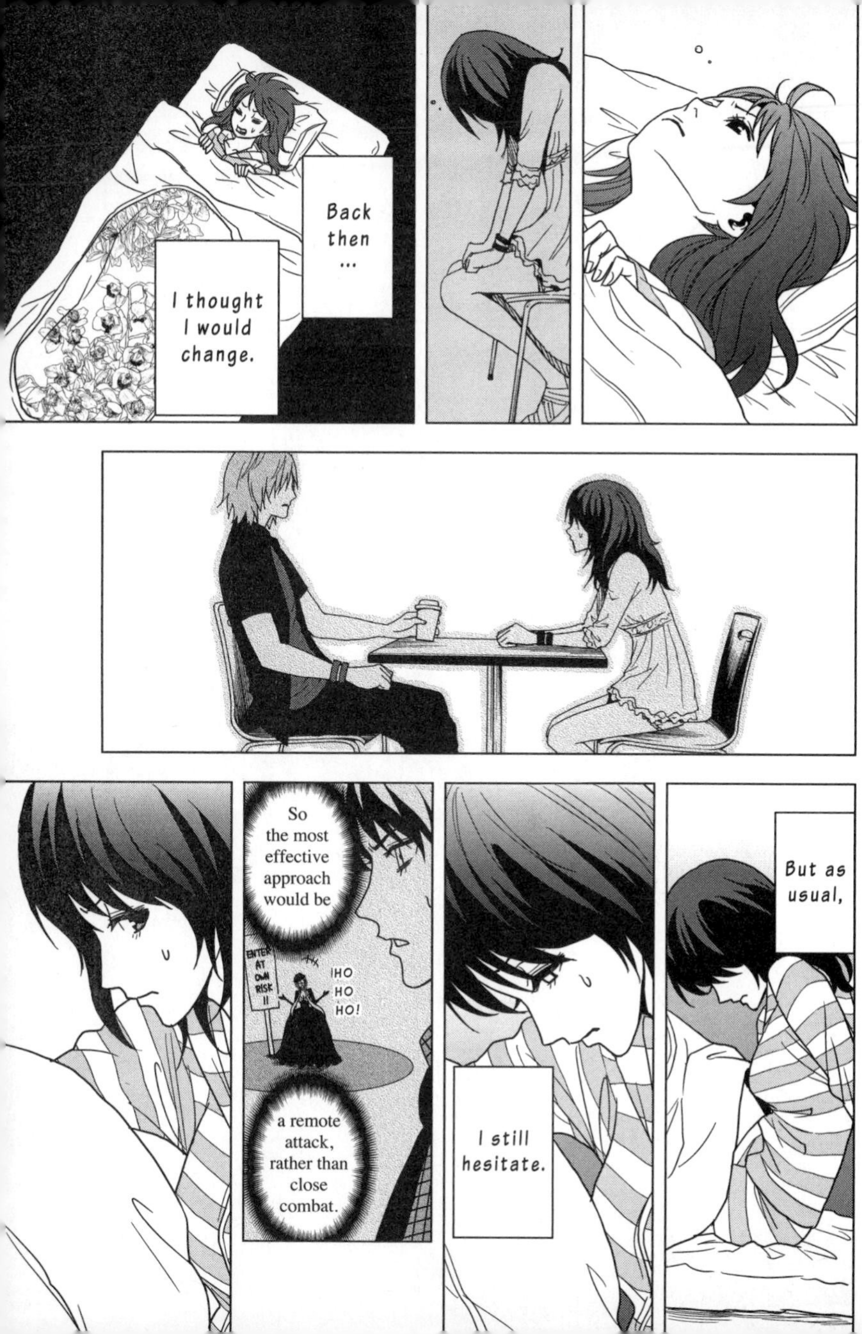
Back then ...
I thought I would change.
But as usual,
I still hesitate.
So the most effective approach would be
HO HO HO!
ENTER AT OWN RISK !!
a remote attack, rather than close combat.

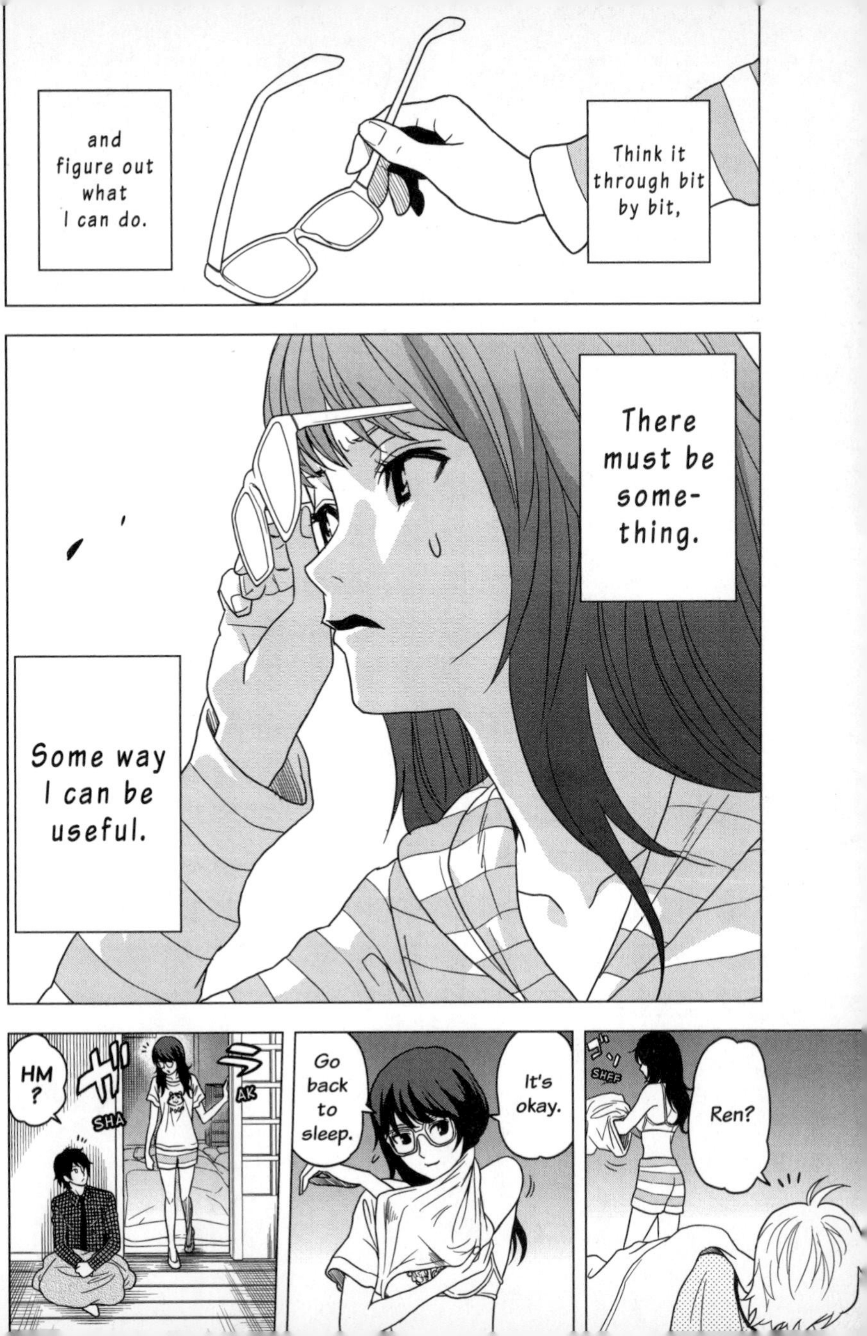
Think it through bit by bit,
and figure out what I can do.
There must be some-thing.
Some way I can be useful.
SHFF
Ren?
It's okay.
Go back to sleep.
AK
HM ?
SHA

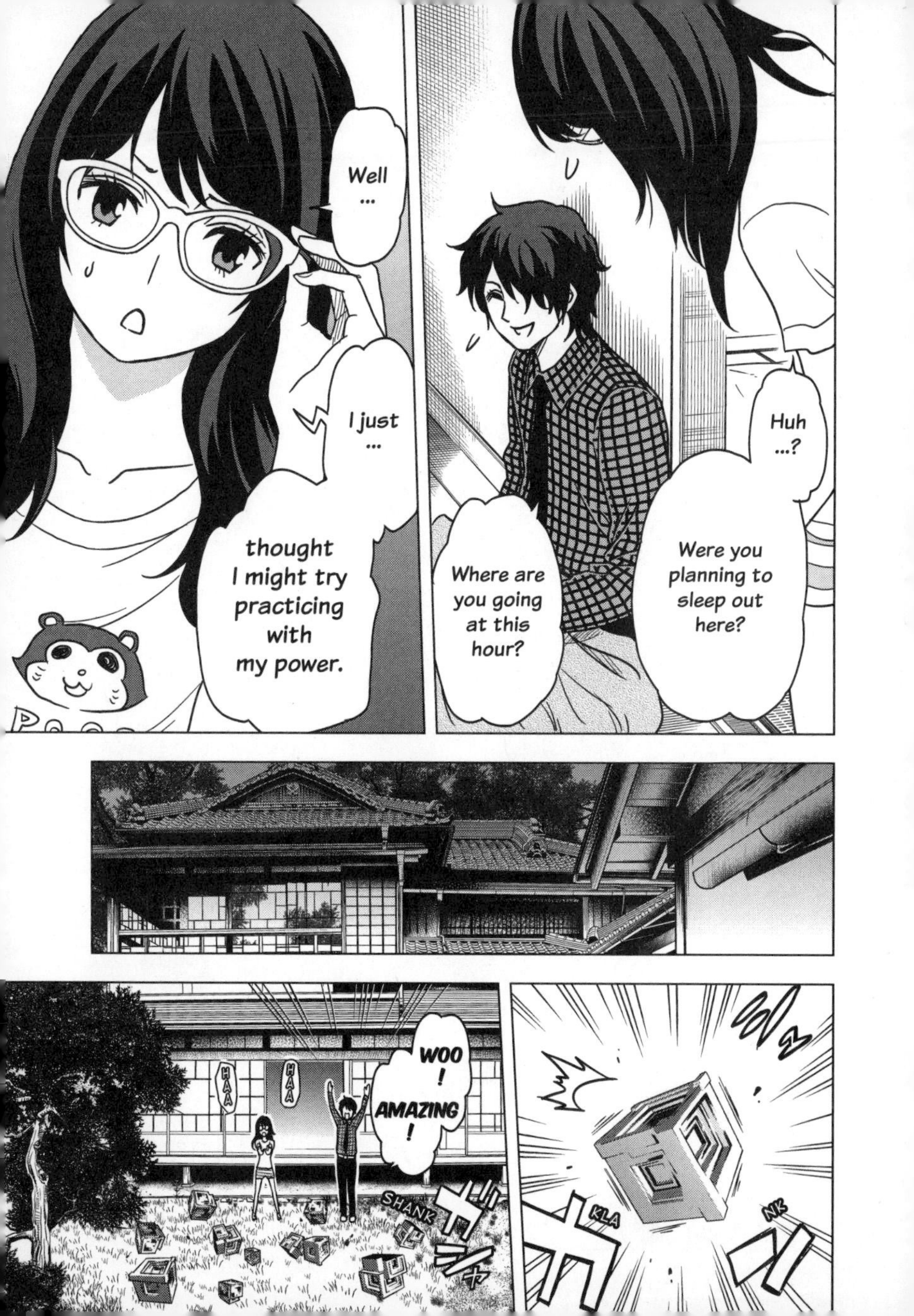
Huh ...?
Were you planning to sleep out here?
Where are you going at this hour?
Well ...
I just ...
thought I might try practicing with my power.
KLA
NK
WOO! AMAZING!
HAA
HAA
SHANK

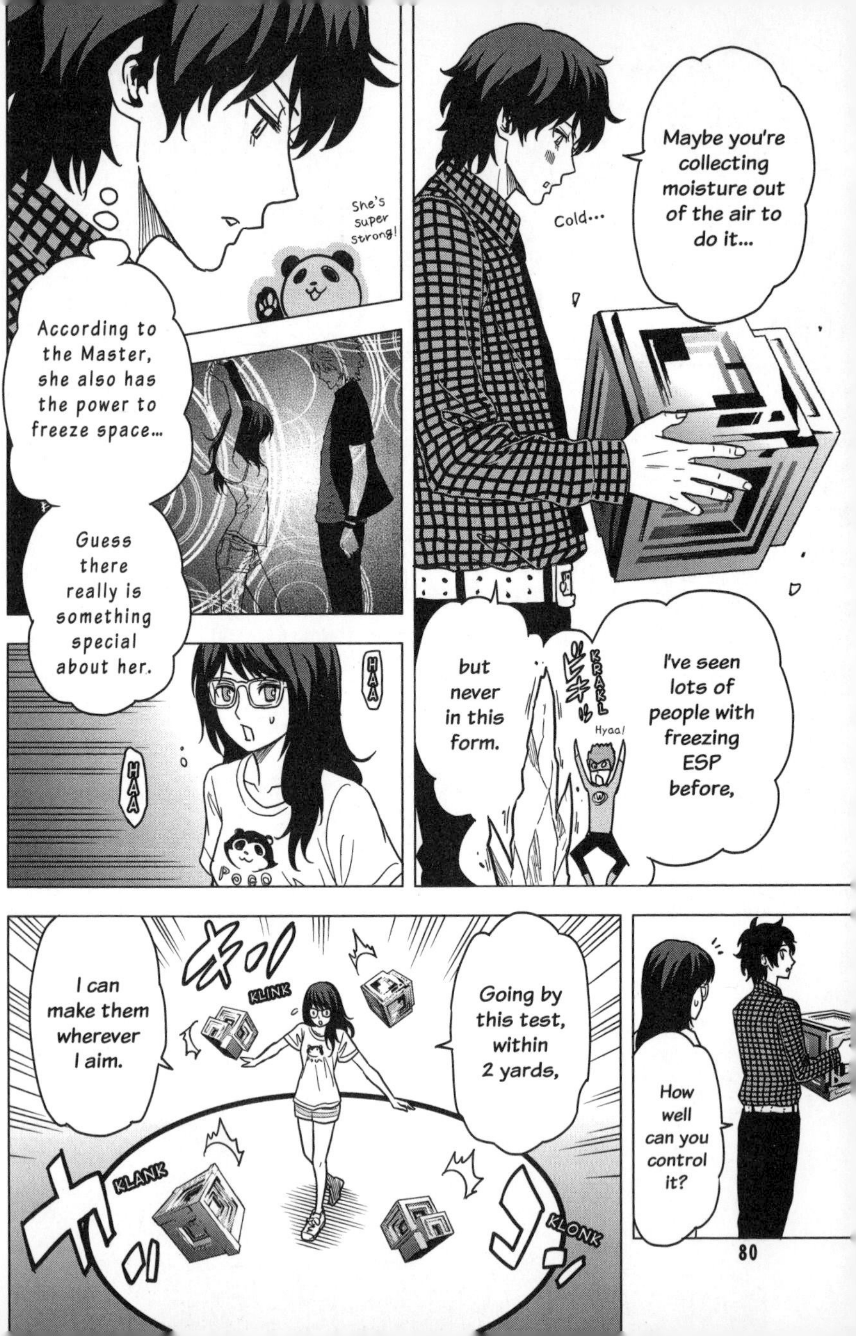
Maybe you're collecting moisture out of the air to do it...
Cold...
I've seen lots of people with freezing ESP before,
KRAKL
Hyaa!
but never in this form.
She's super strong!
According to the Master, she also has the power to freeze space...
Guess there really is something special about her.
HAA
HAA
How well can you control it?
Going by this test, within 2 yards,
I can make them wherever I aim.
KLINK
KLANK
KLONK

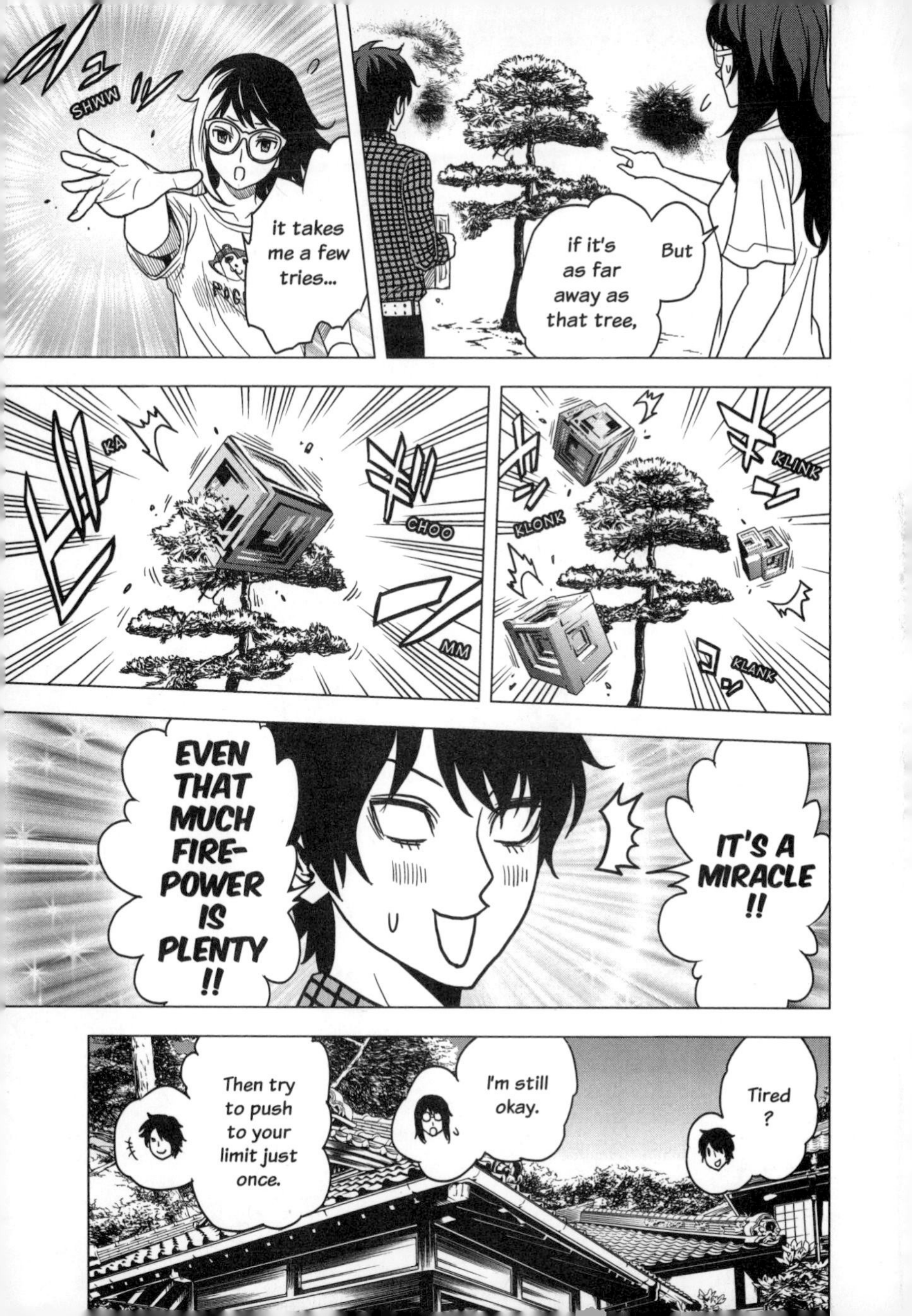
But
if it's as far away as that tree,
it takes me a few tries...
SHWW
KLINK
KLONK
KLANK
KA
CHOO
MM
IT'S A MIRACLE!!
EVEN THAT MUCH FIRE-POWER IS PLENTY!!
Tired?
I'm still okay.
Then try to push to your limit just once.

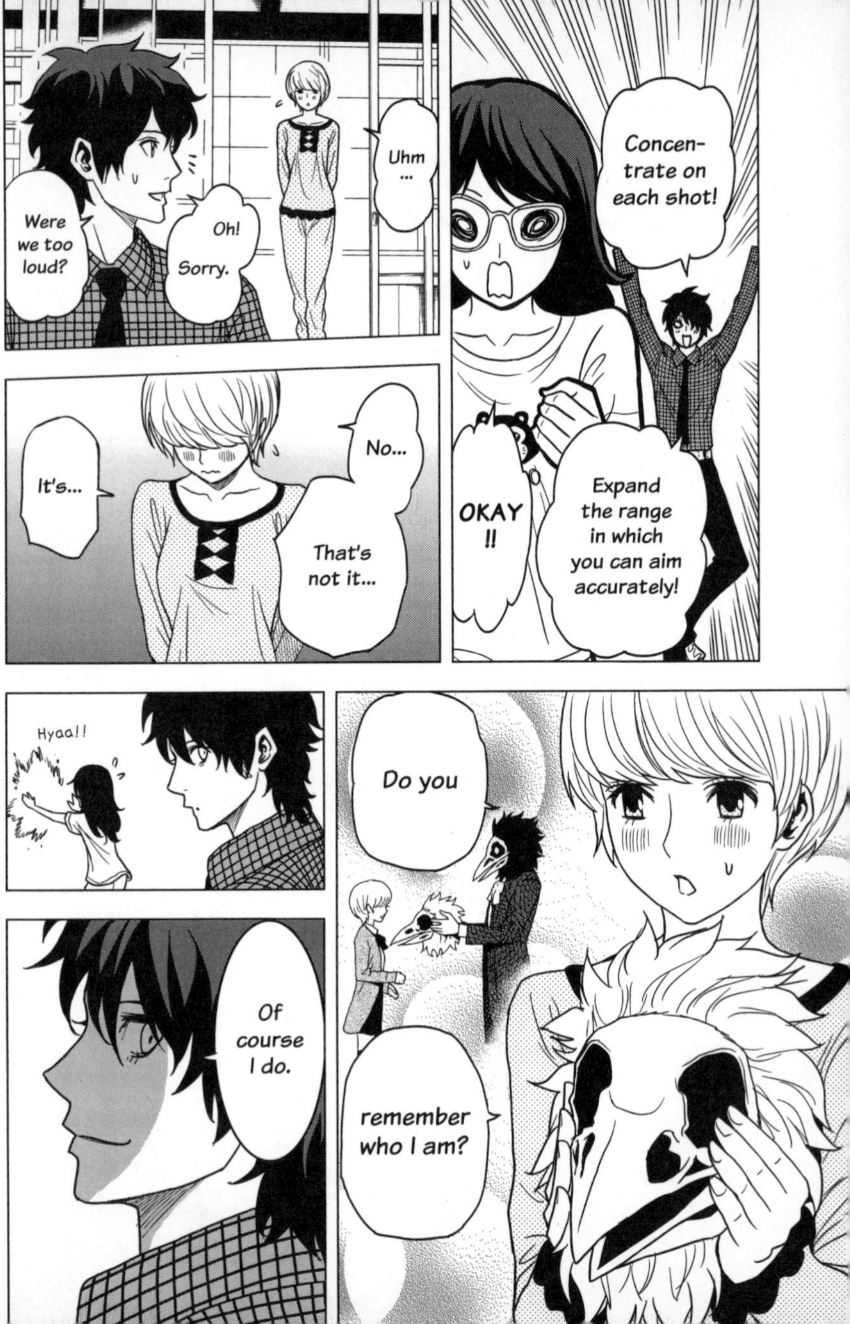
Concen-trate on each shot!
Expand the range in which you can aim accurately!
OKAY !!
Uhm ...
Oh! Sorry.
Were we too loud?
No...
That's not it...
It's...
Do you
remember who I am?
Hyaa!!
Of course I do.

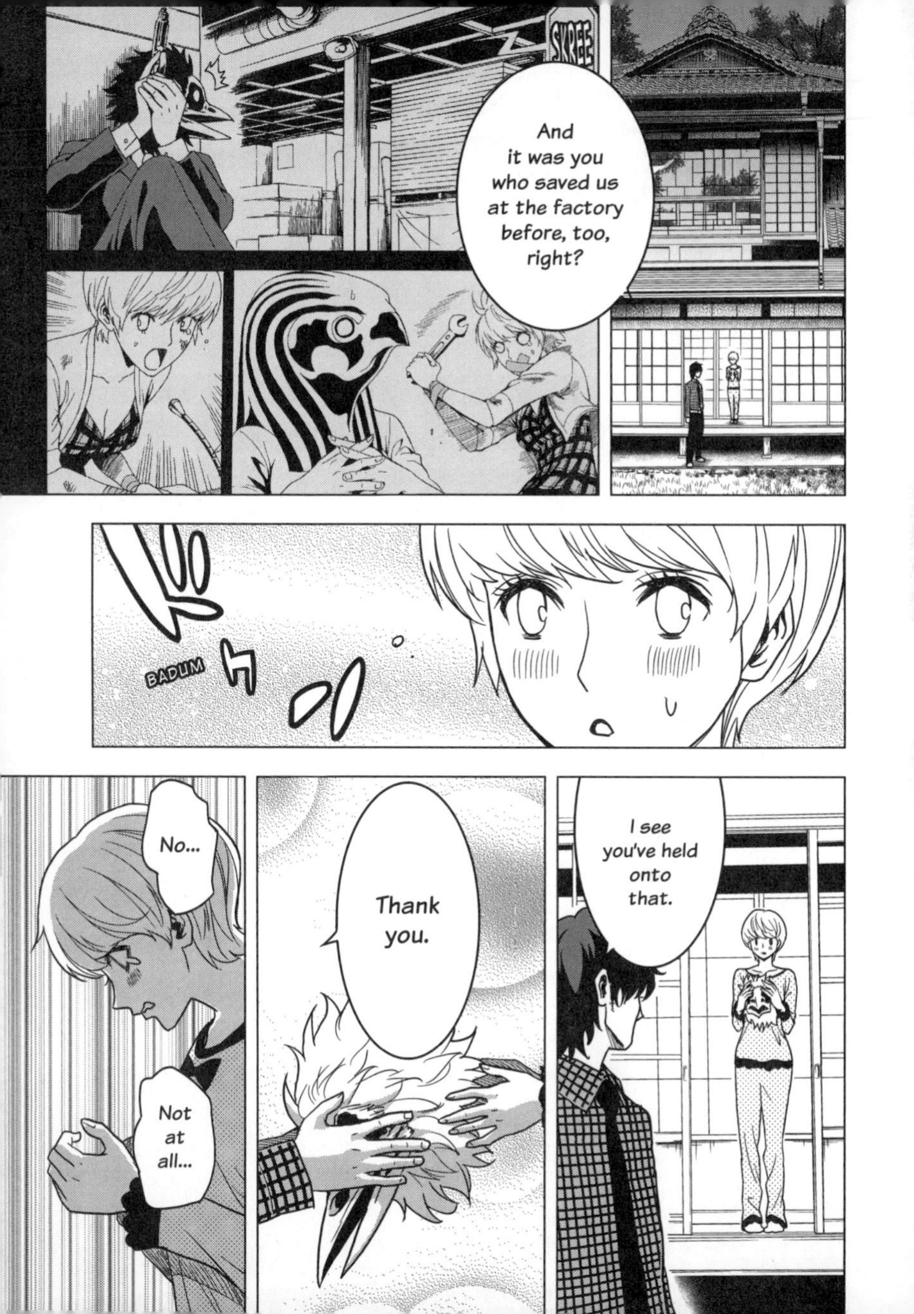
And it was you who saved us at the factory before, too, right?
SKREE
BADUM
I see you've held onto that.
Thank you.
No...
Not at all...

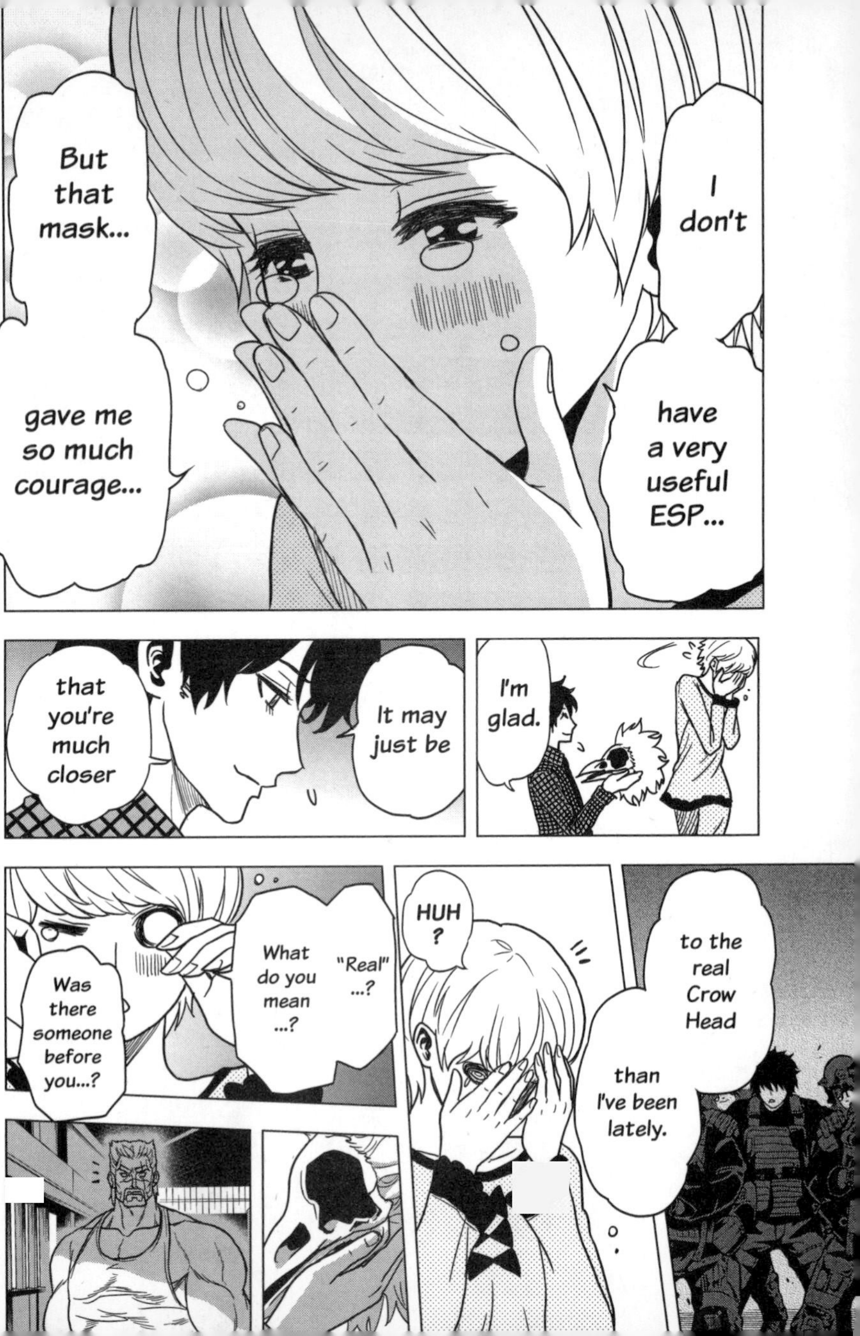
I don't have a very useful ESP...
But that mask... gave me so much courage...
I'm glad.
It may just be
that you're much closer
to the real Crow Head
than I've been lately.
HUH ?
"Real" ...?
What do you mean ...?
Was there someone before you...?

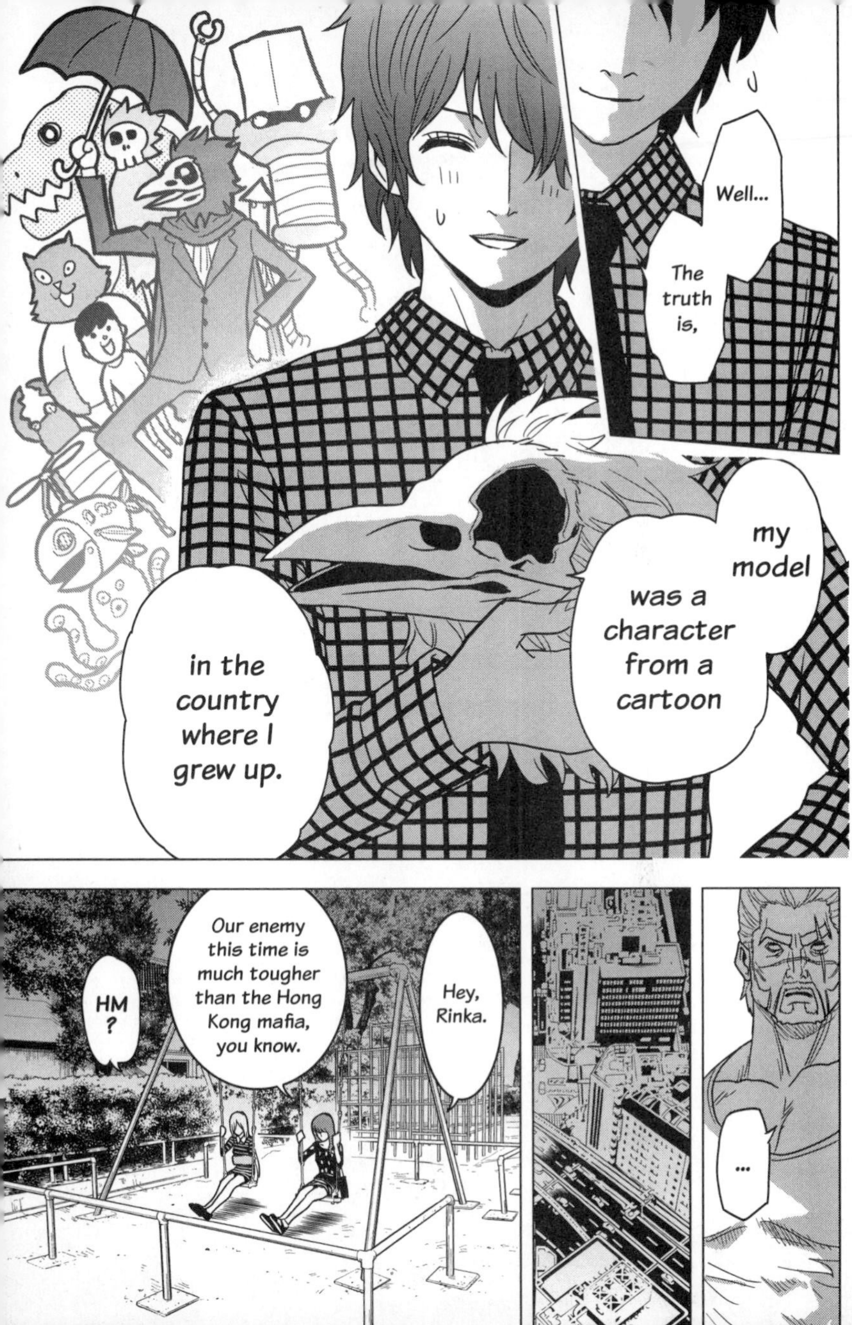
Well...
The truth is,
my model was a character from a cartoon
in the country where I grew up.
...
Hey, Rinka.
Our enemy this time is much tougher than the Hong Kong mafia, you know.
HM?

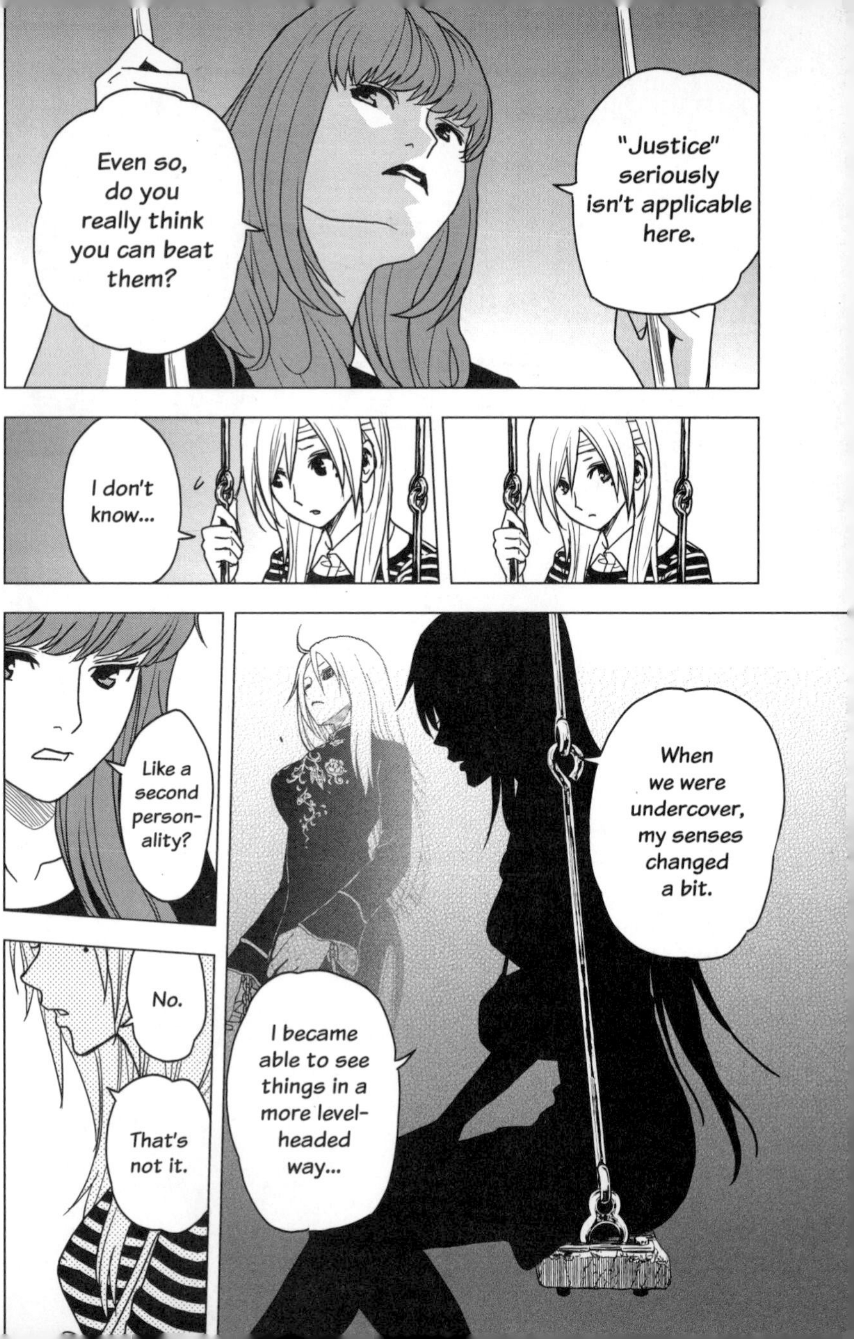
"Justice" seriously isn't applicable here.
Even so, do you really think you can beat them?
I don't know...
When we were undercover, my senses changed a bit.
I became able to see things in a more level-headed way...
Like a second personality?
No.
That's not it.

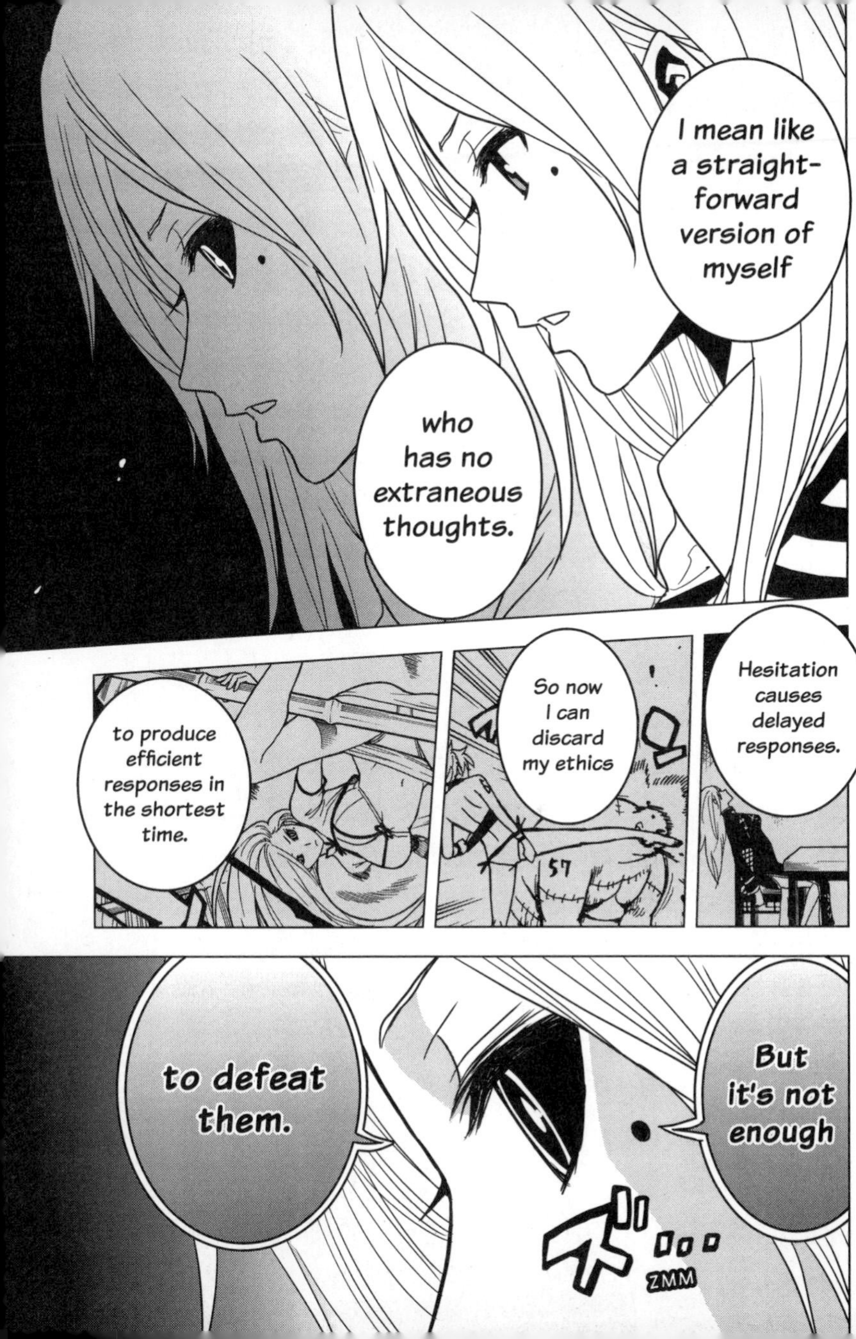
I mean like a straight-forward version of myself
who has no extraneous thoughts.
Hesitation causes delayed responses.
So now I can discard my ethics
to produce efficient responses in the shortest time.
But it's not enough
to defeat them.
ZMM

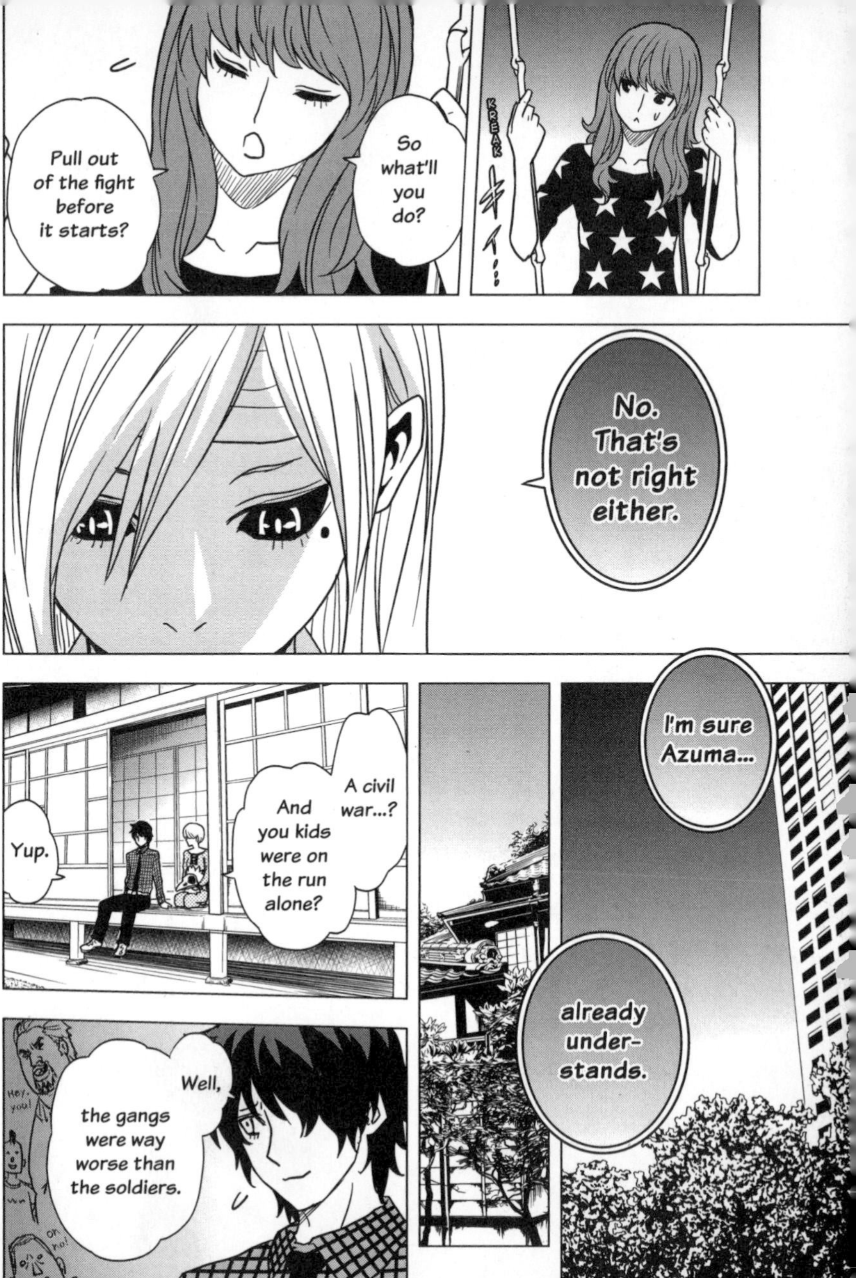
KREAK
キィ…
So what'll you do?
Pull out of the fight before it starts?
No. That's not right either.
I'm sure Azuma...
already under-stands.
A civil war...?
And you kids were on the run alone?
Yup.
Well, the gangs were way worse than the soldiers.
Hey. you!
Oh no!

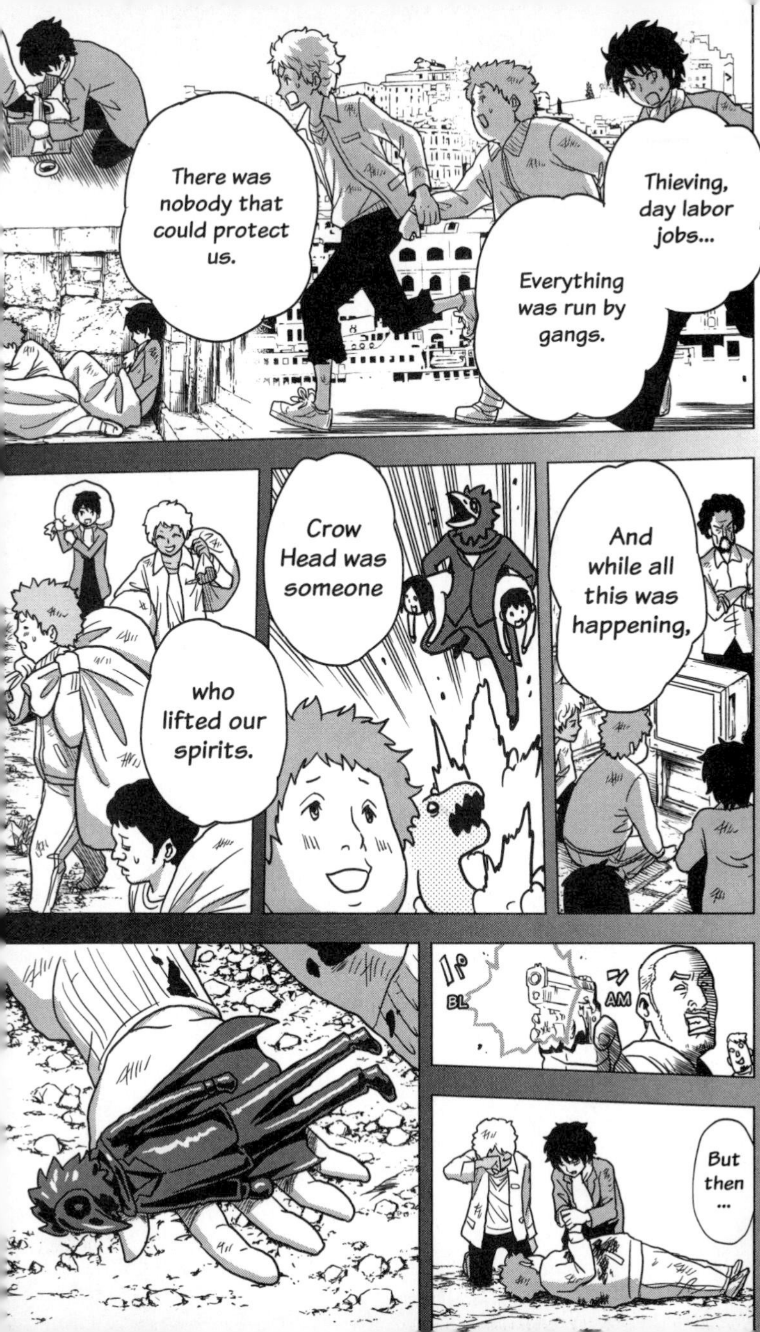

Thieving, day labor jobs...
Everything was run by gangs.
There was nobody that could protect us.
And while all this was happening,
Crow Head was someone
who lifted our spirits.
BL
AM
But then ...

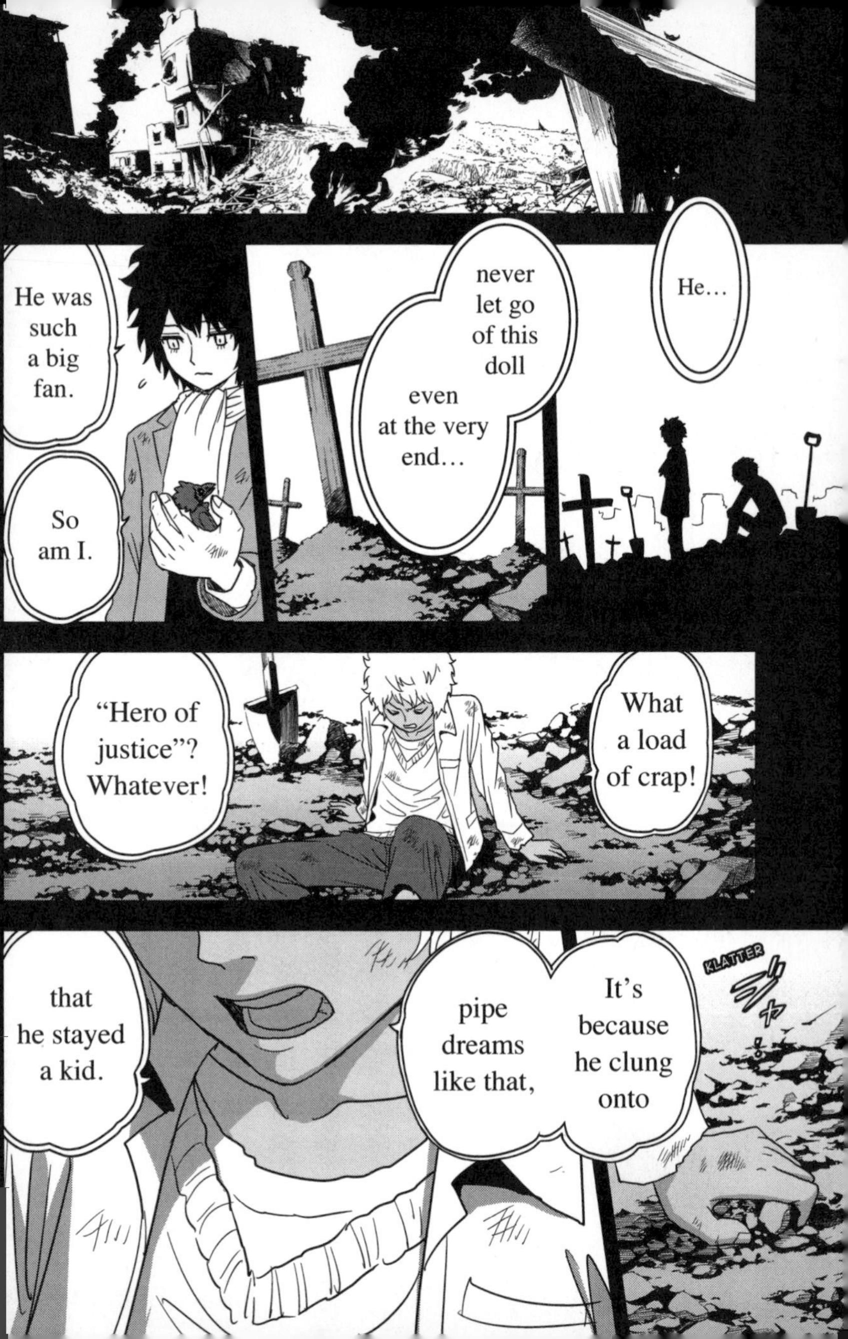
He…
never let go of this doll even at the very end…
He was such a big fan.
So am I.
What a load of crap!
“Hero of justice”? Whatever!
KLATTER
It’s because he clung onto
pipe dreams like that,
that he stayed a kid.

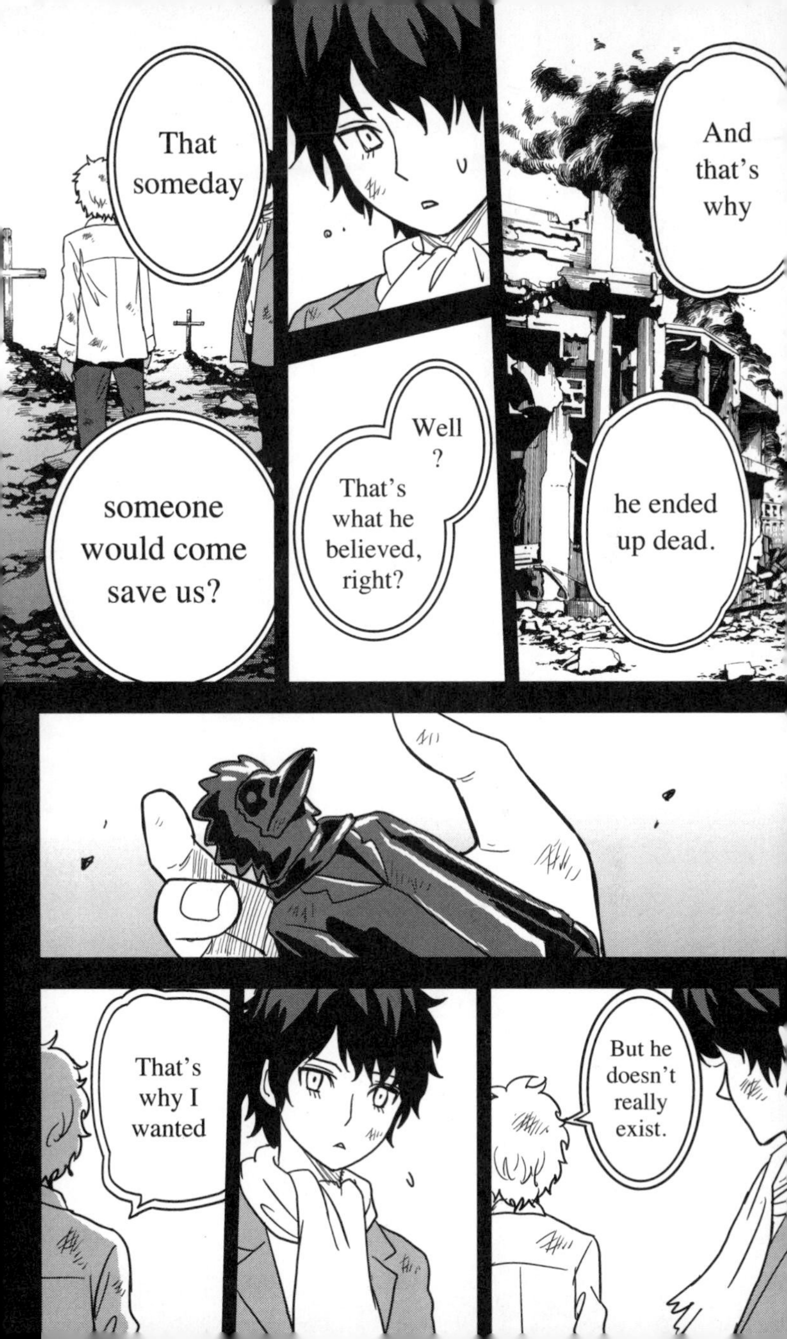
And that's why
he ended up dead.
Well? That's what he believed, right?
That someday
someone would come save us?
But he doesn't really exist.
That's why I wanted

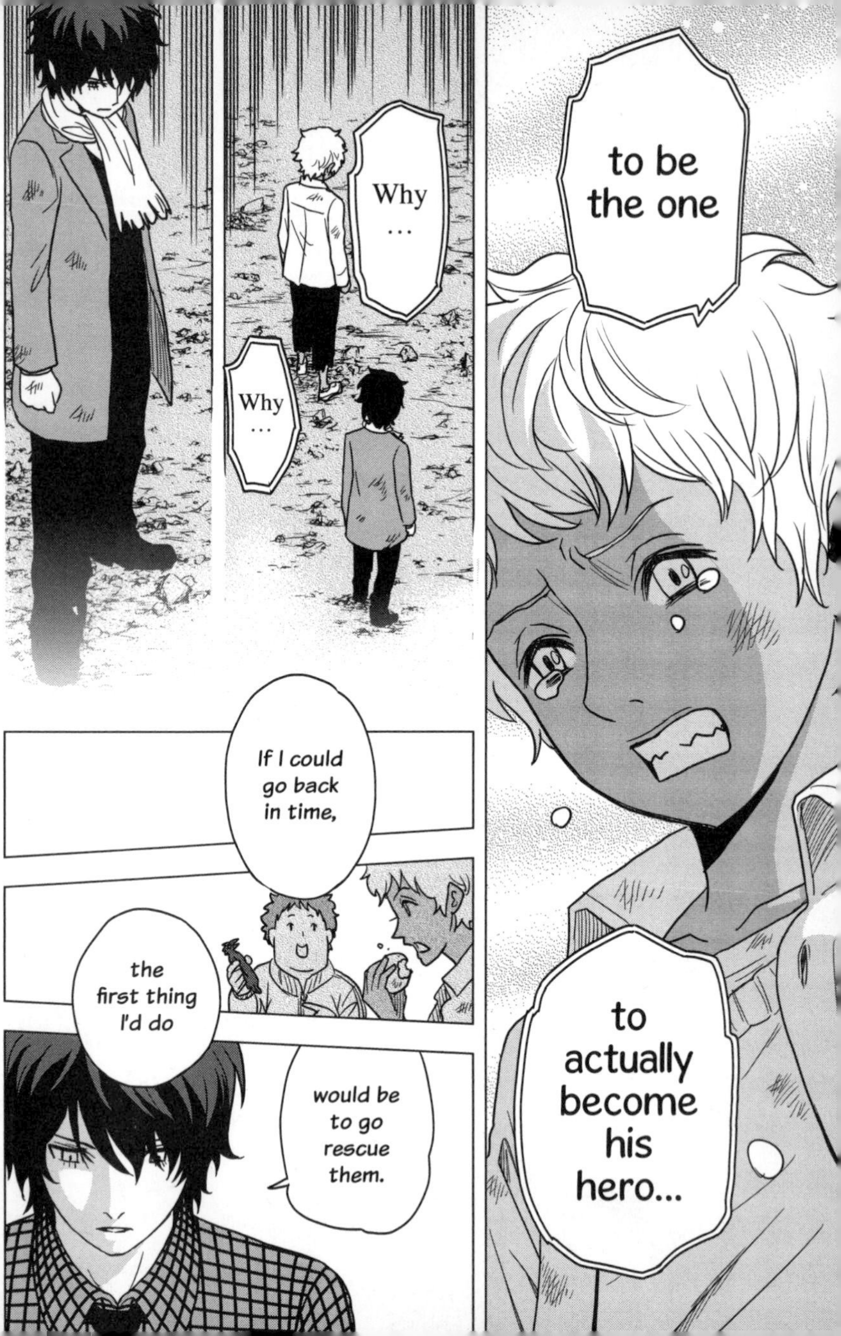
to be the one
to actually become his hero...
Why ...
Why ...
If I could go back in time,
the first thing I'd do
would be to go rescue them.

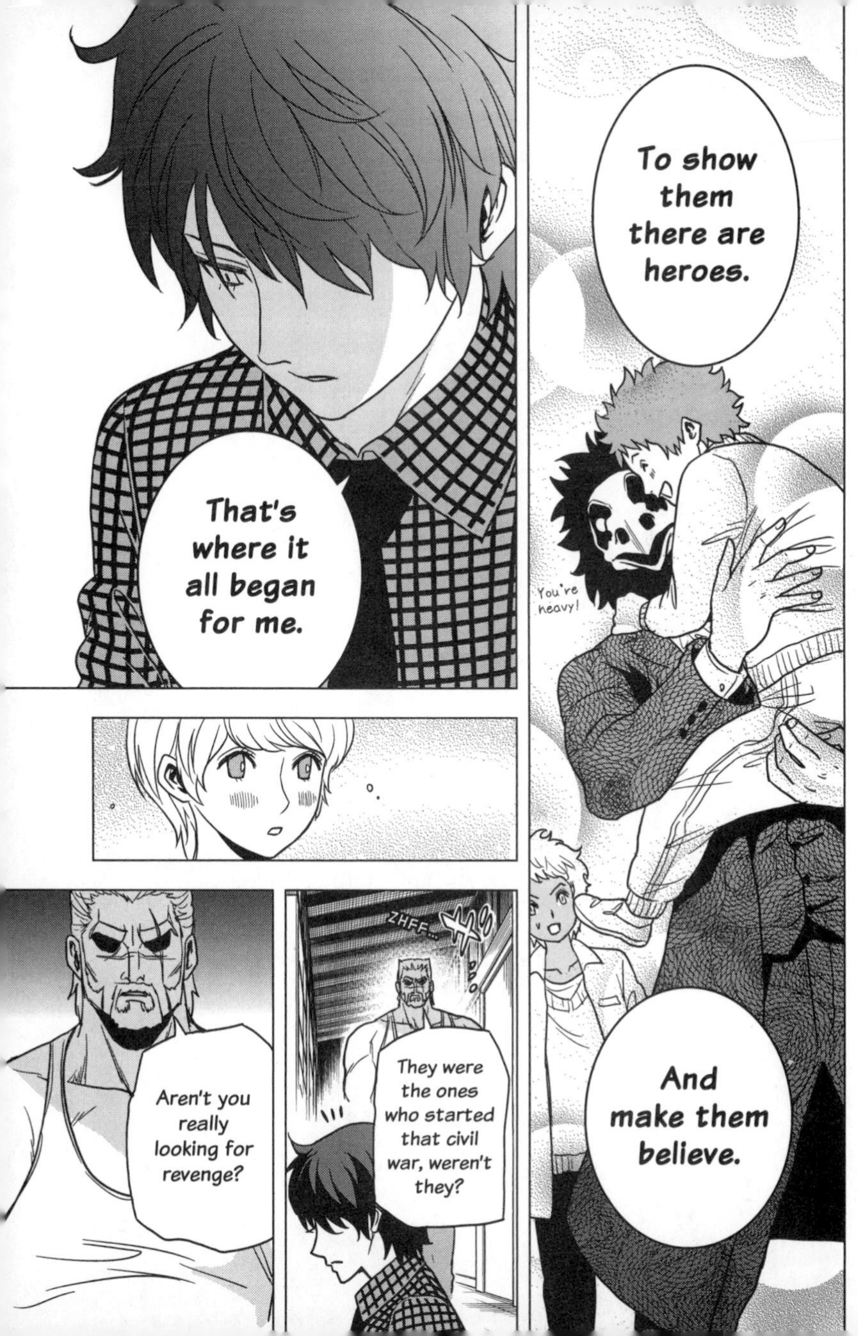
To show them there are heroes.
You're heavy!
And make them believe.
That's where it all began for me.
ZHFF...
They were the ones who started that civil war, weren't they?
Aren't you really looking for revenge?

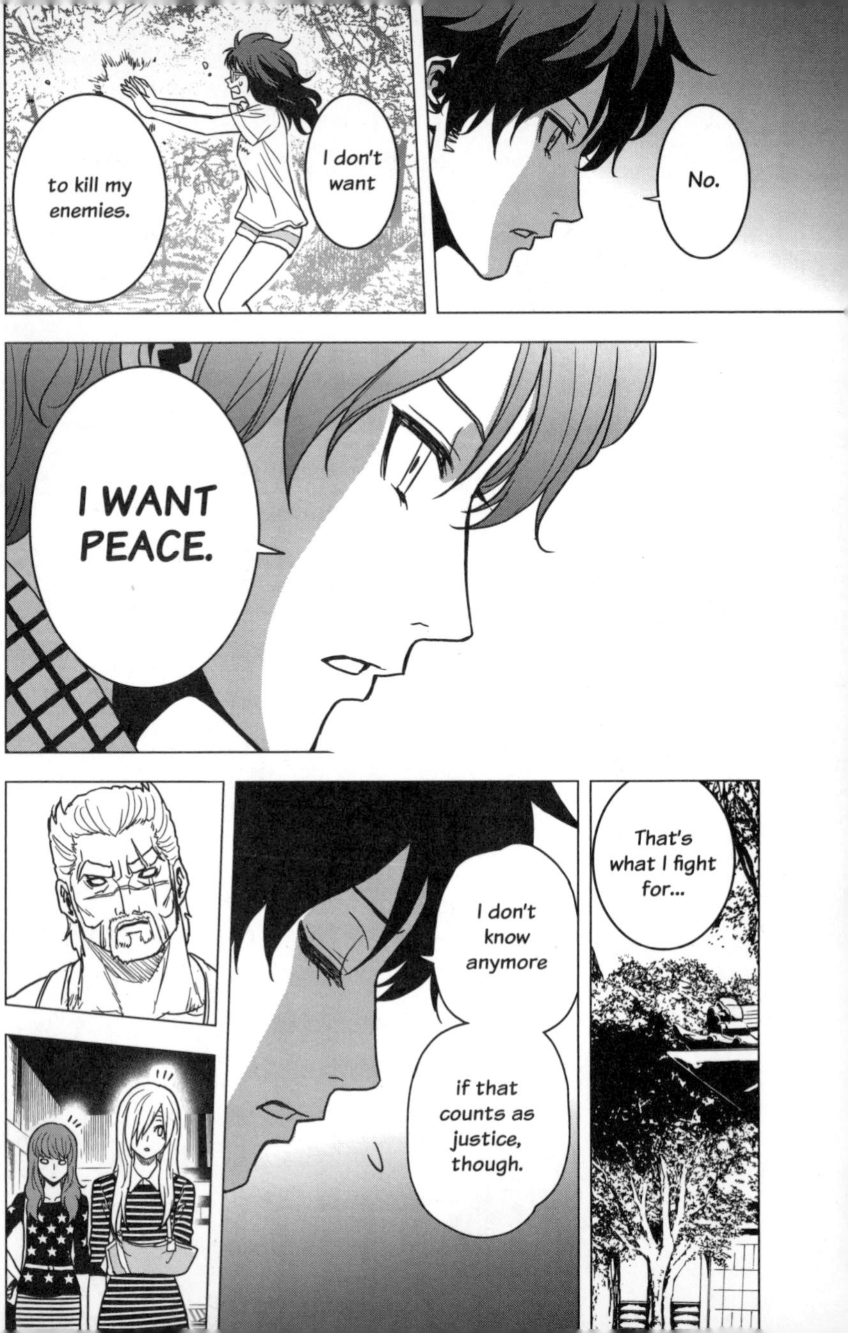
No.
I don't want
to kill my enemies.
I WANT PEACE.
That's what I fight for...
I don't know anymore
if that counts as justice, though.

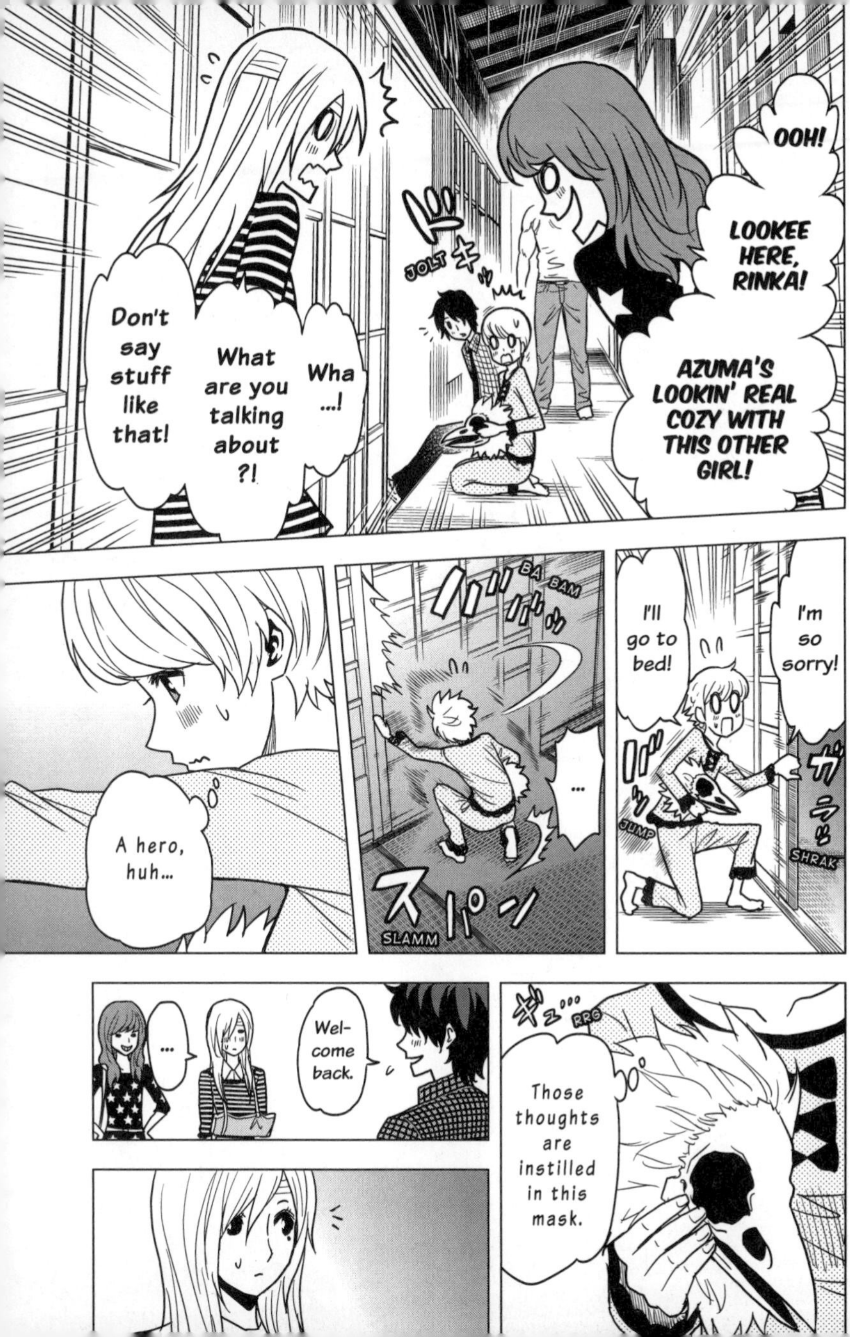
OOH!
LOOKEE HERE, RINKA!
AZUMA'S LOOKIN' REAL COZY WITH THIS OTHER GIRL!
JOLT
Wha...!
What are you talking about?!
Don't say stuff like that!
I'm so sorry!
I'll go to bed!
JUMP
SHRAK
BA BAM
...
SLAMM
A hero, huh...
RRG
Those thoughts are instilled in this mask.
Wel-come back.
...

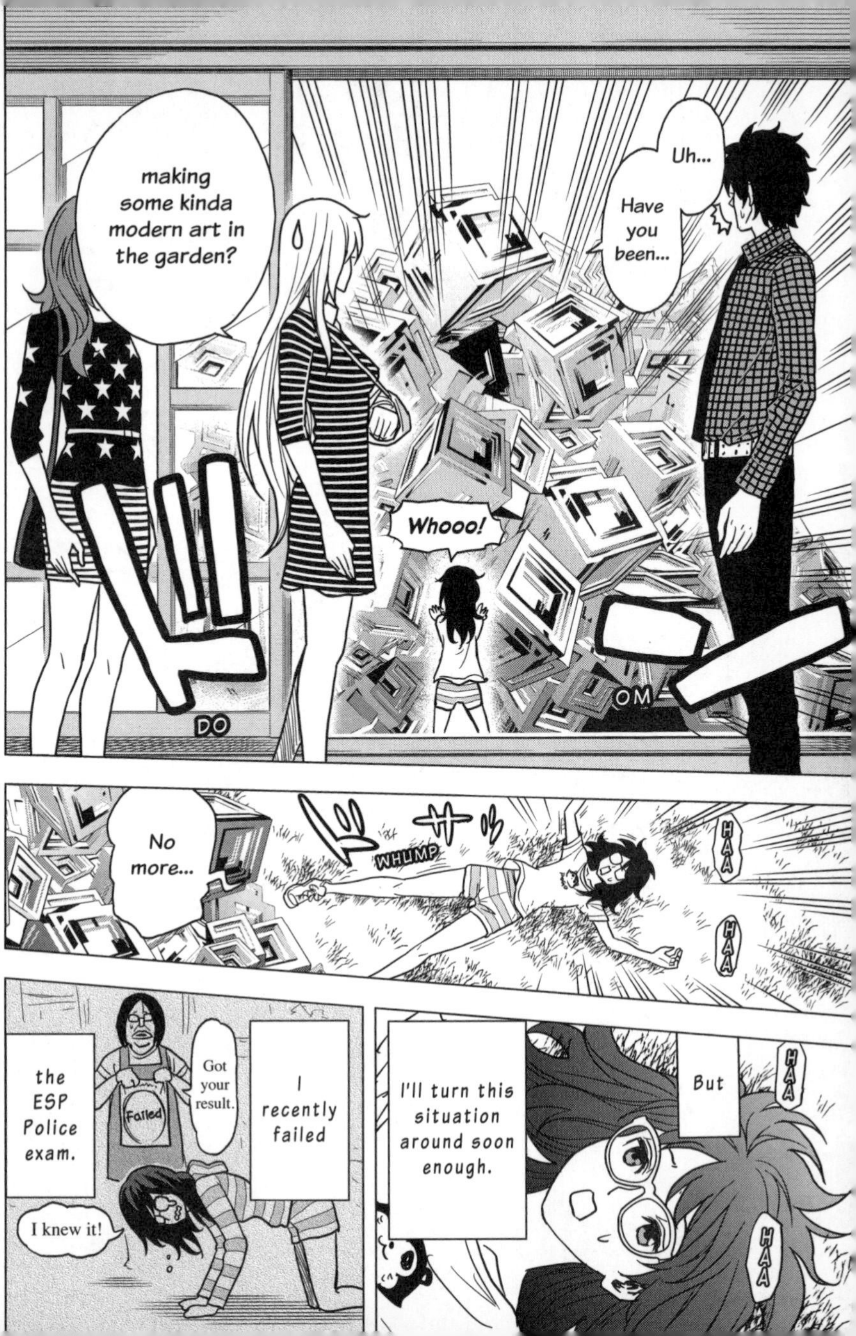

Uh...
Have you been...
making some kinda modern art in the garden?
Whooo!
OM
DO
HAA HAA
WHUMP
No more...
HAA HAA
But
I'll turn this situation around soon enough.
I recently failed
Got your result.
the ESP Police exam.
Failed
I knew it!

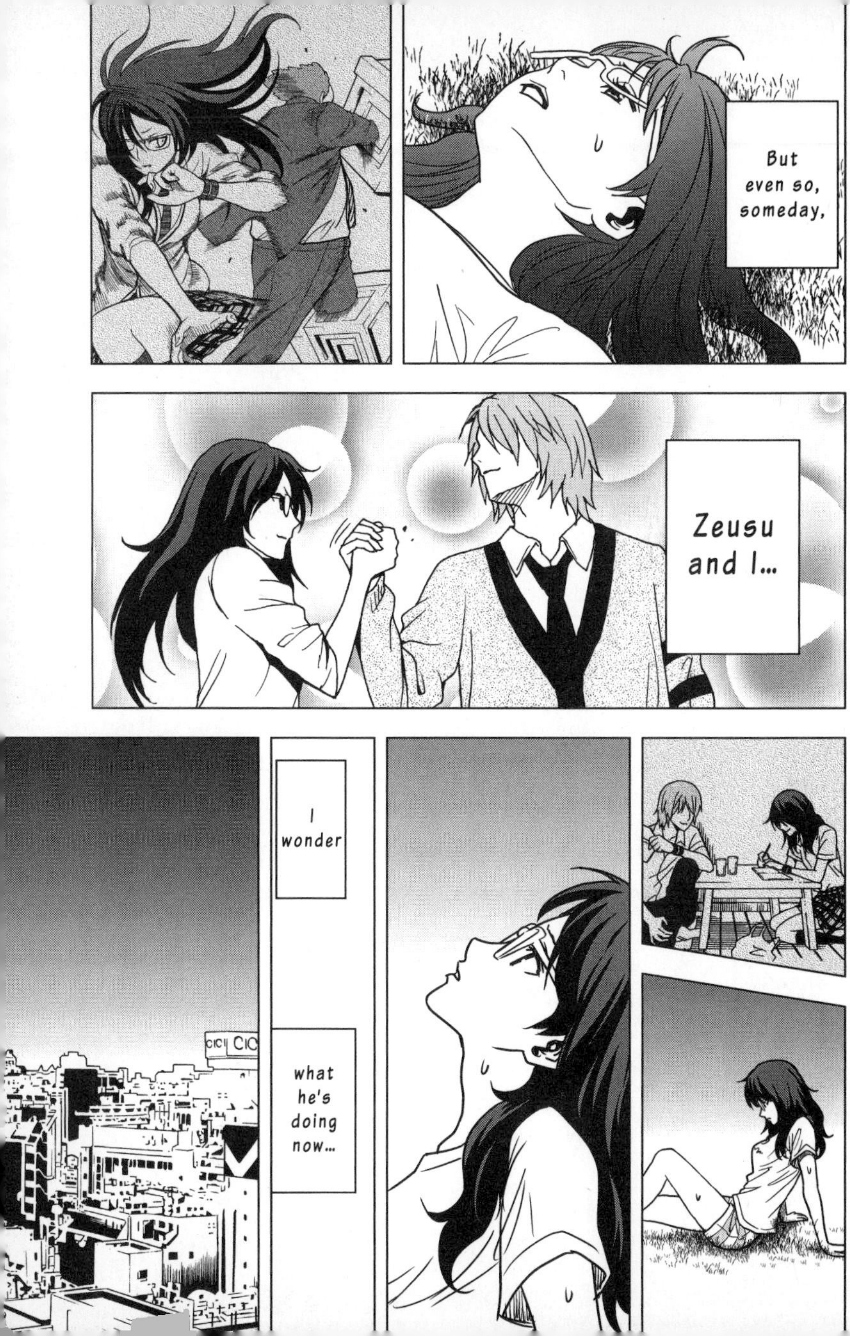
But even so, someday,
Zeusu and I...
I wonder
what he's doing now...

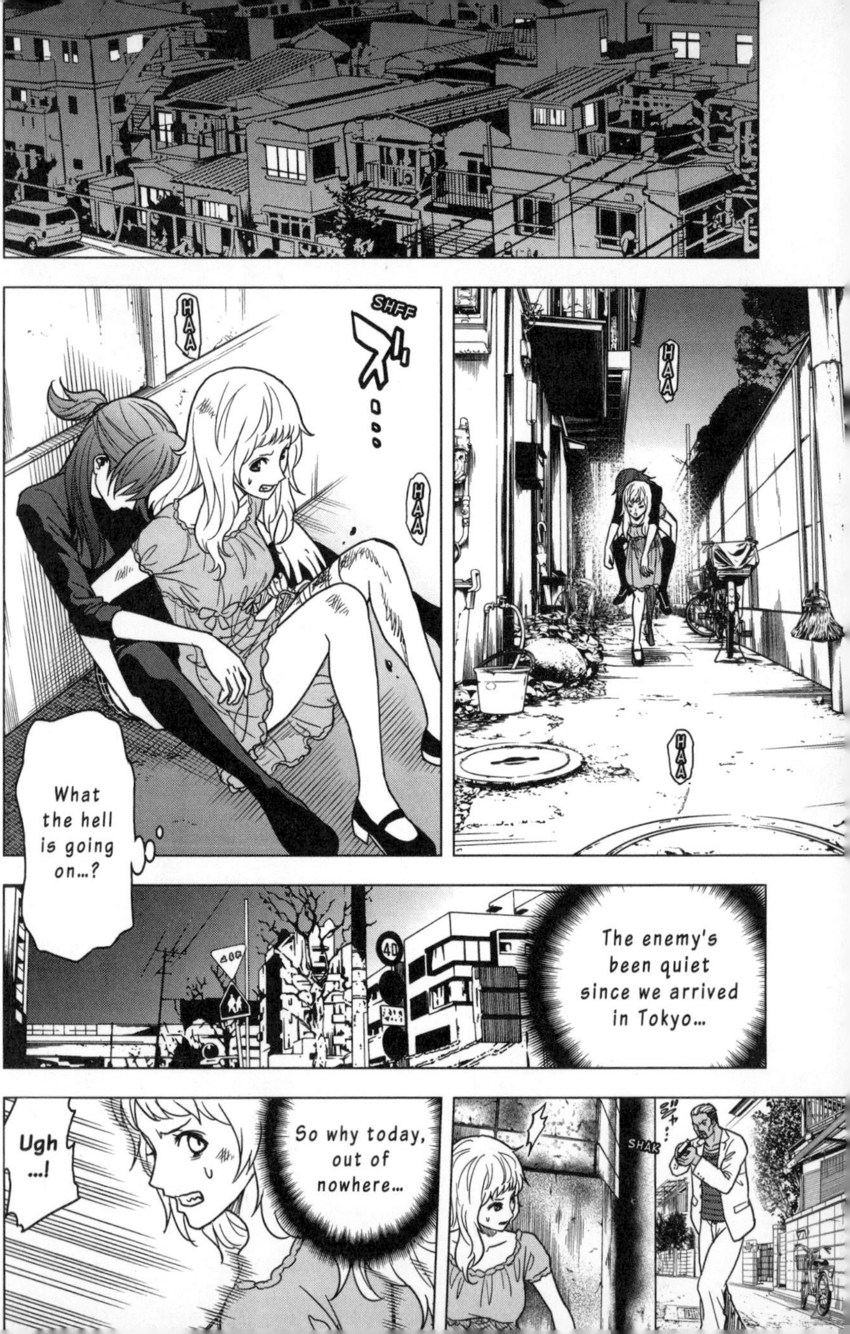
HAA
HAA
SHFF
HAA
HAA
What the hell is going on...?
The enemy's been quiet since we arrived in Tokyo...
SHAK
So why today, out of nowhere...
Ugh ...!

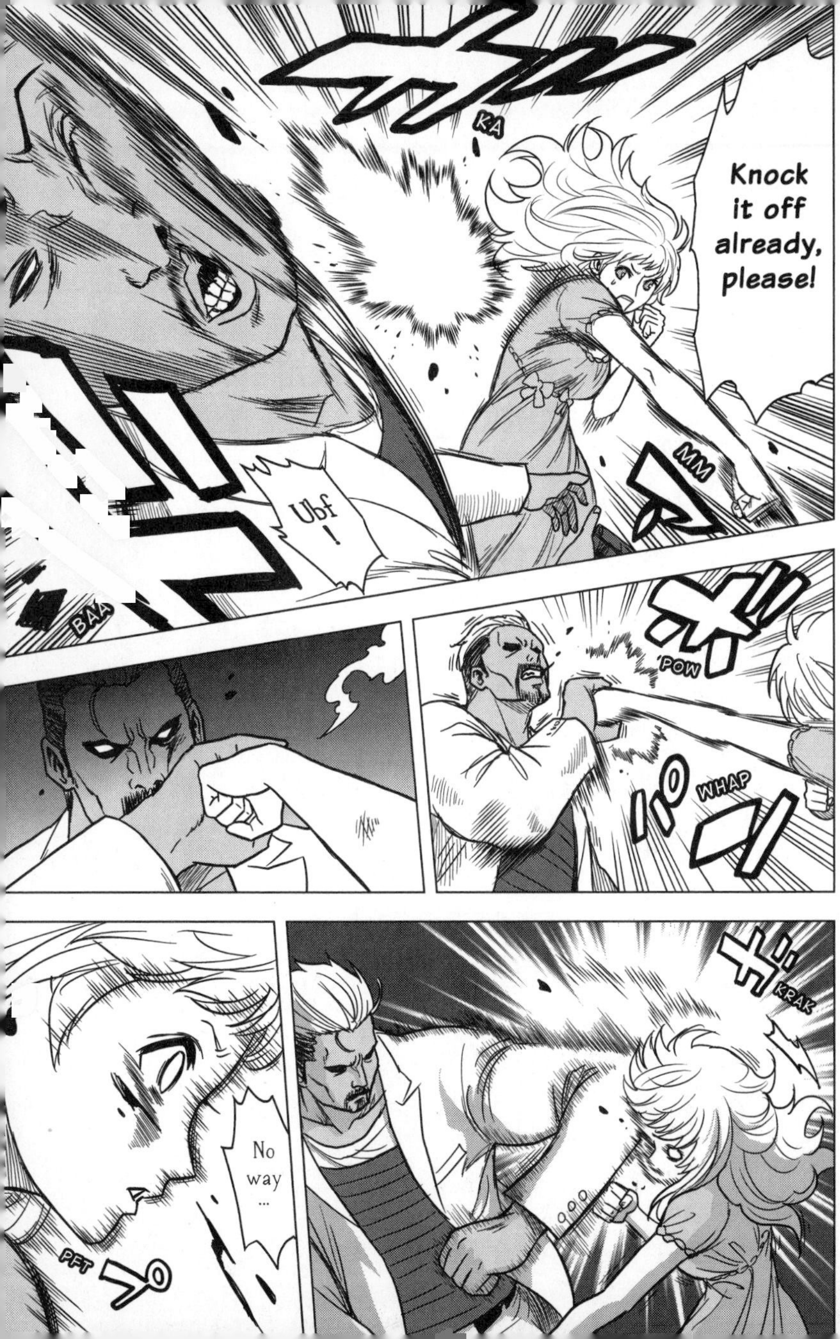
Knock it off already, please!
KA
MM
Ubf!
BAA
POW
WHAP
KRAK
No way ...
PFT

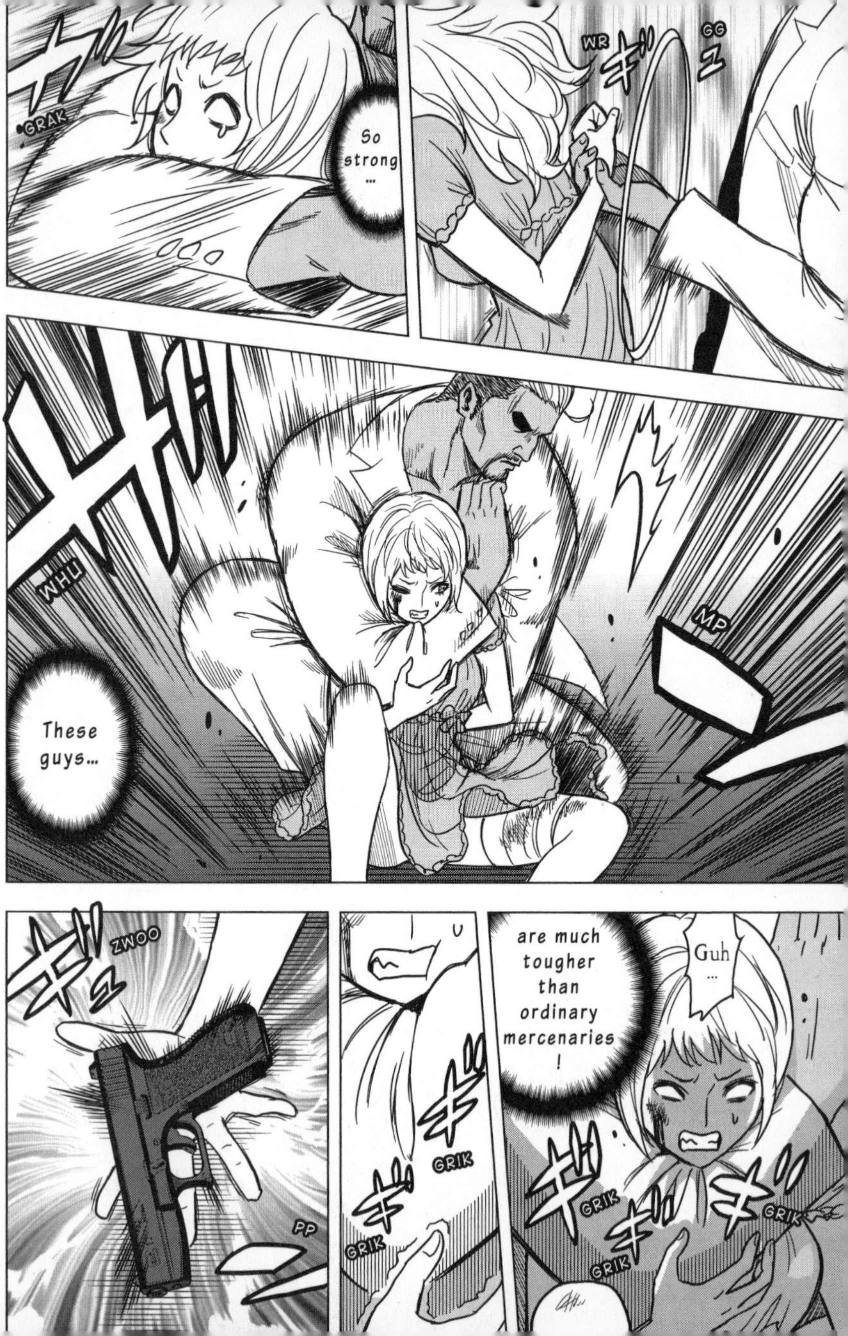
WR
GG
GRAK
So strong ...
WHU
MP
These guys...
are much tougher than ordinary mercenaries !
Guh ...
GRIK
GRIK
GRIK
U
GRIK
GRIK
ZWOO
PP

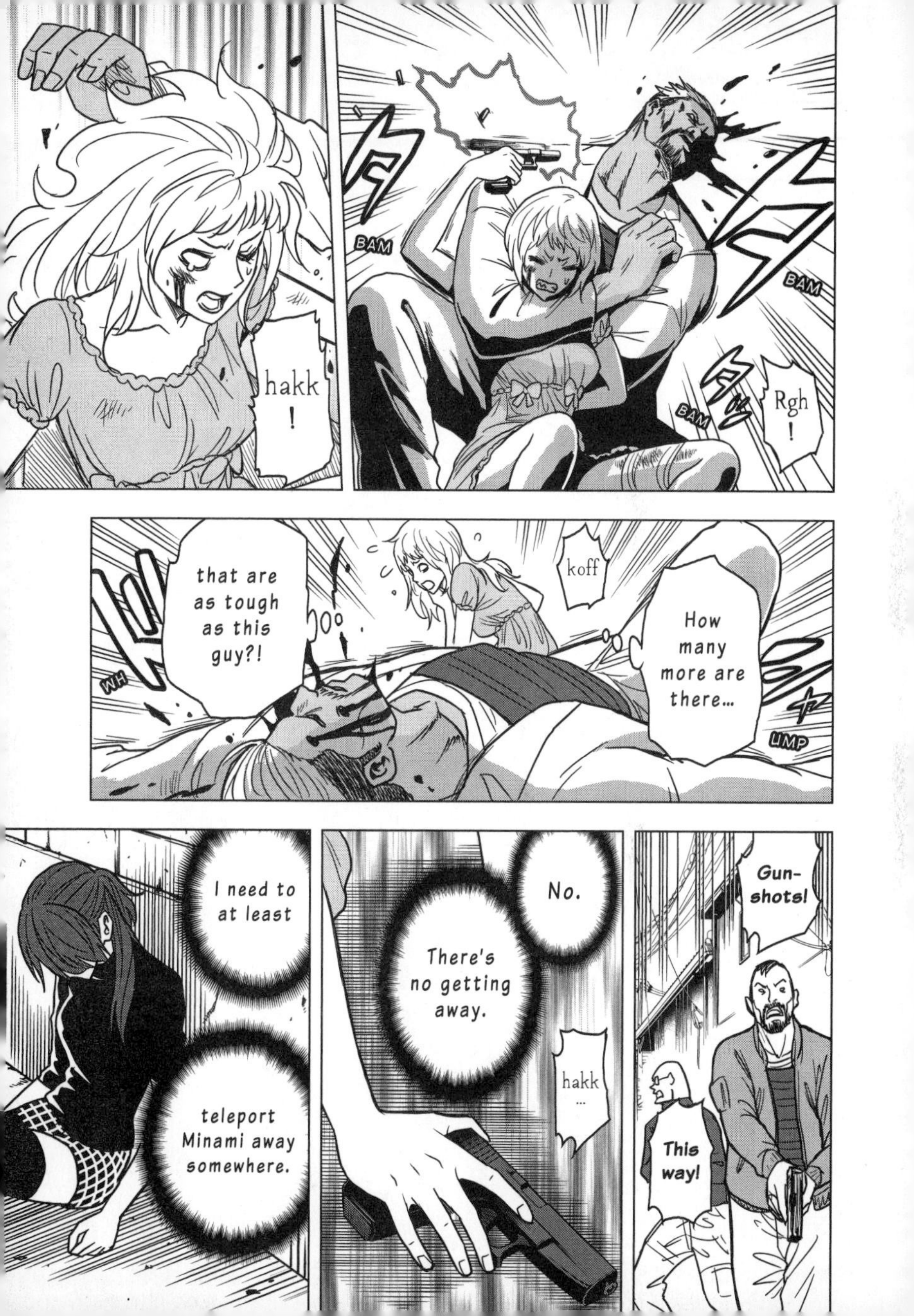
BAM
BAM
BAM
Rgh!
hakk!
koff
How many more are there…
that are as tough as this guy?!
WH
UMP
Gun-shots!
This way!
No.
There's no getting away.
hakk…
I need to at least
teleport Minami away somewhere.

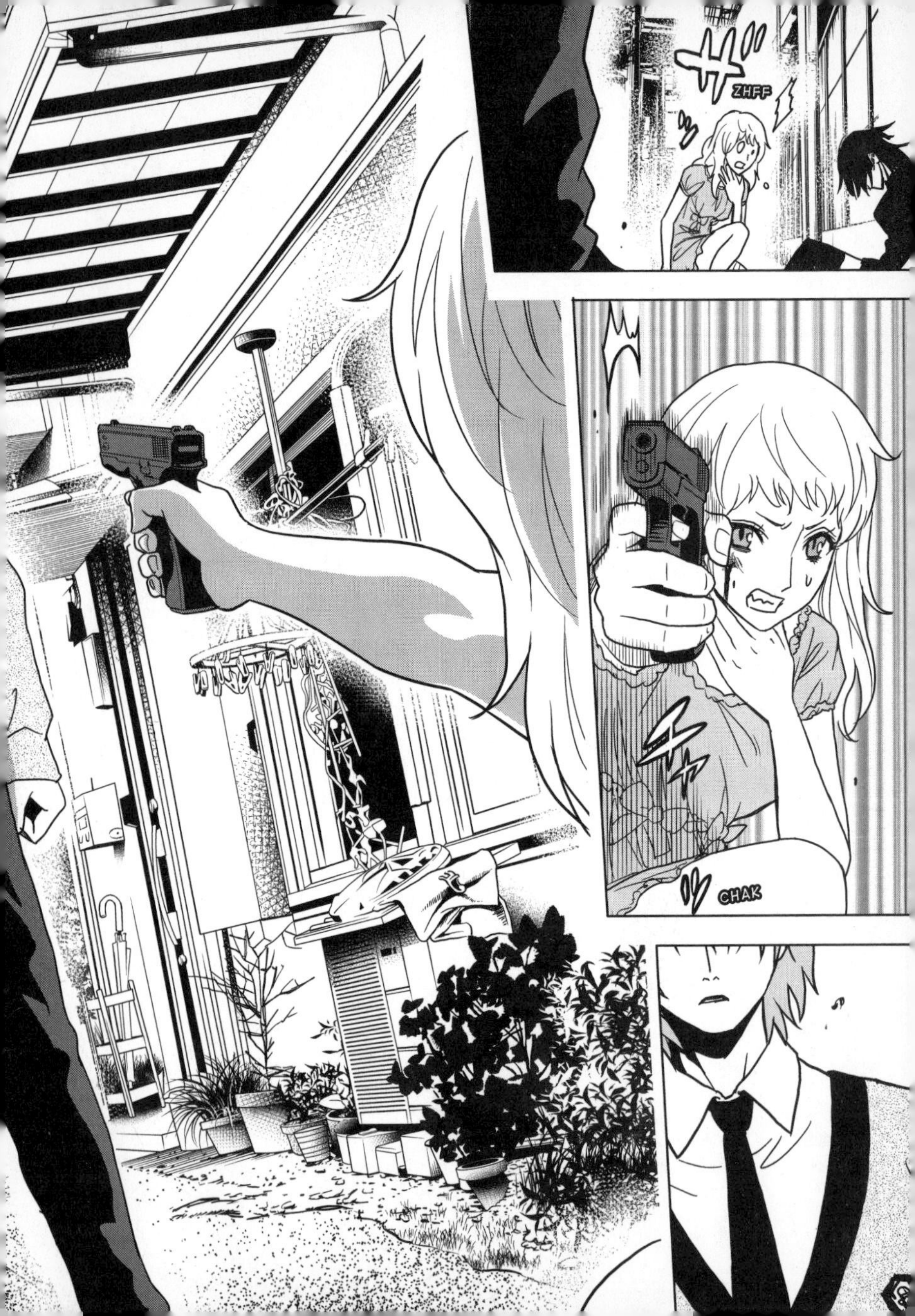
ZHFF
CHAK

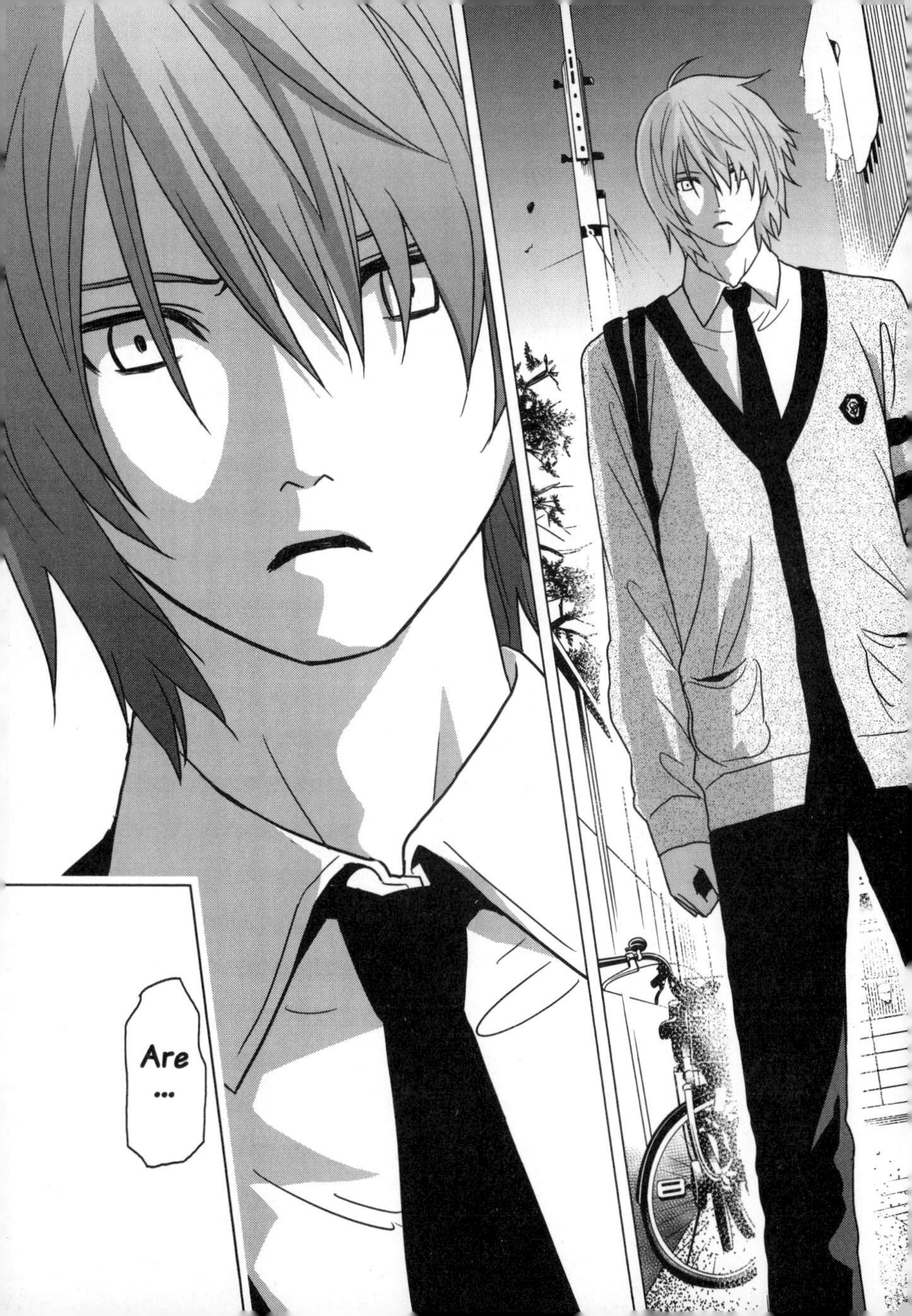
Are ...

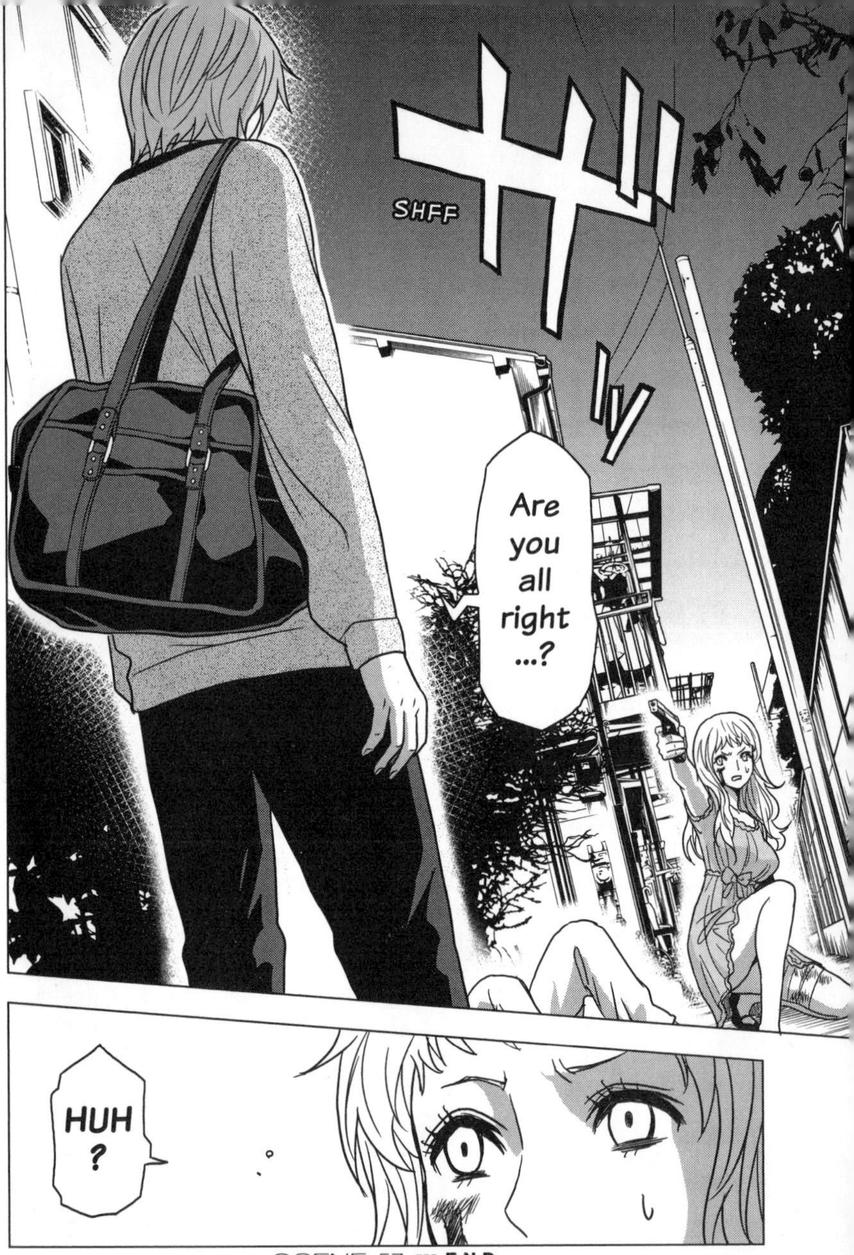
SHFF
Are you all right ...?
HUH ?

SCENE 57 /// END

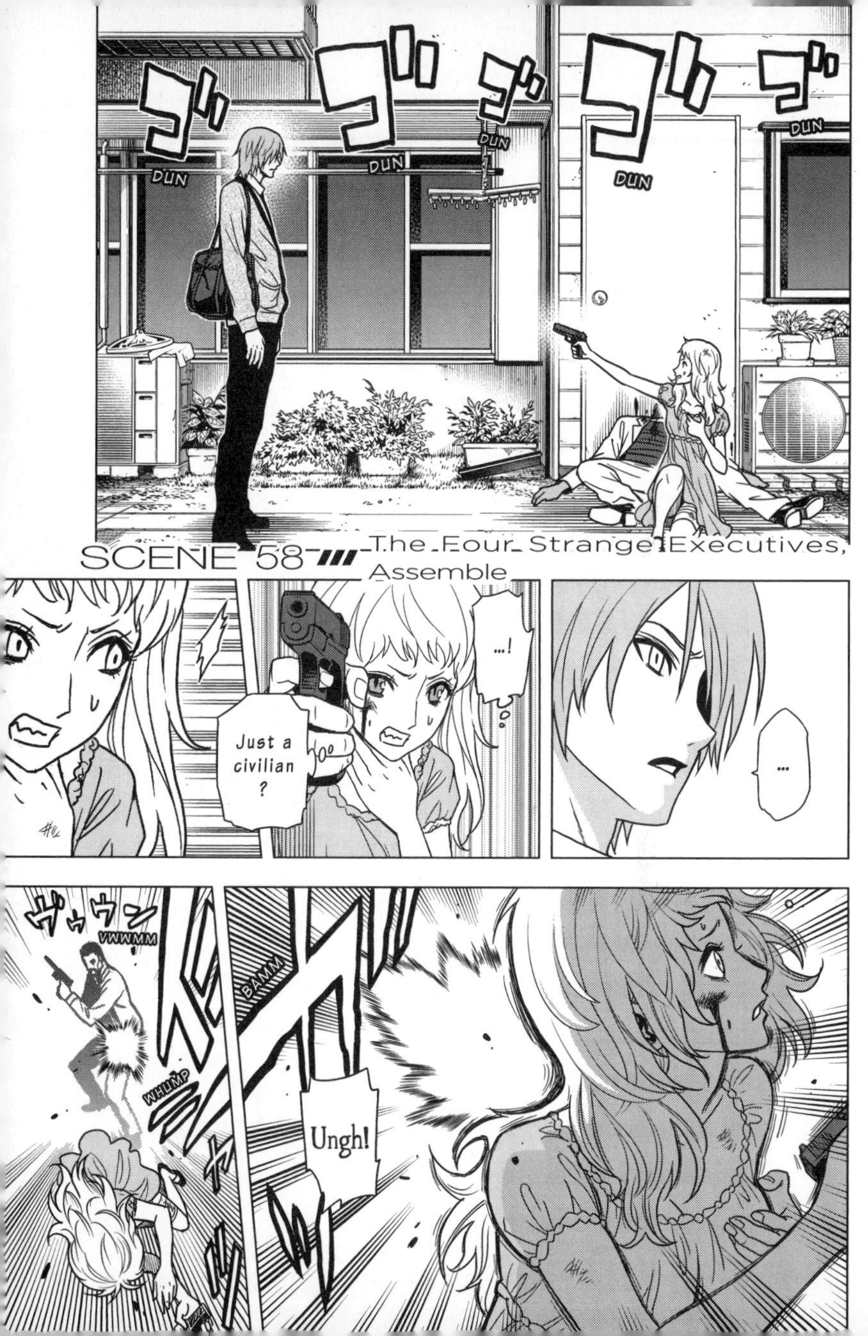
ゴゴゴゴゴゴ
DUN
DUN
DUN
DUN
DUN
DUN
SCENE 58 /// The Four Strange Executives, Assemble
...
...!
Just a civilian ?
BAMM
Ungh!
ヴゥウン
VWWMM
WHUMP

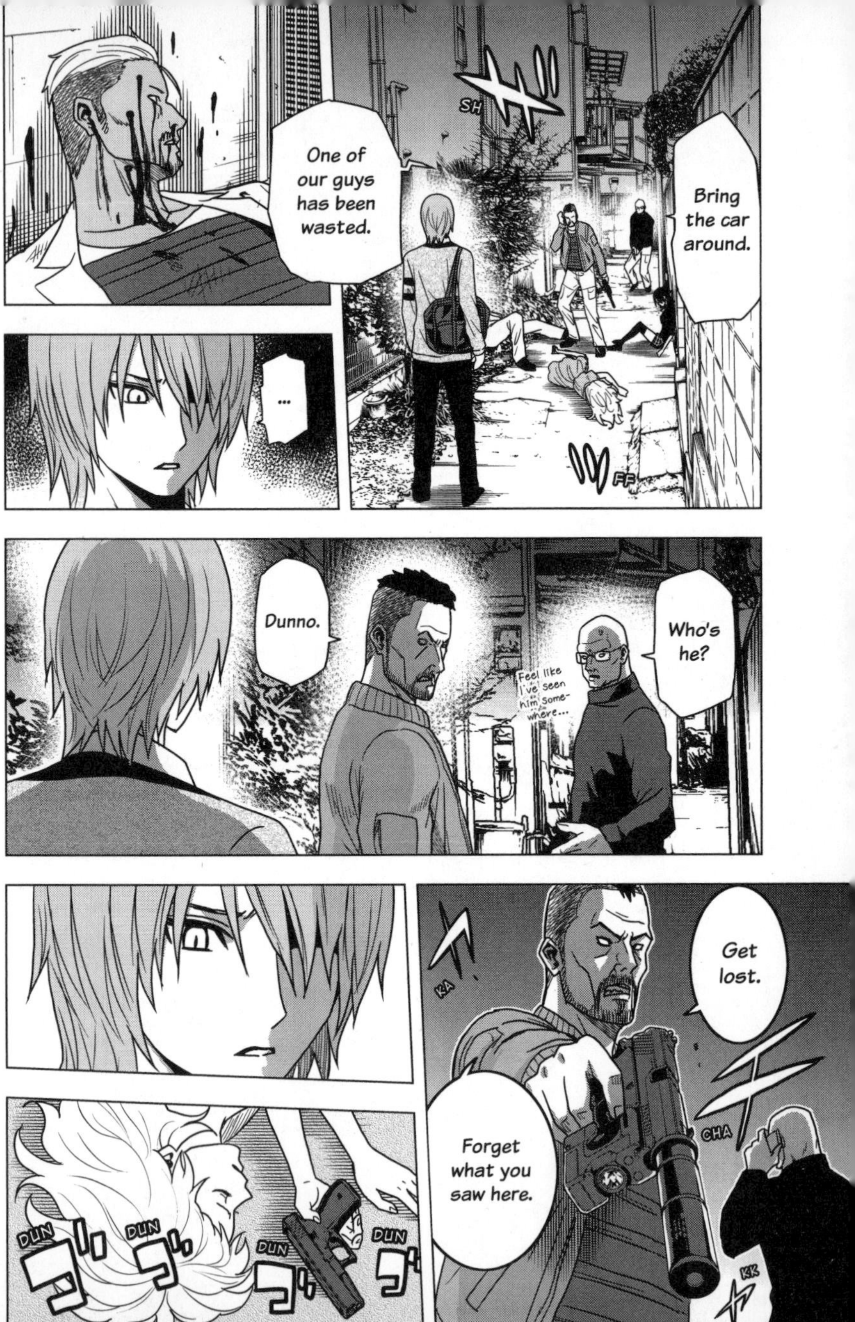
SH
One of our guys has been wasted.
Bring the car around.
FF
...
Who's he?
Feel like I've seen him some-where...
Dunno.
KA
Get lost.
CHA
Forget what you saw here.
KK
DUN
DUN
DUN
DUN

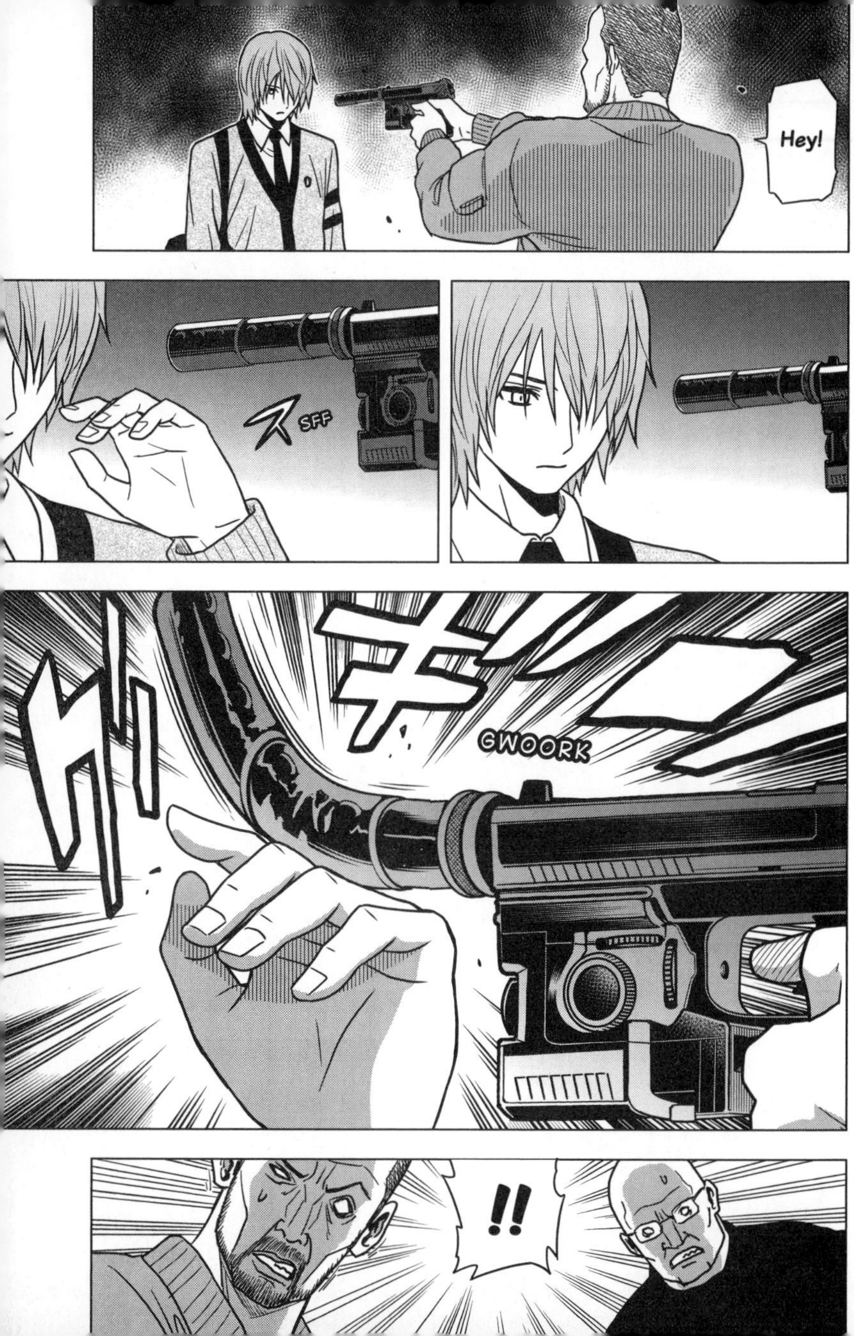
Hey!
ス
SFF
GWOORK
!!

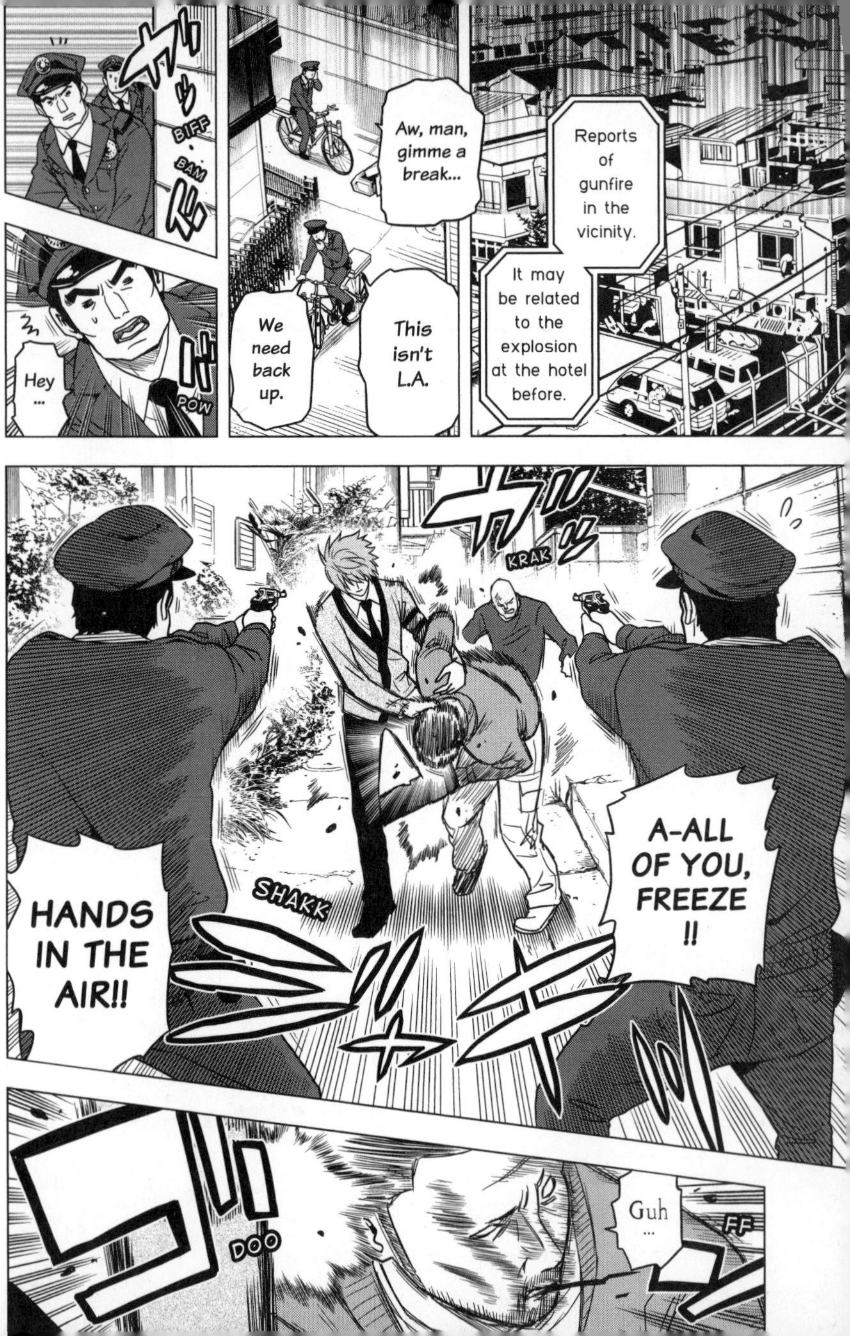
Reports of gunfire in the vicinity.
It may be related to the explosion at the hotel before.
Aw, man, gimme a break...
This isn't L.A.
We need back up.
BIFF
BAM
Hey ...
POW
KRAK
A-ALL OF YOU, FREEZE !!
SHAKK
HANDS IN THE AIR!!
Guh ...
FF
DOO

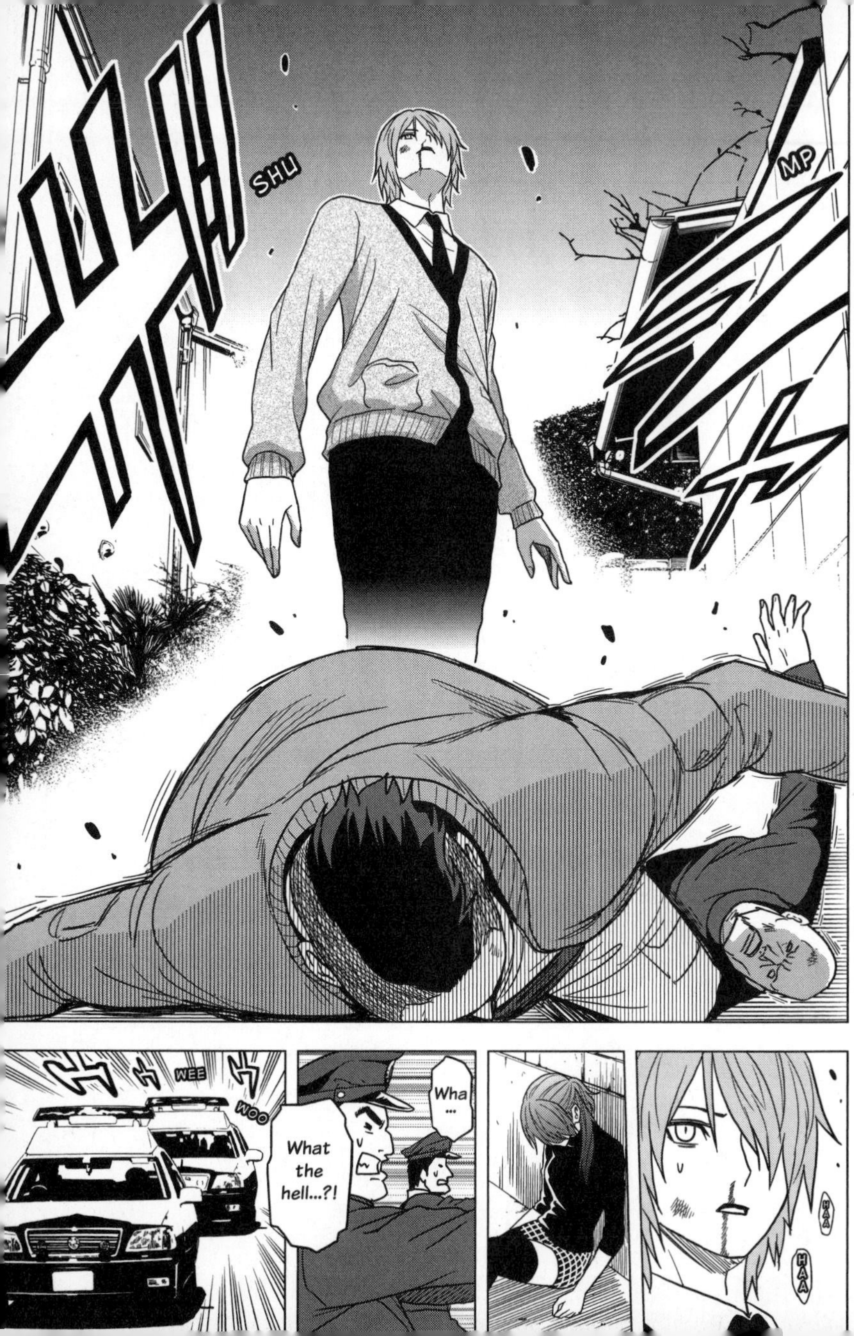
SHU
MP
HAA
HAA
Wha ...
What the hell...?!
WEE
WOO

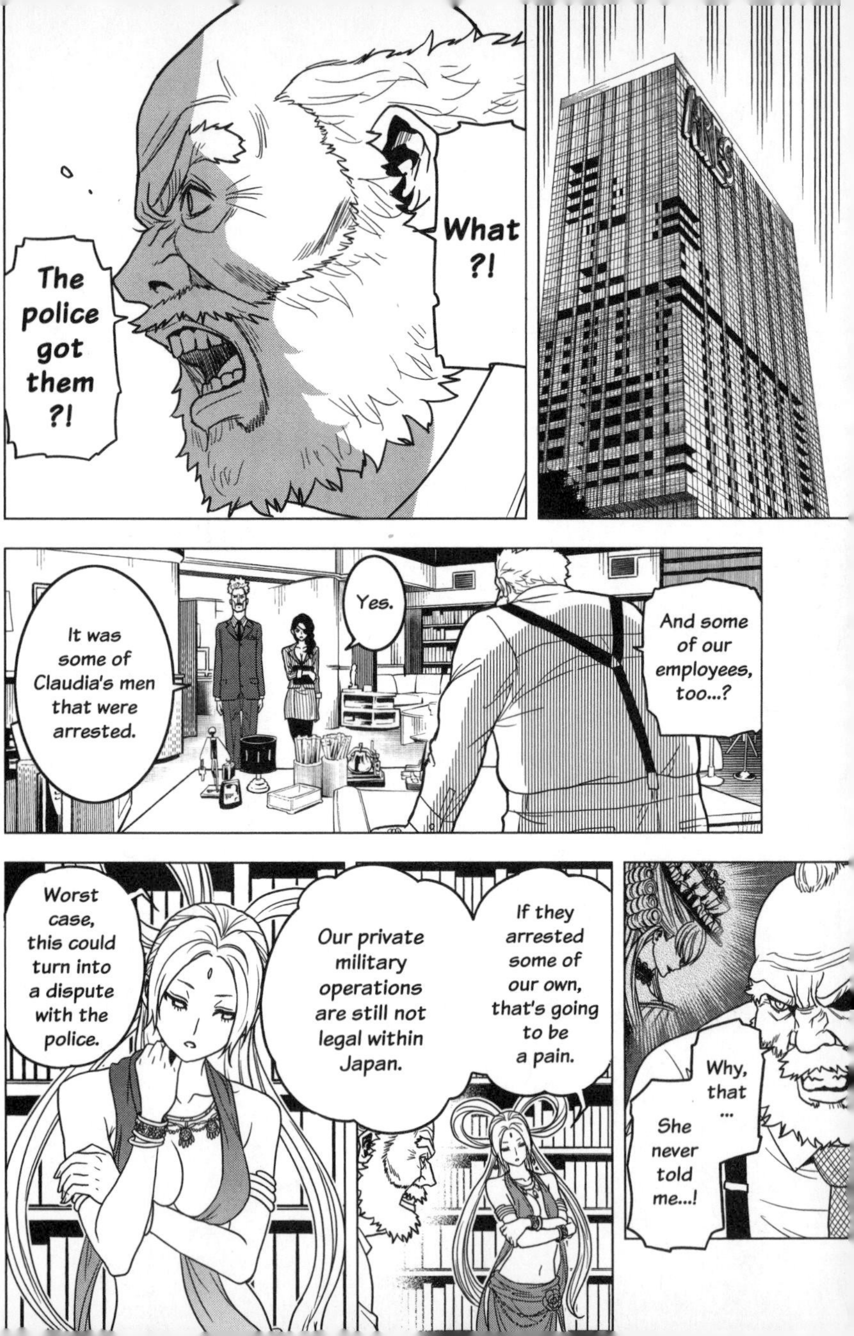
What ?!
The police got them ?!
And some of our employees, too...?
Yes.
It was some of Claudia's men that were arrested.
Why, that ...
She never told me...!
If they arrested some of our own, that's going to be a pain.
Our private military operations are still not legal within Japan.
Worst case, this could turn into a dispute with the police.

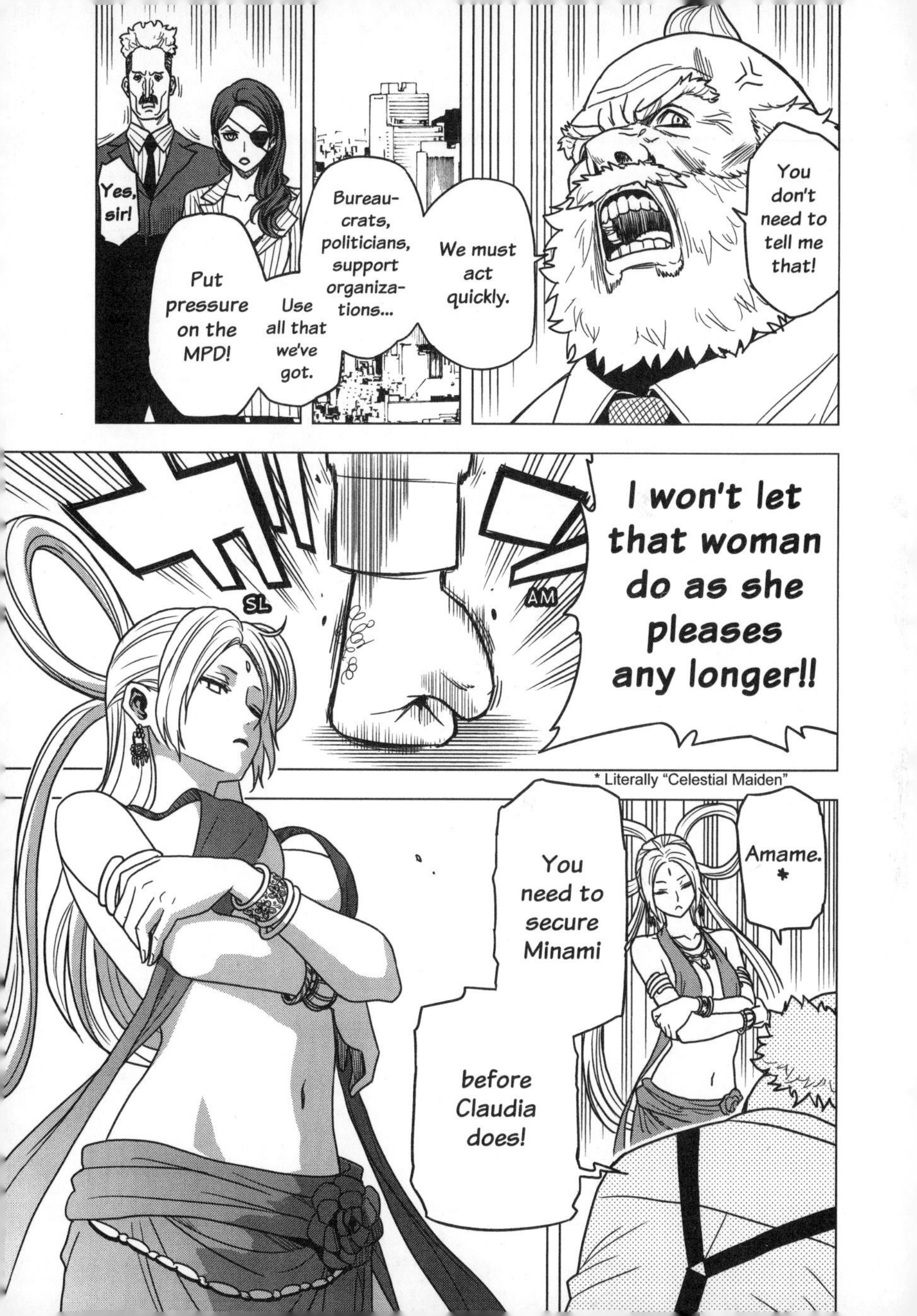
You don't need to tell me that!
We must act quickly.
Bureau-crats, politicians, support organiza-tions...
Use all that we've got.
Put pressure on the MPD!
Yes, sir!
I won't let that woman do as she pleases any longer!!
SL
AM
Amame. *
You need to secure Minami
before Claudia does!

* Literally "Celestial Maiden"

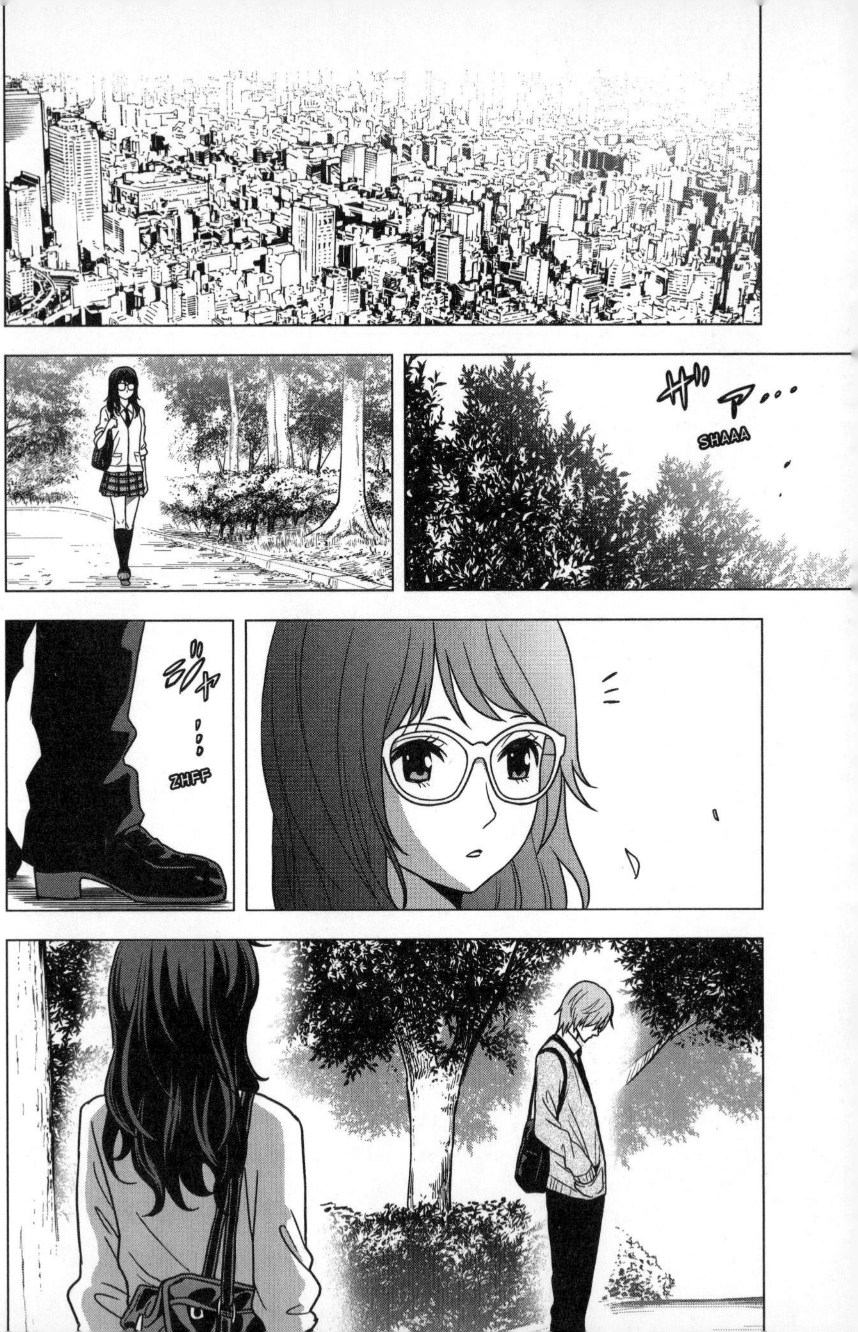
ザァ…
SHAAA
ジャ…
ZHFF

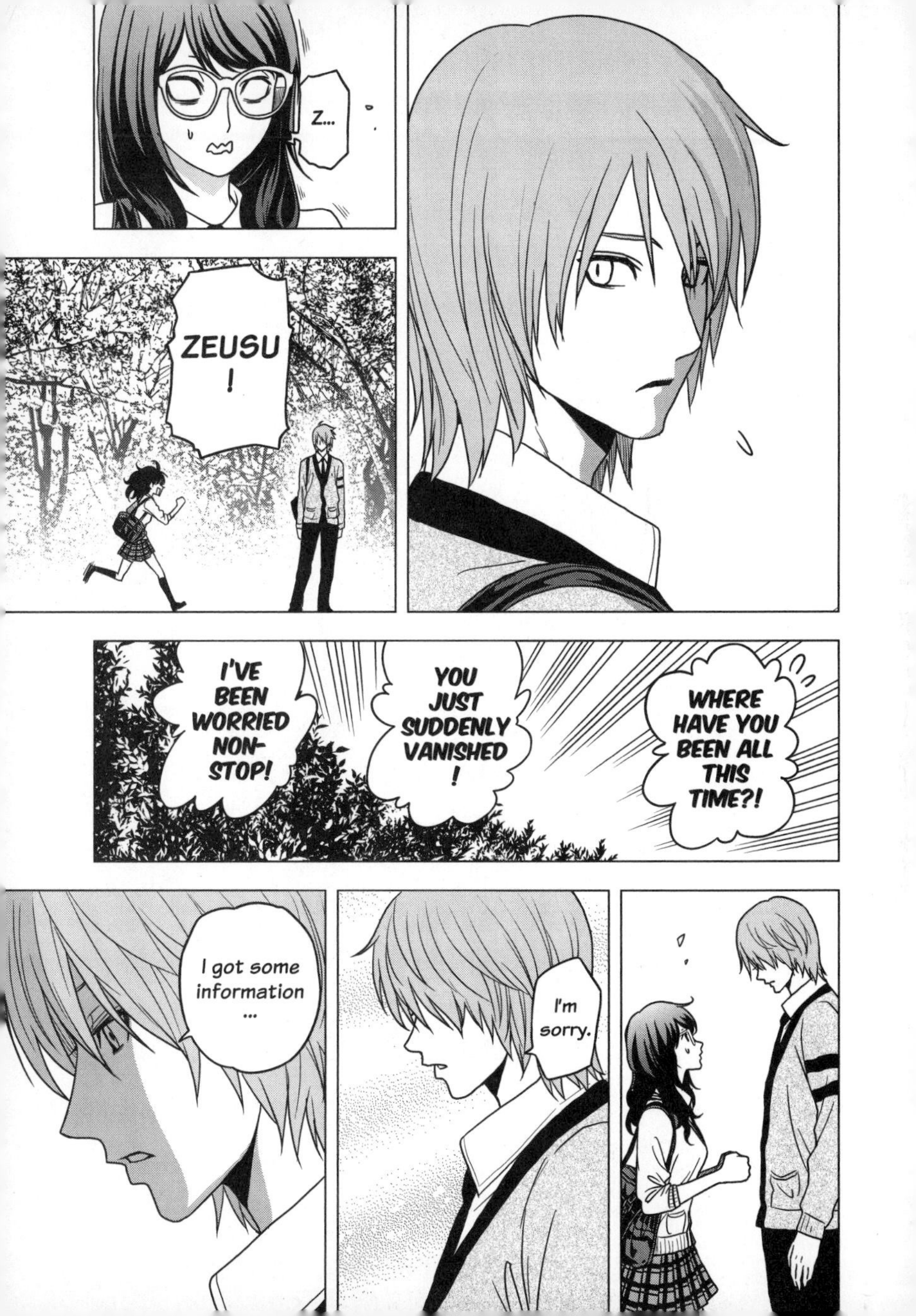
Z...
ZEUSU !
WHERE HAVE YOU BEEN ALL THIS TIME?!
YOU JUST SUDDENLY VANISHED !
I'VE BEEN WORRIED NON-STOP!
I'm sorry.
I got some information ...

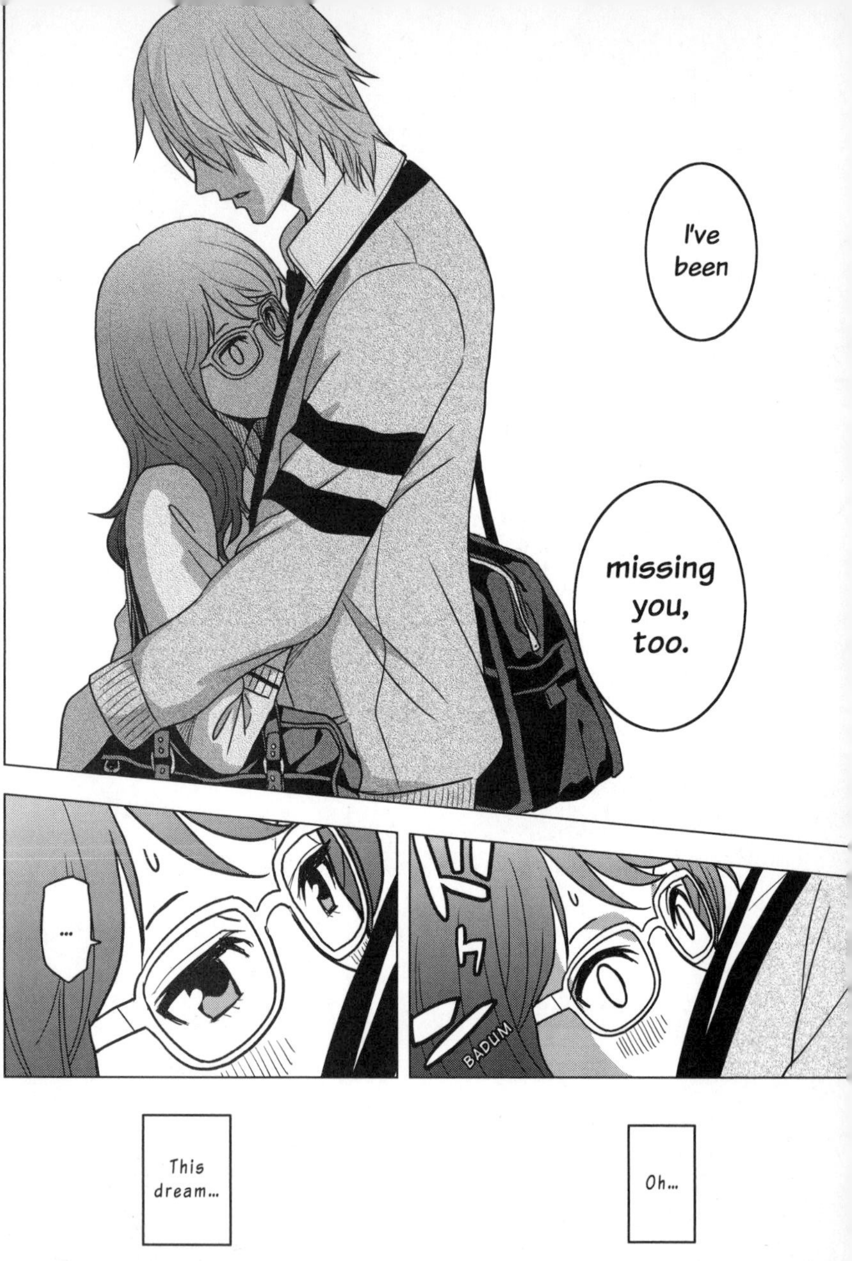
I've been
missing you, too.
BADUM
...
Oh...
This dream...

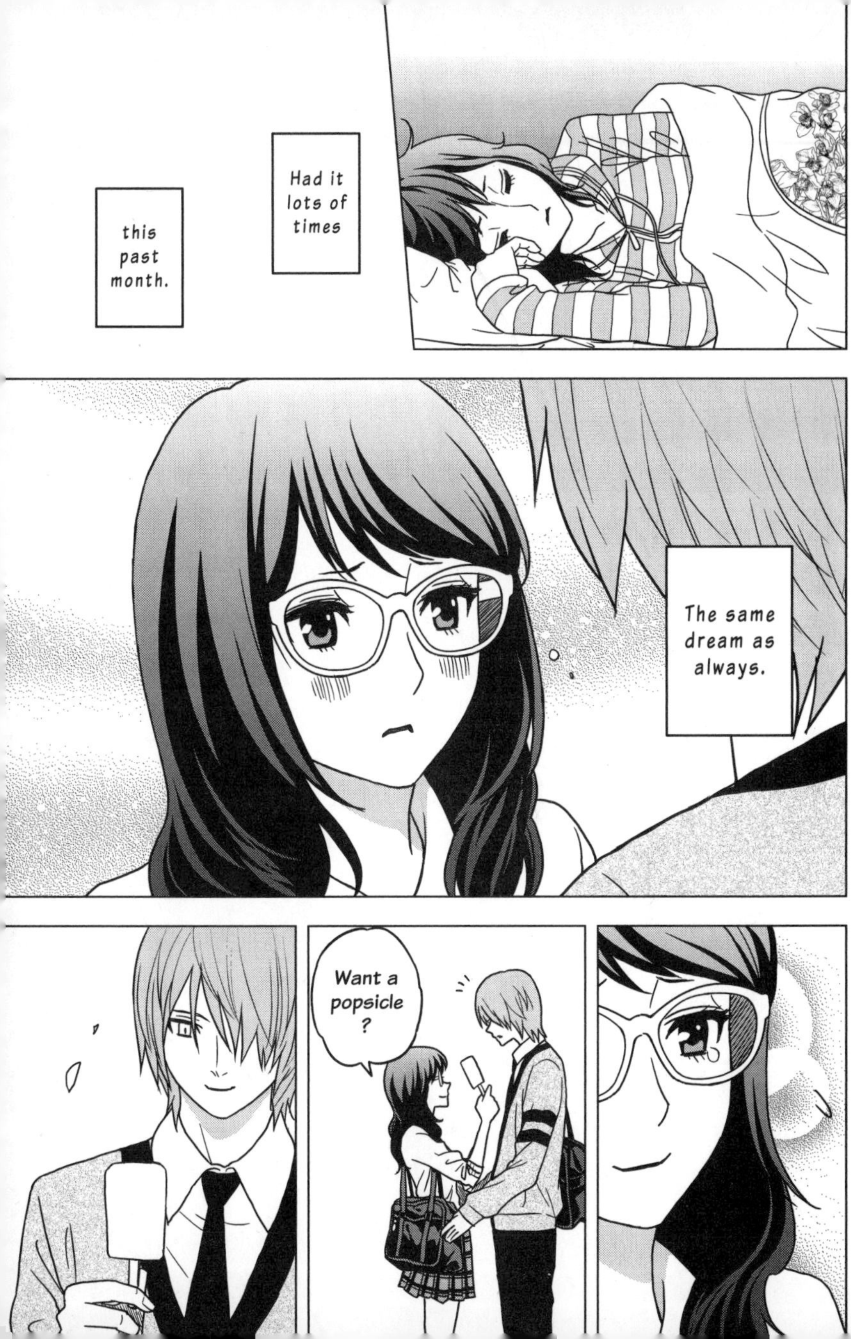
Had it lots of times
this past month.
The same dream as always.
Want a popsicle?

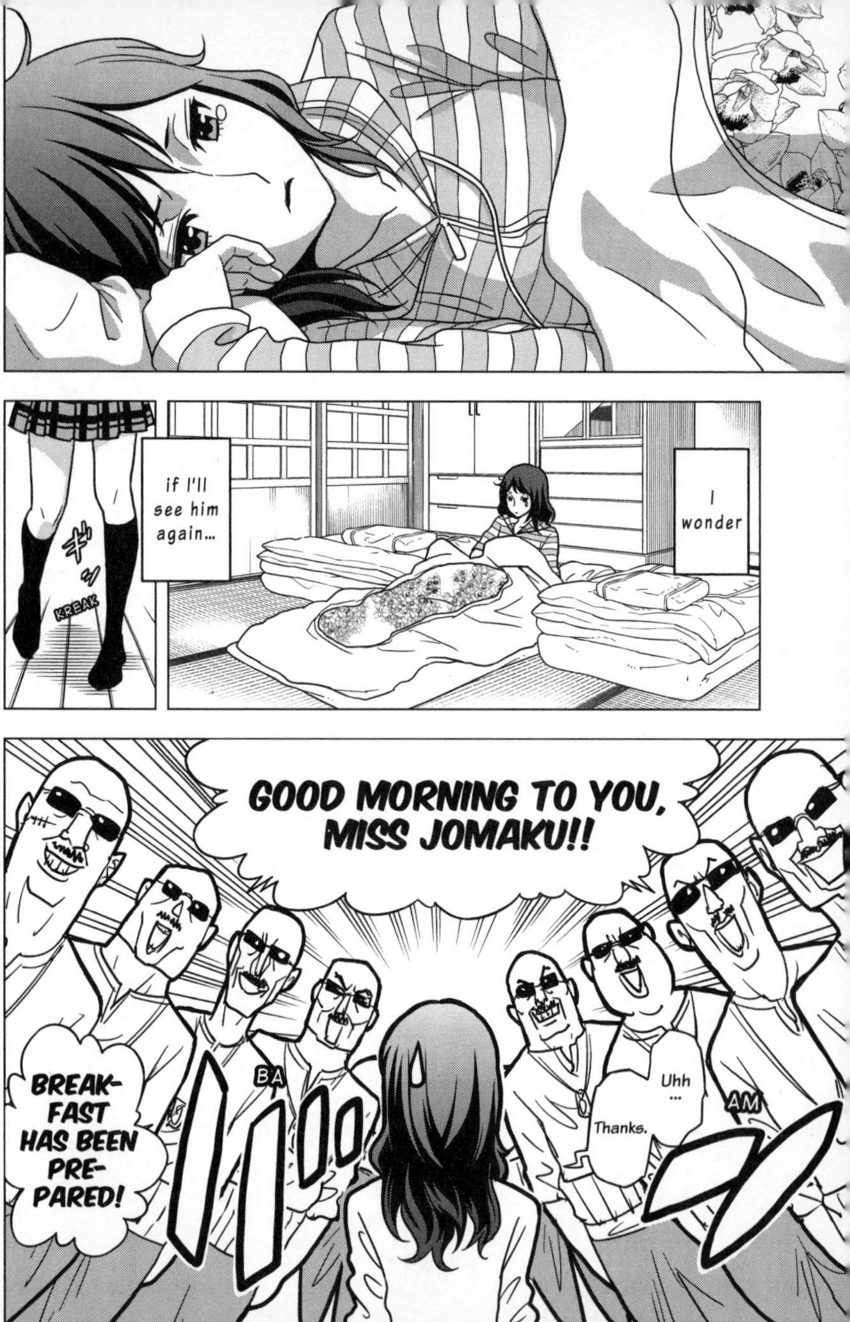
I wonder
if I'll see him again...
ギシ
KREAK
GOOD MORNING TO YOU, MISS JOMAKU!!
Uhh ...
Thanks.
AM
BA
BREAK-FAST HAS BEEN PRE-PARED!

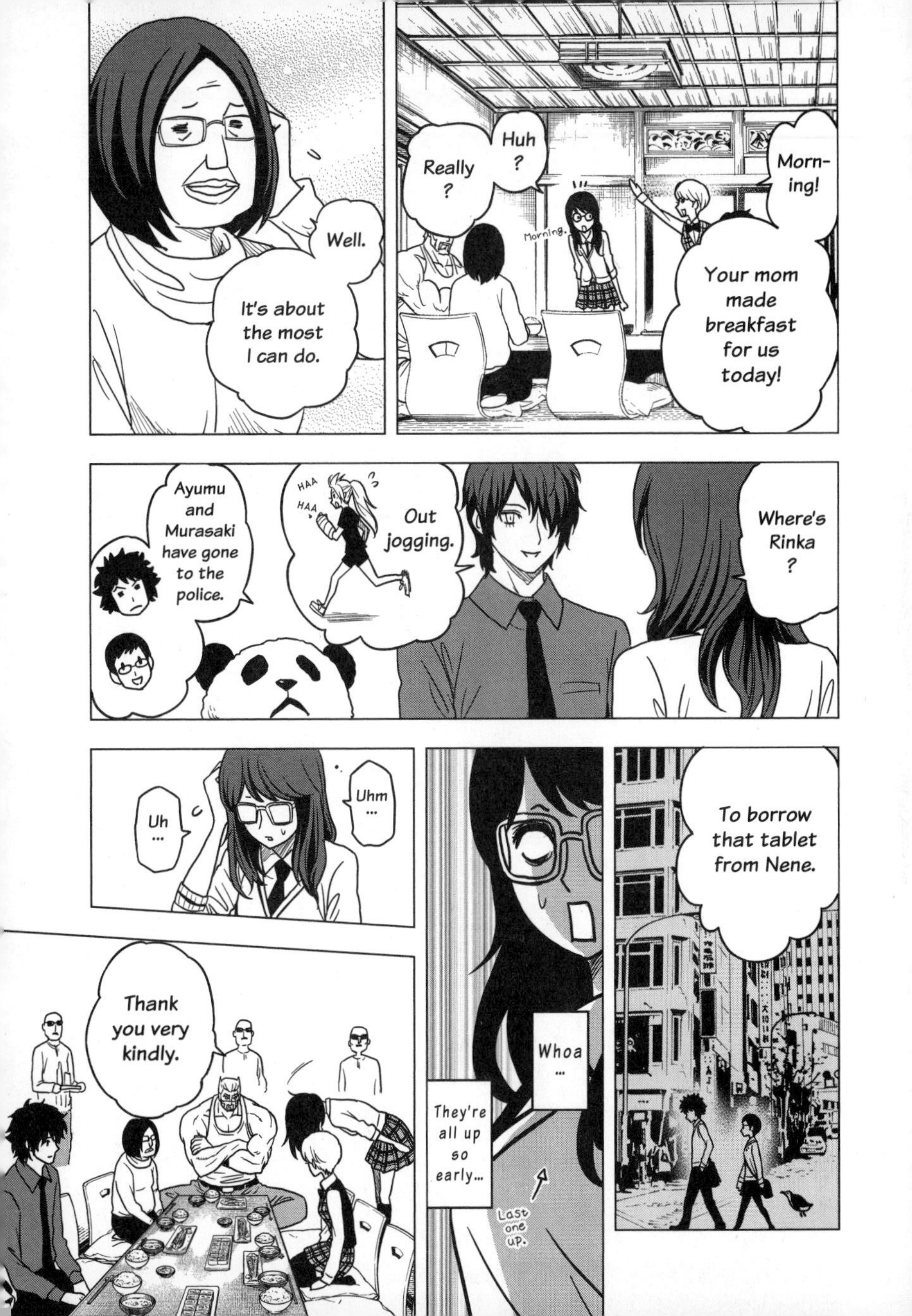

Morn-ing!
Your mom made breakfast for us today!
Morning.
Huh?
Really?
Well.
It's about the most I can do.
Where's Rinka?
Out jogging.
HAA HAA
Ayumu and Murasaki have gone to the police.
To borrow that tablet from Nene.
Whoa...
They're all up so early...
Last one up.
Uhm...
Uh...
Thank you very kindly.

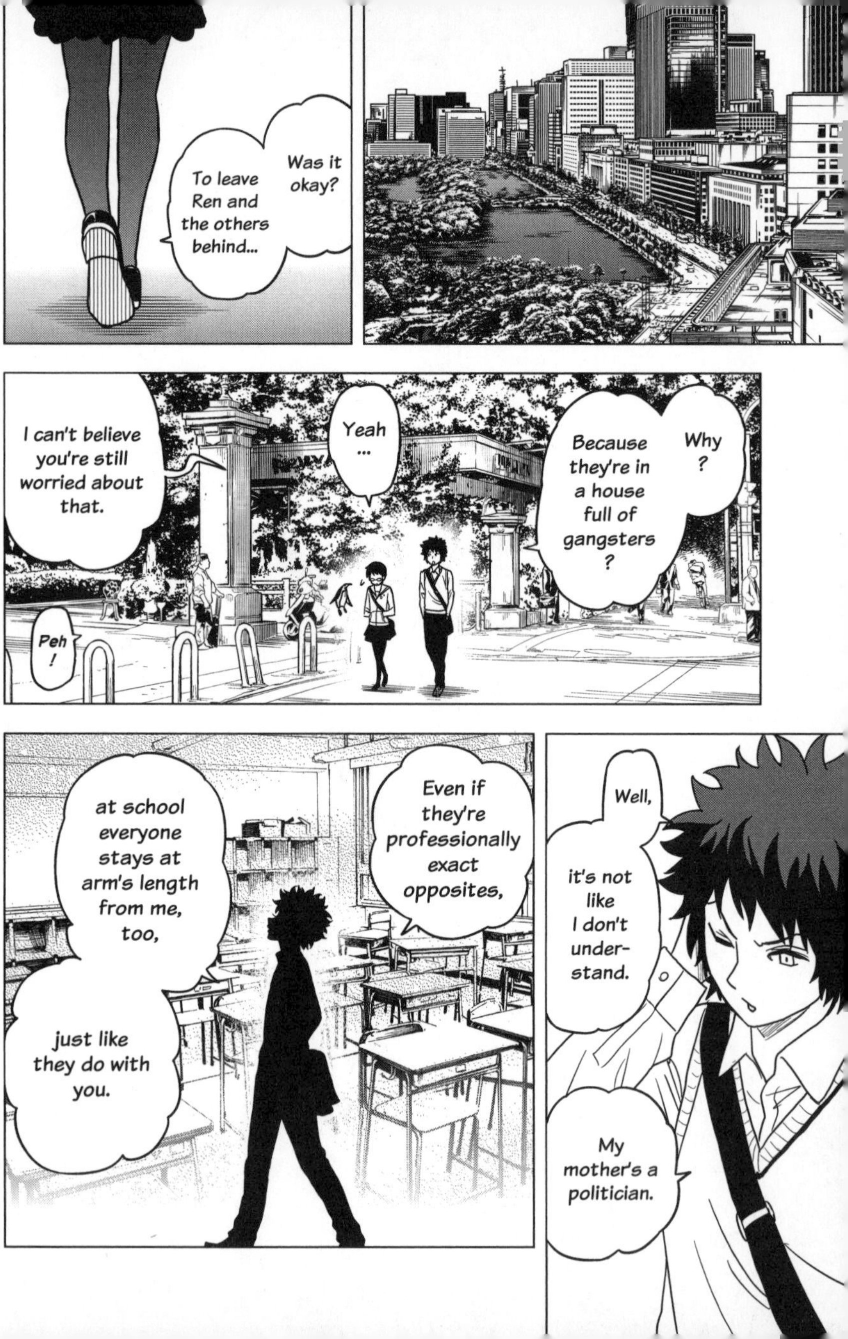
Was it okay?
To leave Ren and the others behind...
Why?
Because they're in a house full of gangsters?
Yeah...
I can't believe you're still worried about that.
Peh!
Well,
it's not like I don't under-stand.
My mother's a politician.
Even if they're professionally exact opposites,
at school everyone stays at arm's length from me, too,
just like they do with you.

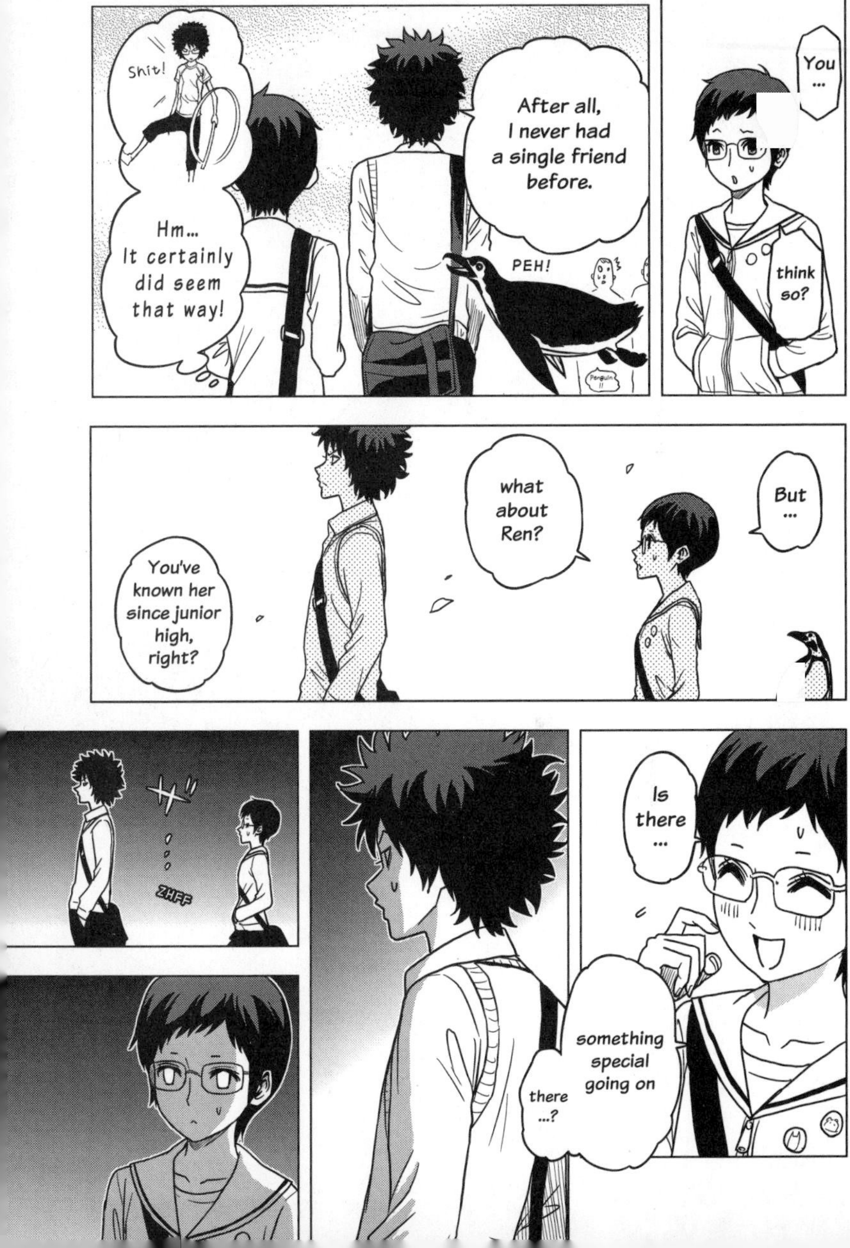
You ...
think so?
After all, I never had a single friend before.
PEH!
Penguin !!
Shit!
Hm... It certainly did seem that way!
But ...
what about Ren?
You've known her since junior high, right?
Is there ...
something special going on
there ...?
ZHFF

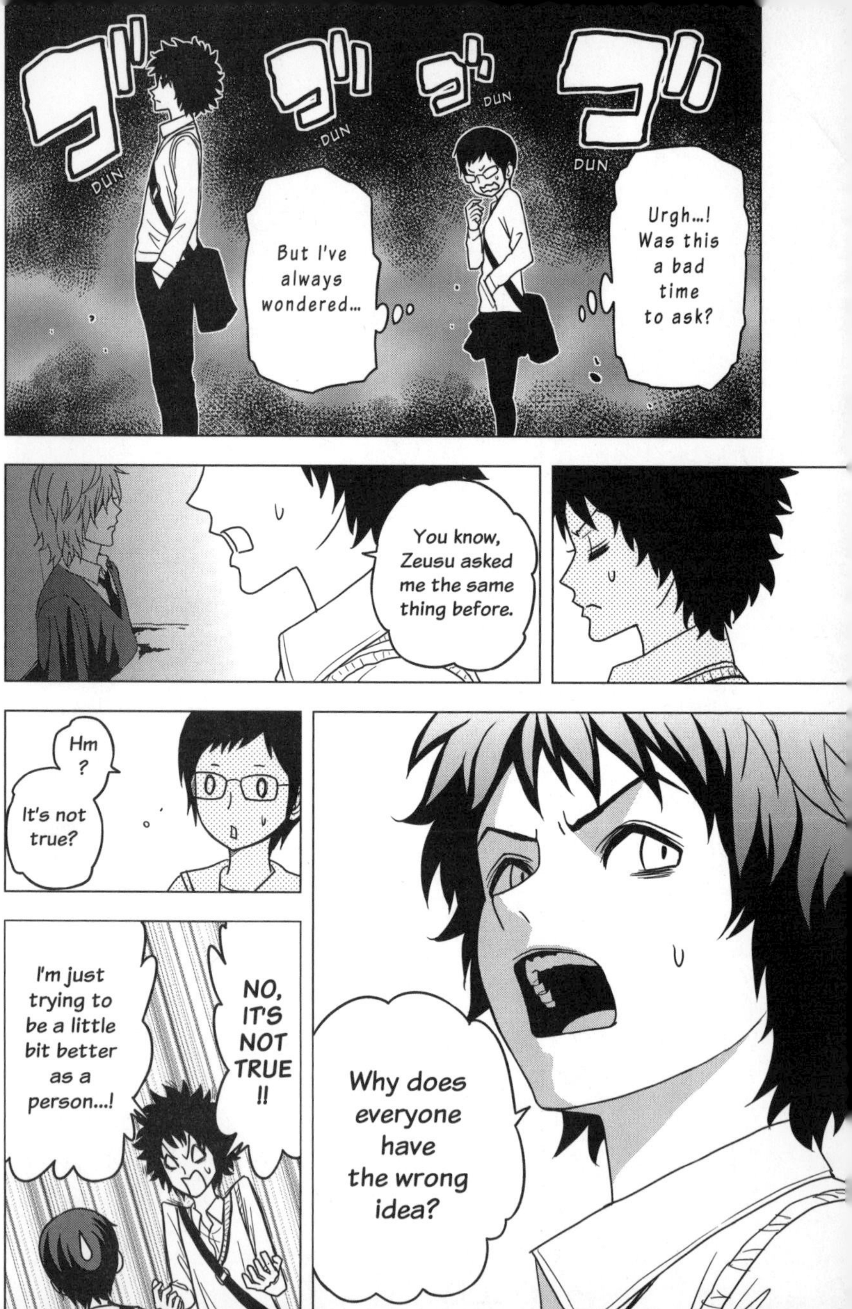
DUN
DUN
DUN
DUN
Urgh...! Was this a bad time to ask?
But I've always wondered...
You know, Zeusu asked me the same thing before.
Why does everyone have the wrong idea?
Hm?
It's not true?
NO, IT'S NOT TRUE!!
I'm just trying to be a little bit better as a person...!

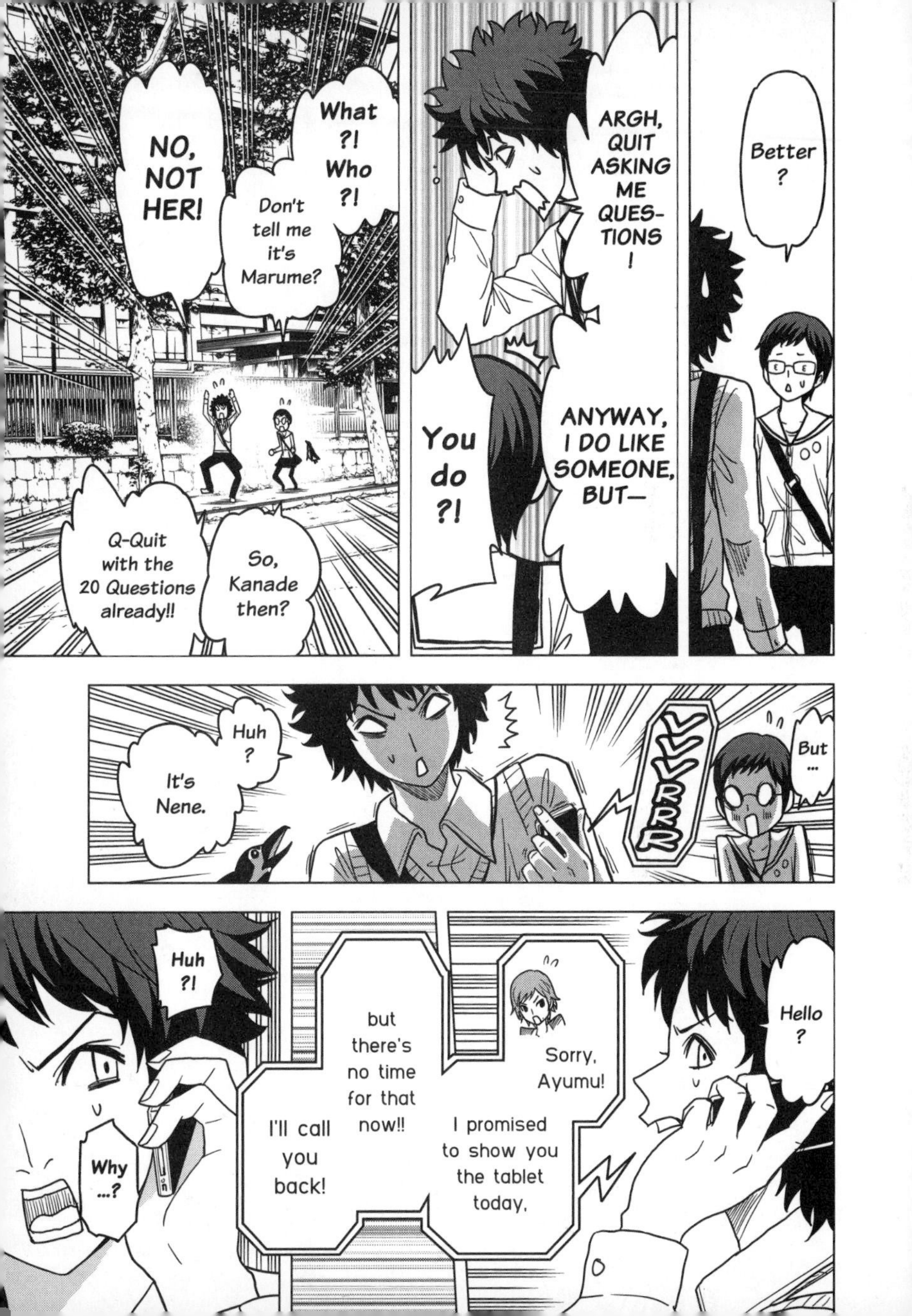
Better ?
ARGH, QUIT ASKING ME QUES- TIONS !
ANYWAY, I DO LIKE SOMEONE, BUT—
You do ?!
What ?! Who ?!
Don't tell me it's Marume?
NO, NOT HER!
So, Kanade then?
Q-Quit with the 20 Questions already!!
But ...
VVVRRR
Huh ?
It's Nene.
Hello ?
Sorry, Ayumu!
I promised to show you the tablet today,
but there's no time for that now!!
I'll call you back!
Huh ?!
Why ...?

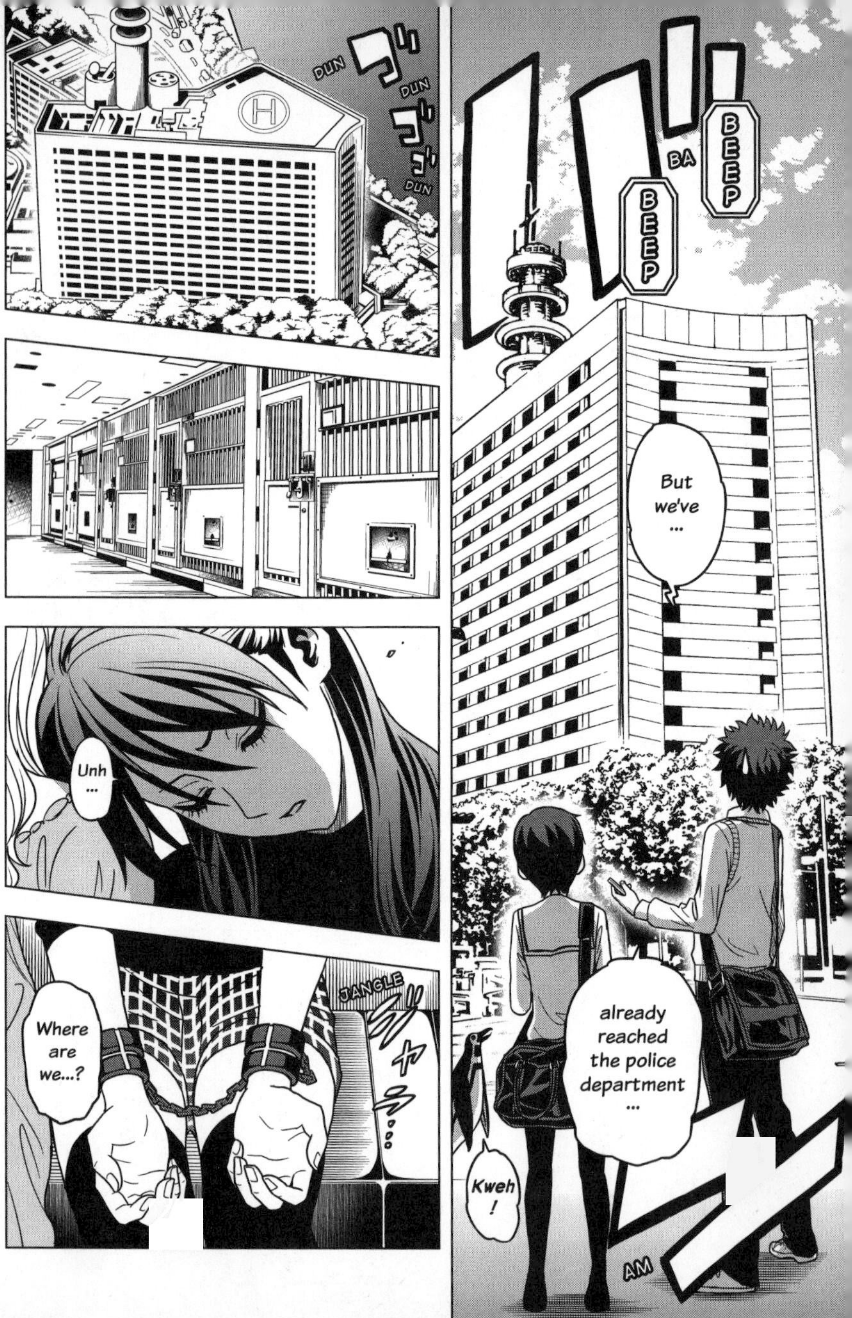
BEEP
BA
BEEP
But we've ...
already reached the police department ...
Kweh!
AM
DUN
DUN
DUN
Unh ...
JANGLE
Where are we...?

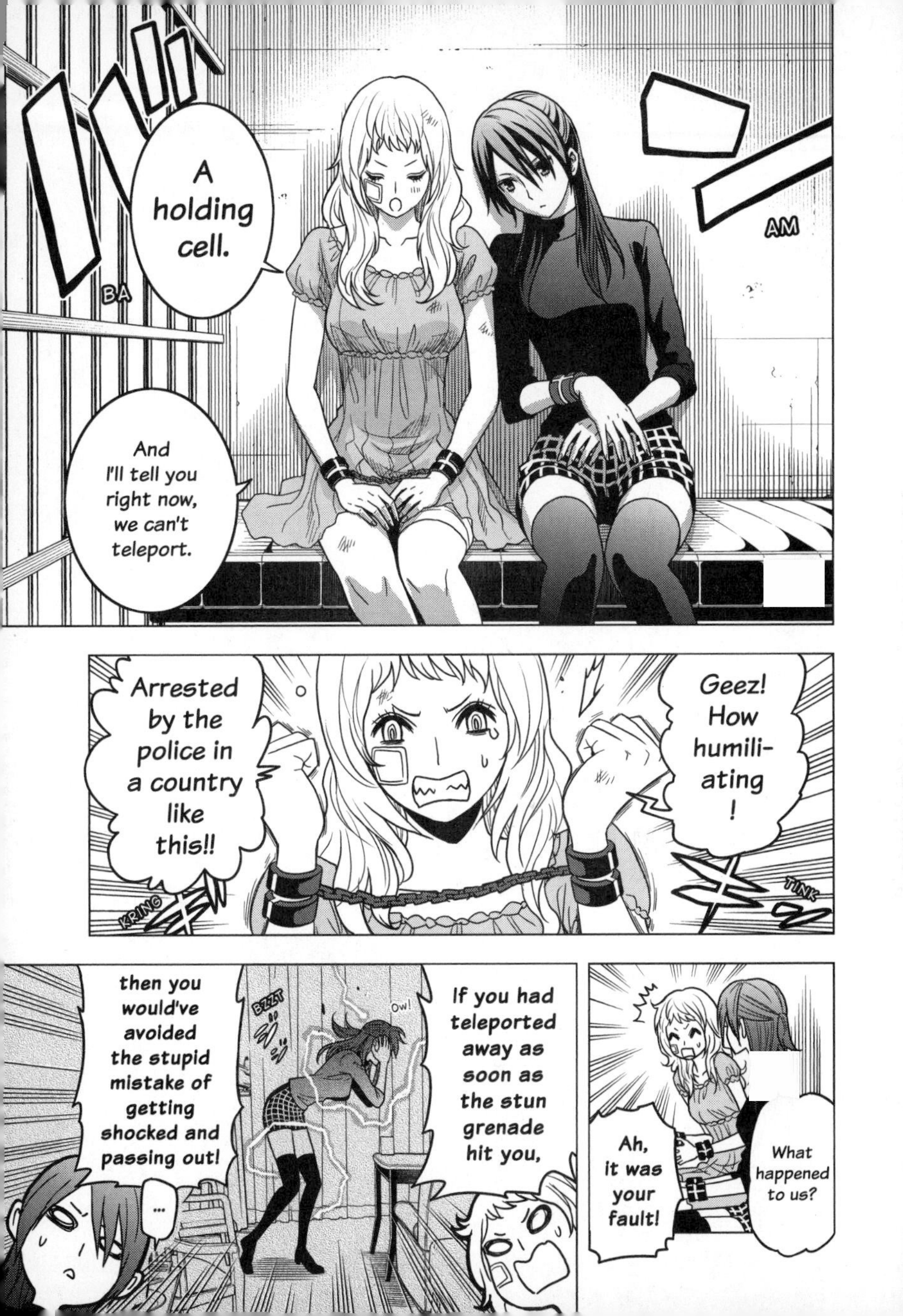
BA
AM
A holding cell.
And I'll tell you right now, we can't teleport.
Geez! How humili-ating!
Arrested by the police in a country like this!!
TINK
KRING
What happened to us?
Ah, it was your fault!
If you had teleported away as soon as the stun grenade hit you,
BZZZT
Ow!
then you would've avoided the stupid mistake of getting shocked and passing out!
...

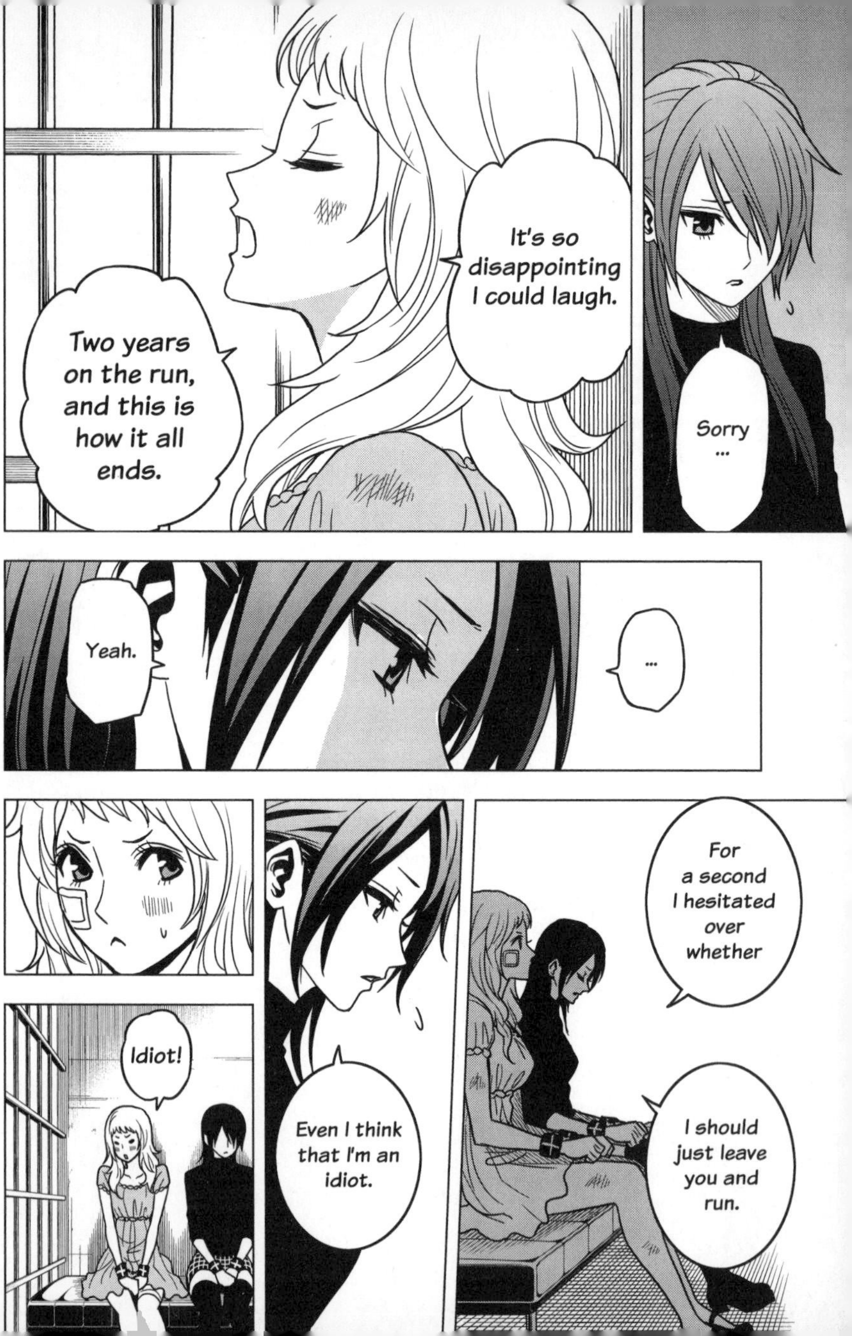
Sorry ...
It's so disappointing I could laugh.
Two years on the run, and this is how it all ends.
...
Yeah.
For a second I hesitated over whether
I should just leave you and run.
Even I think that I'm an idiot.
Idiot!

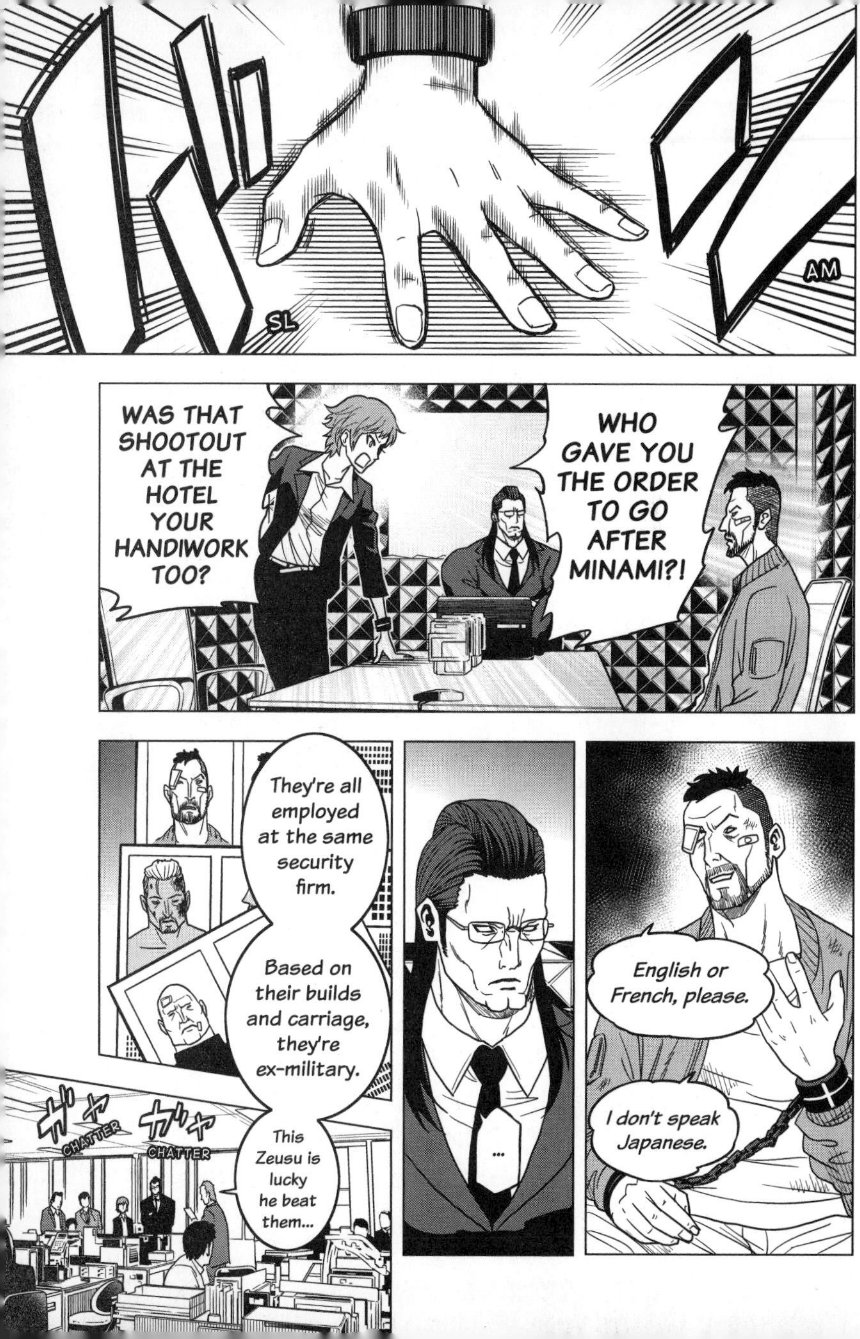
SL
AM
WHO GAVE YOU THE ORDER TO GO AFTER MINAMI?!
WAS THAT SHOOTOUT AT THE HOTEL YOUR HANDIWORK TOO?
English or French, please.
I don't speak Japanese.
...
They're all employed at the same security firm.
Based on their builds and carriage, they're ex-military.
This Zeusu is lucky he beat them...
ガヤ CHATTER
ガヤ CHATTER

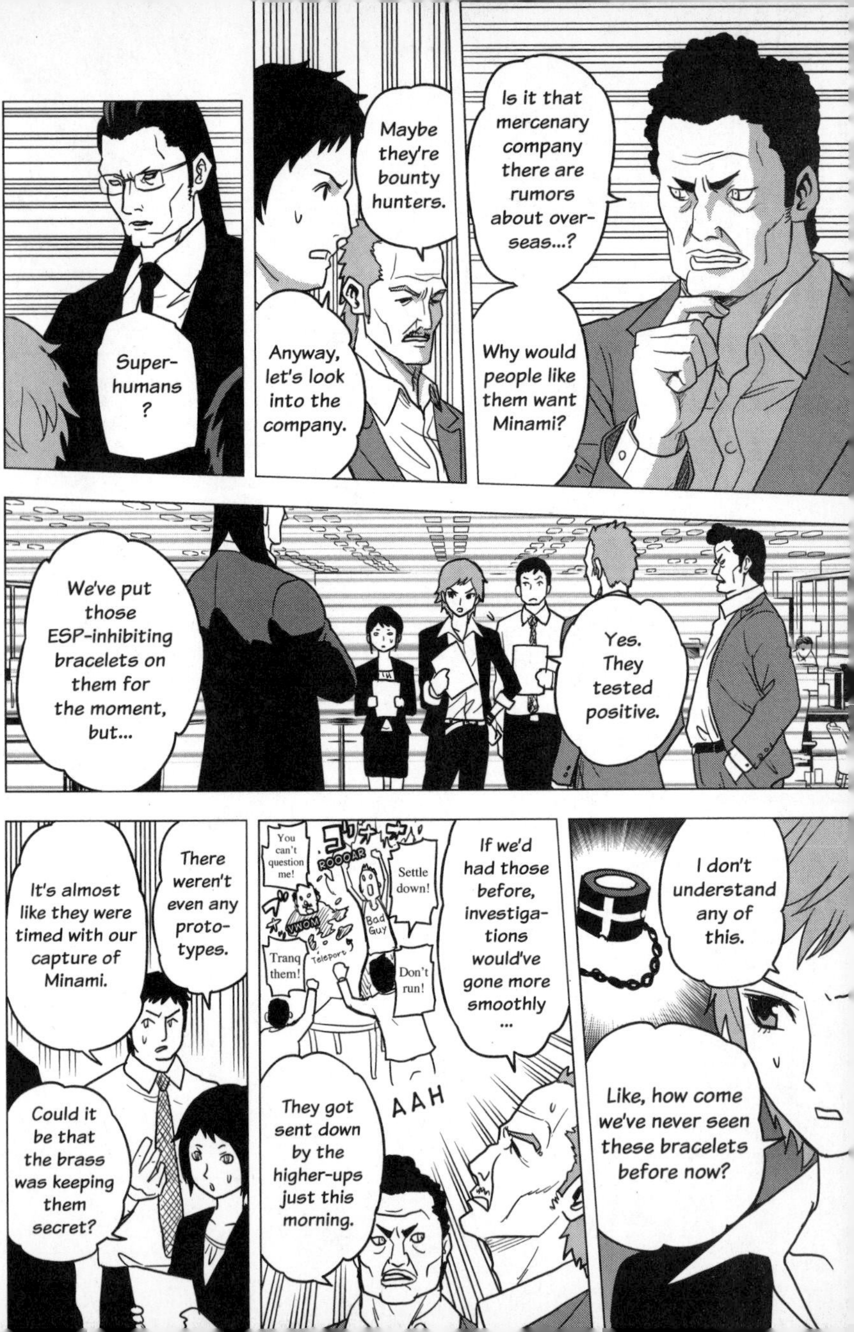
Is it that mercenary company there are rumors about over-seas...?
Why would people like them want Minami?
Maybe they're bounty hunters.
Anyway, let's look into the company.
Super-humans?
Yes. They tested positive.
We've put those ESP-inhibiting bracelets on them for the moment, but...
I don't understand any of this.
Like, how come we've never seen these bracelets before now?
If we'd had those before, investiga-tions would've gone more smoothly...
You can't question me!
ROOOAR
Settle down!
Bad Guy
VWOM
Tranq them!
Teleport
Don't run!
AAH
They got sent down by the higher-ups just this morning.
There weren't even any proto-types.
It's almost like they were timed with our capture of Minami.
Could it be that the brass was keeping them secret?

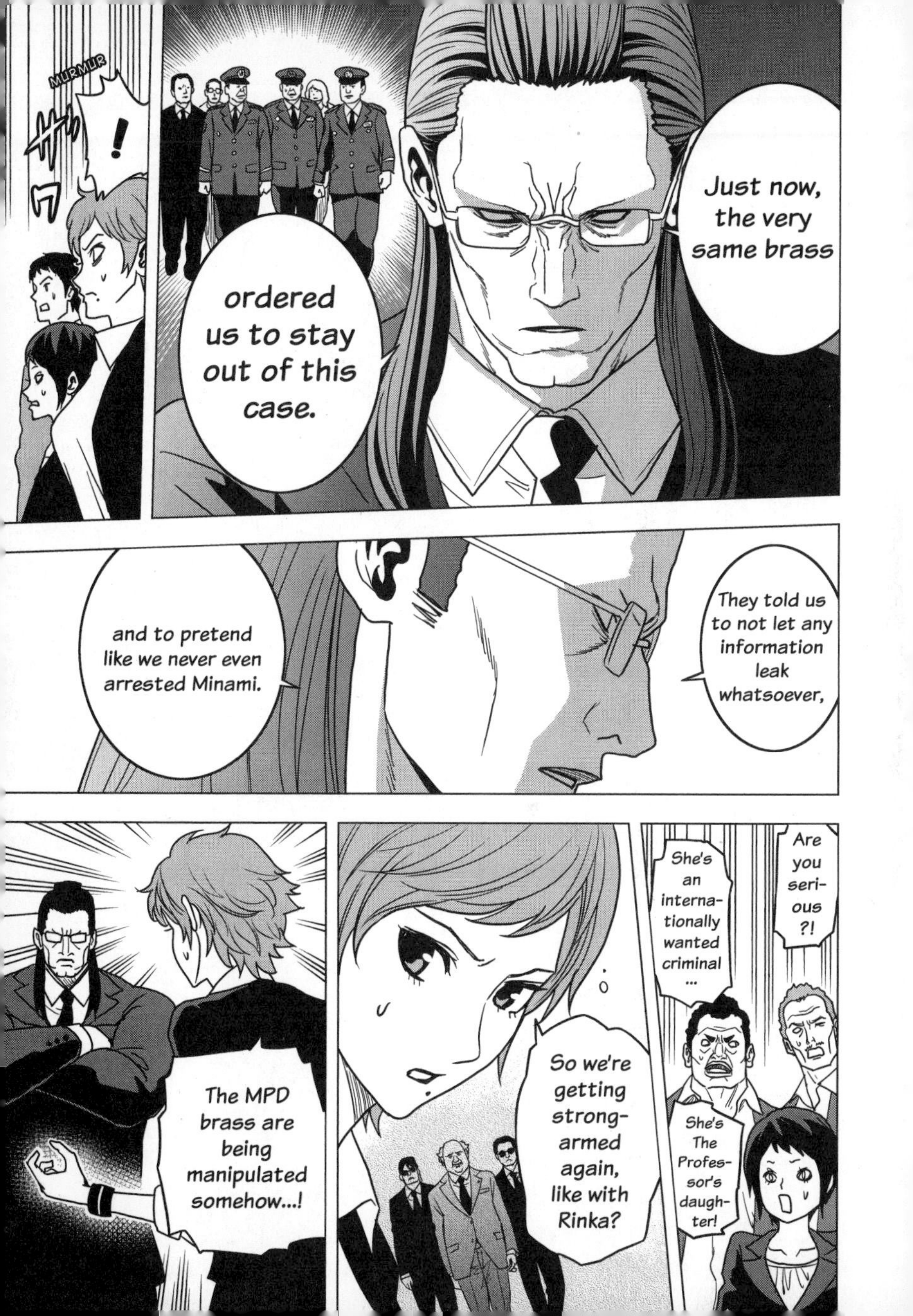
Just now, the very same brass
ordered us to stay out of this case.
MURMUR
!
They told us to not let any information leak whatsoever,
and to pretend like we never even arrested Minami.
Are you seri- ous ?!
She's an interna- tionally wanted criminal ...
She's The Profes- sor's daugh- ter!
So we're getting strong- armed again, like with Rinka?
The MPD brass are being manipulated somehow...!

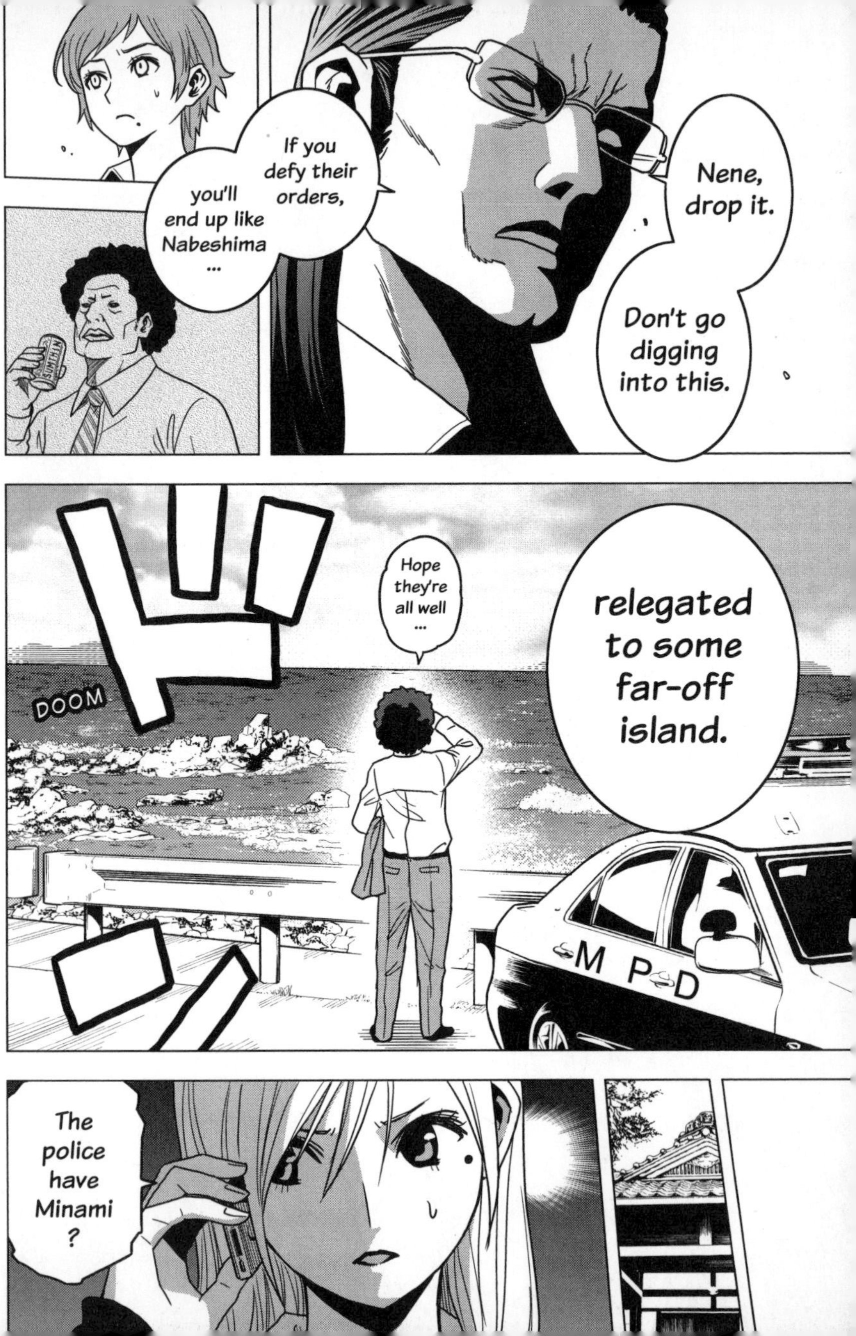
Nene, drop it.
Don't go digging into this.
If you defy their orders, you'll end up like Nabeshima ...
relegated to some far-off island.
Hope they're all well ...
DOOM
The police have Minami?

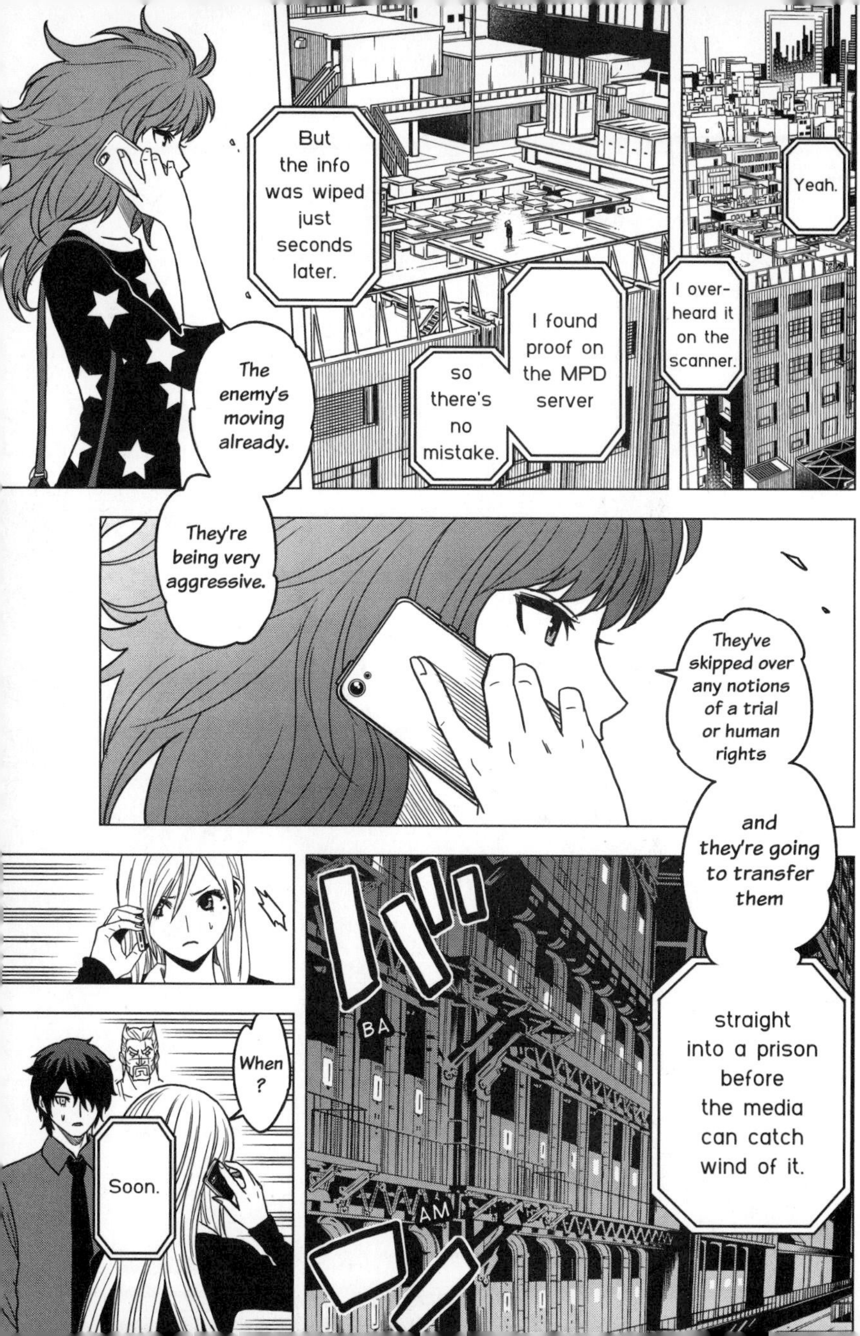
Yeah.
I over-heard it on the scanner.
I found proof on the MPD server
so there's no mistake.
But the info was wiped just seconds later.
The enemy's moving already.
They're being very aggressive.
They've skipped over any notions of a trial or human rights
and they're going to transfer them
straight into a prison before the media can catch wind of it.
BA
AM
When ?
Soon.

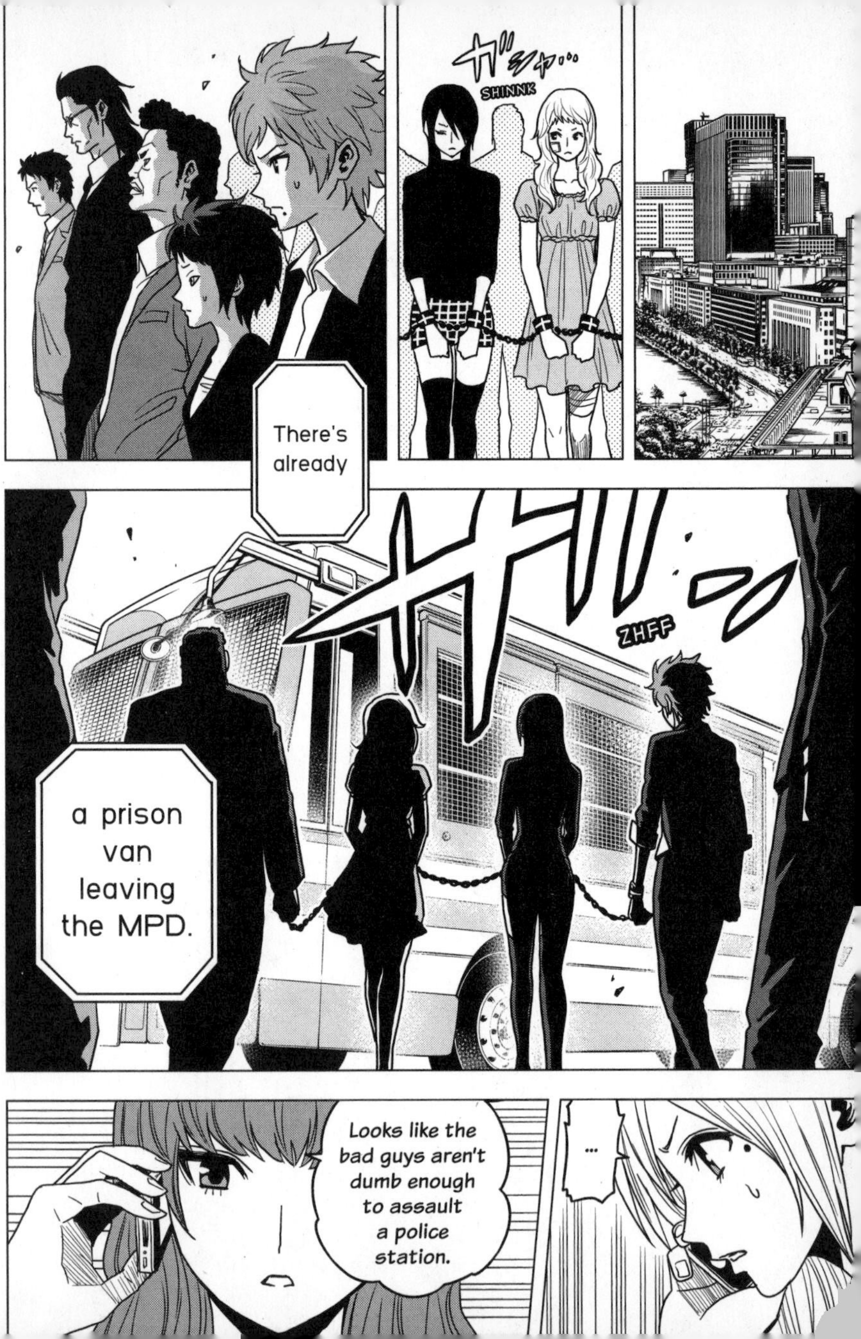
SHINNK
There's already
ZHFF
a prison van leaving the MPD.
...
Looks like the bad guys aren't dumb enough to assault a police station.

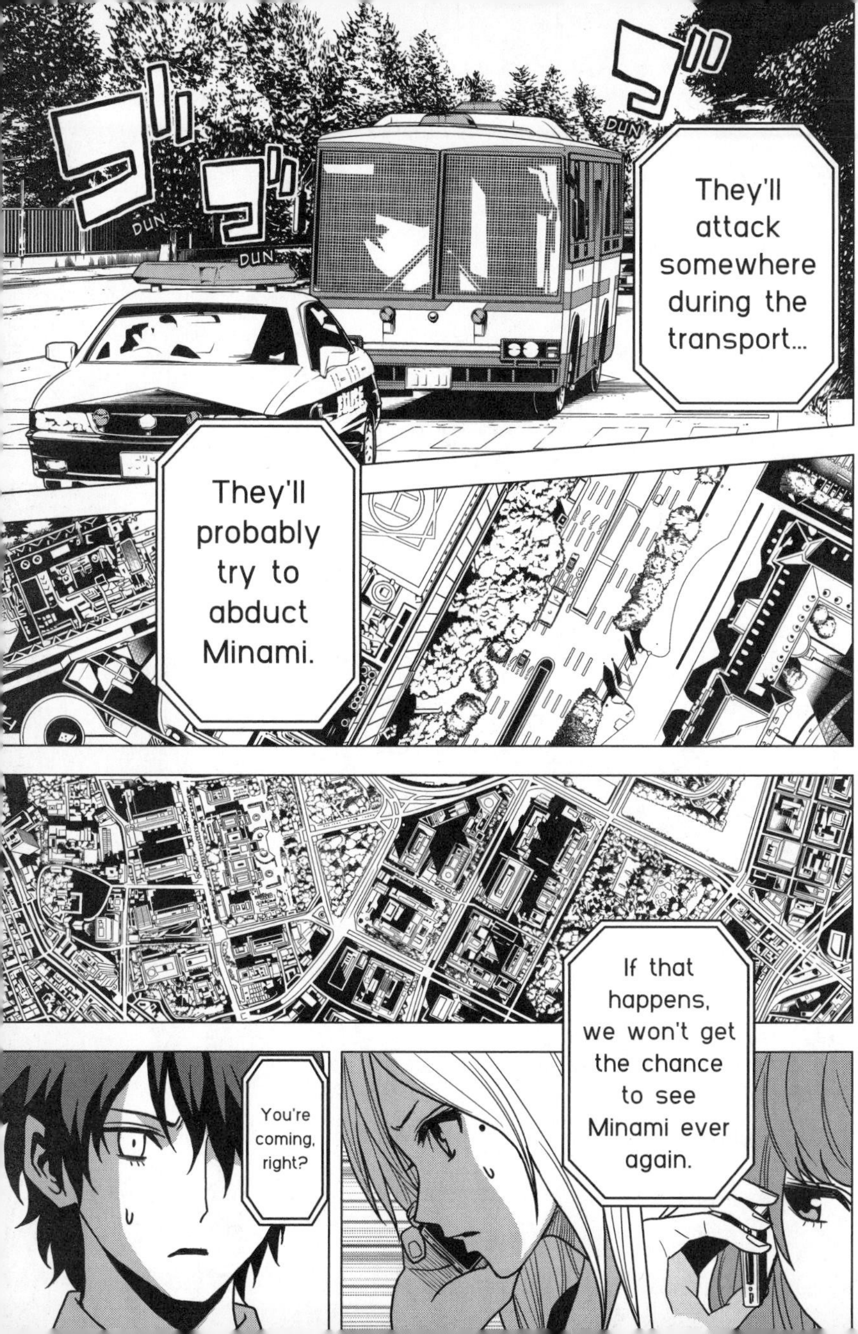
DUN
They'll attack somewhere during the transport...
DUN
DUN
They'll probably try to abduct Minami.
If that happens, we won't get the chance to see Minami ever again.
You're coming, right?

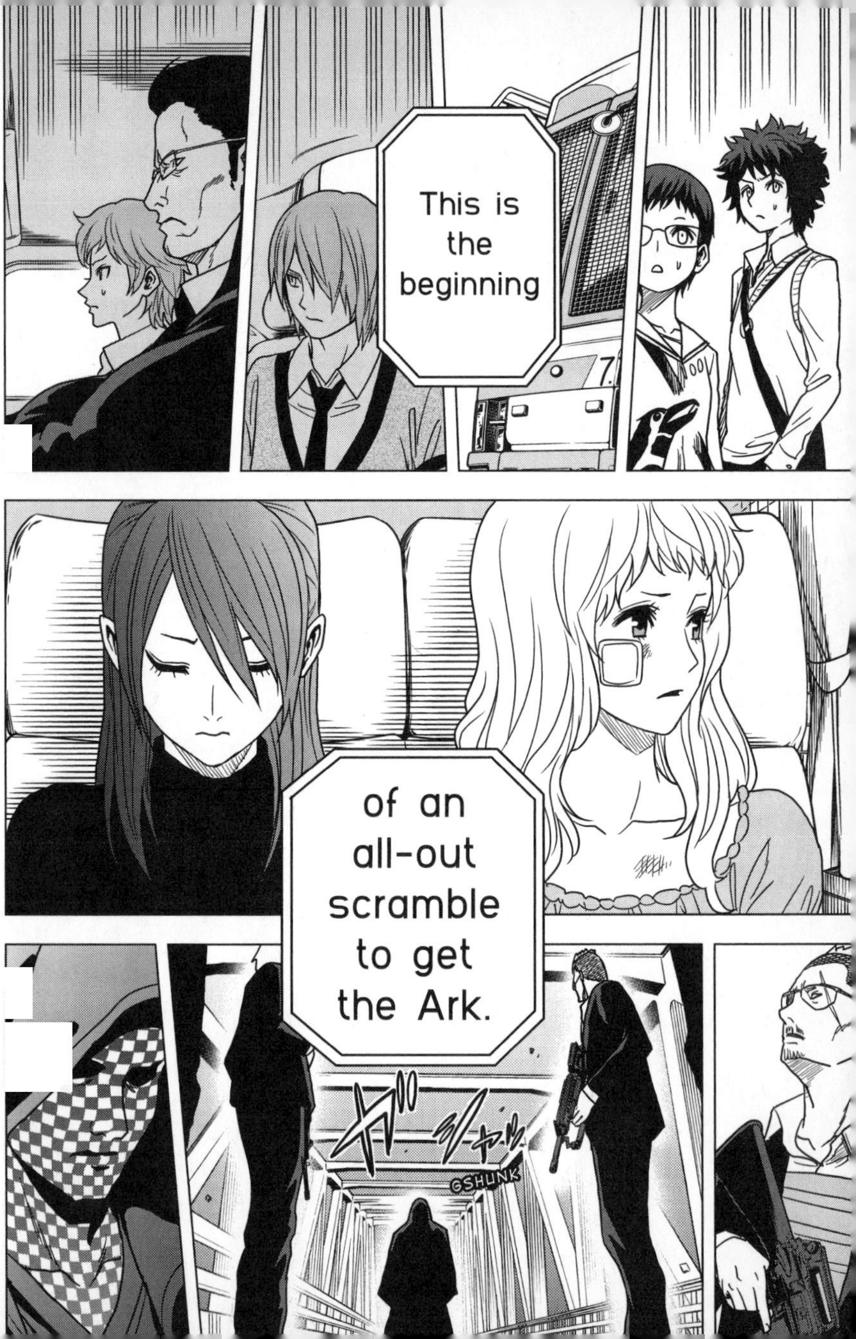
This is the beginning
of an all-out scramble to get the Ark.
GSHUNK

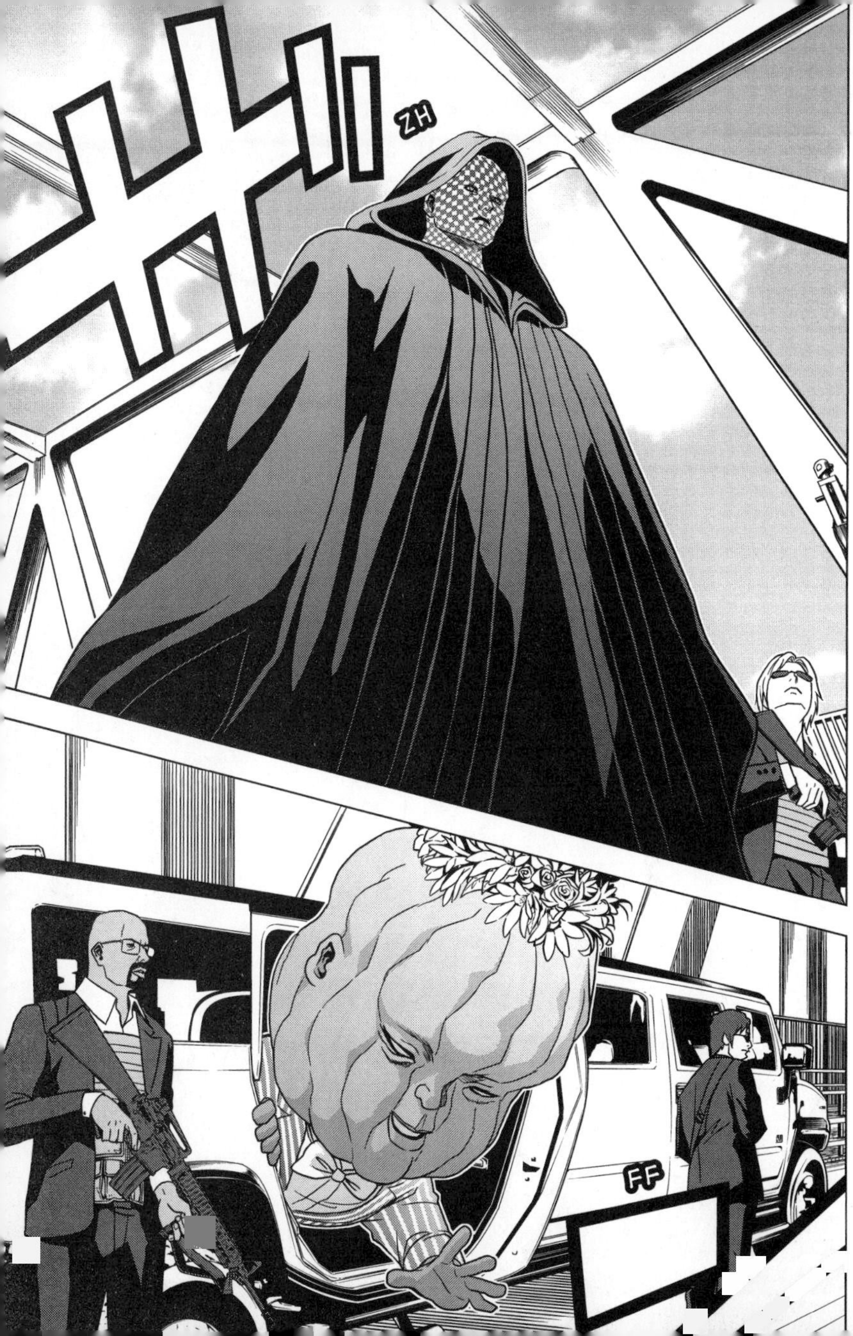
ZH
FF

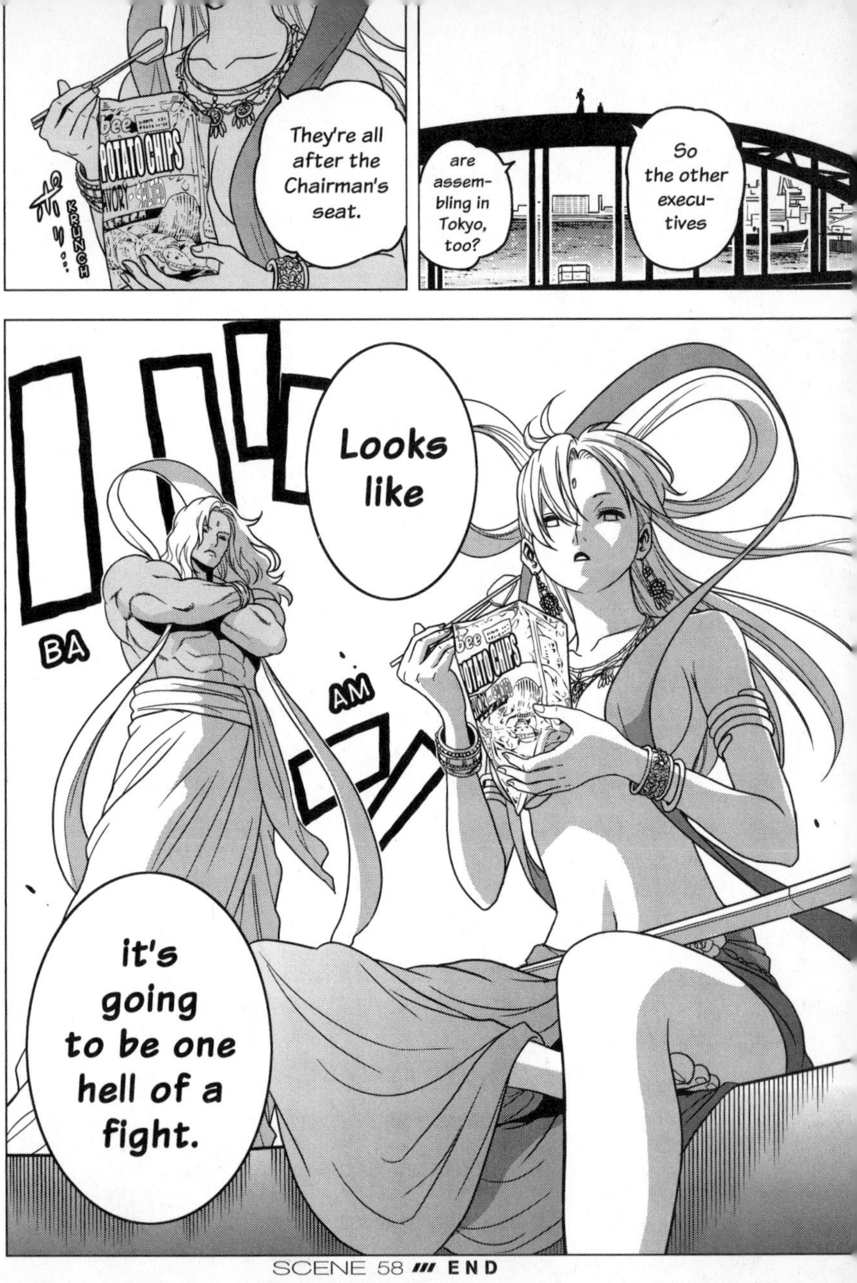
So the other executives
are assembling in Tokyo, too?
They're all after the Chairman's seat.
KRUNCH
POTATO CHIPS
Looks like
BA
AM
it's going to be one hell of a fight.

SCENE 58 /// END

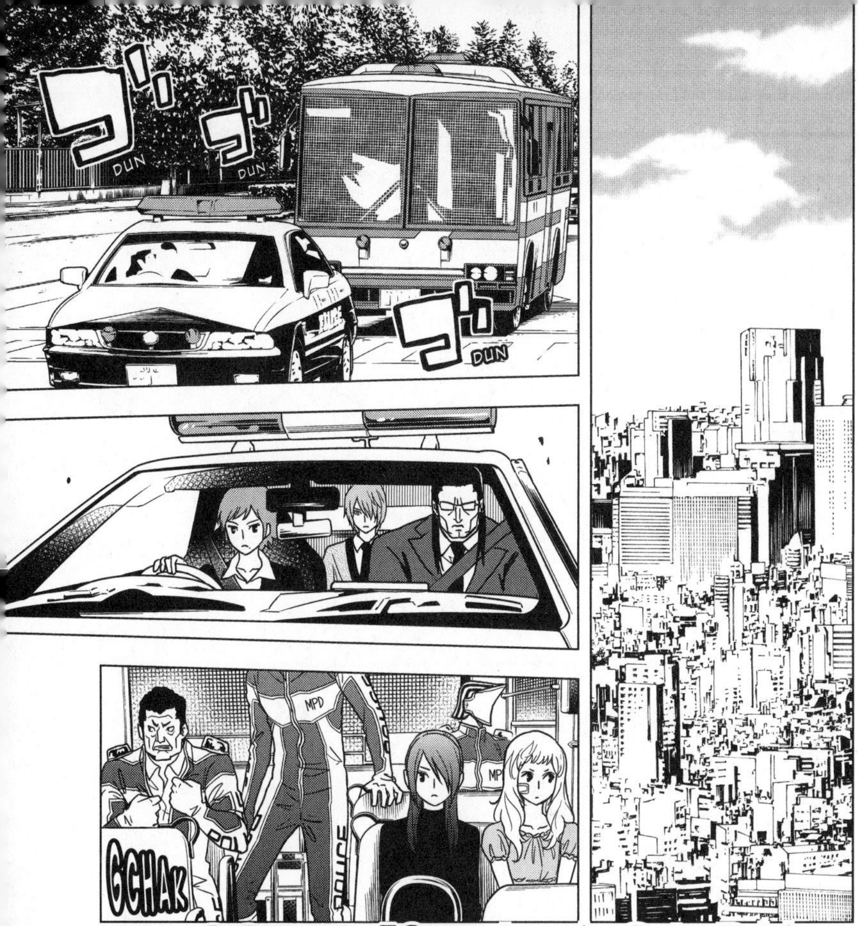
DUN
DUN
DUN
GCHAK

SCENE 59 /// Jungle Gate Bridge

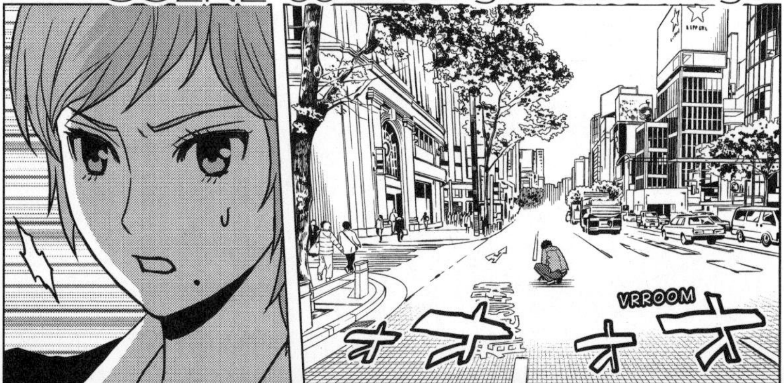
VRROOM

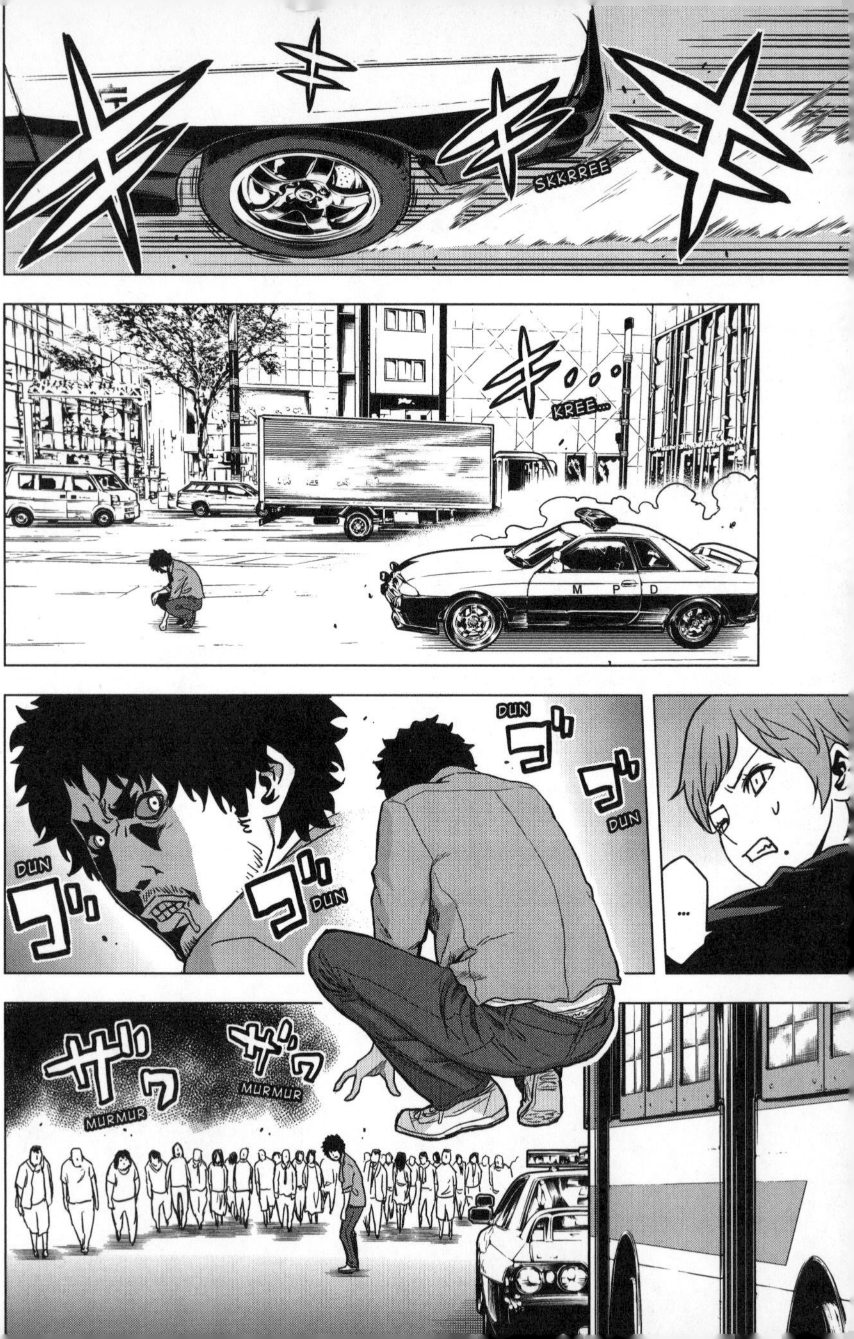

SKKRREE
KREE...
...
DUN
DUN
DUN
DUN
MURMUR
MURMUR

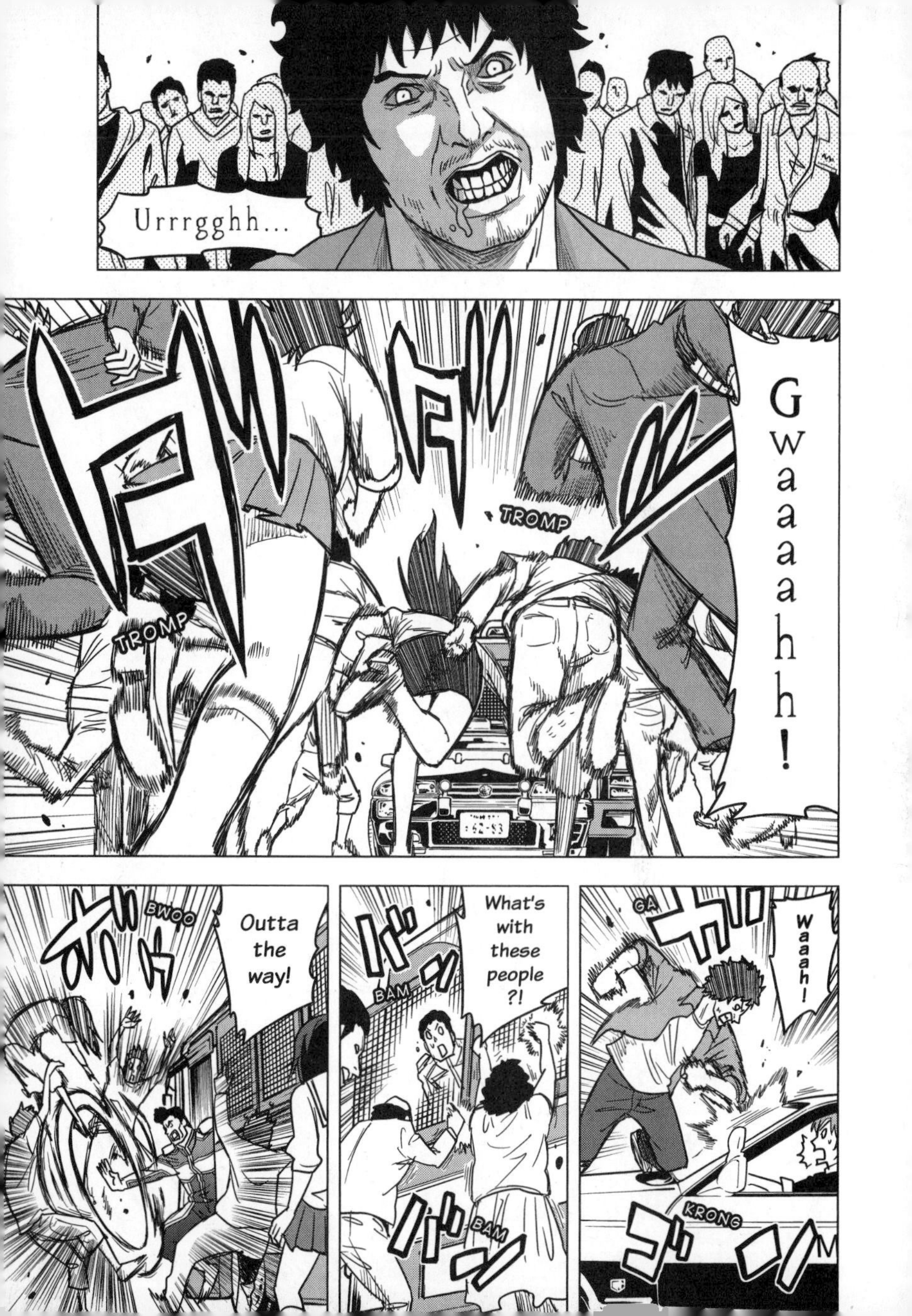
Urrrgghh...
Gwaaaaahh!
TROMP
TROMP
GA
Waaah!
KRONG
What's with these people?!
BAM
BAM
BWOO
Outta the way!

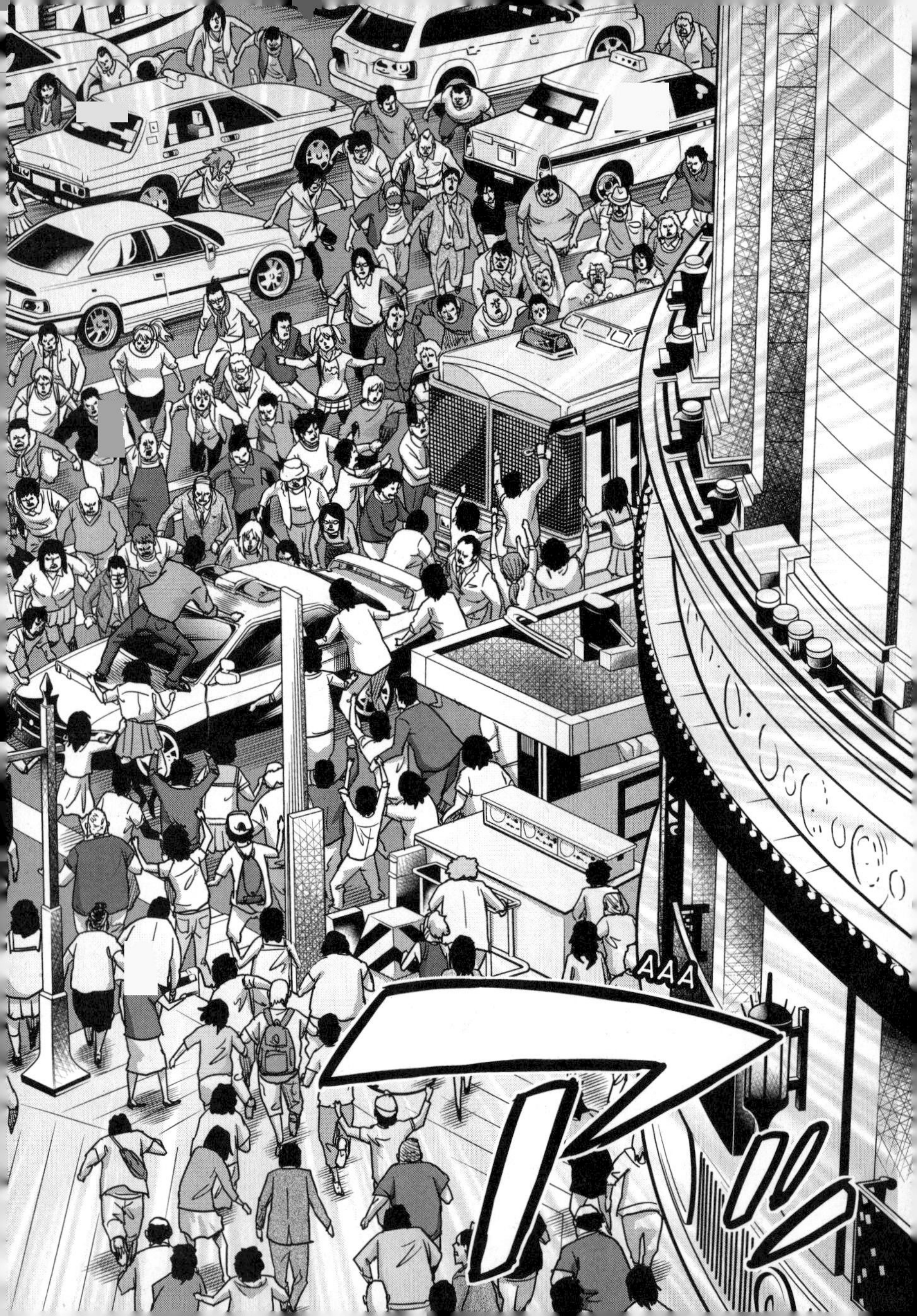
AAA
アッ

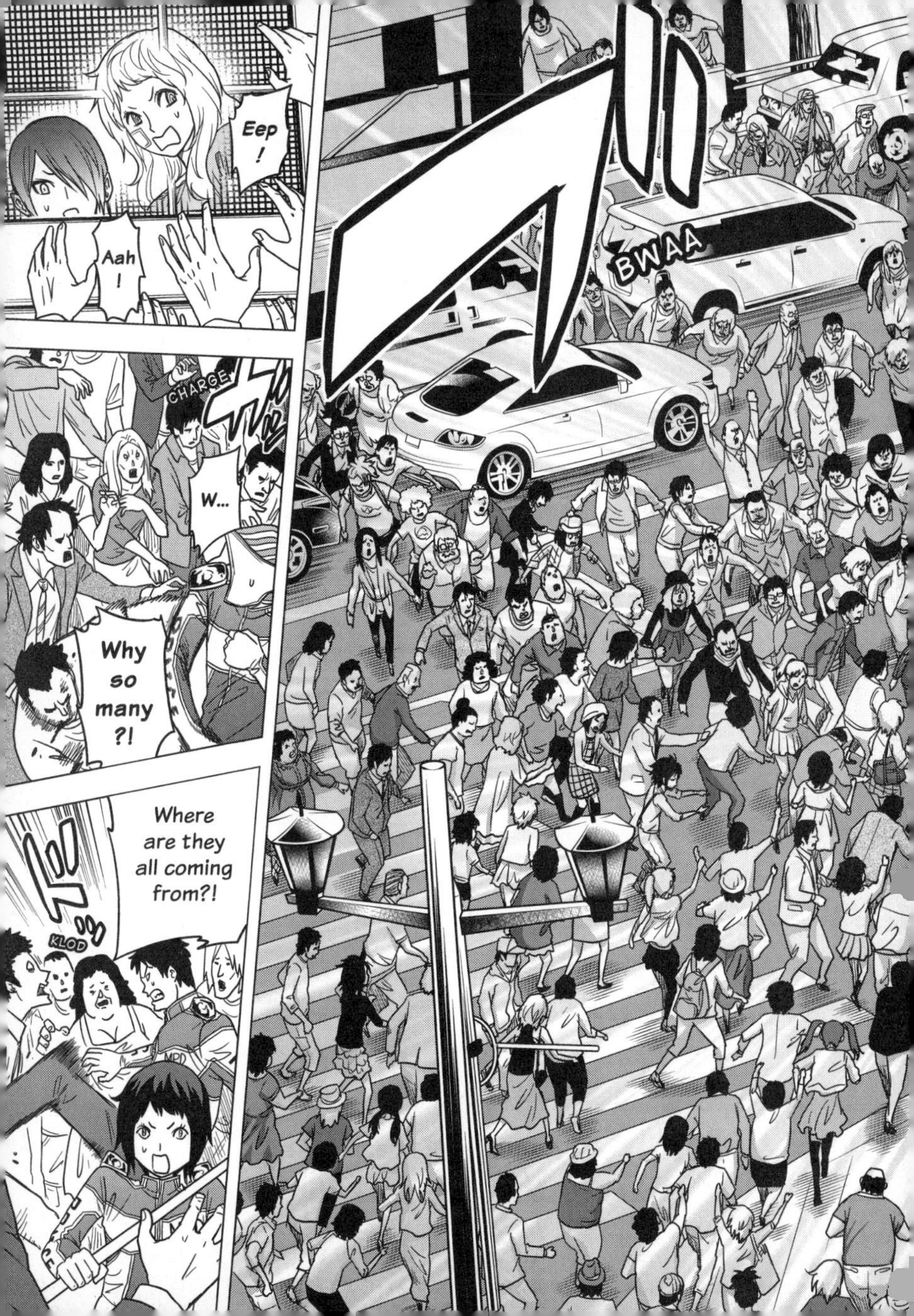
BWAA
Eep!
Aah!
CHARGE
W...
Why so many?!
Where are they all coming from?!
KLOD

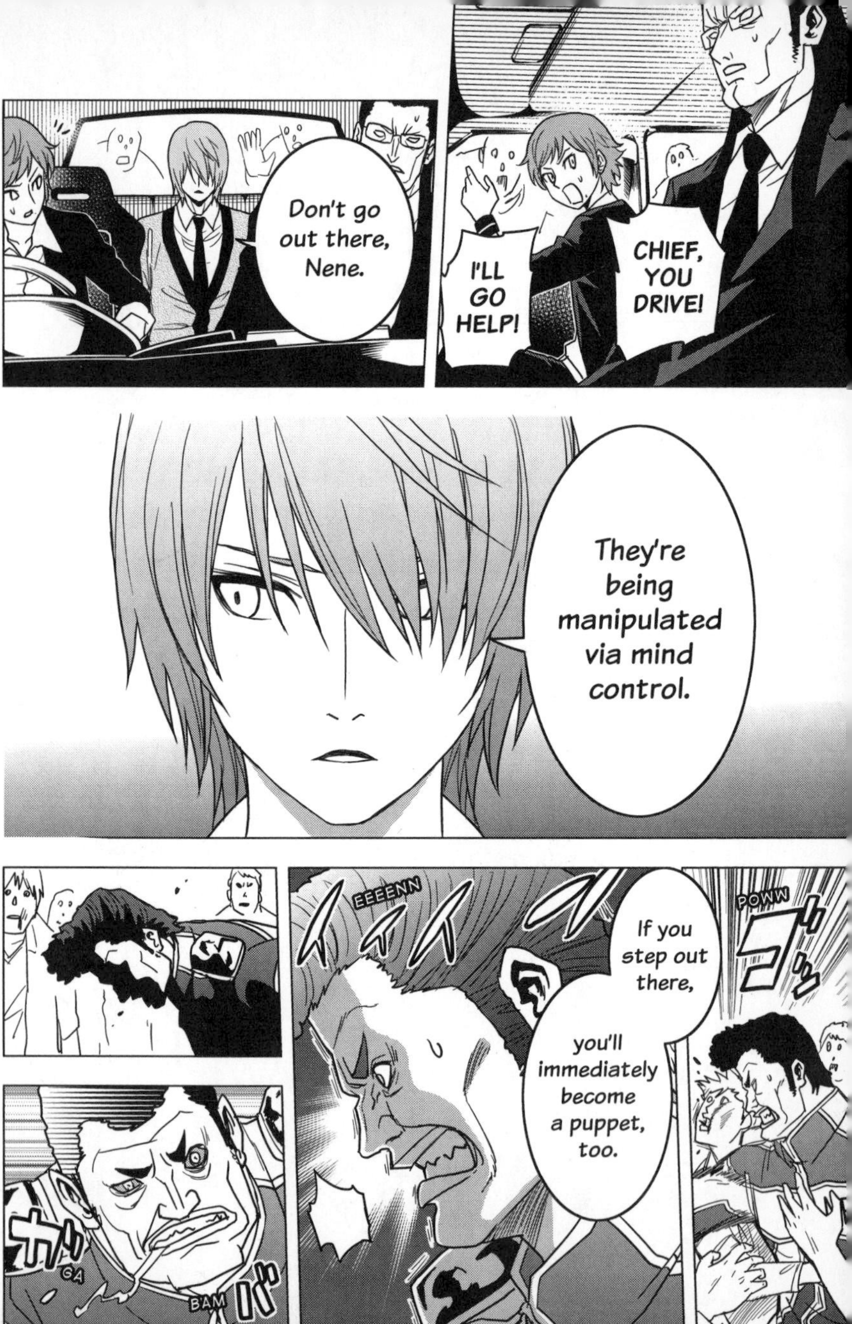
CHIEF, YOU DRIVE!
I'LL GO HELP!
Don't go out there, Nene.
They're being manipulated via mind control.
POWW
EEEENN
If you step out there,
you'll immediately become a puppet, too.
GA
BAM

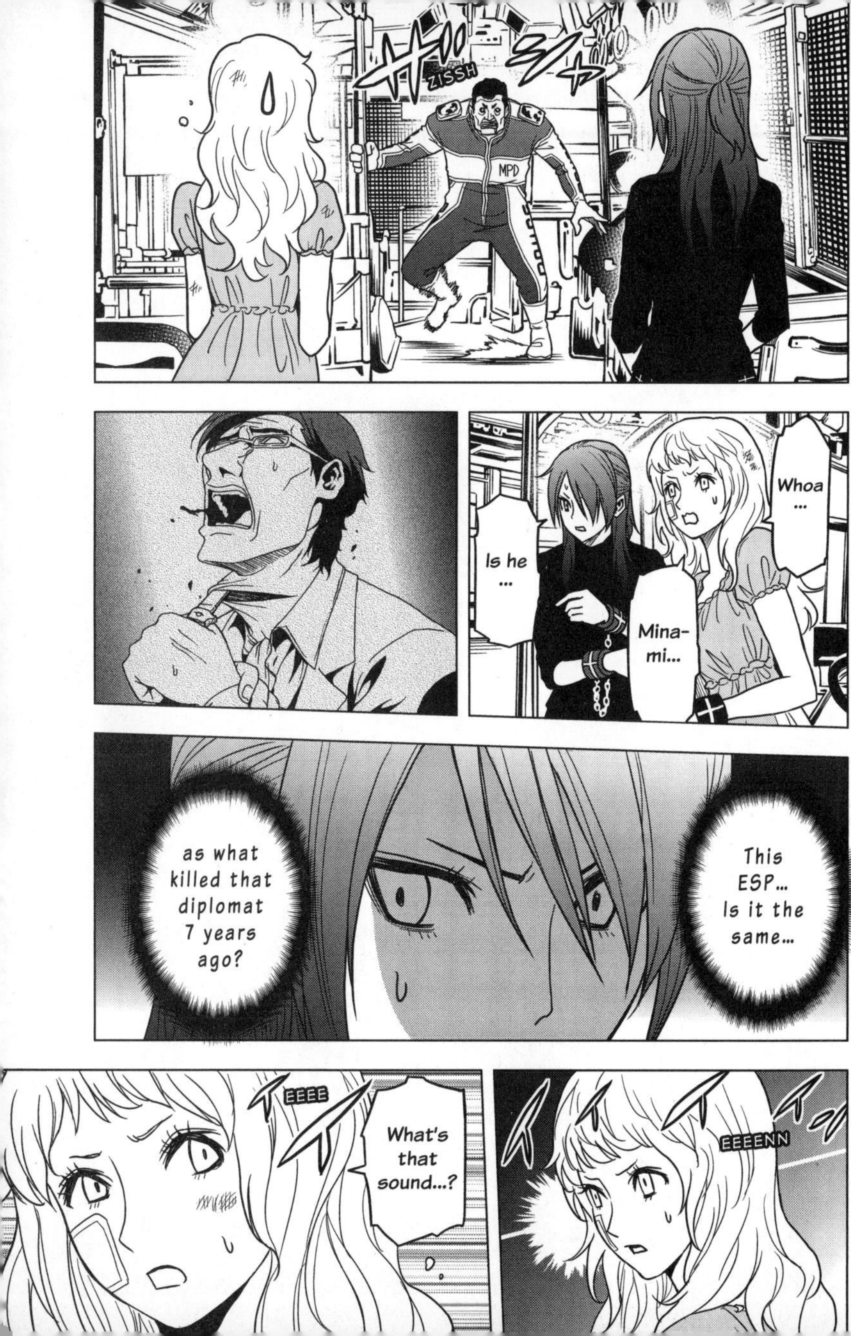
ZISSH
Whoa ...
Is he ...
Mina-mi...
This ESP... Is it the same...
as what killed that diplomat 7 years ago?
EEEENN
EEEE
What's that sound...?

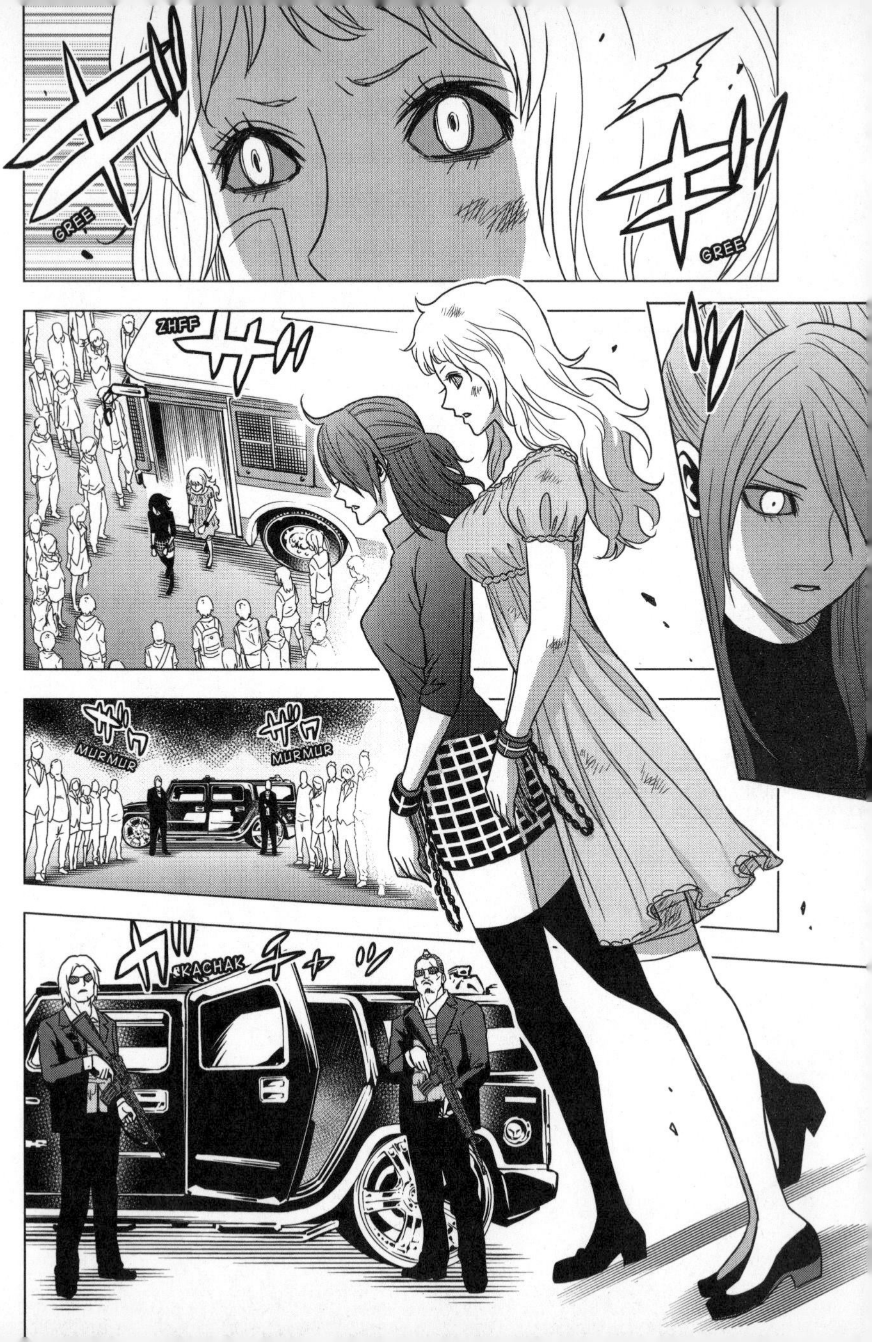
GREE
GREE
ZHFF
MURMUR
MURMUR
KACHAK

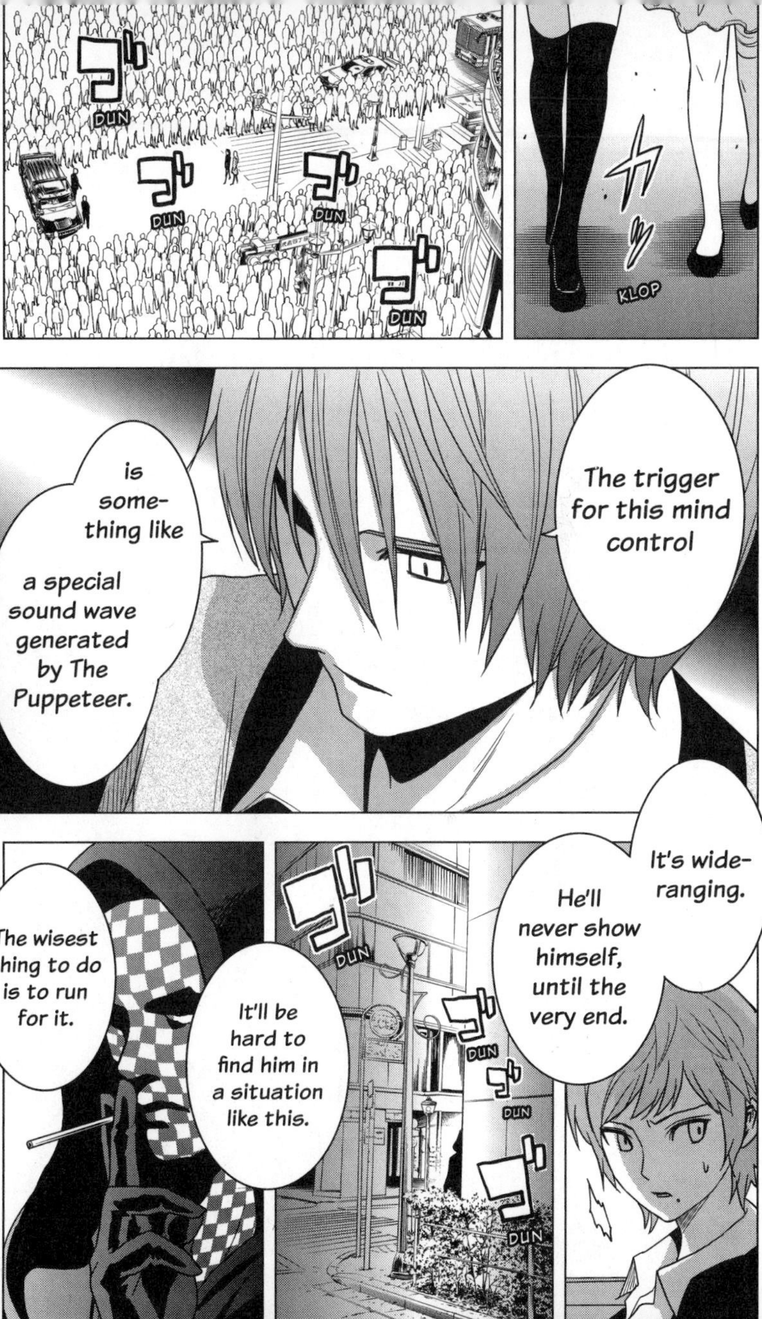
KLOP
DUN
DUN
DUN
DUN
The trigger for this mind control
is some-thing like a special sound wave generated by The Puppeteer.
It's wide-ranging.
He'll never show himself, until the very end.
DUN
DUN
DUN
DUN
It'll be hard to find him in a situation like this.
The wisest thing to do is to run for it.

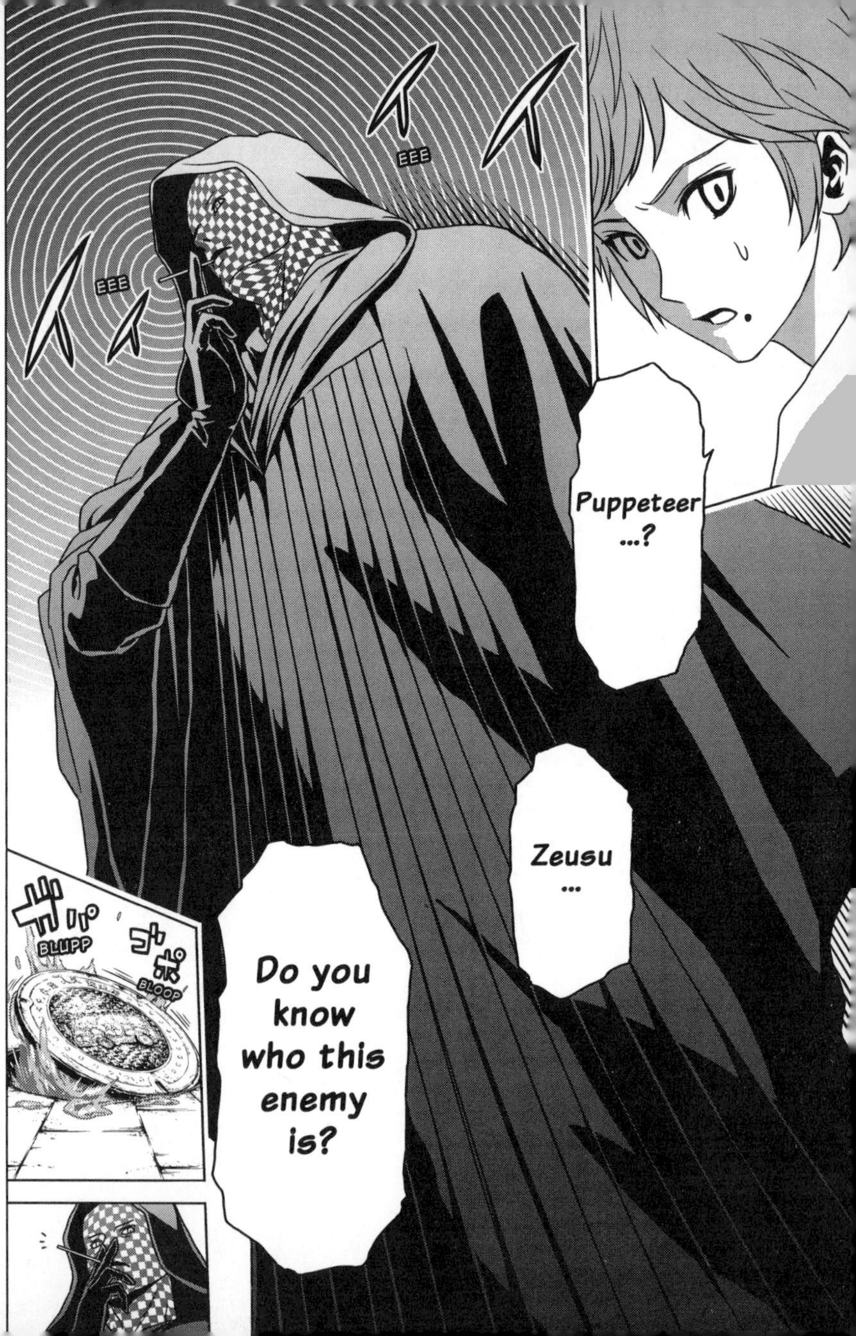
EEE
EEE
Puppeteer ...?
Zeusu ...
Do you know who this enemy is?
BLUPP
BLOOP

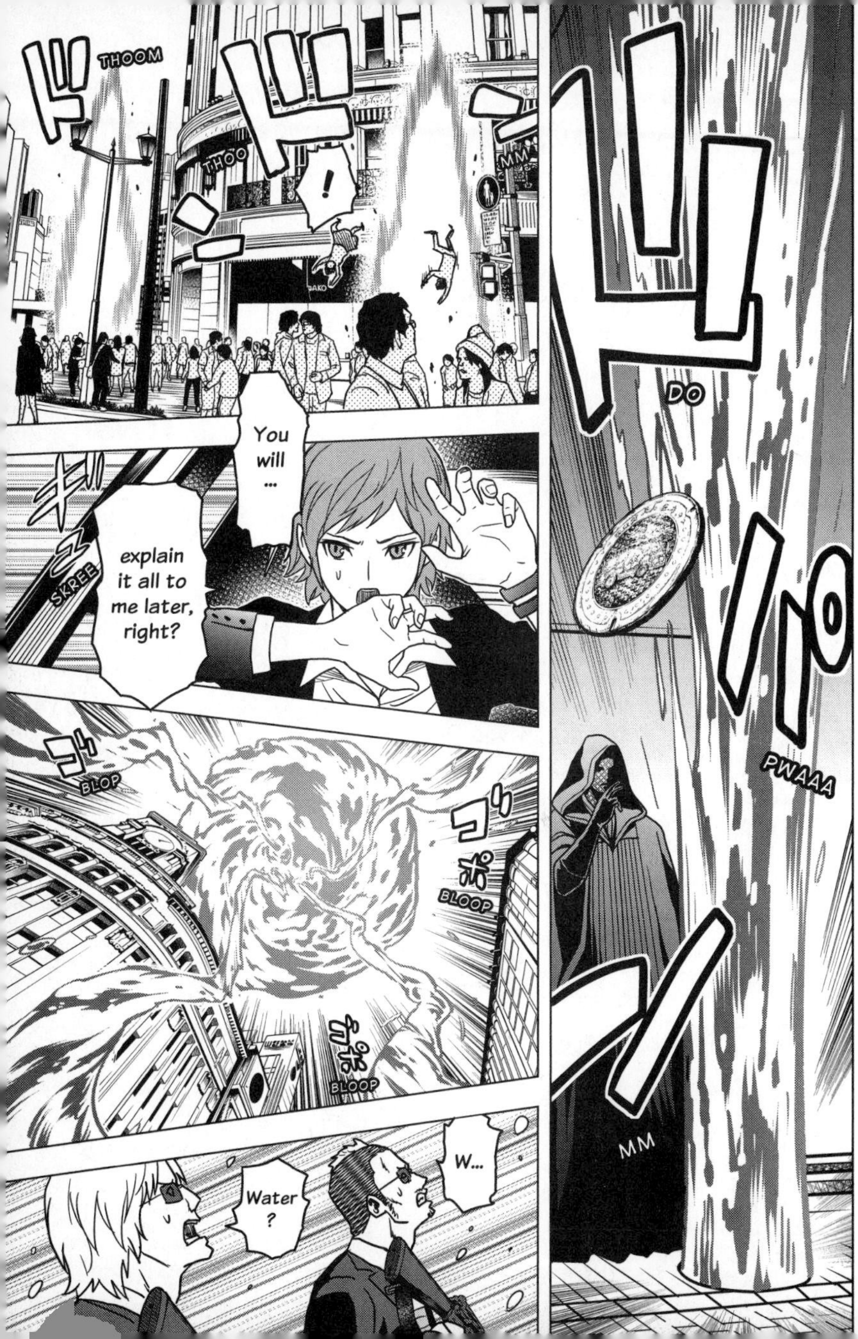
DO
PWAAA
MM
THOOM
THOO
MM
!
You will ...
explain it all to me later, right?
SKREE
BLOOP
BLOOP
BLOP
W...
Water?

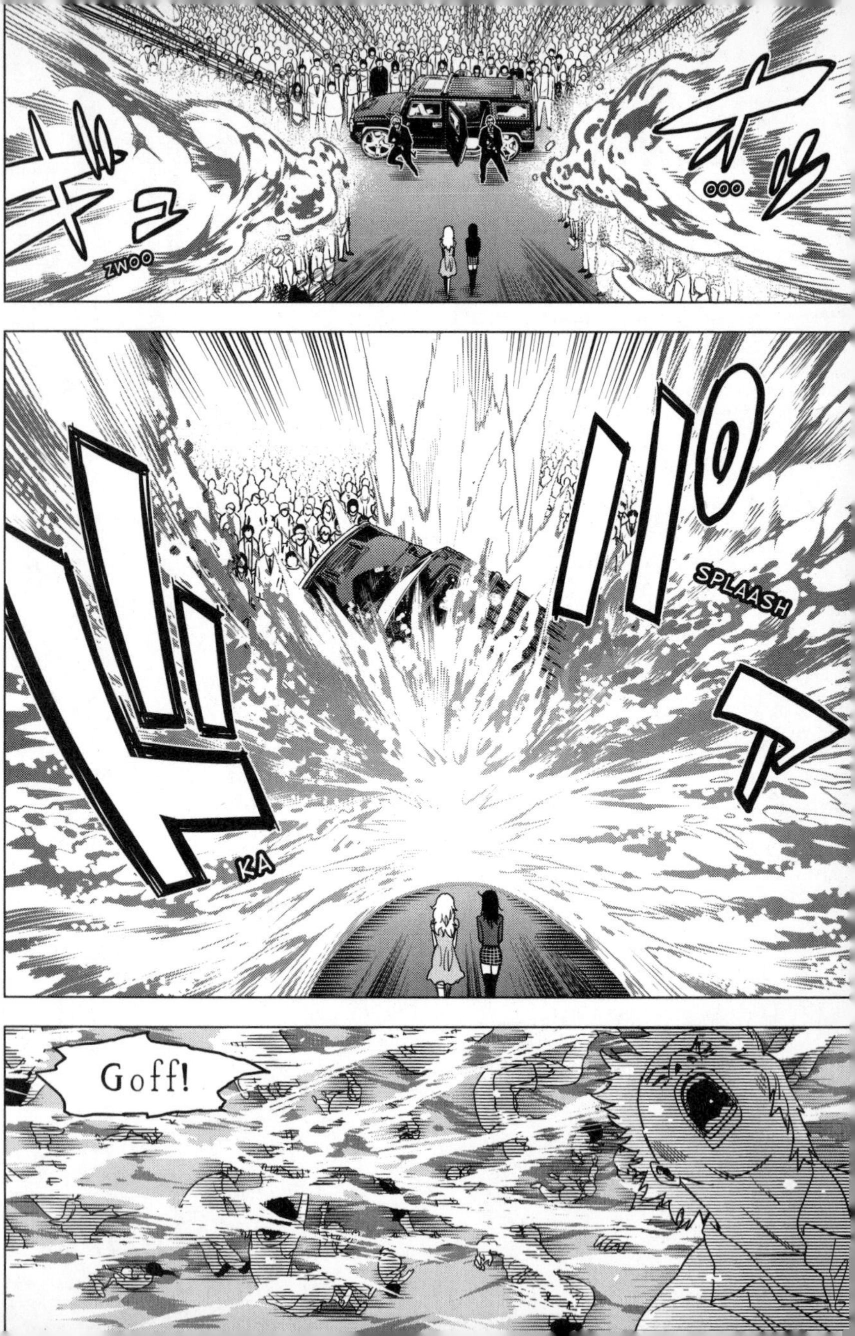
ooo
ZWOO
SPLAASH
KA
Goff!

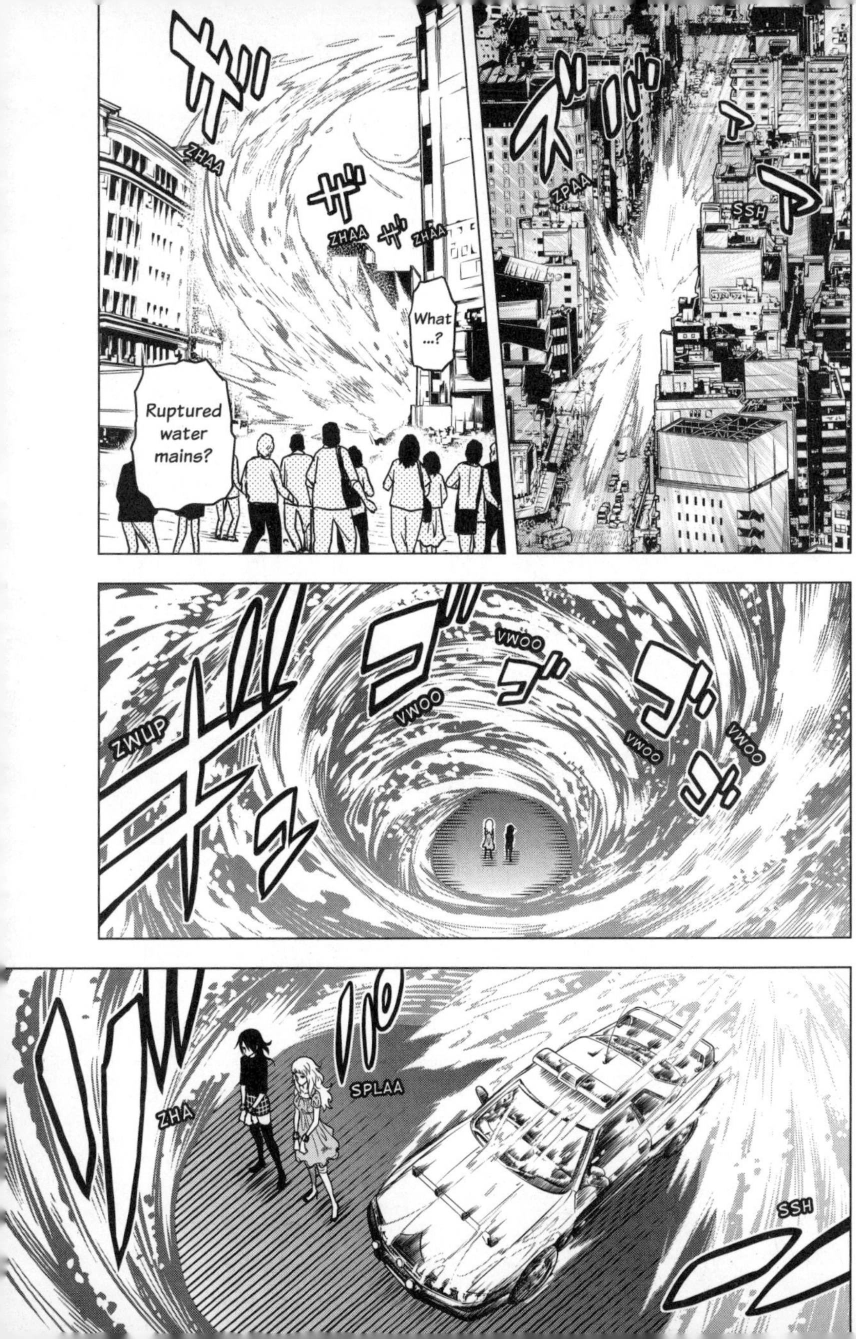
SSH
ZPAA
ZHAA
ZHAA
What ...?
ZHAA
Ruptured water mains?
VWOO
VWOO
VWOO
VWOO
ZWUP
SSH
SPLAA
ZHA

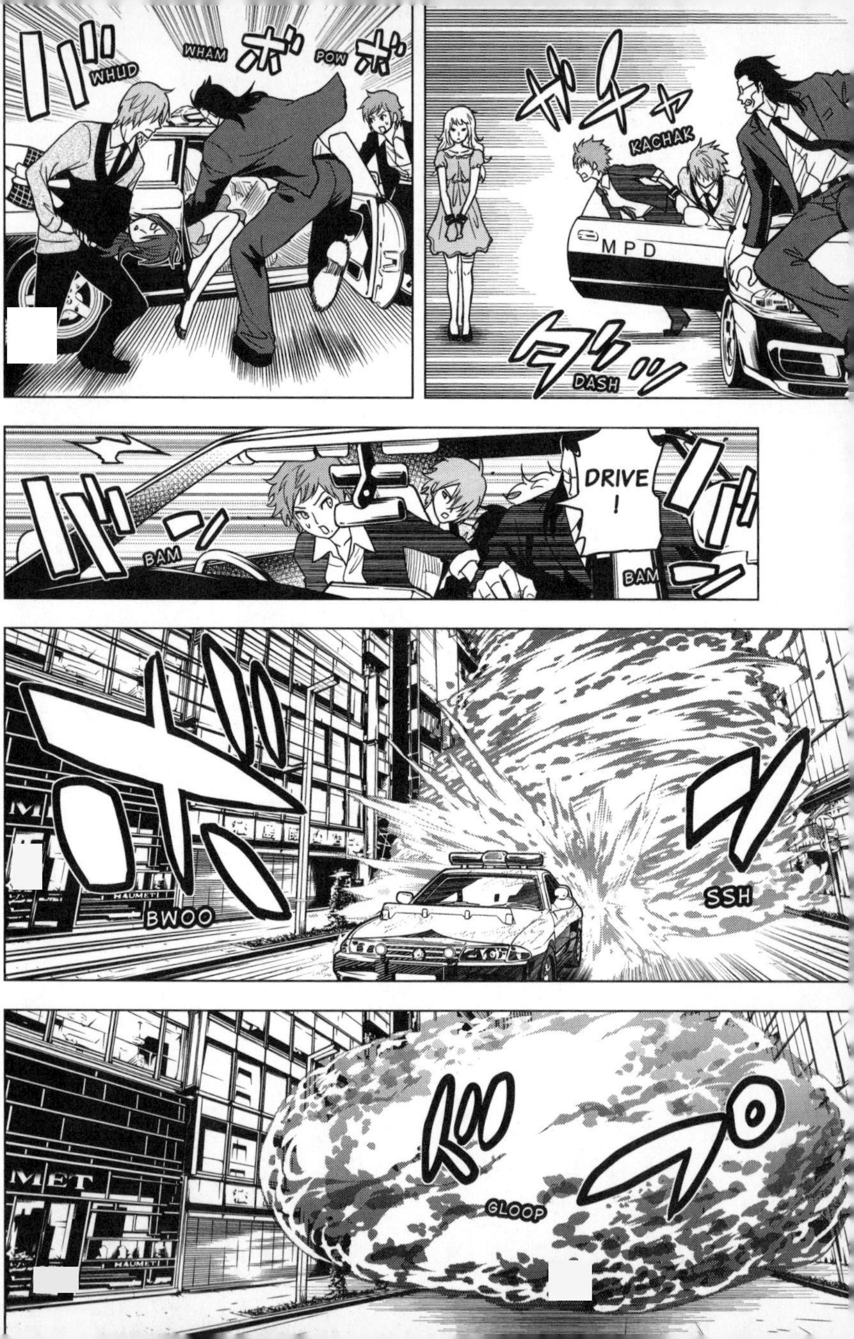
KACHAK
DASH
POW
WHAM
WHUD
DRIVE!
BAM
BAM
SSH
BWOO
GLOOP

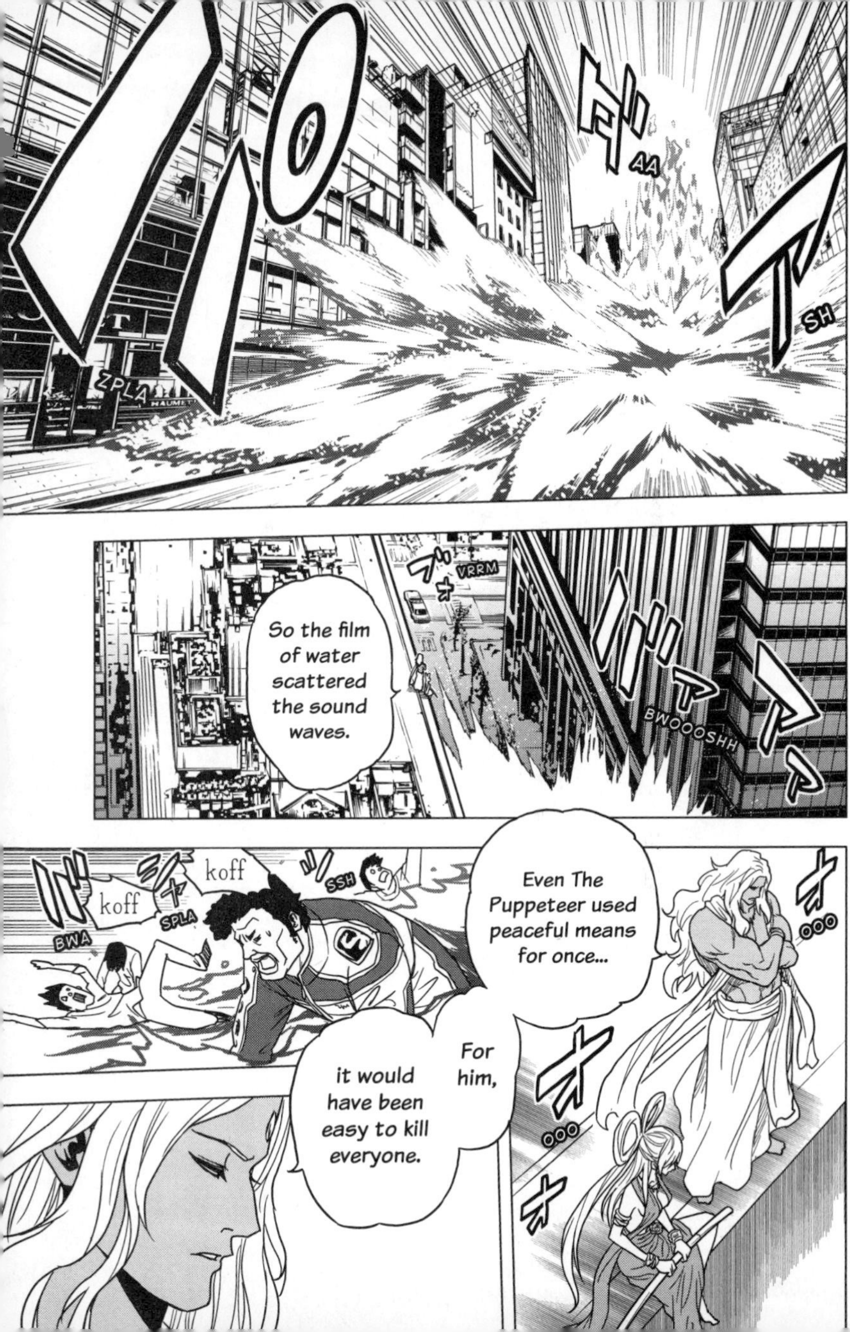

AA
SH
ZPLA
BWOOOSHH
VRRM
So the film of water scattered the sound waves.
OOO
Even The Puppeteer used peaceful means for once...
OOO
SSH
koff
SPLA
koff
BWA
For him,
it would have been easy to kill everyone.

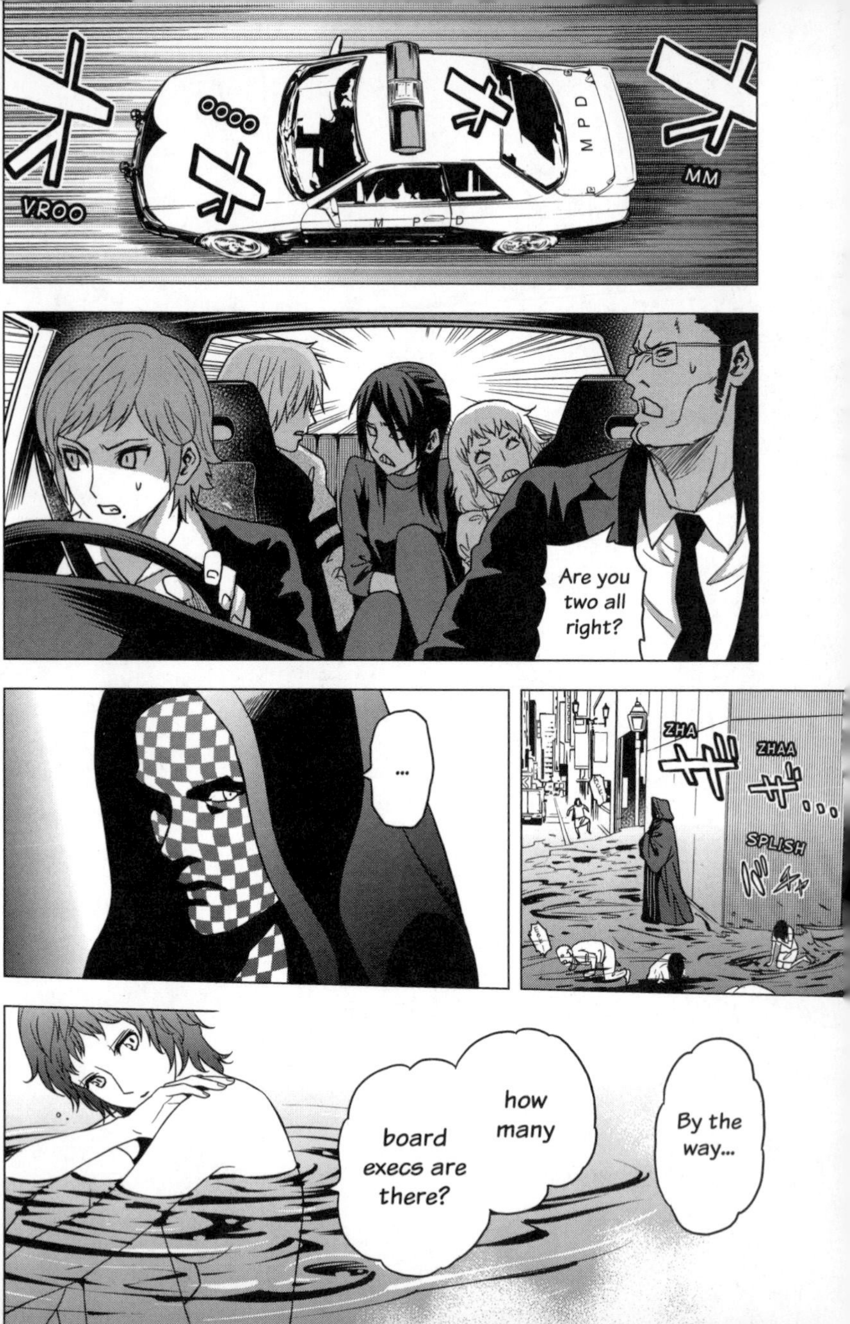
VROO
oooo
MM
Are you two all right?
ZHA
ZHAA
SPLISH
...
By the way...
how many
board execs are there?

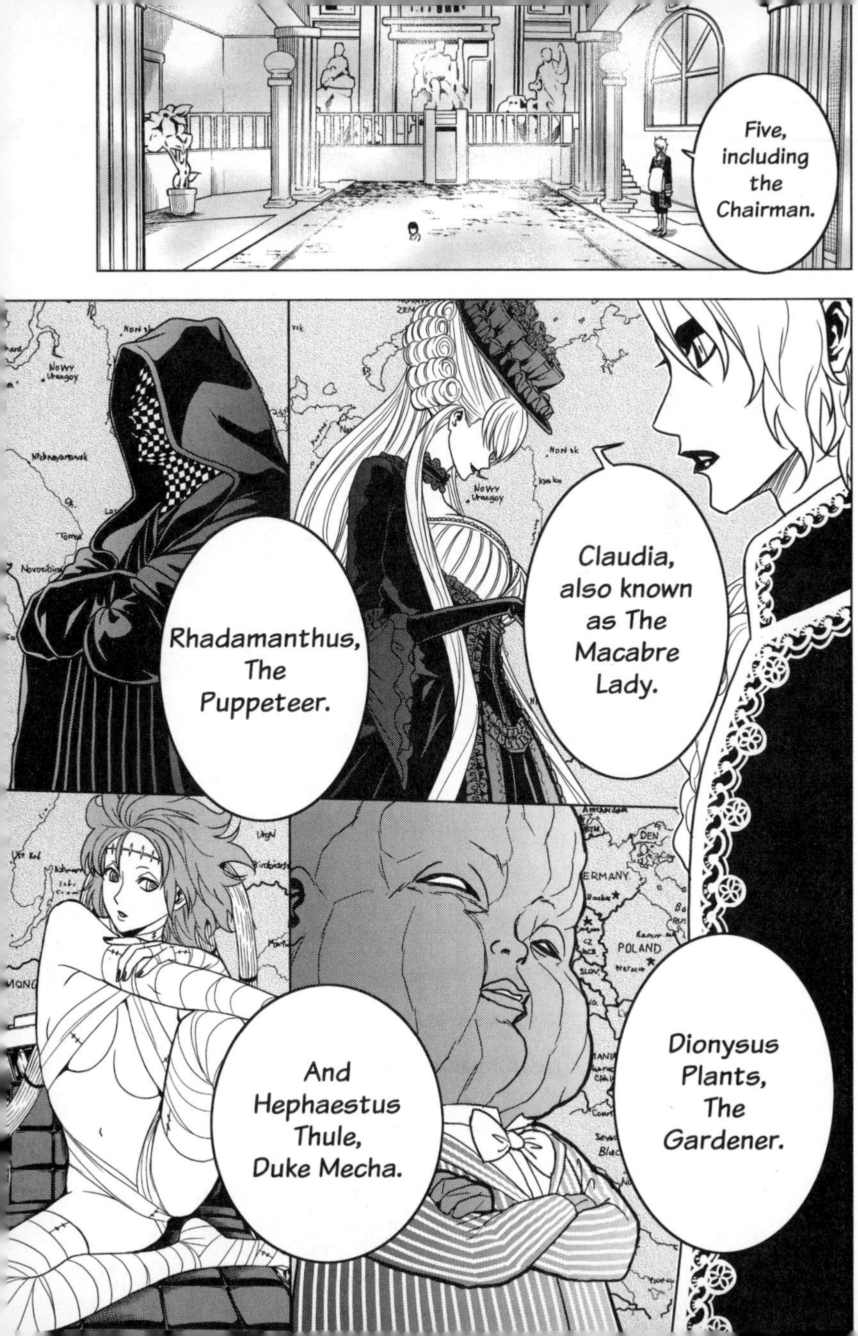
Five, including the Chairman.
Claudia, also known as The Macabre Lady.
Rhadamanthus, The Puppeteer.
Dionysus Plants, The Gardener.
And Hephaestus Thule, Duke Mecha.

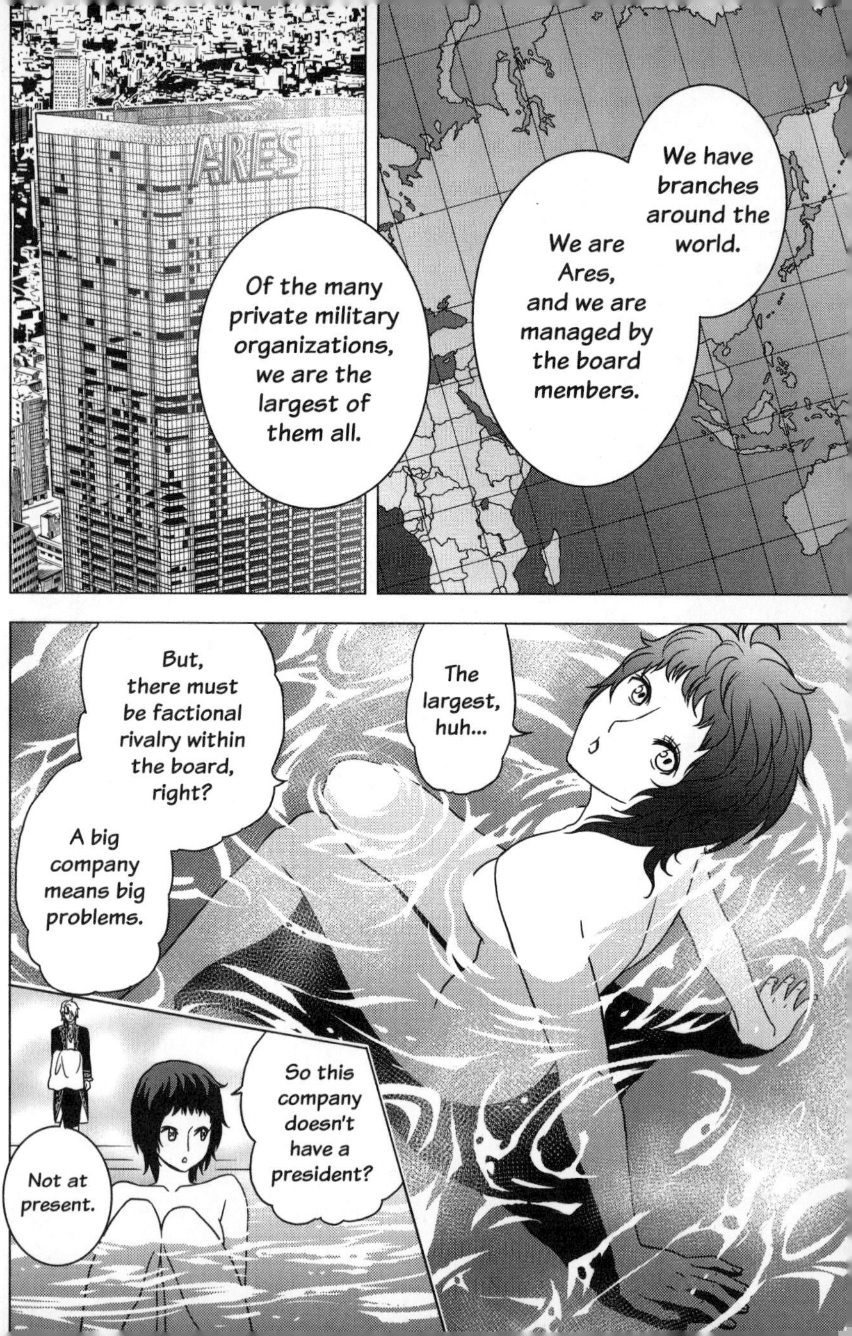
We have branches around the world.
We are Ares, and we are managed by the board members.
ARES
Of the many private military organizations, we are the largest of them all.
The largest, huh...
But, there must be factional rivalry within the board, right?
A big company means big problems.
So this company doesn't have a president?
Not at present.

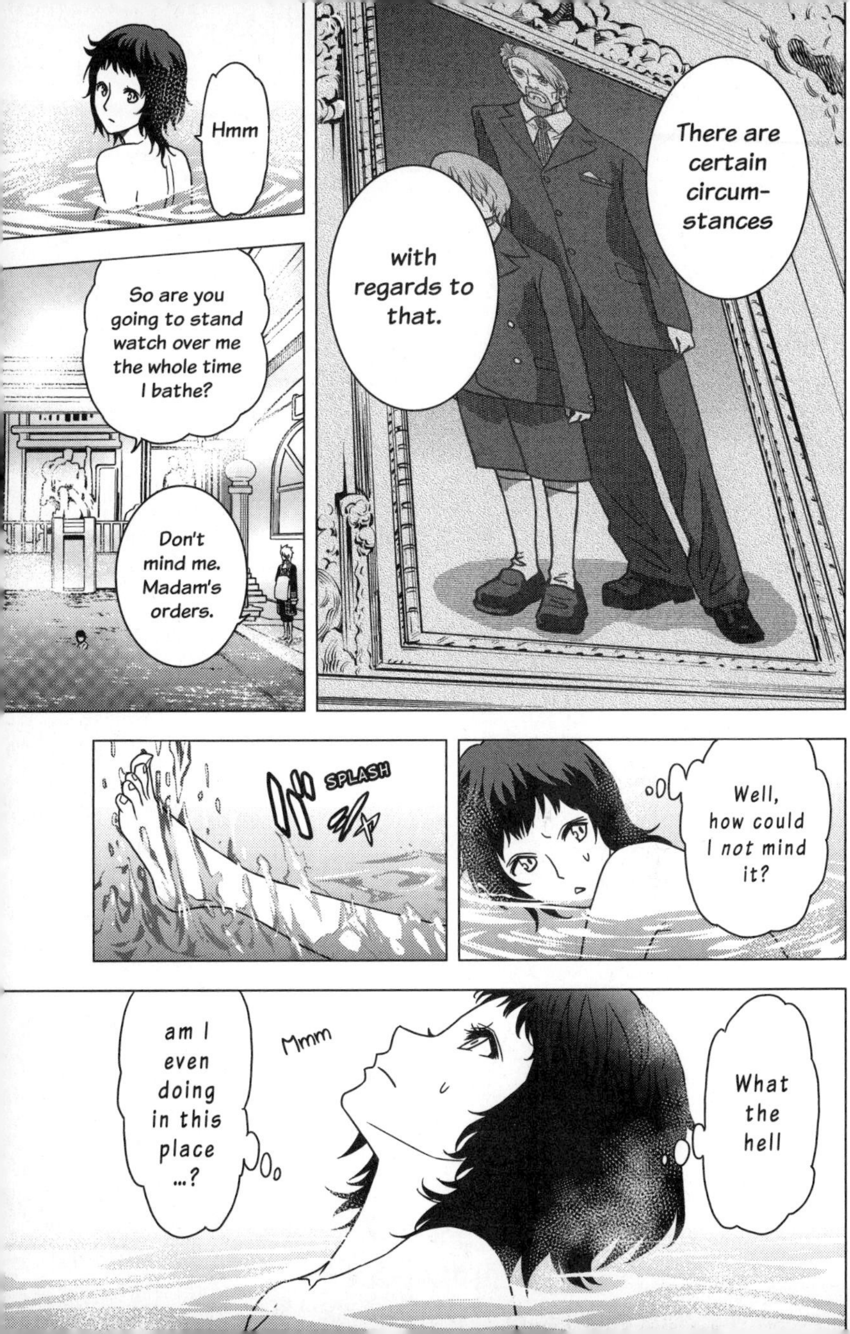
There are certain circum-stances
with regards to that.
Hmm
So are you going to stand watch over me the whole time I bathe?
Don't mind me. Madam's orders.
Well, how could I *not* mind it?
SPLASH
What the hell
Mmm
am I even doing in this place ...?

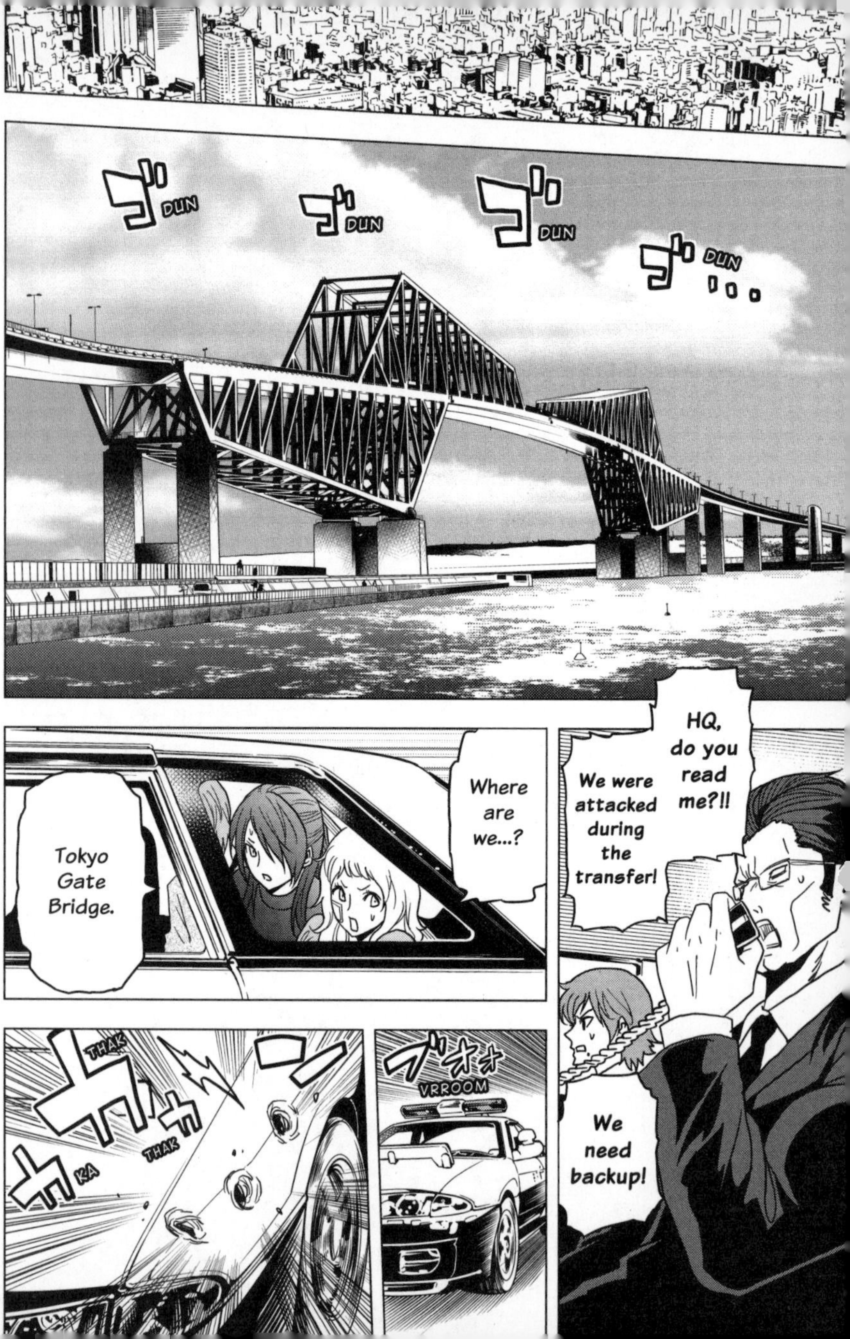
ゴ DUN
ゴ DUN
ゴ DUN
ゴ DUN
HQ, do you read me?!!
We were attacked during the transfer!
We need backup!
Where are we...?
Tokyo Gate Bridge.
VRROOM
THAK
THAK
KA

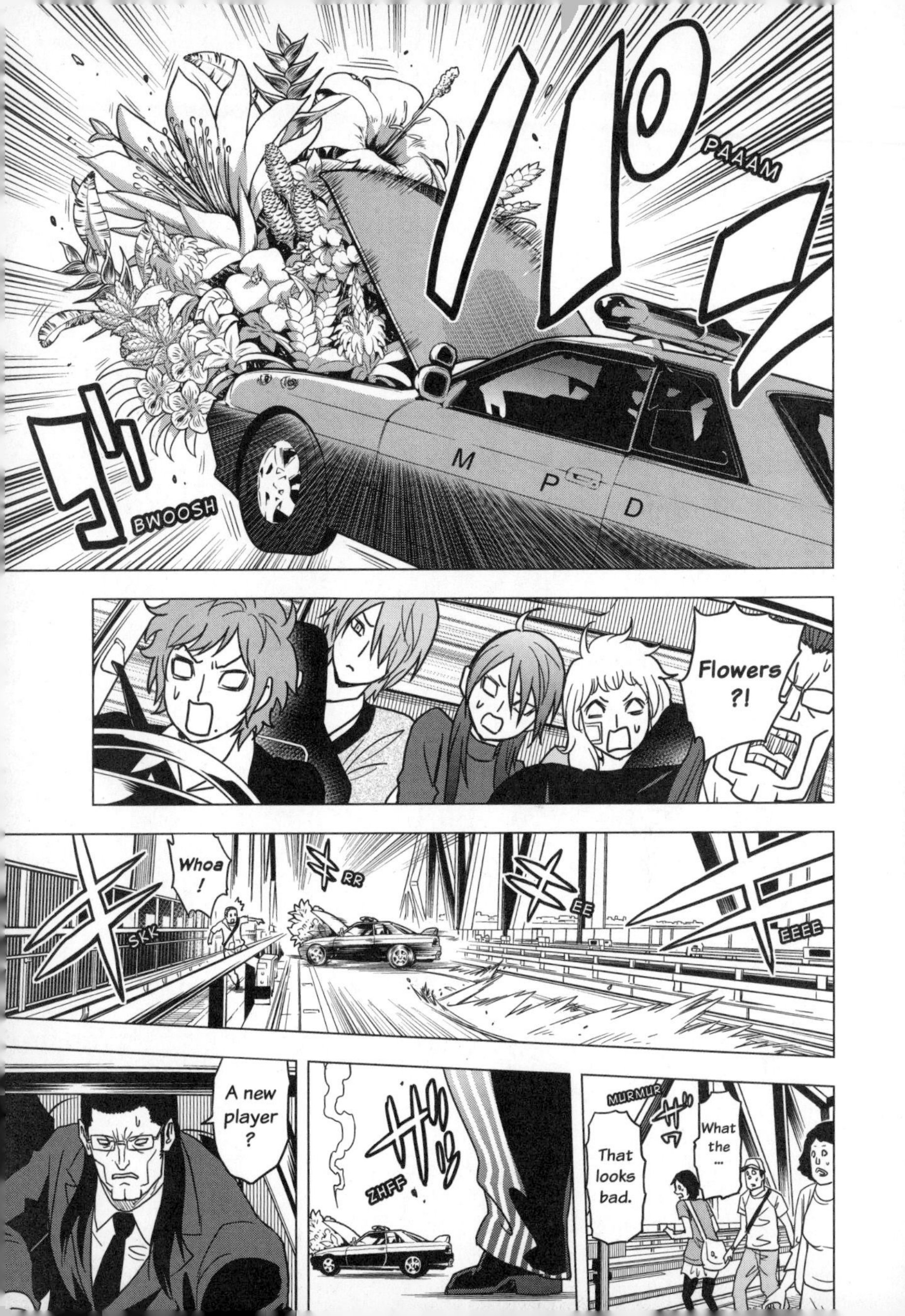
PAAAM
BWOOSH
Flowers ?!
EEEE
EE
RR
Whoa!
SKK
MURMUR
What the ...
That looks bad.
ZHFF
A new player?

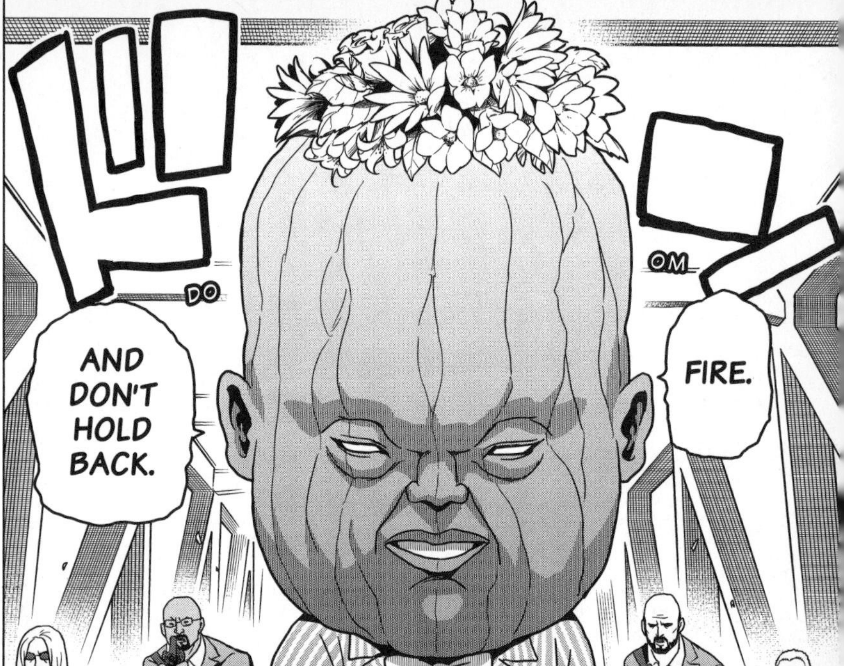
DO
OM
FIRE.
AND DON'T HOLD BACK.

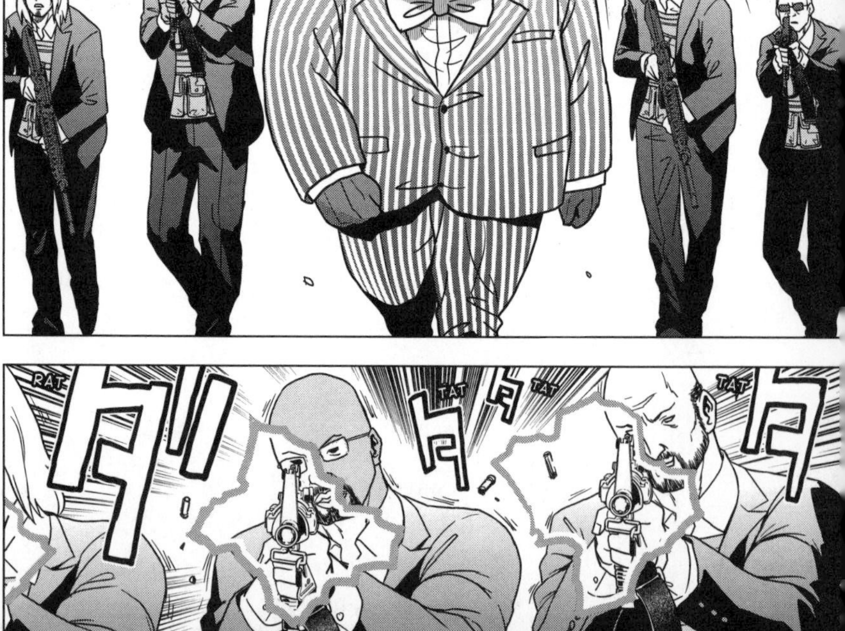
TAT
TAT
TAT
RAT

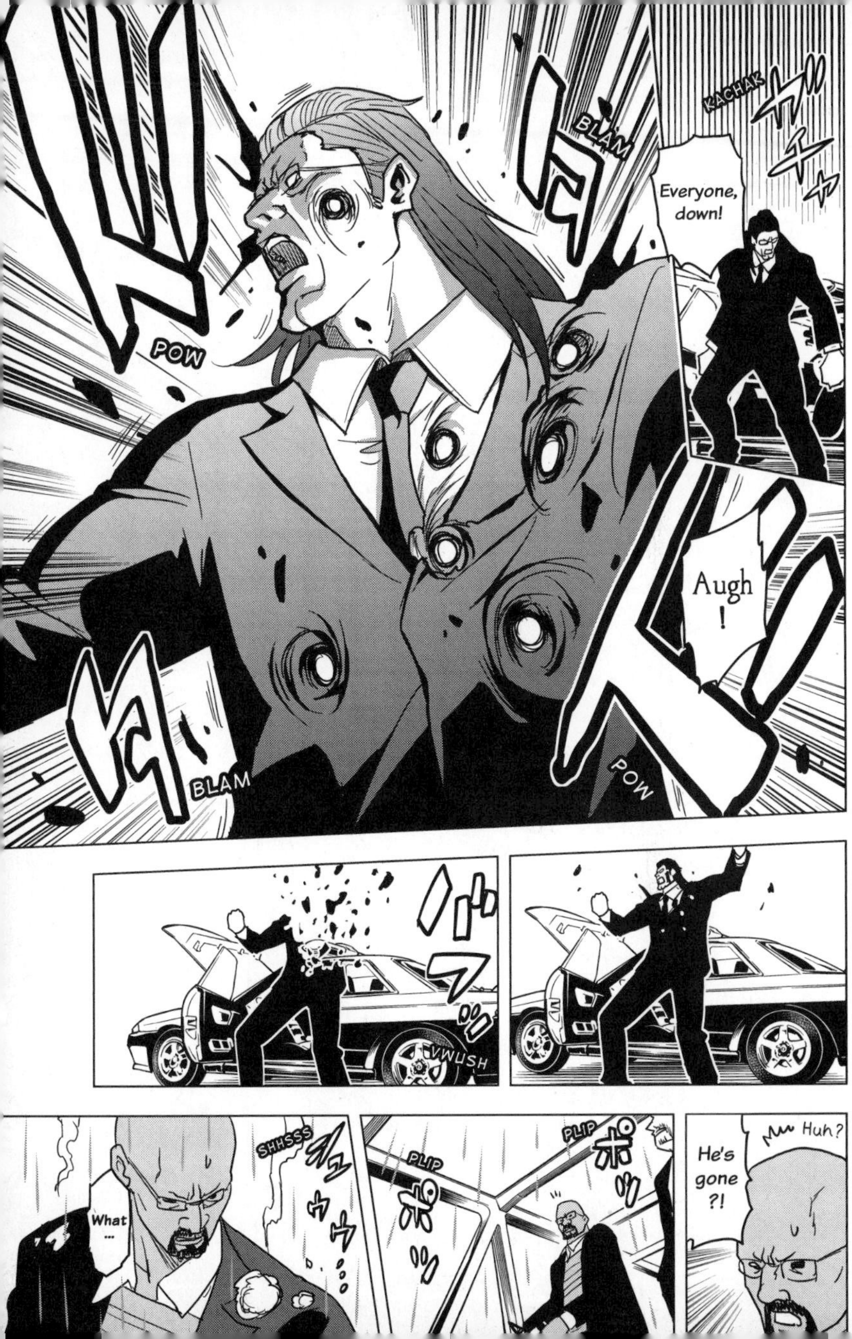
KACHAK
Everyone, down!
BLAM
Augh!
POW
BLAM
POW
VWUSH
Huh?
He's gone?!
PLIP
PLIP
SHHSSS
What...

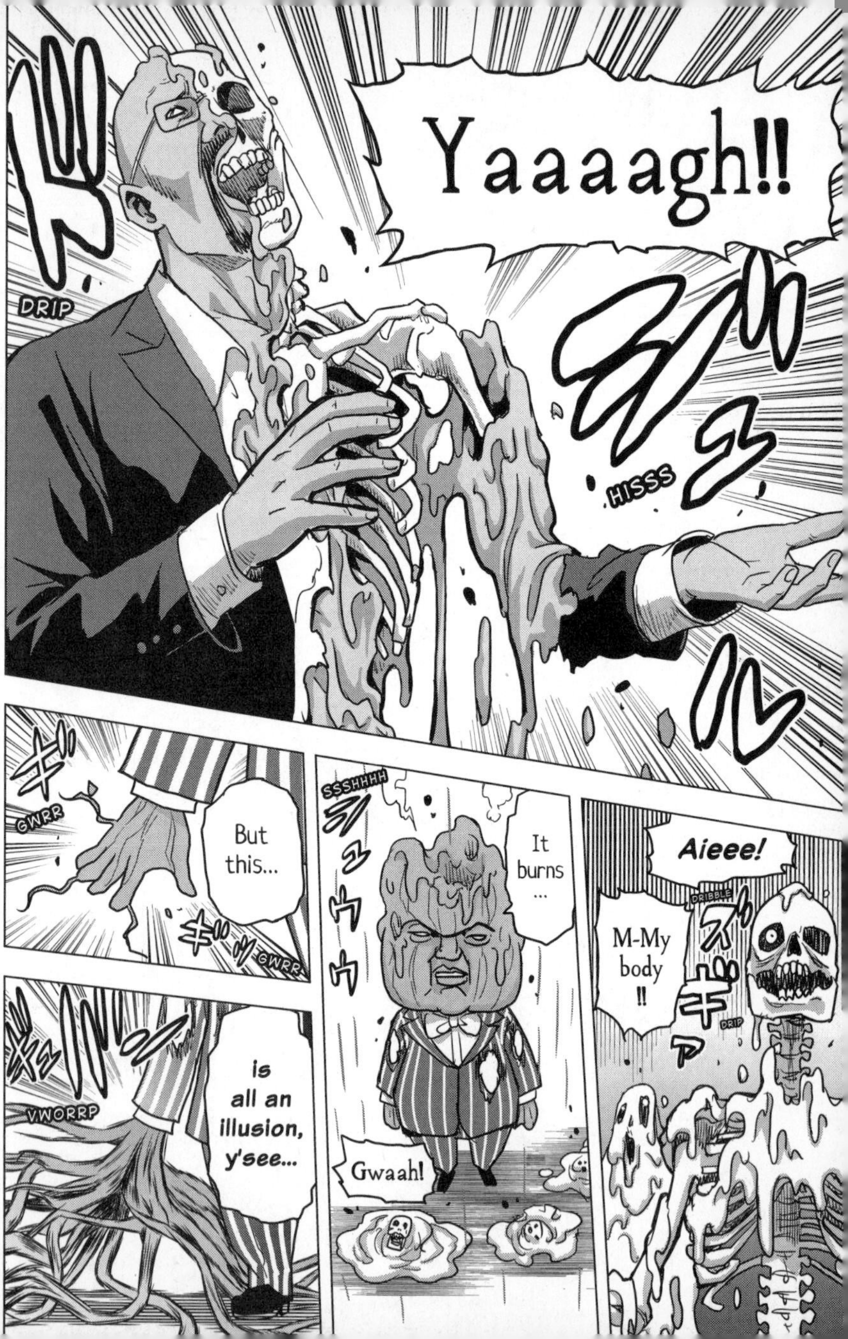
Yaaaagh!!
HISSS
DRIP
Aieee!
DRIBBLE
M-My body !!
DRIP
SSSHHHH
It burns ...
Gwaah!
But this...
GWRR
GWRR
is all an illusion, y'see...
VWORRP

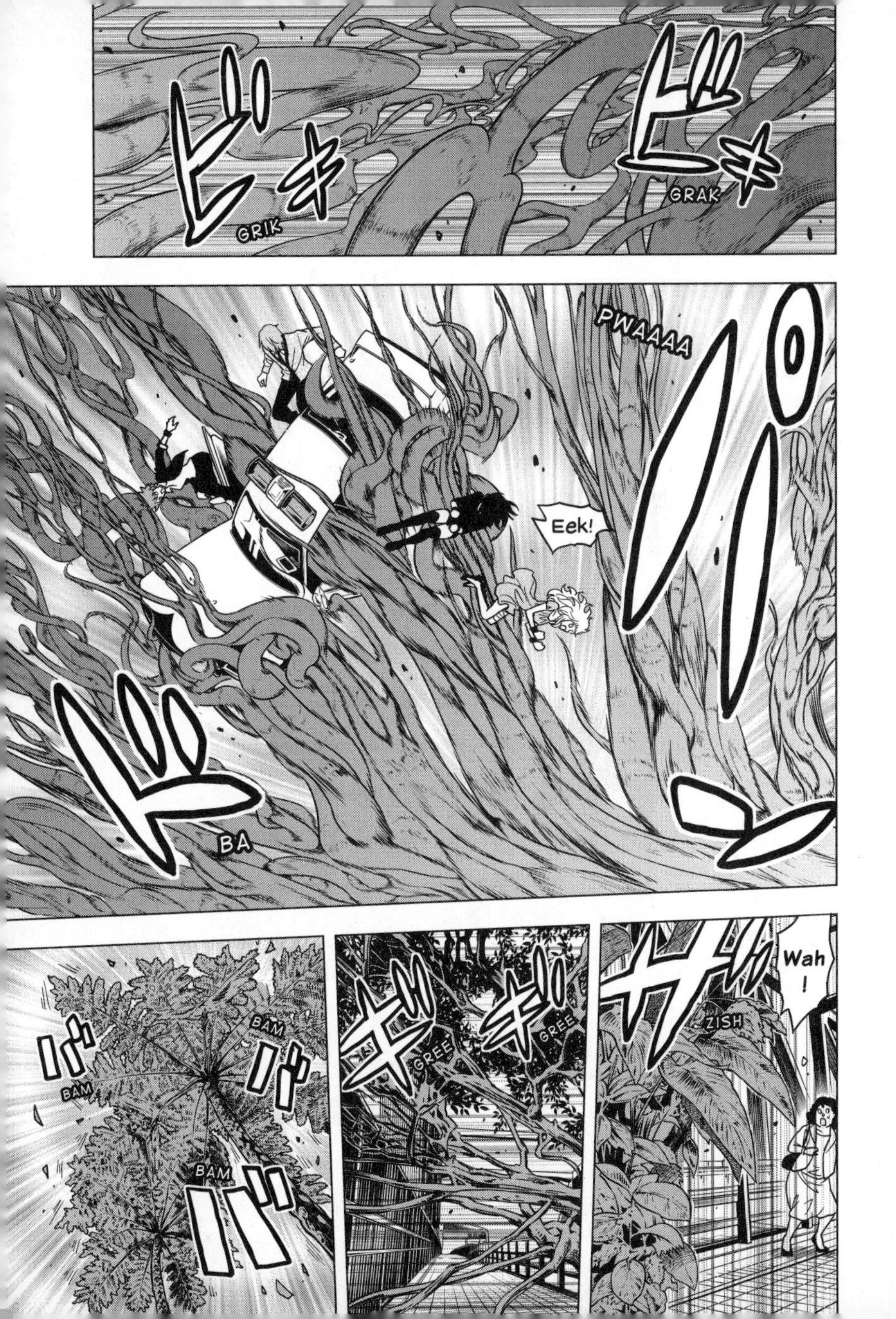
GRAK
GRIK
PWAAAA
Eek!
BA
Wah!
ZISH
GREE
GREE
BAM
BAM
BAM

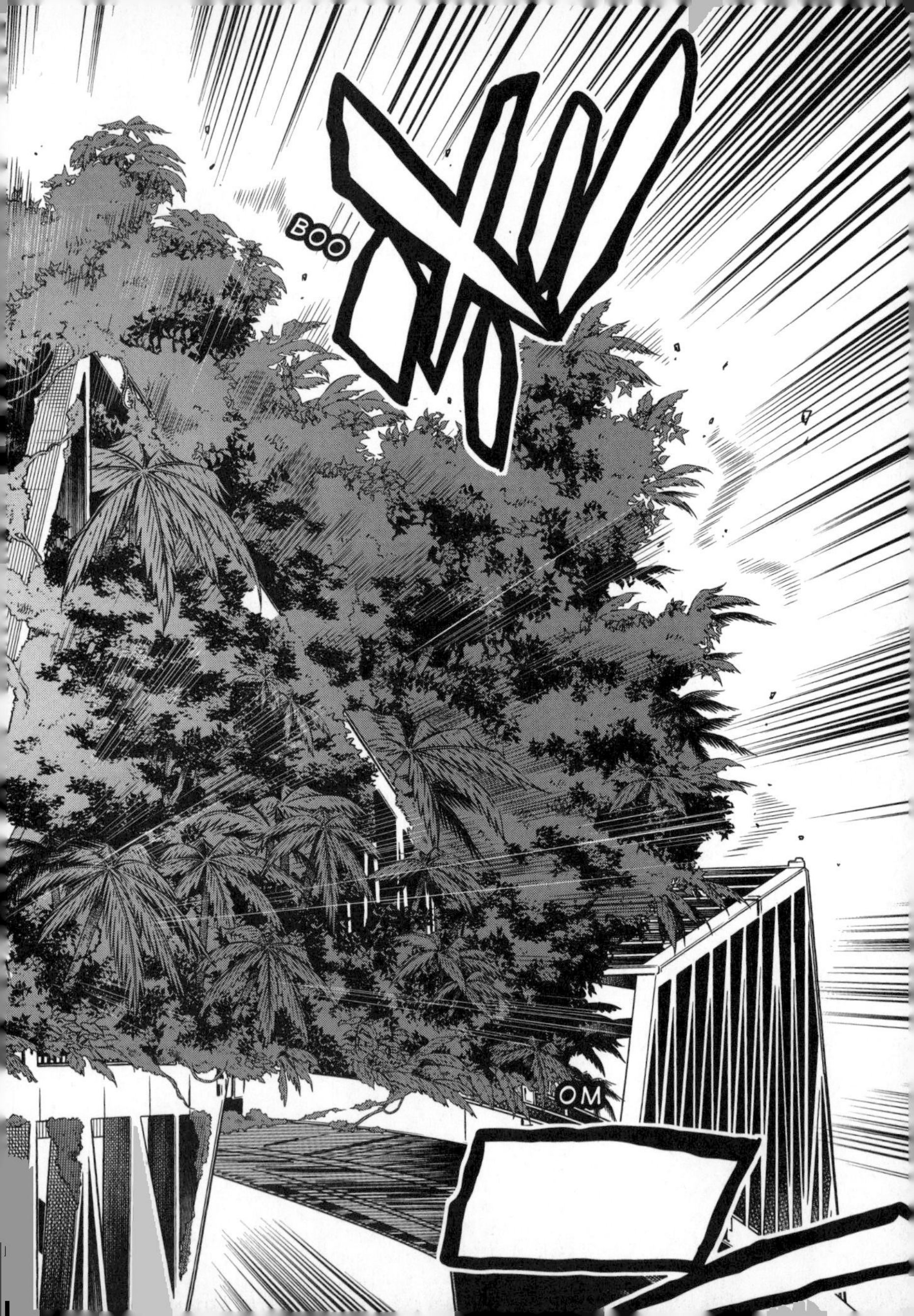
BOO
OM

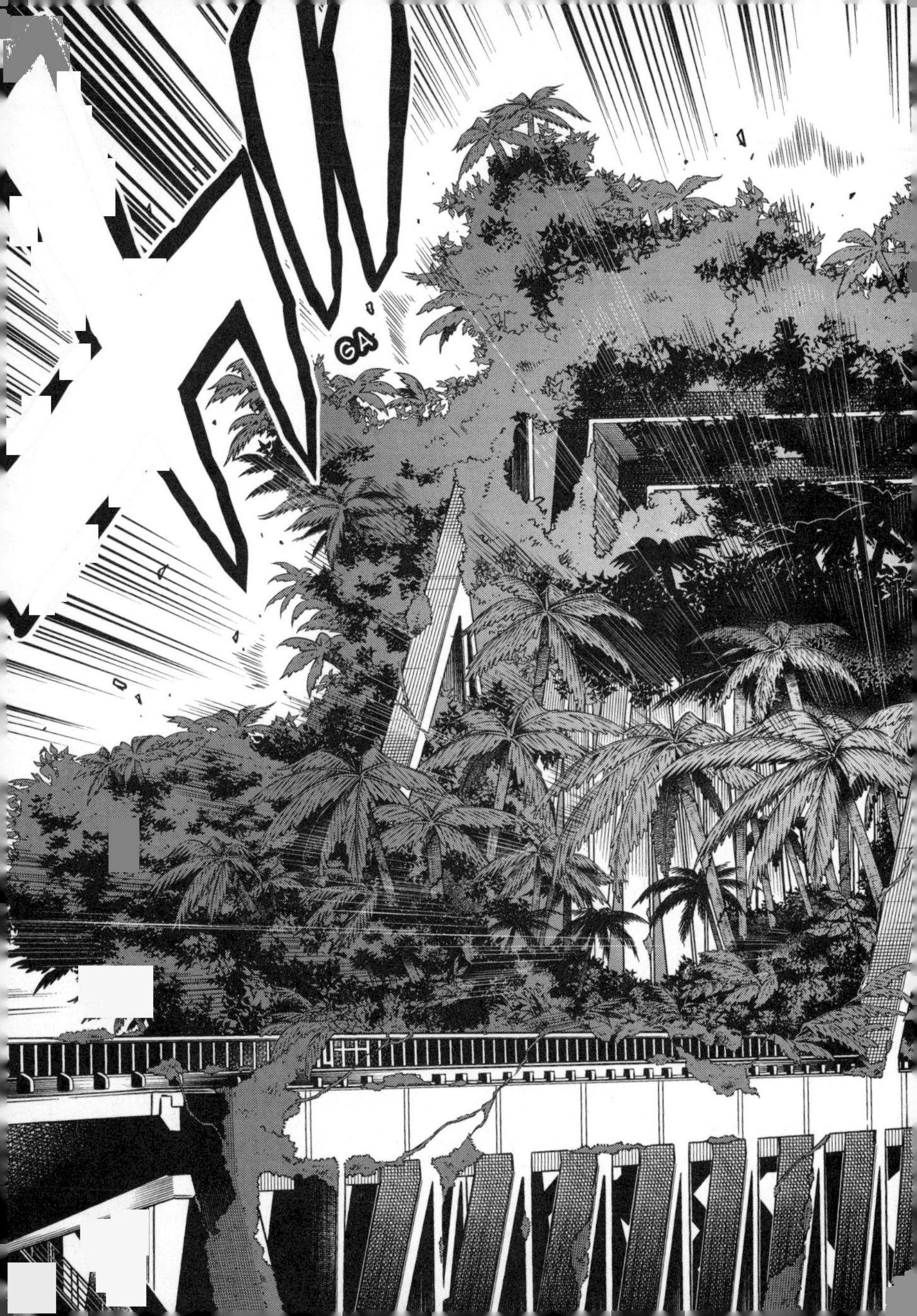
GA

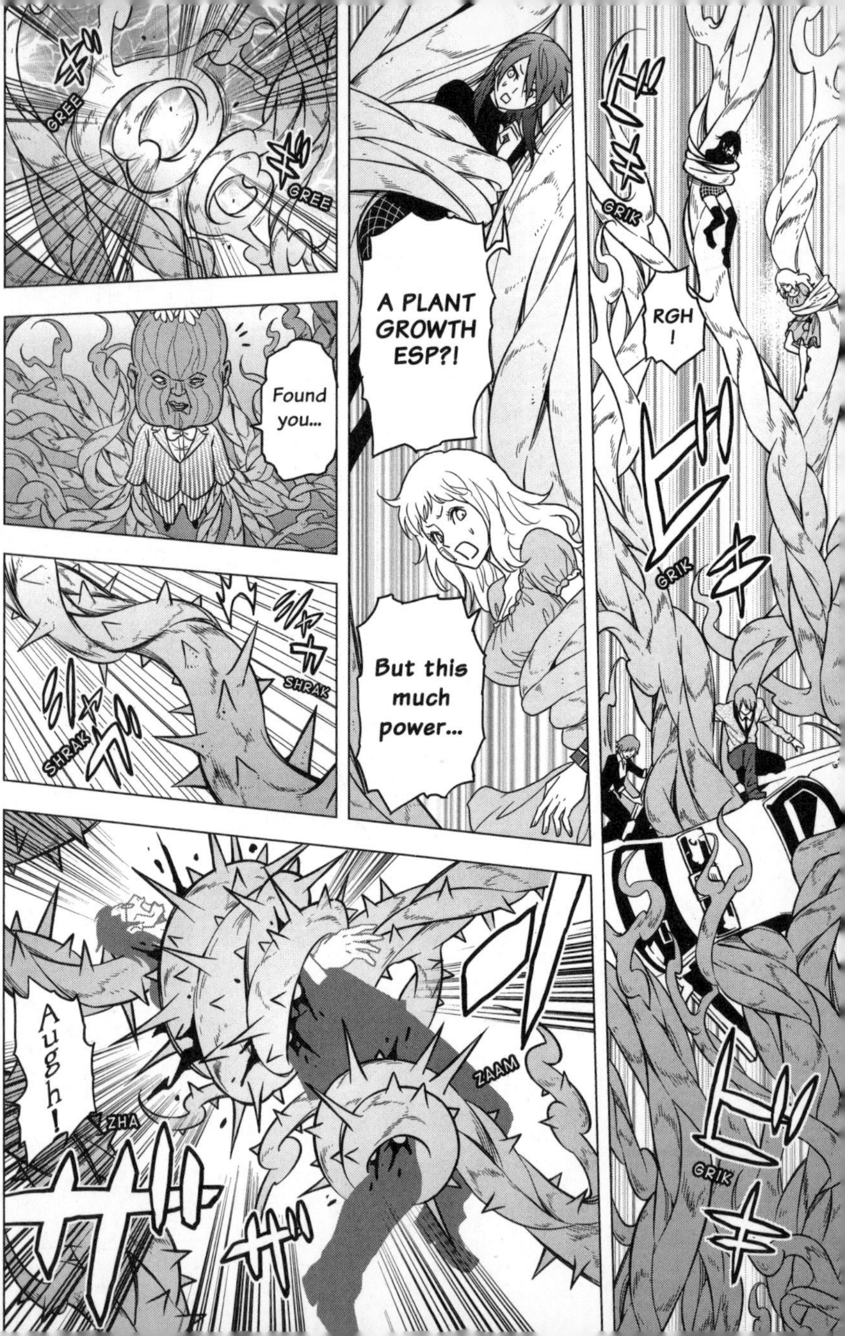
GRIK
RGH!
GRIK
GRIK
A PLANT GROWTH ESP?!
But this much power...
GREE
GREE
Found you...
SHRAK
SHRAK
ZAAM
Augh!
ZHA

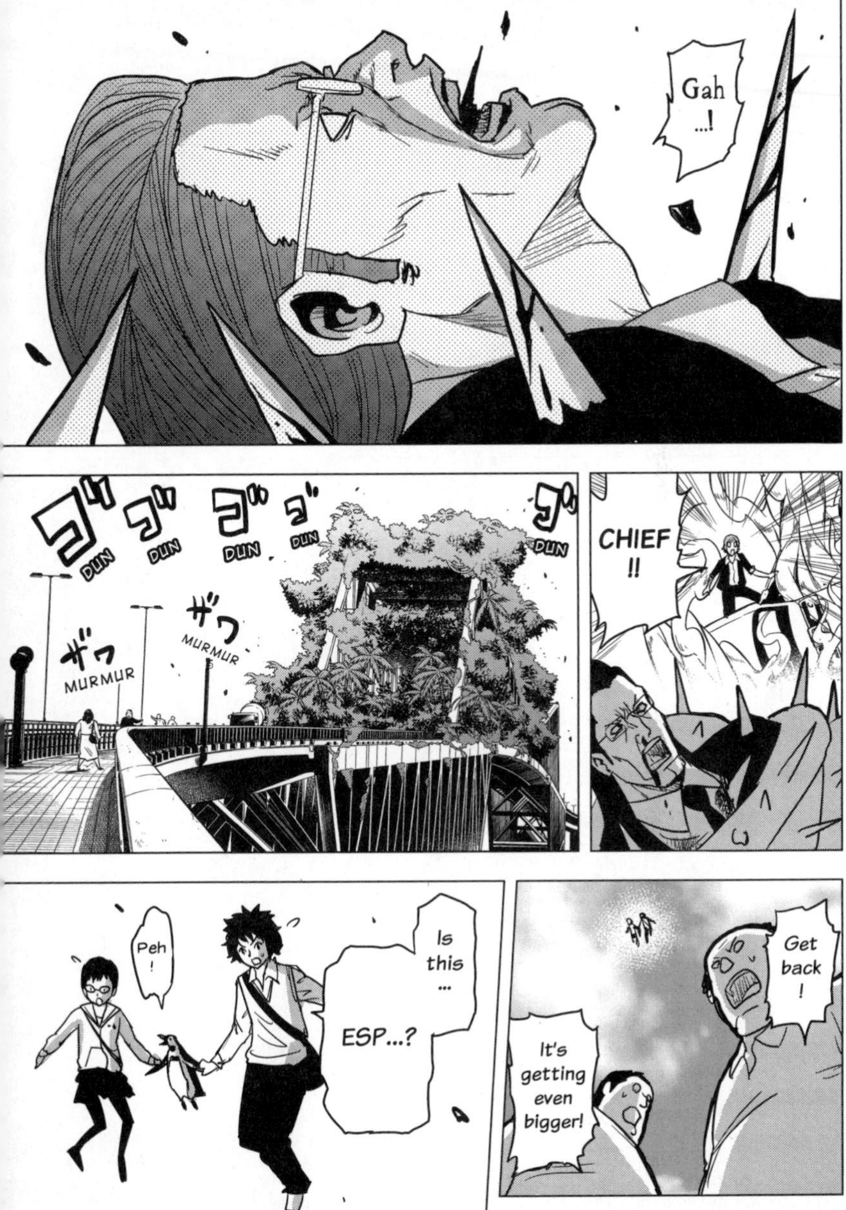

Gah ...!
CHIEF !!
ゴ DUN
ゴ DUN
ゴ DUN
ゴ DUN
ゴ DUN
ザワ MURMUR
ザワ MURMUR
Get back!
It's getting even bigger!
Is this ...
ESP...?
Peh!

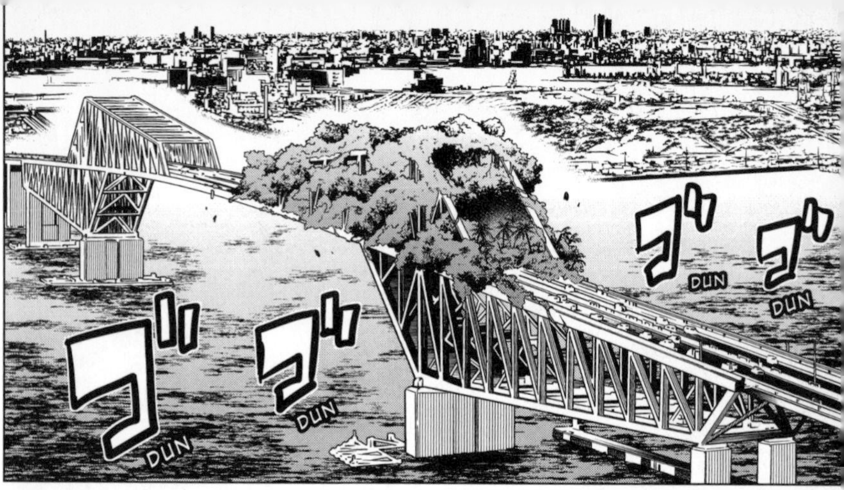
ゴ
DUN
ゴ
DUN
ゴ
DUN
ゴ
DUN

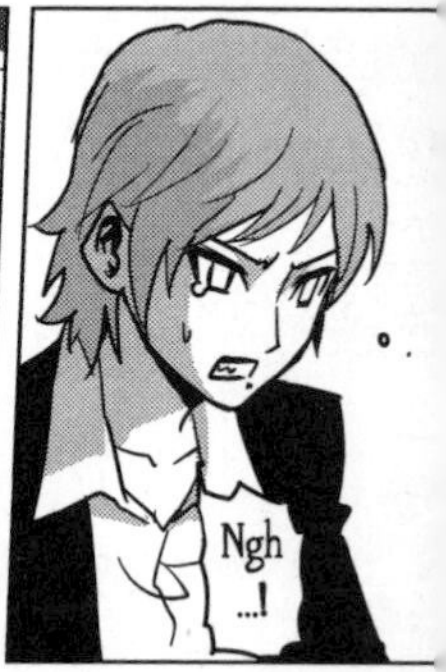
Ngh ...!

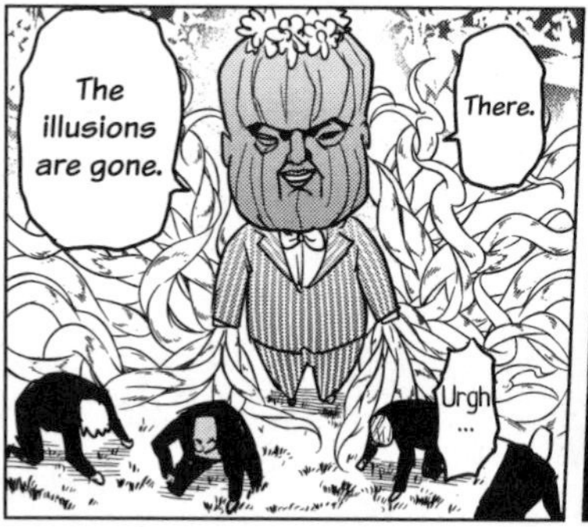
There.
The illusions are gone.
Urgh ...

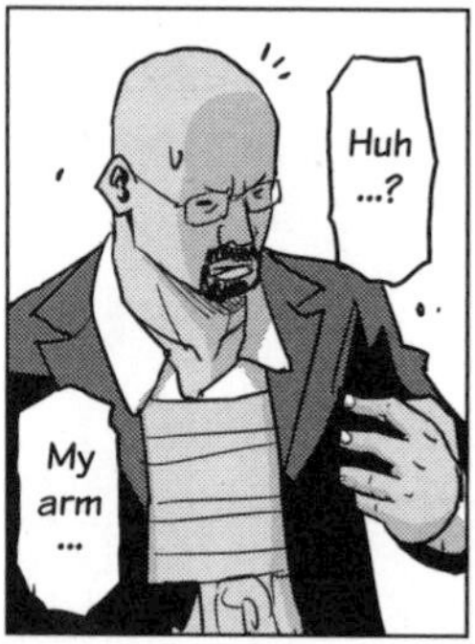
Huh ...?
My arm ...

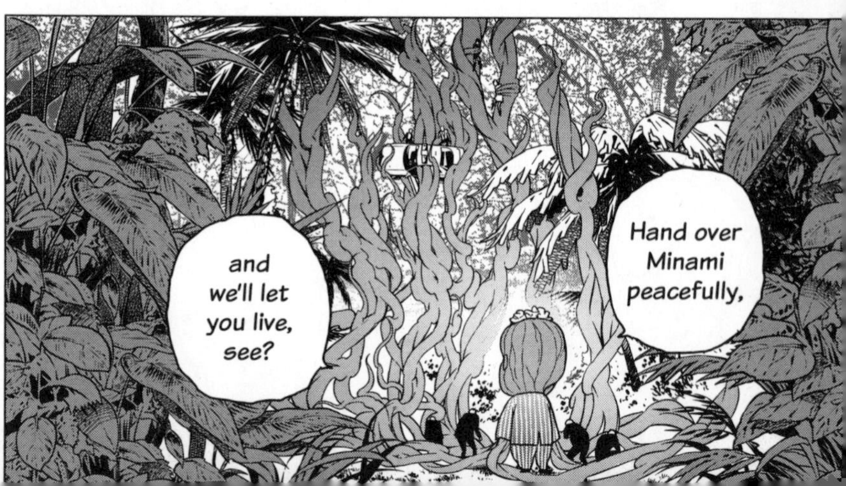
Hand over Minami peacefully,
and we'll let you live, see?

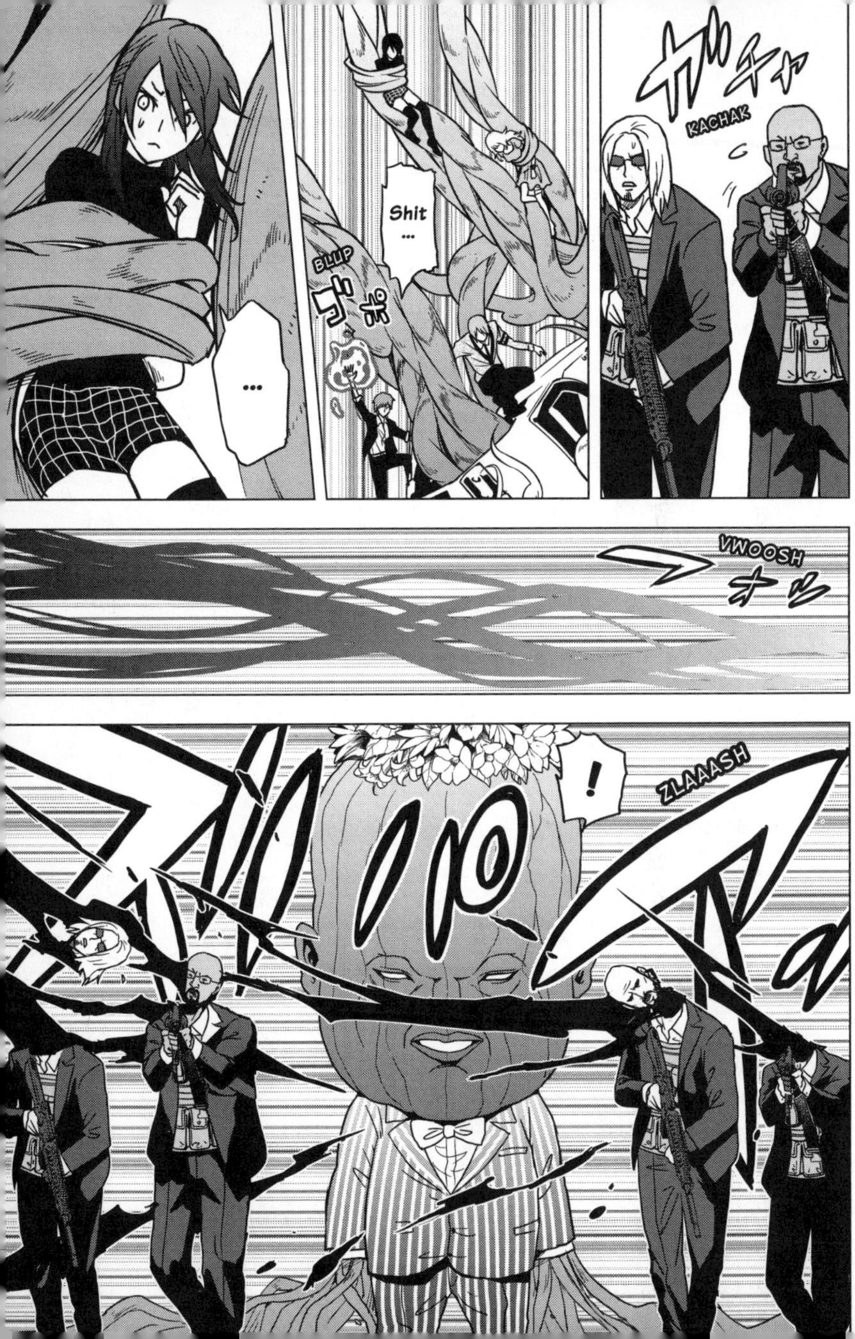
KACHAK
Shit
...
BLUP
ゴポ
...
VWOOSH
ZLAAASH
!

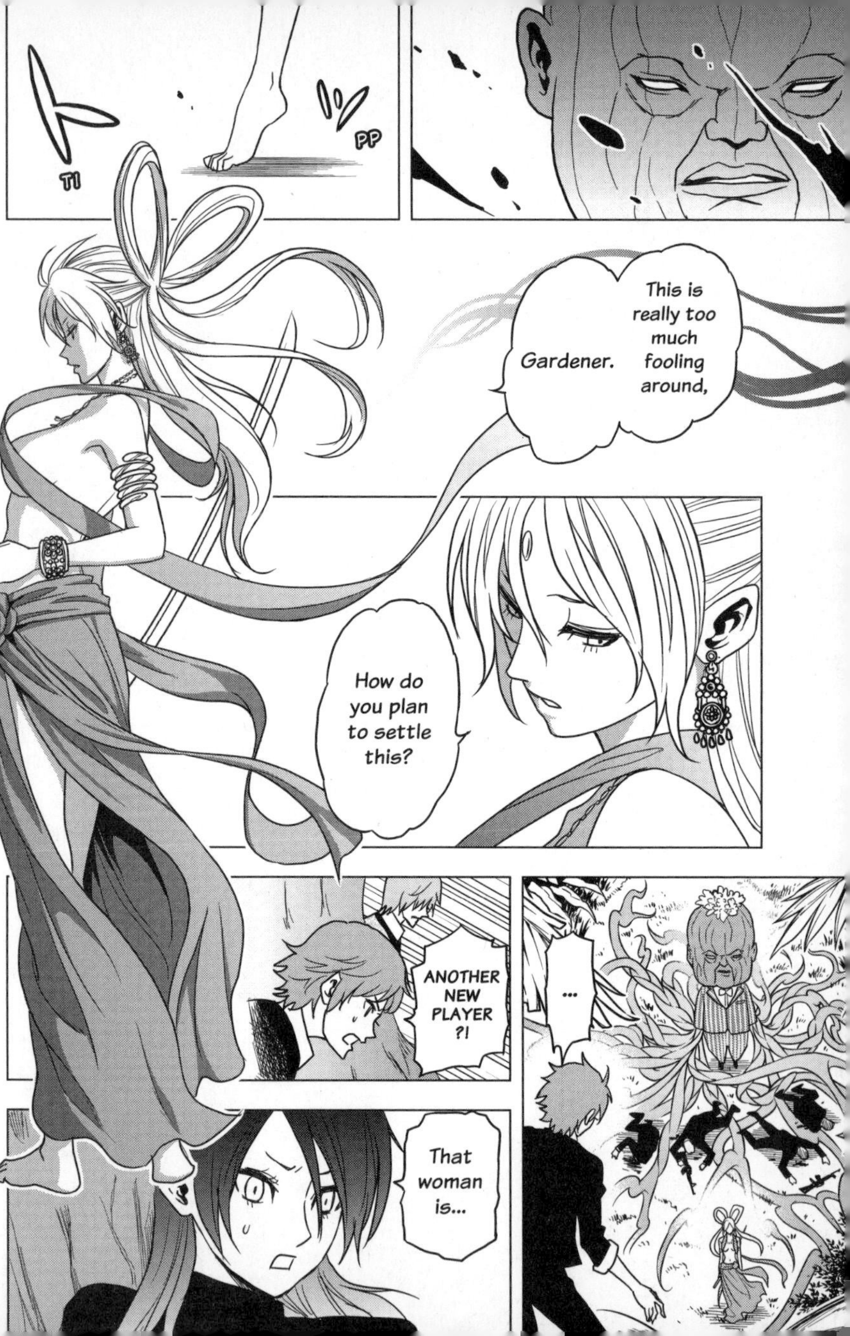
TI
PP
This is really too much fooling around, Gardener.
How do you plan to settle this?
...
ANOTHER NEW PLAYER ?!
That woman is...

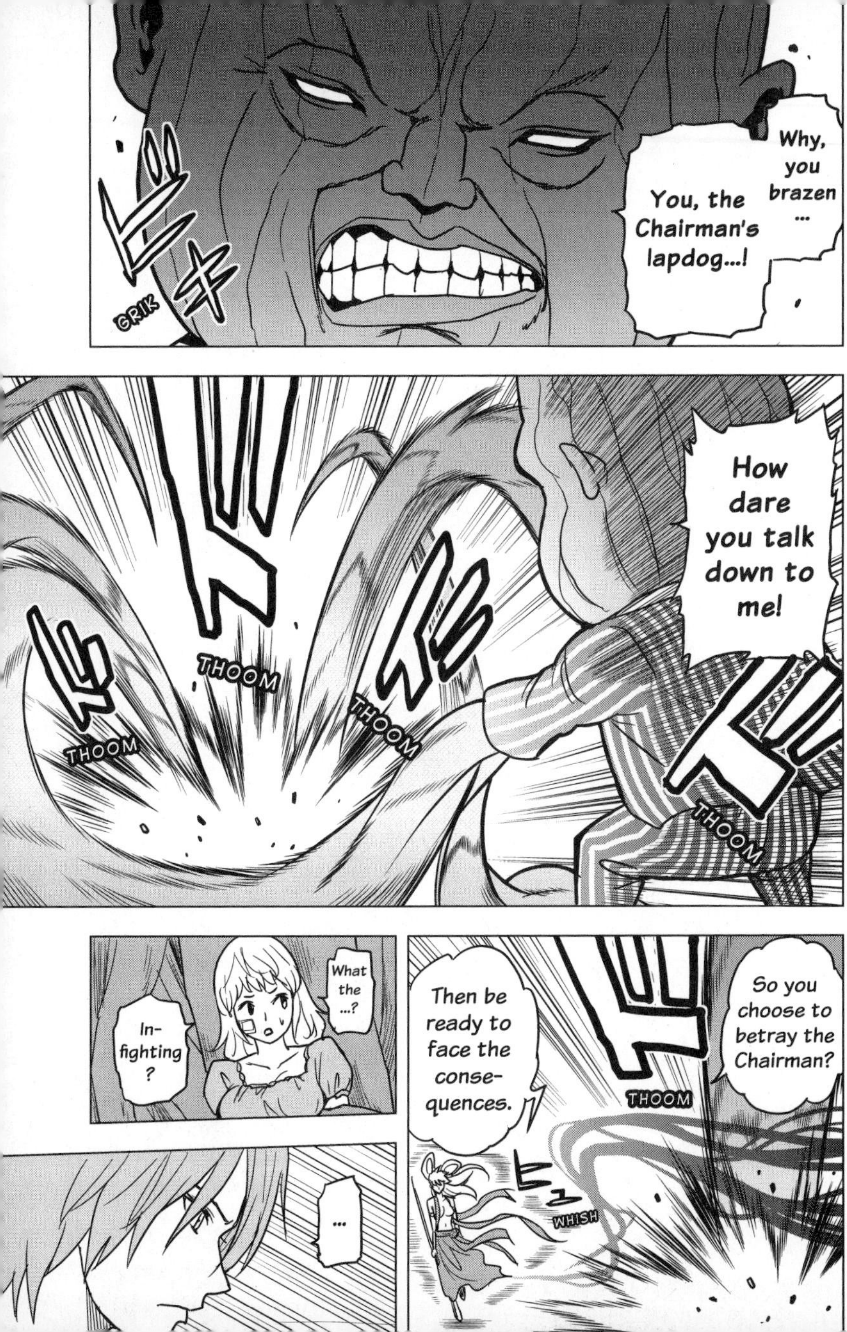
Why, you brazen ...
You, the Chairman's lapdog...!
GRIK
How dare you talk down to me!
THOOM
THOOM
THOOM
THOOM
So you choose to betray the Chairman?
Then be ready to face the conse-quences.
THOOM
WHISH
What the ...?
In-fighting ?
...

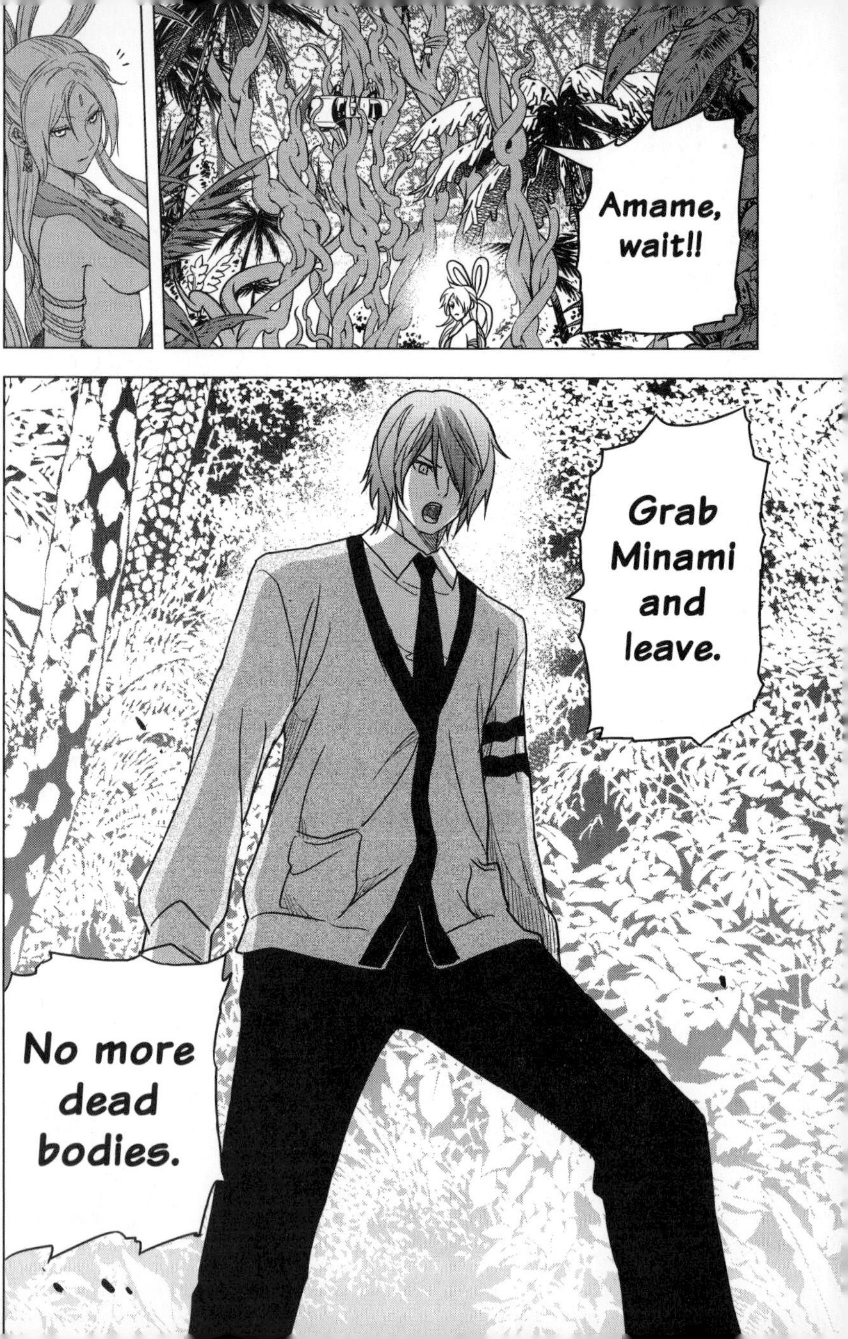
Amame, wait!!
Grab Minami and leave.
No more dead bodies.

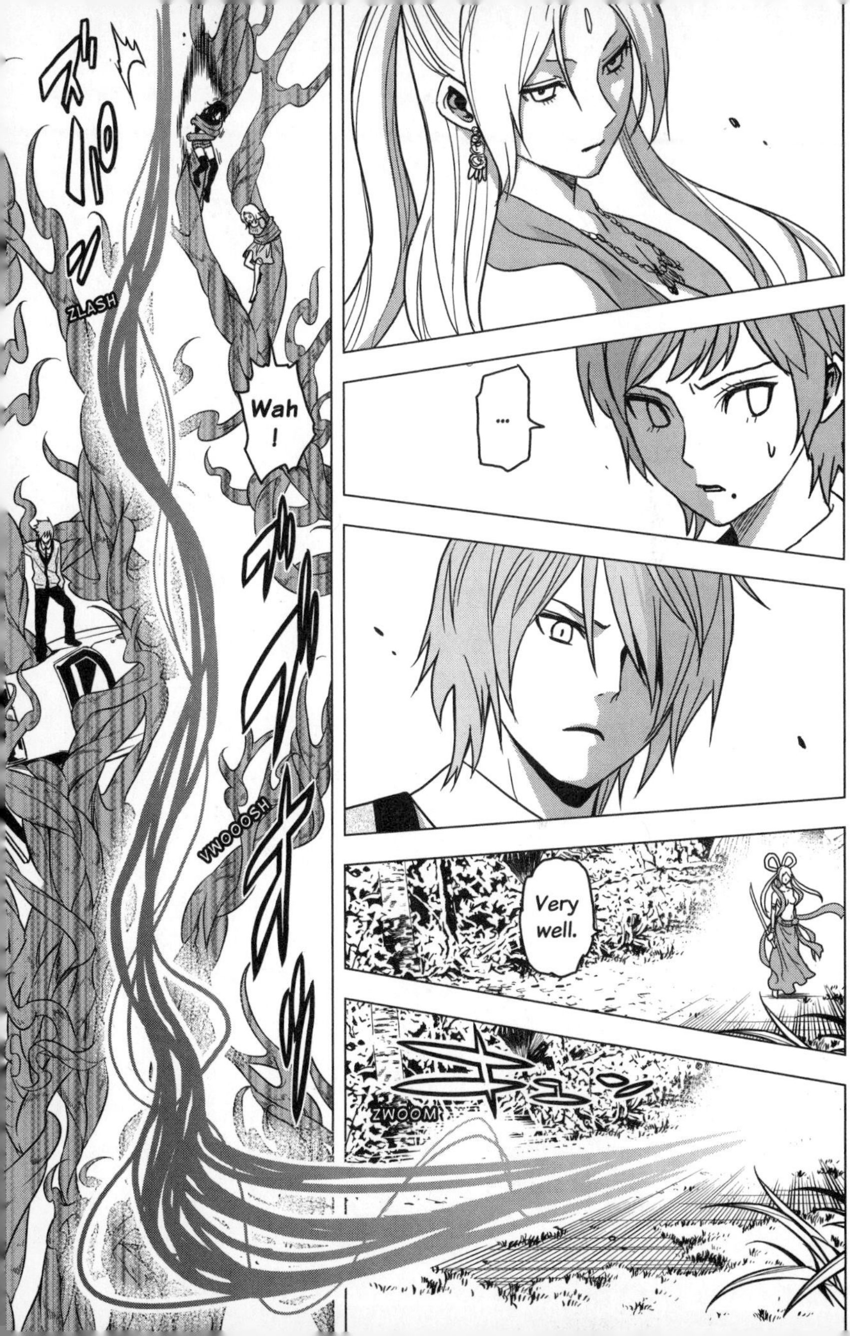
...
Very well.
ZWOOM
ZLASH
Wah!
VWOOOSH

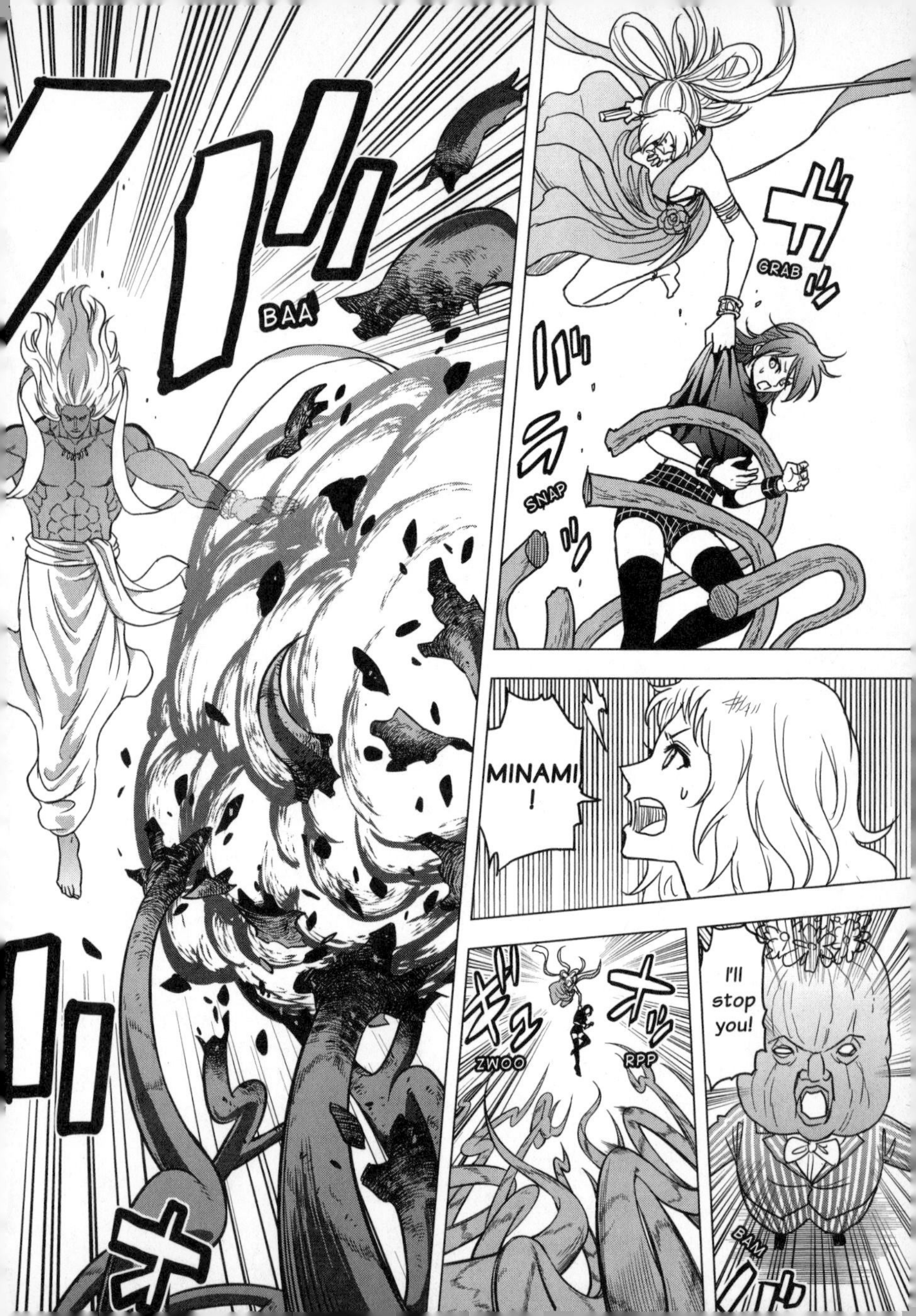
GRAB
SNAP
MINAMI!
I'll stop you!
BAM
RPP
ZWOO
BAA

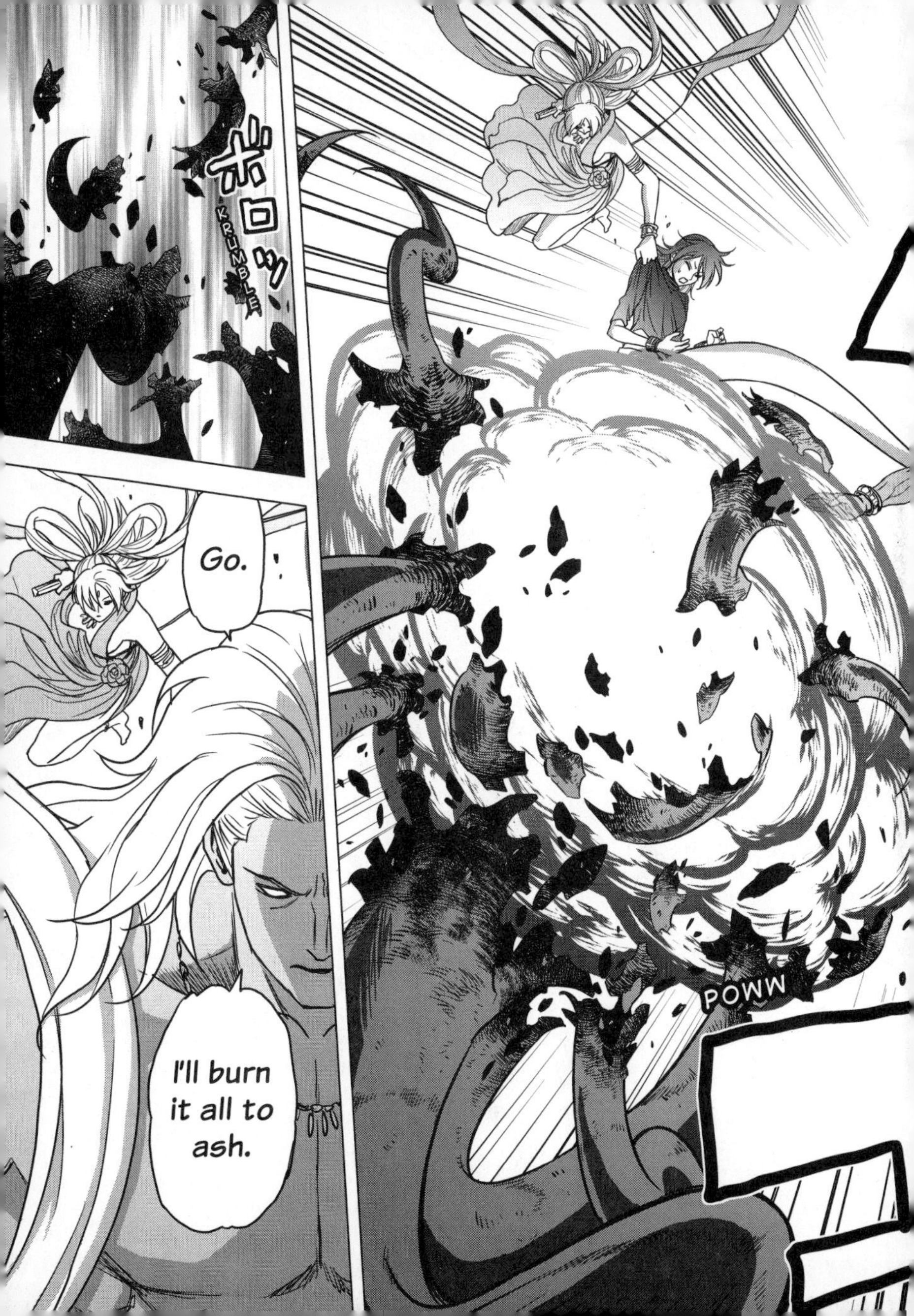
POWW
ボロッ
KRUMBLE
Go.
I'll burn it all to ash.

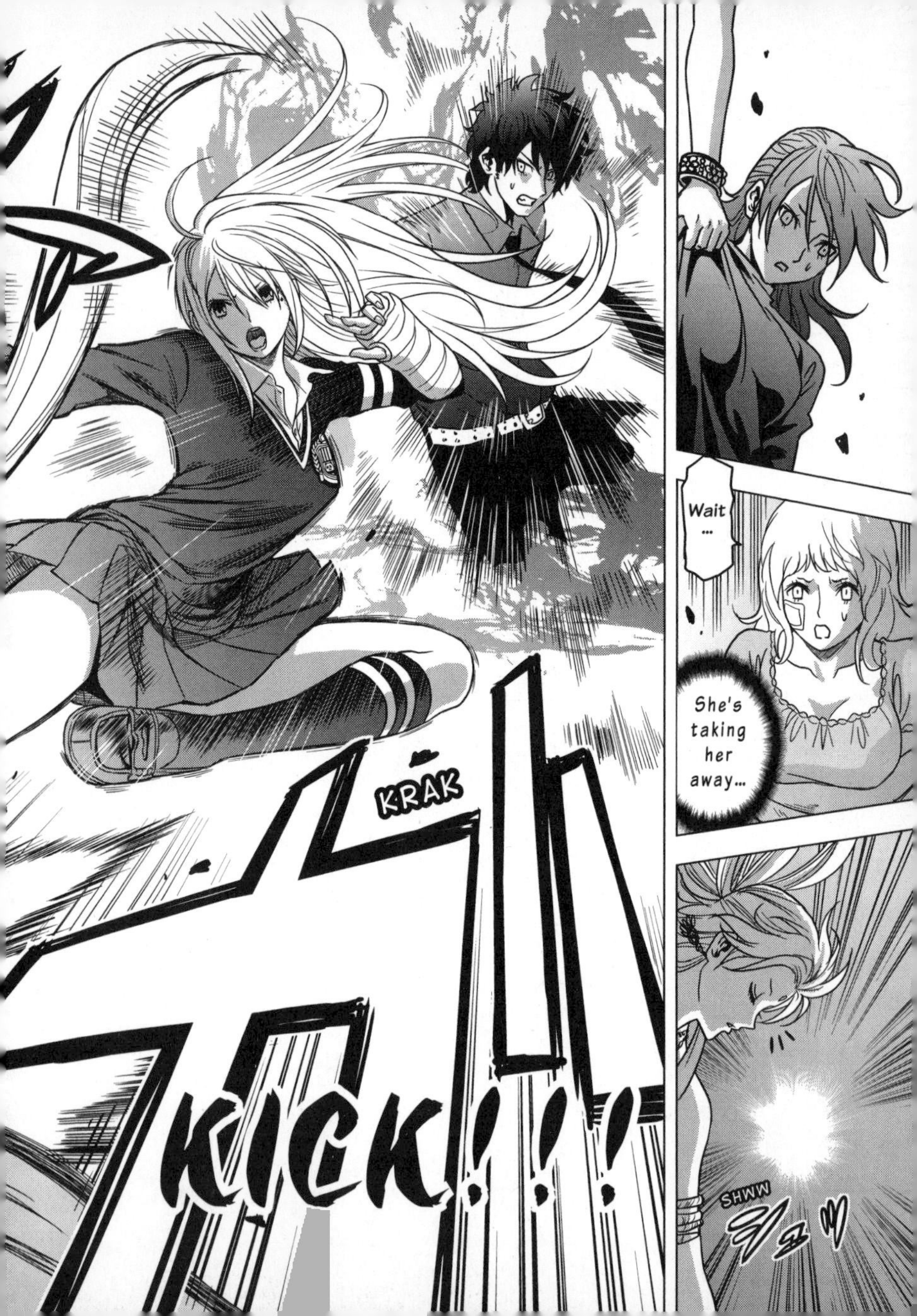
Wait ...
She's taking her away...
SHWW
KRAK
KICK!!!

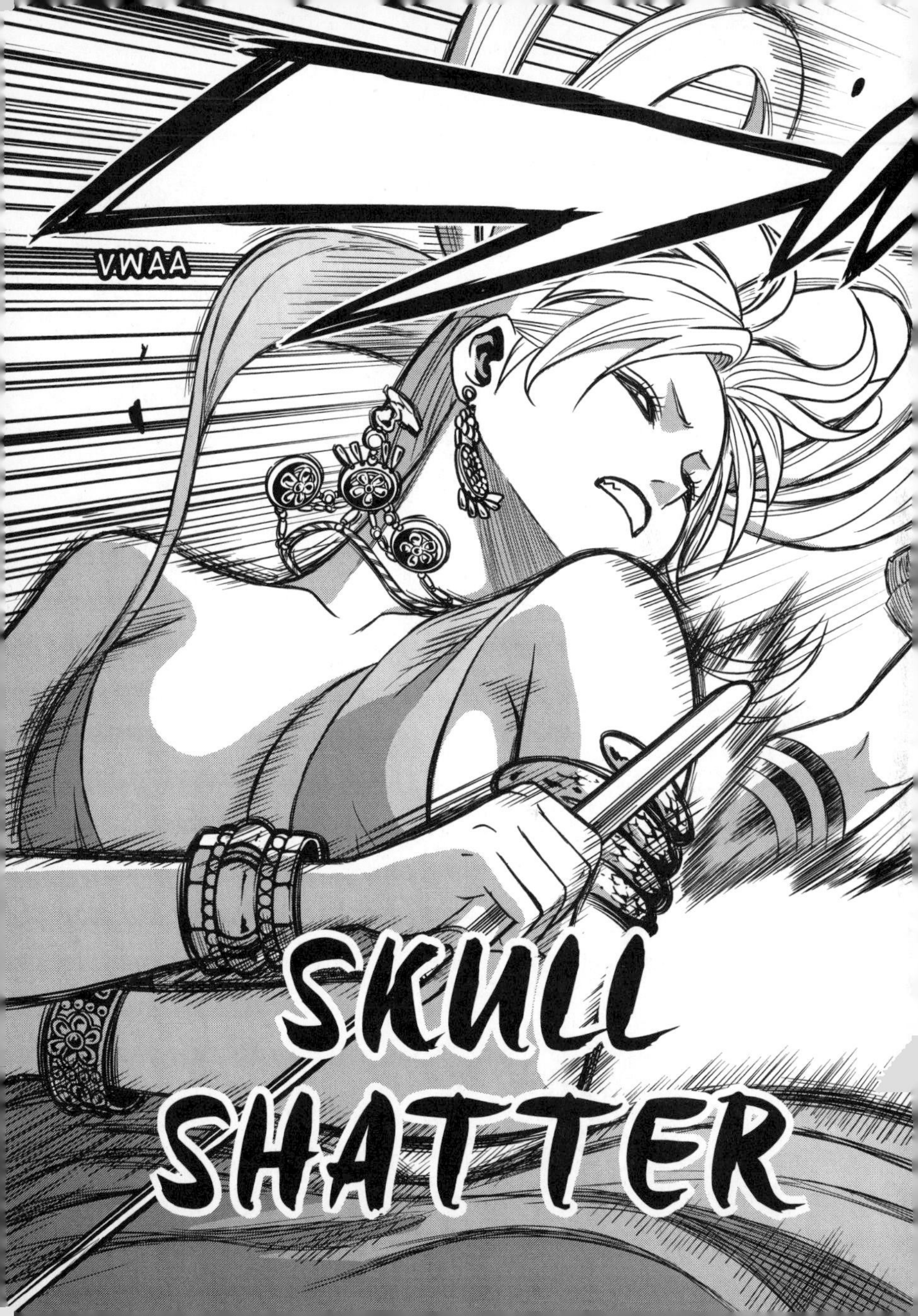
VWAA
SKULL SHATTER

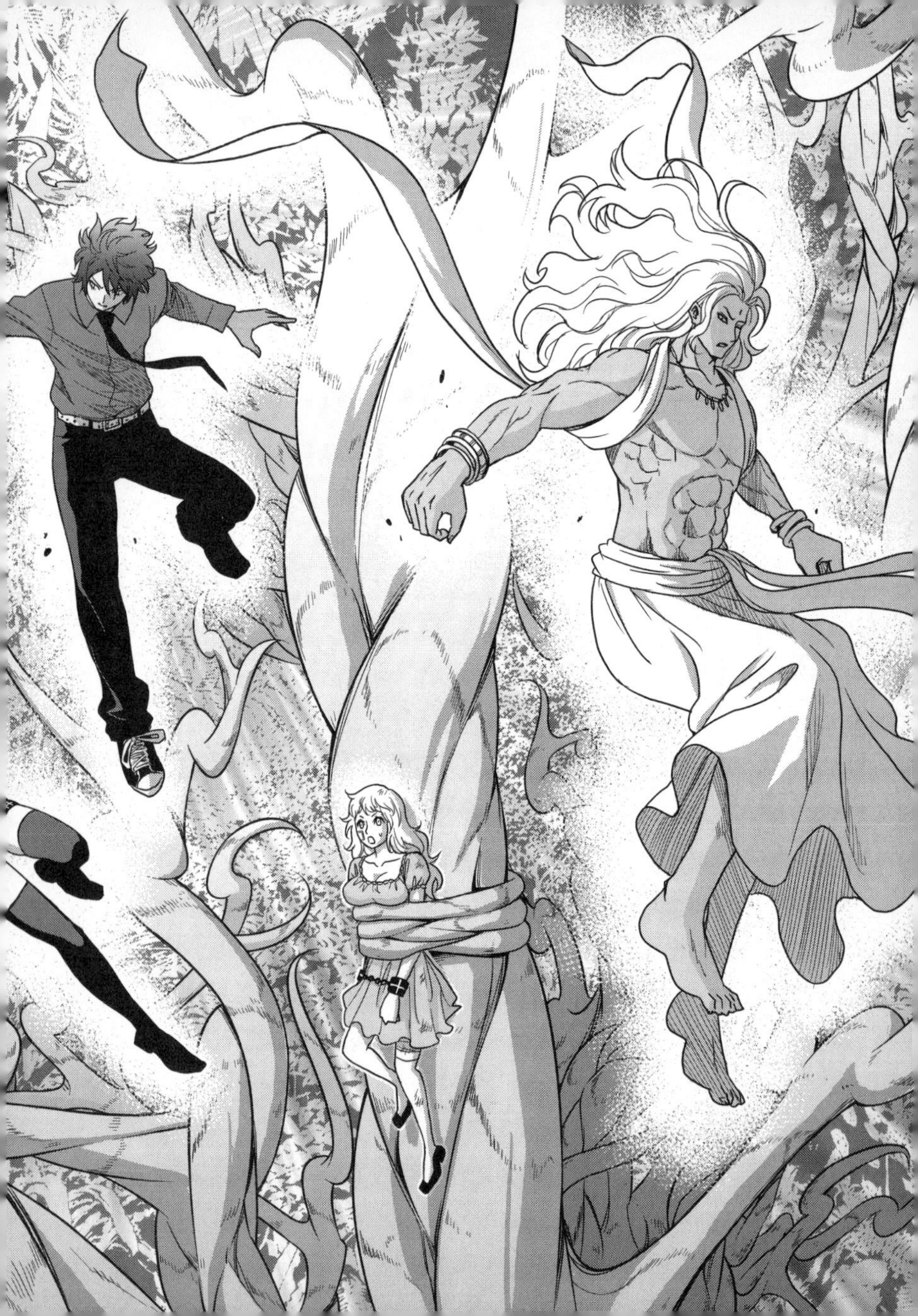

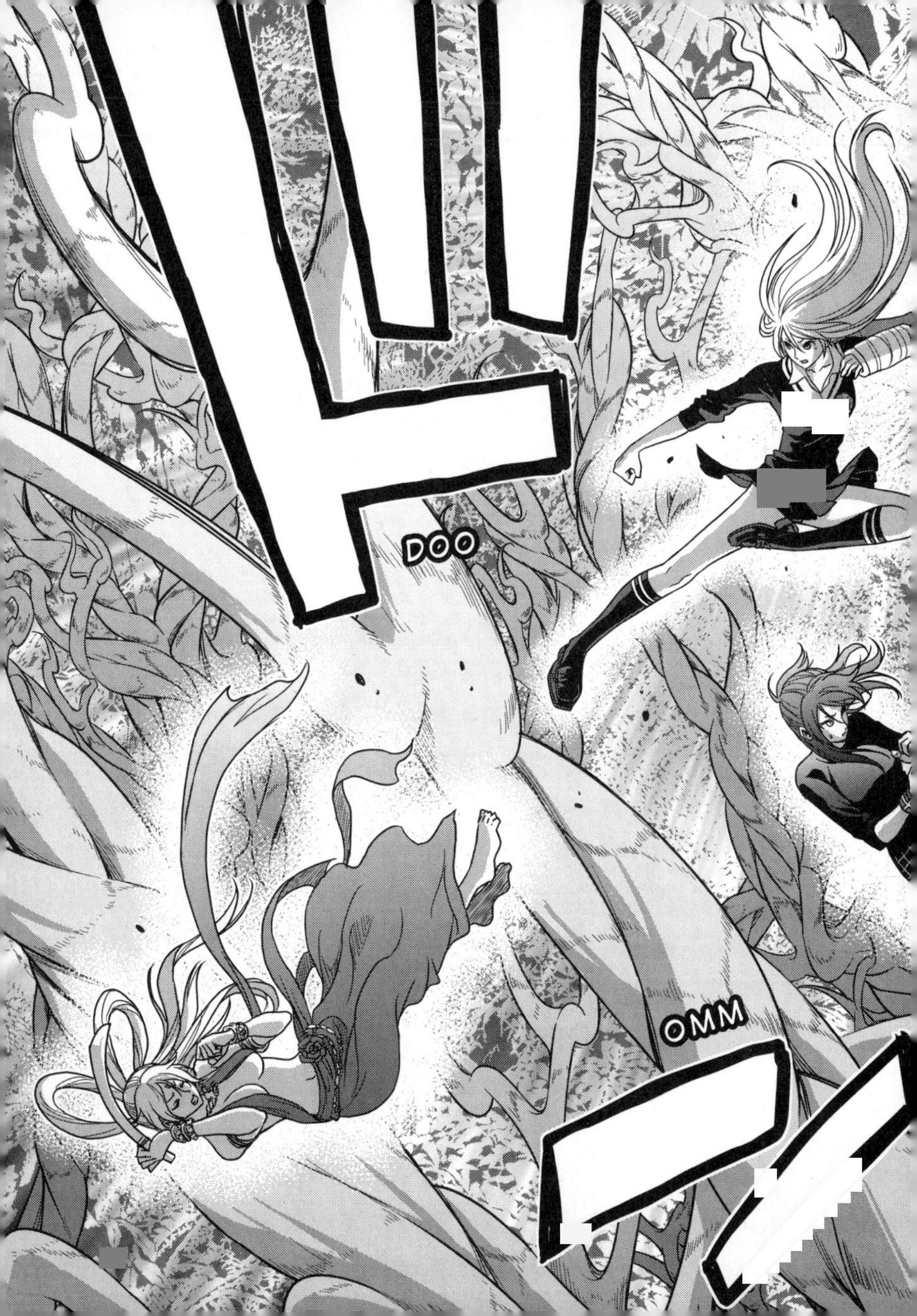
DOO
OMM

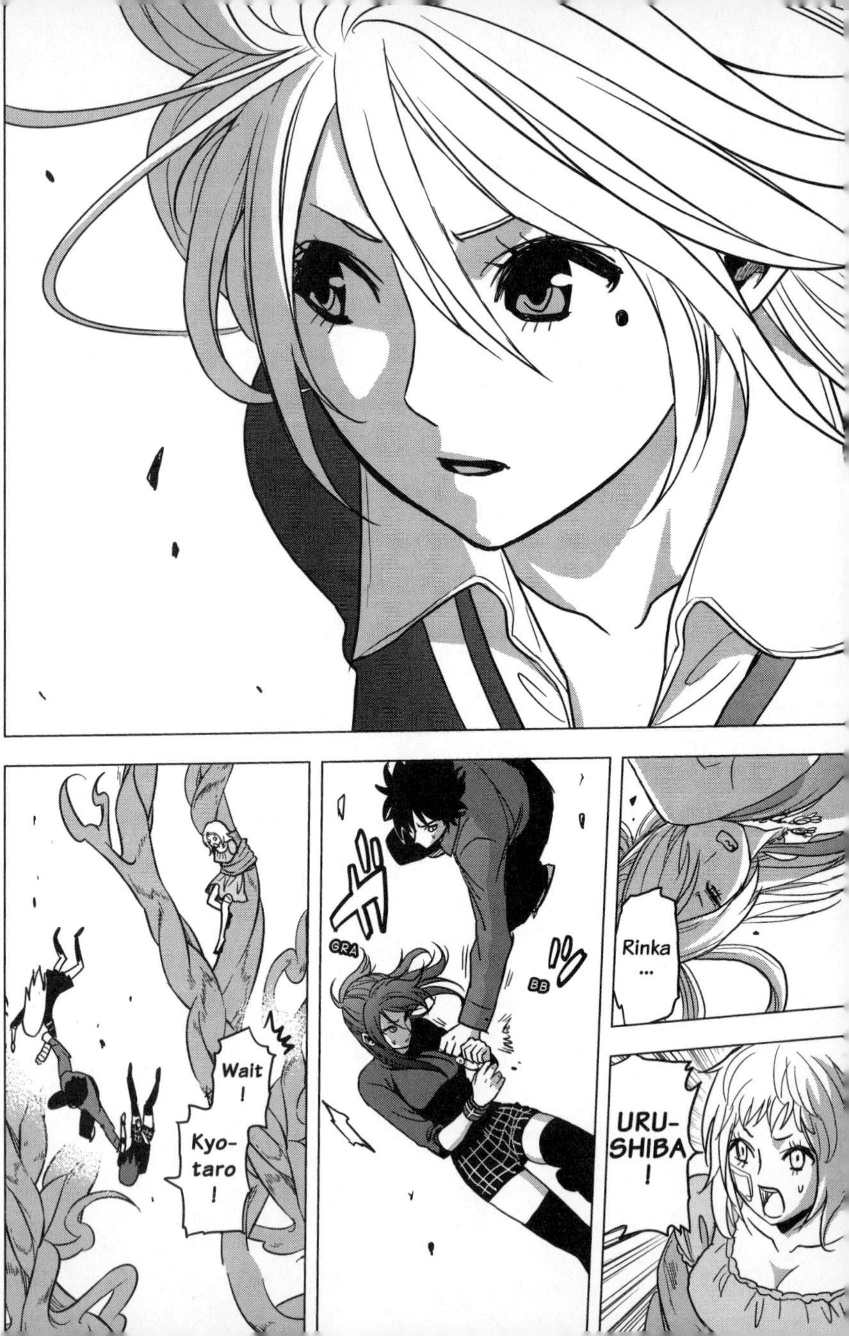

Rinka ...
URU-SHIBA!
GRA
BB
Wait! Kyo-taro!

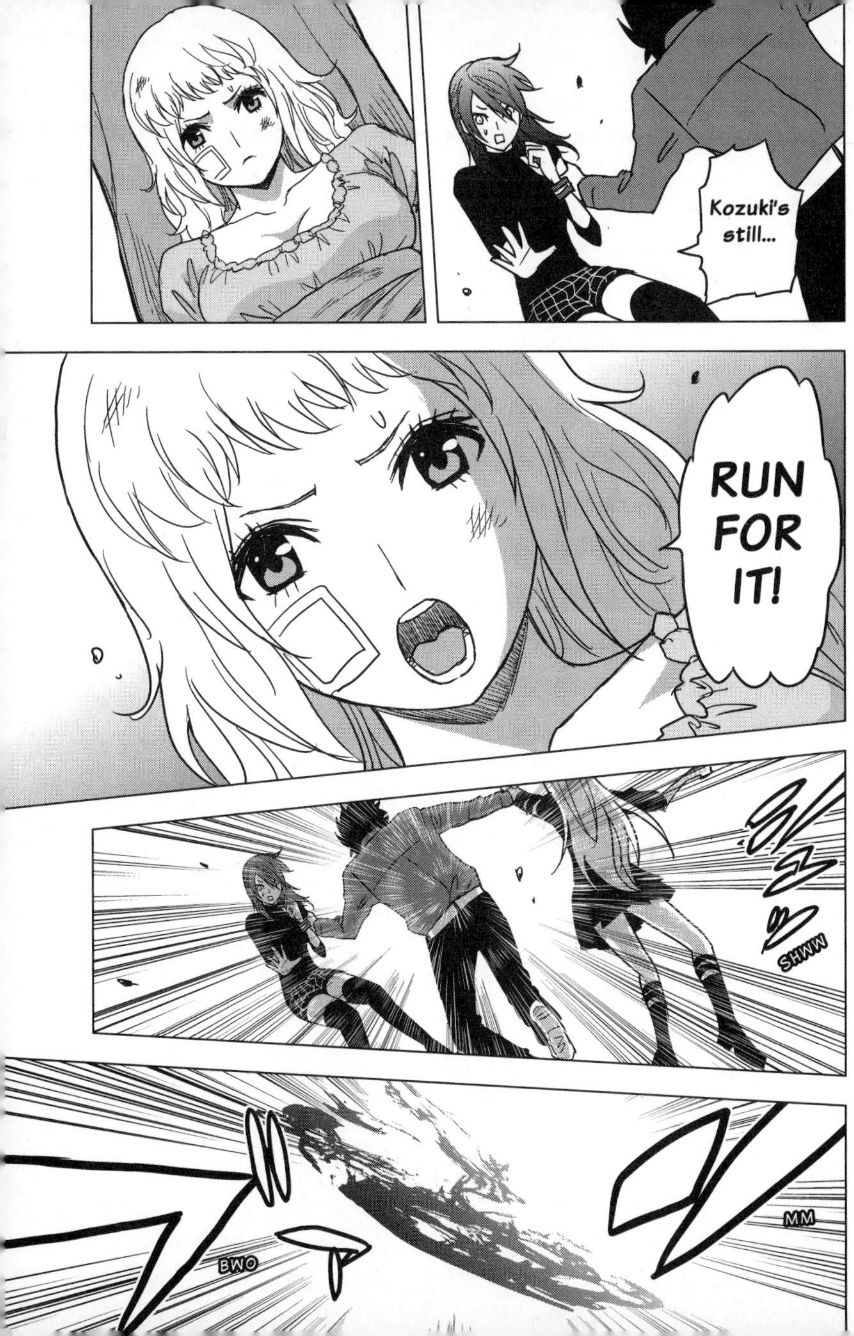
Kozuki's still...
RUN FOR IT!
SHWW
MM
BWO

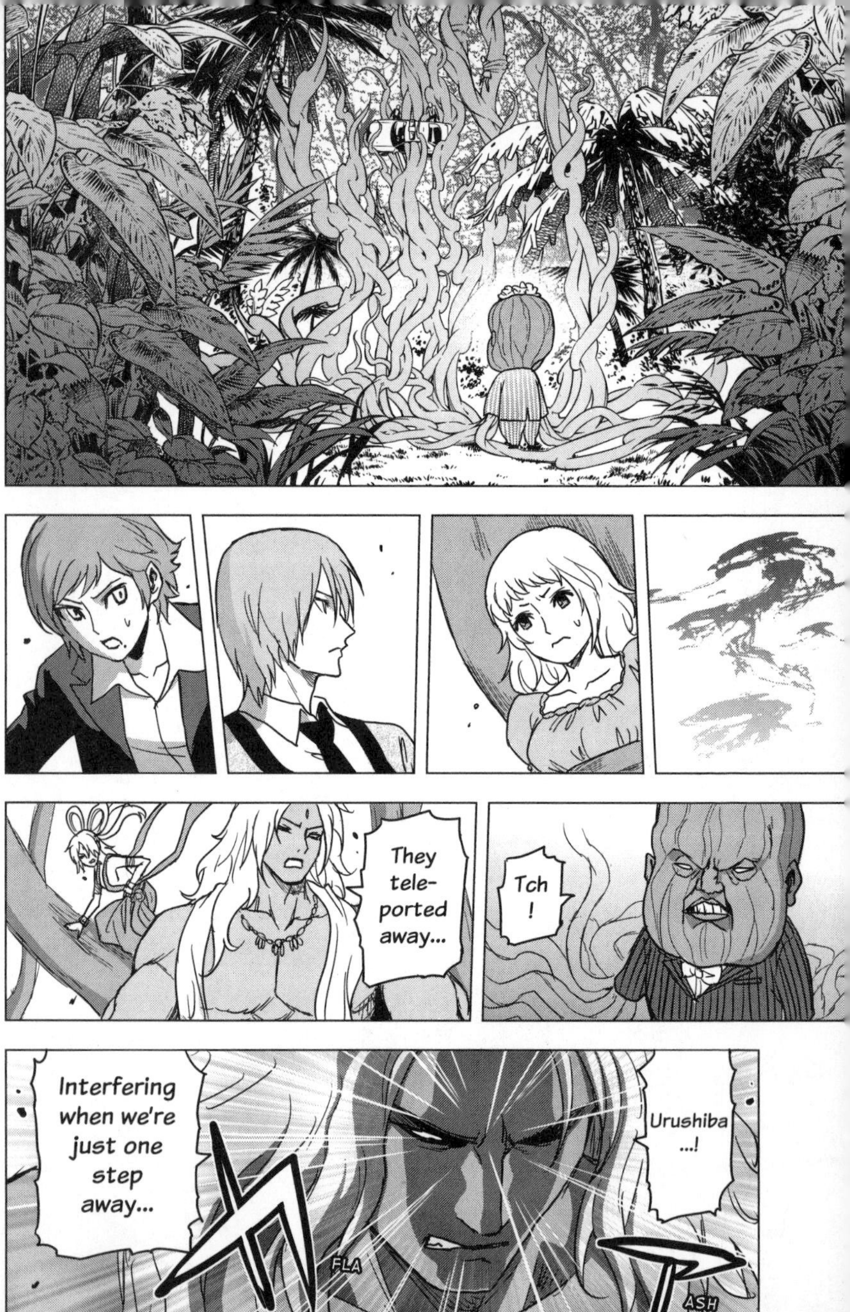
Tch!
They teleported away...
Urushiba ...!
Interfering when we're just one step away...
FLA
ASH

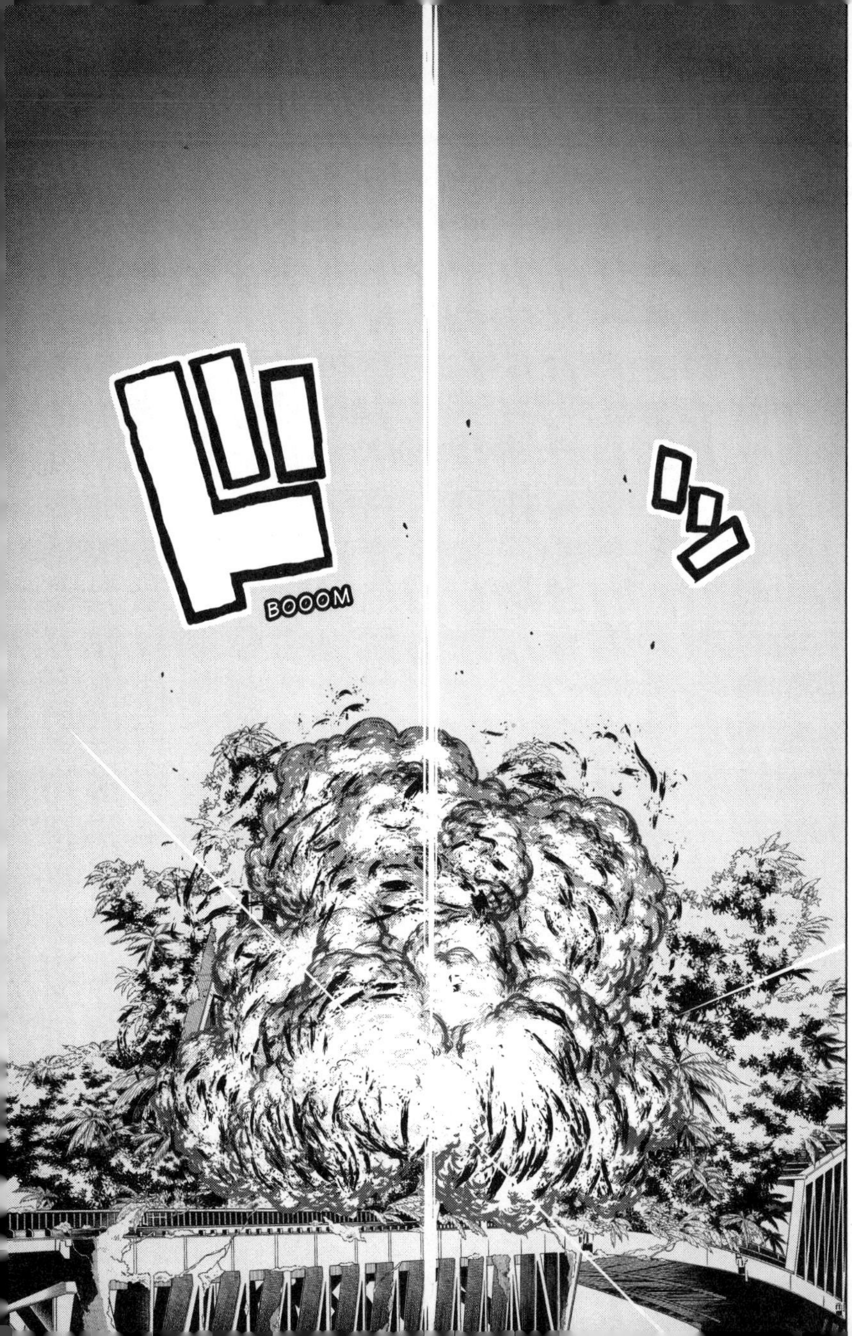
ドッ
BOOOM

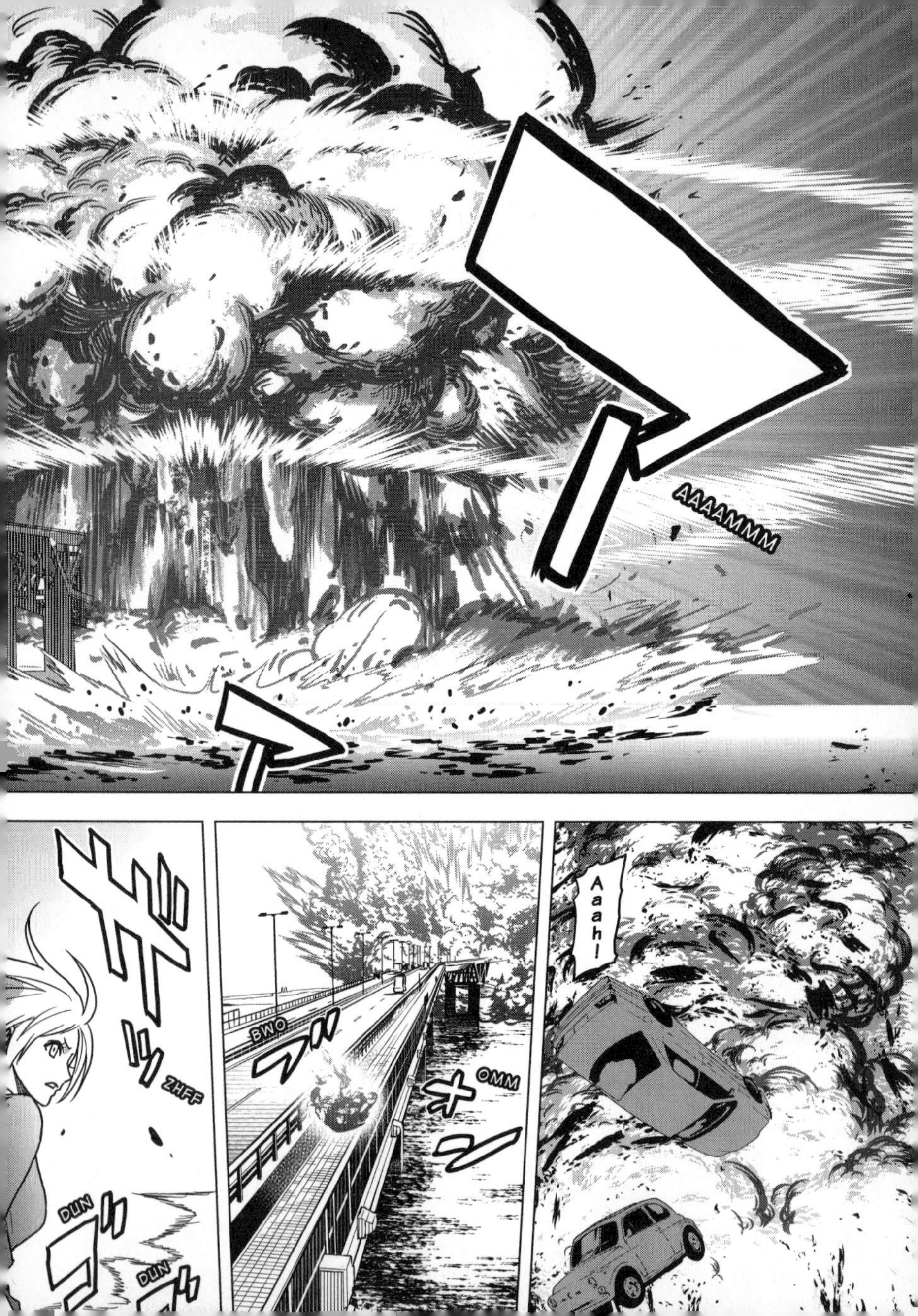
AAAAMMMM
Aaah!
BWO
OMM
ZHFF
DUN
DUN

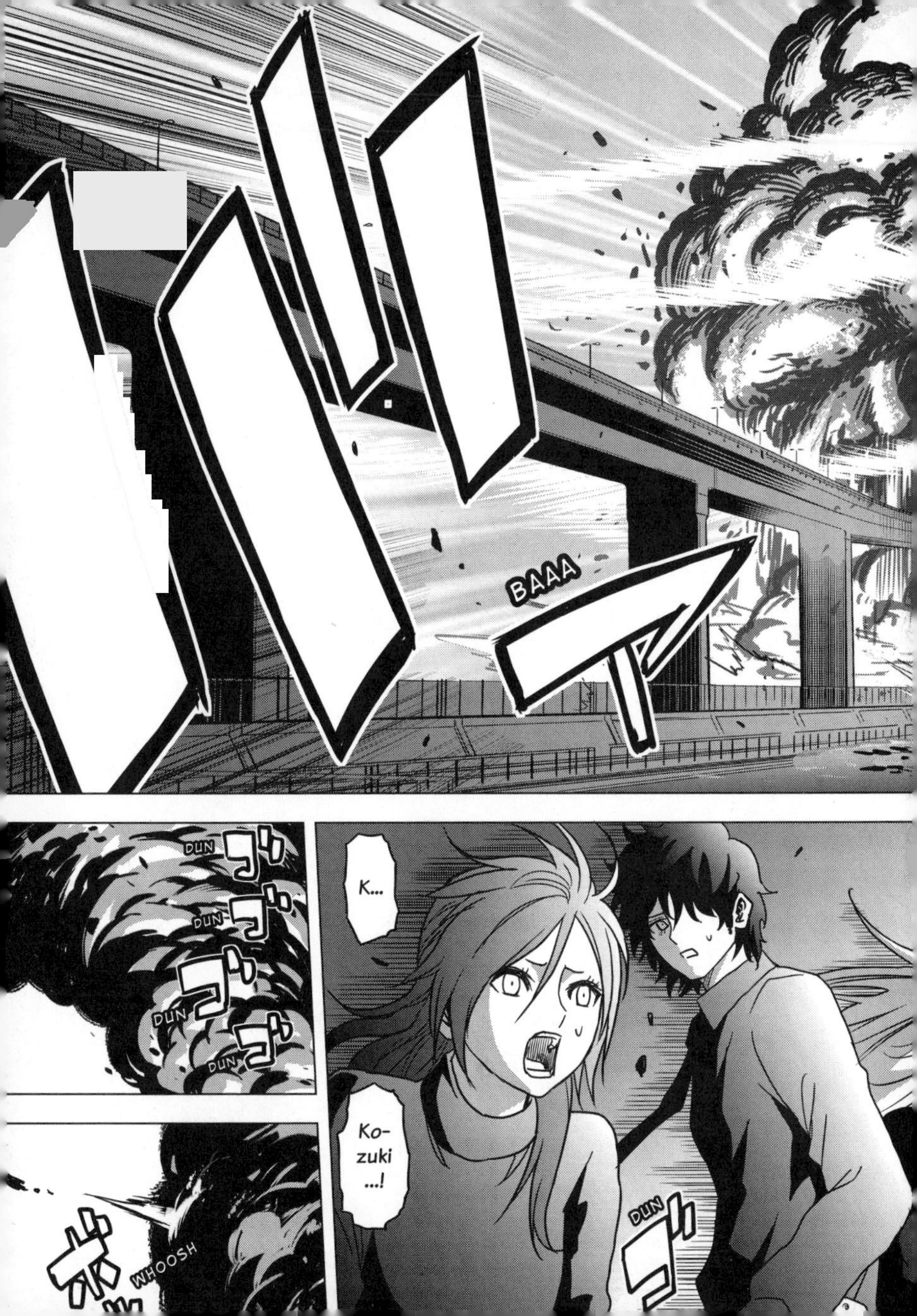
BAAA
K...
Ko-zuki ...!
DUN
DUN
DUN
DUN
DUN
WHOOSH

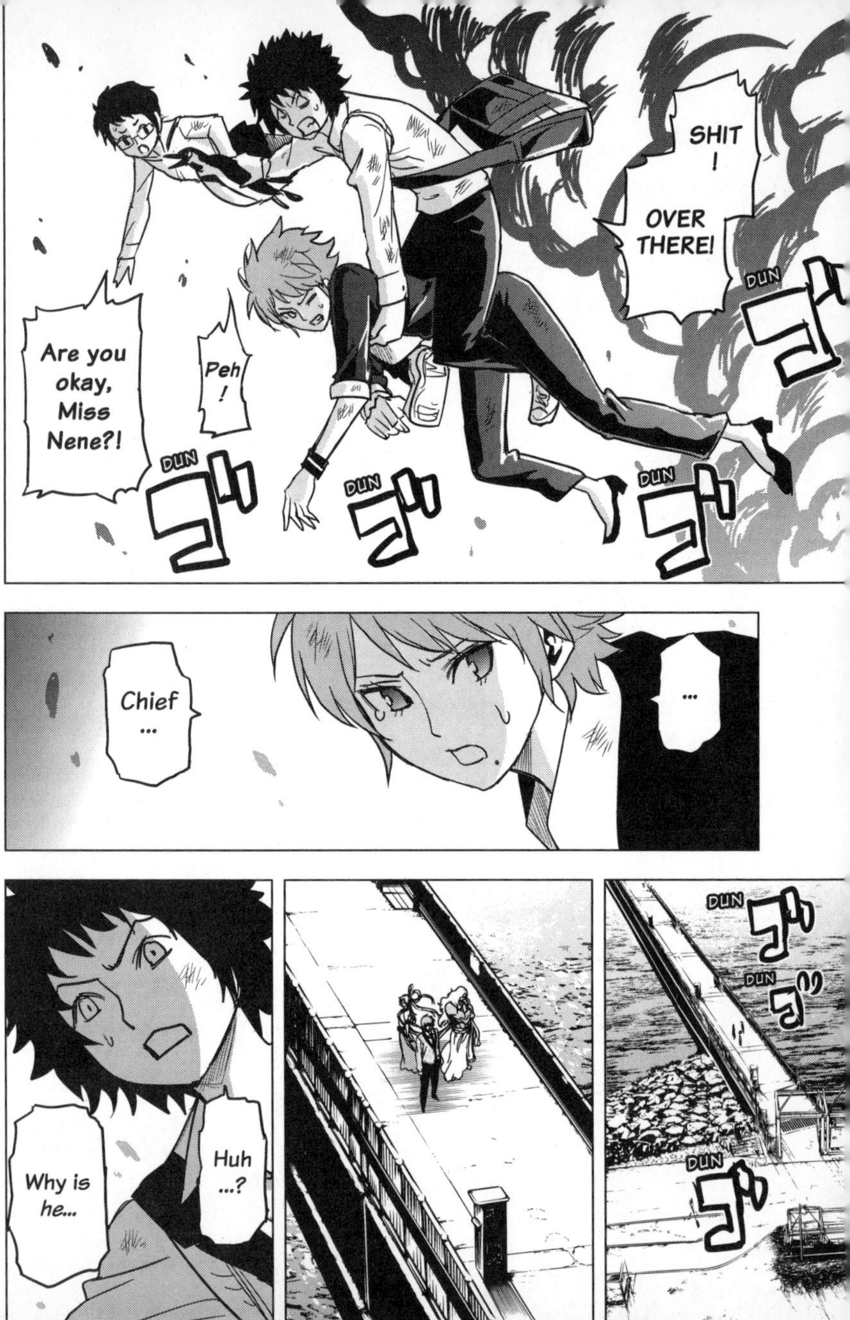

SHIT! OVER THERE!
DUN ゴ
DUN ゴ
Peh!
DUN ゴ
Are you okay, Miss Nene?!
DUN ゴ
...
Chief ...
DUN ゴ
DUN ゴ
DUN ゴ
Huh ...?
Why is he...

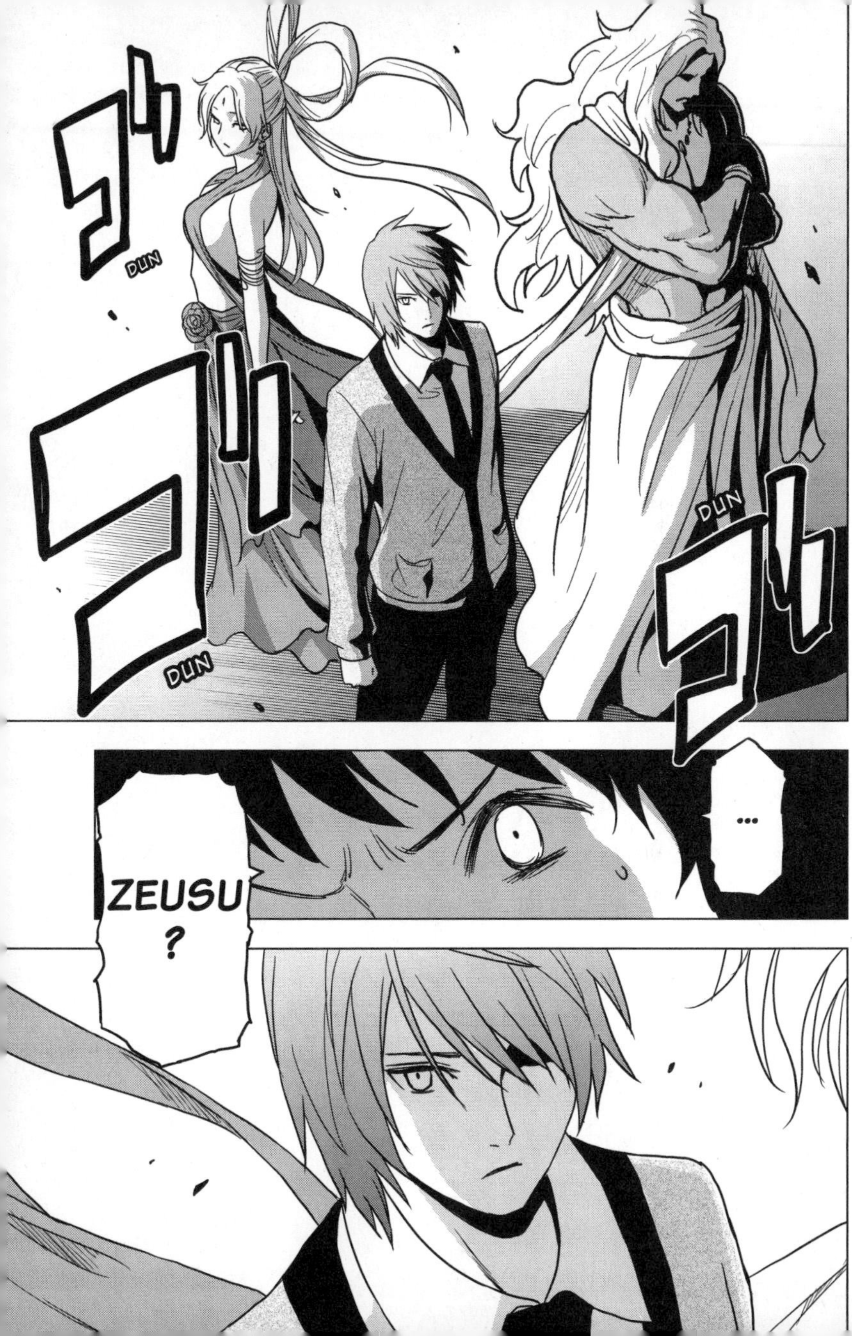
DUN
DUN
DUN
...
ZEUSU ?

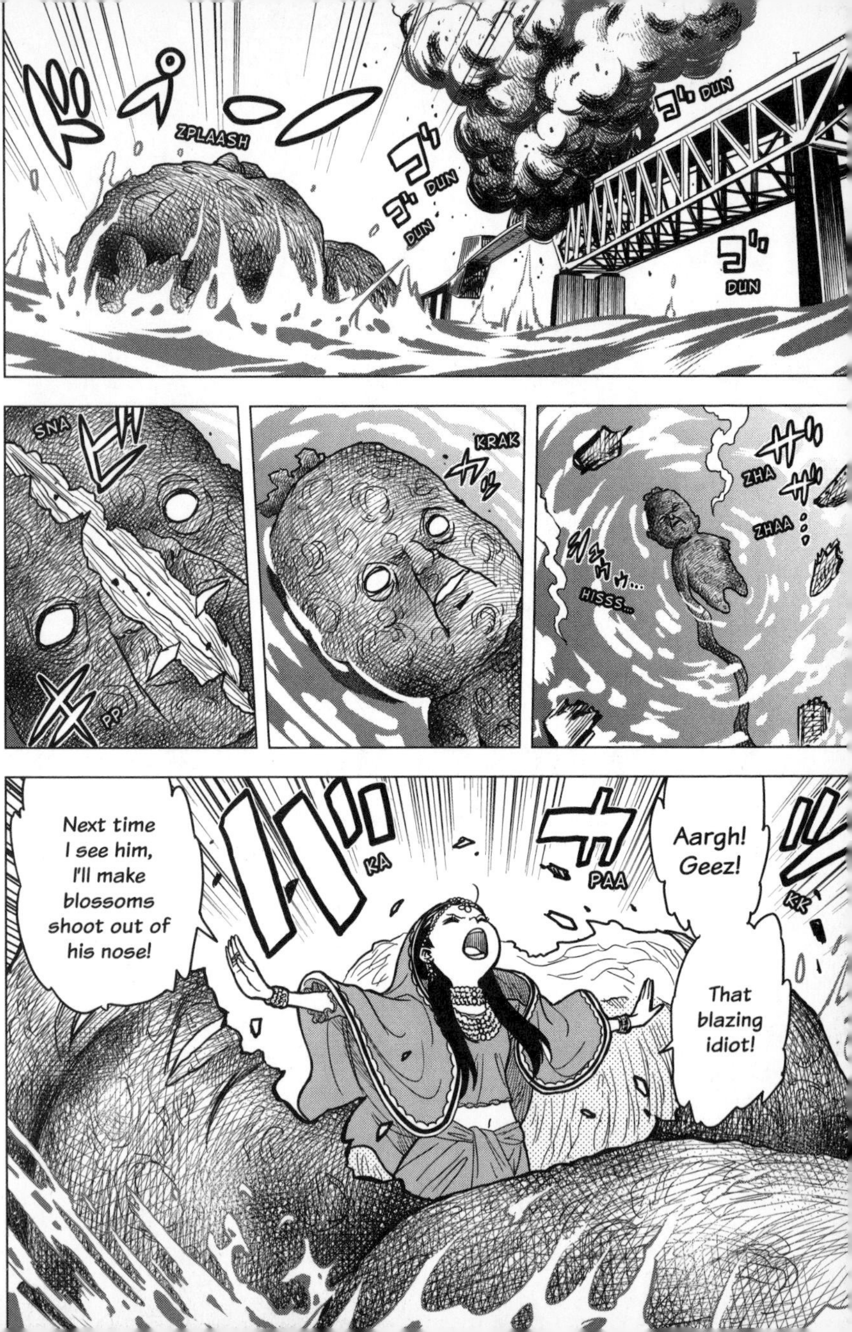
DUN
DUN
DUN
DUN
ZPLAASH
ZHA
ZHAA
HISSS...
KRAK
SNA
PP
Aargh! Geez!
That blazing idiot!
KK
PAA
KA
Next time I see him, I'll make blossoms shoot out of his nose!

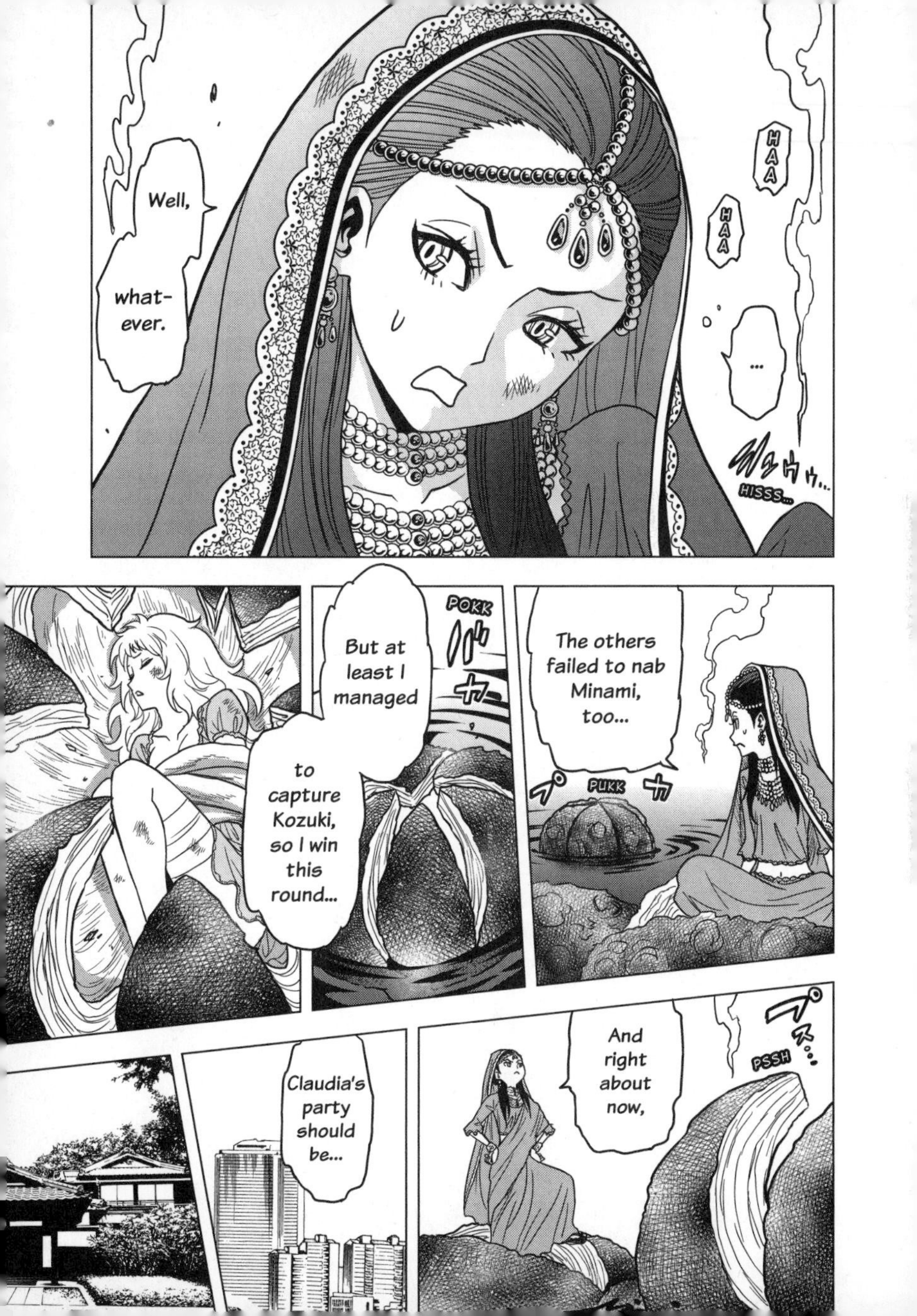
HAA
HAA
...
Well, whatever.
HISSS...
The others failed to nab Minami, too...
PUKK
POKK
But at least I managed
to capture Kozuki, so I win this round...
PSSH
And right about now,
Claudia's party should be...

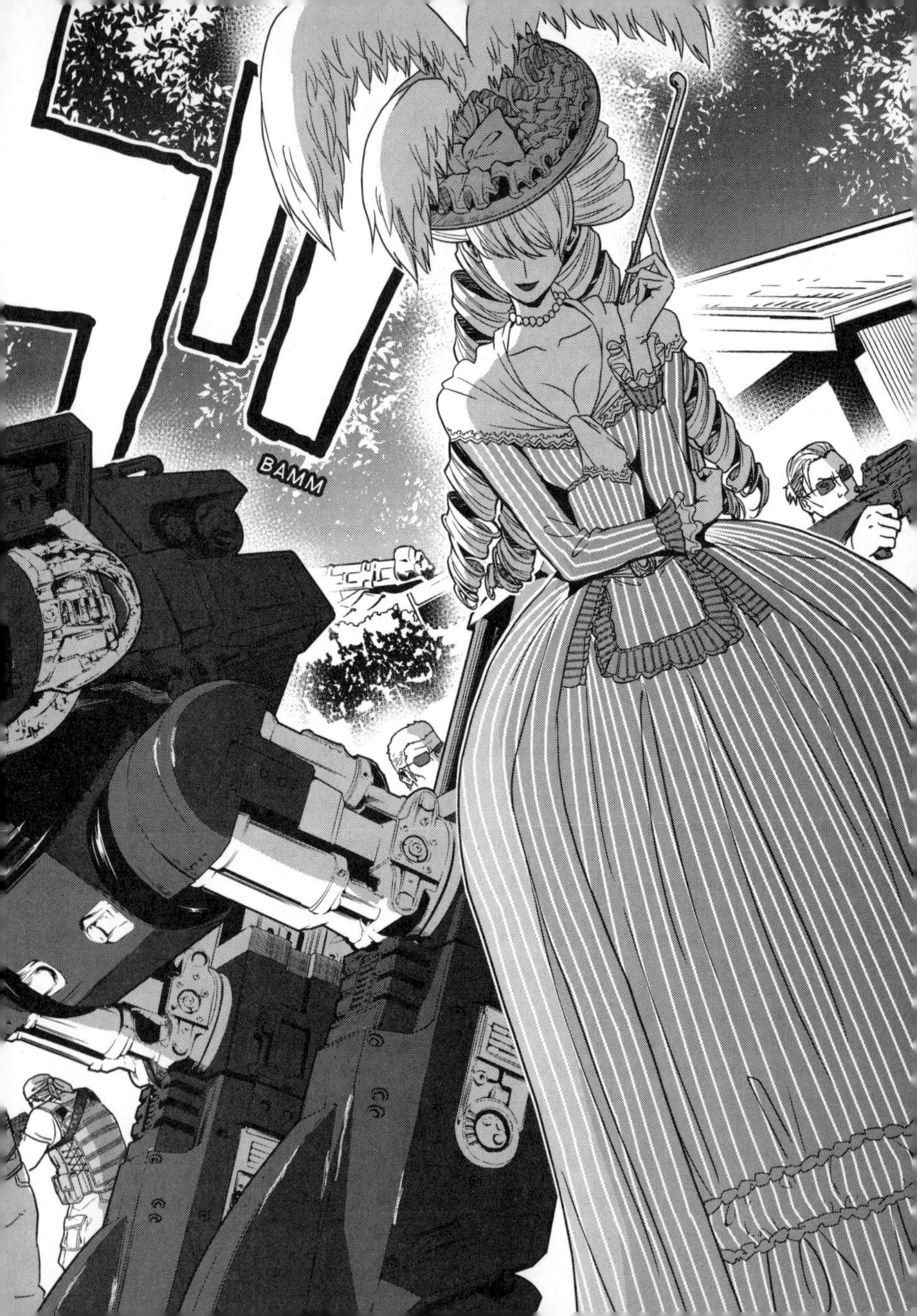
BAMM

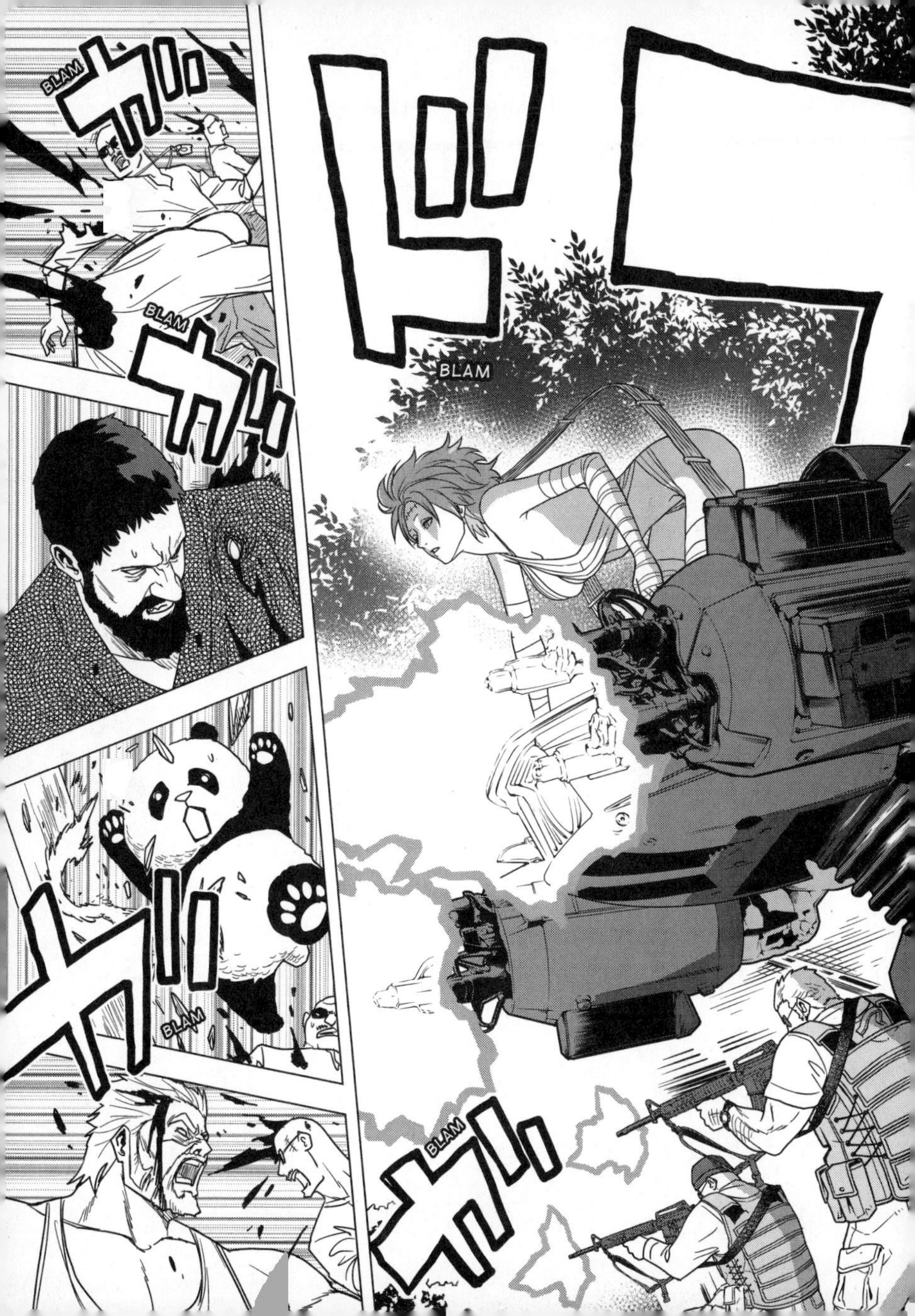

BLAM
BLAM
BLAM
BLAM
BLAM

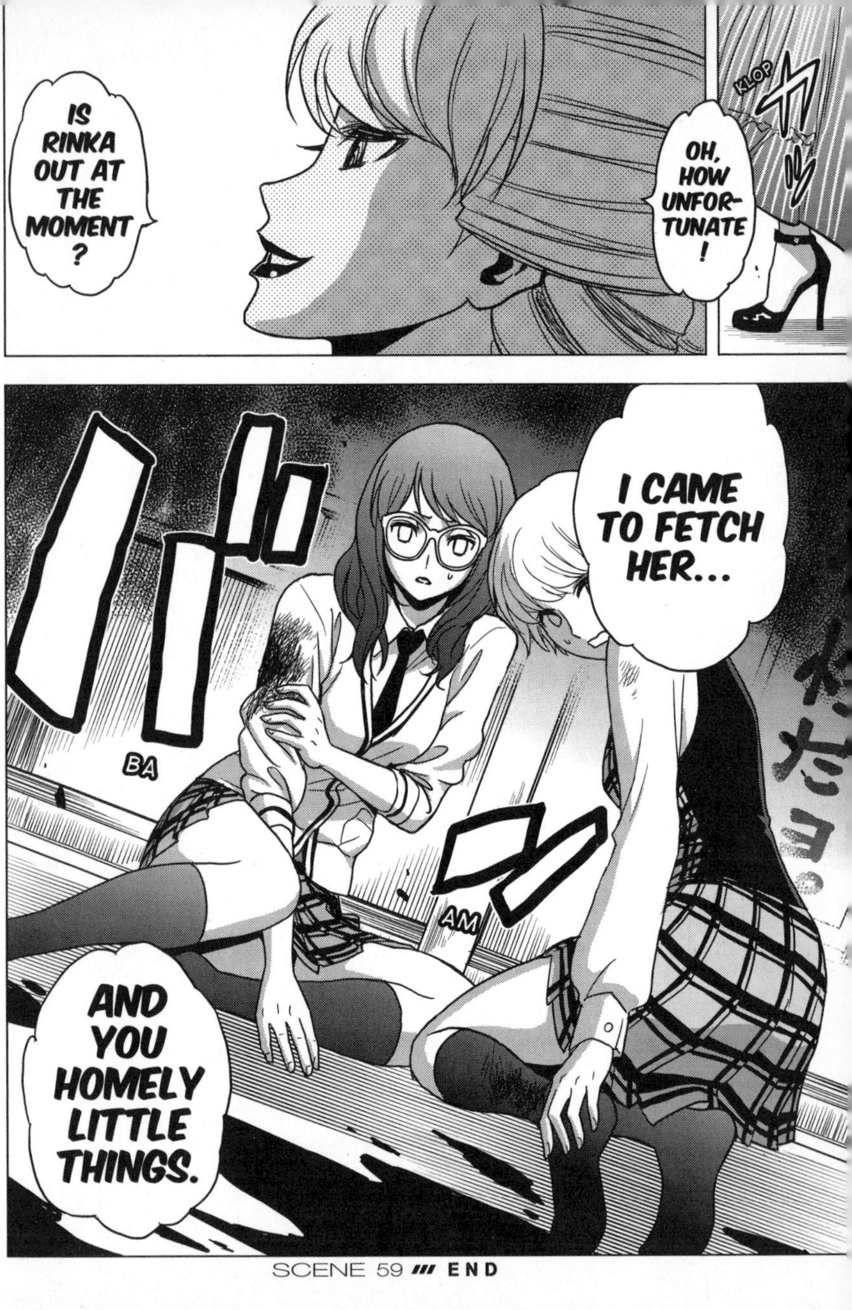
KLOP
OH, HOW UNFOR-TUNATE!
IS RINKA OUT AT THE MOMENT?
I CAME TO FETCH HER...
BA
AM
AND YOU HOMELY LITTLE THINGS.

SCENE 59 /// END

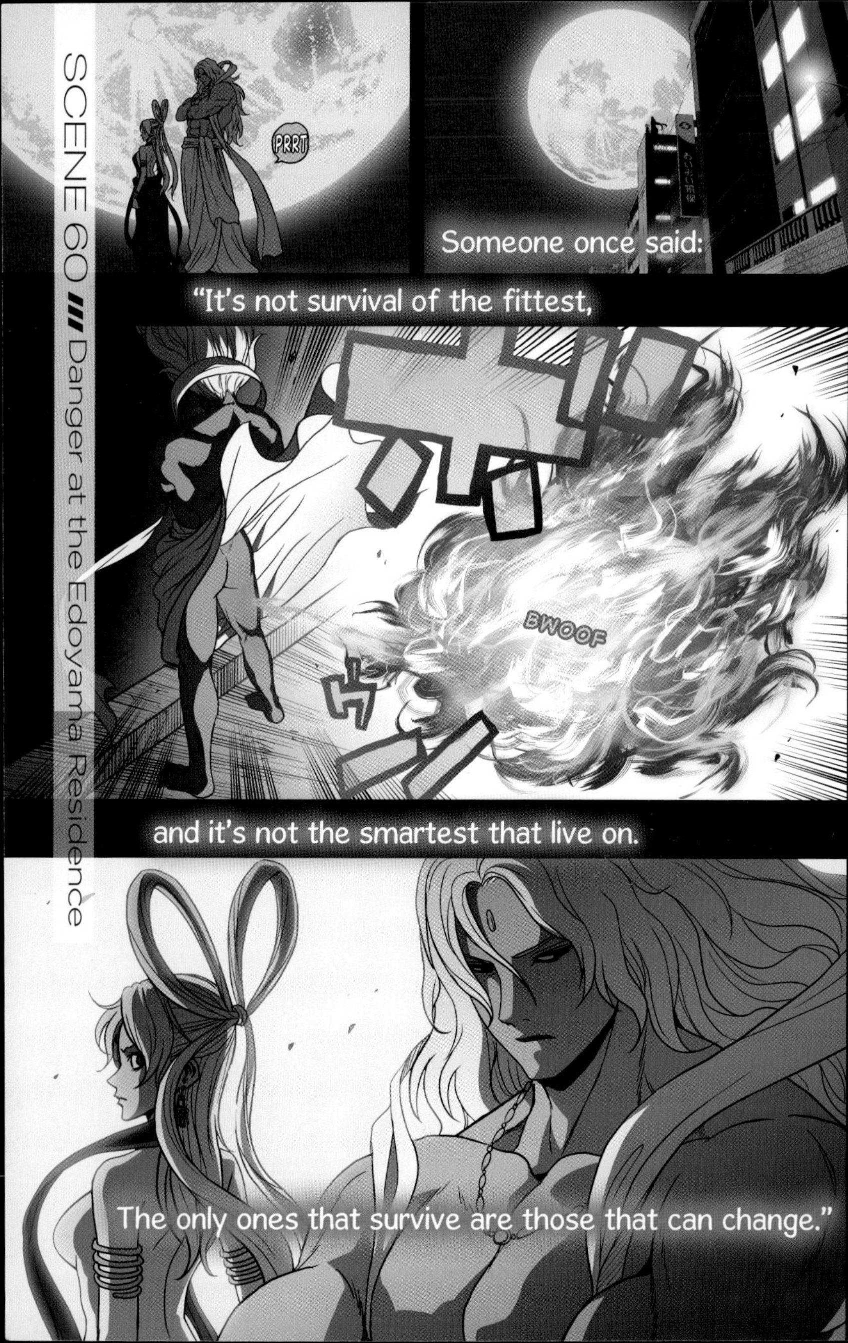
SCENE 60 /// Danger at the Edoyama Residence
Someone once said:
PRRT
"It's not survival of the fittest,
BWOOF
and it's not the smartest that live on.
The only ones that survive are those that can change."

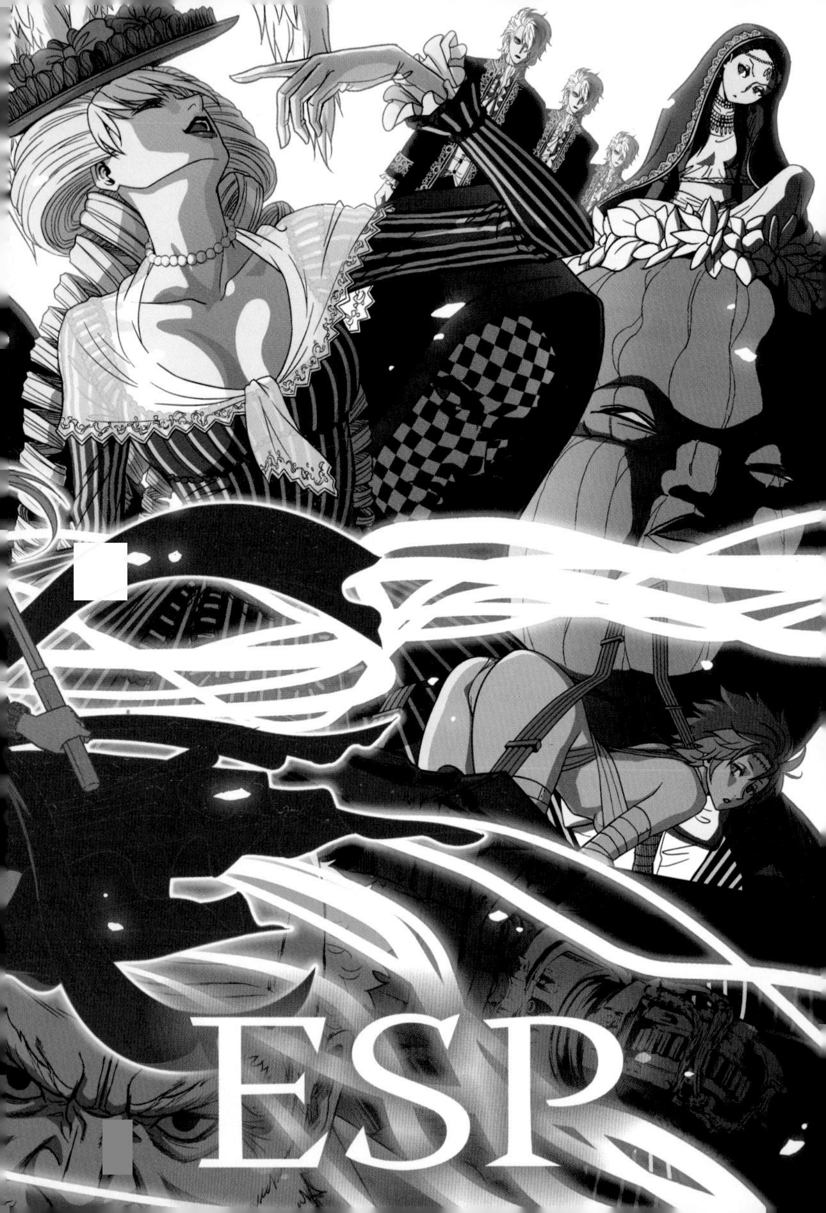
ESP

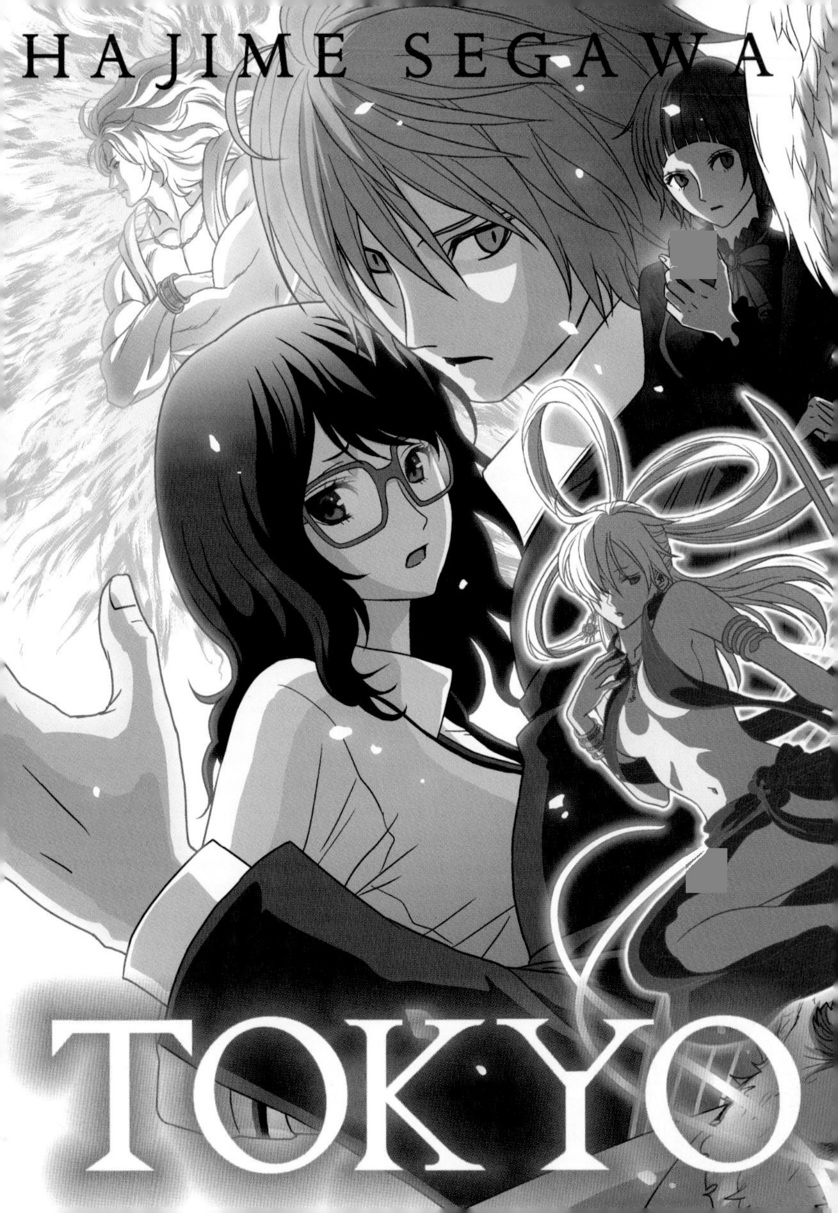
HAJIME SEGAWA
TOKYO

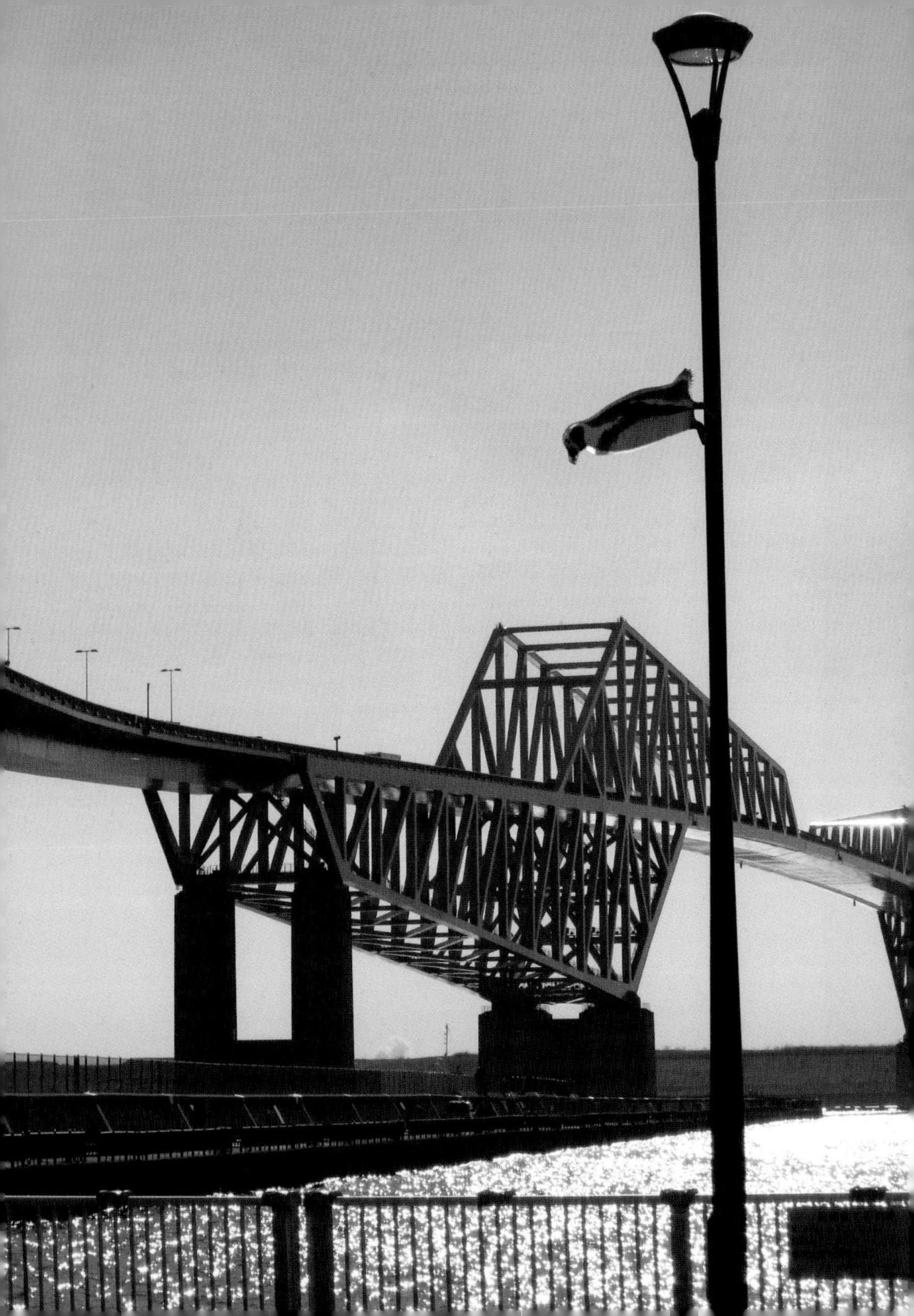

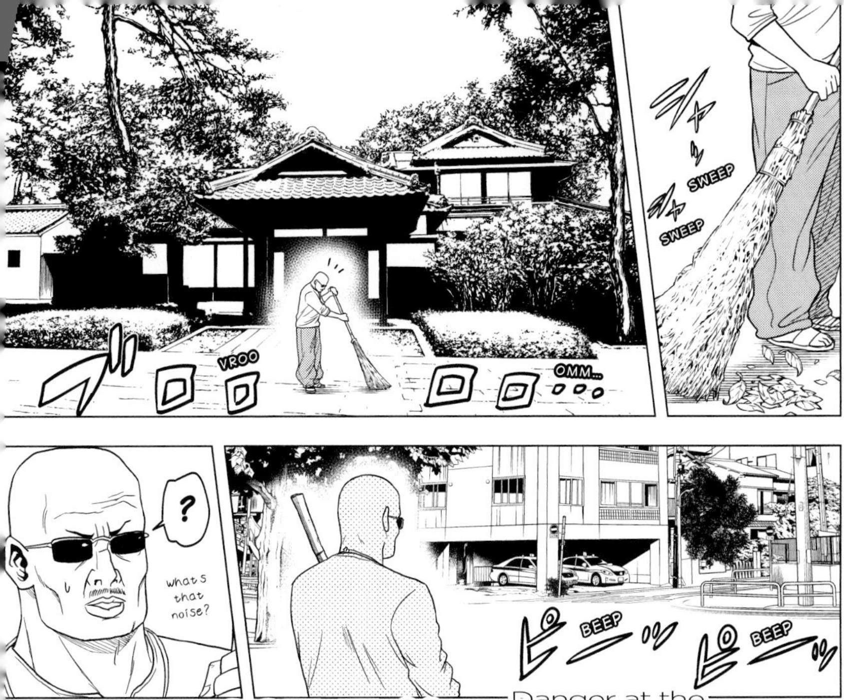
SWEEP
SWEEP
VROO
OMM...
BEEP
BEEP
?
whats that noise?

SCENE_60 /// Danger at the Edoyama Residence

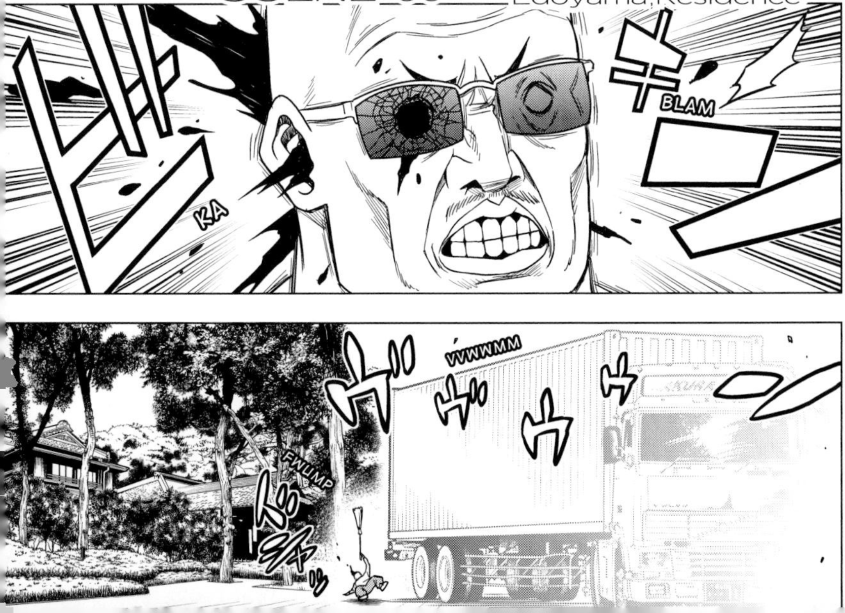
BLAM
KA
VVWMM
FWUMP

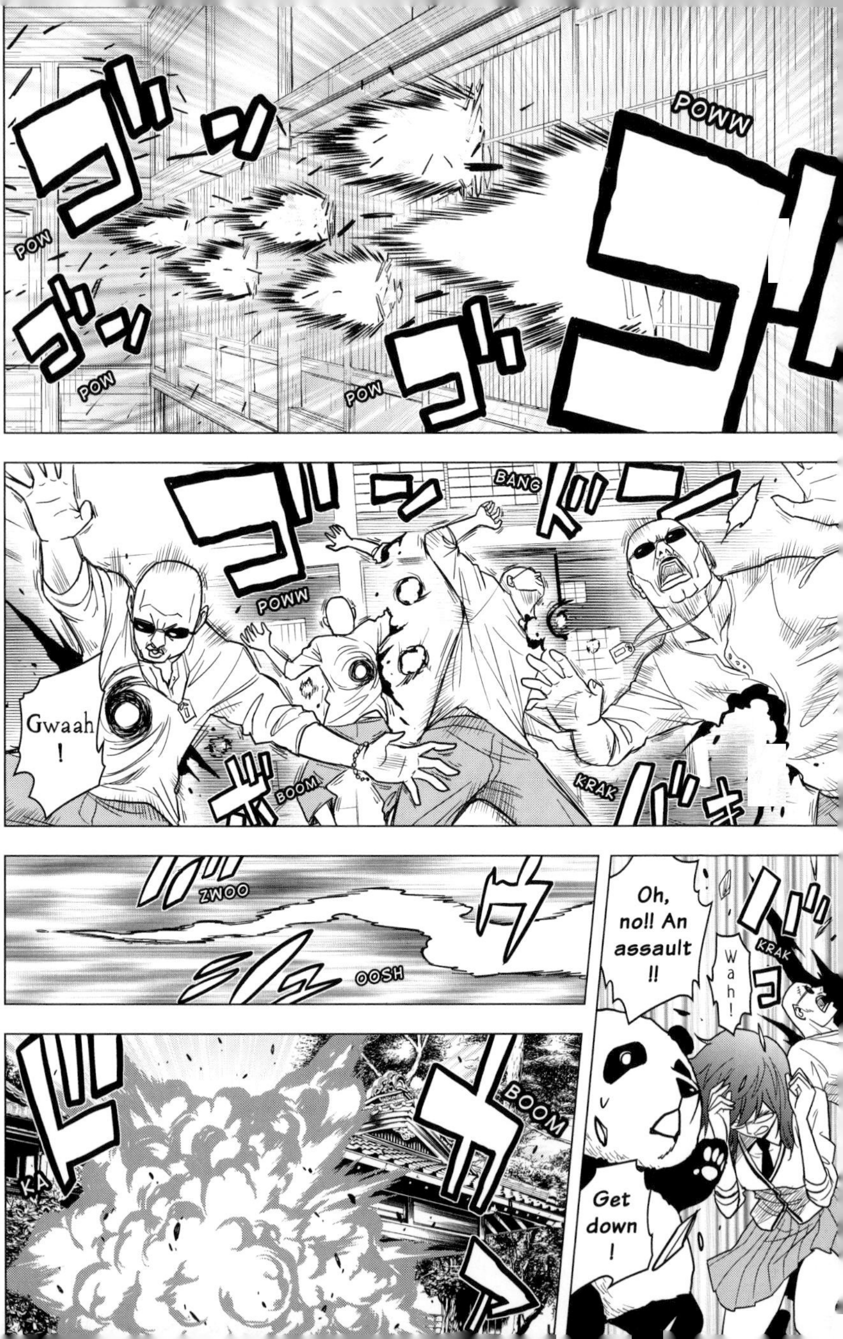
POWW
POW
POW
POW
BANG
POWW
KRAK
BOOM
Gwaah!
KRAK
Wah!
Oh, no!! An assault!!
Get down!
ZWOO
OOSH
BOOM
KA

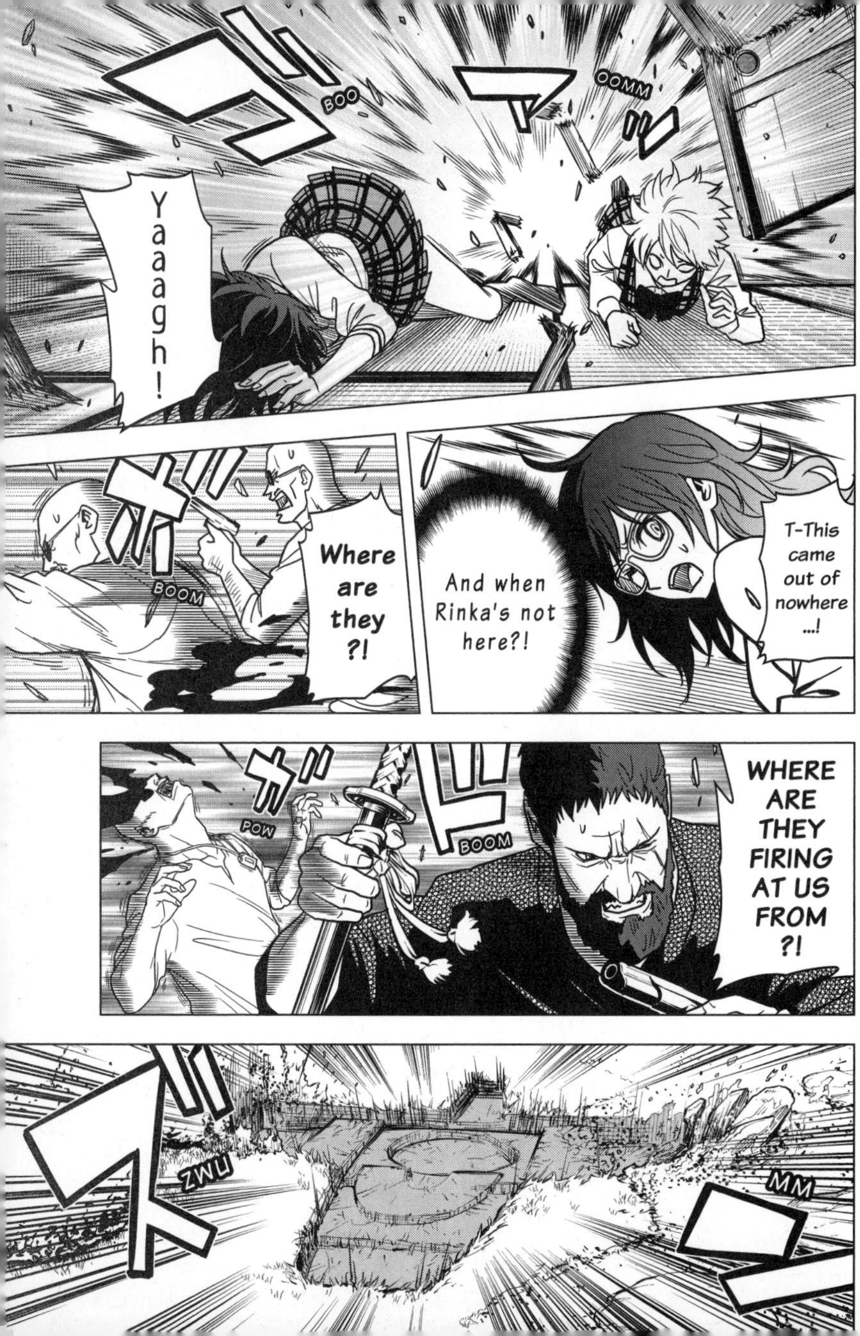
BOO
OOMM
Yaaaagh!
T-This came out of nowhere ...!
And when Rinka's not here?!
Where are they ?!
BOOM
WHERE ARE THEY FIRING AT US FROM ?!
BOOM
POW
ZWU
MM

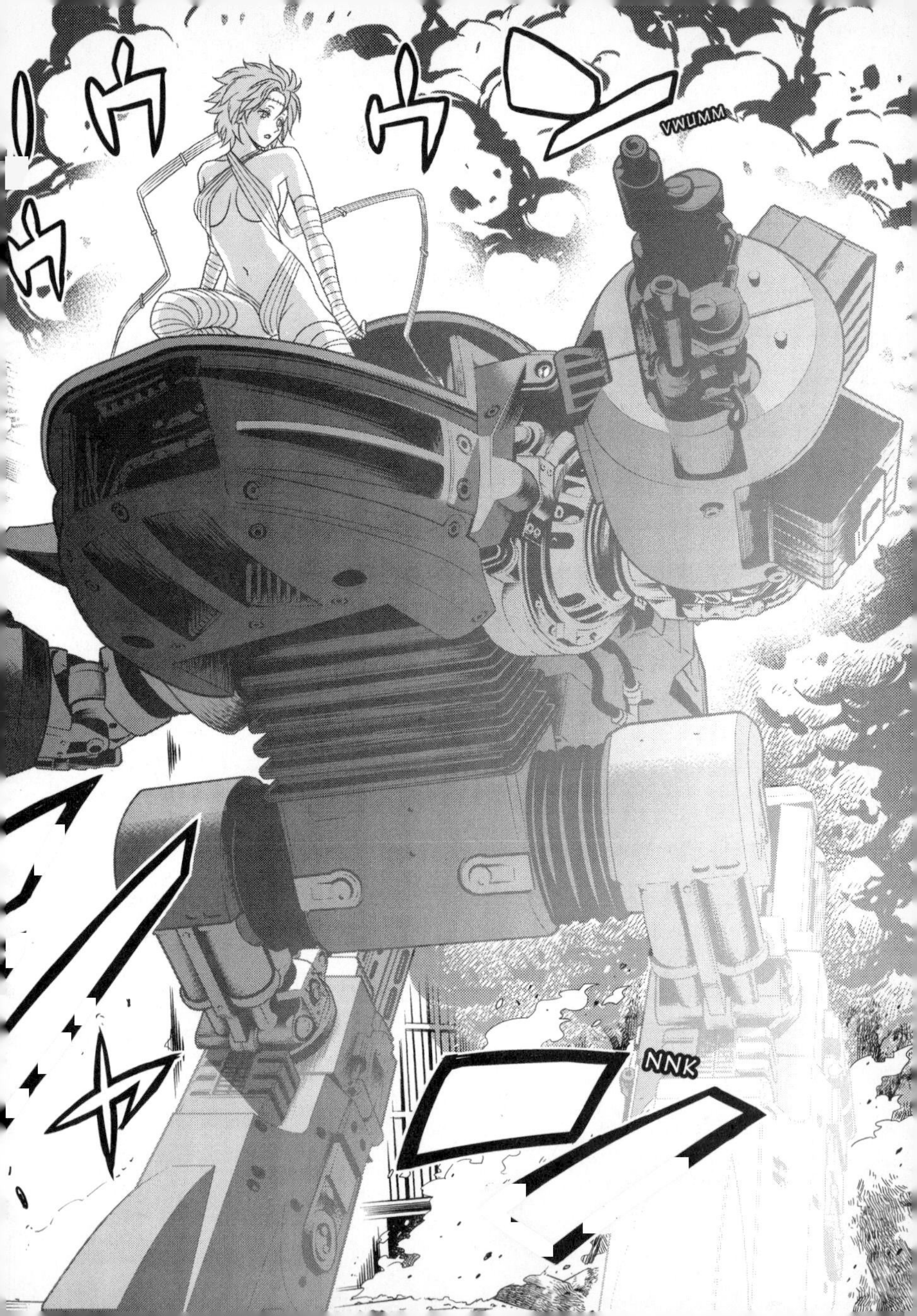
VWUMM
NNK

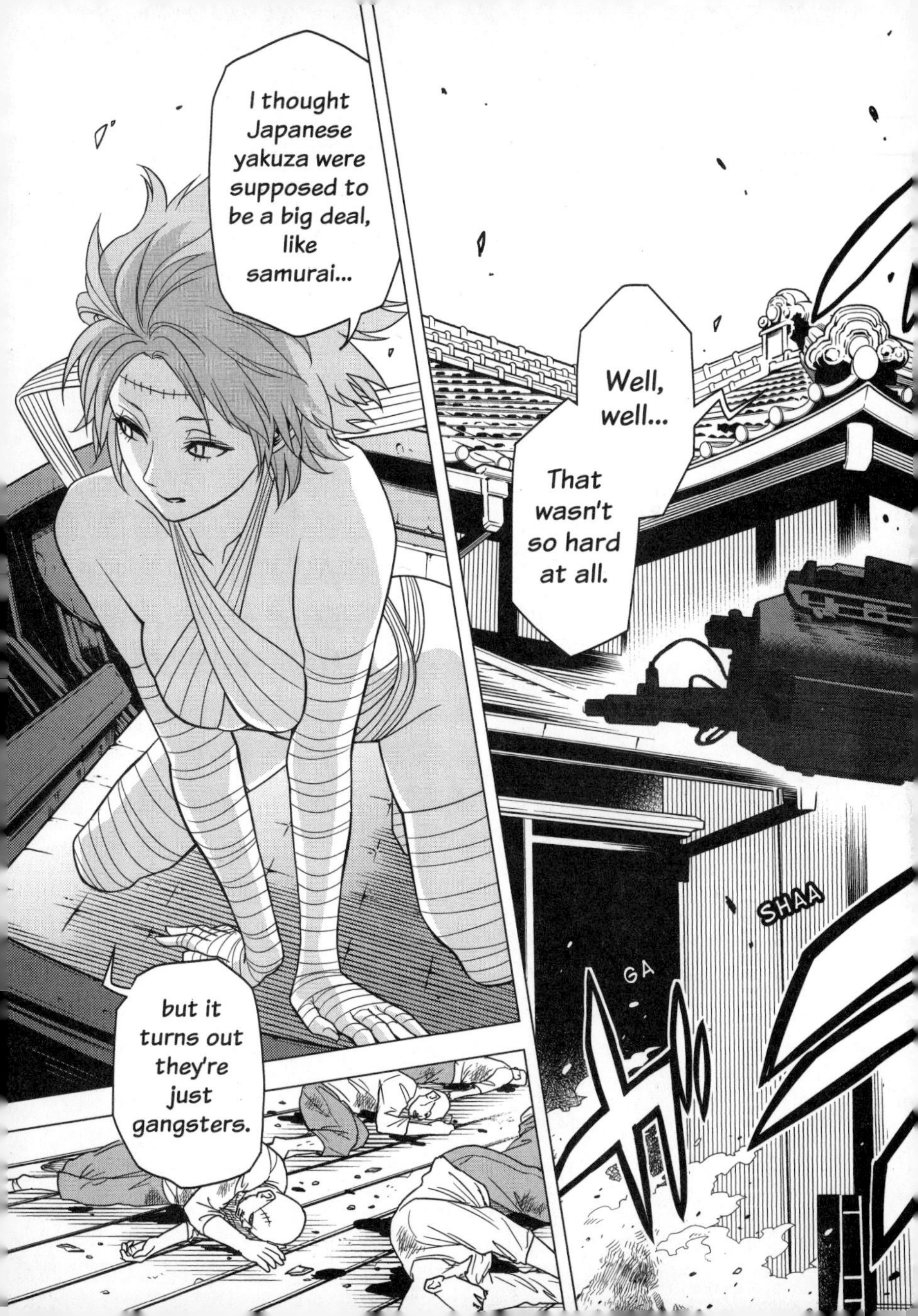
Well, well...
That wasn't so hard at all.
SHAA
GA
I thought Japanese yakuza were supposed to be a big deal, like samurai...
but it turns out they're just gangsters.

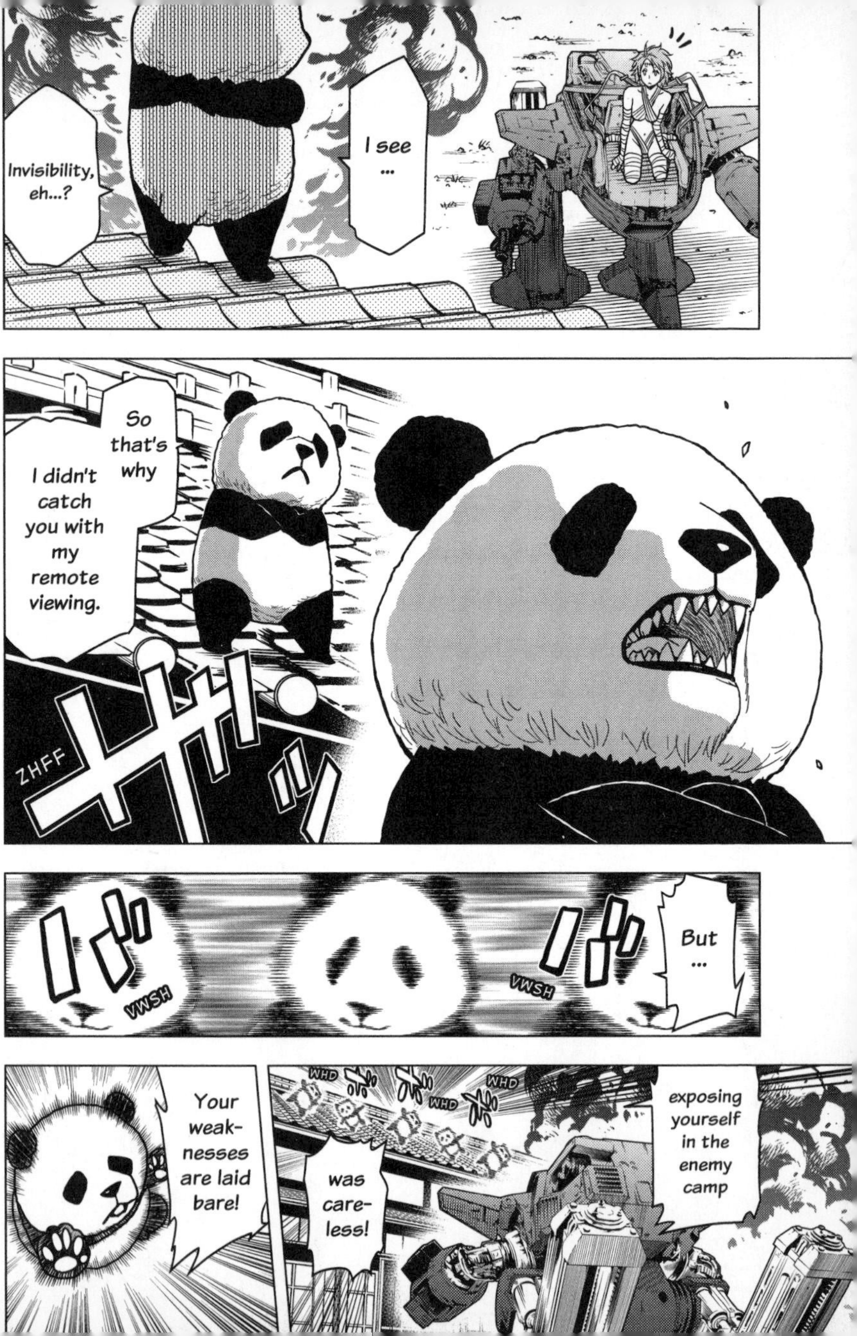
I see ...
Invisibility, eh...?
So that's why I didn't catch you with my remote viewing.
ZHFF
VWSH
VWSH
But ...
WHD
WHD
WHD
exposing yourself in the enemy camp
was care-less!
Your weak-nesses are laid bare!

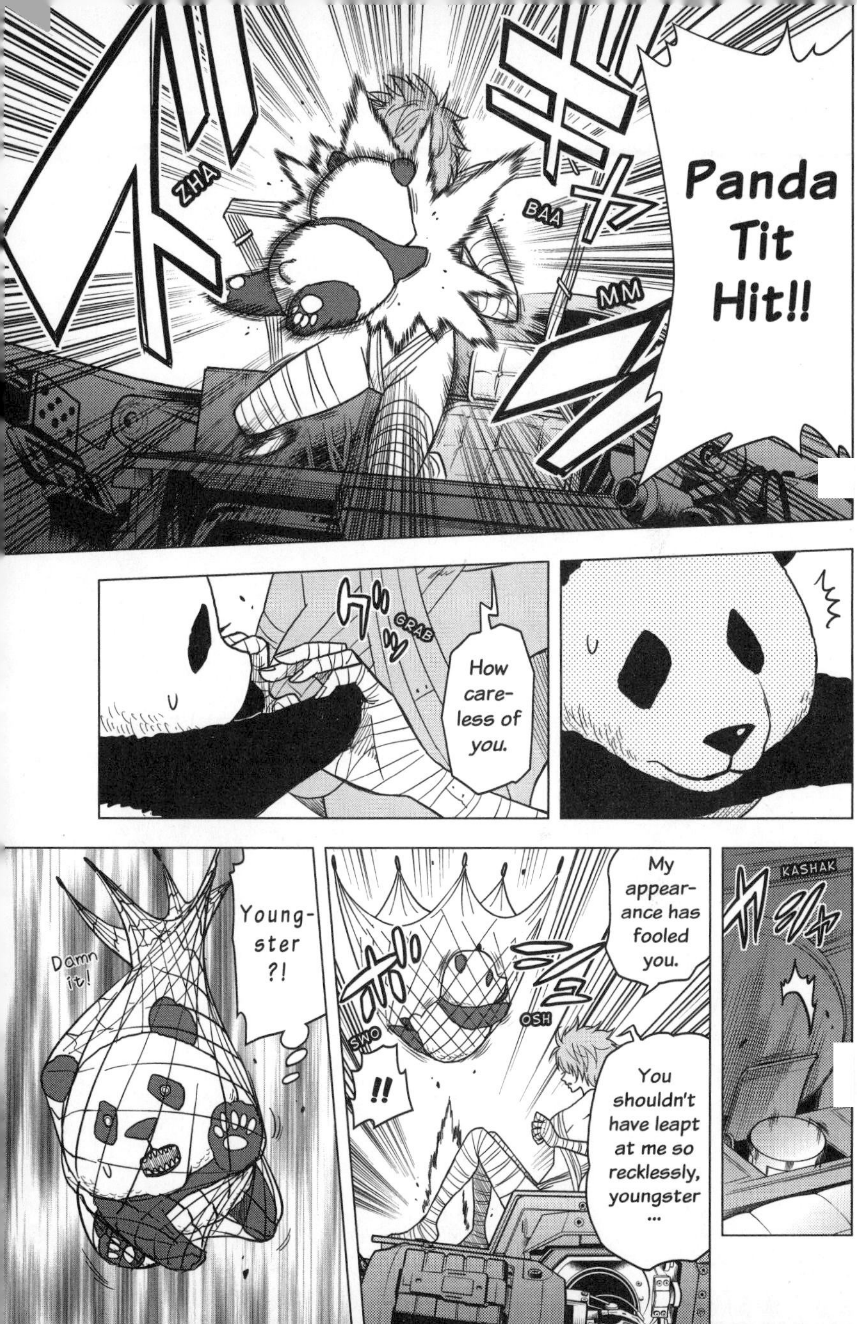
Panda Tit Hit!!
MM
BAA
ZHA
GRAB
How careless of you.
KASHAK
My appearance has fooled you.
SWO
OSH
!!
You shouldn't have leapt at me so recklessly, youngster...
Youngster?!
Damn it!

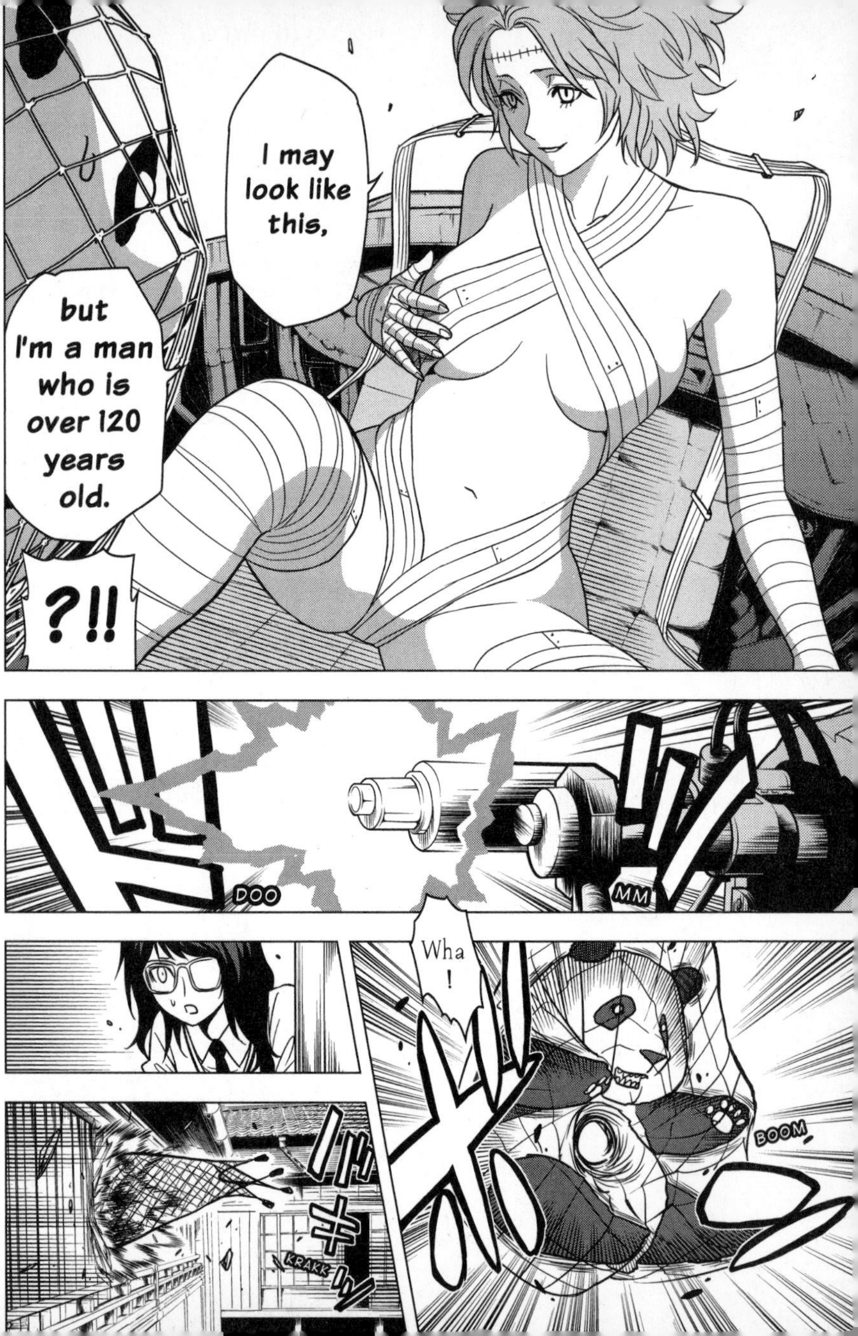
I may look like this,
but I'm a man who is over 120 years old.
?!!
DOO
MM
Wha!
BOOM
KRAKK

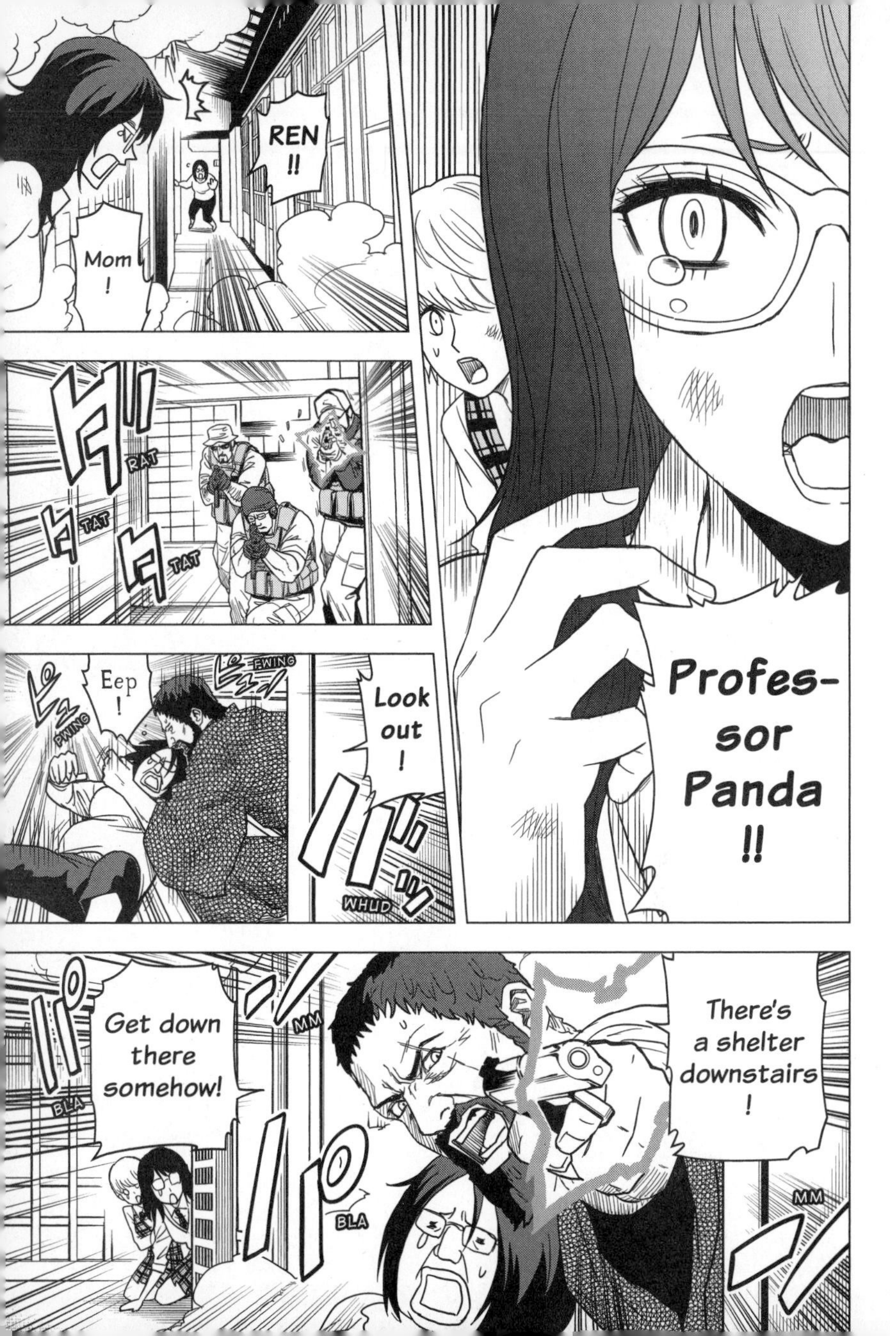
Profes-
sor
Panda
!!
REN
!!
Mom
!
RAT
TAT
TAT
Look
out
!
FWING
Eep
!
PWING
WHUD
There's
a shelter
downstairs
!
MM
Get down
there
somehow!
BLA
BLA
MM

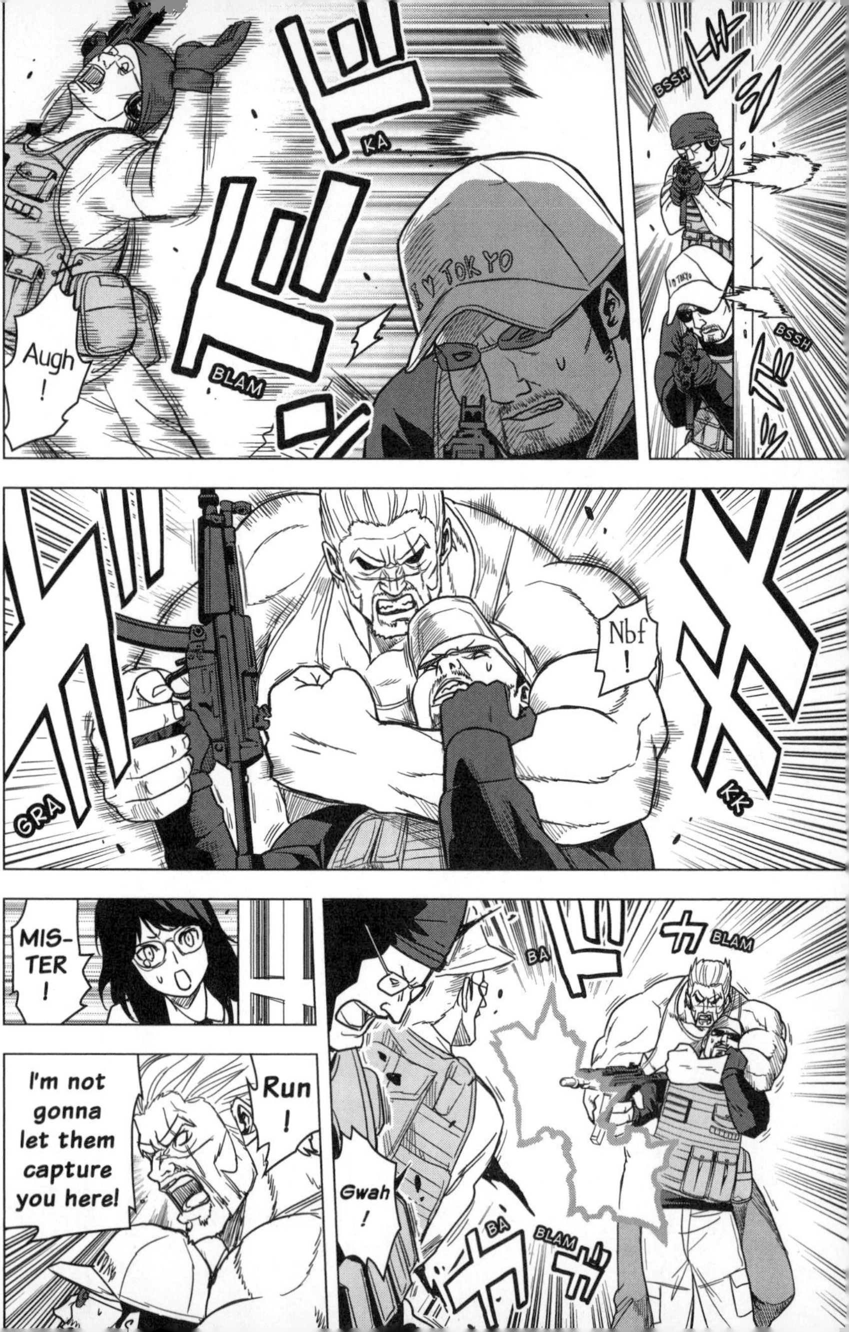
BSSH
BSSH
KA
I ♥ TOKYO
BLAM
Augh!
Nbf!
KK
GRA
BLAM
BA
Gwah!
BA BLAM
MIS-TER!
Run!
I'm not gonna let them capture you here!

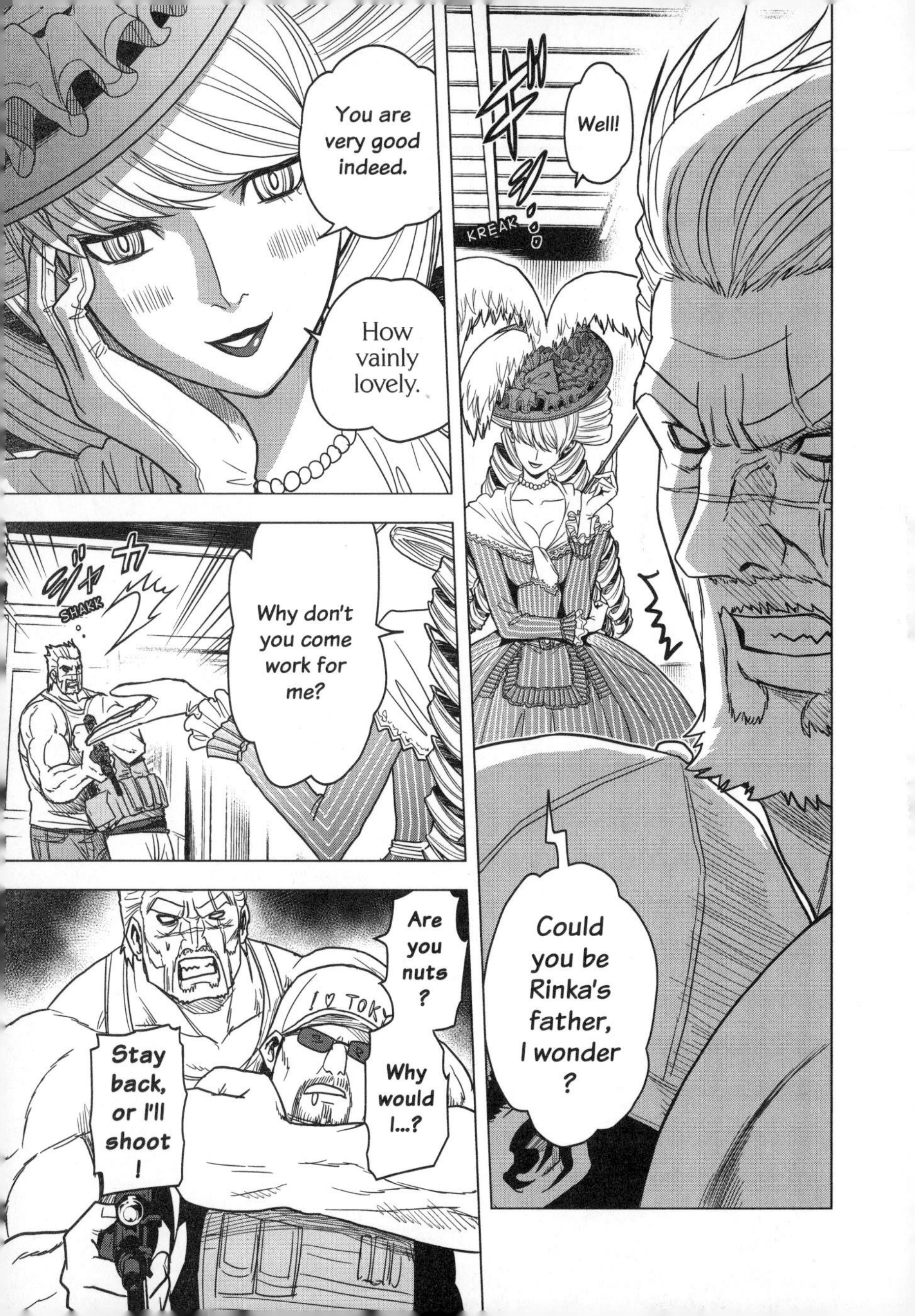
Well!
KREAK
Could you be Rinka's father, I wonder?
You are very good indeed.
How vainly lovely.
SHAKK
Why don't you come work for me?
Are you nuts?
Why would I...?
Stay back, or I'll shoot!
I ♡ TOKY

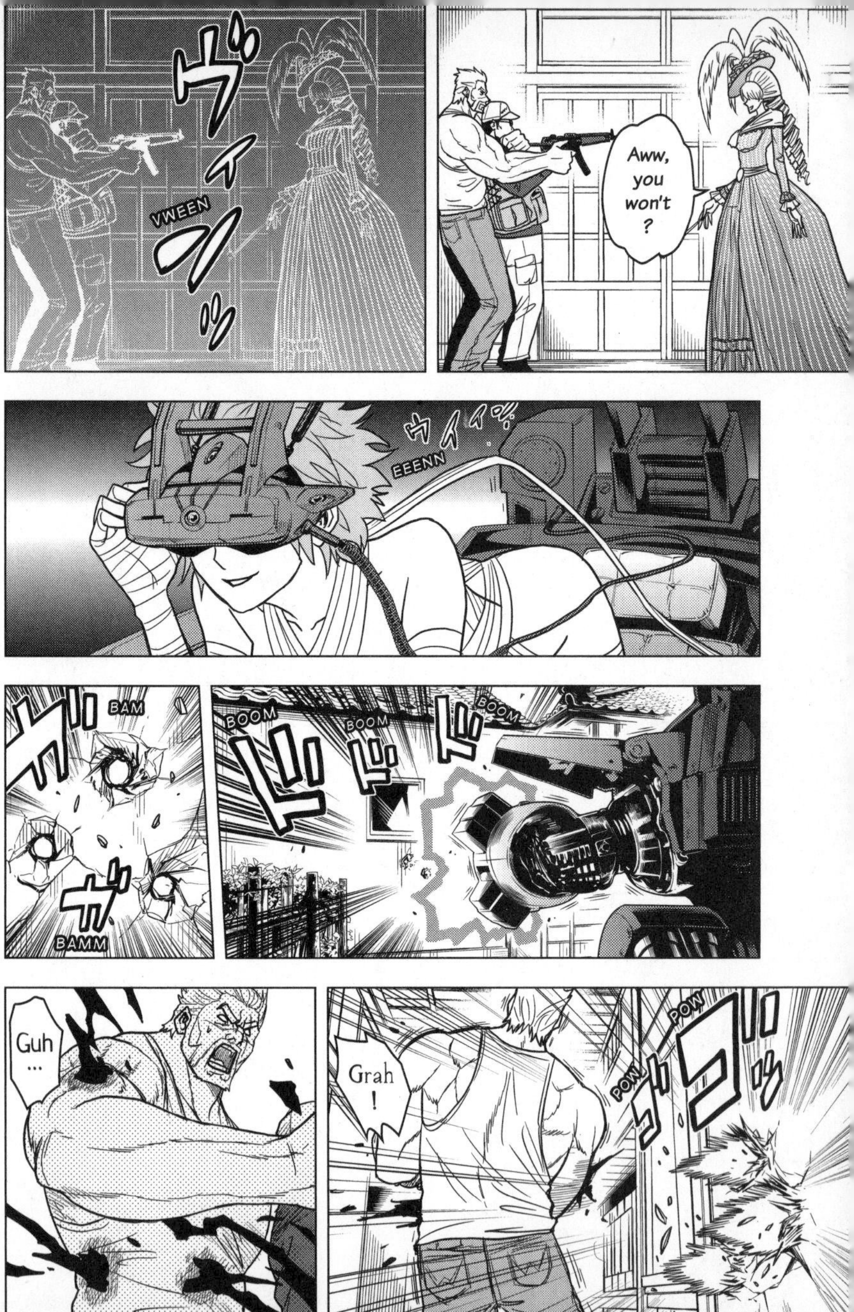
Aww, you won't?
VWEEN
EEENN
BOOM
BOOM
BOOM
BAM
BAMM
POW
POW
Grah!
Guh...

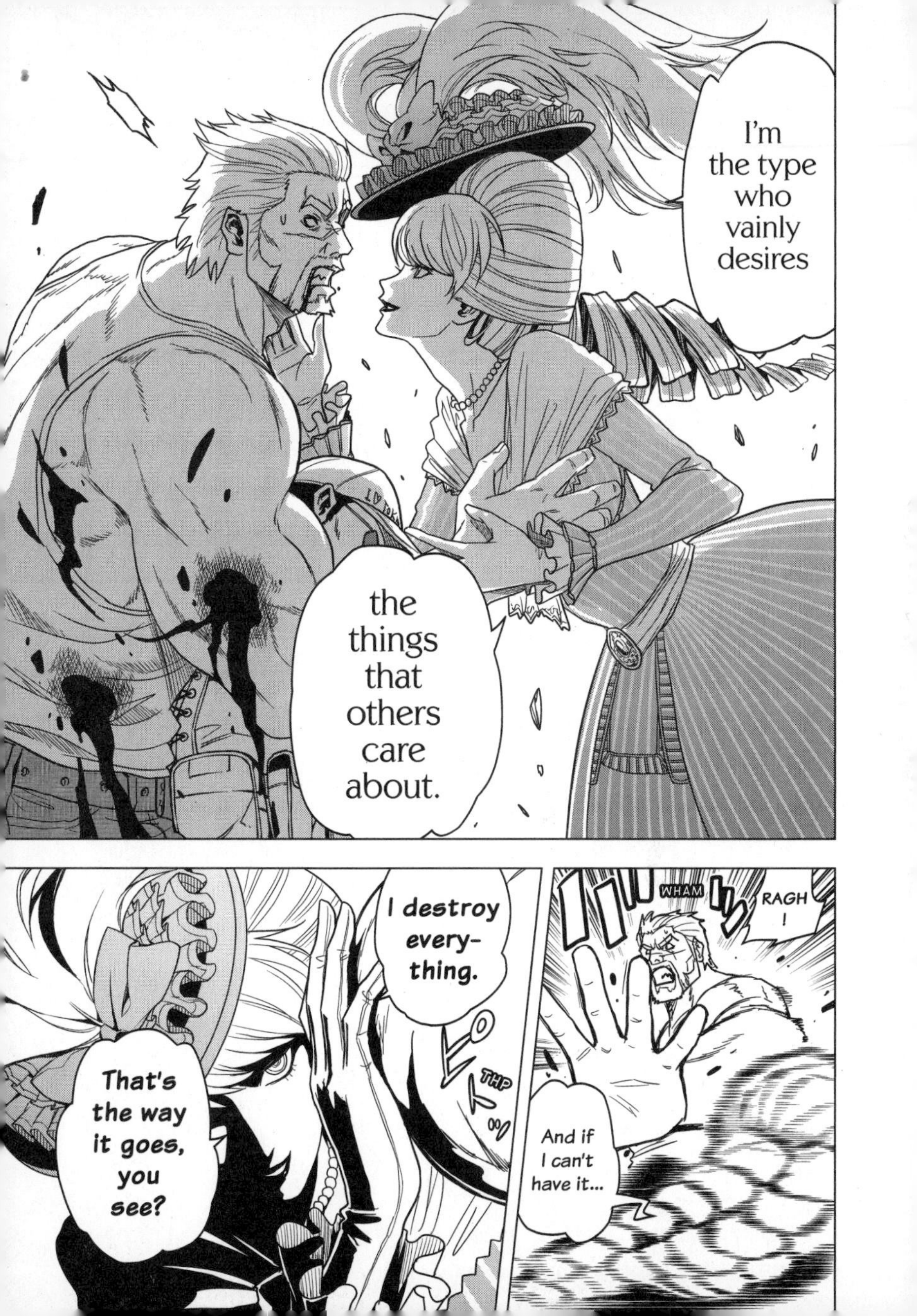
I'm the type who vainly desires
the things that others care about.
RAGH !
WHAM
And if I can't have it...
I destroy every-thing.
THP
That's the way it goes, you see?

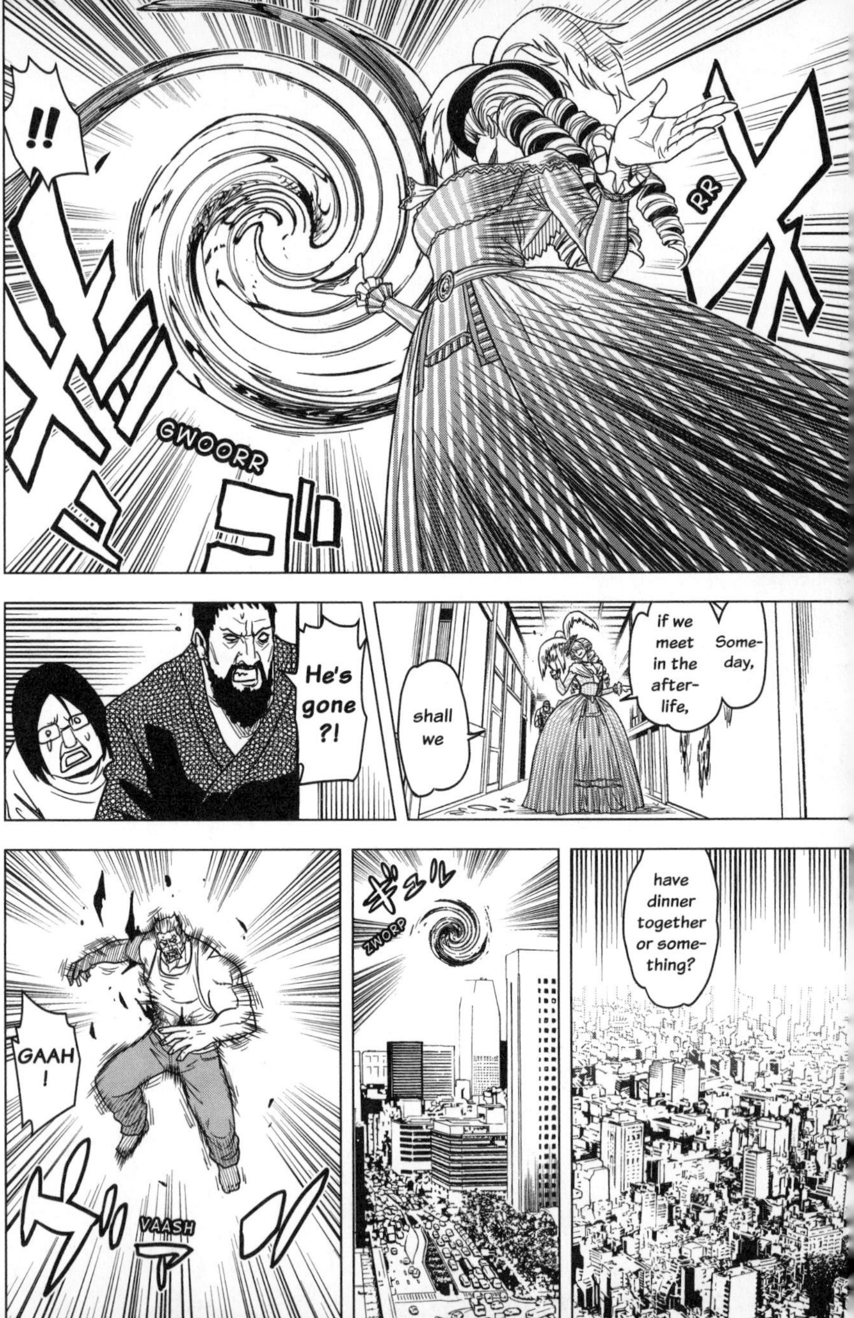
RR
!!
GWOORR
Some-day,
if we meet in the after-life,
shall we
He's gone ?!
have dinner together or some-thing?
ZWORP
GAAH !
VAASH

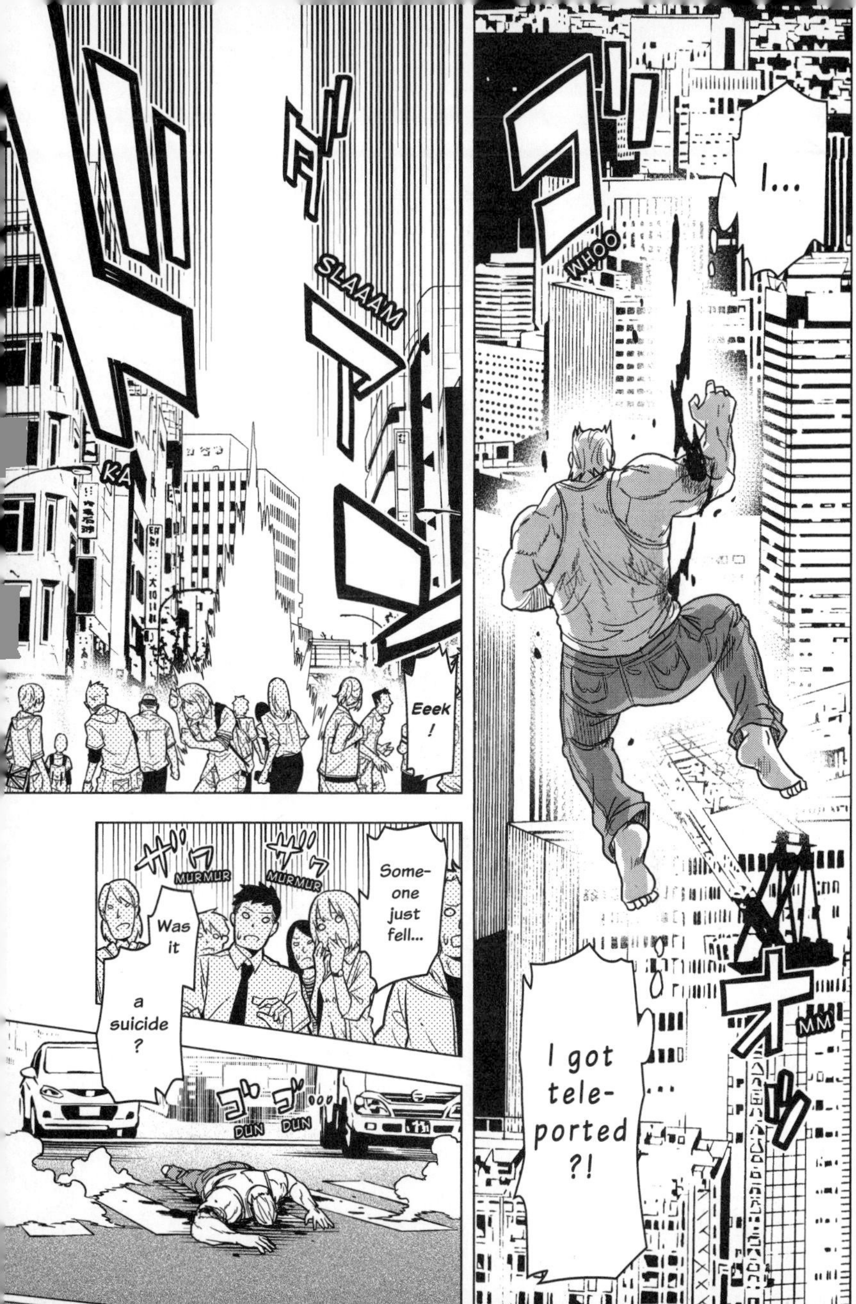
I...
WHOO
MM
I got tele-ported?!
SLAAAM
KA
Eeek!
MURMUR
MURMUR
Some-one just fell...
Was it a suicide?
DUN
DUN

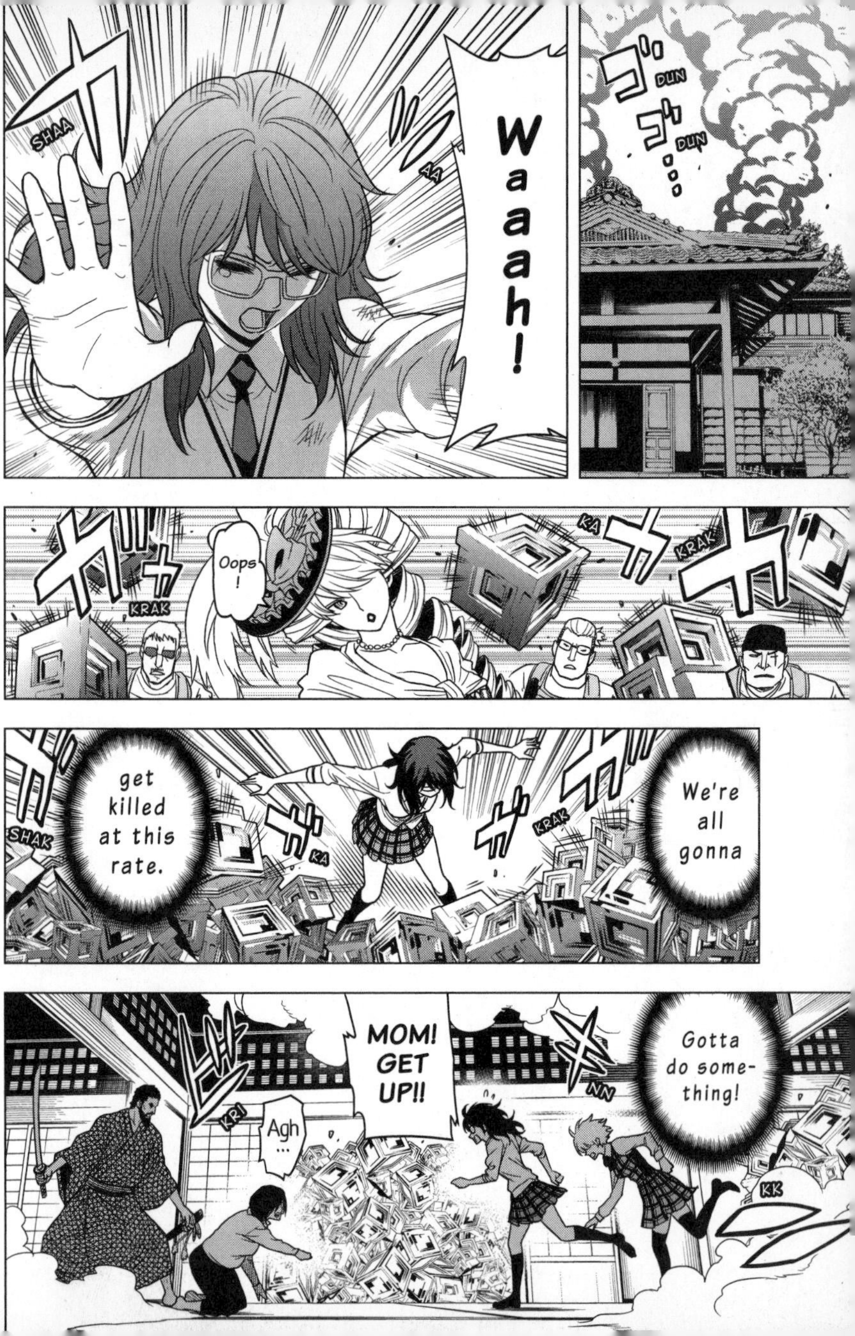
DUN
DUN
Waaaah!
AA
SHAA
KRAK
KA
Oops!
KRAK
We're all gonna
KRAK
KA
get killed at this rate.
SHAK
Gotta do some-thing!
KK
NN
MOM! GET UP!!
KRI
Agh...

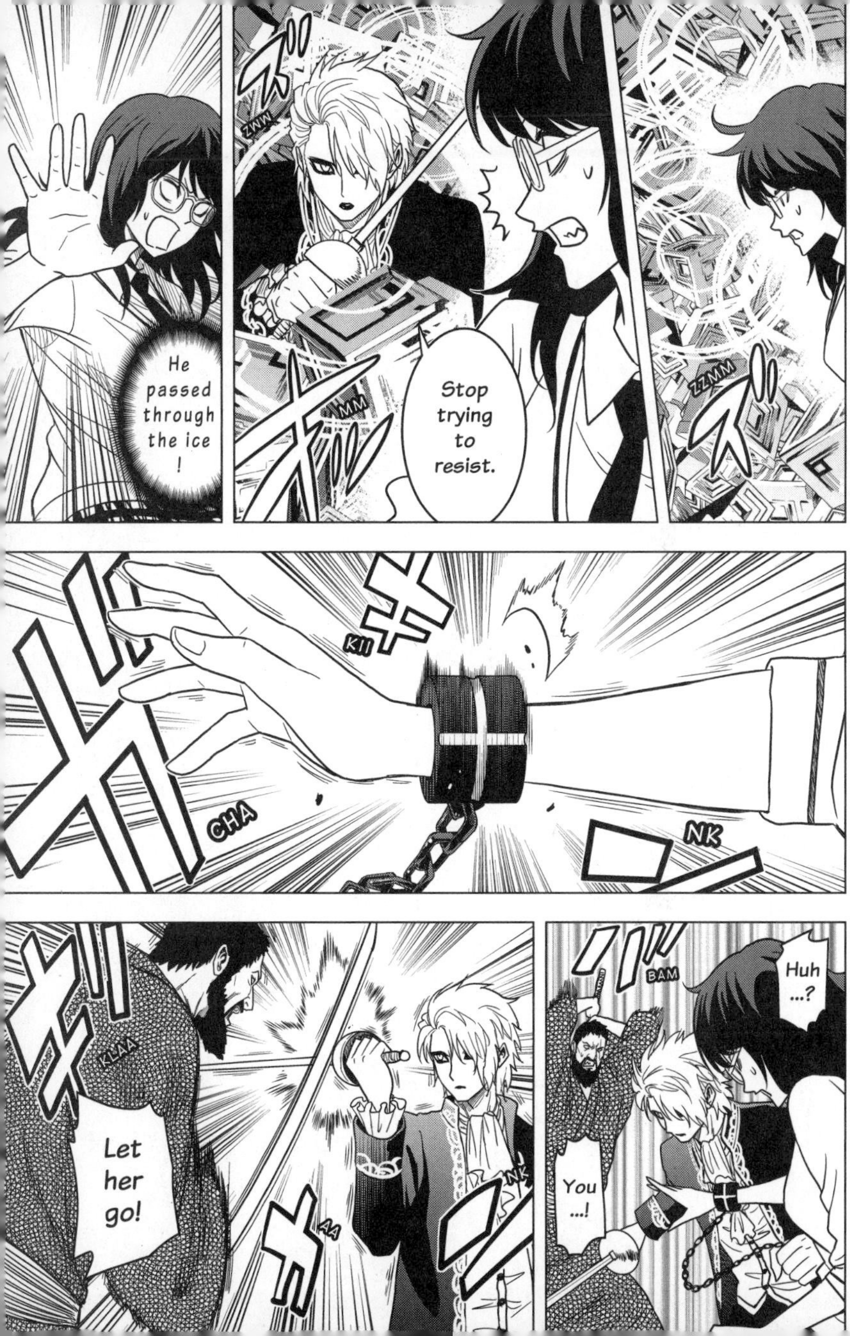
ZZMM
Stop trying to resist.
ZWMM
MM
He passed through the ice!
KII
CHA
NK
BAM
Huh ...?
You ...!
KLAA
Let her go!
NK
AA

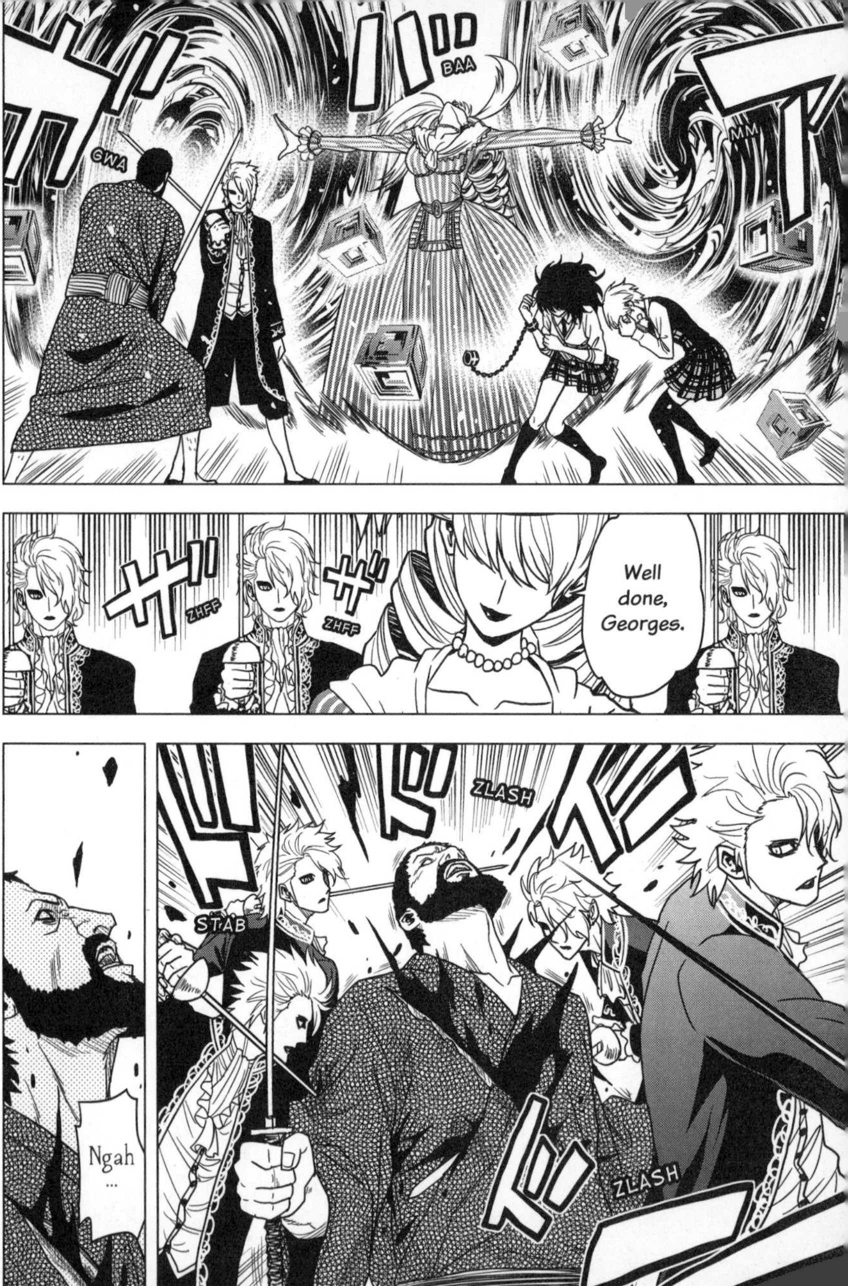
MM
BAA
GWA
Well done, Georges.
ZHFF
ZHFF
ZLASH
STAB
ZLASH
Ngah …

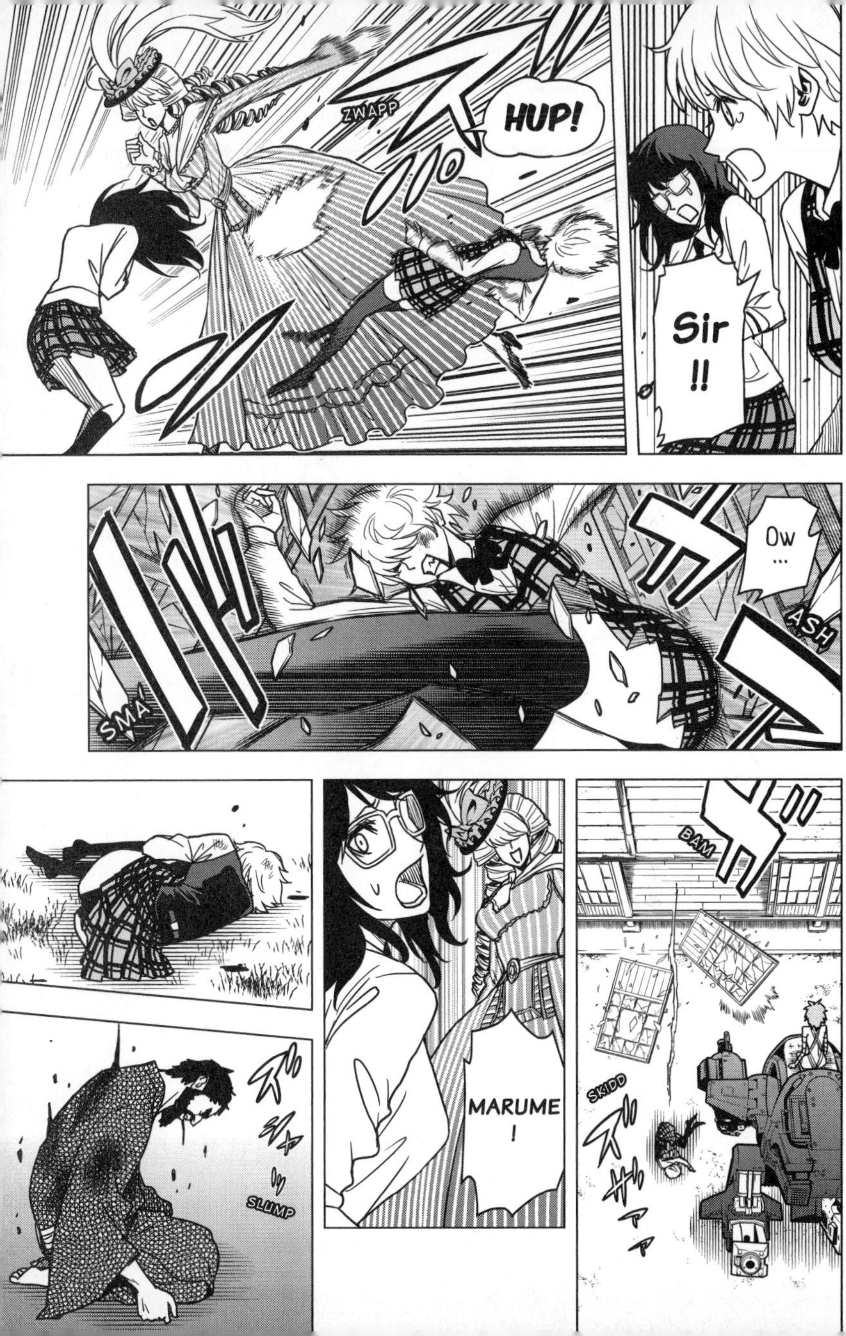
Sir !!
HUP!
ZWAPP
Ow ...
ASH
SMA
BAM
SKIDD
MARUME !
SLUMP

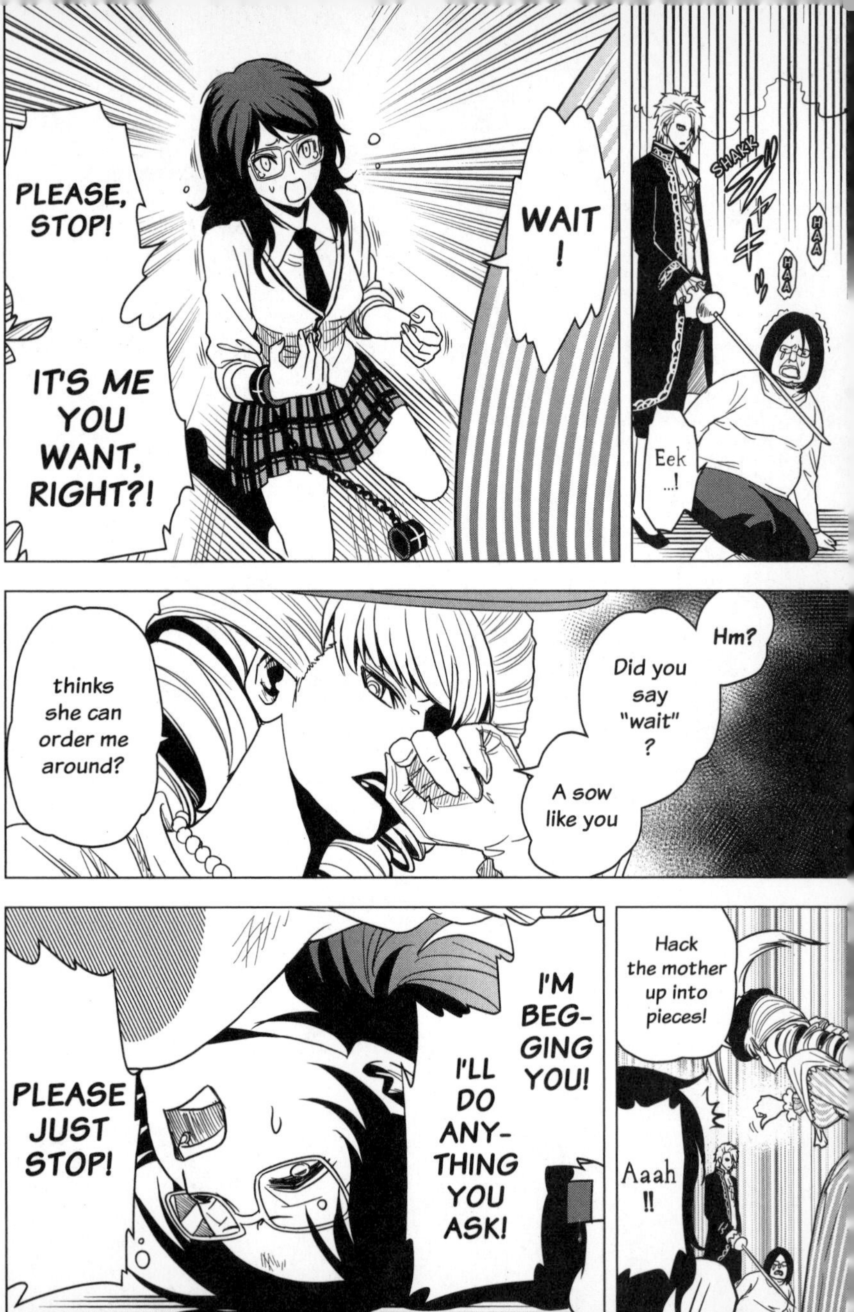
SHAKK
HAA
HAA
Eek ...!
WAIT!
PLEASE, STOP!
IT'S ME YOU WANT, RIGHT?!
Hm?
Did you say "wait"?
A sow like you
thinks she can order me around?
Hack the mother up into pieces!
Aaah!!
I'M BEG-GING YOU!
I'LL DO ANY-THING YOU ASK!
PLEASE JUST STOP!

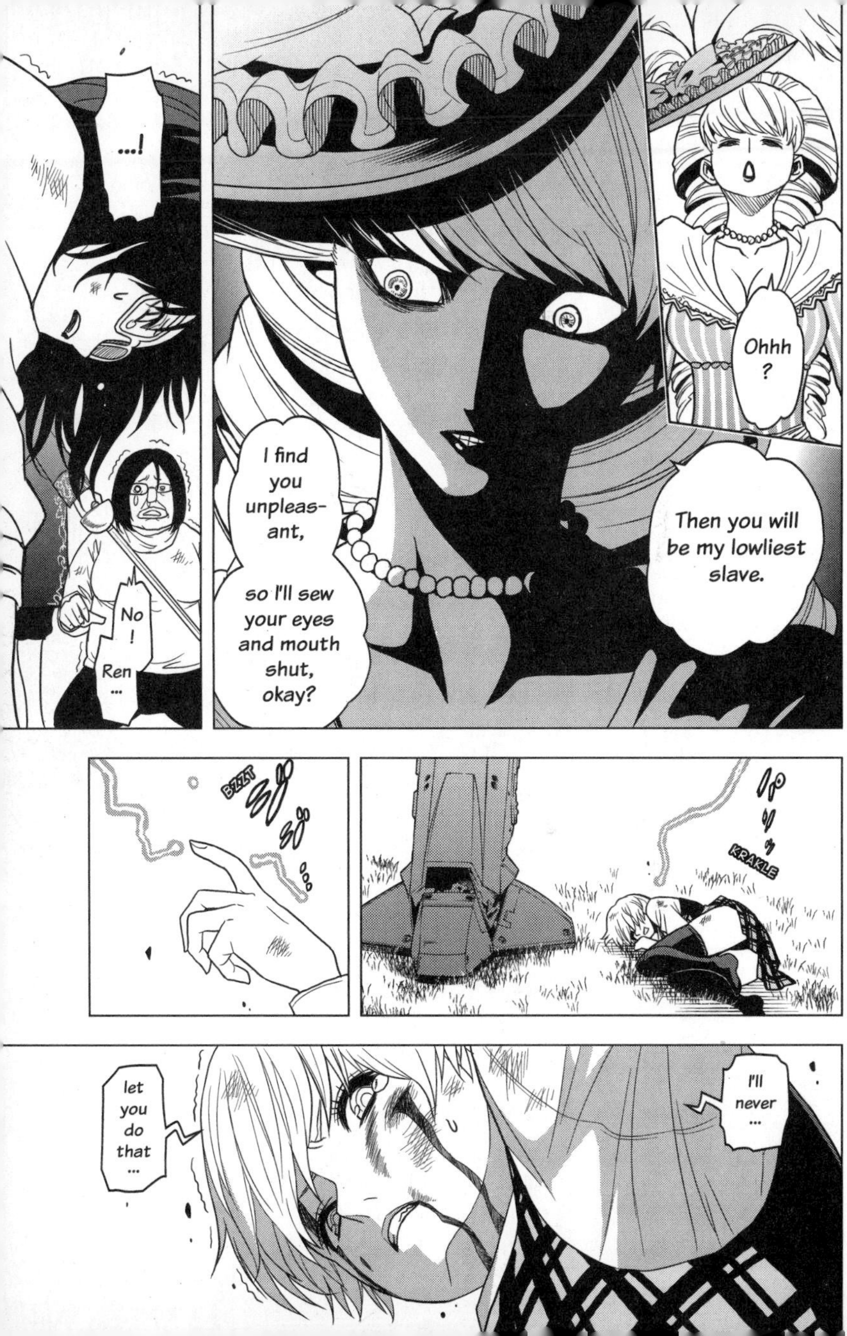

Ohhh?
I find you unpleasant,
so I'll sew your eyes and mouth shut, okay?
Then you will be my lowliest slave.
...!
No! Ren...
KRAKLE
BZZT
I'll never...
let you do that...

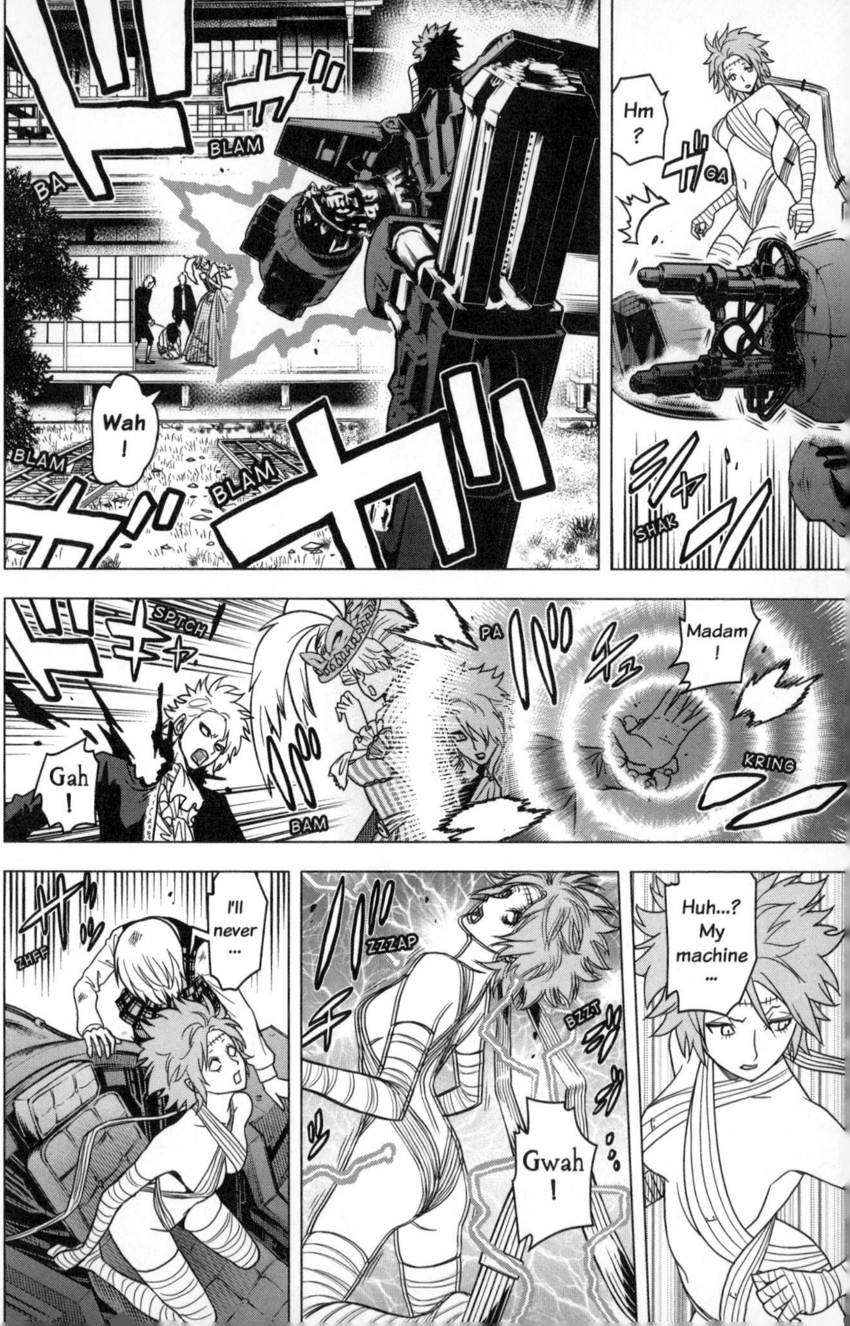
Hm ?
GA
SHAK
BLAM
BA
Wah !
BLAM
BLAM
Madam !
KRING
PA
SPTCH
Gah !
BAM
Huh...? My machine ...
ZZZAP
BZZT
Gwah !
I'll never ...
ZHFF

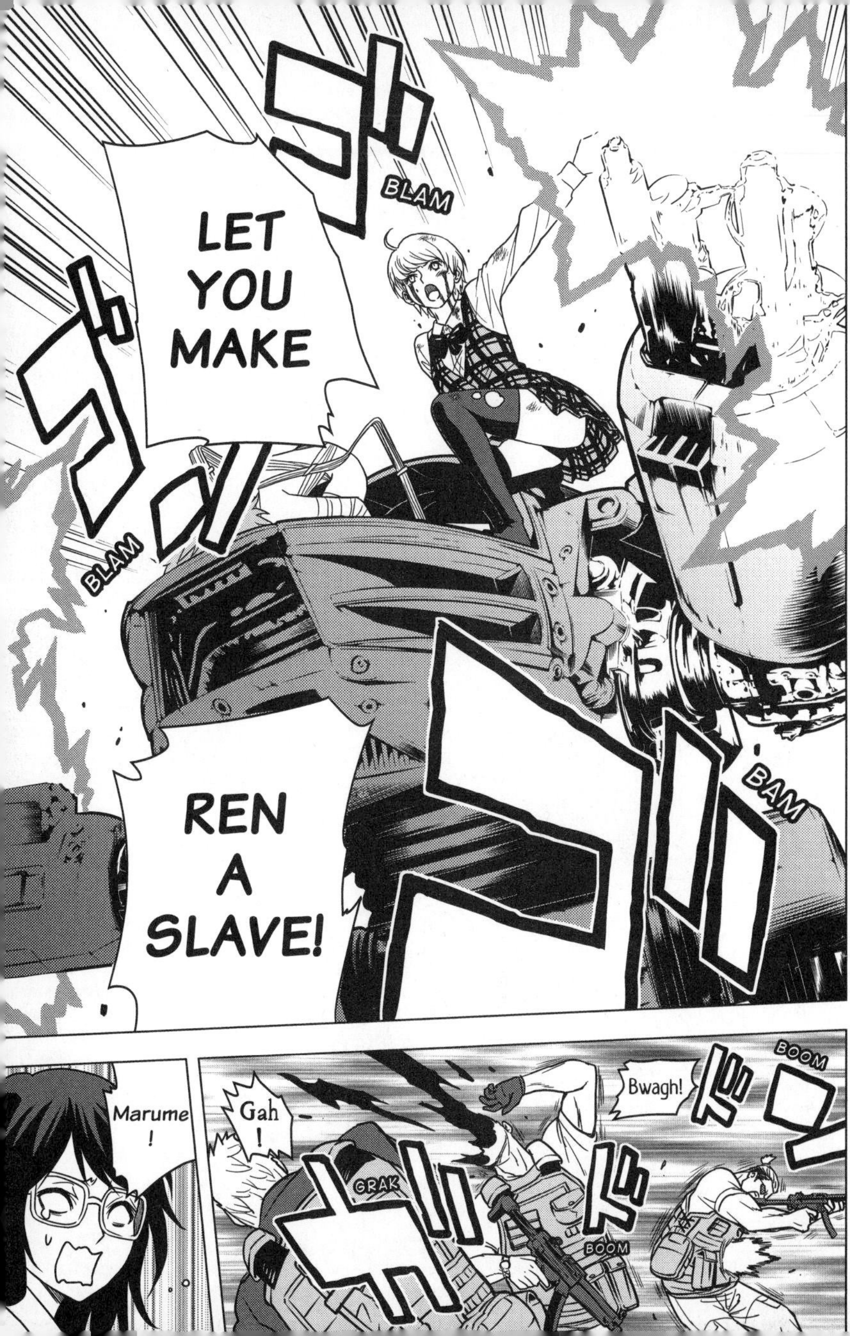
BLAM
LET YOU MAKE
BLAM
BAM
REN A SLAVE!
BOOM
Bwagh!
Gah!
GRAK
BOOM
Marume!

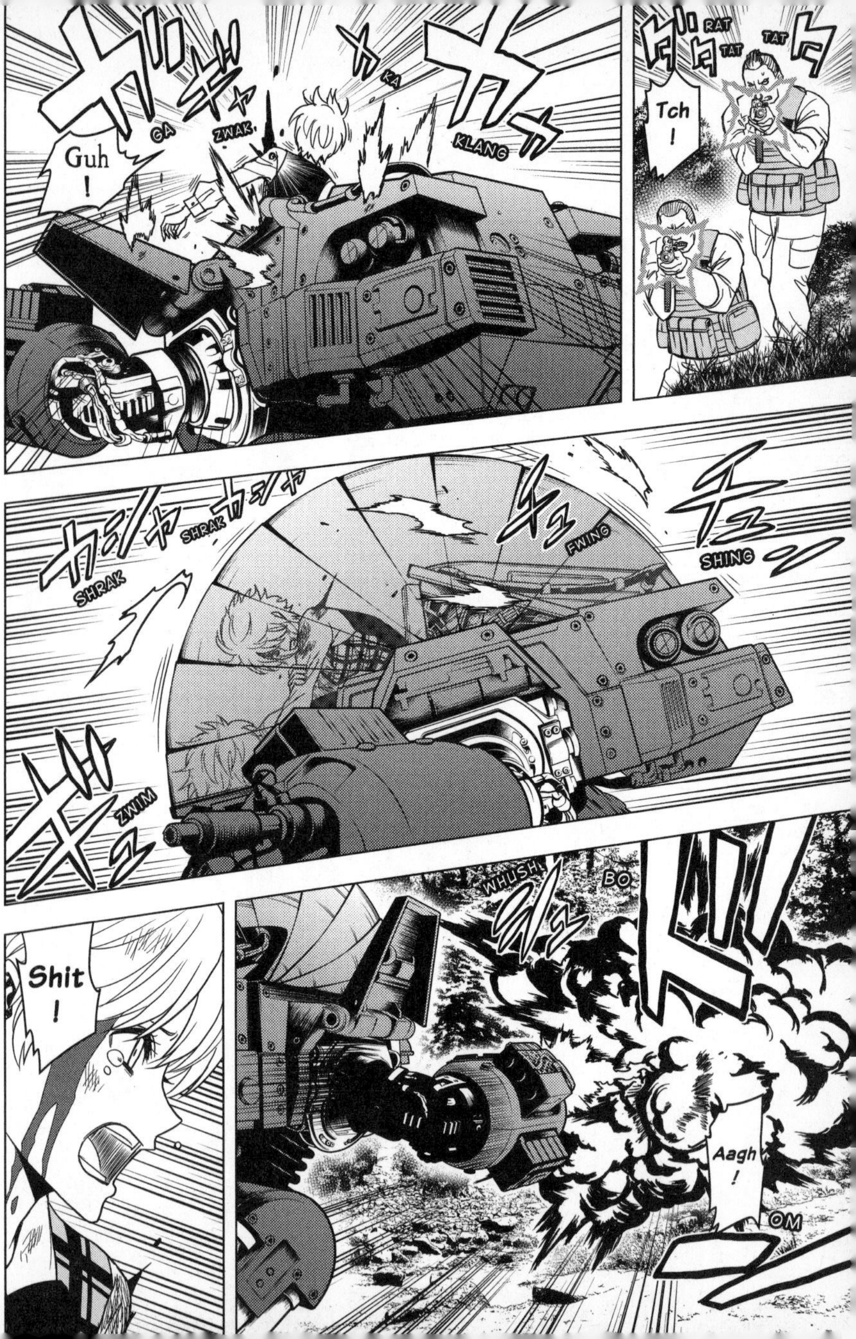
RAT
TAT
TAT
Tch!
KLANG
KA
ZWAK
GA
Guh!
SHING
FWING
SHRAK
SHRAK
ZWIM
BO
WHUSH
Aagh!
OM
Shit!

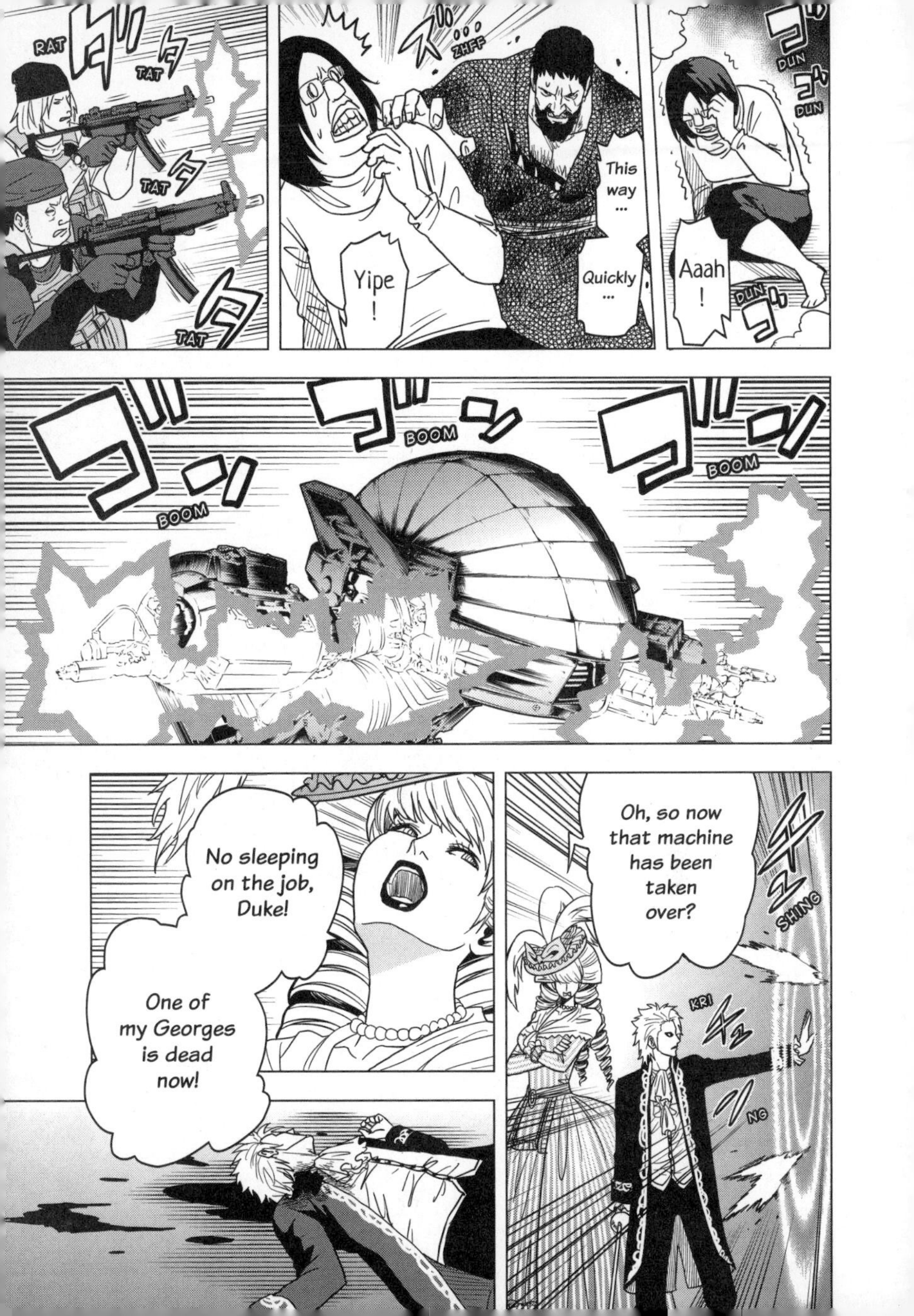
DUN
DUN
Aaah!
DUN
ZHFF
This way...
Quickly...
Yipe!
RAT
TAT
TAT
TAT
BOOM
BOOM
BOOM
Oh, so now that machine has been taken over?
SHING
KRI
NG
No sleeping on the job, Duke!
One of my Georges is dead now!

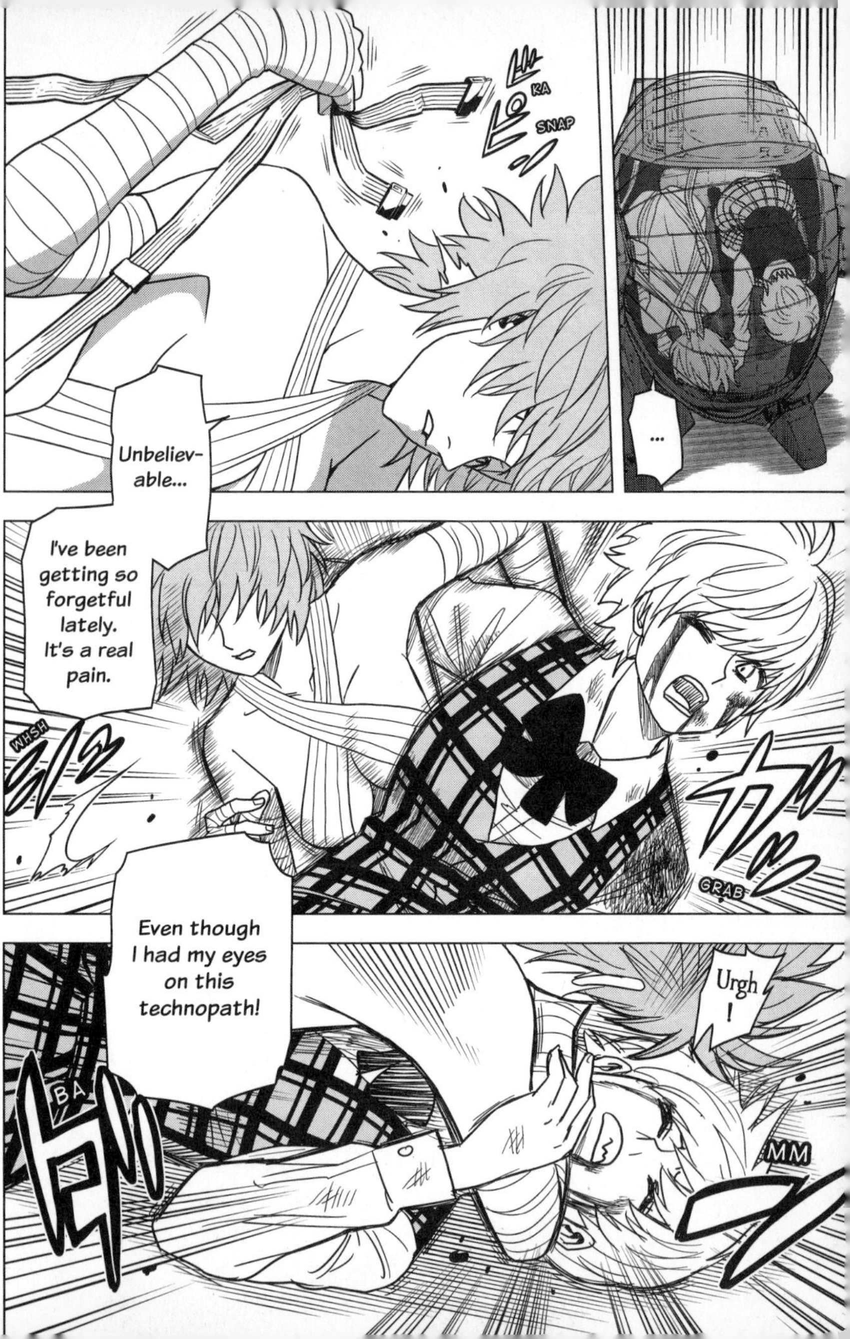
...
KA
SNAP
Unbeliev-
able...
I've been getting so forgetful lately. It's a real pain.
GRAB
WHSH
Urgh
!
Even though I had my eyes on this technopath!
MM
BA

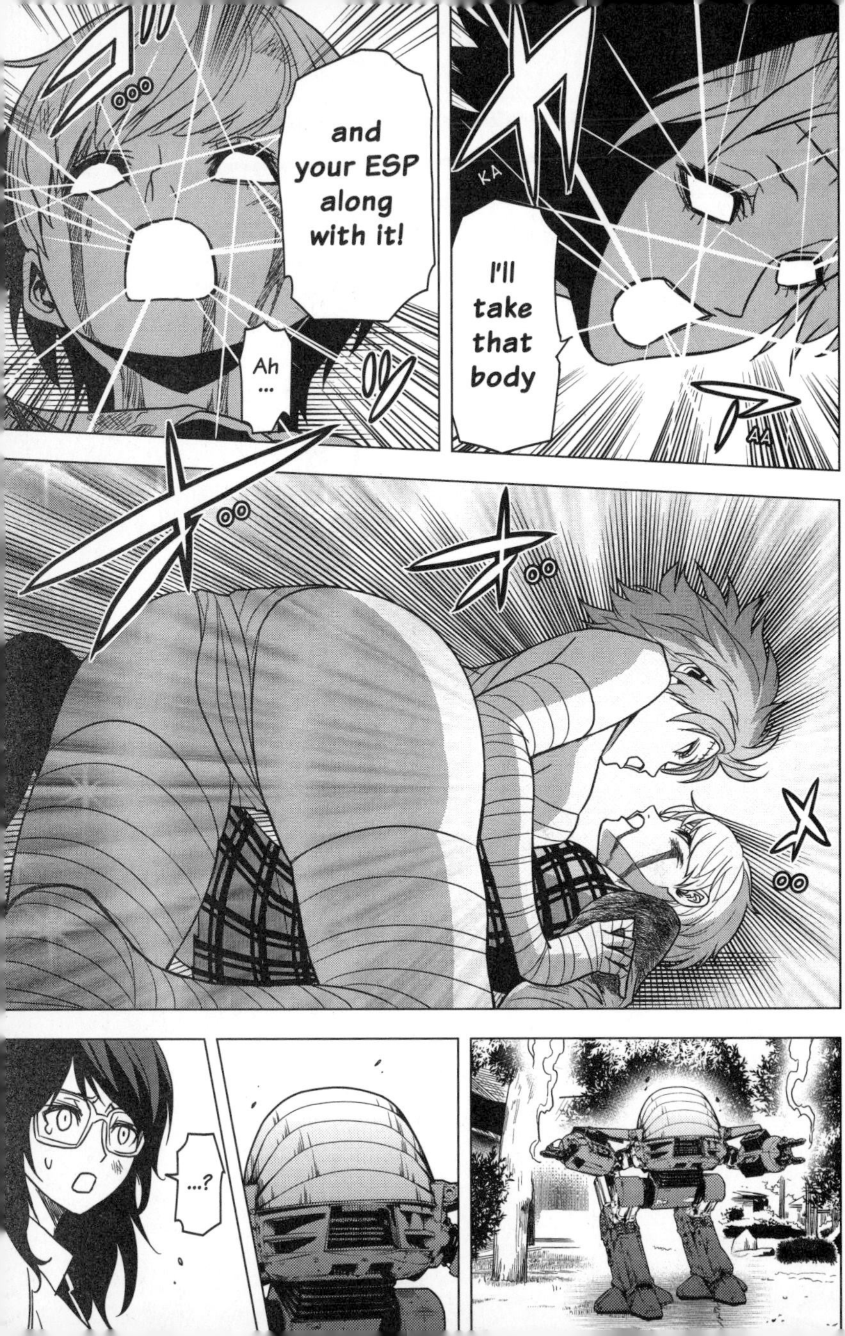
KA
I'll take that body
AA
and your ESP along with it!
Ah ...
...?

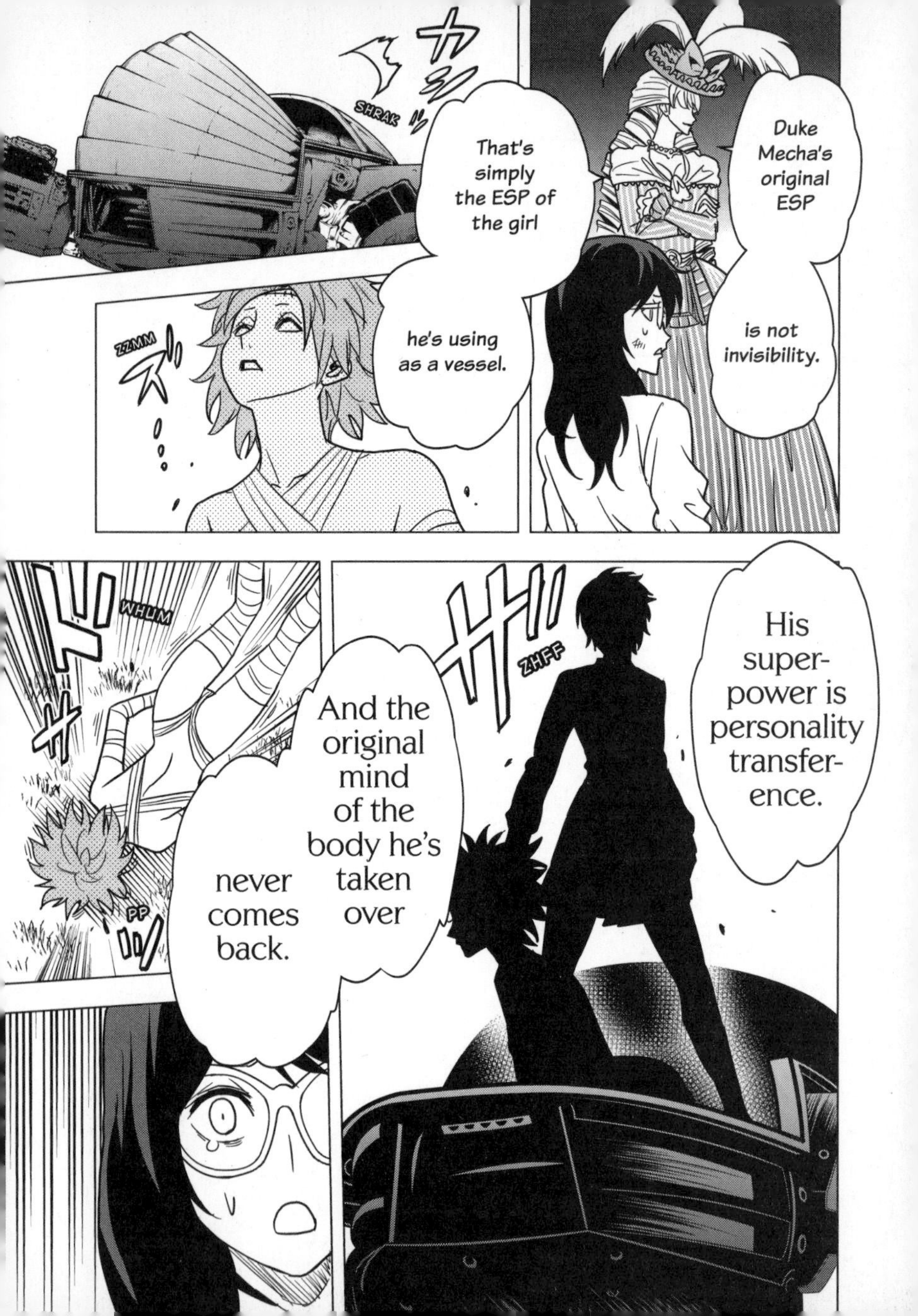
Duke Mecha's original ESP
is not invisibility.
SHRAK
That's simply the ESP of the girl
he's using as a vessel.
ZZMM
ZHFF
His super-power is personality transference.
And the original mind of the body he's taken over never comes back.
WHUM
PP

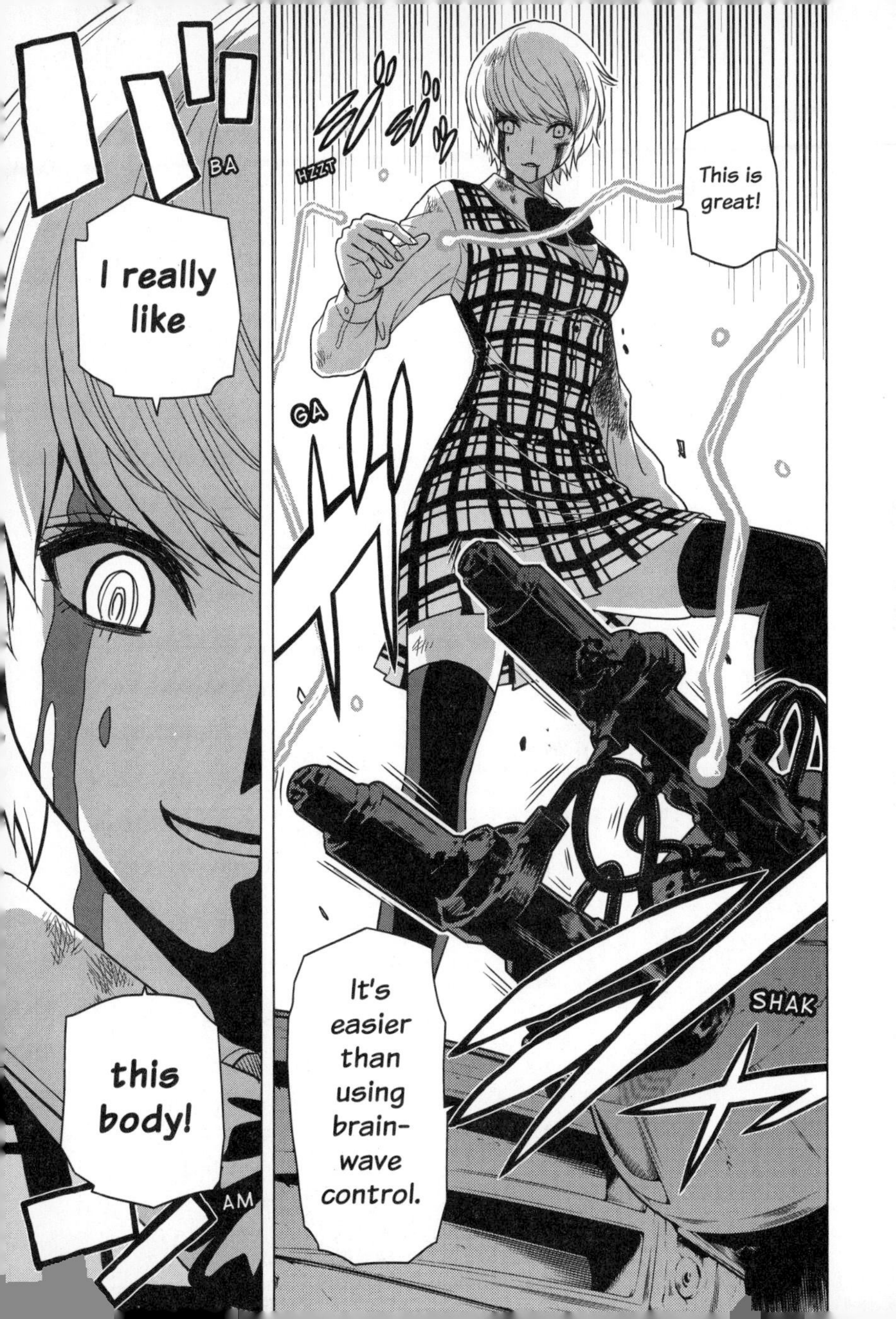
This is great!
HZZT
GA
SHAK
It's easier than using brain-wave control.
BA
I really like
this body!
AM

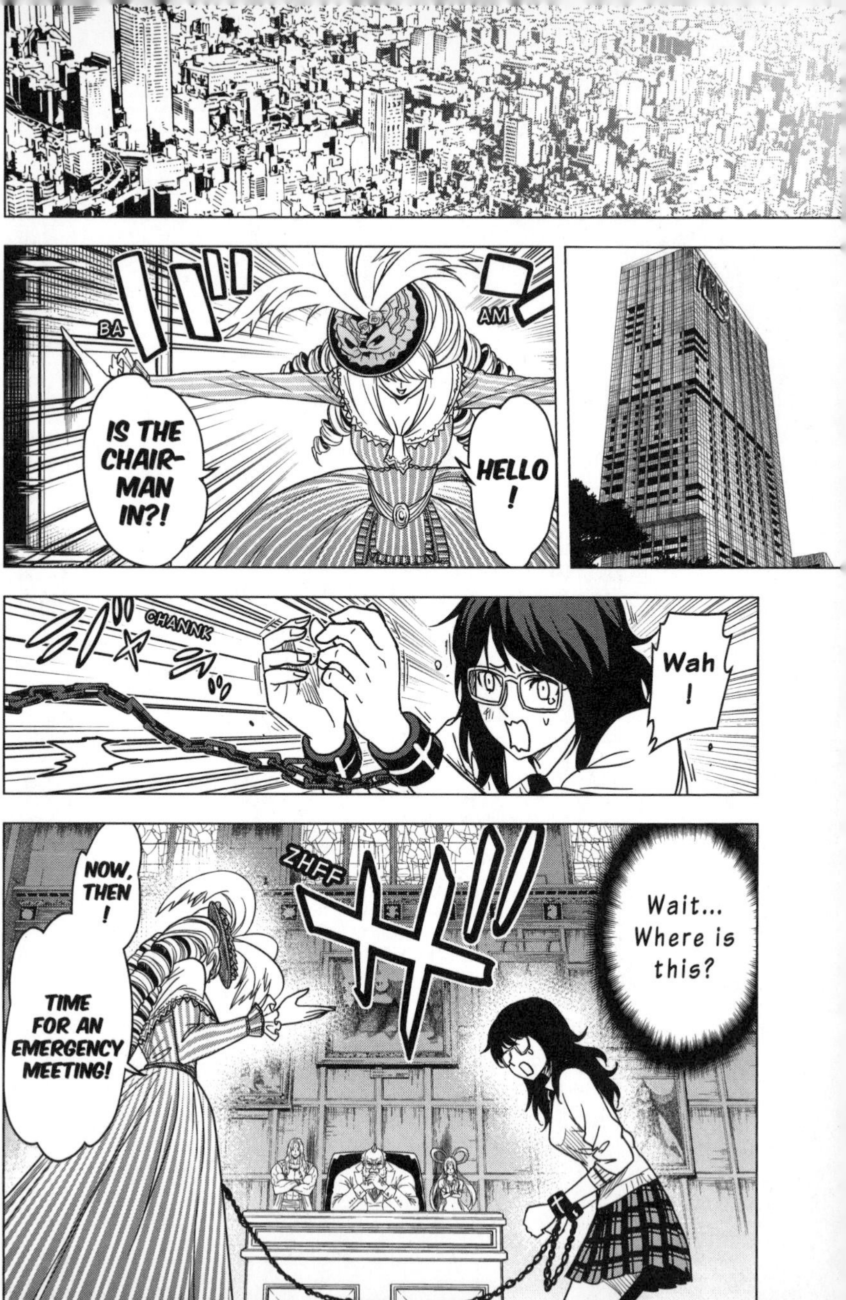
BA
AM
HELLO!
IS THE CHAIR-MAN IN?!
Wah!
CHANNK
Wait... Where is this?
ZHFF
NOW, THEN!
TIME FOR AN EMERGENCY MEETING!

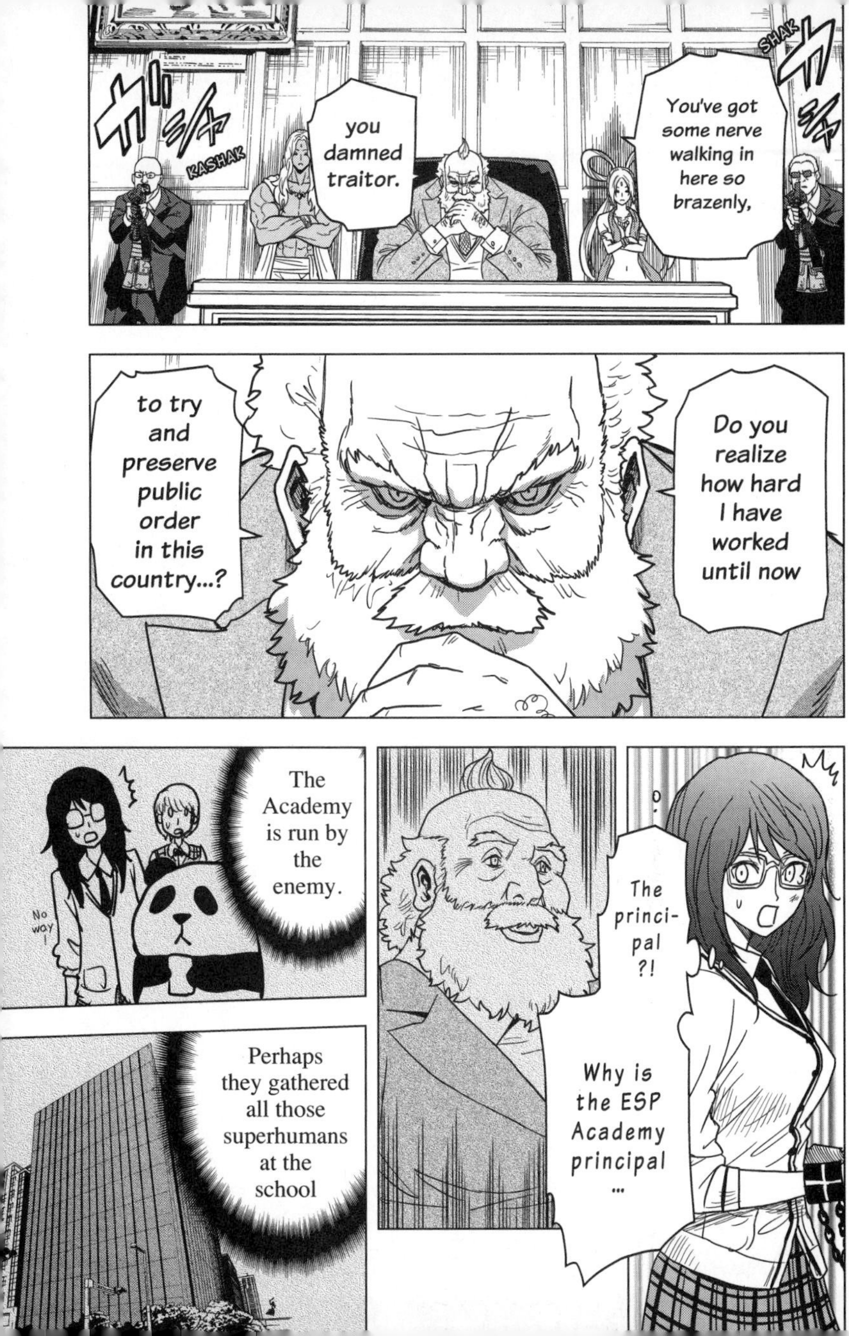
SHAK
You've got some nerve walking in here so brazenly,
you damned traitor.
KASHAK
Do you realize how hard I have worked until now
to try and preserve public order in this country...?
The principal?!
Why is the ESP Academy principal ...
The Academy is run by the enemy.
No way!
Perhaps they gathered all those superhumans at the school

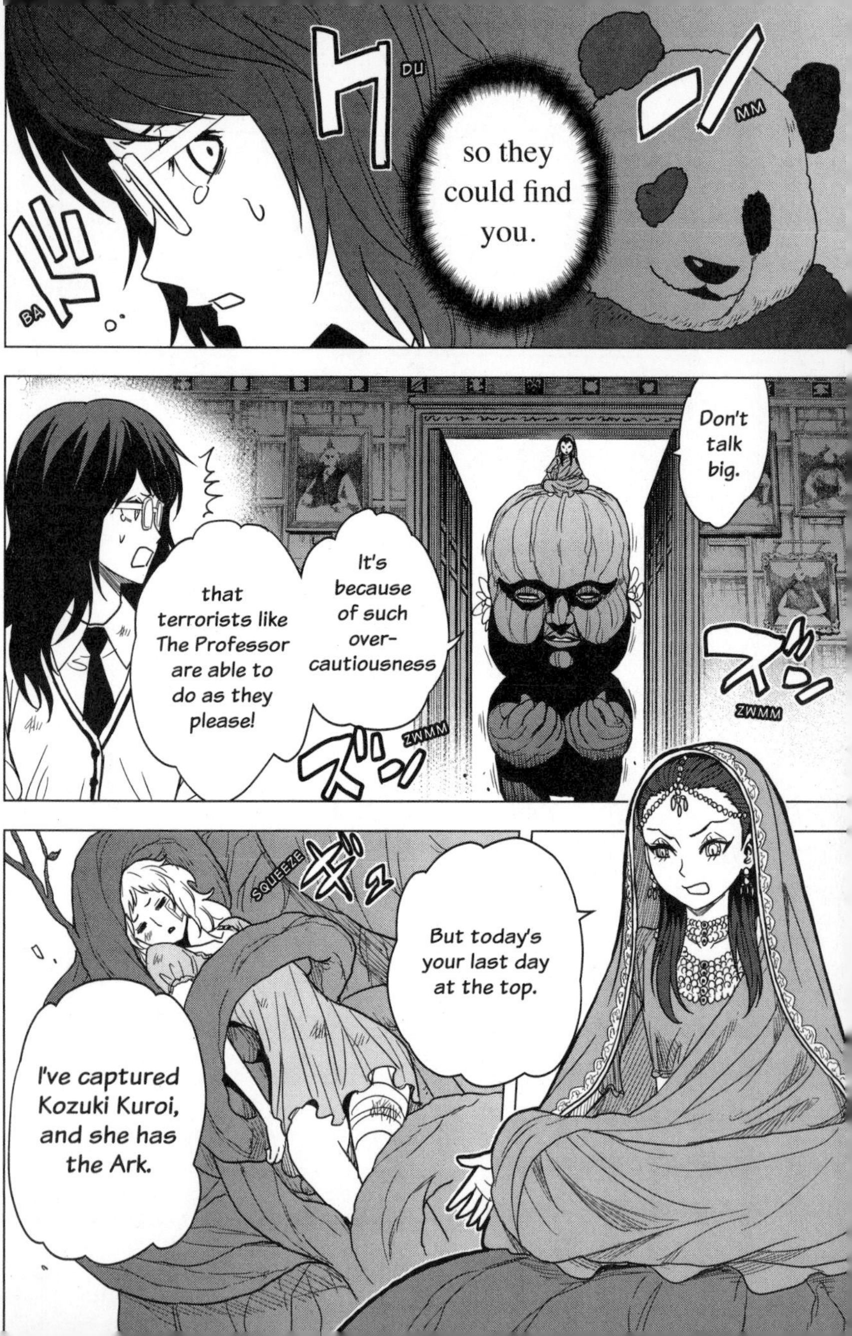
MM
DU
so they could find you.
BA
Don't talk big.
ZWMM
It's because of such over-cautiousness
that terrorists like The Professor are able to do as they please!
ZWMM
But today's your last day at the top.
I've captured Kozuki Kuroi, and she has the Ark.
SQUEEZE

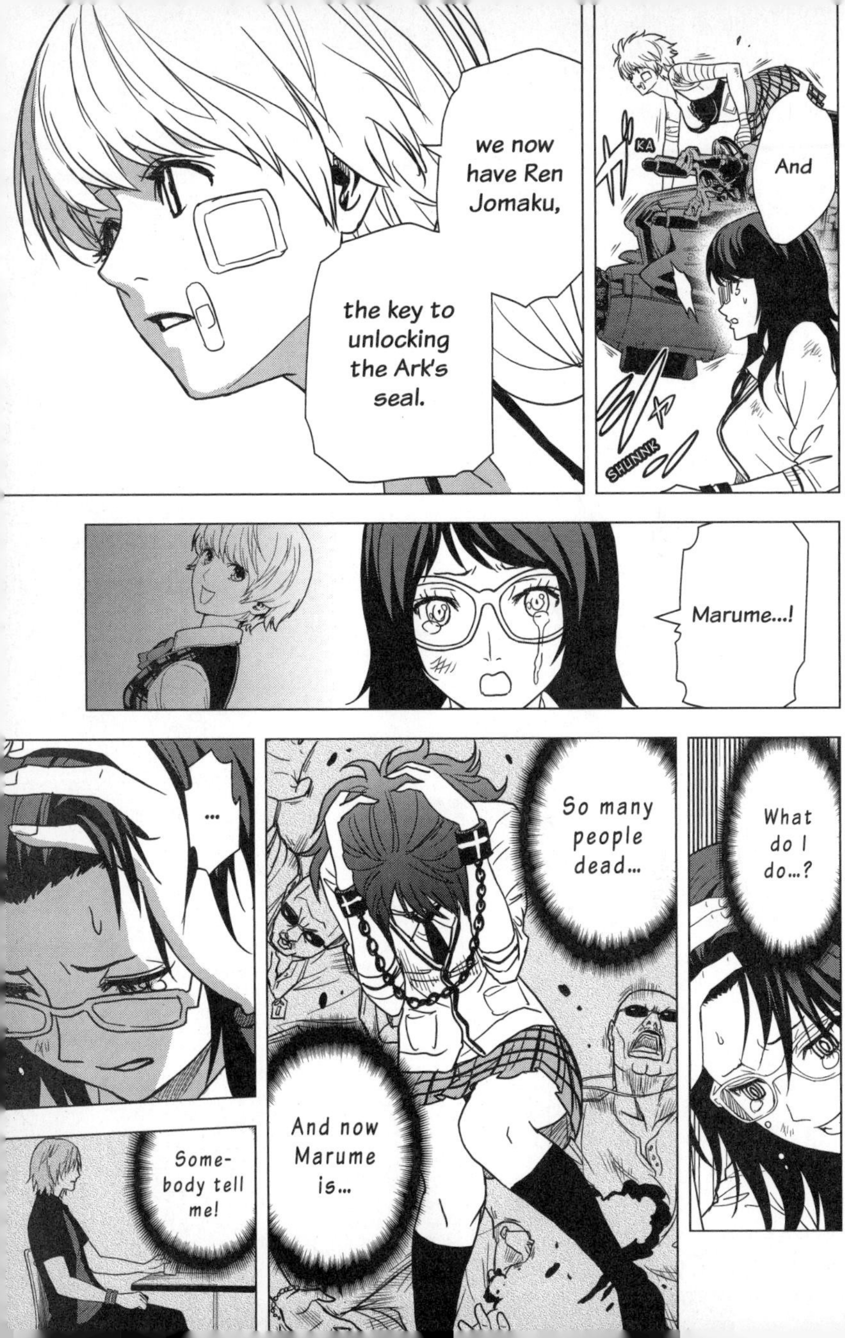
KA
And
SHUNNK
we now have Ren Jomaku,
the key to unlocking the Ark's seal.
Marume...!
What do I do...?
So many people dead...
And now Marume is...
...
Some-body tell me!

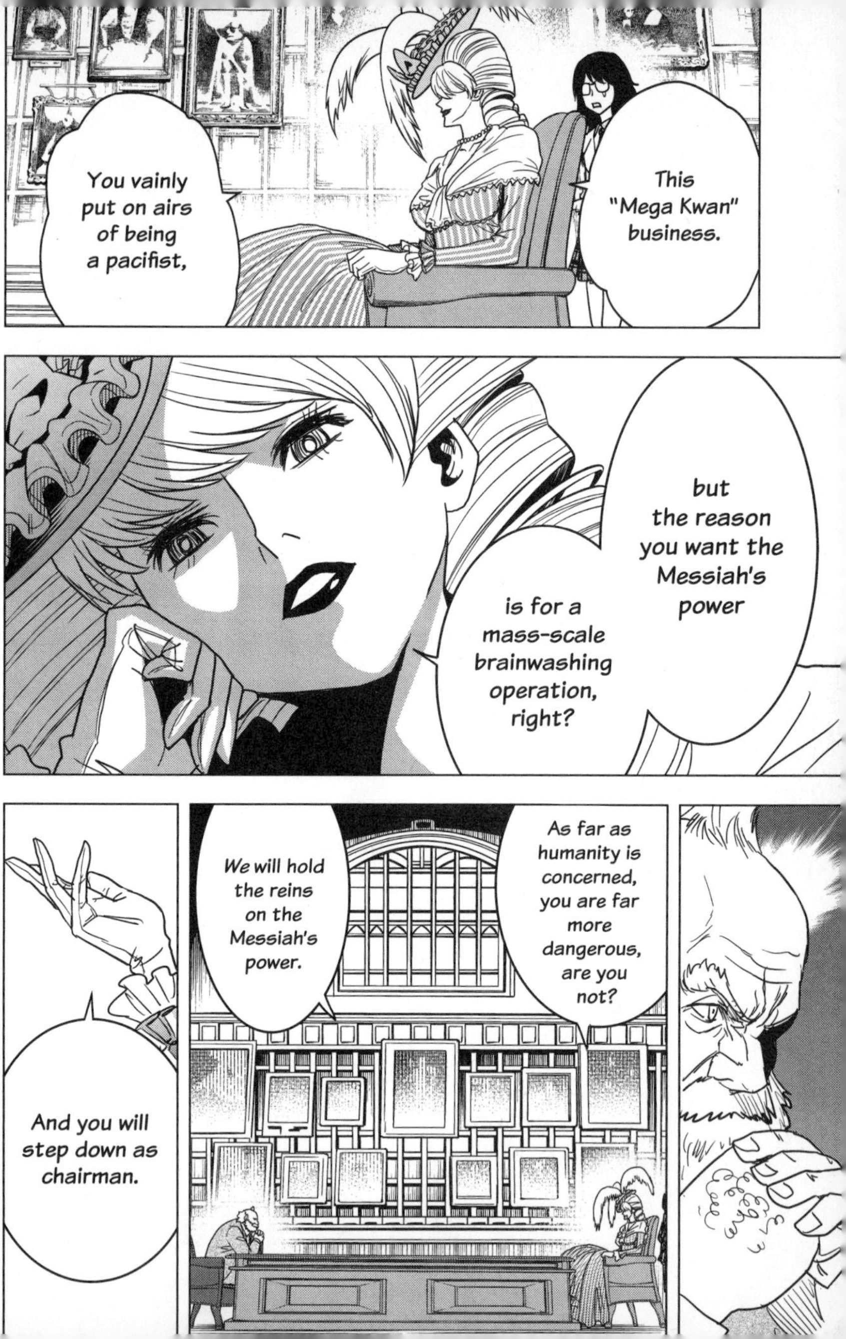
This "Mega Kwan" business.
You vainly put on airs of being a pacifist,
but the reason you want the Messiah's power
is for a mass-scale brainwashing operation, right?
As far as humanity is concerned, you are far more dangerous, are you not?
We will hold the reins on the Messiah's power.
And you will step down as chairman.

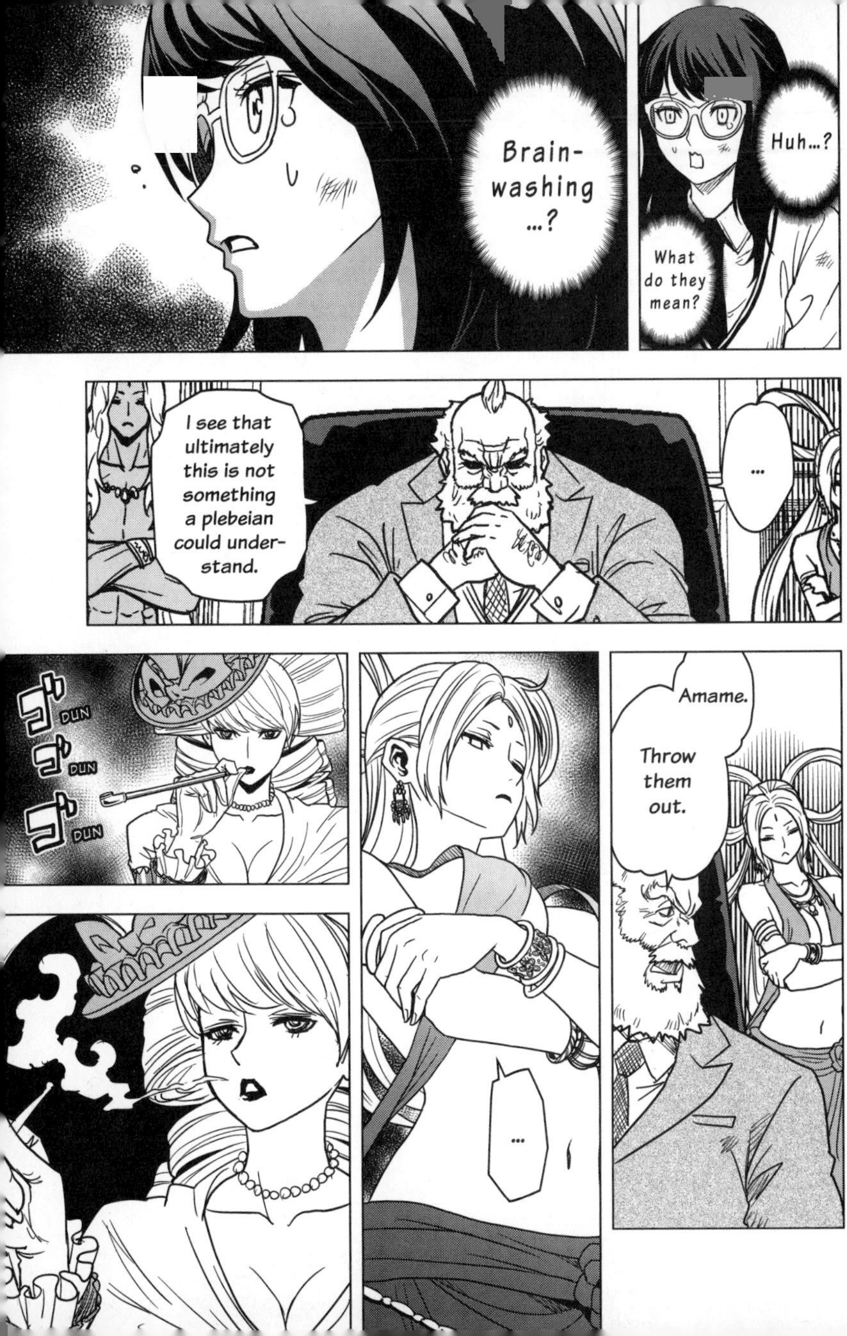
Huh...?
What do they mean?
Brain-washing ...?
...
I see that ultimately this is not something a plebeian could under-stand.
Amame.
Throw them out.
...
ゴ DUN
ゴ DUN
ゴ DUN

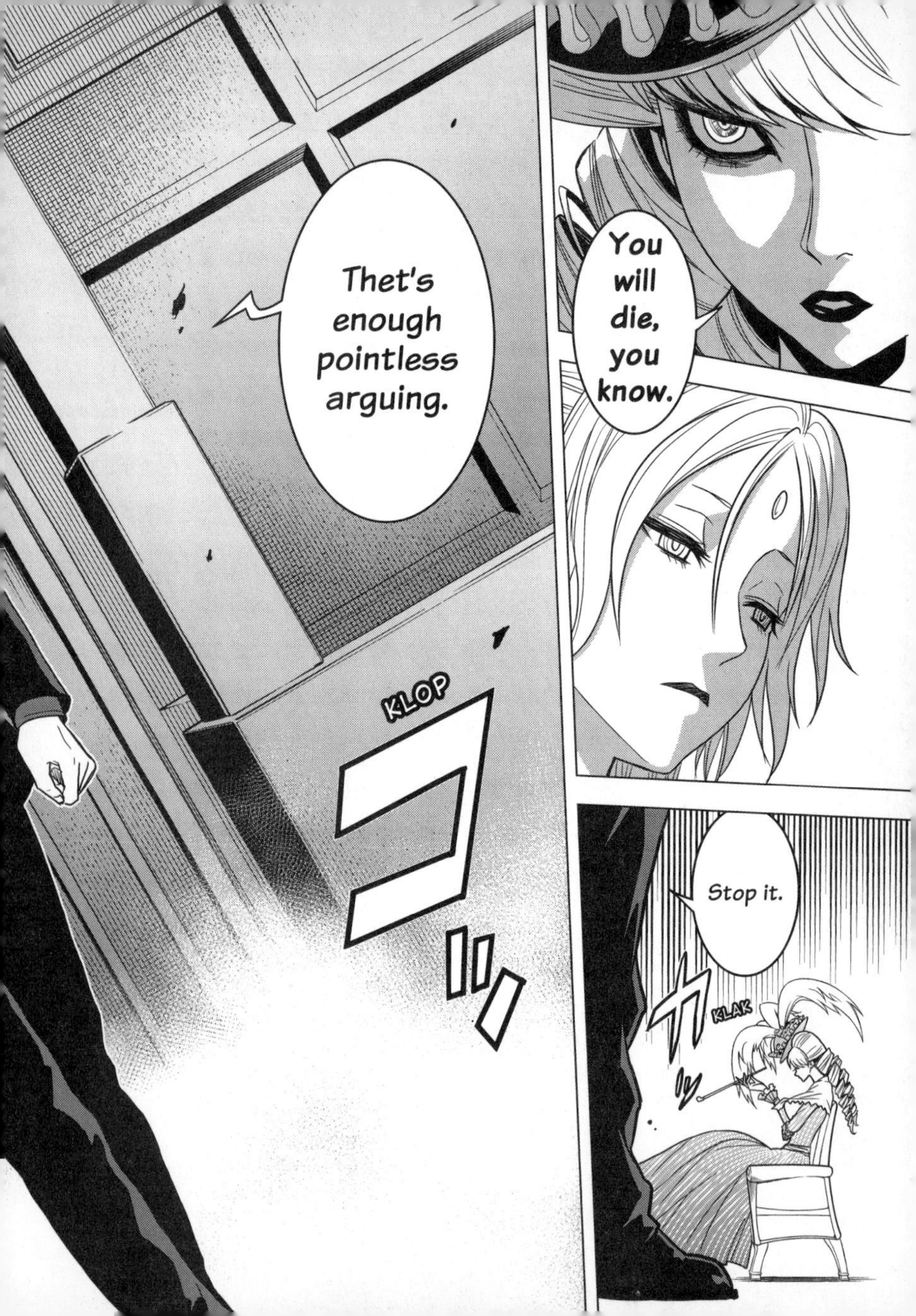
You will die, you know.
Stop it.
KLAK
Thet's enough pointless arguing.
KLOP

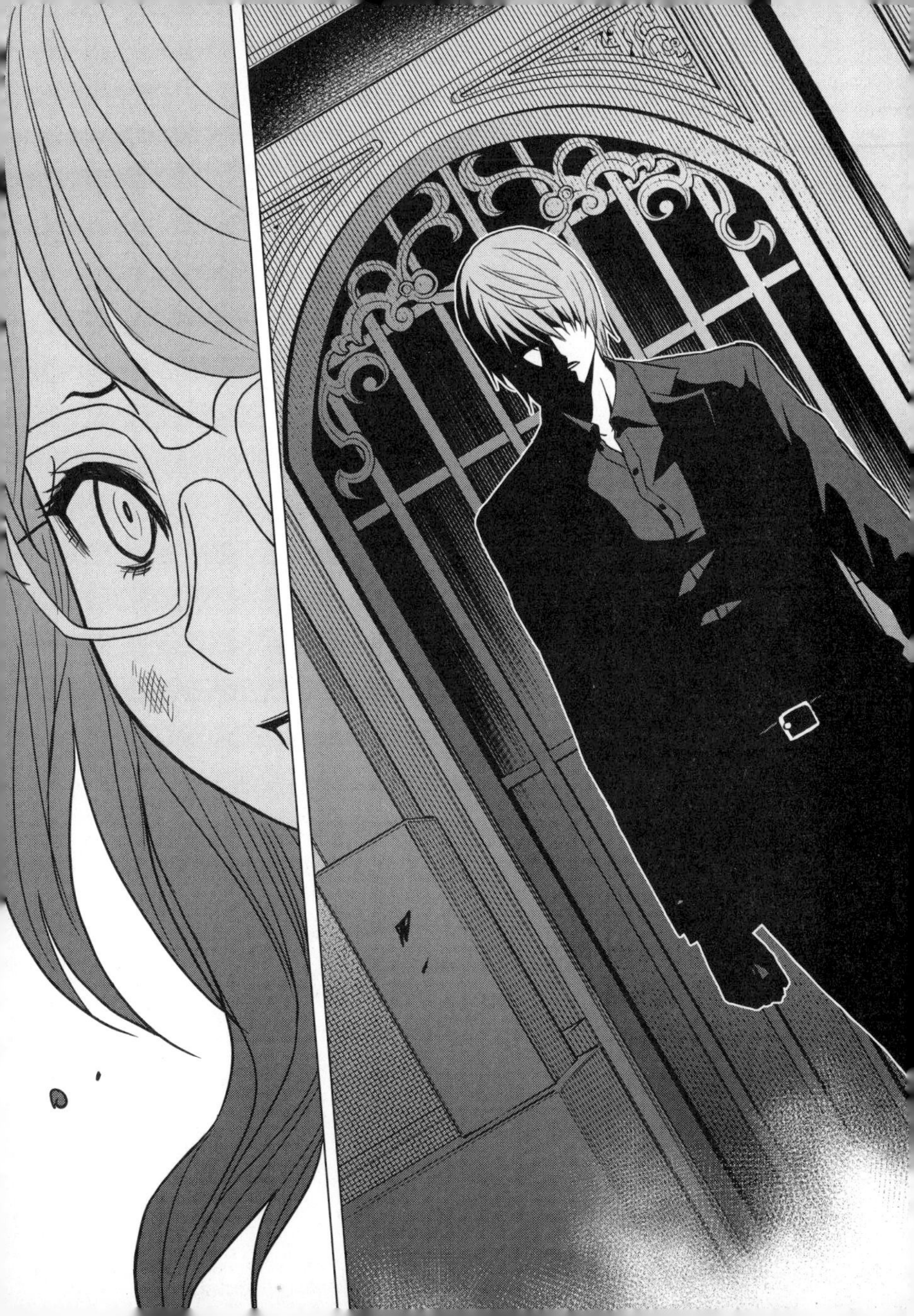

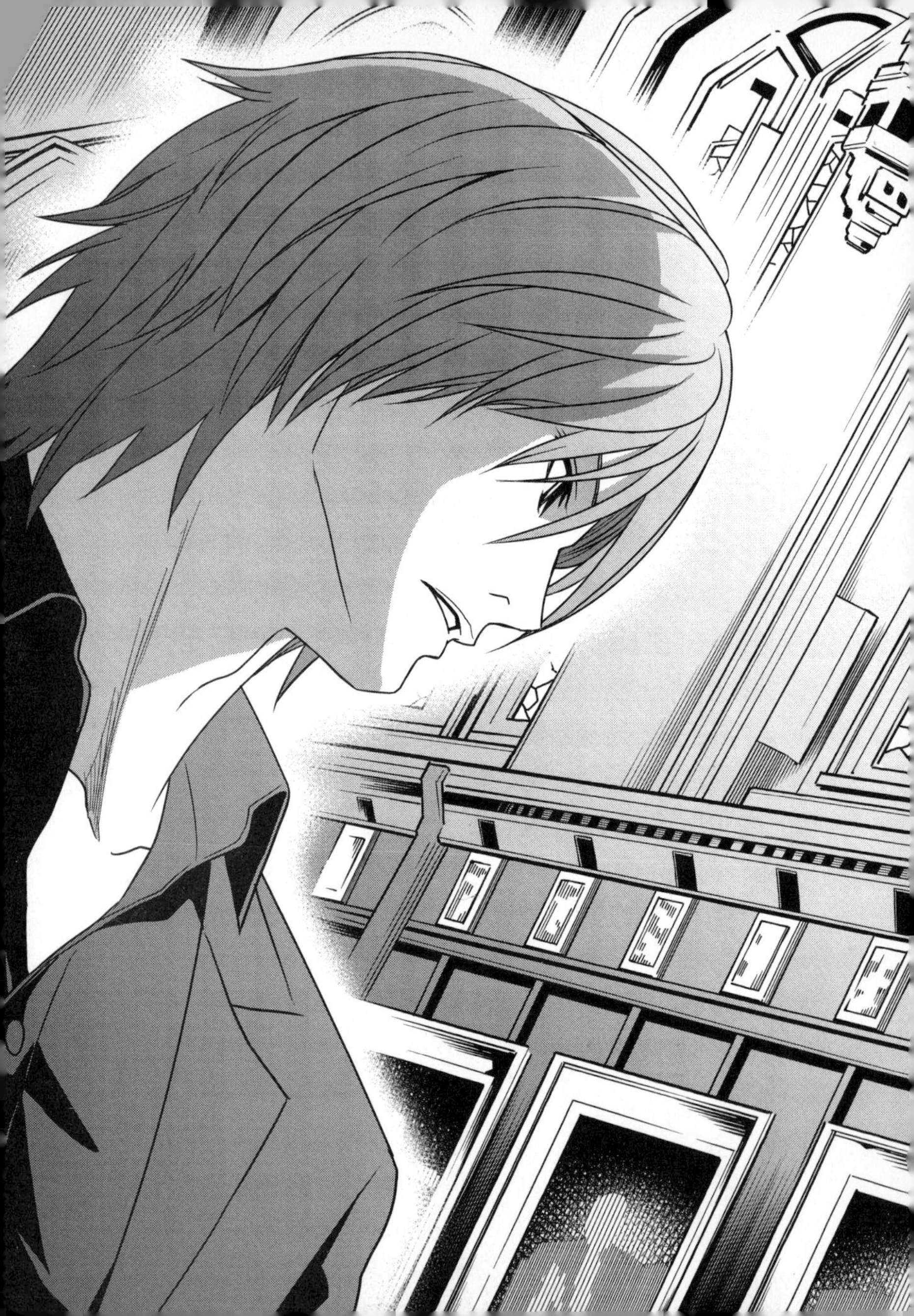

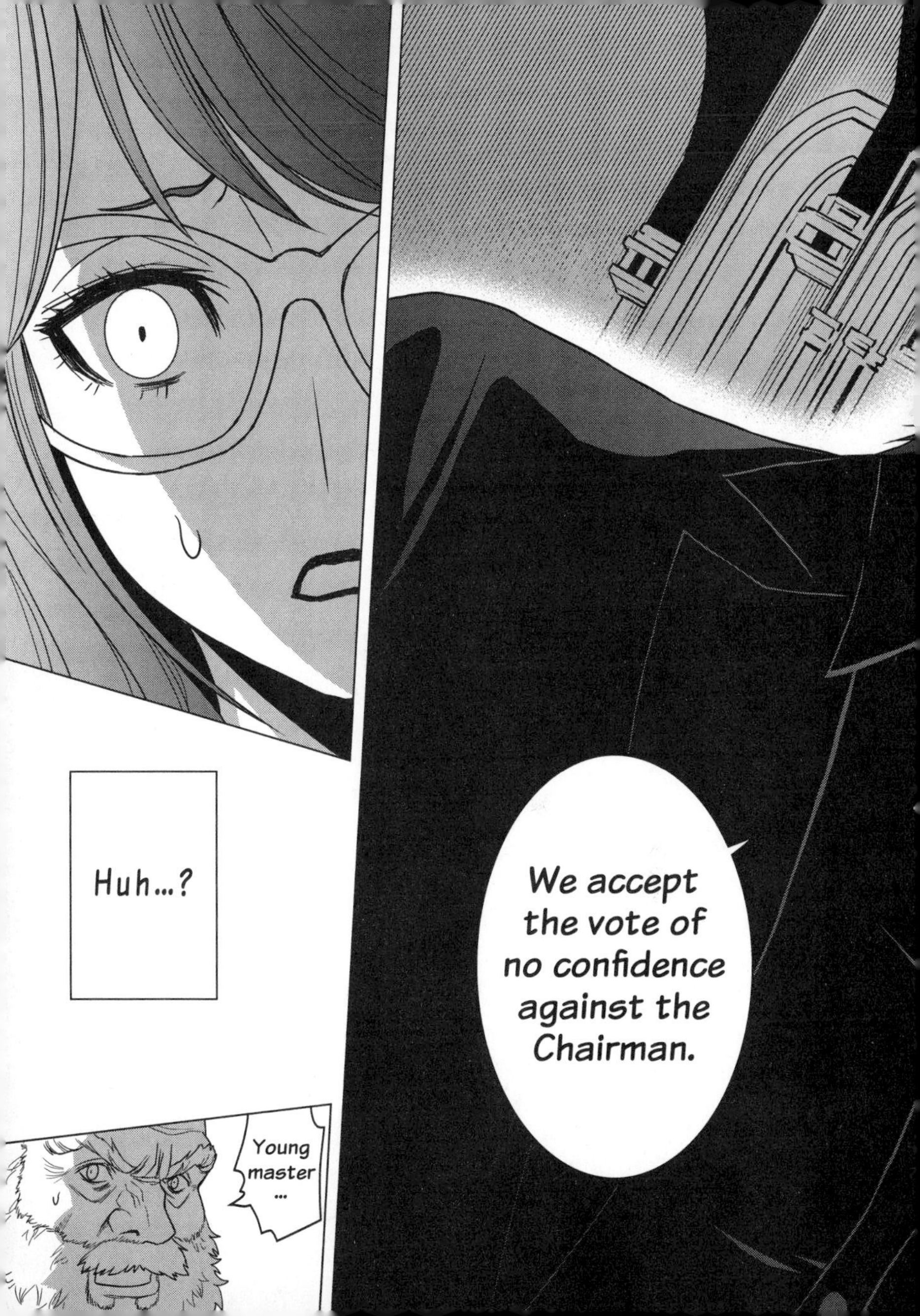
We accept the vote of no confidence against the Chairman.
Huh...?
Young master ...

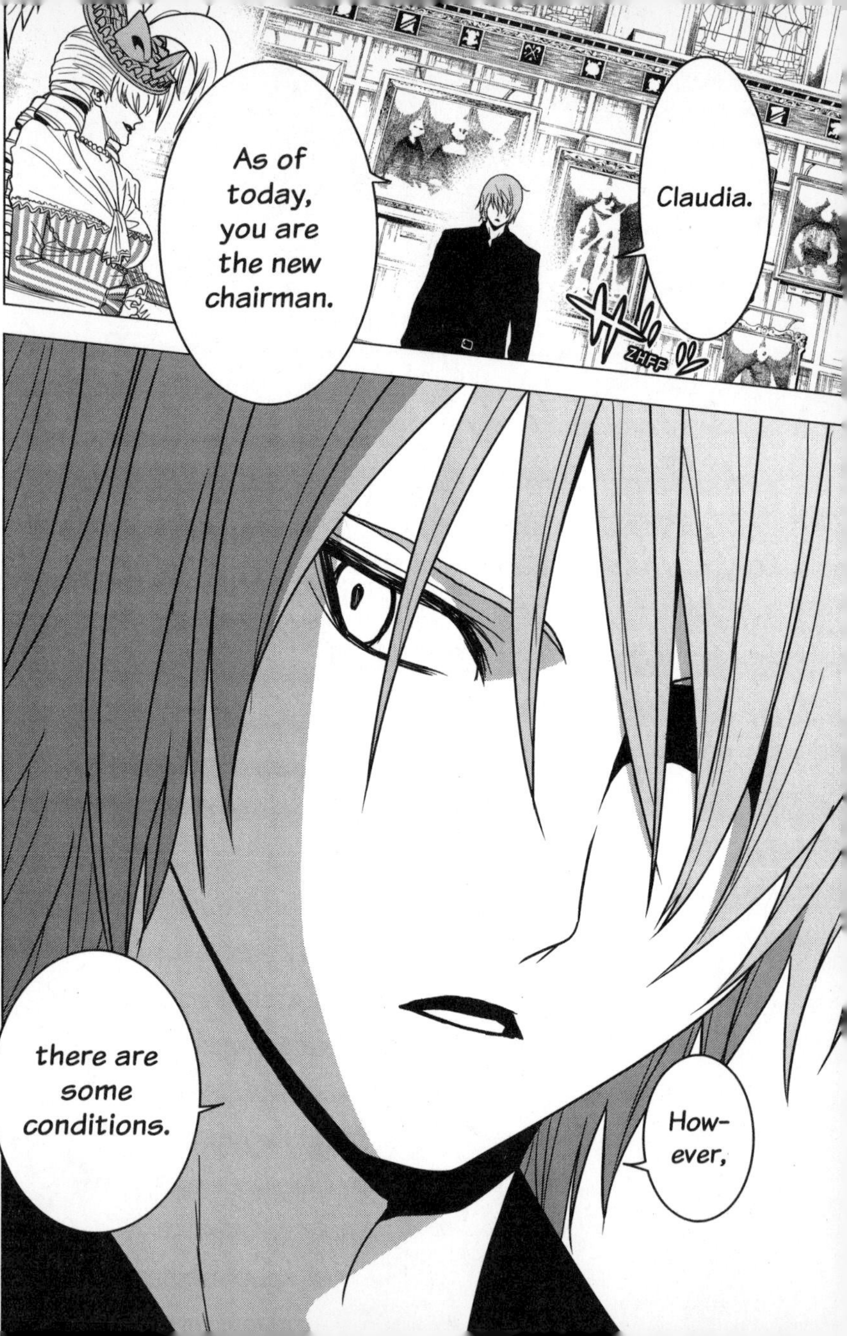
Claudia.
As of today, you are the new chairman.
ZHFF
However,
there are some conditions.

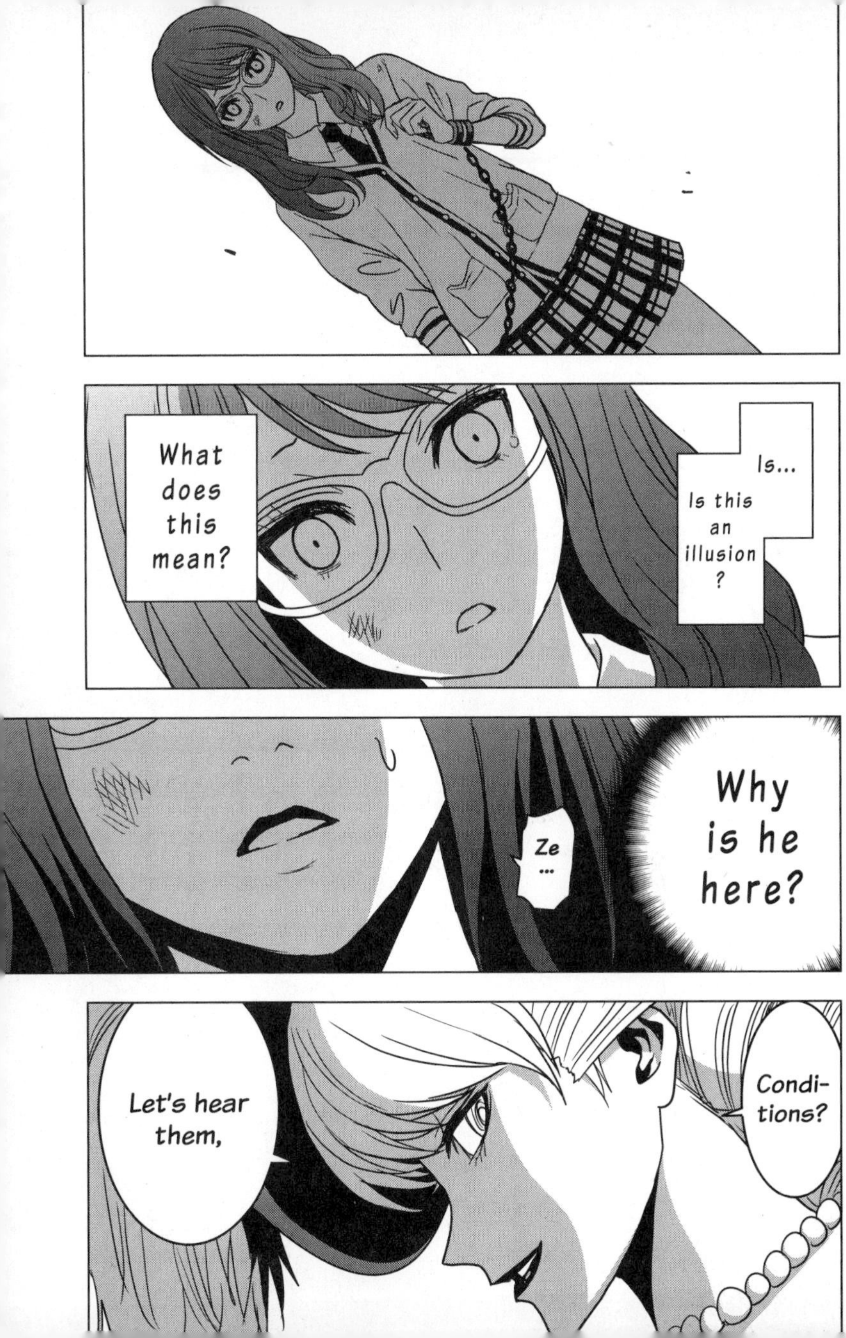
Is...
Is this an illusion?
What does this mean?
Why is he here?
Ze...
Condi-tions?
Let's hear them,

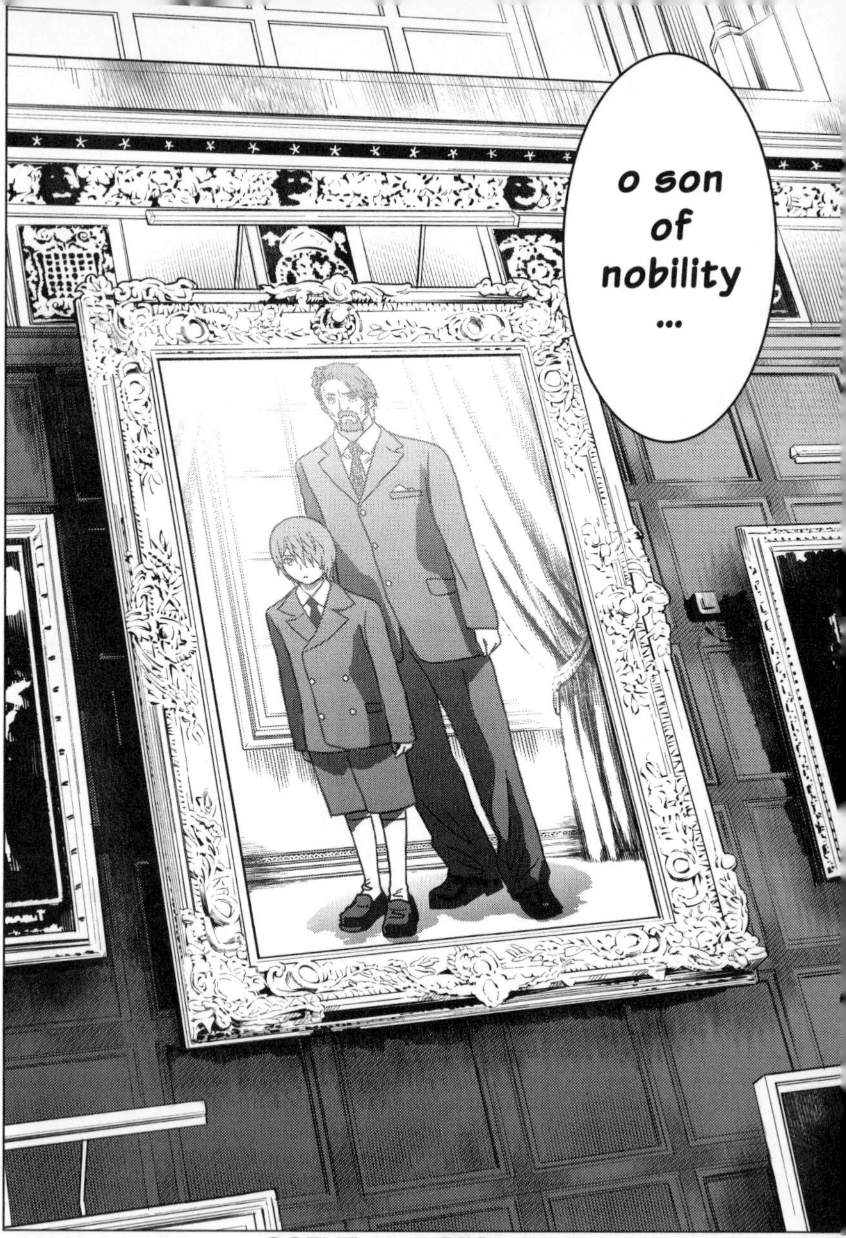
o son of nobility ...

SCENE 60 /// END

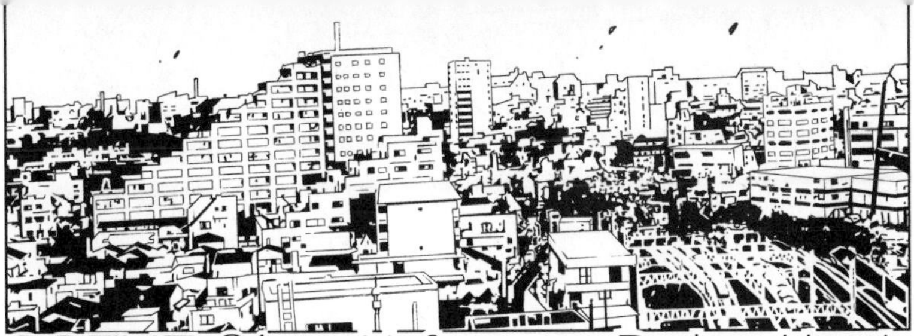

SCENE 61 /// Unforeseen Broken Heart

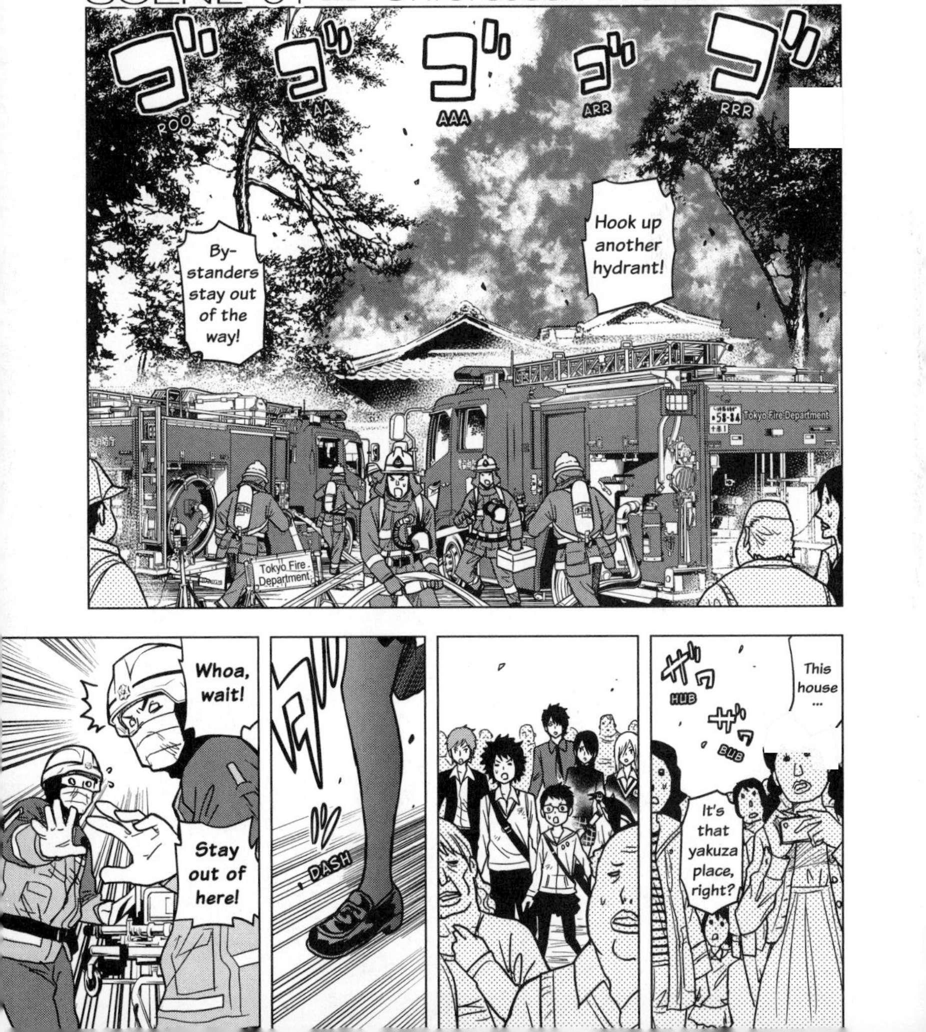
ROO AA AAA ARR RRR
Hook up another hydrant!
By-standers stay out of the way!
Tokyo Fire Department
Tokyo Fire Department
This house ...
HUB BUB
It's that yakuza place, right?
DASH
Whoa, wait!
Stay out of here!

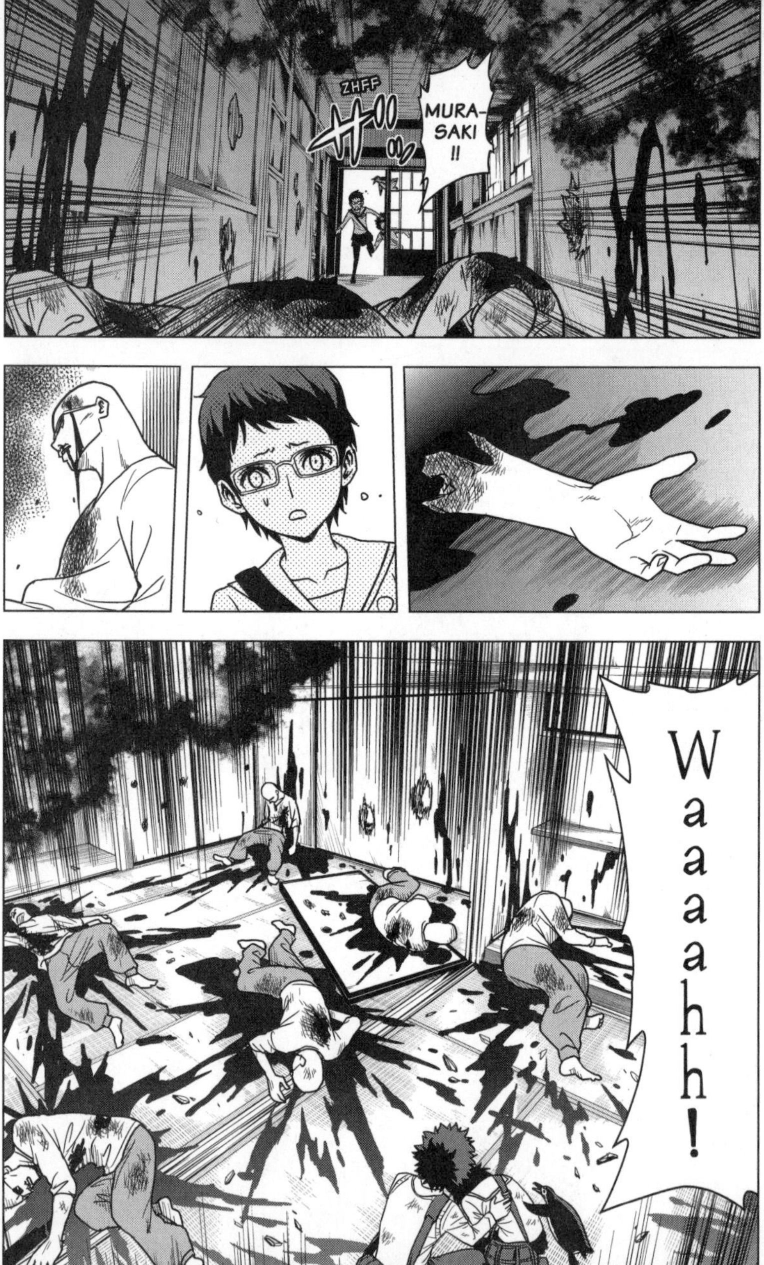
MURA-
SAKI
!!
ZHFF
Waaaaahh!

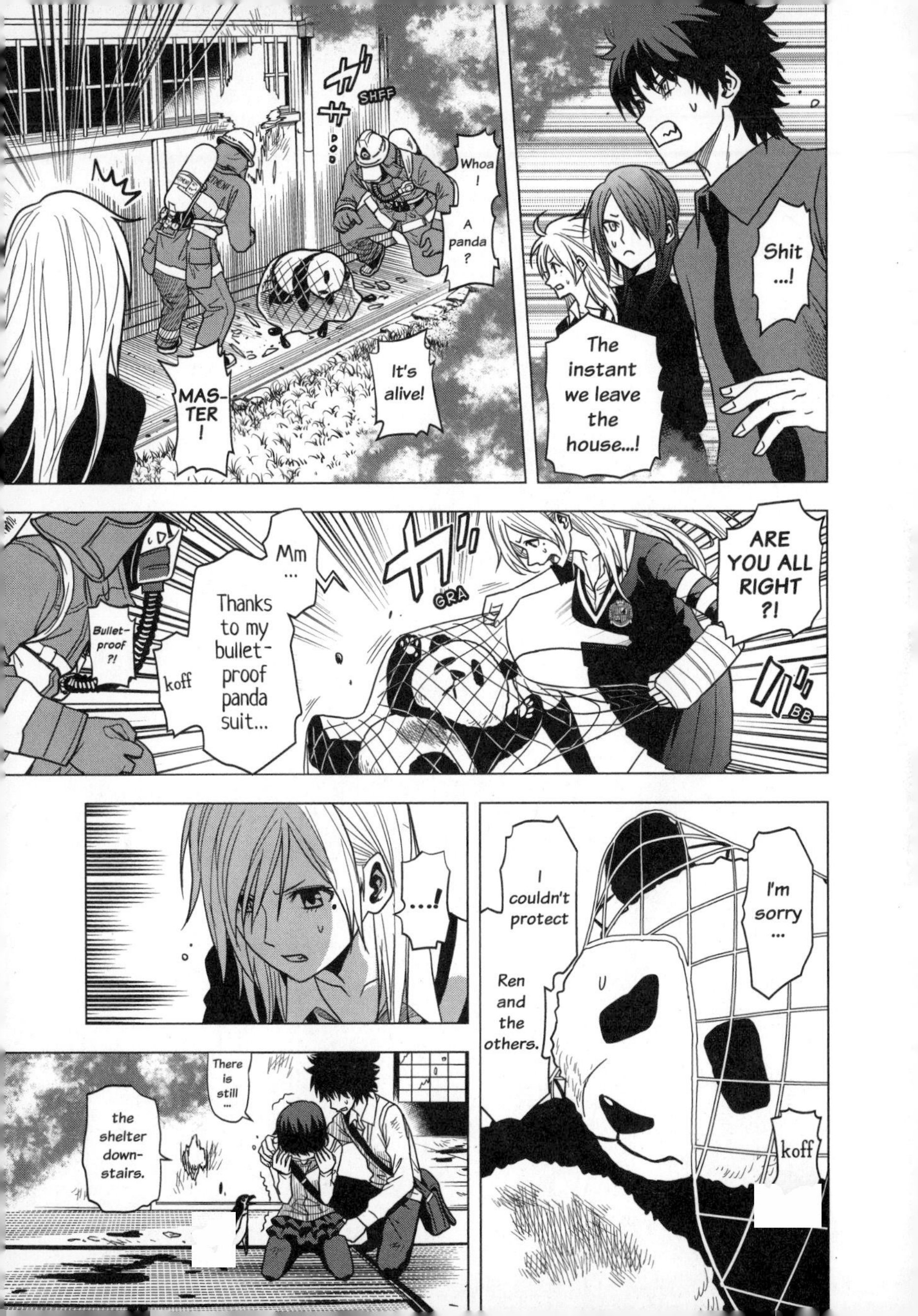
Shit ...!
The instant we leave the house...!
Whoa ! A panda ?
SHFF
It's alive!
MASTER !
ARE YOU ALL RIGHT ?!
BB
GRA
Mm ...
Thanks to my bullet-proof panda suit...
koff
Bullet-proof ?!
I'm sorry ...
I couldn't protect Ren and the others.
koff
...!
There is still ...
the shelter down-stairs.

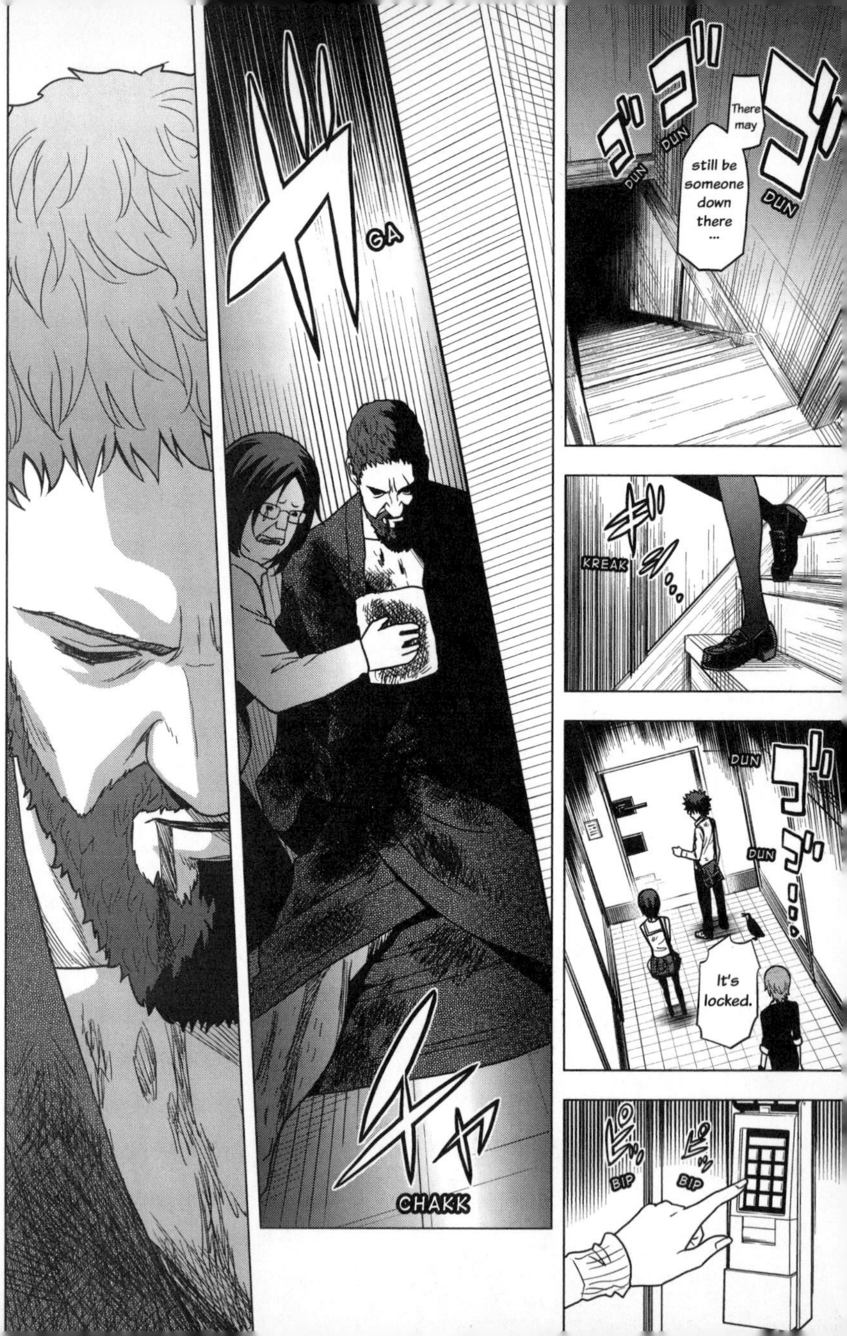
DUN
DUN
There may still be someone down there ...
DUN
KREAK
DUN
DUN
It's locked.
BIP
BIP
GA
CHAKK

I'm sorry...

There was nothing I could do...

...

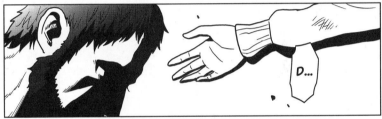

D...

Dad!

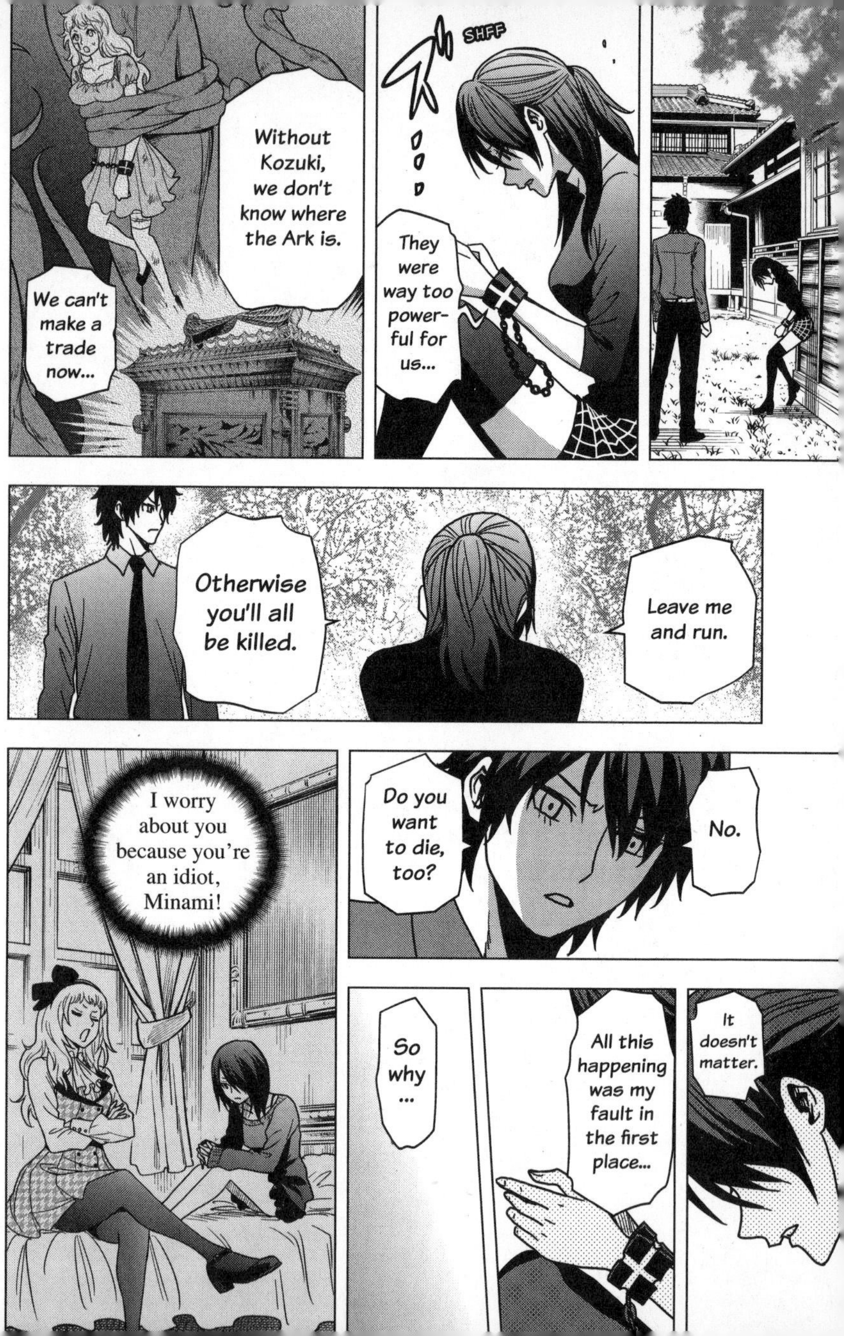
SHFF
They were way too powerful for us...
Without Kozuki, we don't know where the Ark is.
We can't make a trade now...
Leave me and run.
Otherwise you'll all be killed.
No.
Do you want to die, too?
It doesn't matter.
All this happening was my fault in the first place...
So why ...
I worry about you because you're an idiot, Minami!

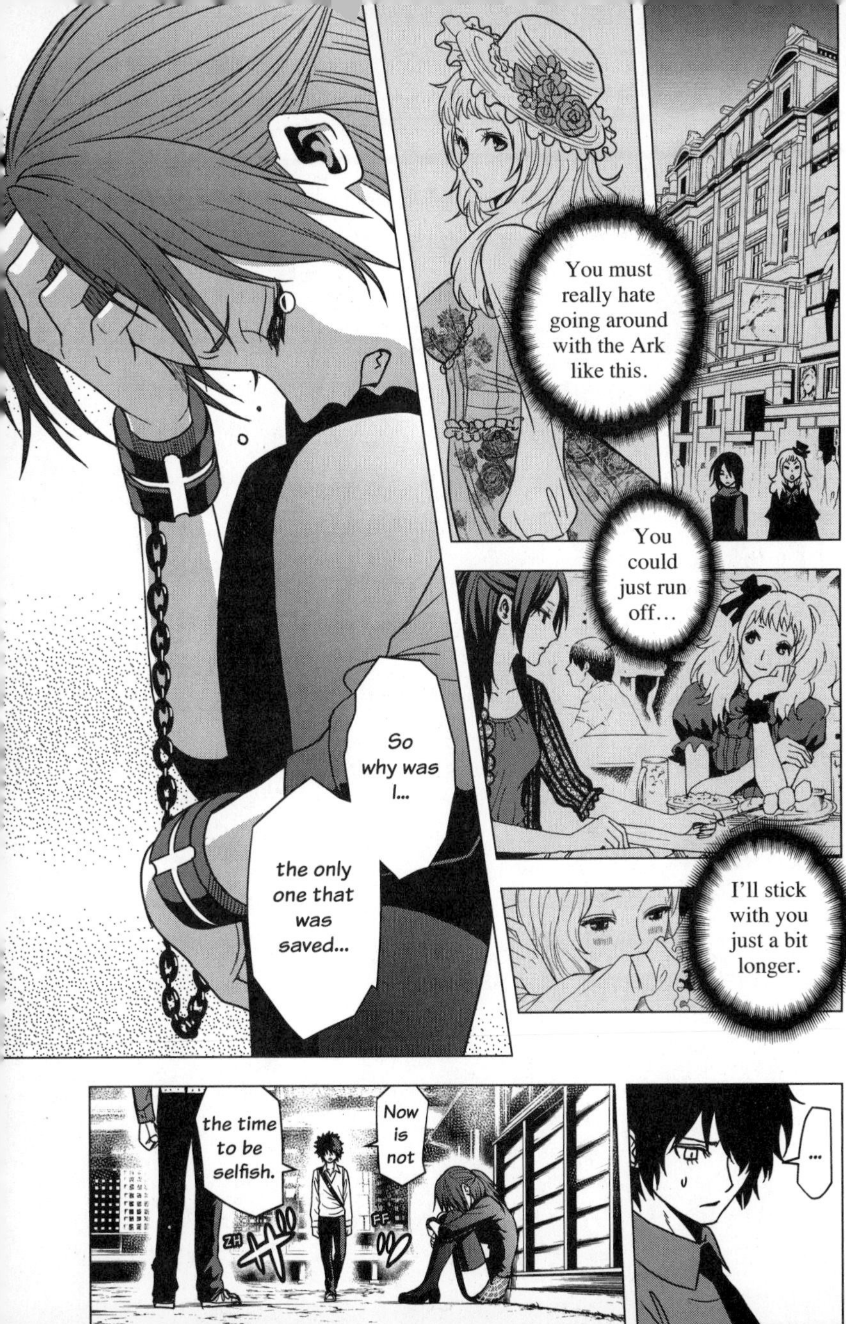
You must really hate going around with the Ark like this.
You could just run off…
I'll stick with you just a bit longer.
So why was I…
the only one that was saved…
…
Now is not
the time to be selfish.
FF
ZH

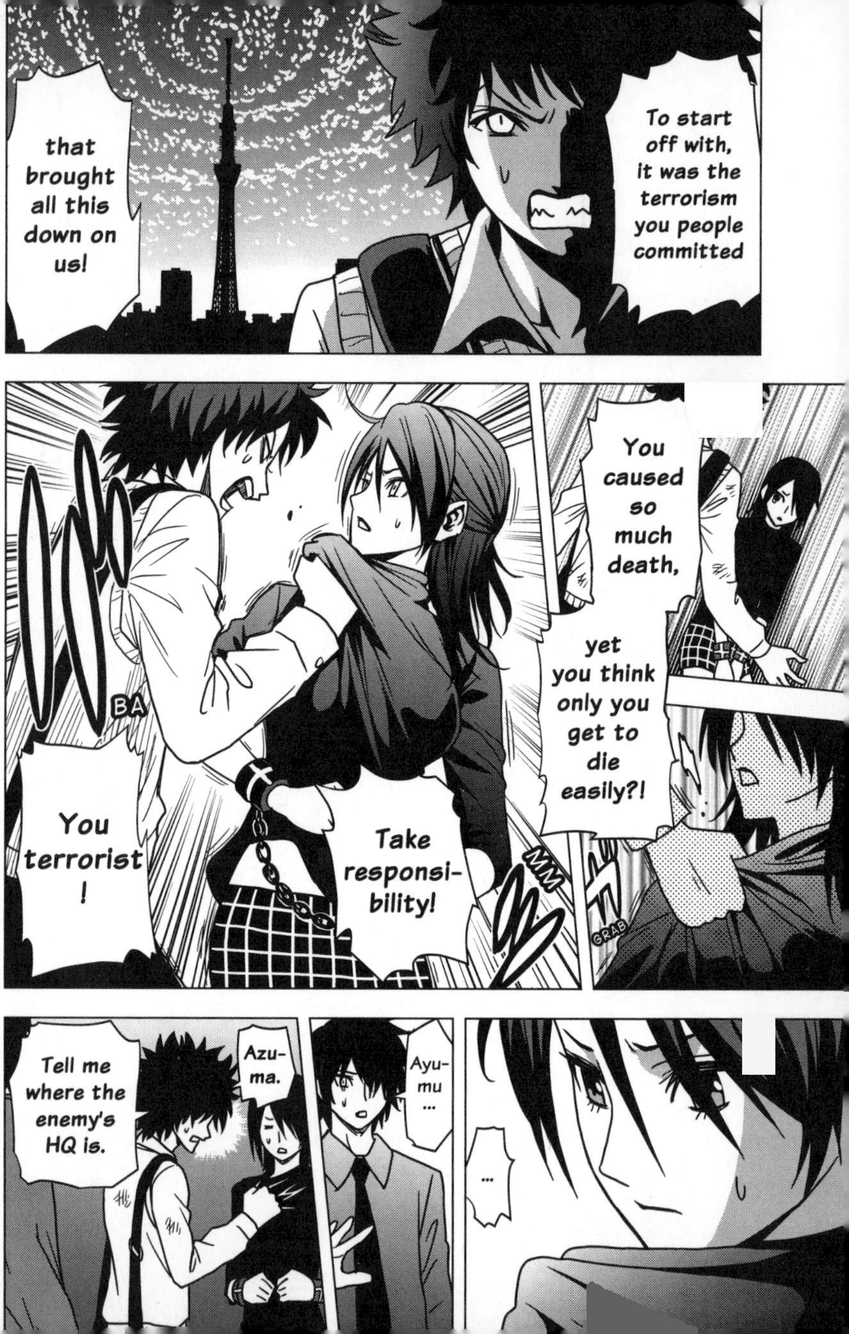
To start off with, it was the terrorism you people committed
that brought all this down on us!
You caused so much death,
yet you think only you get to die easily?!
GRAB
MM
Take responsi-bility!
You terrorist!
BA
...
Ayu-mu...
Azu-ma.
Tell me where the enemy's HQ is.

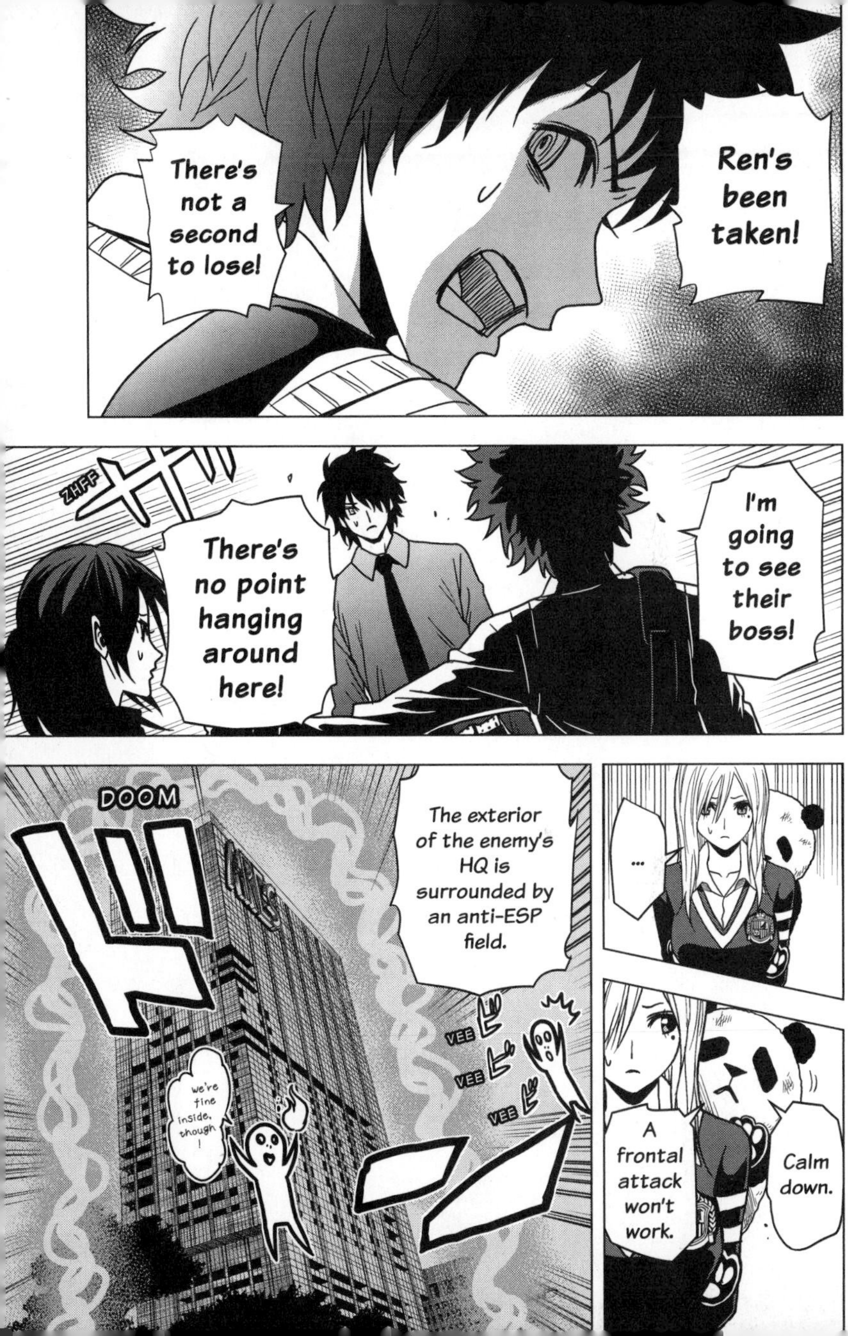
Ren's been taken!
There's not a second to lose!
I'm going to see their boss!
ZHFF
There's no point hanging around here!
...
Calm down.
A frontal attack won't work.
DOOM
The exterior of the enemy's HQ is surrounded by an anti-ESP field.
VEE
VEE
VEE
we're fine inside, though!

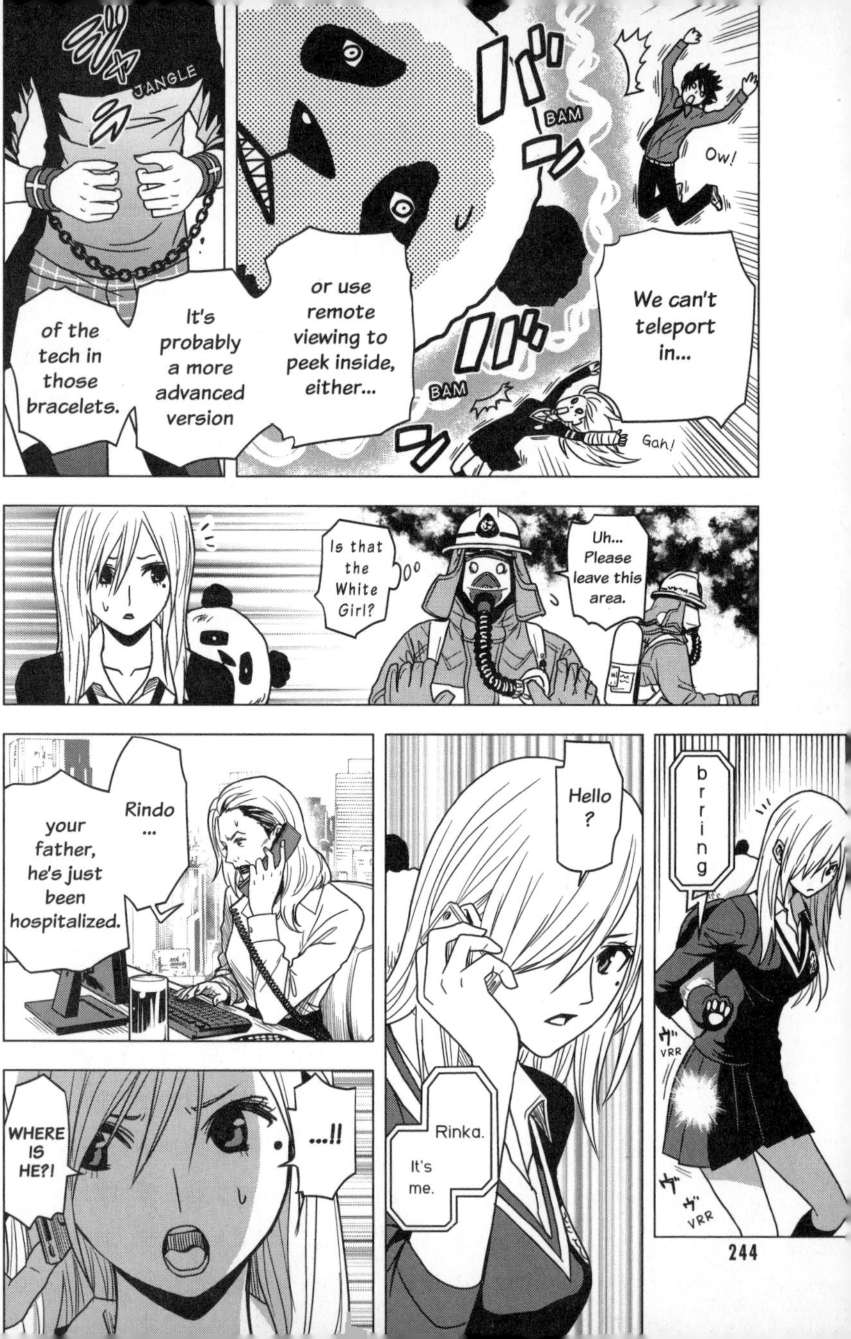
BAM
Ow!
We can't teleport in...
BAM
Gah!
or use remote viewing to peek inside, either...
It's probably a more advanced version
of the tech in those bracelets.
JANGLE
Uh... Please leave this area.
Is that the White Girl?
brring
VRR
VRR
Hello?
Rinka. It's me.
Rindo...
your father, he's just been hospitalized.
...!!
WHERE IS HE?!

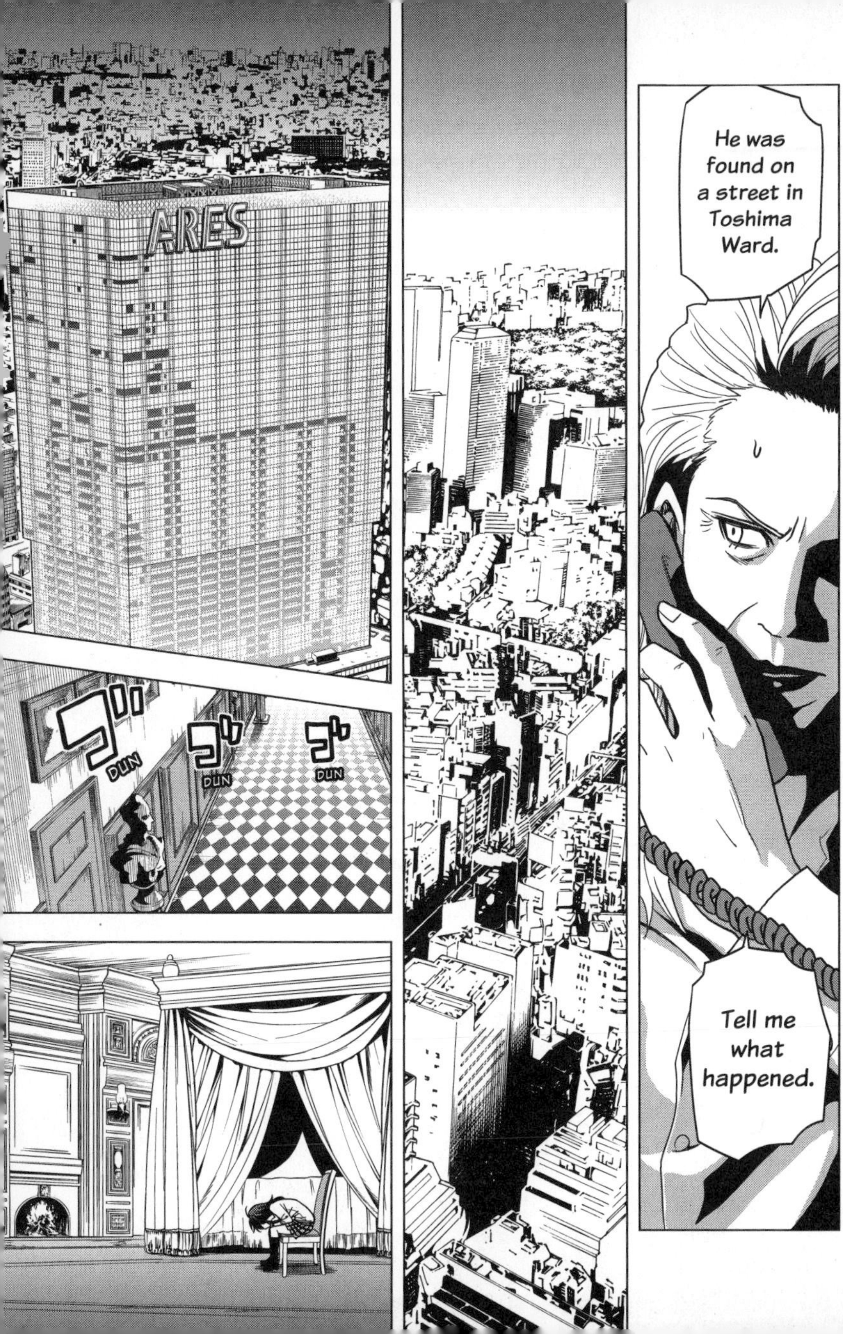
He was found on a street in Toshima Ward.
Tell me what happened.
ARES
DUN
DUN
DUN

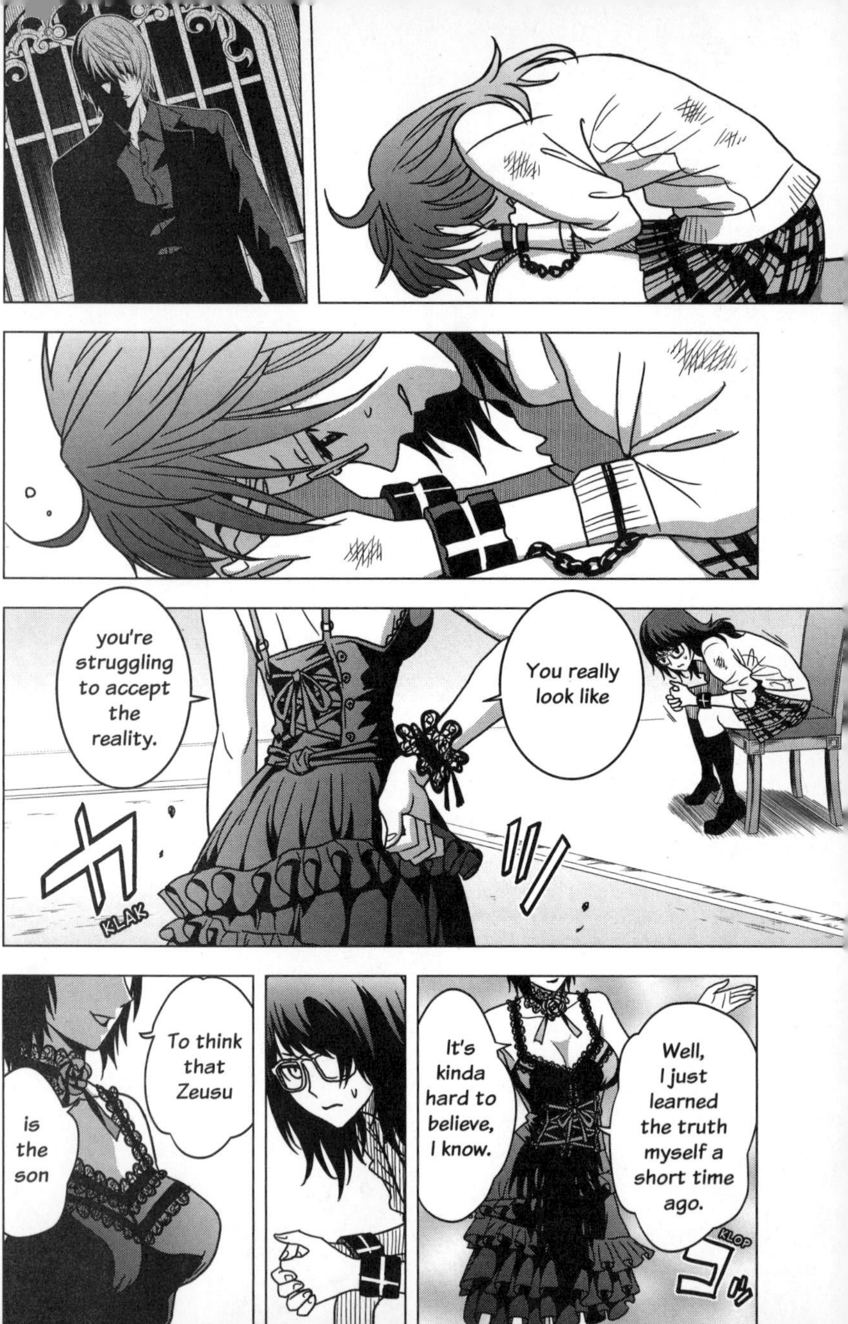
You really look like
you're struggling to accept the reality.
KLAK
Well, I just learned the truth myself a short time ago.
KLOP
It's kinda hard to believe, I know.
To think that Zeusu
is the son

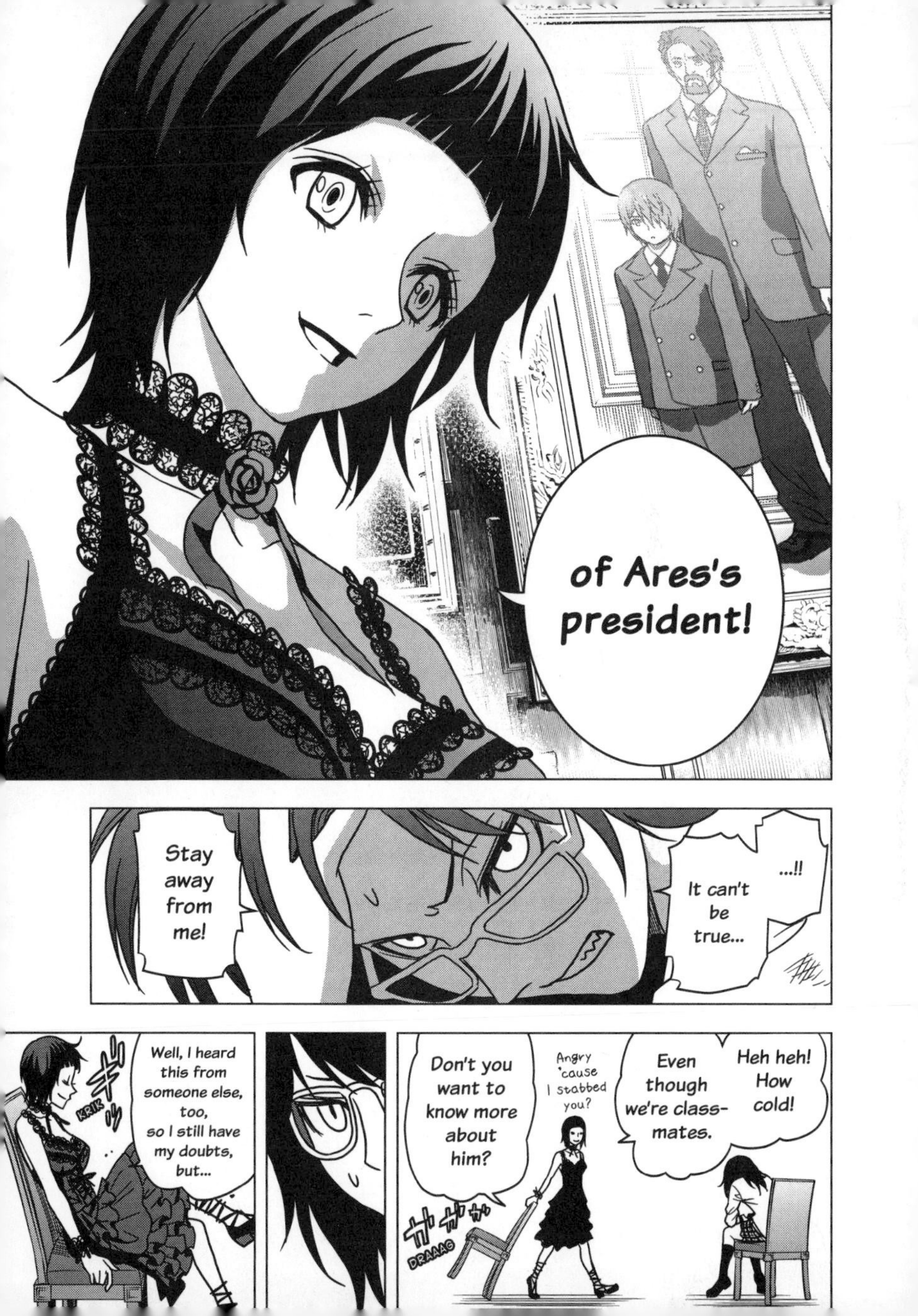
of Ares's president!
...!! It can't be true...
Stay away from me!
Heh heh! How cold!
Even though we're class-mates.
Angry 'cause I stabbed you?
Don't you want to know more about him?
DRAAAG
Well, I heard this from someone else, too, so I still have my doubts, but...
KRIK

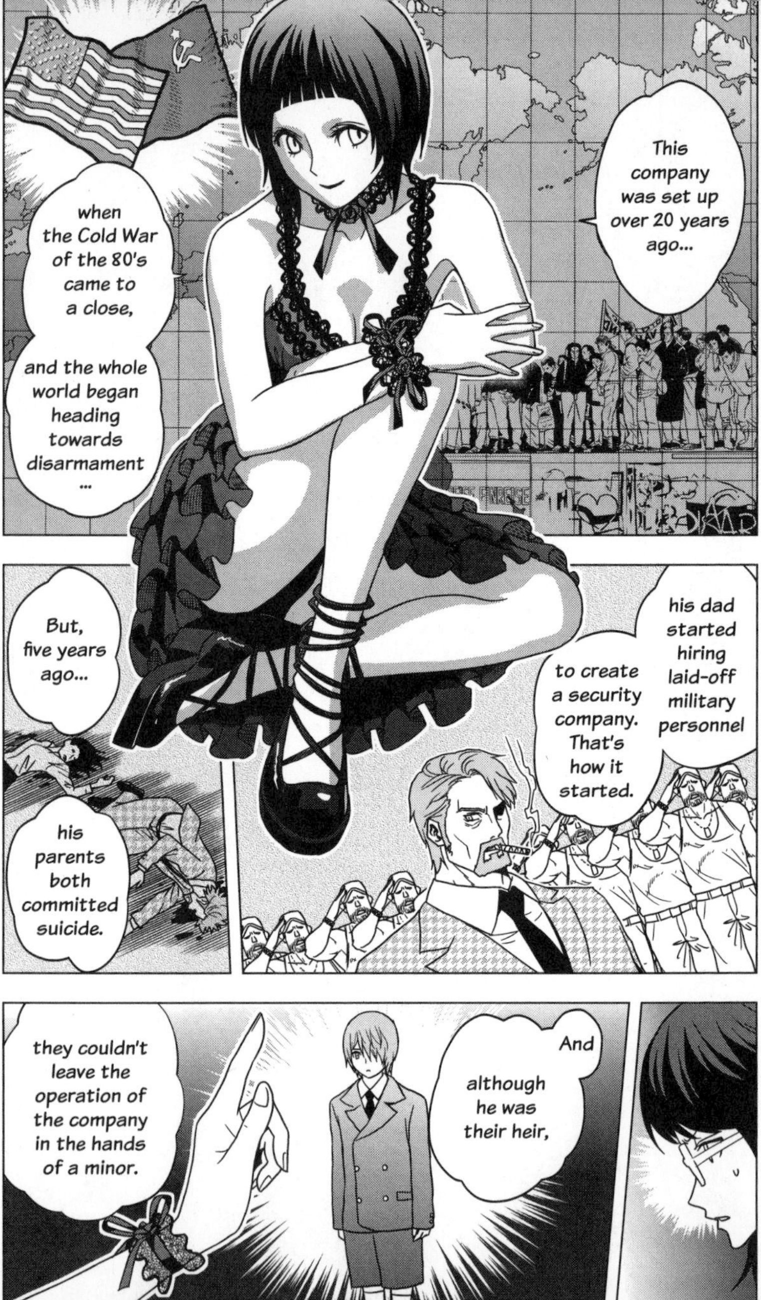

This company was set up over 20 years ago...
when the Cold War of the 80's came to a close,
and the whole world began heading towards disarmament ...
his dad started hiring laid-off military personnel
to create a security company. That's how it started.
But, five years ago...
his parents both committed suicide.
And
although he was their heir,
they couldn't leave the operation of the company in the hands of a minor.

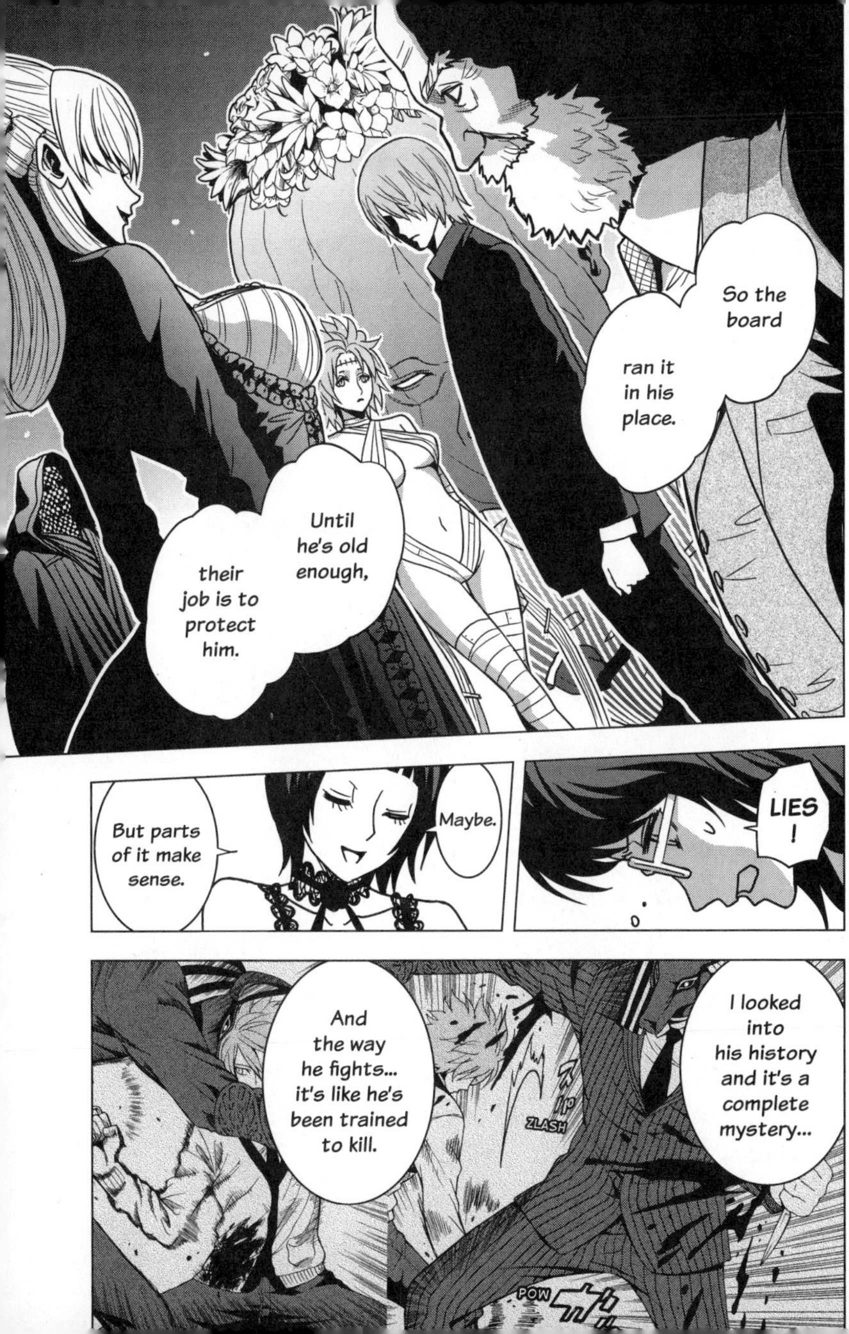
So the board ran it in his place.
Until he's old enough, their job is to protect him.
LIES!
Maybe.
But parts of it make sense.
I looked into his history and it's a complete mystery...
And the way he fights... it's like he's been trained to kill.
ZLASH
POW

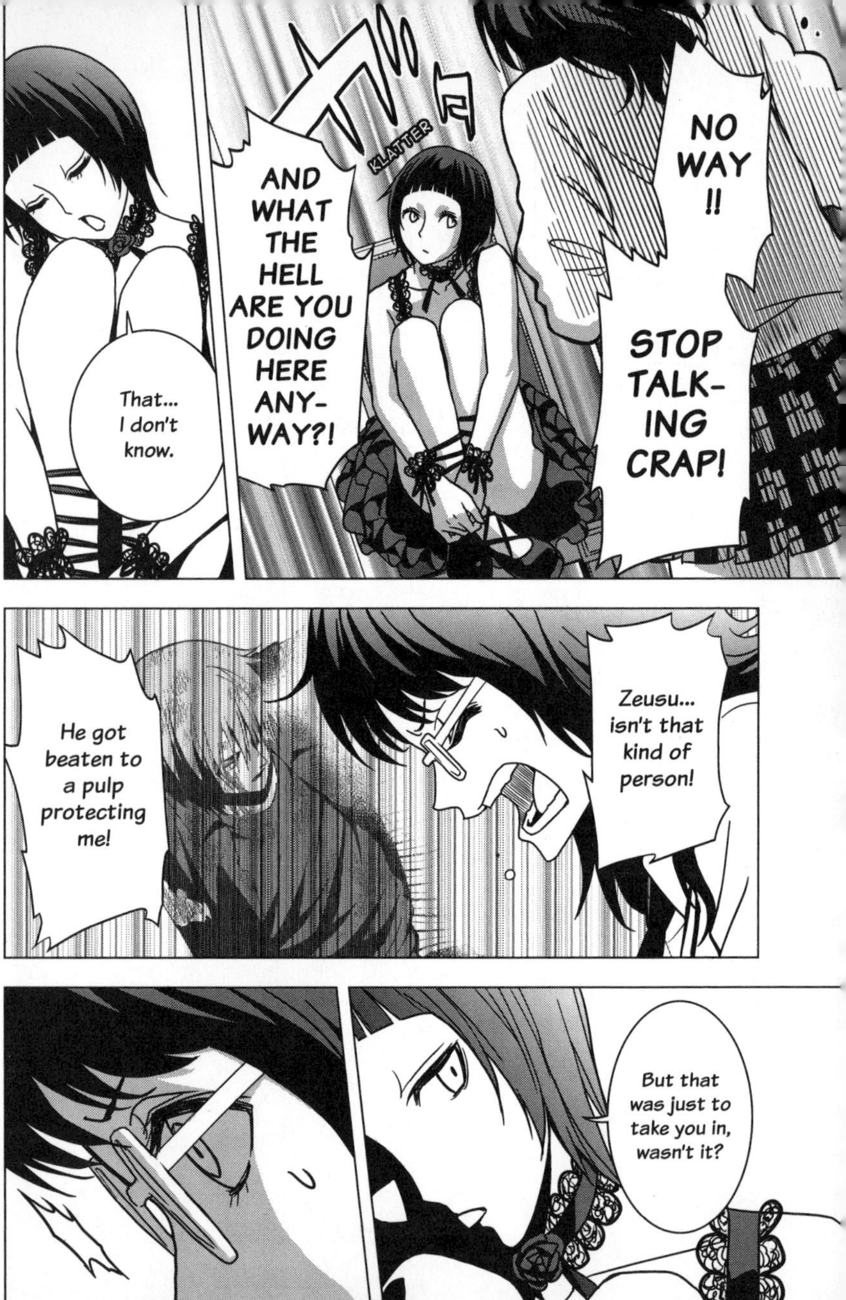
NO WAY !!
STOP TALK-ING CRAP!
KLATTER
AND WHAT THE HELL ARE YOU DOING HERE ANY-WAY?!
That... I don't know.
Zeusu... isn't that kind of person!
He got beaten to a pulp protecting me!
But that was just to take you in, wasn't it?

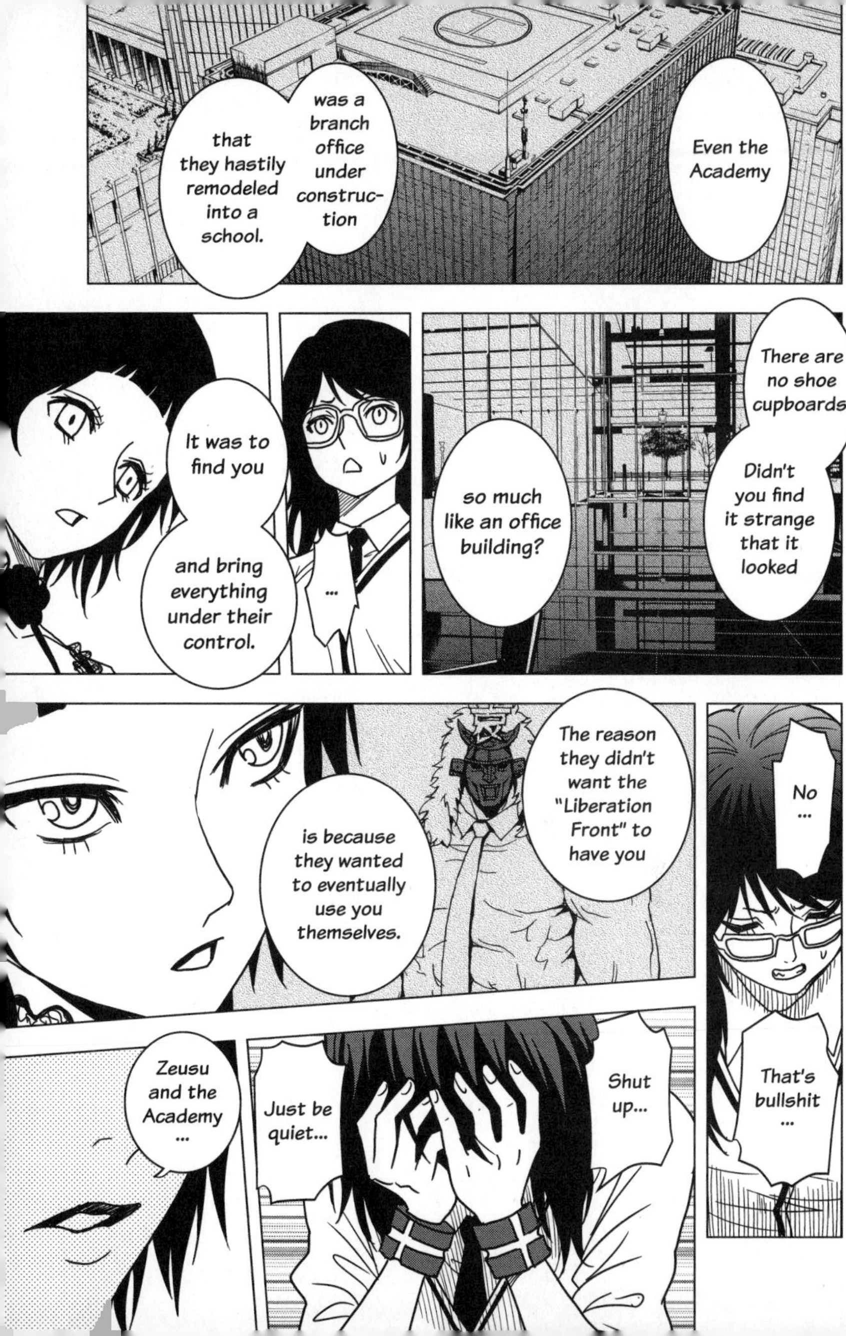
Even the Academy
was a branch office under construction
that they hastily remodeled into a school.
There are no shoe cupboards.
Didn't you find it strange that it looked
so much like an office building?
...
It was to find you
and bring everything under their control.
No ...
That's bullshit ...
The reason they didn't want the "Liberation Front" to have you
is because they wanted to eventually use you themselves.
Shut up...
Just be quiet...
Zeusu and the Academy ...

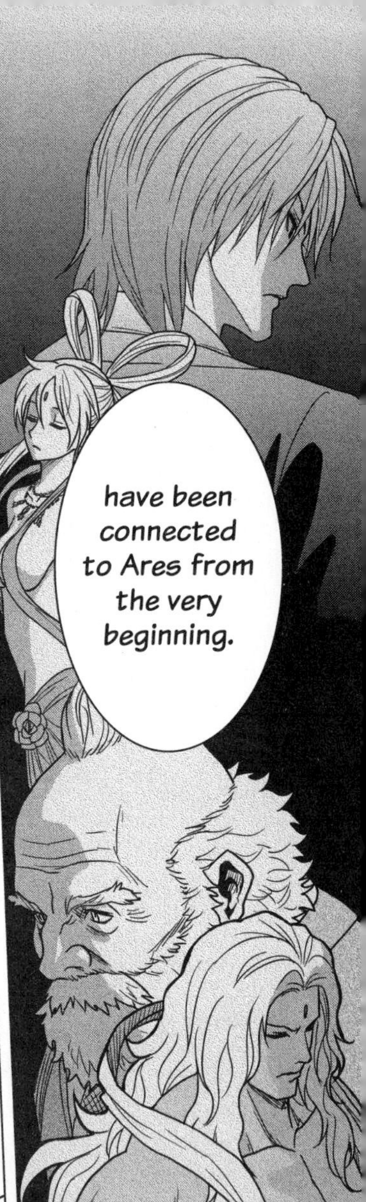
have been connected to Ares from the very beginning.

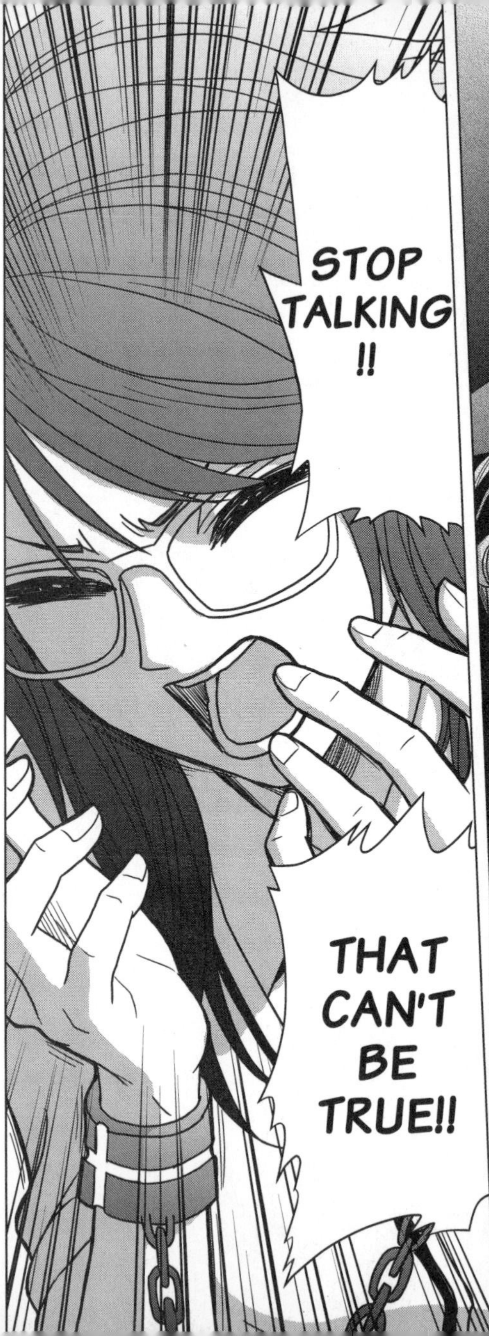
STOP TALKING!!
THAT CAN'T BE TRUE!!

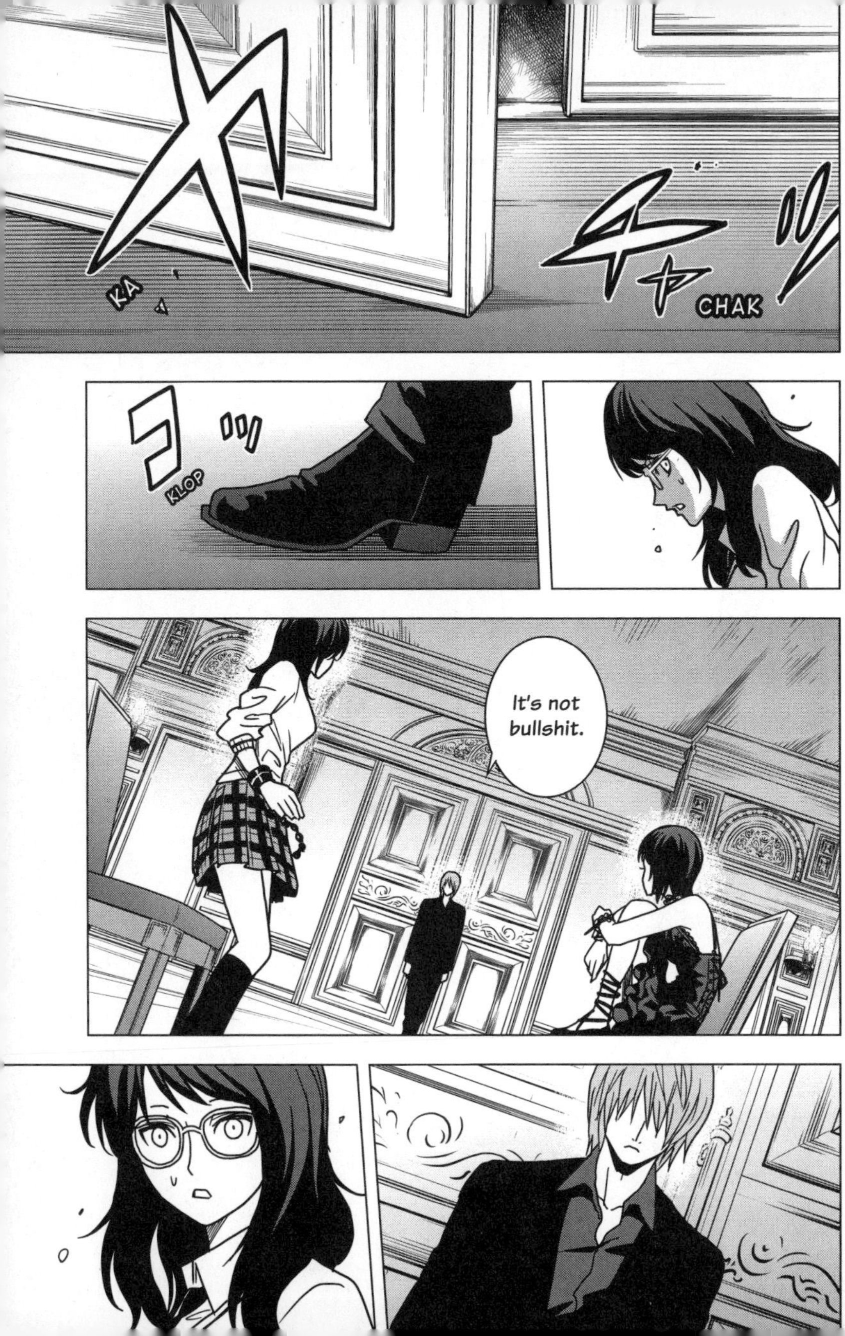
CHAK
KA
KLOP
It's not bullshit.

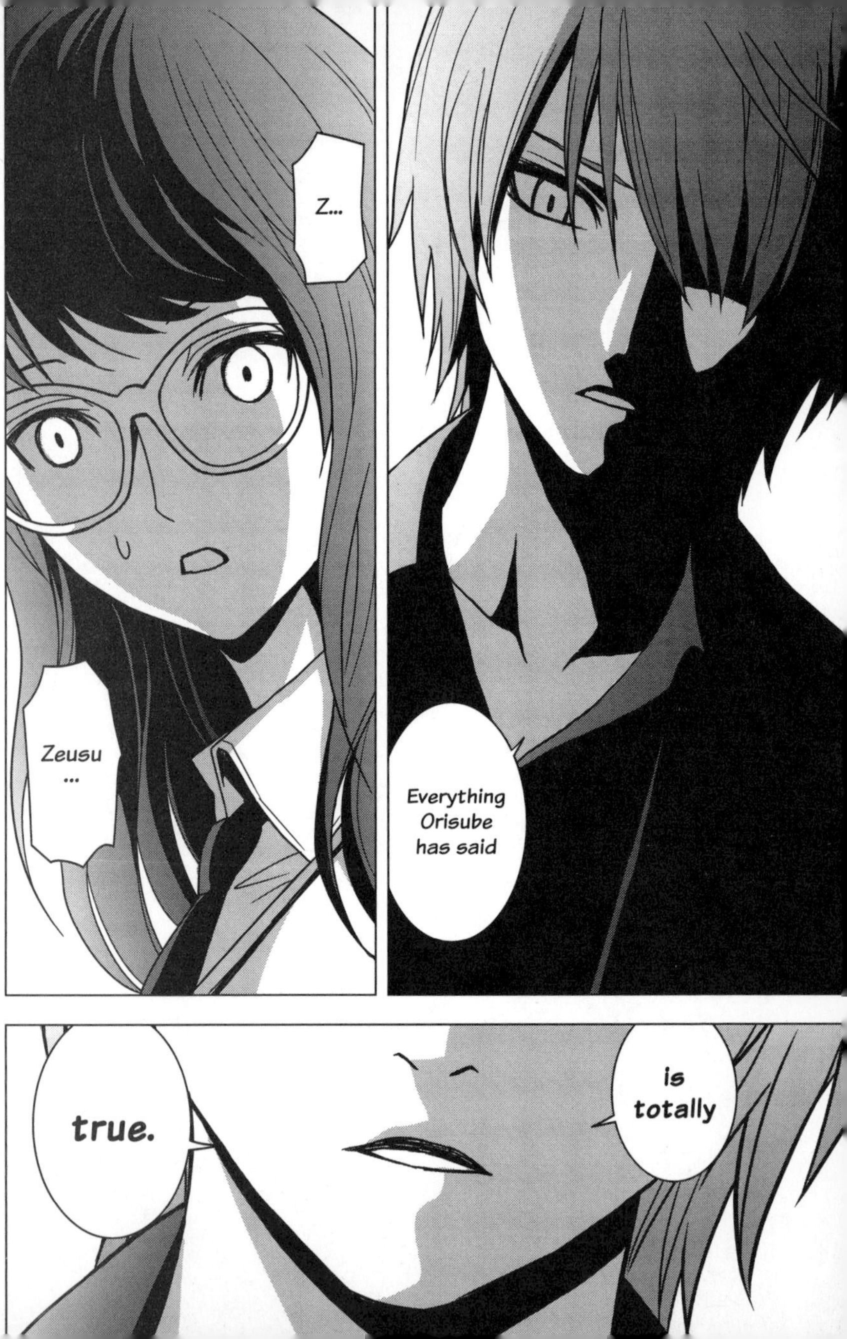
Everything Orisube has said
Z...
Zeusu ...
is totally
true.

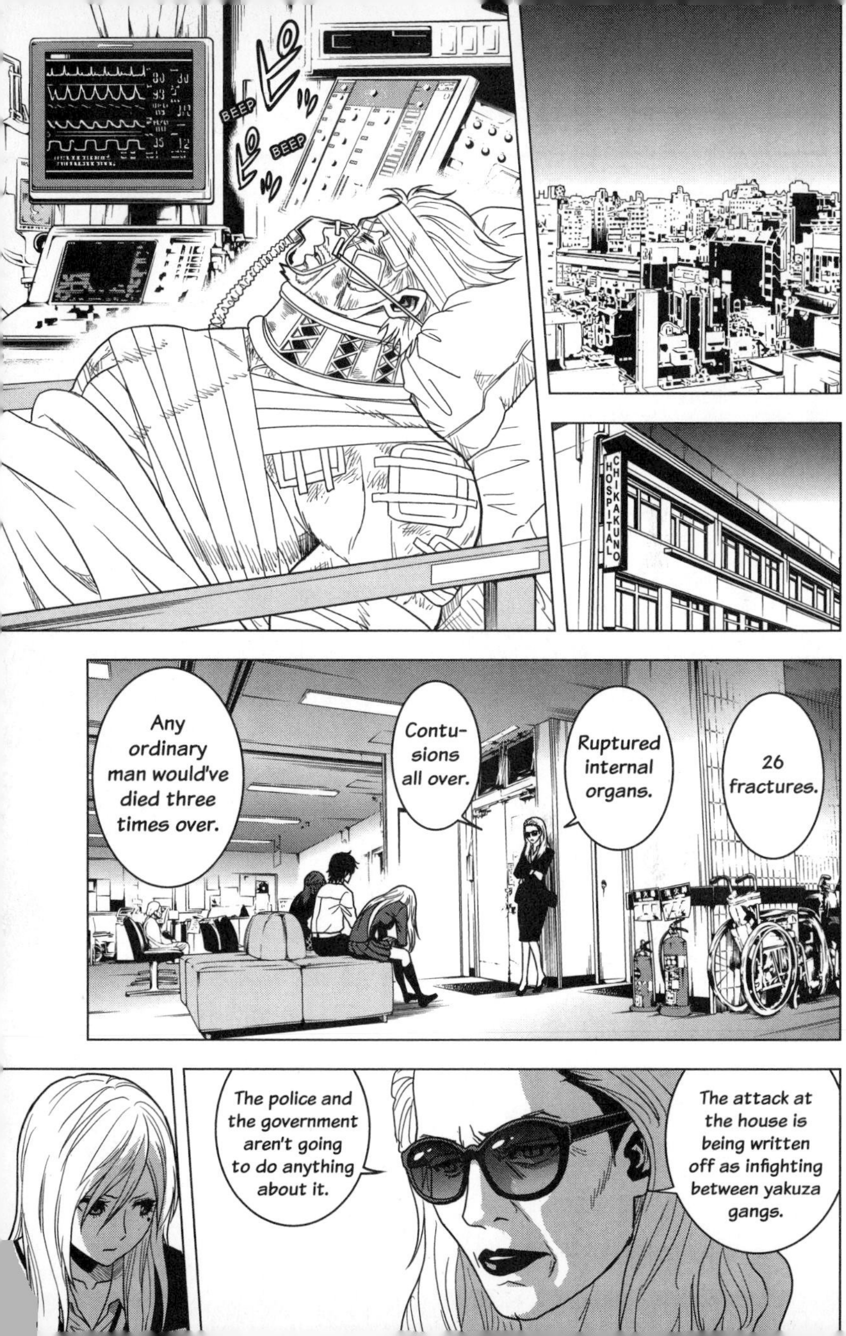
CHIKAKUNO HOSPITAL
BEEP
BEEP
26 fractures.
Ruptured internal organs.
Contusions all over.
Any ordinary man would've died three times over.
The attack at the house is being written off as infighting between yakuza gangs.
The police and the government aren't going to do anything about it.

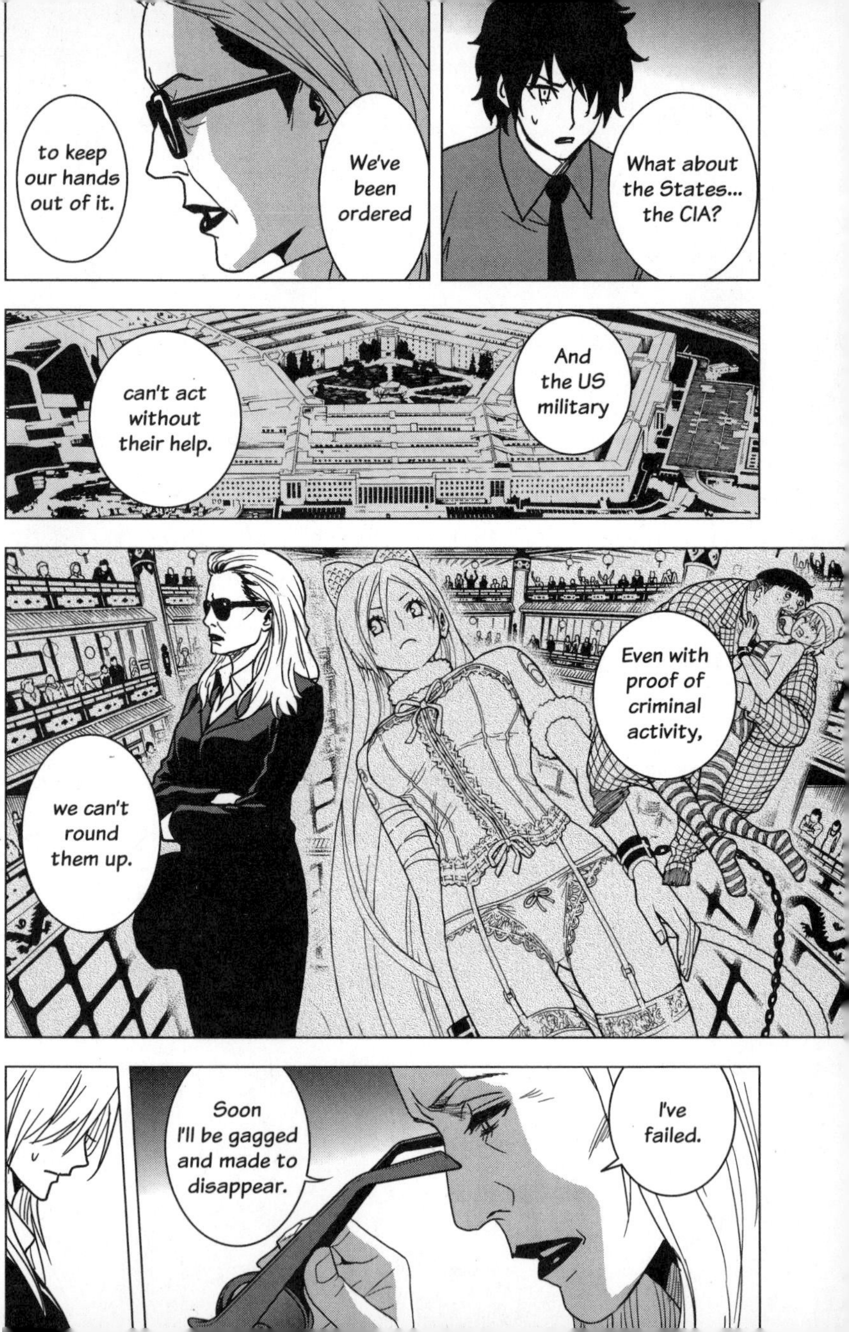
What about the States... the CIA?
We've been ordered
to keep our hands out of it.
And the US military
can't act without their help.
Even with proof of criminal activity,
we can't round them up.
I've failed.
Soon I'll be gagged and made to disappear.

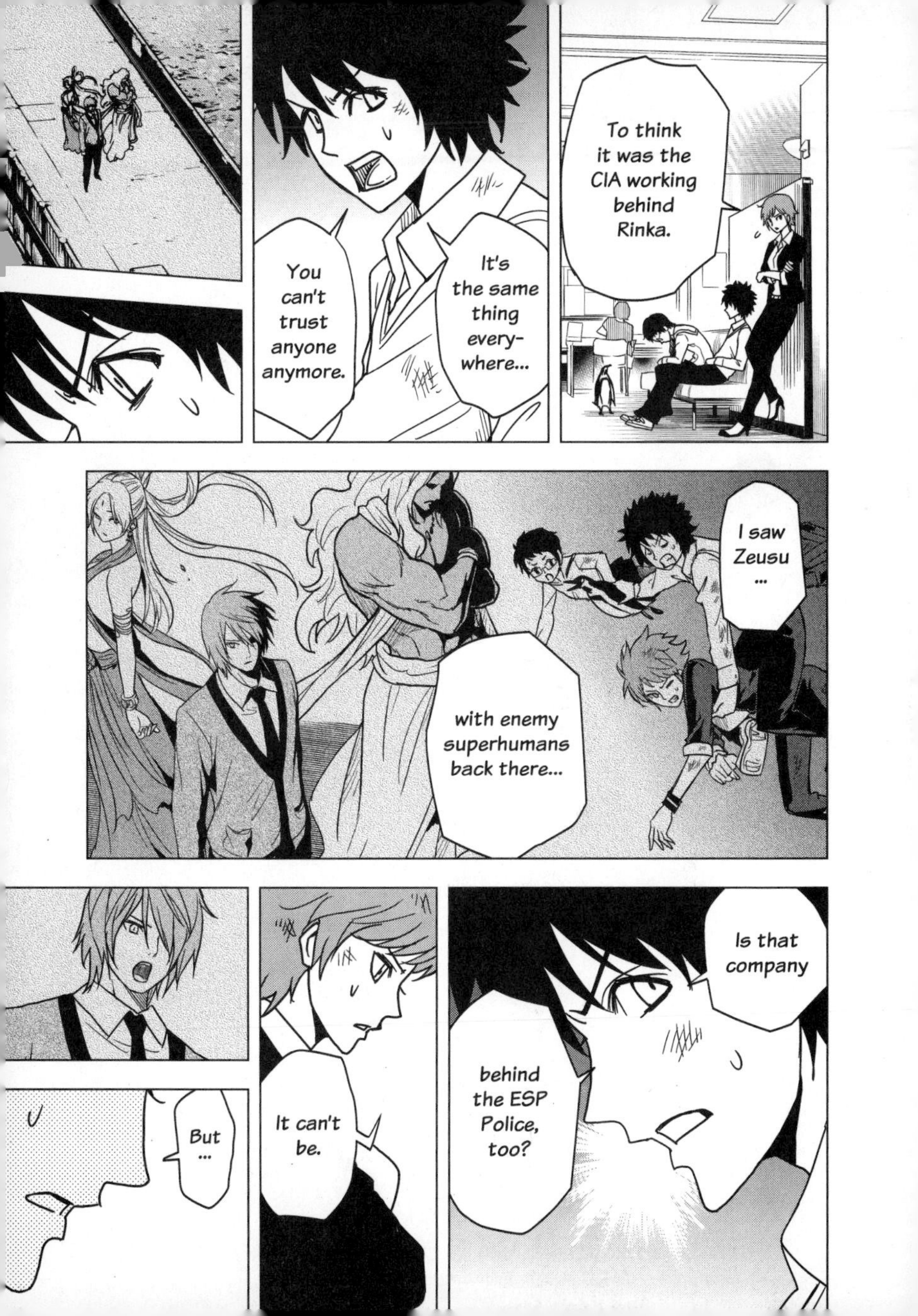
To think it was the CIA working behind Rinka.
It's the same thing every-where...
You can't trust anyone anymore.
I saw Zeusu ...
with enemy superhumans back there...
Is that company
behind the ESP Police, too?
It can't be.
But ...

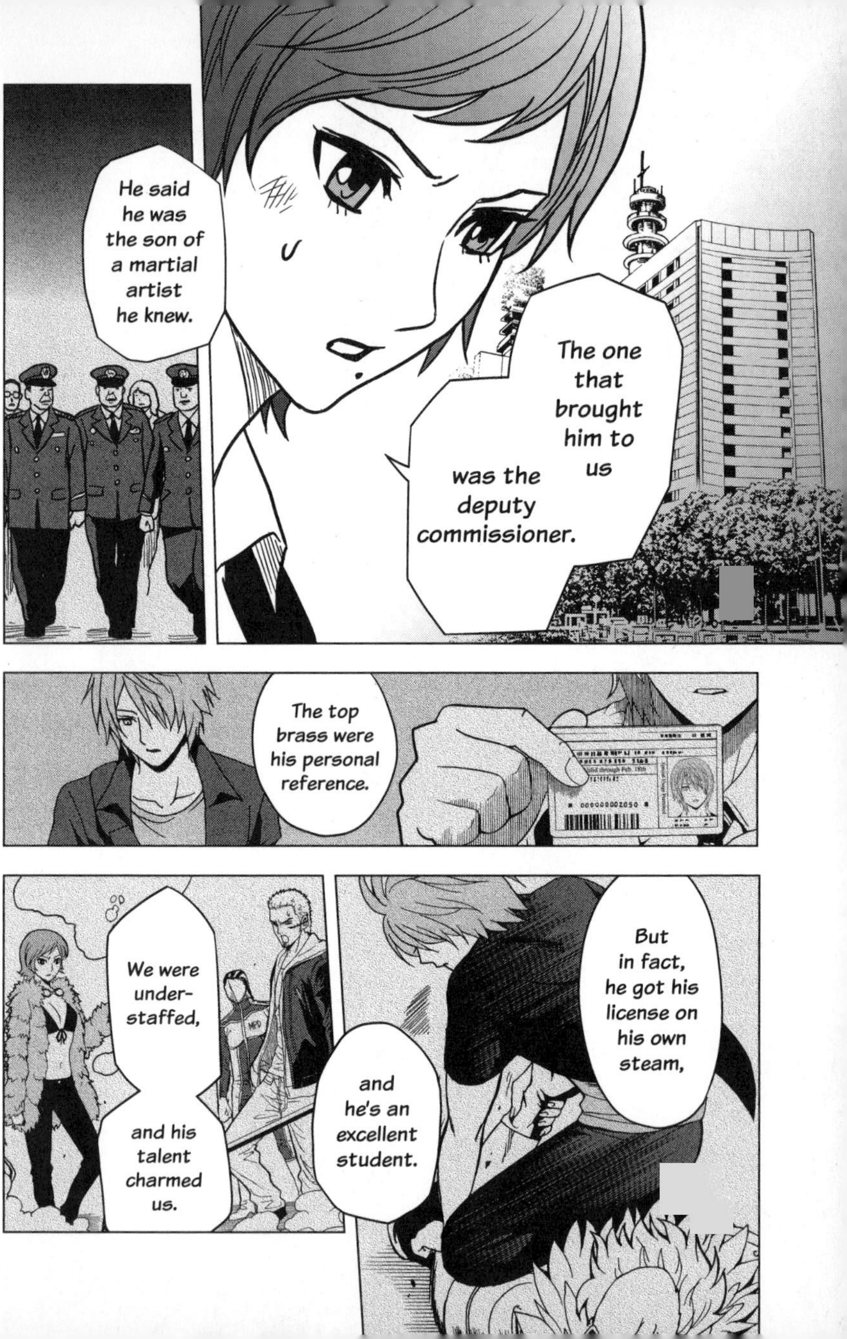
The one that brought him to us
was the deputy commissioner.
He said he was the son of a martial artist he knew.
The top brass were his personal reference.
But in fact, he got his license on his own steam,
and he's an excellent student.
We were under-staffed,
and his talent charmed us.

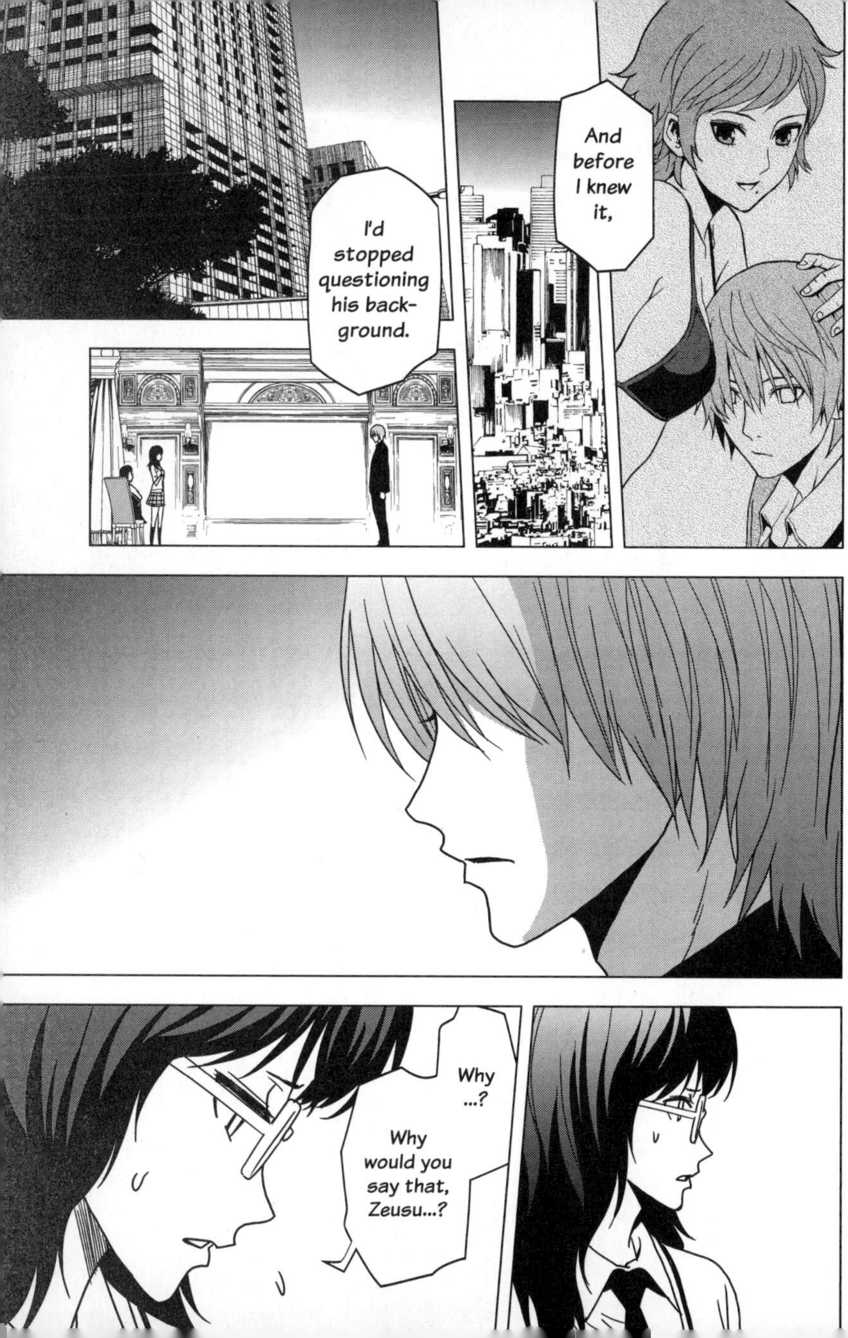
And before I knew it,
I'd stopped questioning his back-ground.
Why ...?
Why would you say that, Zeusu...?

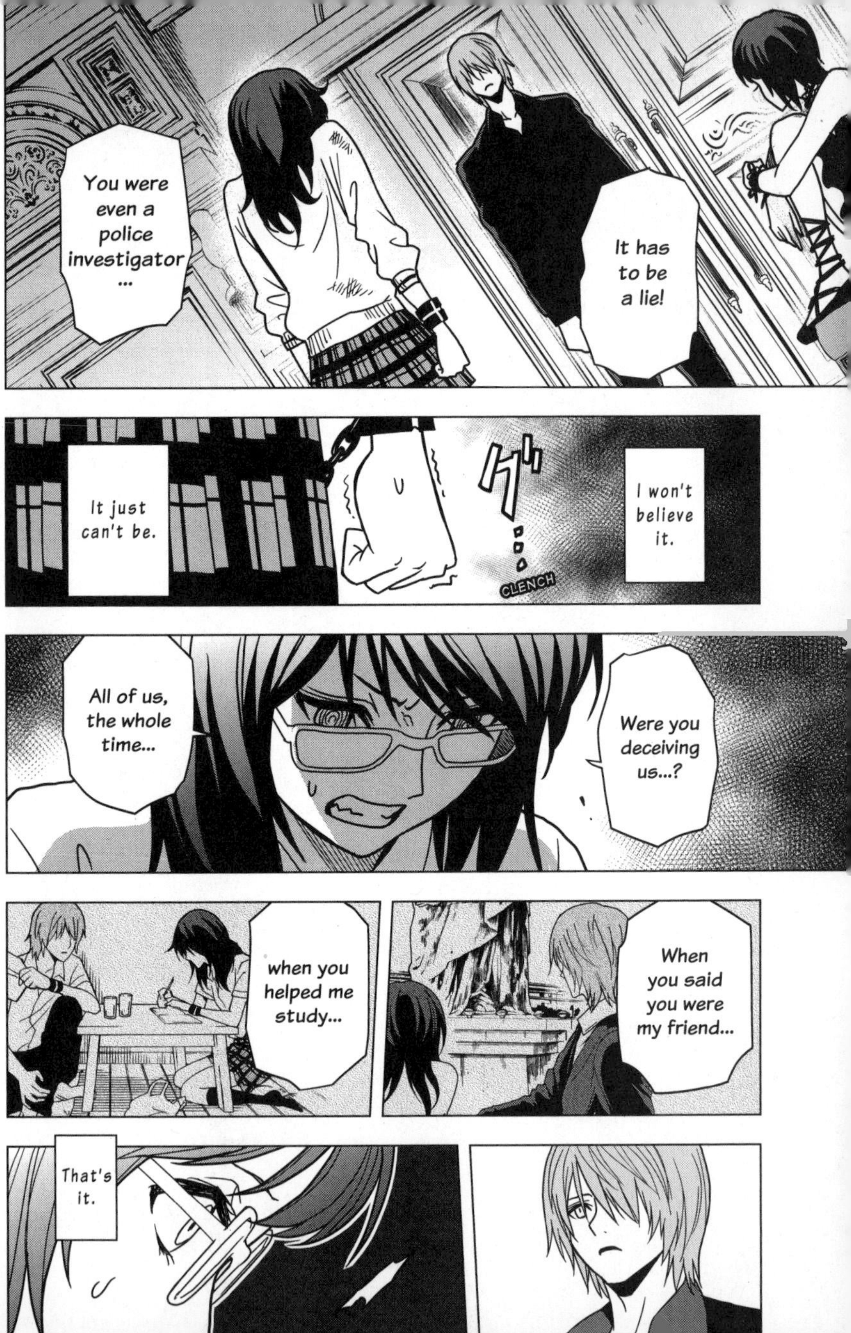
It has to be a lie!
You were even a police investigator...
I won't believe it.
グッ
CLENCH
It just can't be.
Were you deceiving us...?
All of us, the whole time...
When you said you were my friend...
when you helped me study...
That's it.

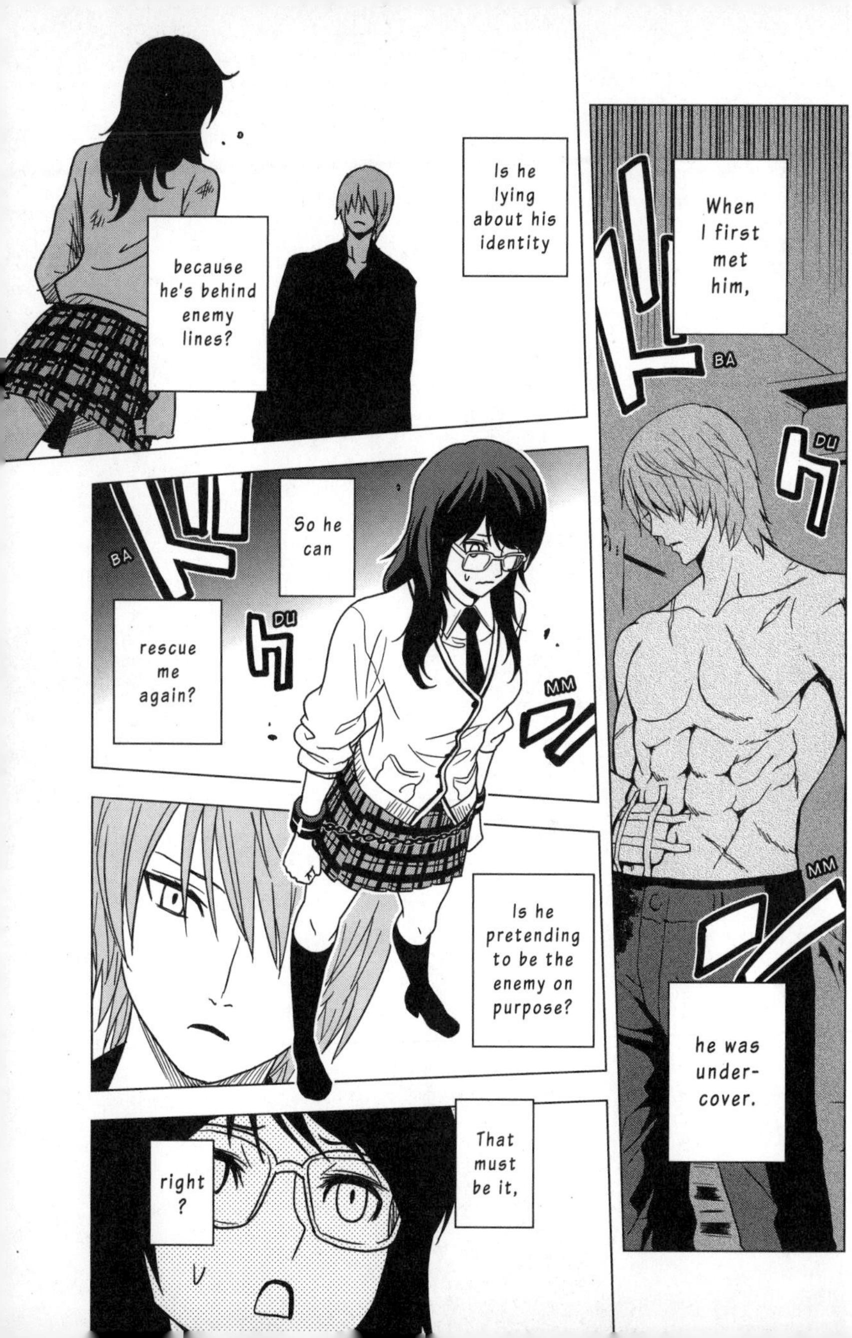
When I first met him,
BA
DU
MM
he was under-cover.
Is he lying about his identity
because he's behind enemy lines?
So he can
BA
rescue me again?
DU
MM
Is he pretending to be the enemy on purpose?
That must be it,
right?

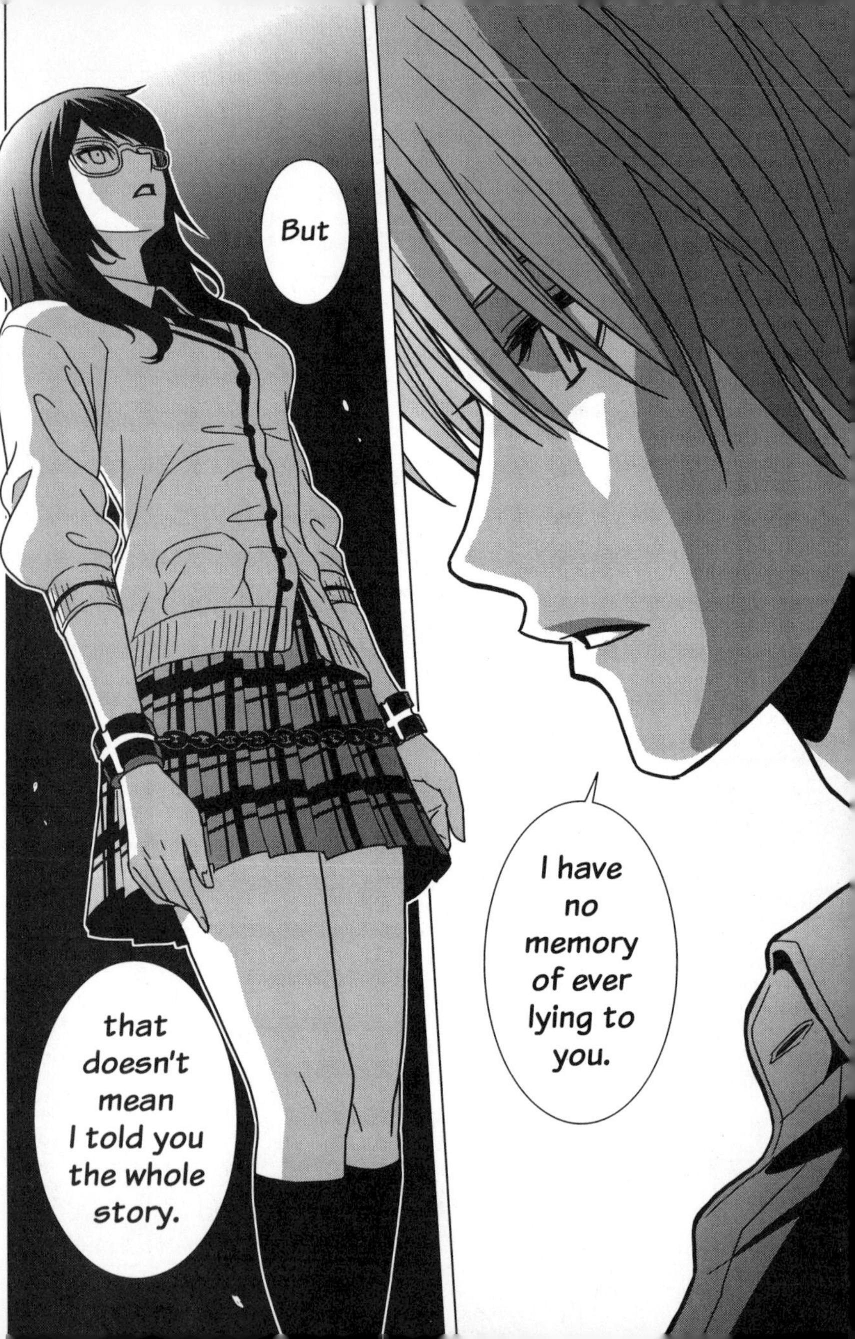
I have no memory of ever lying to you.
But
that doesn't mean I told you the whole story.

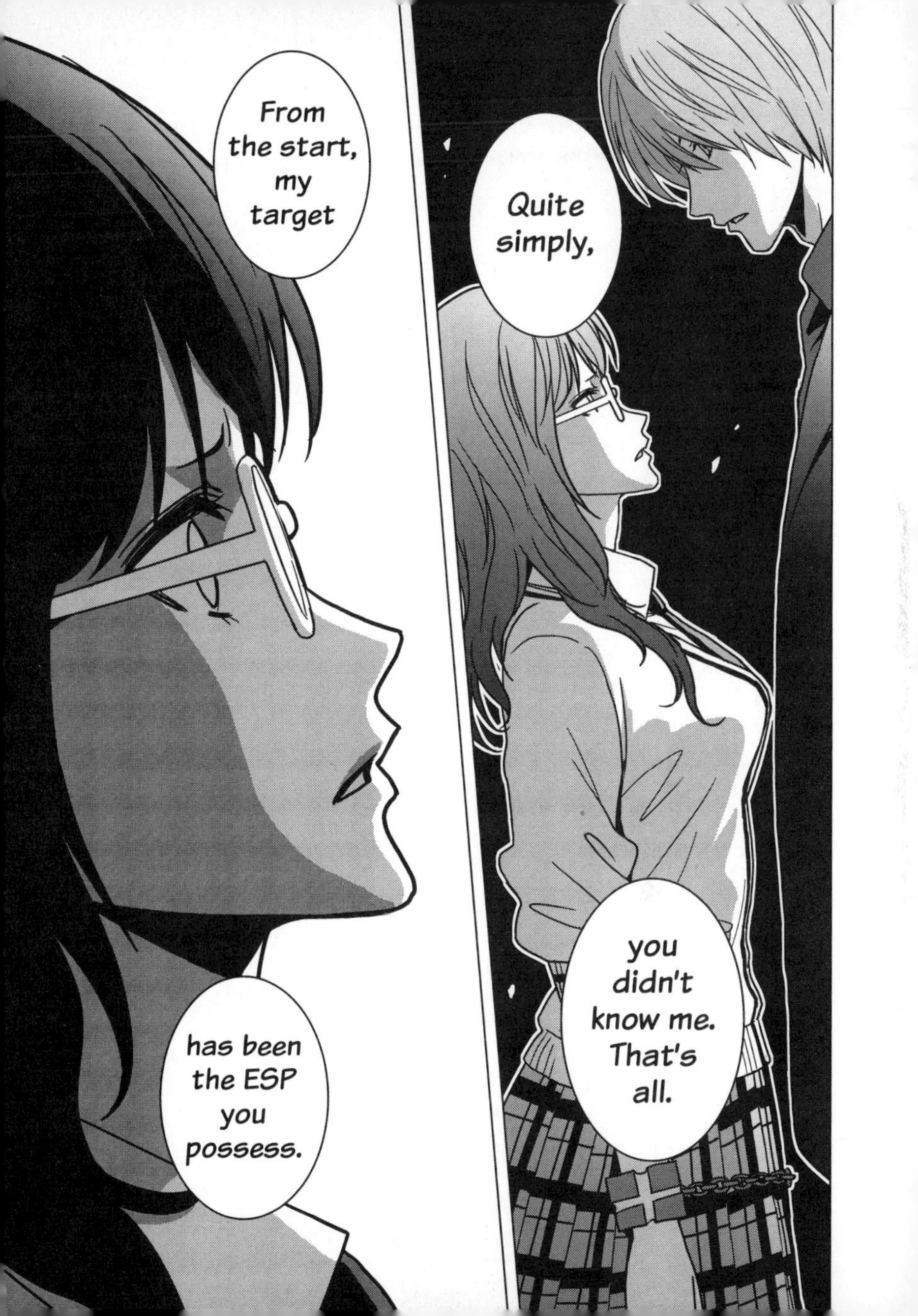
Quite simply,
you didn't know me. That's all.
From the start, my target
has been the ESP you possess.

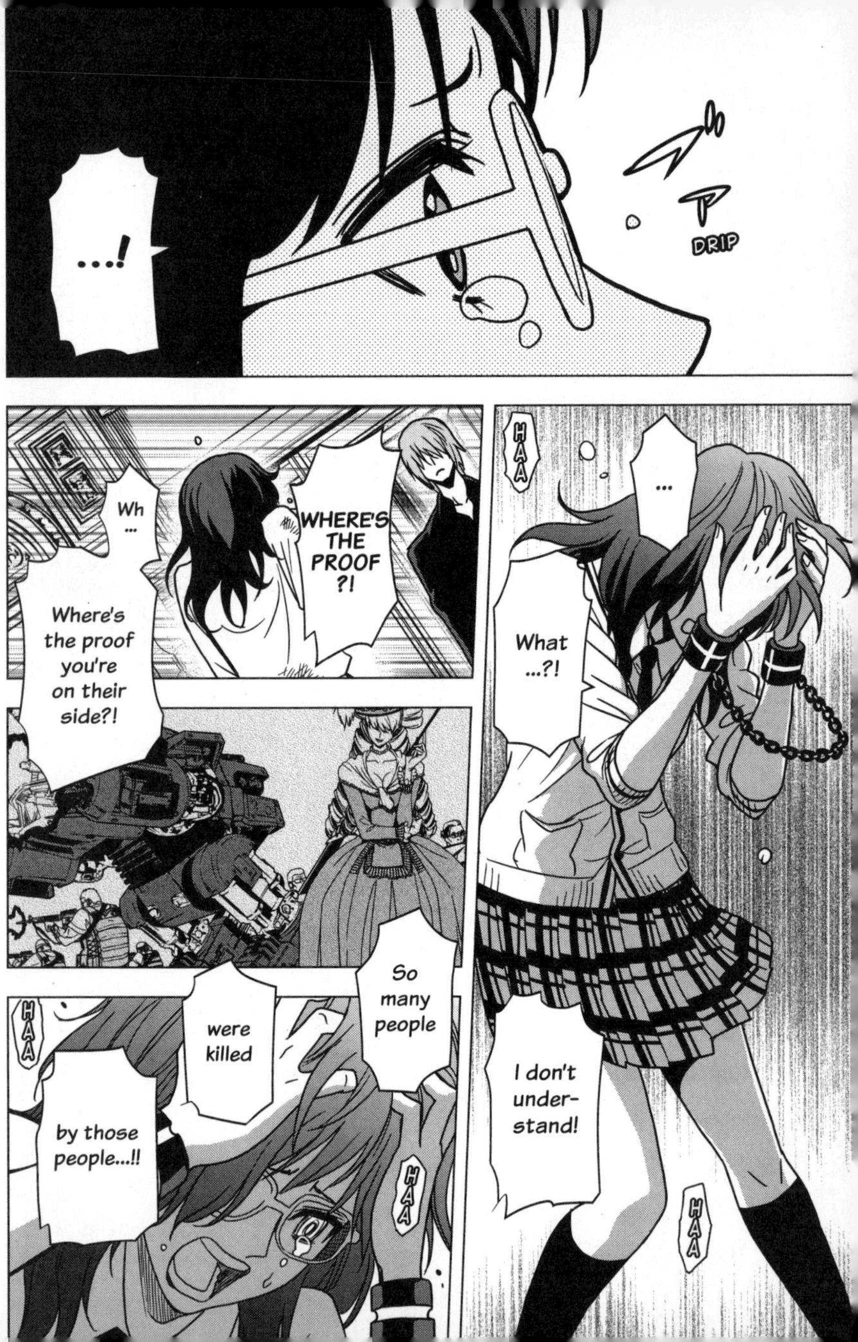
...!
DRIP
HAA
...
What ...?!
I don't under-stand!
HAA
WHERE'S THE PROOF ?!
Wh ...
Where's the proof you're on their side?!
HAA
So many people
were killed
by those people...!!
HAA

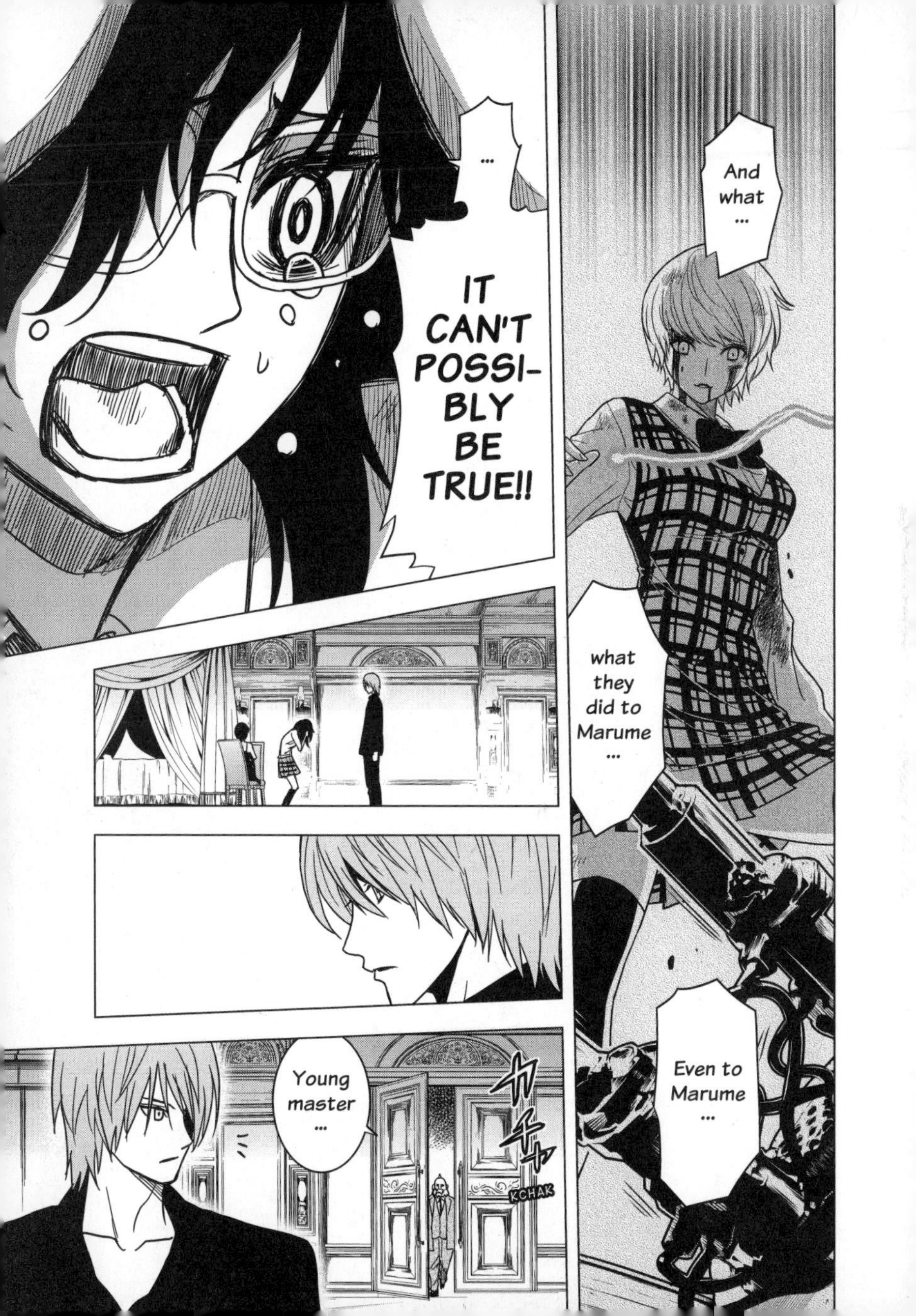

And what ...
what they did to Marume ...
Even to Marume ...
...
IT CAN'T POSSIBLY BE TRUE!!
Young master ...
KCHAK

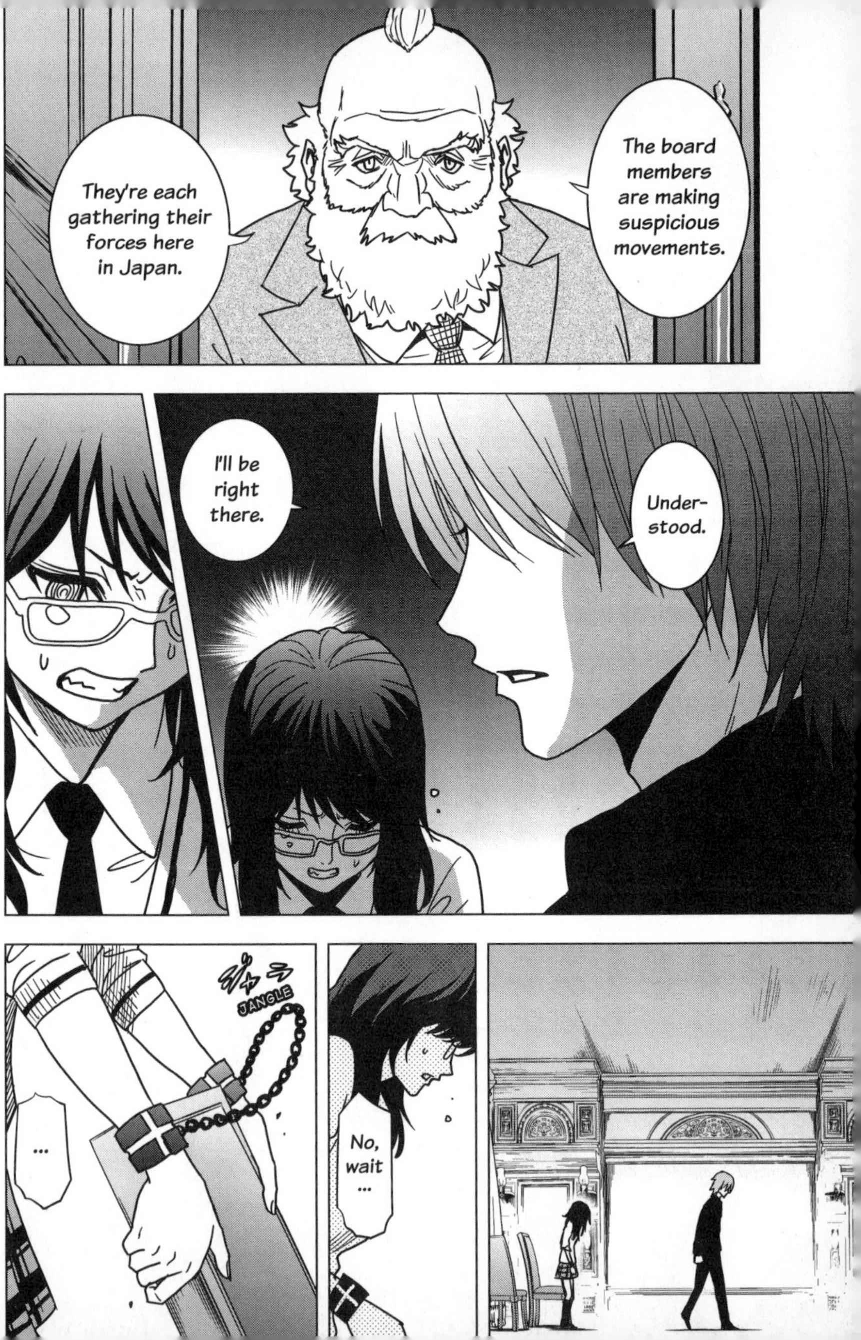
The board members are making suspicious movements.
They're each gathering their forces here in Japan.
Under-stood.
I'll be right there.
No, wait ...
ジャラ
JANGLE
...

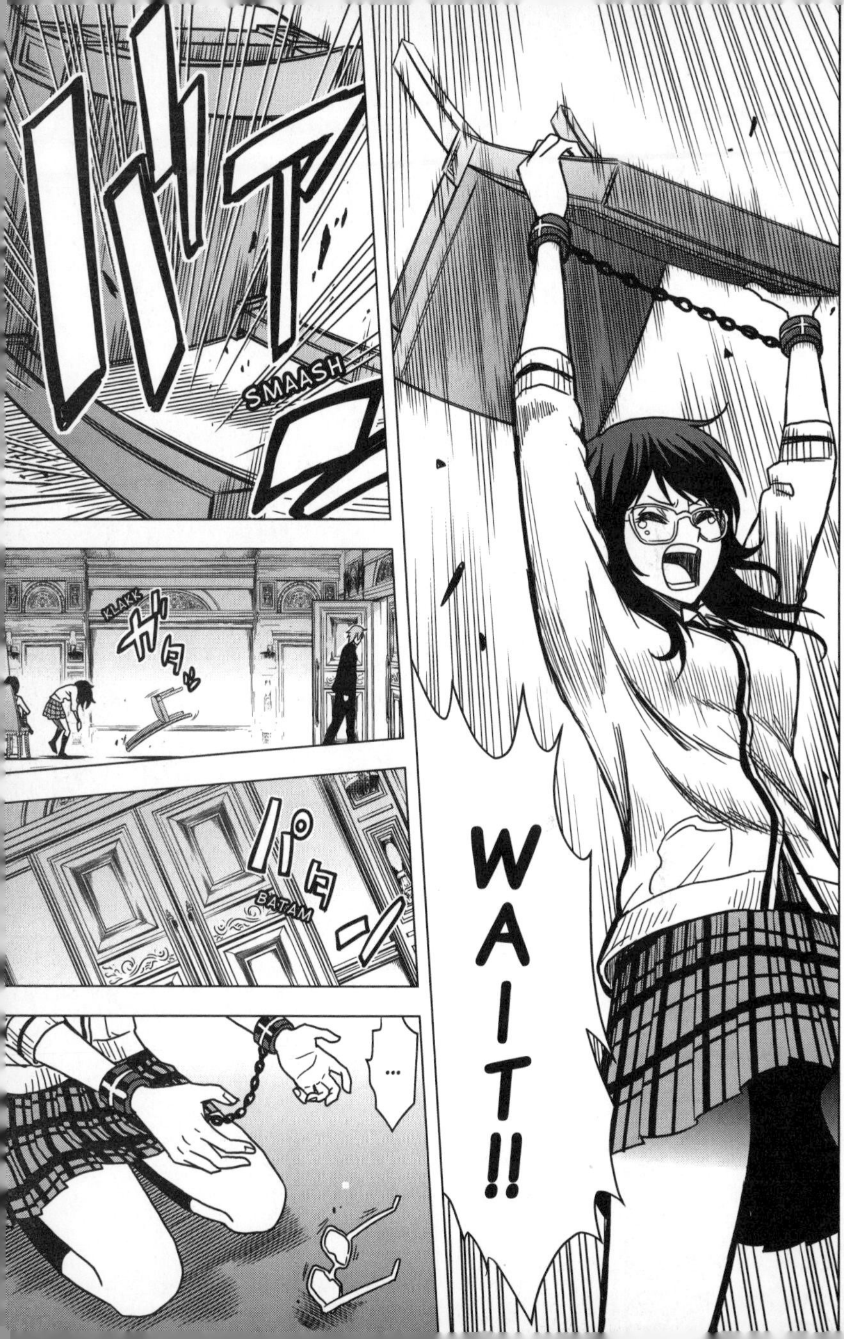
WAIT!!
SMAASH
KLAKK
BATAM
...

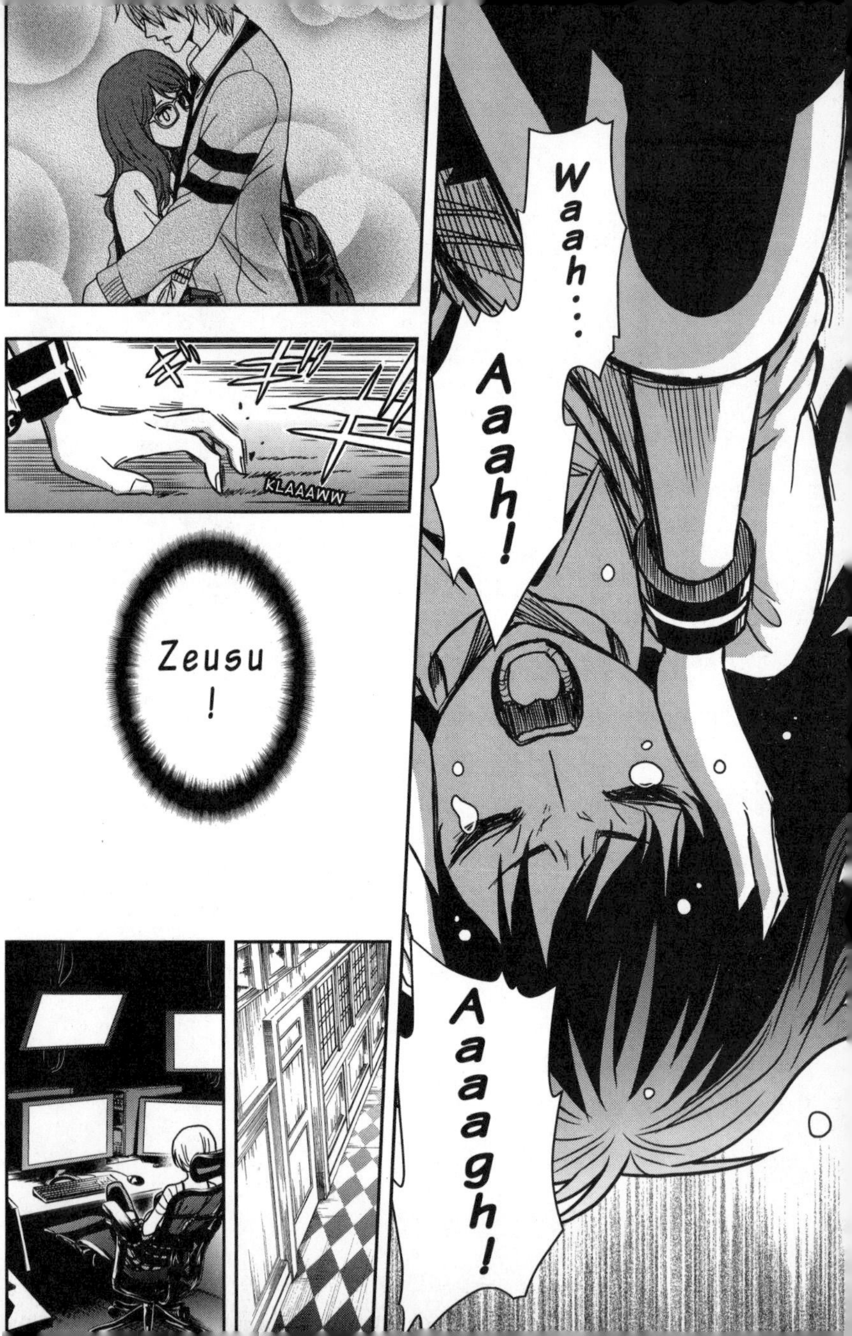
Waaah... Aaaah!
Aaaaagh!
KLAAAWW
Zeusu!

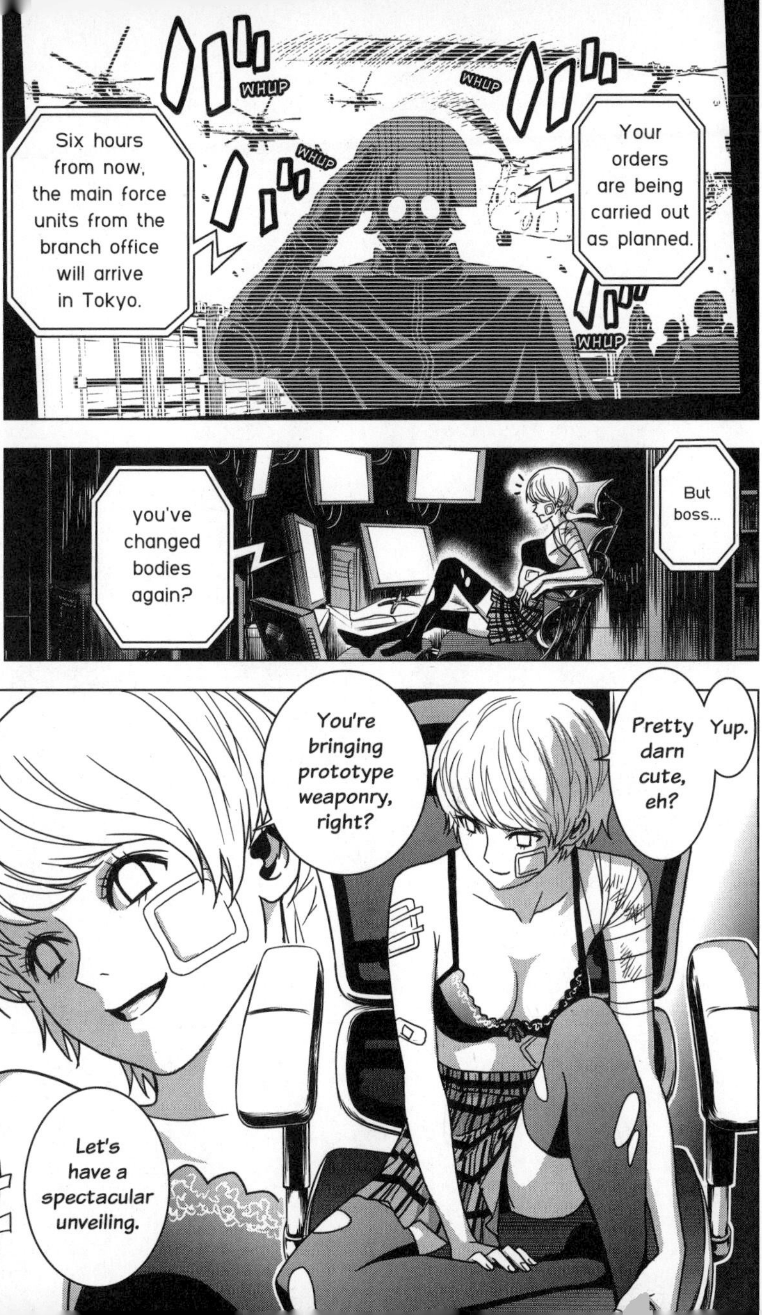
WHUP
WHUP
WHUP
WHUP
Your orders are being carried out as planned.
Six hours from now, the main force units from the branch office will arrive in Tokyo.
But boss...
you've changed bodies again?
Yup.
Pretty darn cute, eh?
You're bringing prototype weaponry, right?
Let's have a spectacular unveiling.

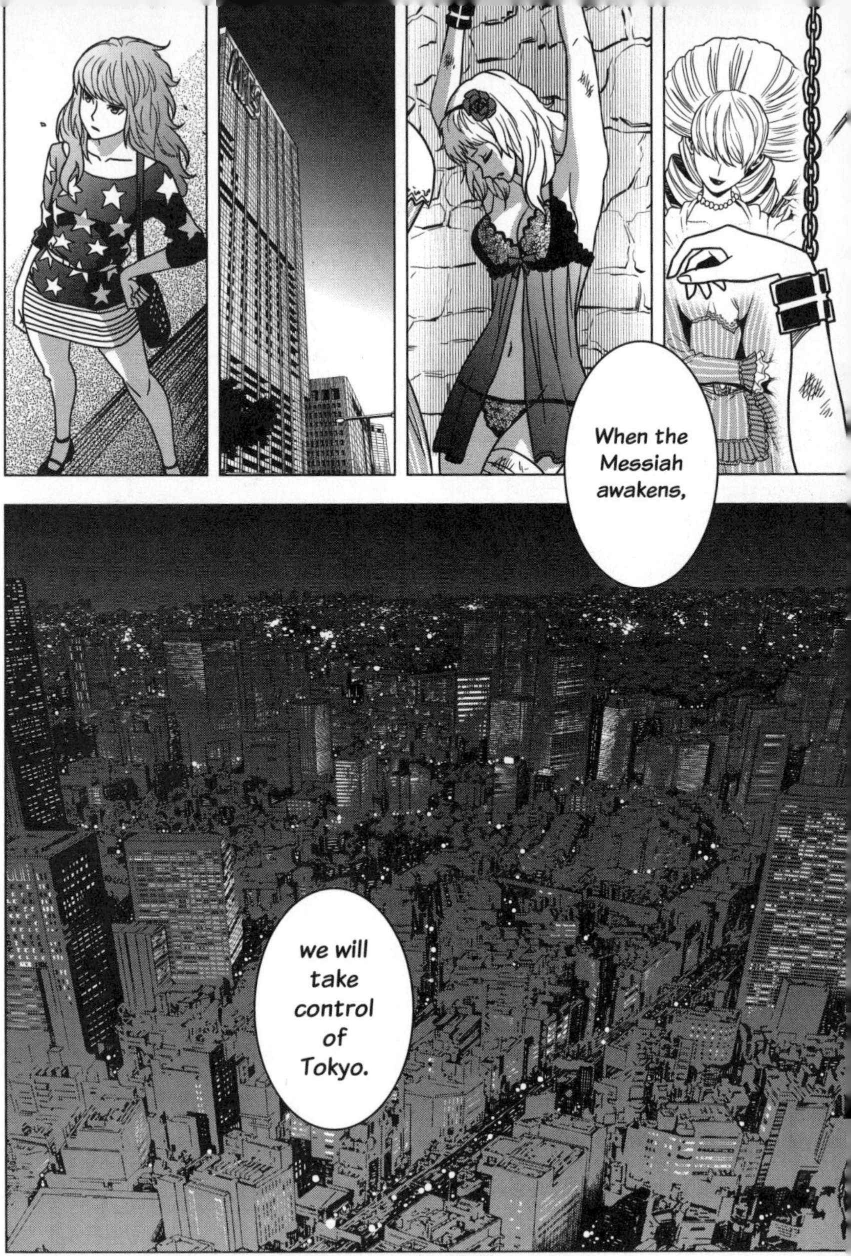
When the Messiah awakens,
we will take control of Tokyo.

SCENE 61 /// END

SCENE 62 /// The Forms of Bonds

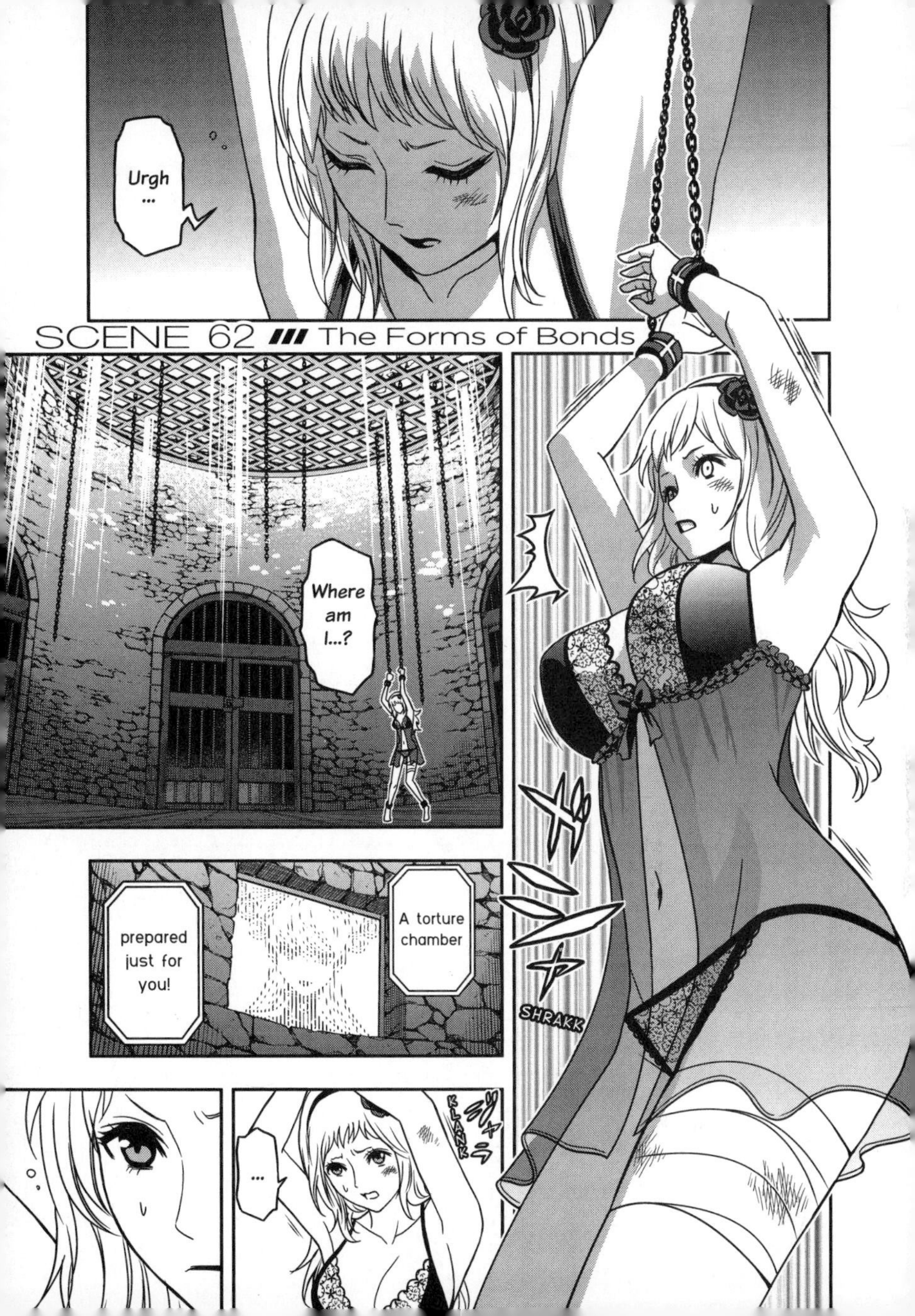

Urgh ...
SHRAKK
Where am I...?
A torture chamber
prepared just for you!
KLANK
...

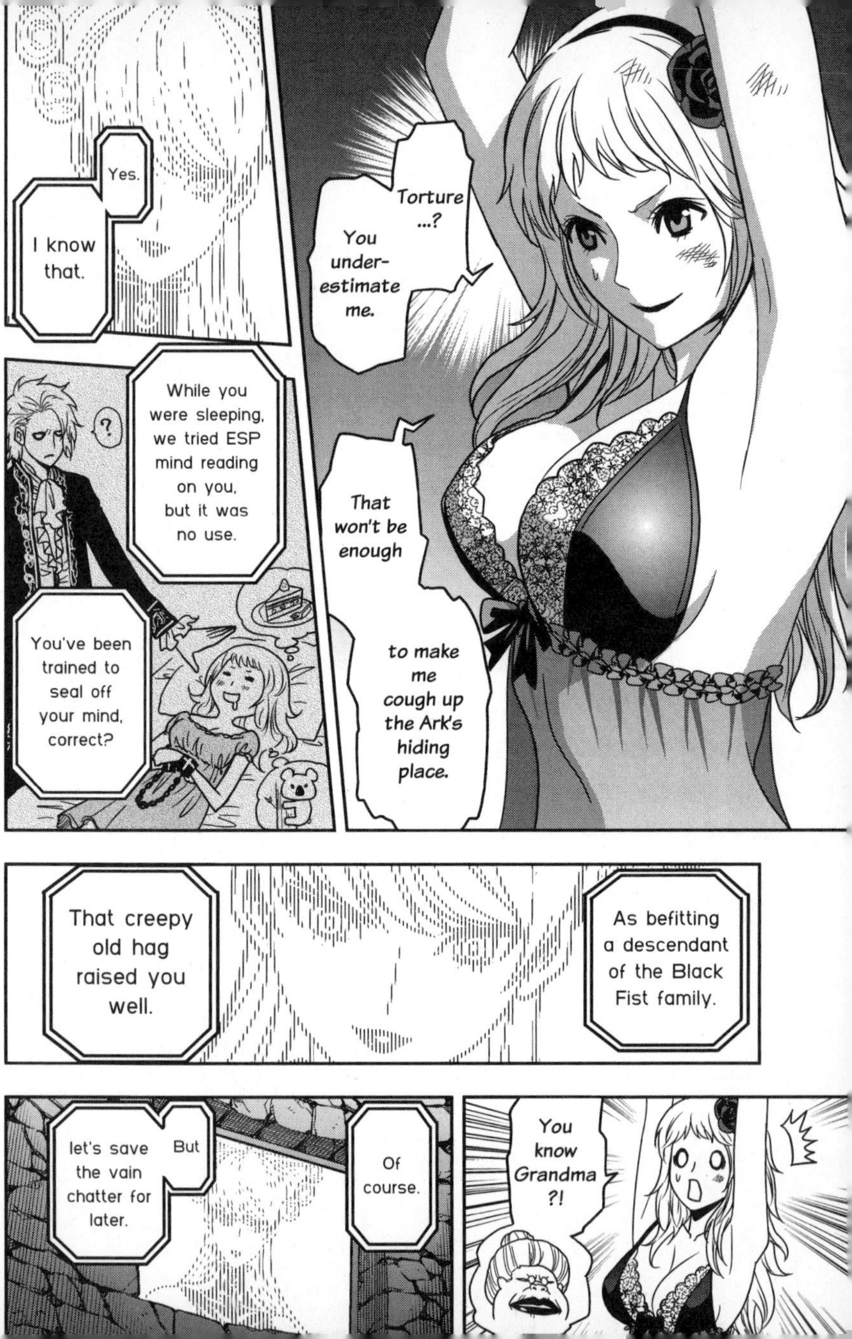
Torture ...? You underestimate me.
That won't be enough
to make me cough up the Ark's hiding place.
Yes.
I know that.
While you were sleeping, we tried ESP mind reading on you, but it was no use.
?
You've been trained to seal off your mind, correct?
As befitting a descendant of the Black Fist family.
That creepy old hag raised you well.
You know Grandma ?!
Of course.
But let's save the vain chatter for later.

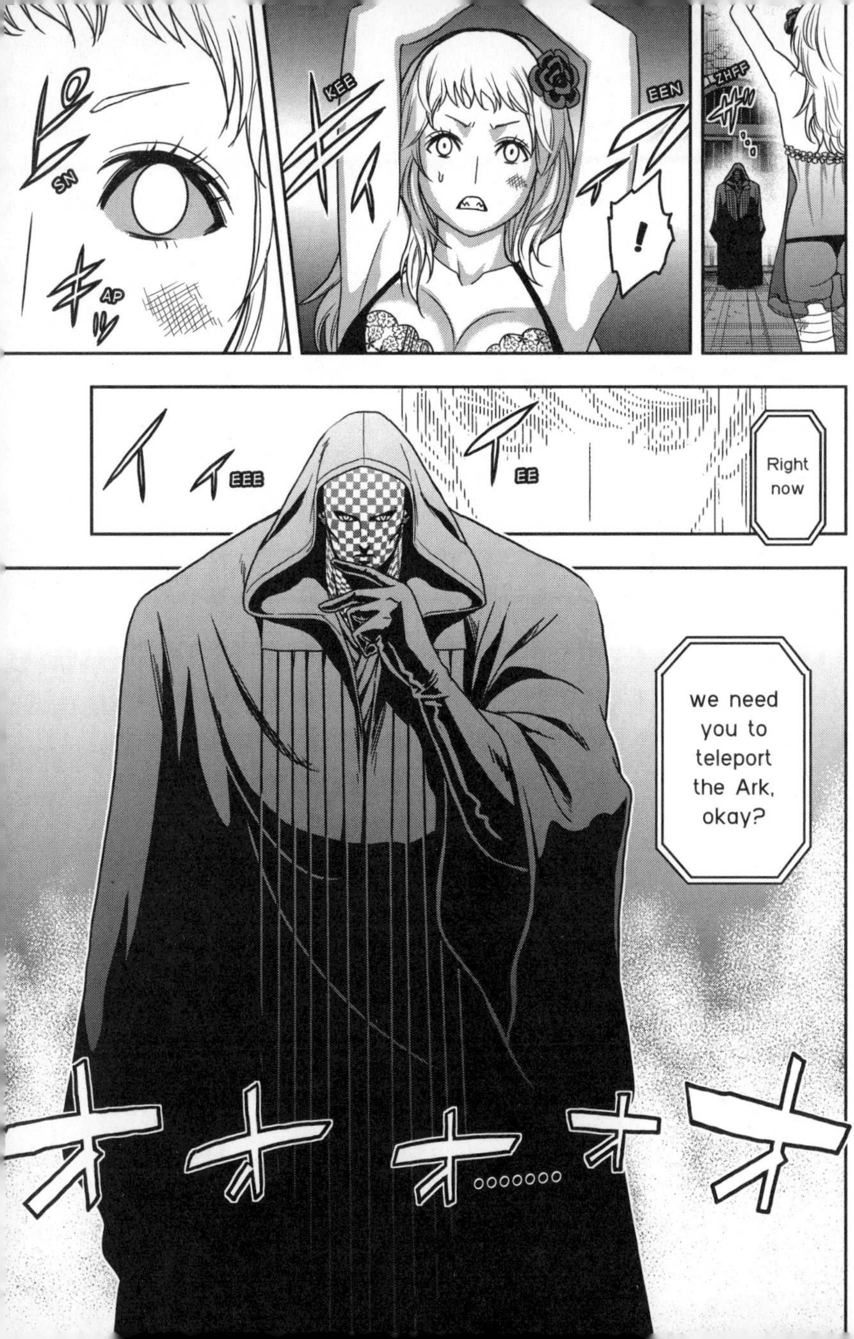
ZHFF
EEN
KEE
!
SN
AP
Right now
EE
EEE
we need you to teleport the Ark, okay?
OOOOOOO

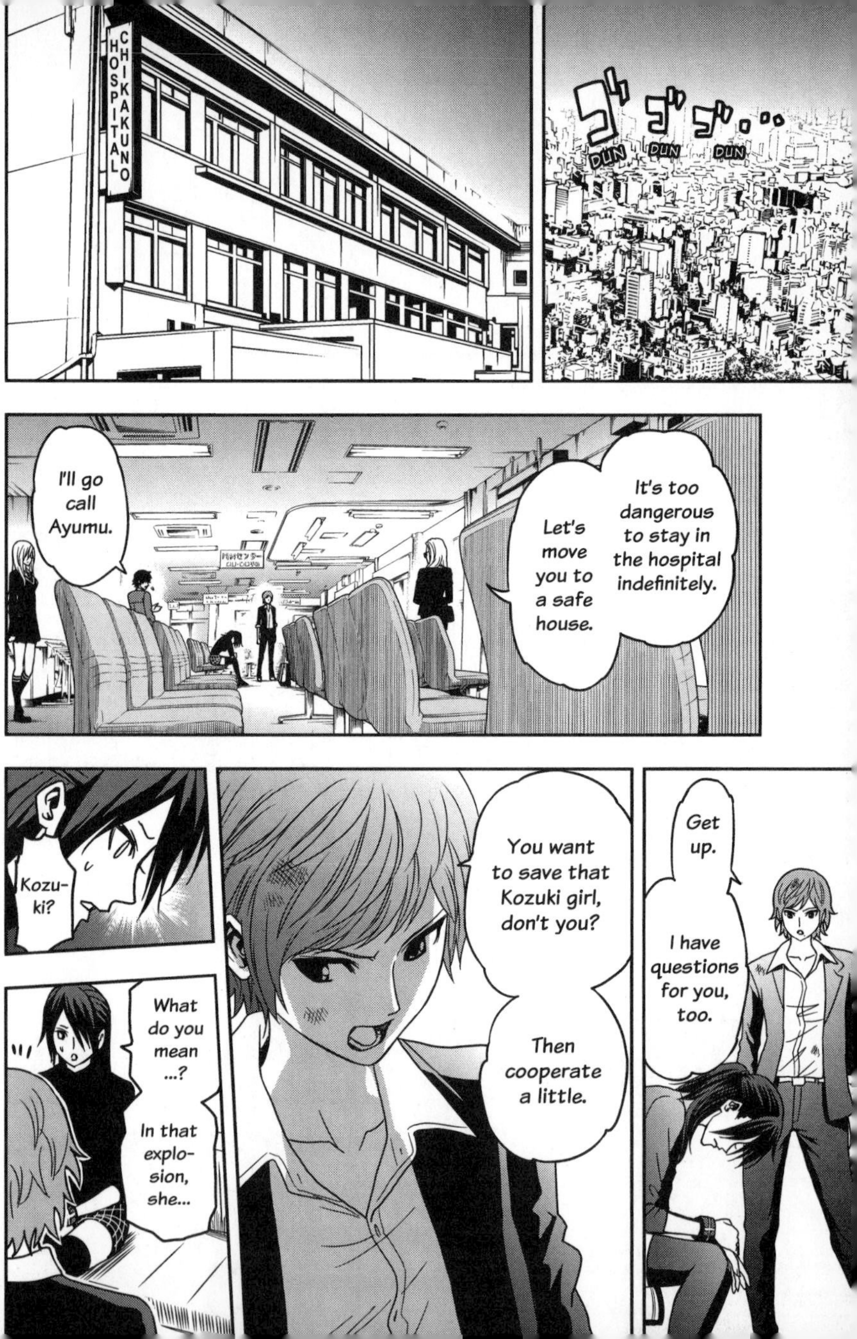
DUN DUN DUN
CHIKAKUNO HOSPITAL
It's too dangerous to stay in the hospital indefinitely.
Let's move you to a safe house.
I'll go call Ayumu.
Get up.
I have questions for you, too.
You want to save that Kozuki girl, don't you?
Then cooperate a little.
Kozuki?
What do you mean ...?
In that explosion, she...

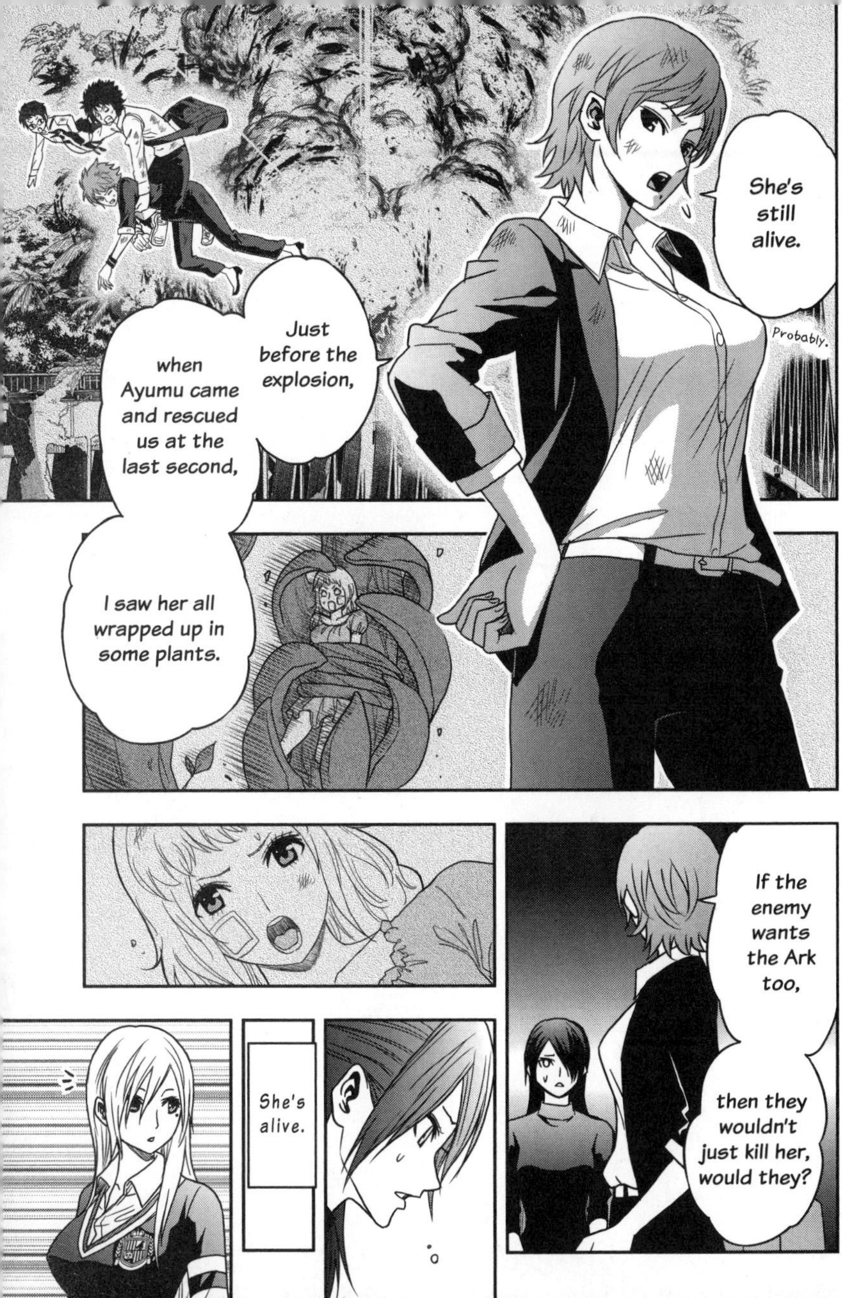
She's still alive.
Probably.
Just before the explosion,
when Ayumu came and rescued us at the last second,
I saw her all wrapped up in some plants.
If the enemy wants the Ark too,
then they wouldn't just kill her, would they?
She's alive.

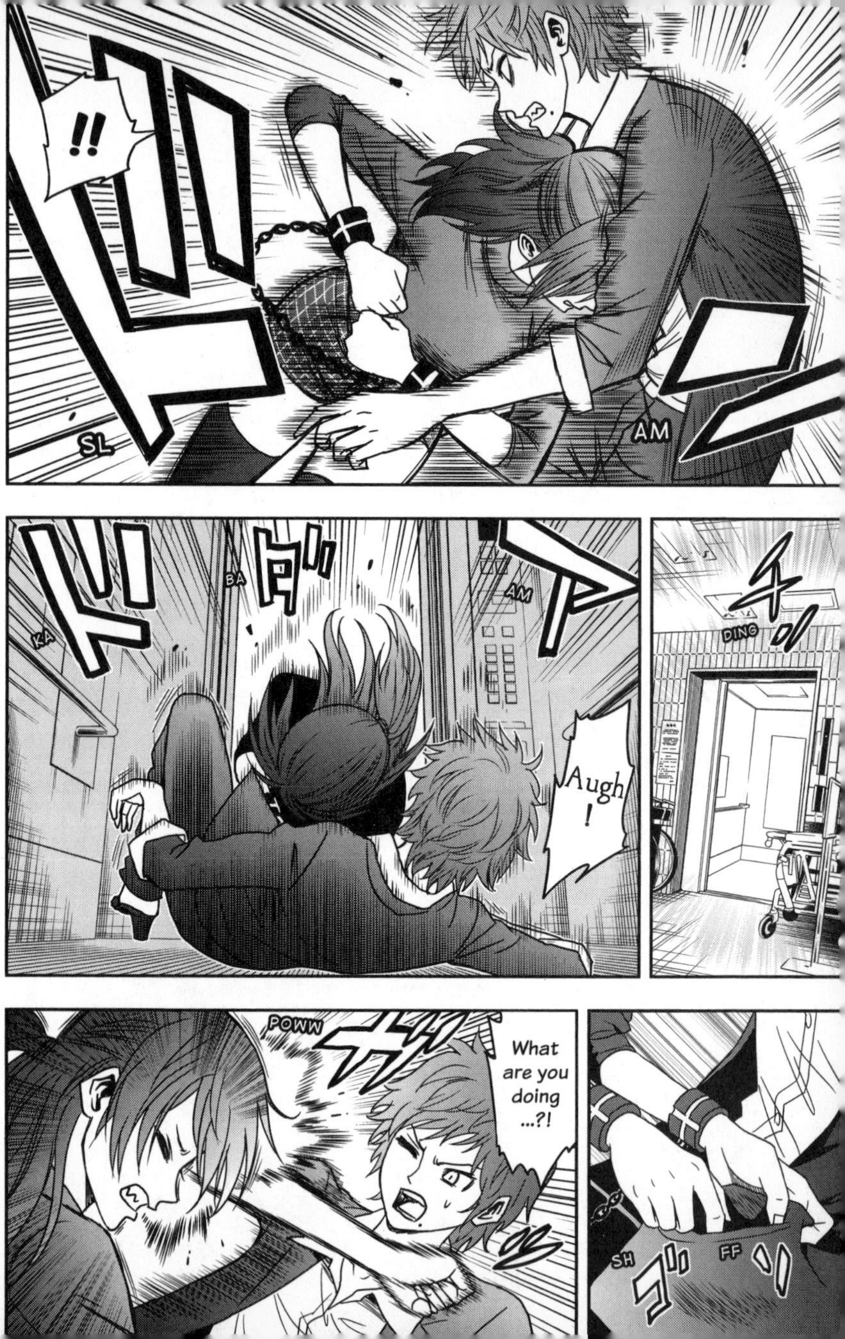
!!
SL
AM
DING
BA
AM
KA
Augh!
SH
FF
What are you doing ...?!
POWW

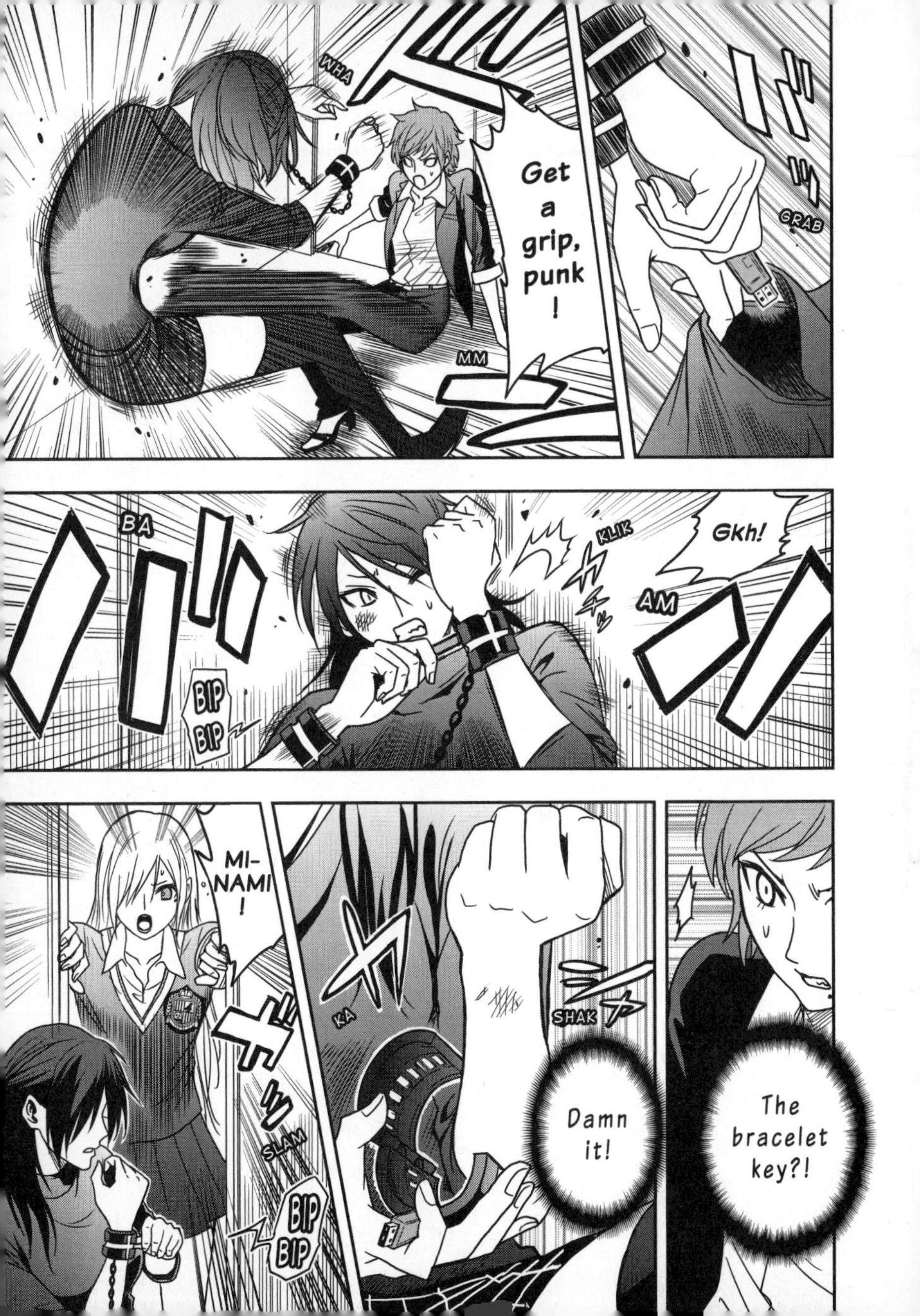
GRAB
Get a grip, punk!
WHA
MM
Gkh!
KLIK
AM
BA
BIP BIP
The bracelet key?!
Damn it!
SHAK
KA
MI-NAMI!
SLAM
BIP BIP

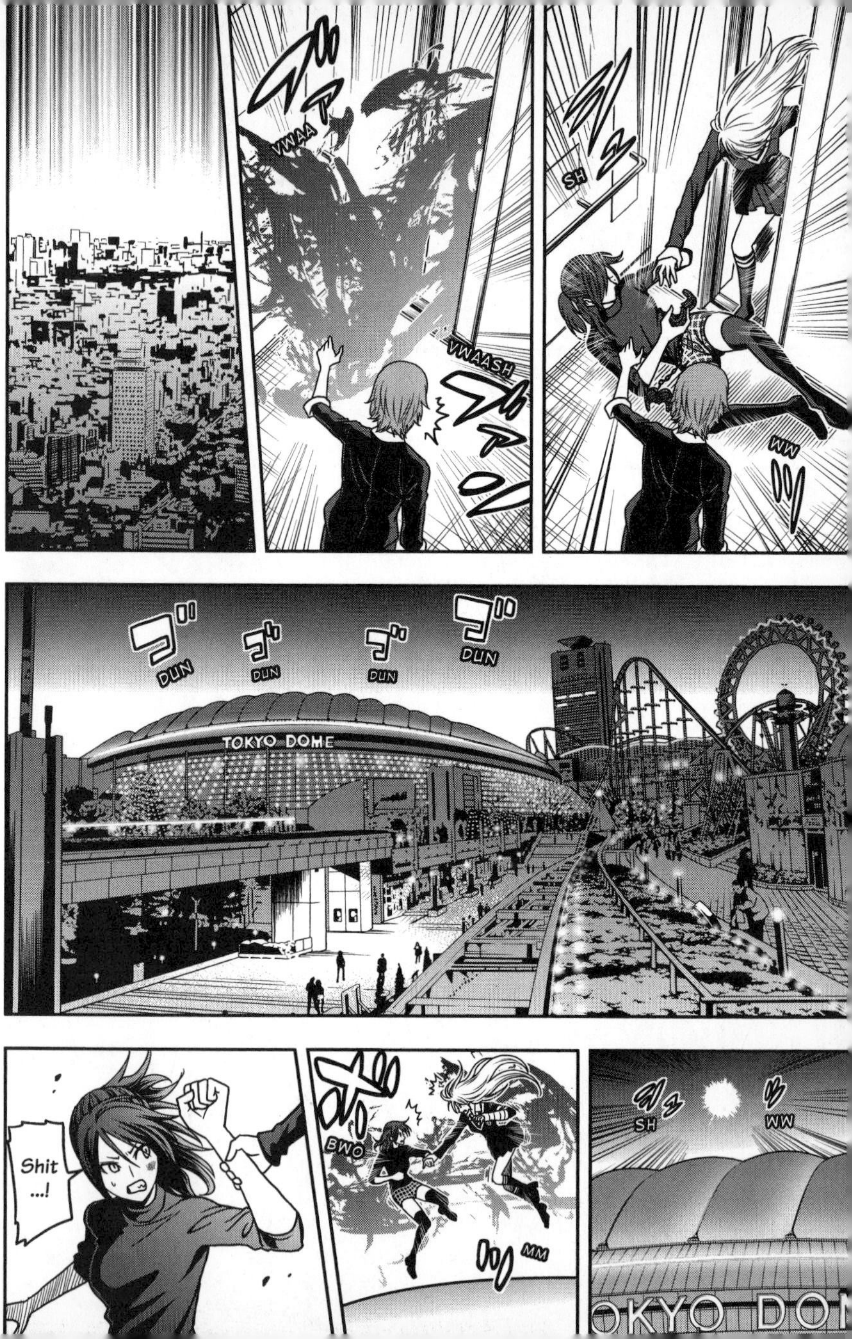
SH
WW
VWAA
VWAASH
DUN
DUN
DUN
DUN
TOKYO DOME
SH
WW
BWO
MM
Shit ...!

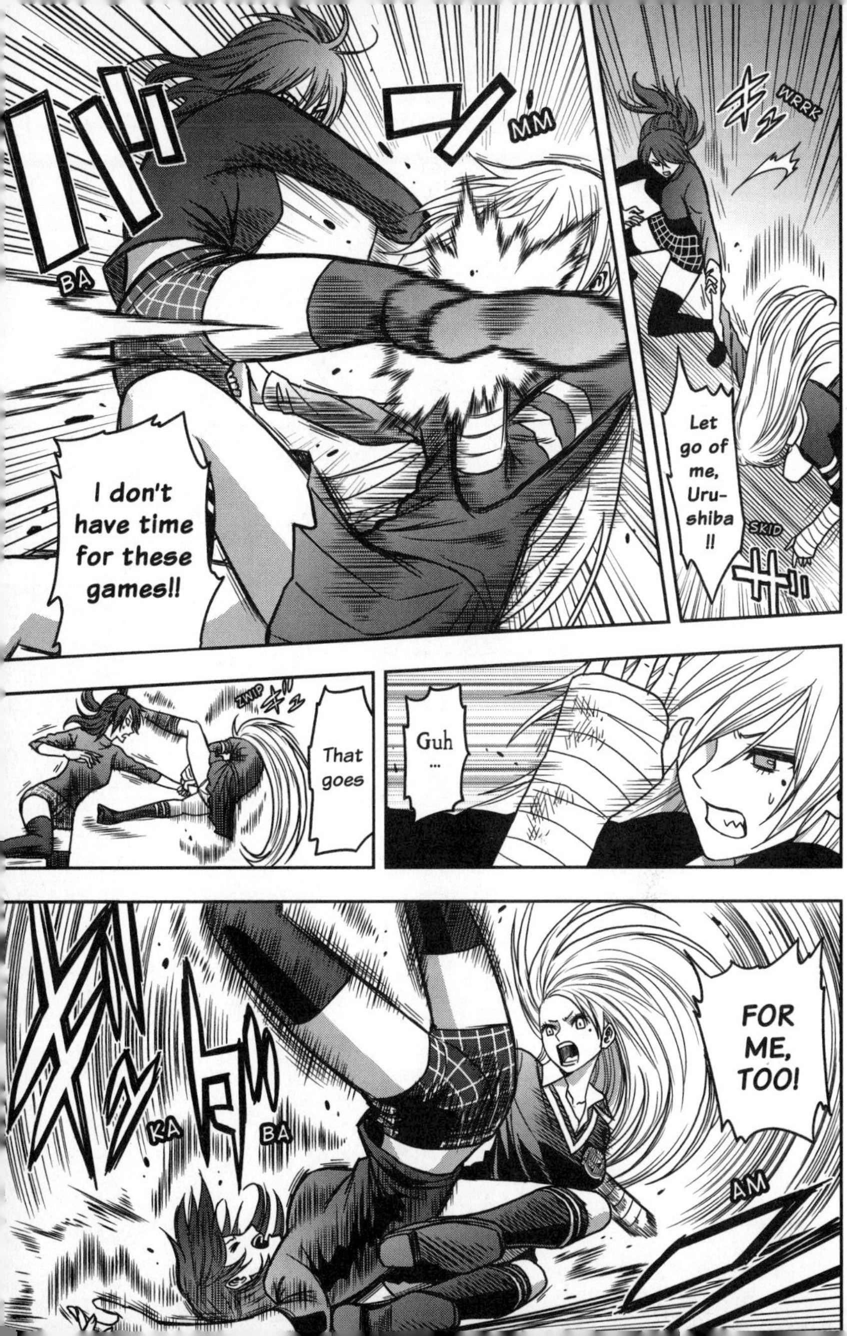
WRRK
Let go of me, Uru-shiba!!
SKID
MM
BA
I don't have time for these games!!
Guh ...
ZWIP
That goes
FOR ME, TOO!
AM
BA
KA

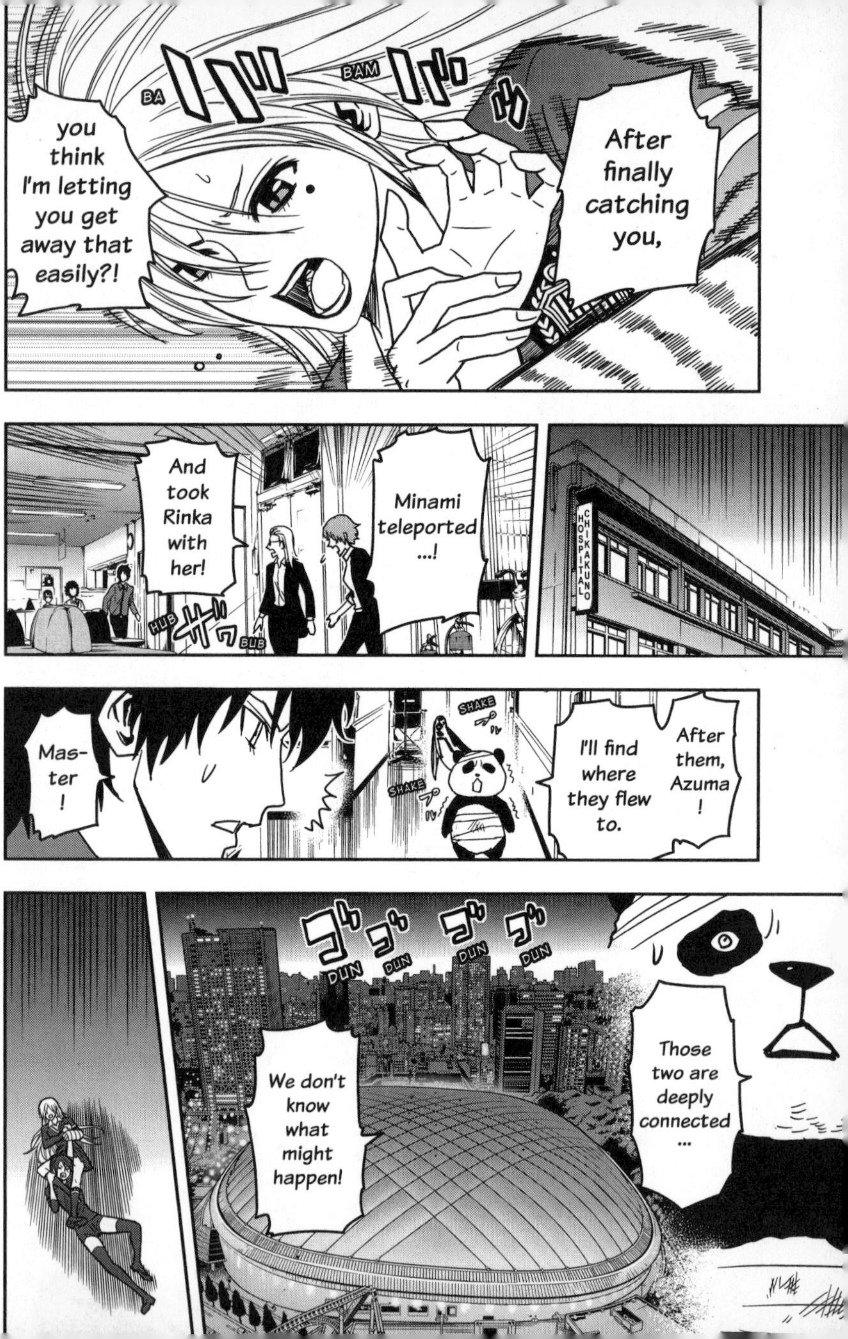
BAM
BA
After finally catching you,
you think I'm letting you get away that easily?!
CHIKAKUNO HOSPITAL
Minami teleported ...!
And took Rinka with her!
HUB BUB
After them, Azuma!
I'll find where they flew to.
SHAKE
SHAKE
Mas-ter!
DUN DUN DUN DUN
Those two are deeply connected ...
We don't know what might happen!

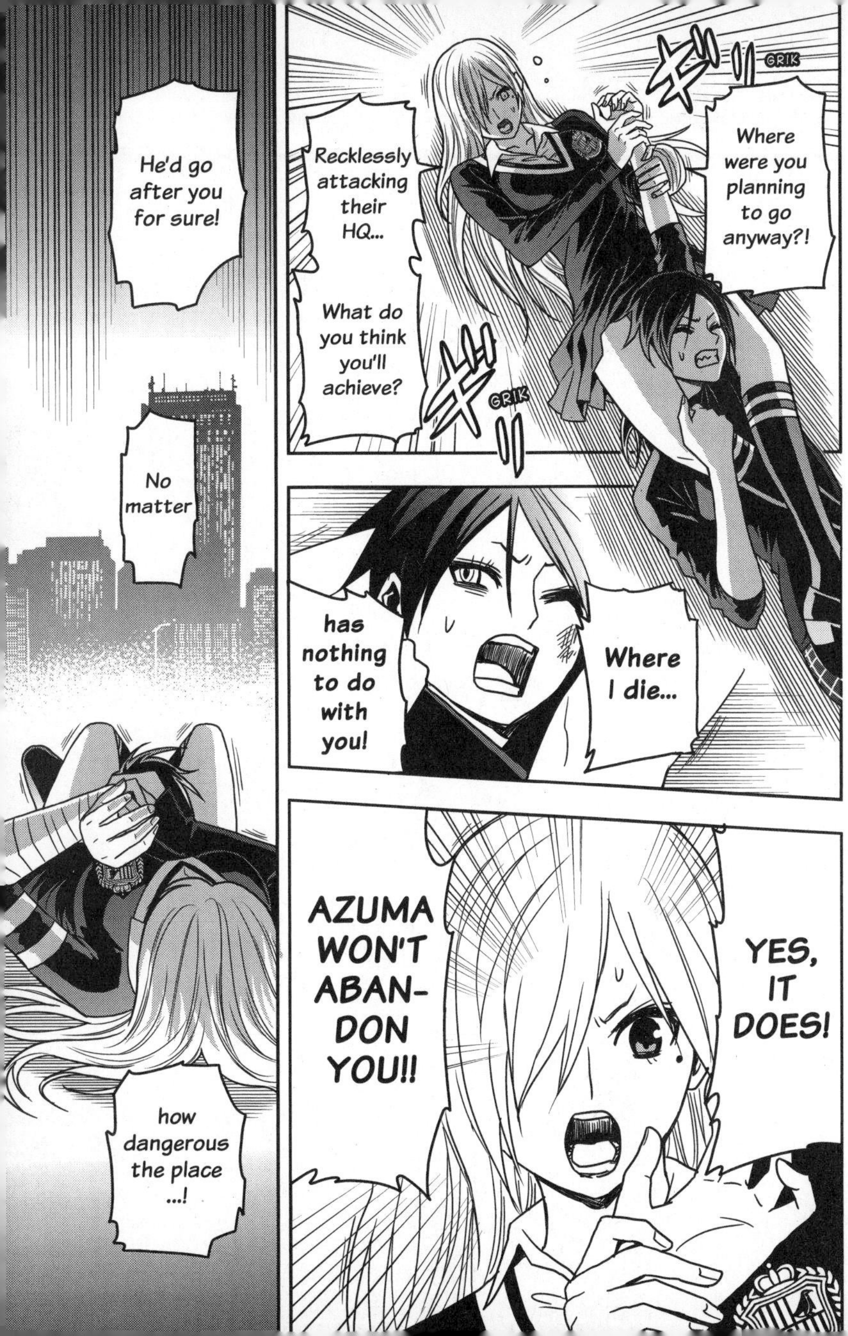
GRIK
Where were you planning to go anyway?!
Recklessly attacking their HQ...
What do you think you'll achieve?
GRIK
Where I die...
has nothing to do with you!
YES, IT DOES!
AZUMA WON'T ABAN-DON YOU!!
He'd go after you for sure!
No matter
how dangerous the place ...!

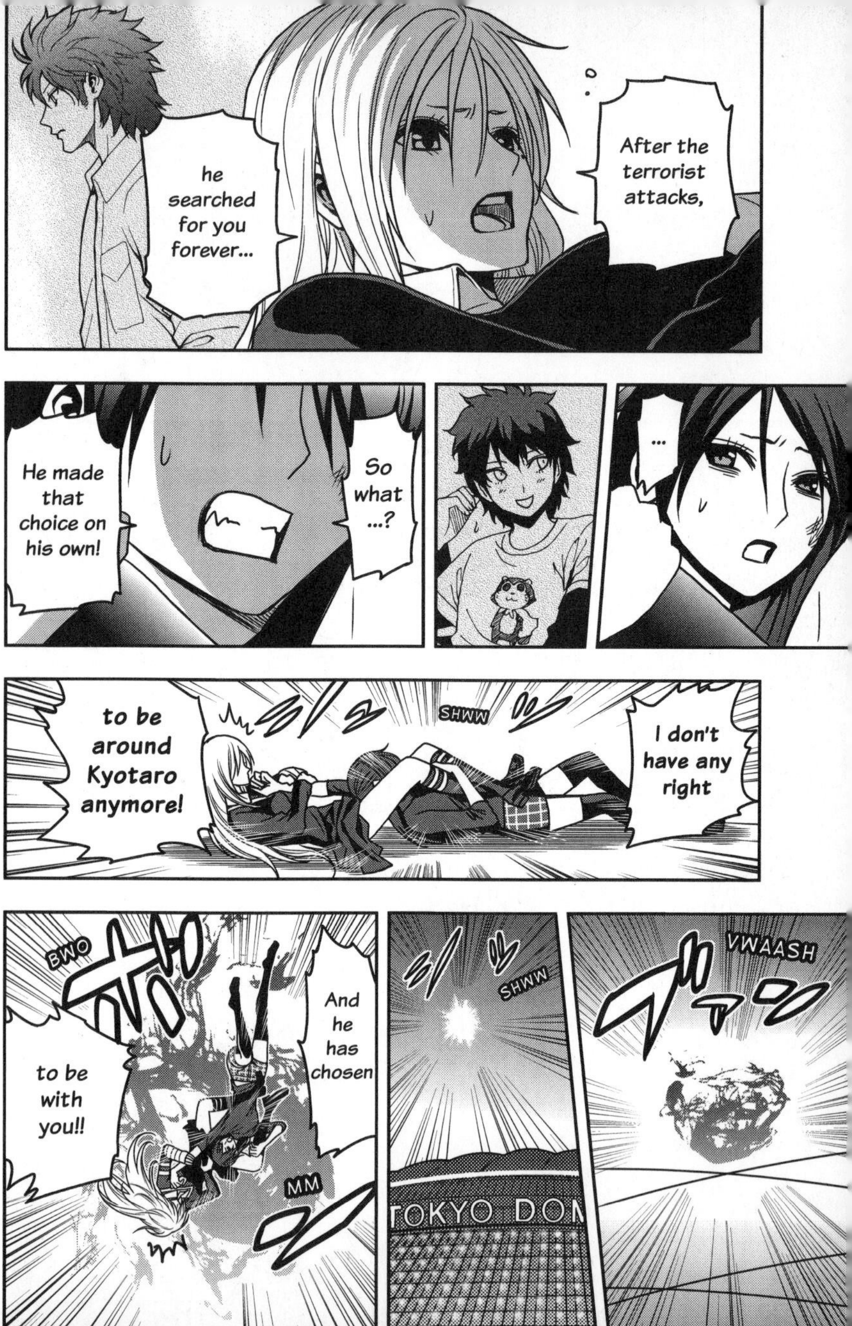
After the terrorist attacks,
he searched for you forever...
...
So what ...?
He made that choice on his own!
I don't have any right
SHWW
to be around Kyotaro anymore!
VWAASH
SHWW
TOKYO DOM
And he has chosen
to be with you!!
BWO
MM

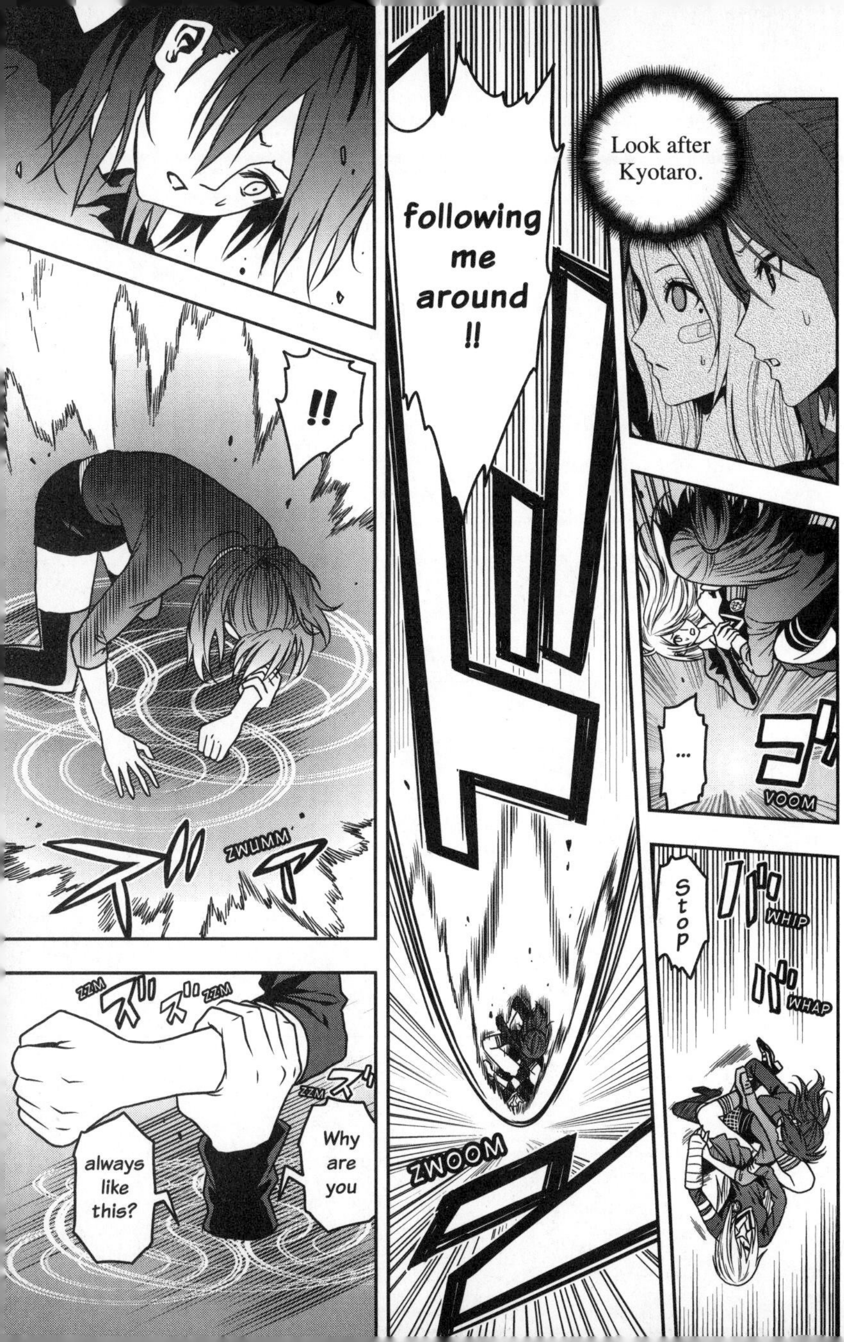

Look after Kyotaro.
...
VOOM
Stop
WHIP
WHAP
following me around!!
ZWOOM
!!
ZWUMM
ZZM
ZZM
ZZM
Why are you
always like this?

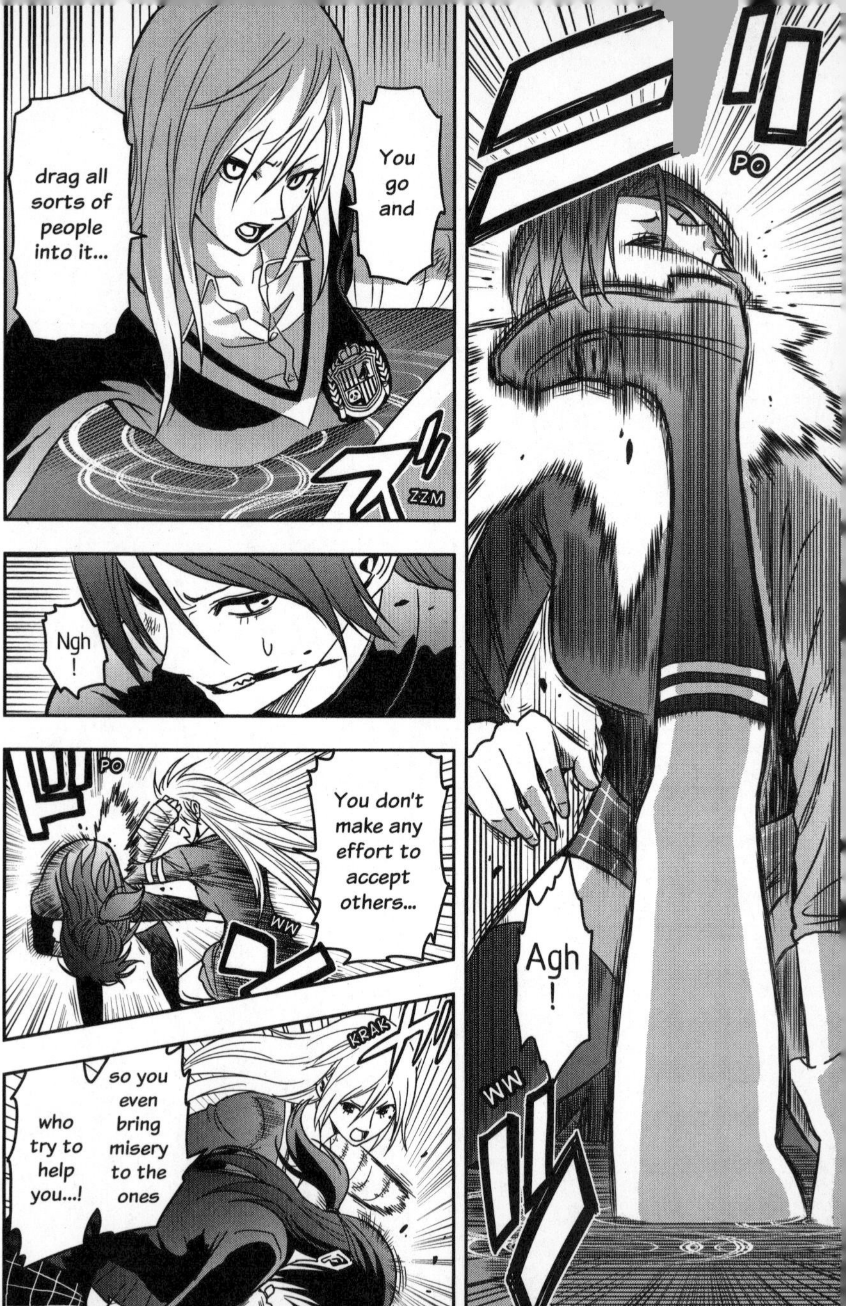
PO
Agh!
WW
You go and
drag all sorts of people into it...
ZZM
Ngh!
PO
You don't make any effort to accept others...
WW
KRAK
so you even bring misery to the ones
who try to help you...!

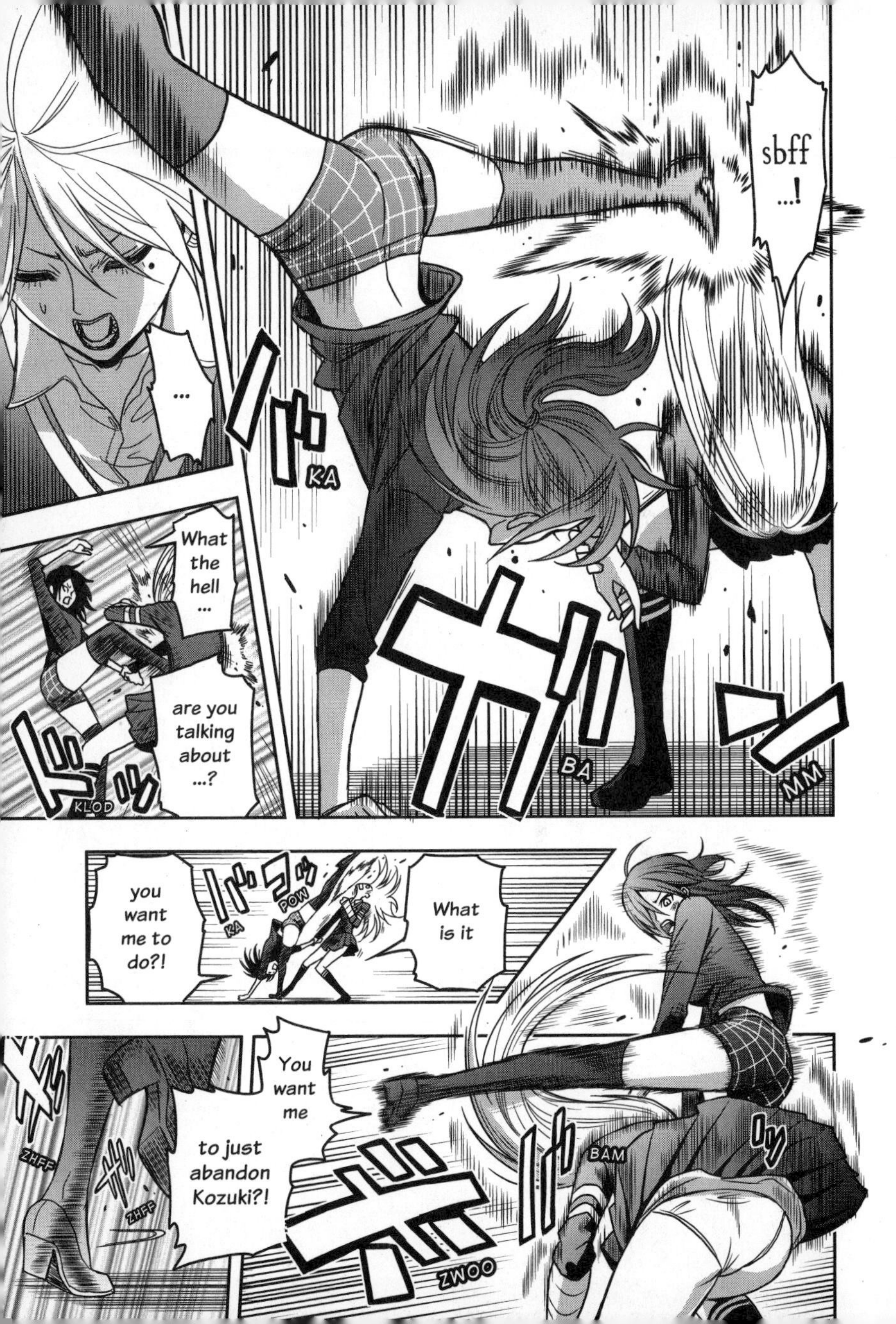
sbff ...!
KA
BA
MM
...
What the hell ...
are you talking about ...?
KLOD
What is it
POW
KA
you want me to do?!
You want me
to just abandon Kozuki?!
BAM
ZWOO
ZHFF
ZHFF

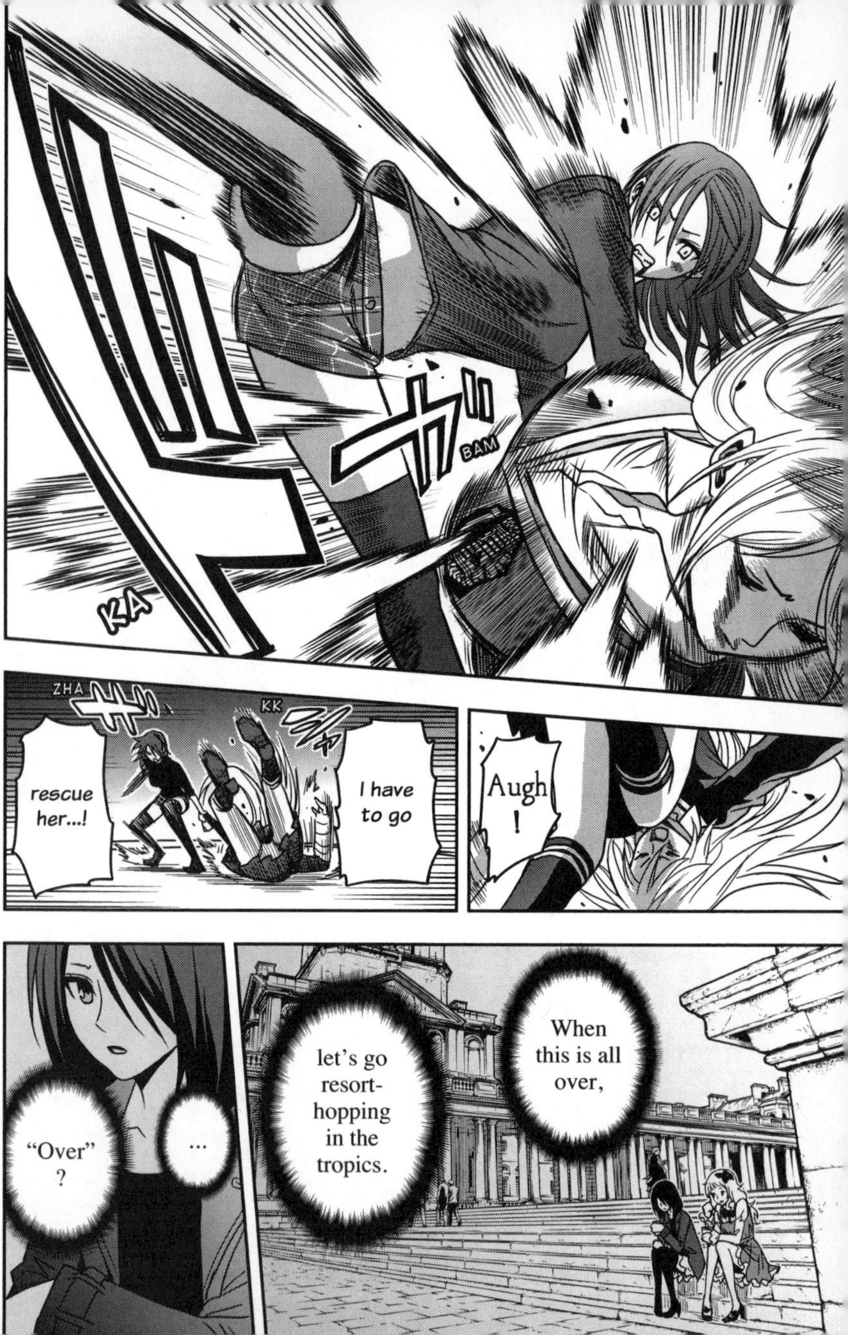
BAM
KA
Augh!
KK
I have to go
ZHA
rescue her...!
When this is all over,
let’s go resort-hopping in the tropics.
...
“Over”?

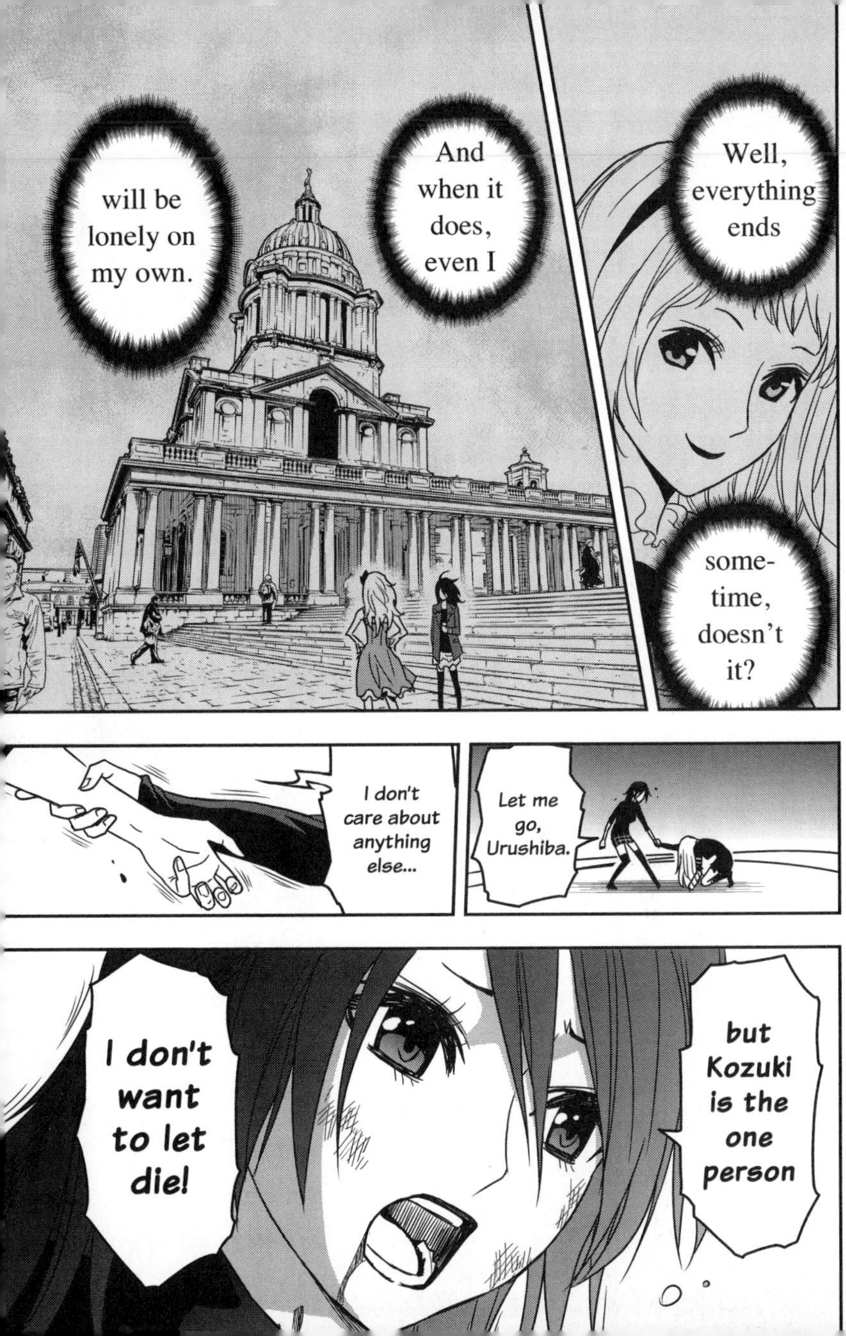
Well, everything ends
sometime, doesn't it?
And when it does, even I
will be lonely on my own.
Let me go, Urushiba.
I don't care about anything else...
but Kozuki is the one person
I don't want to let die!

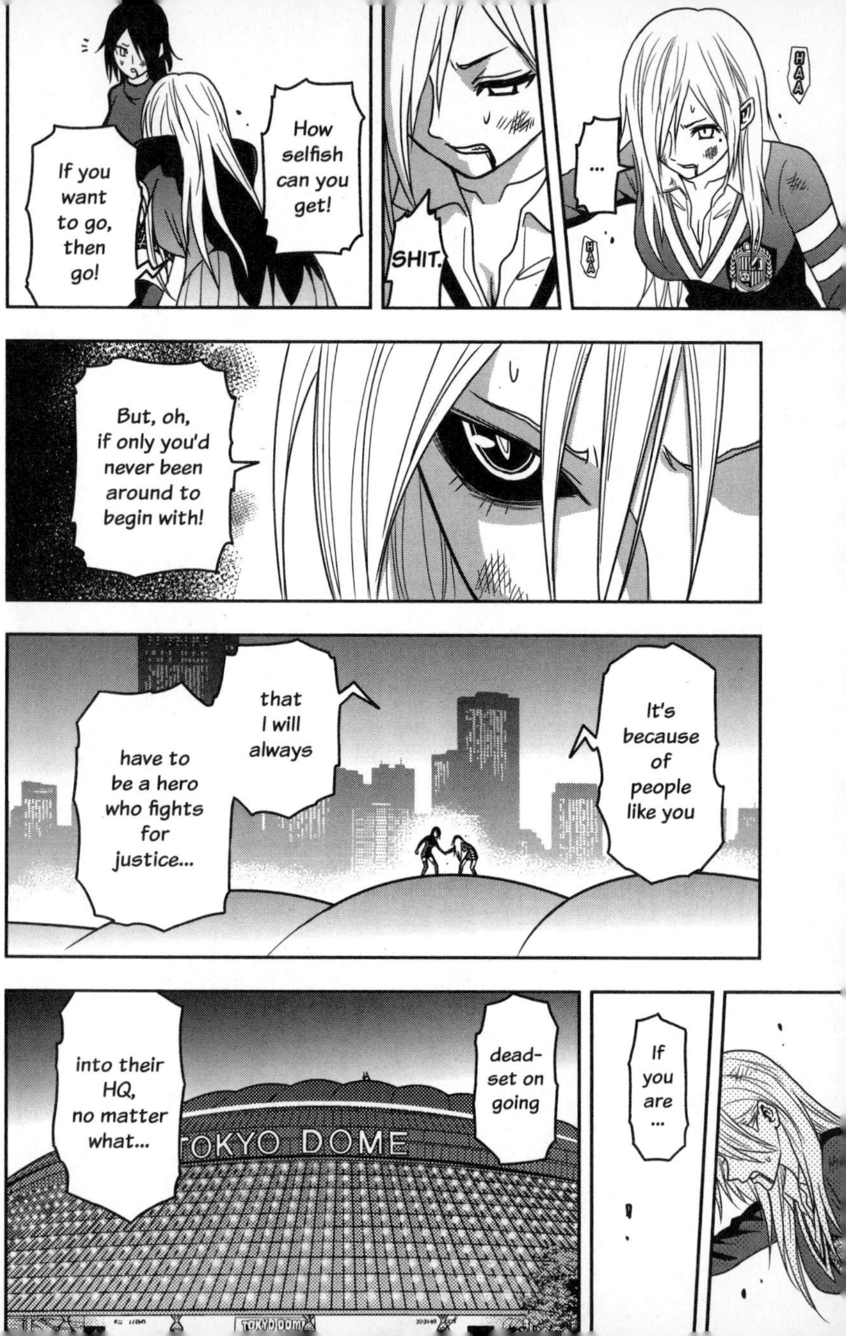
HAA
HAA
...
SHIT.
How selfish can you get!
If you want to go, then go!
But, oh, if only you'd never been around to begin with!
It's because of people like you
that I will always
have to be a hero who fights for justice...
If you are ...
dead-set on going
into their HQ, no matter what...
TOKYO DOME
TOKYO DOME

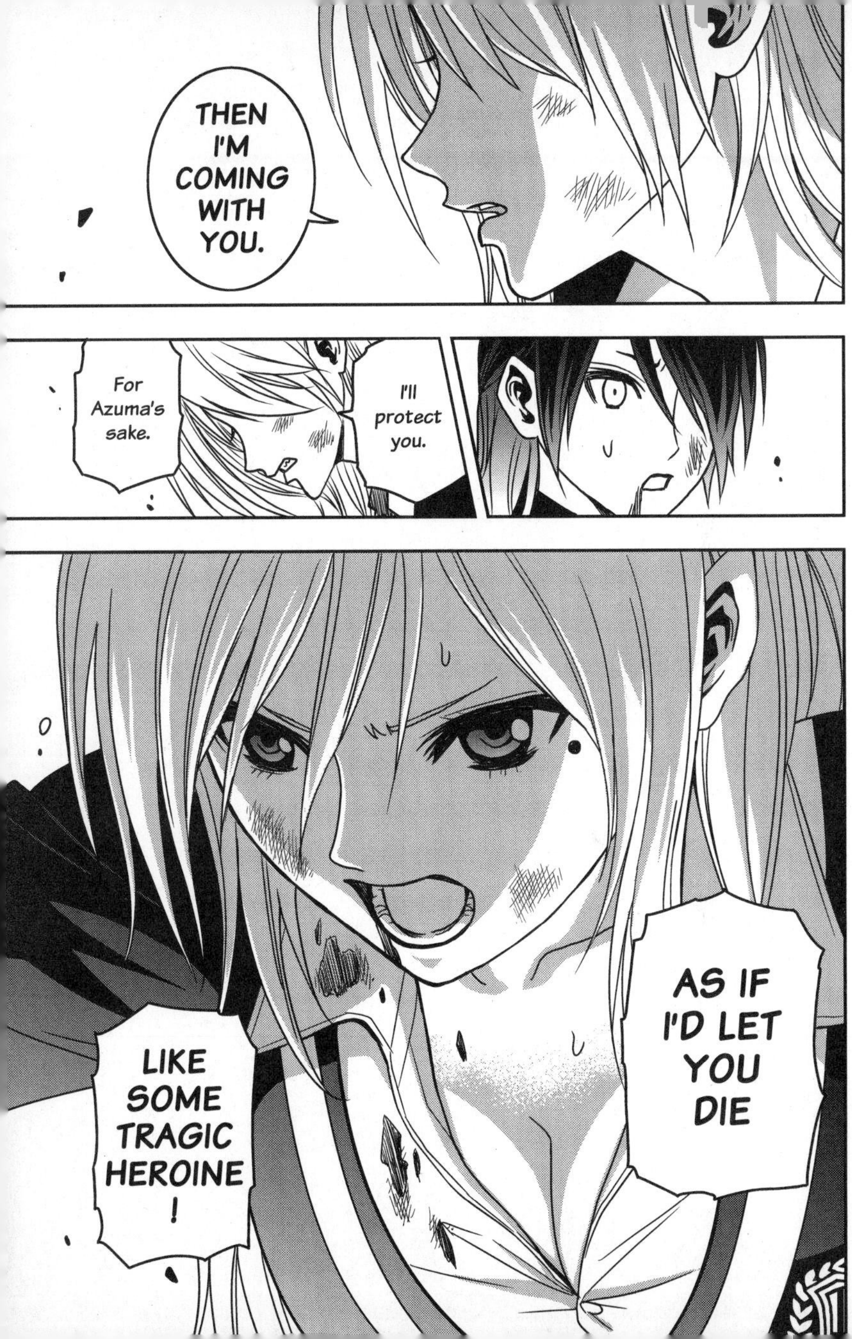
THEN I'M COMING WITH YOU.
I'll protect you.
For Azuma's sake.
AS IF I'D LET YOU DIE
LIKE SOME TRAGIC HEROINE!

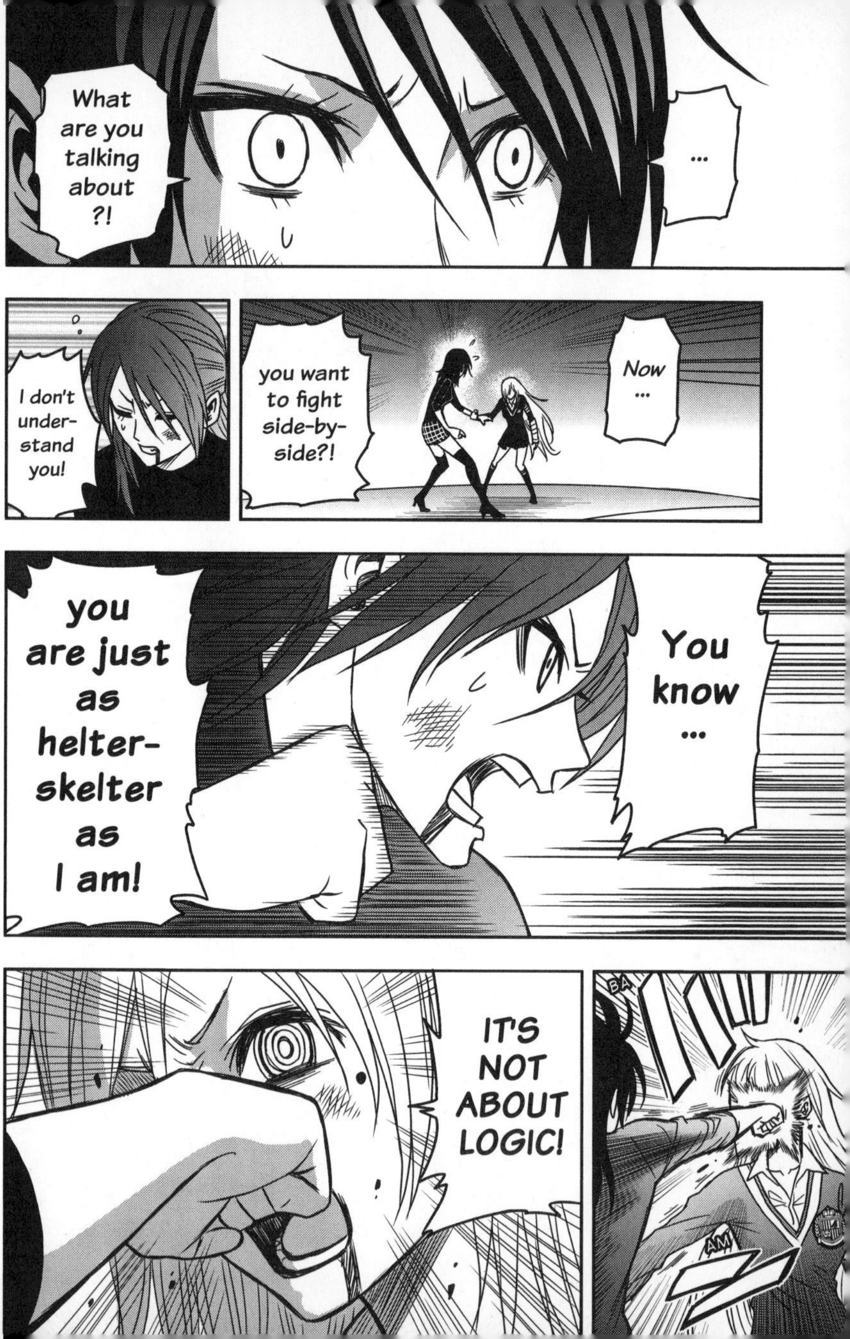
...
What are you talking about?!
Now ...
you want to fight side-by-side?!
I don't under-stand you!
You know ...
you are just as helter-skelter as I am!
BA
AM
IT'S NOT ABOUT LOGIC!

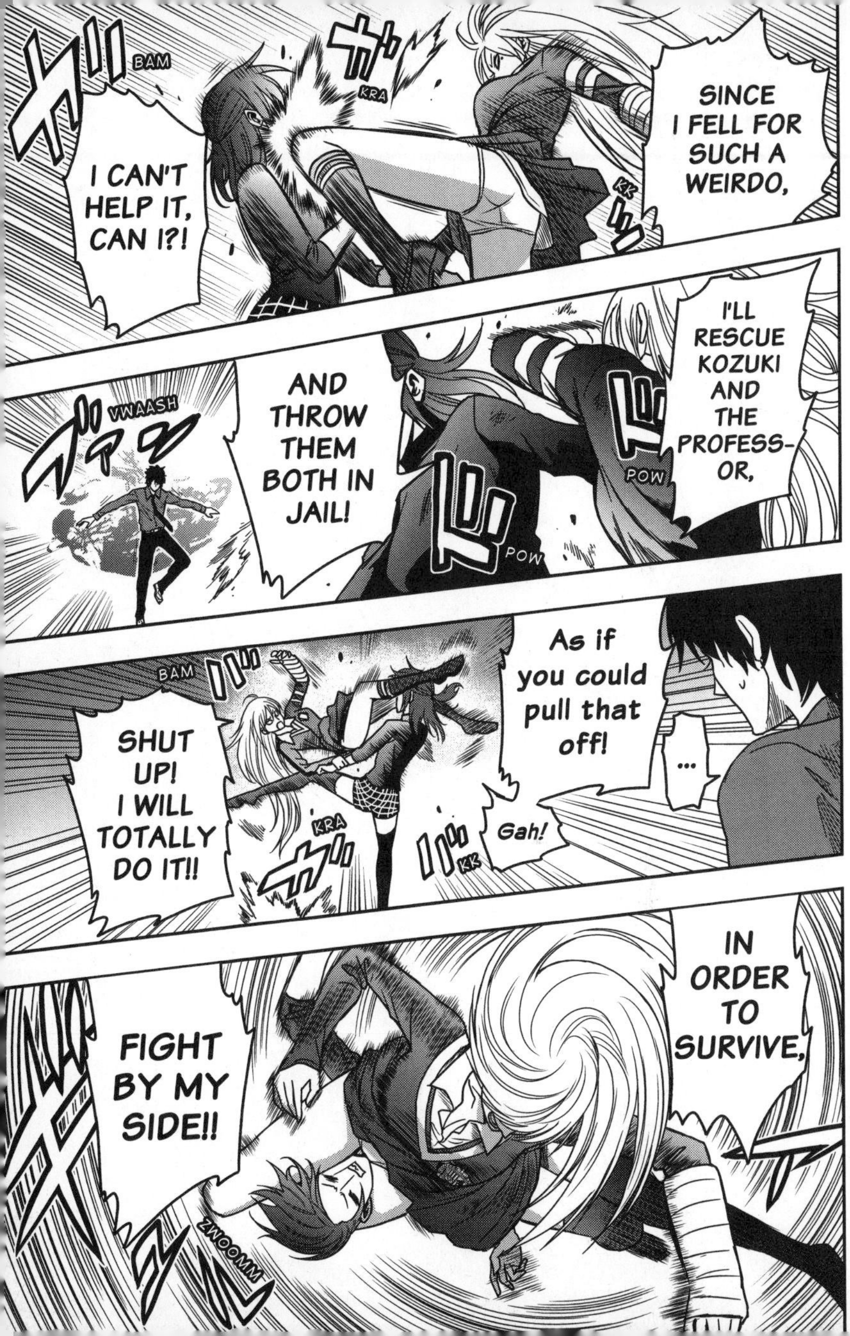
KRA
SINCE I FELL FOR SUCH A WEIRDO,
KK
BAM
I CAN'T HELP IT, CAN I?!
I'LL RESCUE KOZUKI AND THE PROFESS-OR,
POW
AND THROW THEM BOTH IN JAIL!
POW
VWAASH
...
As if you could pull that off!
BAM
Gah!
KK
SHUT UP! I WILL TOTALLY DO IT!!
KRA
IN ORDER TO SURVIVE,
FIGHT BY MY SIDE!!
ZWOOMM

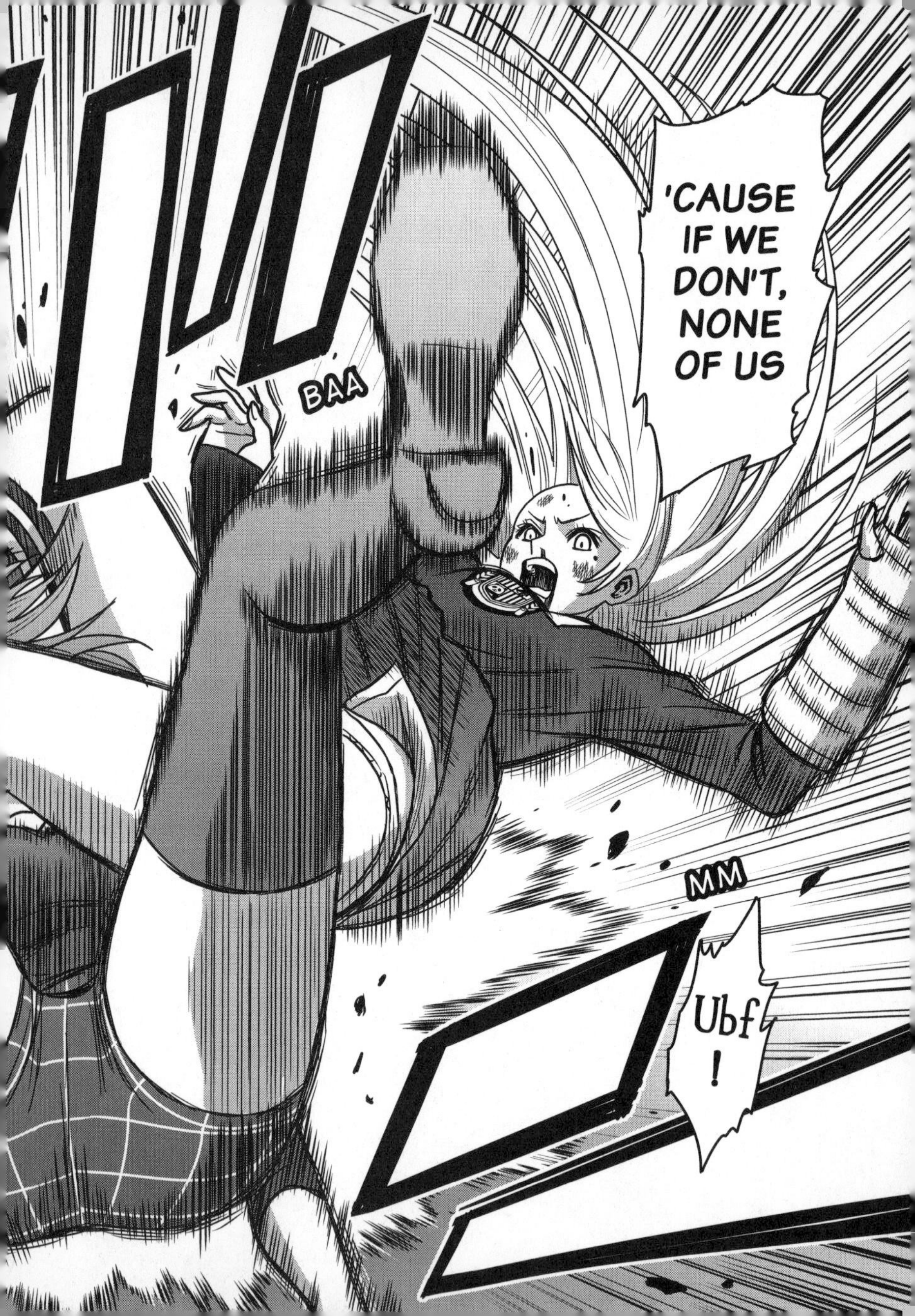
'CAUSE IF WE DON'T, NONE OF US
BAA
MM
Ubf!

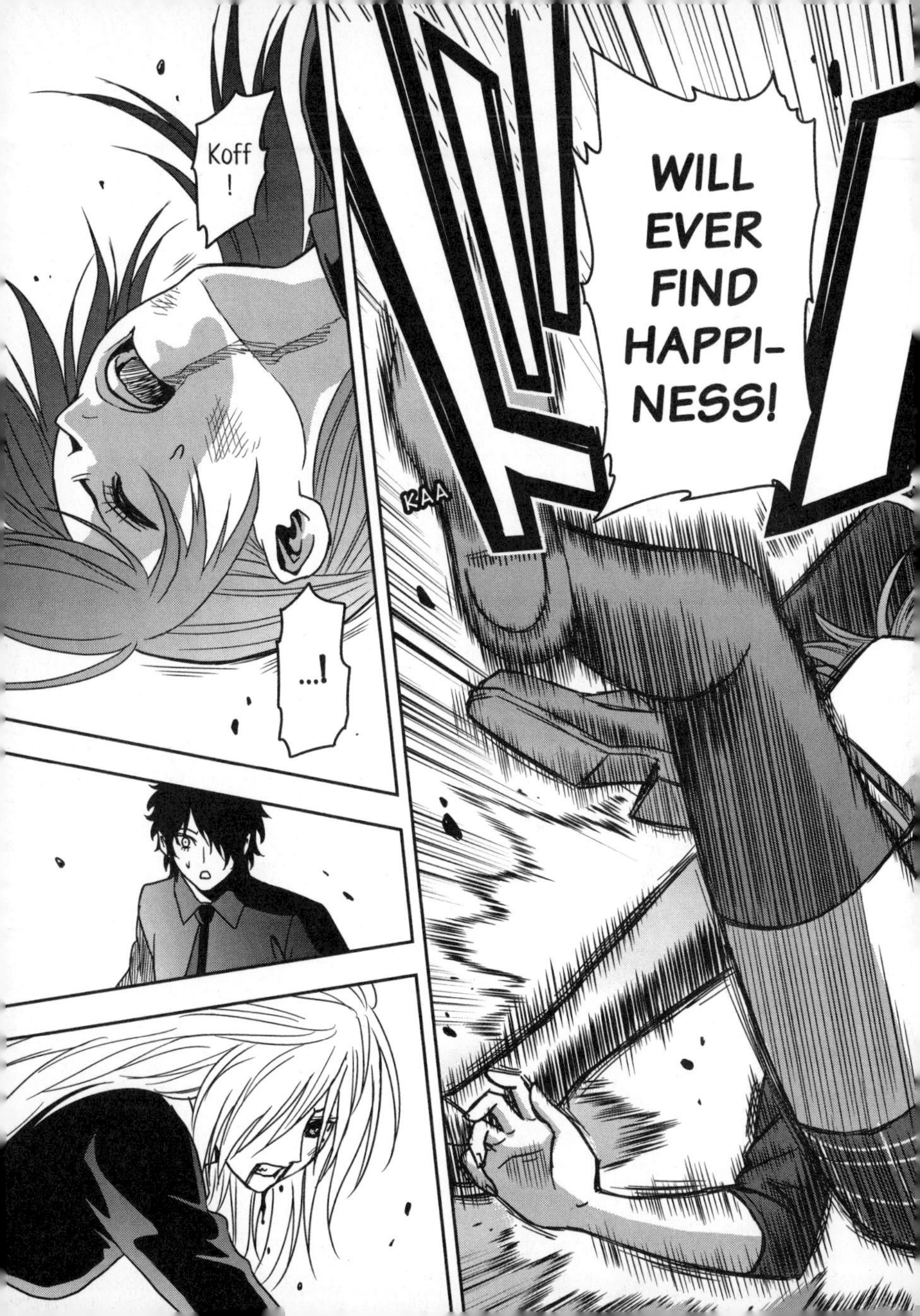
WILL EVER FIND HAPPI-NESS!
KAA
Koff !
...!

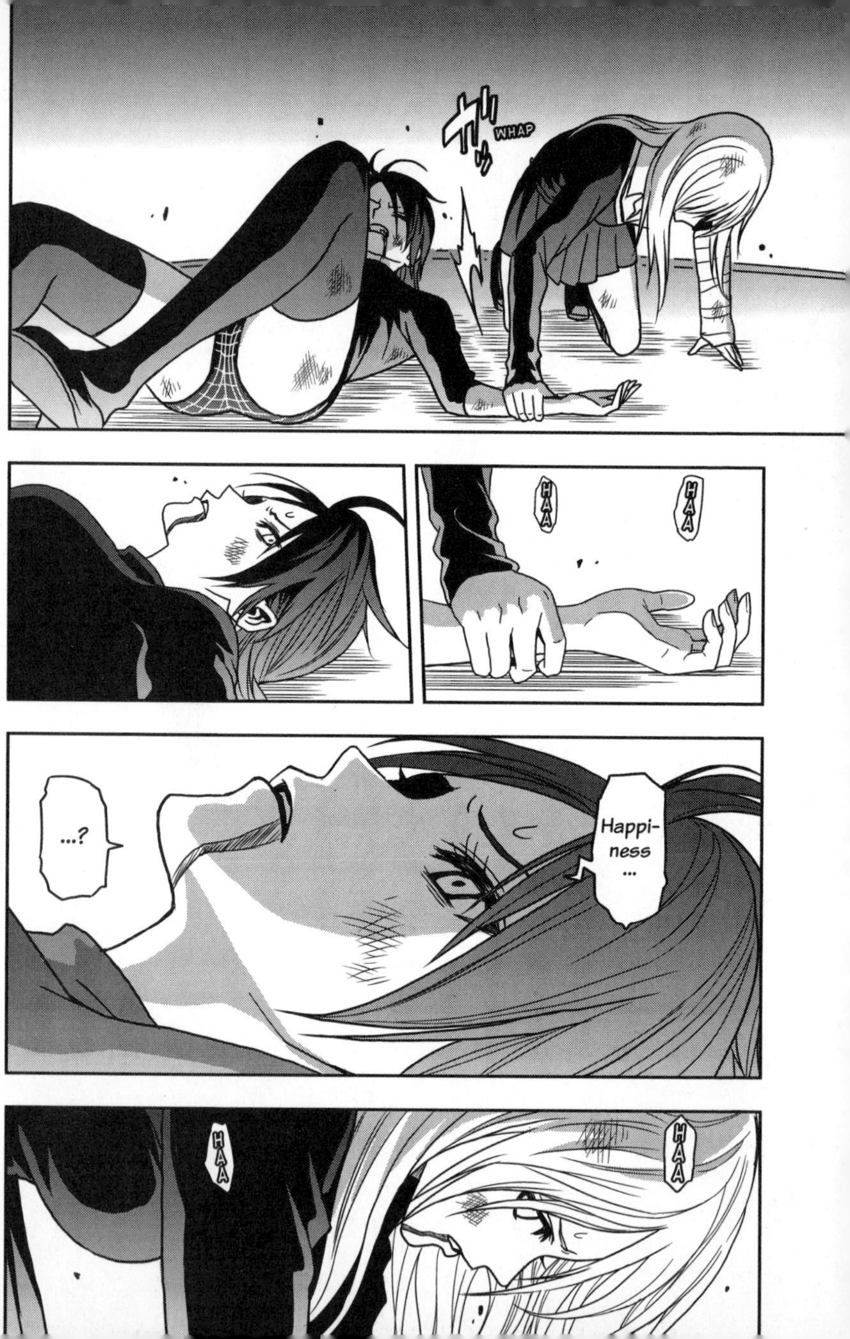
WHAP
HAA
HAA
Happiness ...
...?
HAA
HAA

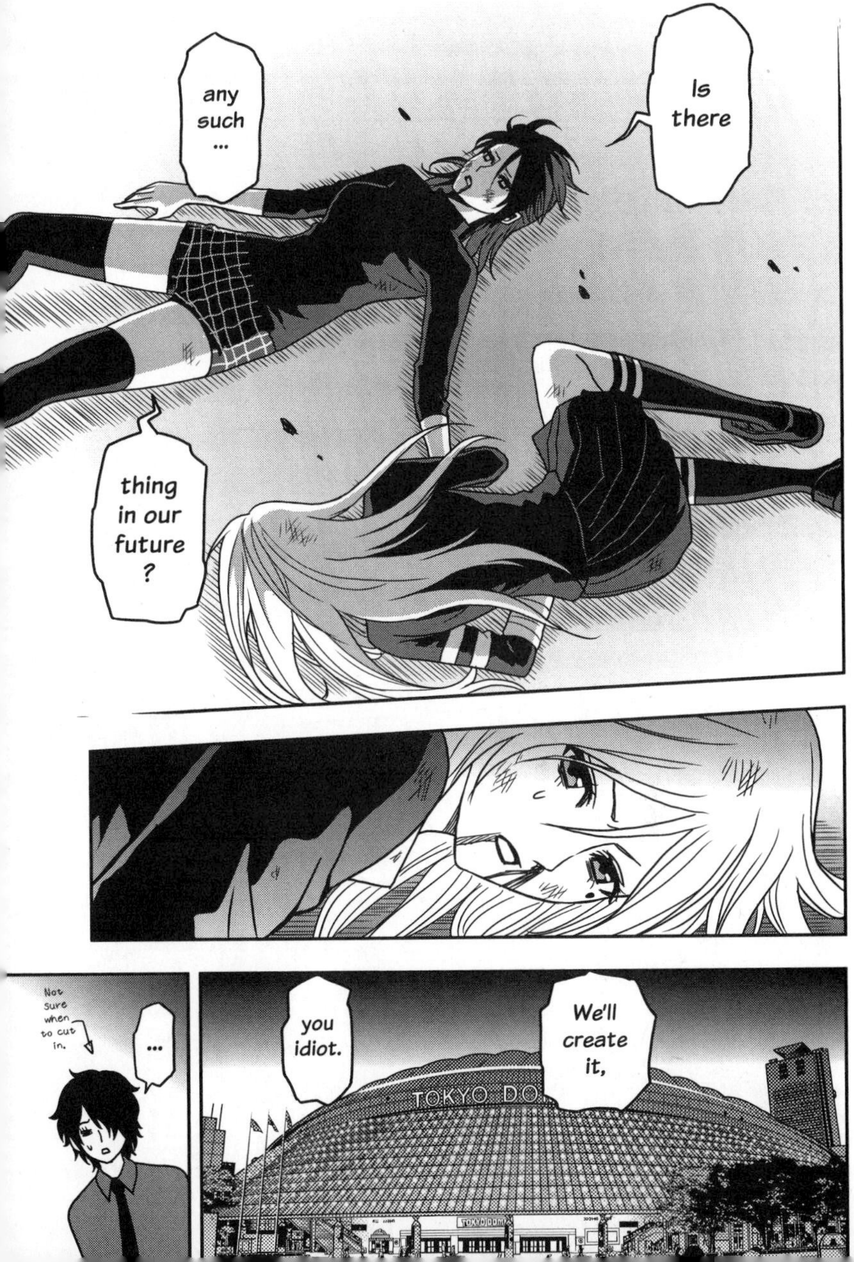
Is there
any such ...
thing in our future ?
We'll create it,
you idiot.
...
Not sure when to cut in.

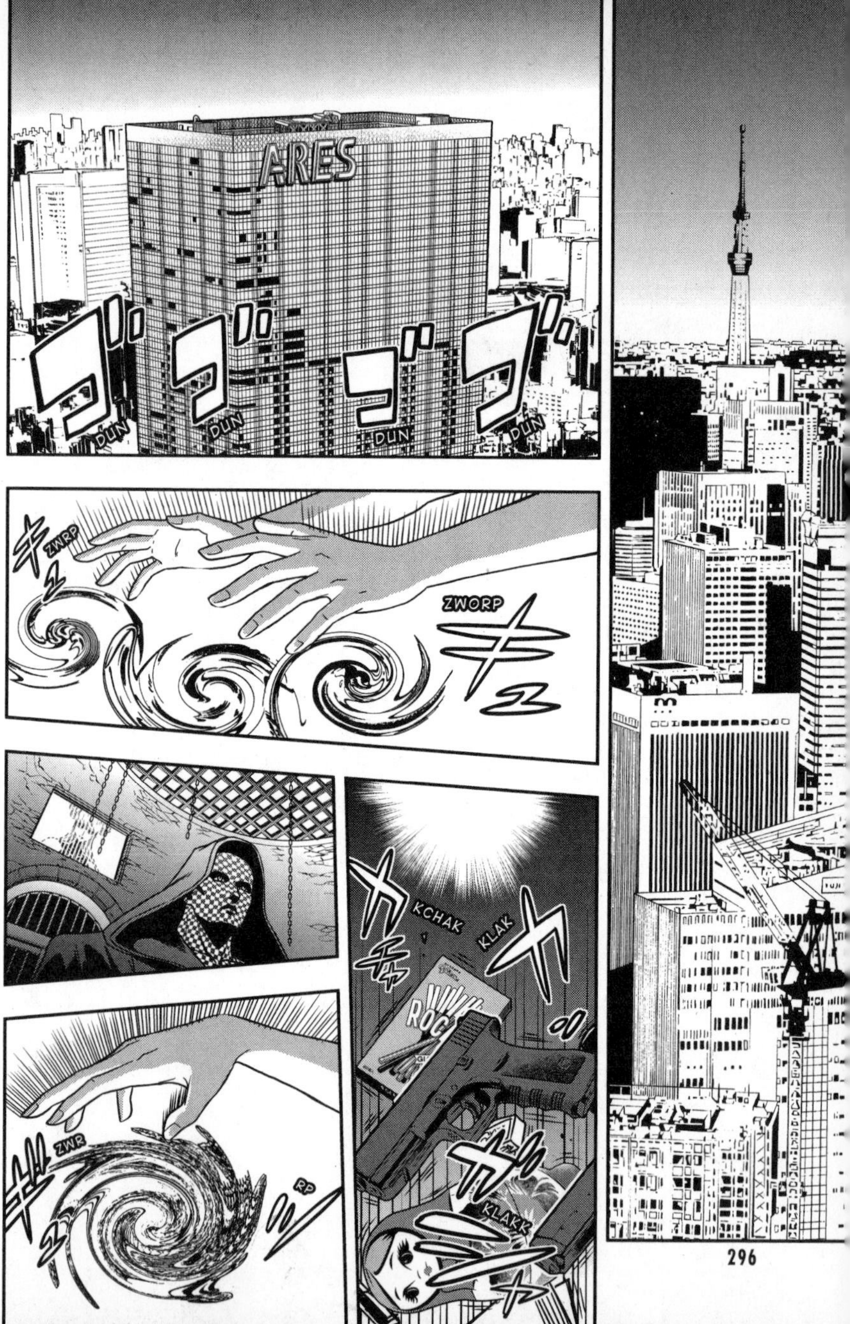
ARES
DUN
DUN
DUN
DUN
ZWRP
ZWORP
KCHAK
KLAK
ROC
KLAKK
ZWR
RP

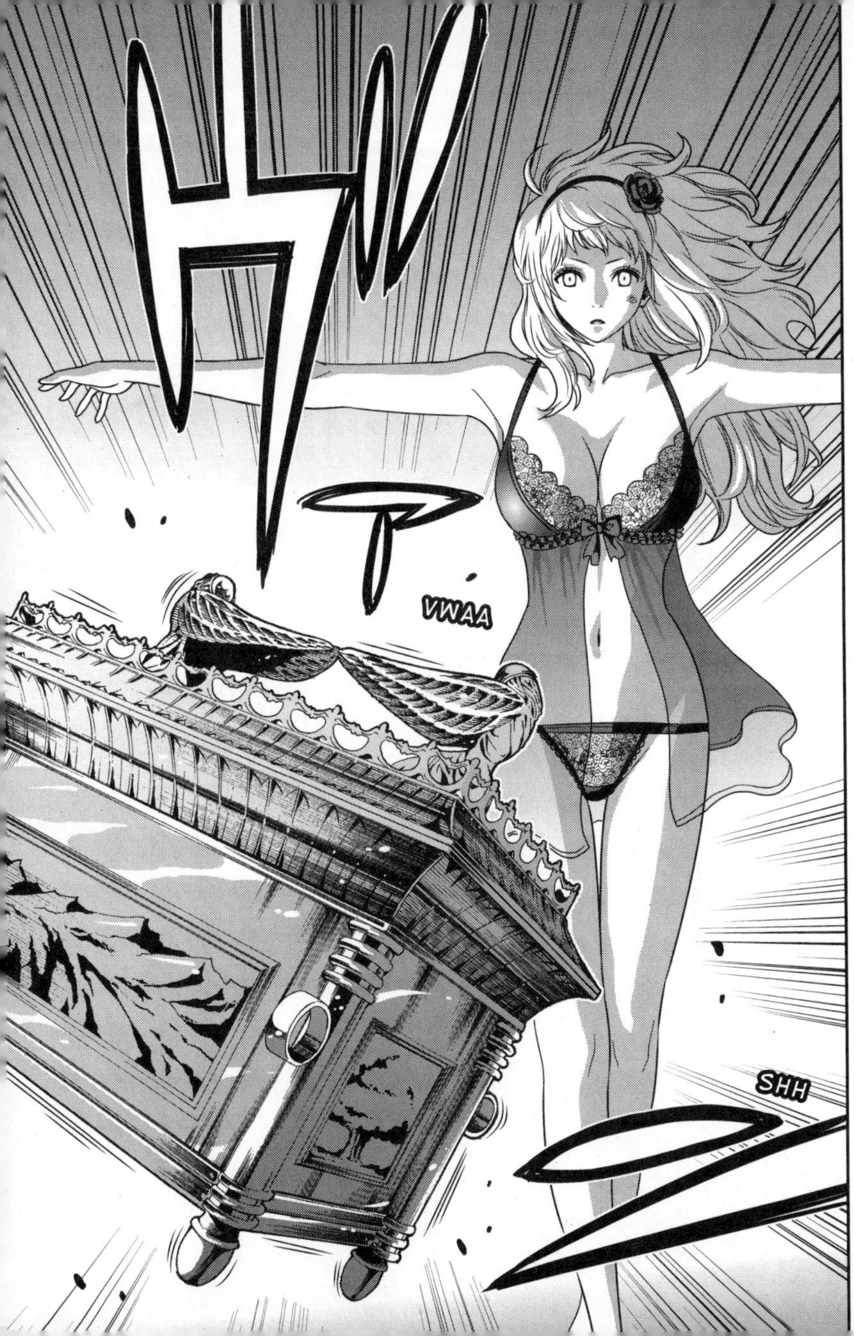
VWAA
SHH

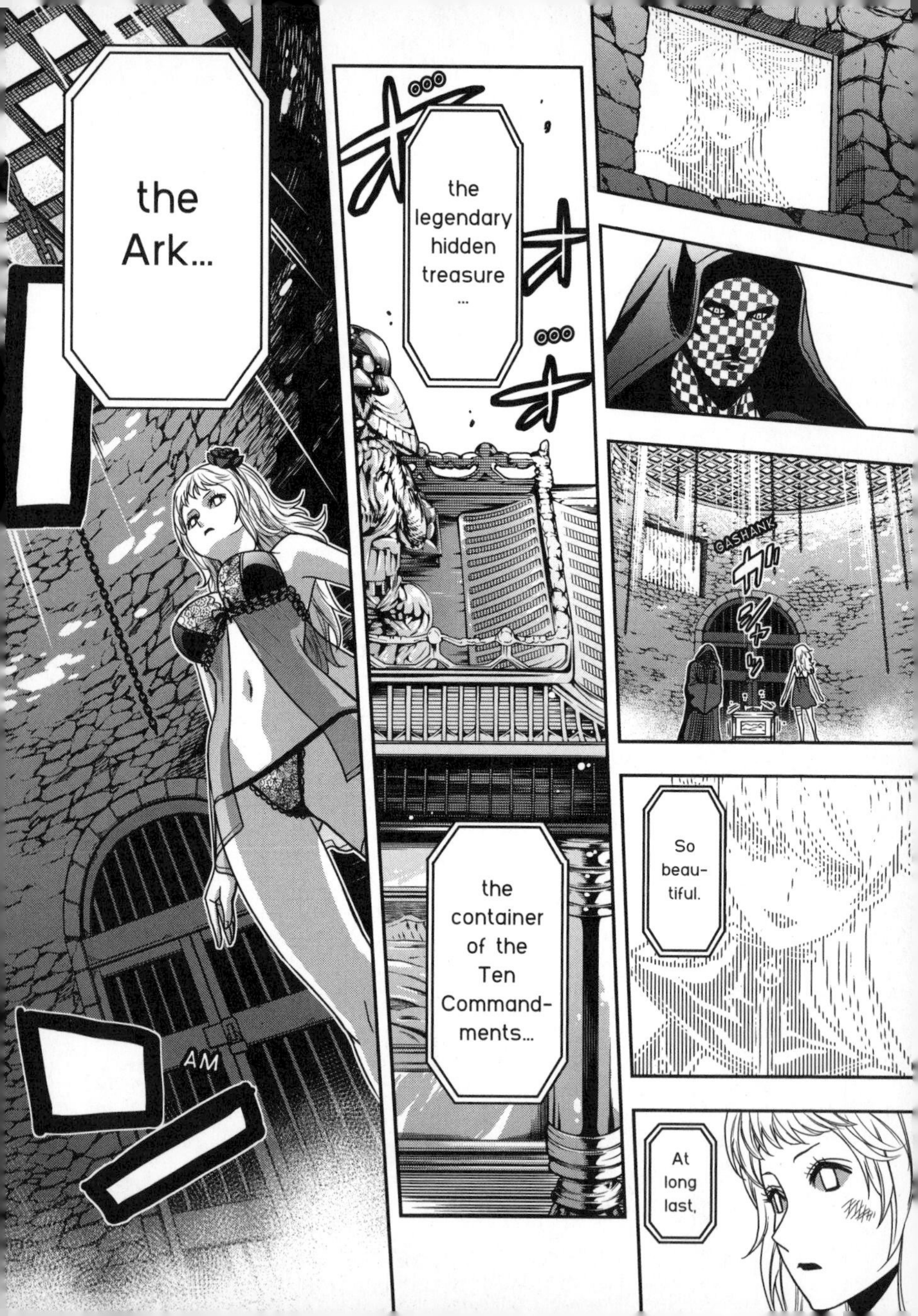
CASHANK
So beau-tiful.
At long last,
the legendary hidden treasure...
the container of the Ten Command-ments...
the Ark...
AM

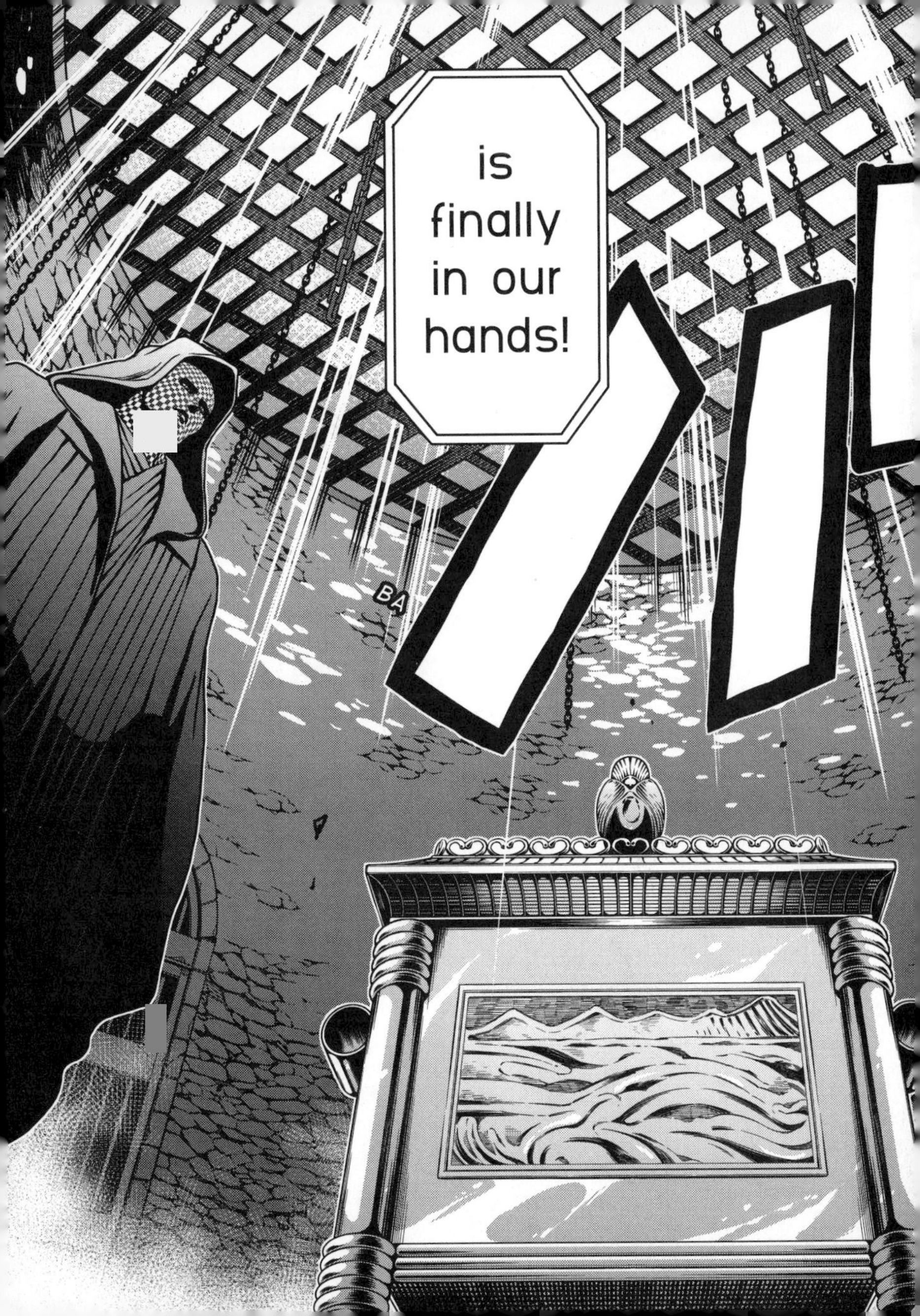
is finally in our hands!
BA

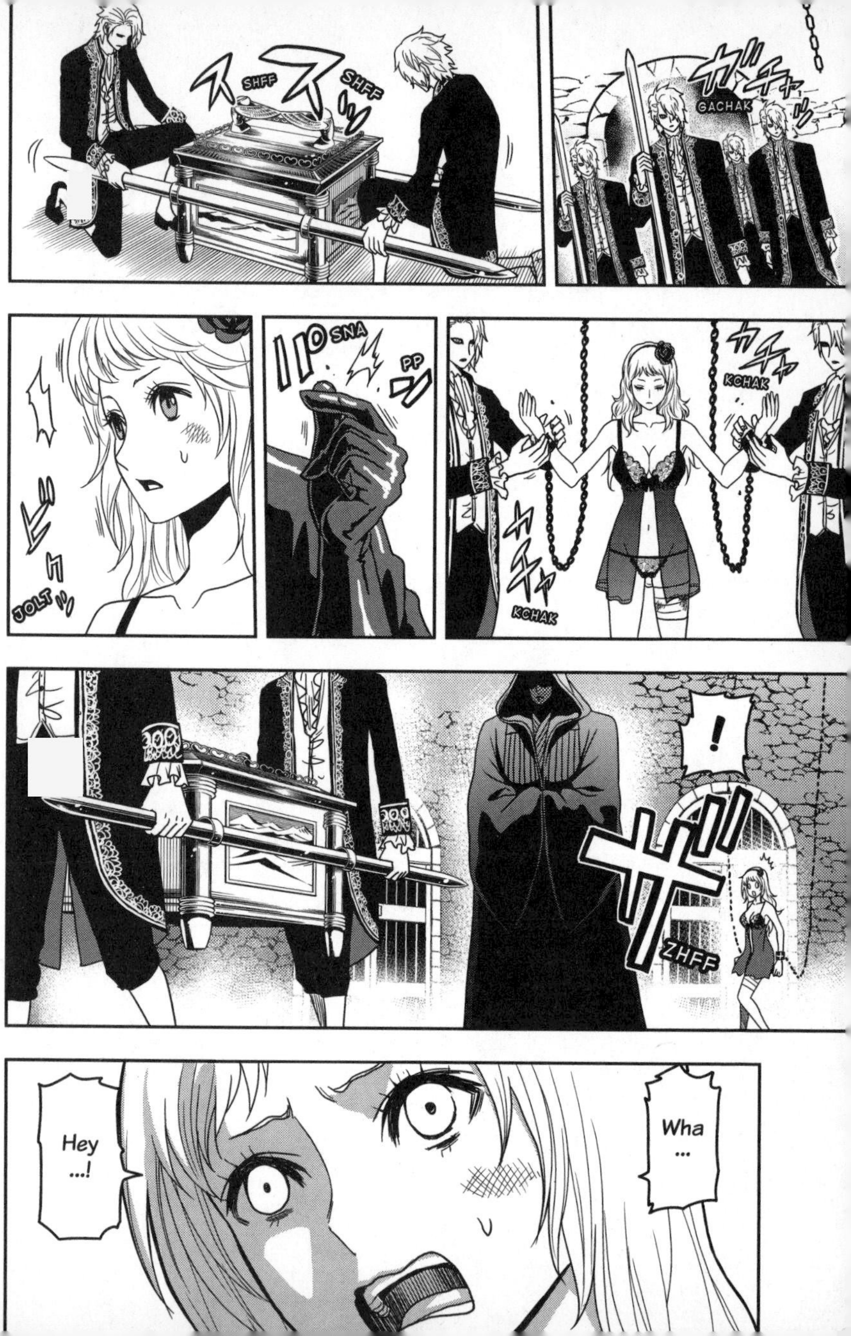
GACHAK
SHFF
SHFF
KCHAK
KCHAK
SNA
PP
JOLT
!
ZHFF
Wha ...
Hey ...!

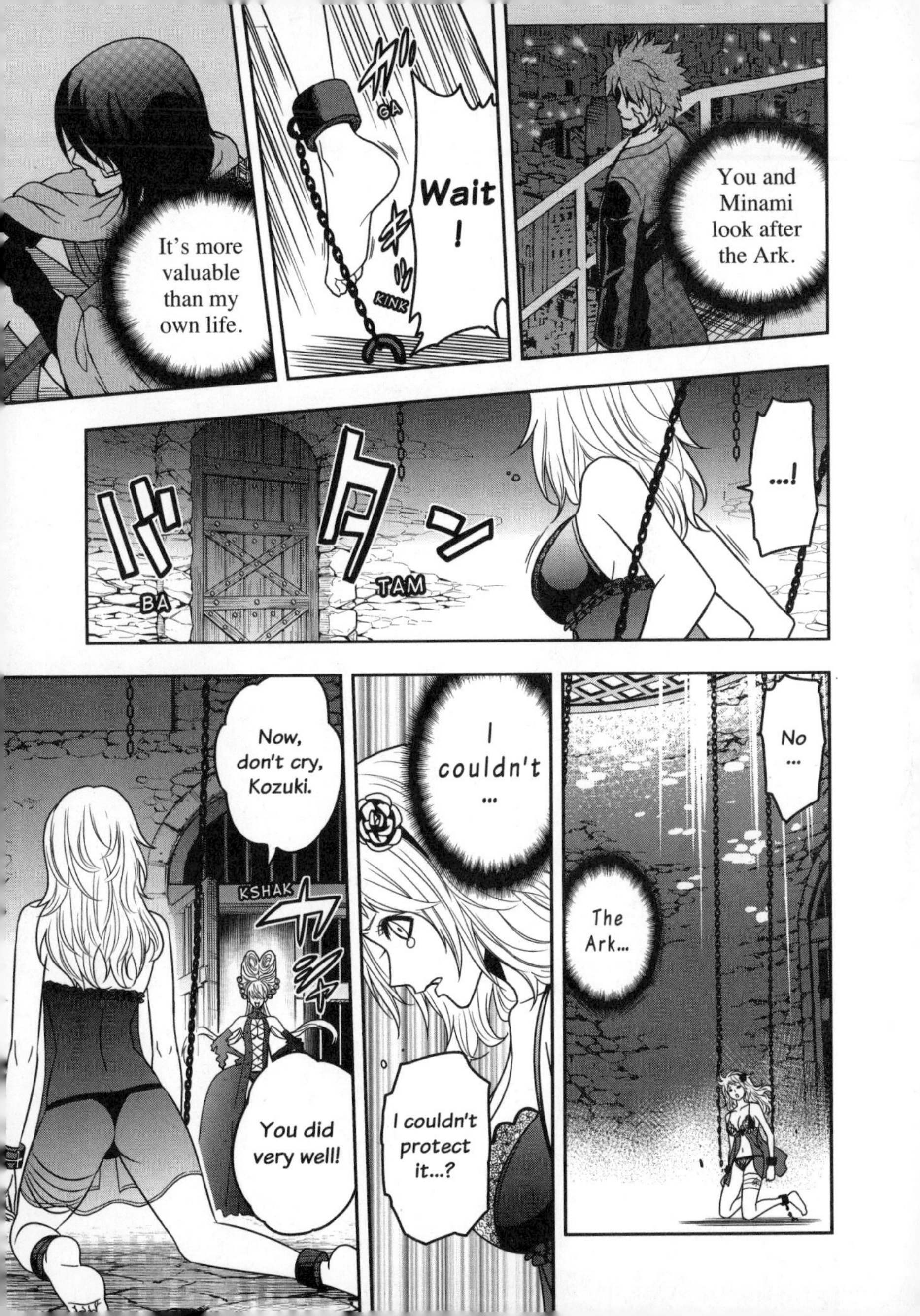
You and Minami look after the Ark.
GA
Wait !
KINK
It's more valuable than my own life.
...!
TAM
BA
No ...
The Ark...
I couldn't ...
I couldn't protect it...?
Now, don't cry, Kozuki.
KSHAK
You did very well!

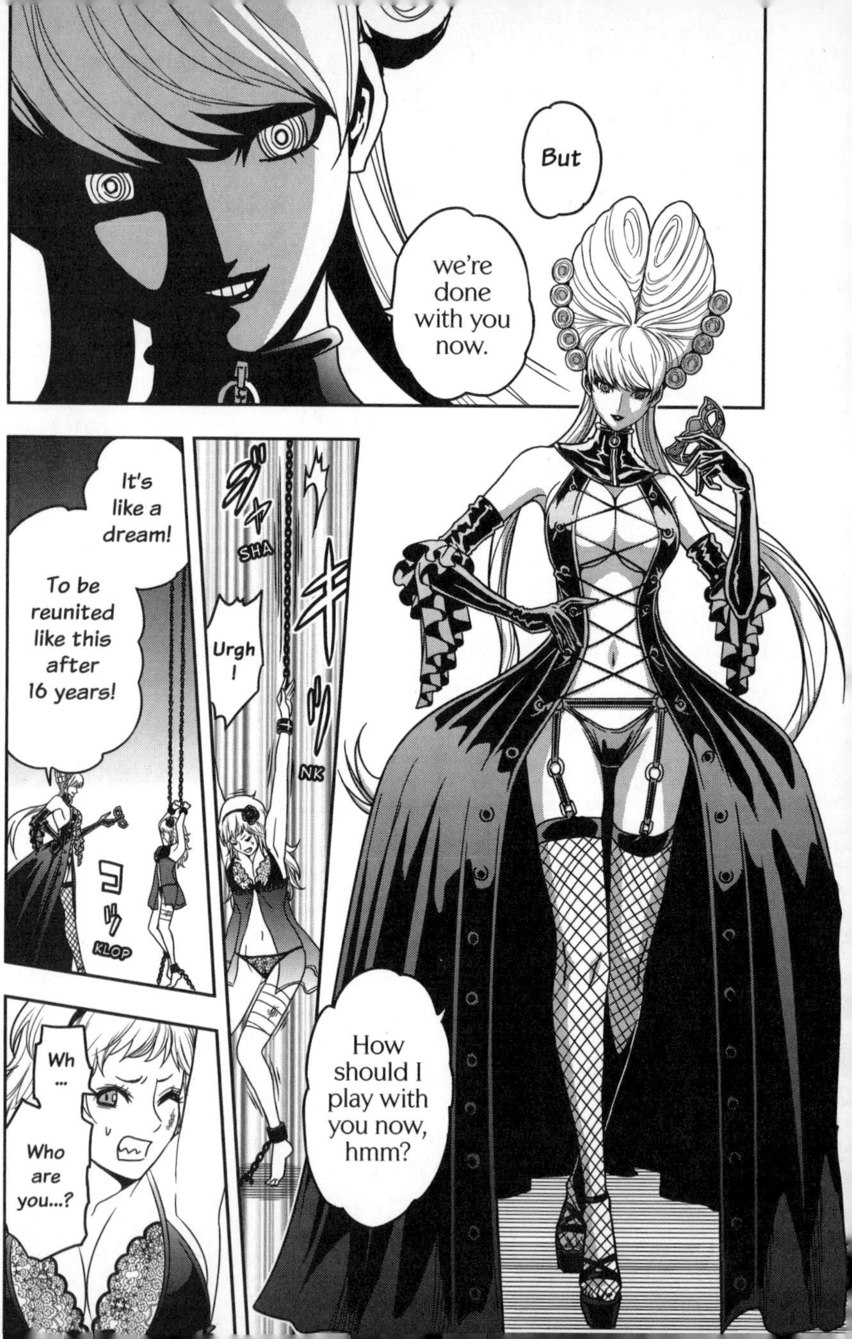
But
we're done with you now.
How should I play with you now, hmm?
SHA
Urgh!
NK
It's like a dream!
To be reunited like this after 16 years!
KLOP
Wh...
Who are you...?

Heh heh!
I can't blame you for not remembering me.
You were still so little back then.
...?
Did you hurt your leg?
Oh, you poor thing.
ZWOO
SZ
PP
STA
BB

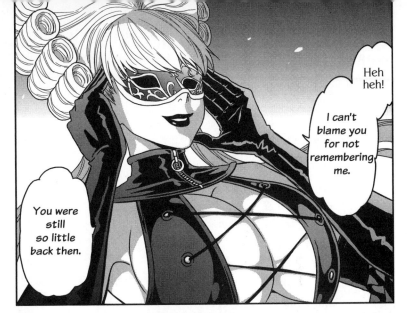

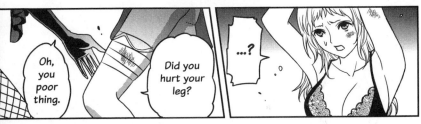

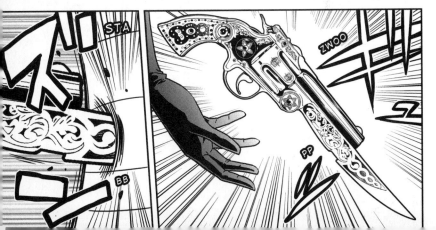

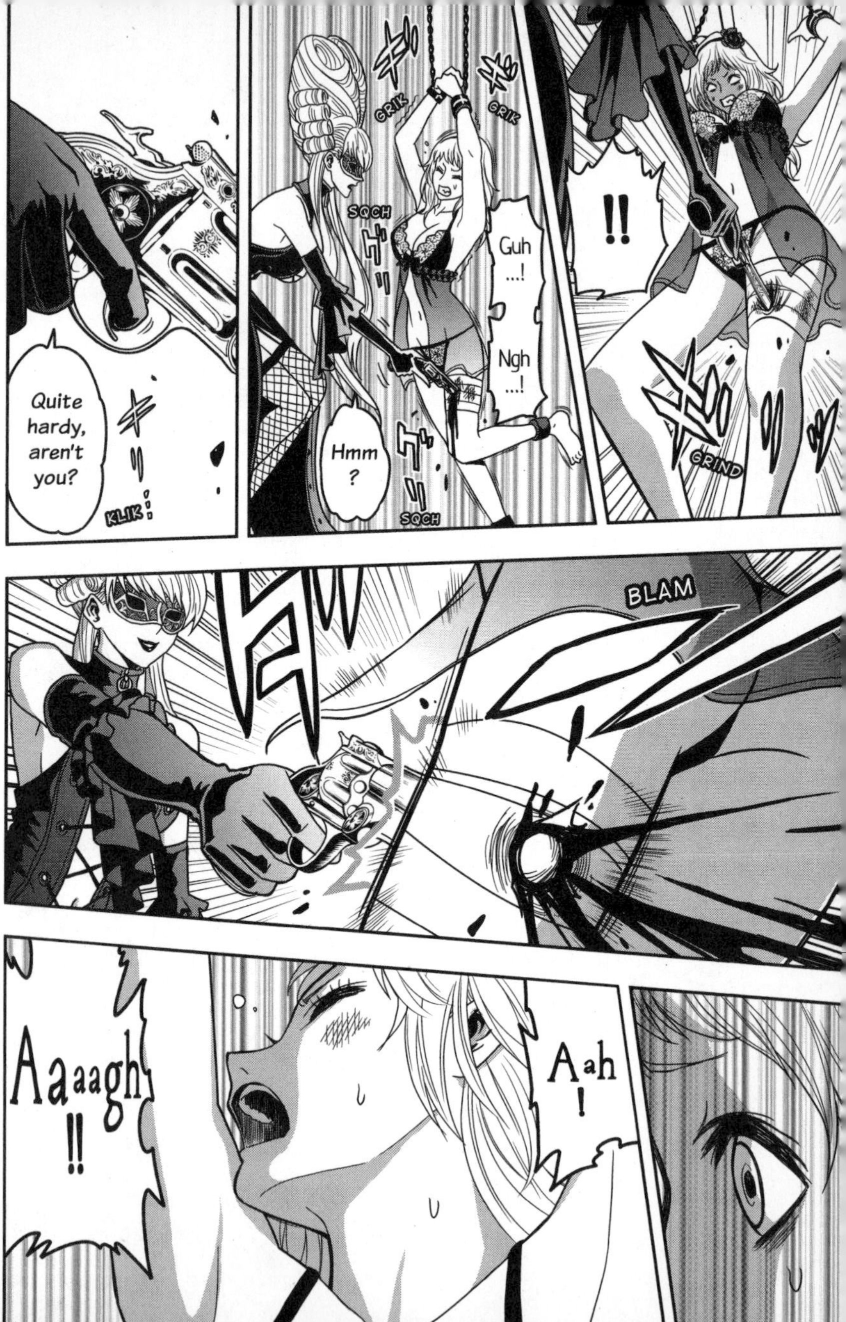
!!
GRIND
GRIK
GRIK
Guh ...!
Ngh ...!
SQCH
Hmm ?
SQCH
Quite hardy, aren't you?
KLIK
BLAM
Aah !
Aaaagh !!

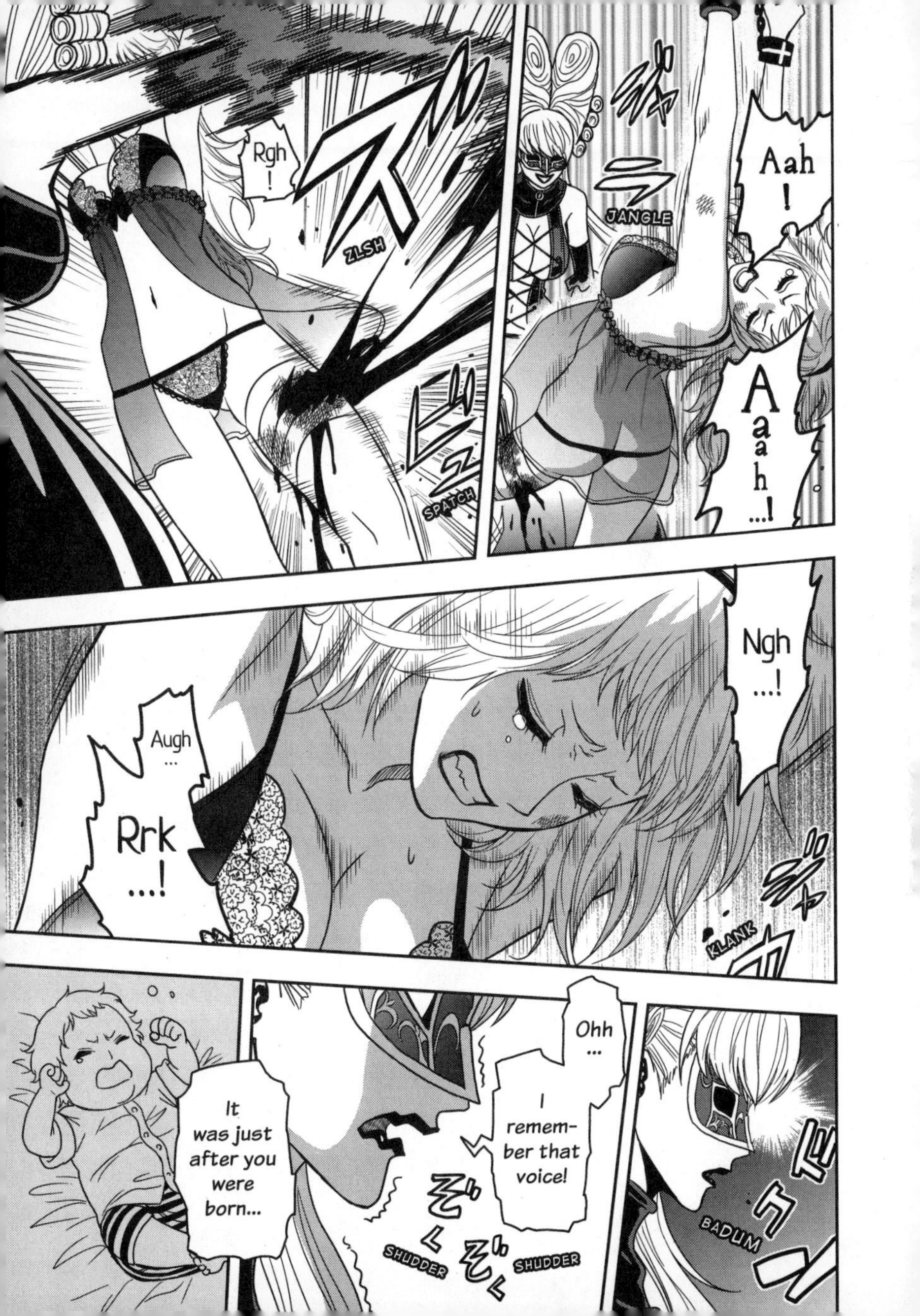
Aah!
JANGLE
Aaah...!
Rgh!
ZLSH
SPATCH
Ngh...!
KLANK
Augh...
Rrk...!
BADUM
Ohh...
I remember that voice!
SHUDDER
SHUDDER
It was just after you were born...

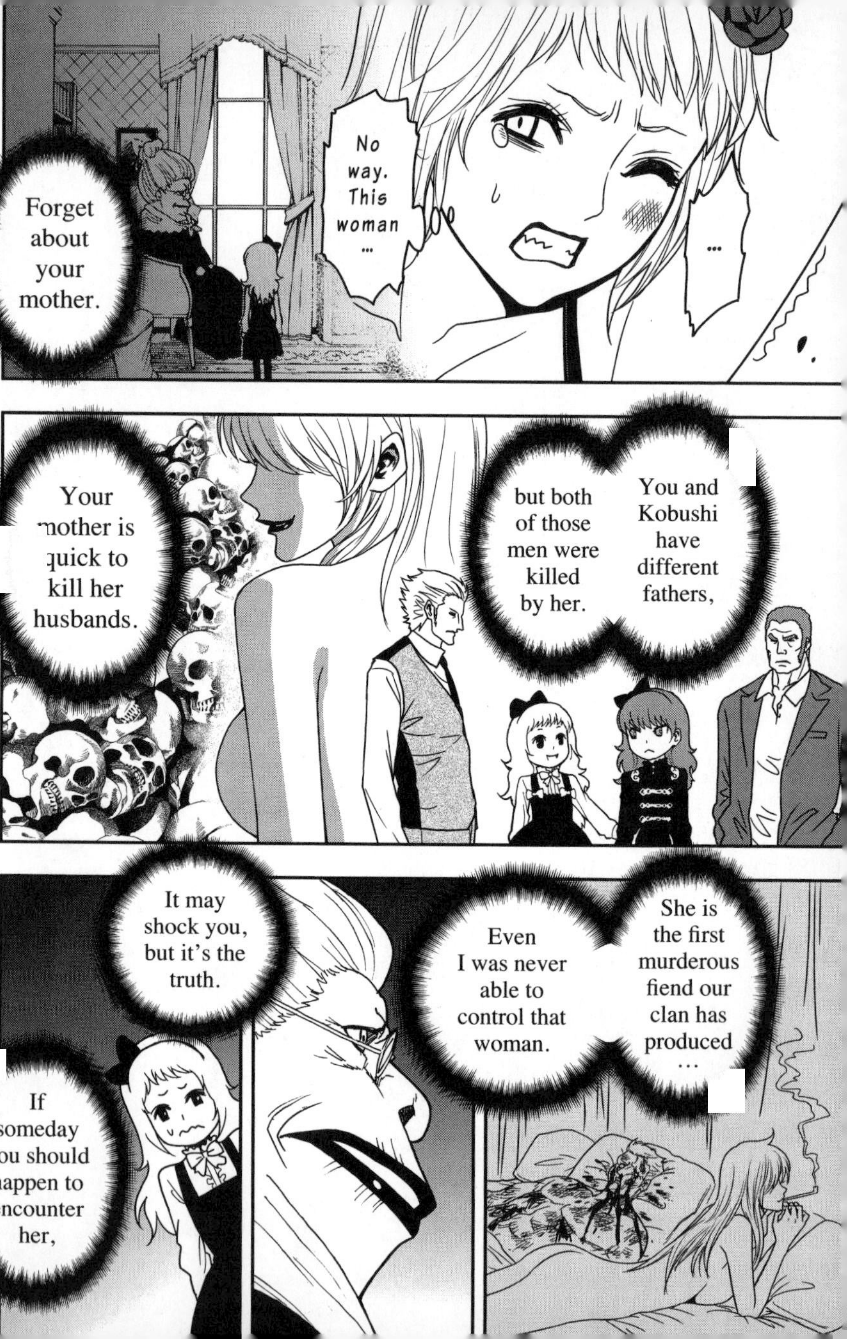
...
No way. This woman ...
Forget about your mother.
You and Kobushi have different fathers,
but both of those men were killed by her.
Your mother is quick to kill her husbands.
She is the first murderous fiend our clan has produced ...
Even I was never able to control that woman.
It may shock you, but it's the truth.
If someday you should happen to encounter her,

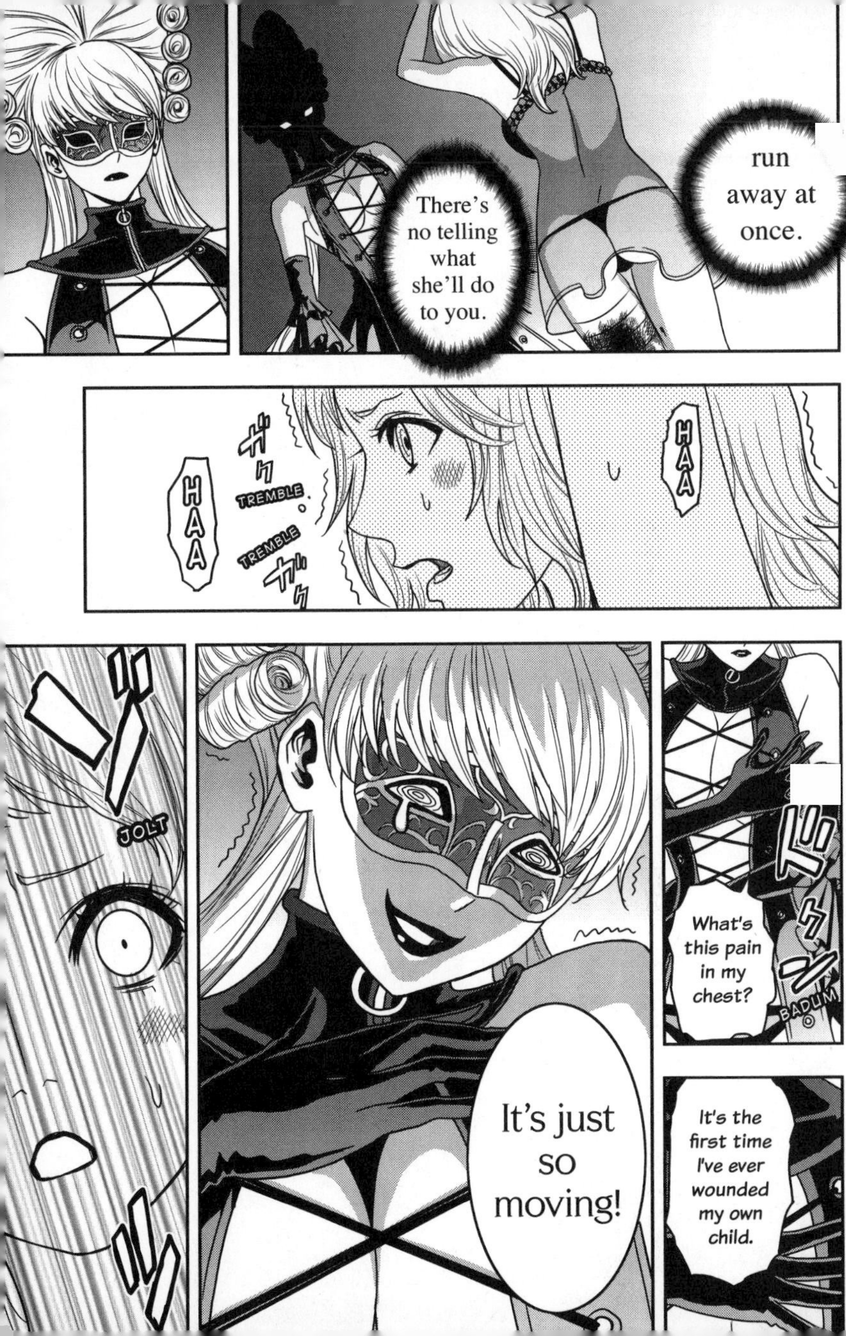
run away at once.
There's no telling what she'll do to you.
HAA
TREMBLE
TREMBLE
HAA
What's this pain in my chest?
BADUM
It's the first time I've ever wounded my own child.
It's just so moving!
JOLT

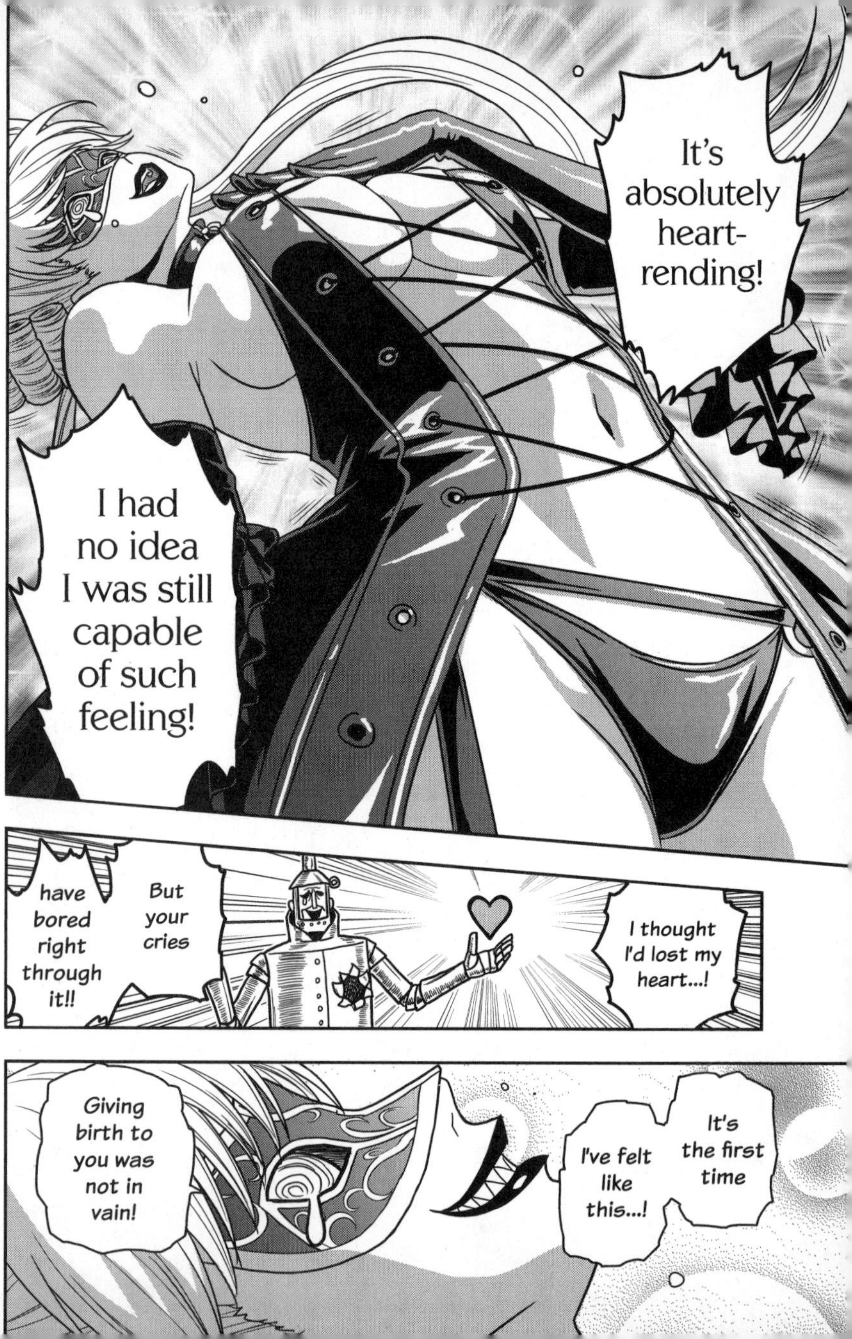
It's absolutely heart-rending!
I had no idea I was still capable of such feeling!
I thought I'd lost my heart...!
But your cries
have bored right through it!!
It's the first time
I've felt like this...!
Giving birth to you was not in vain!

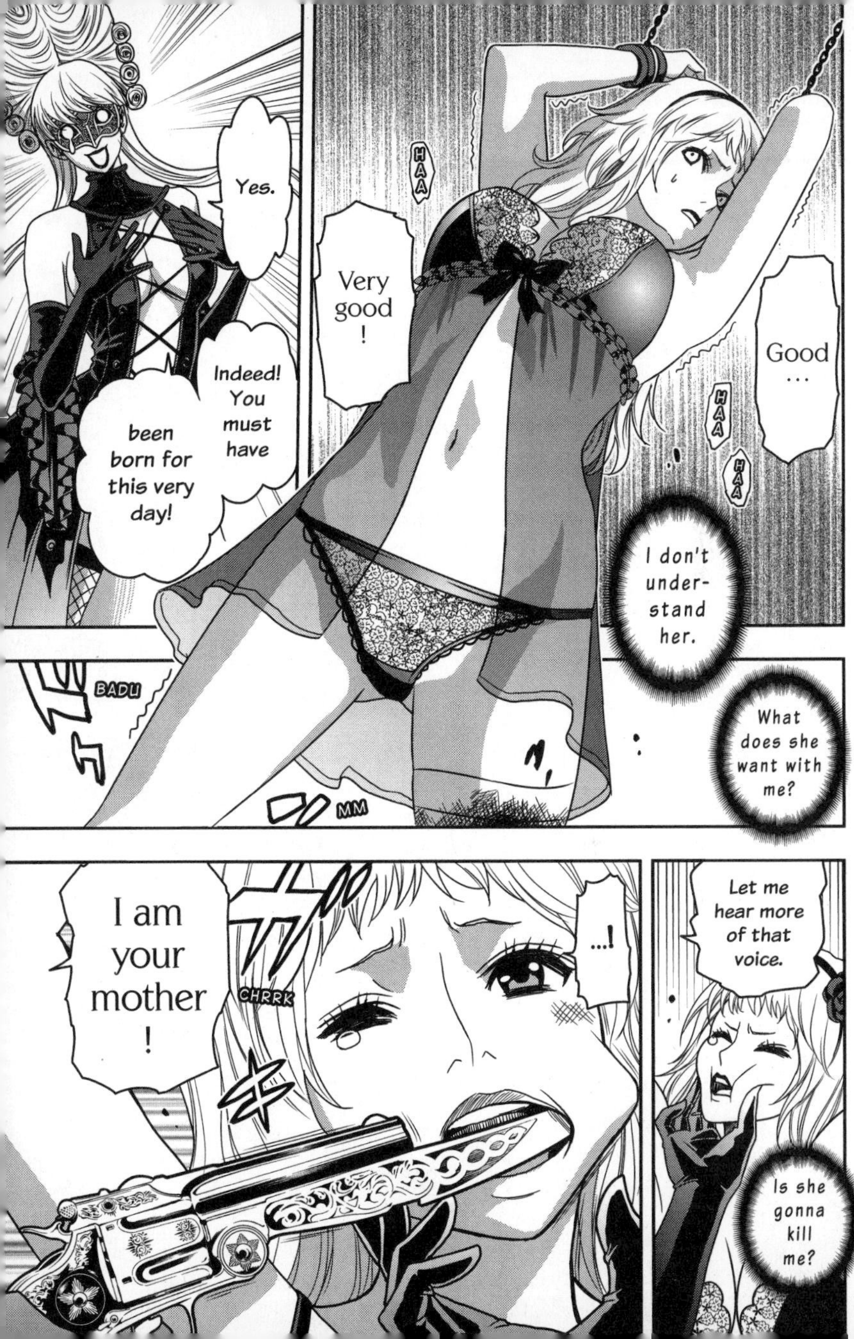
Good...
HAA
HAA
Very good!
HAA
I don't understand her.
What does she want with me?
MM
Yes.
Indeed! You must have been born for this very day!
BADU
Let me hear more of that voice.
Is she gonna kill me?
...!
CHRRK
I am your mother!

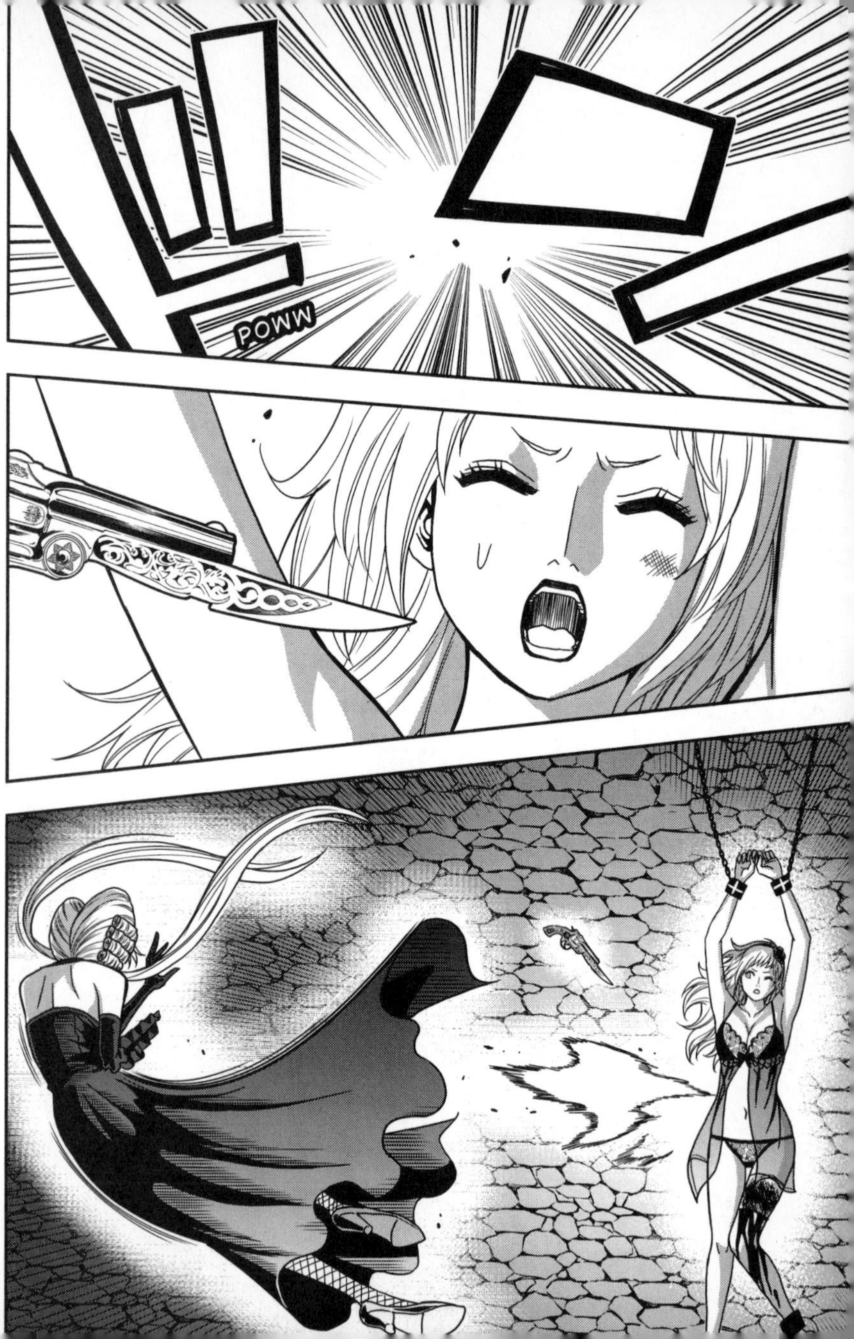
POWW

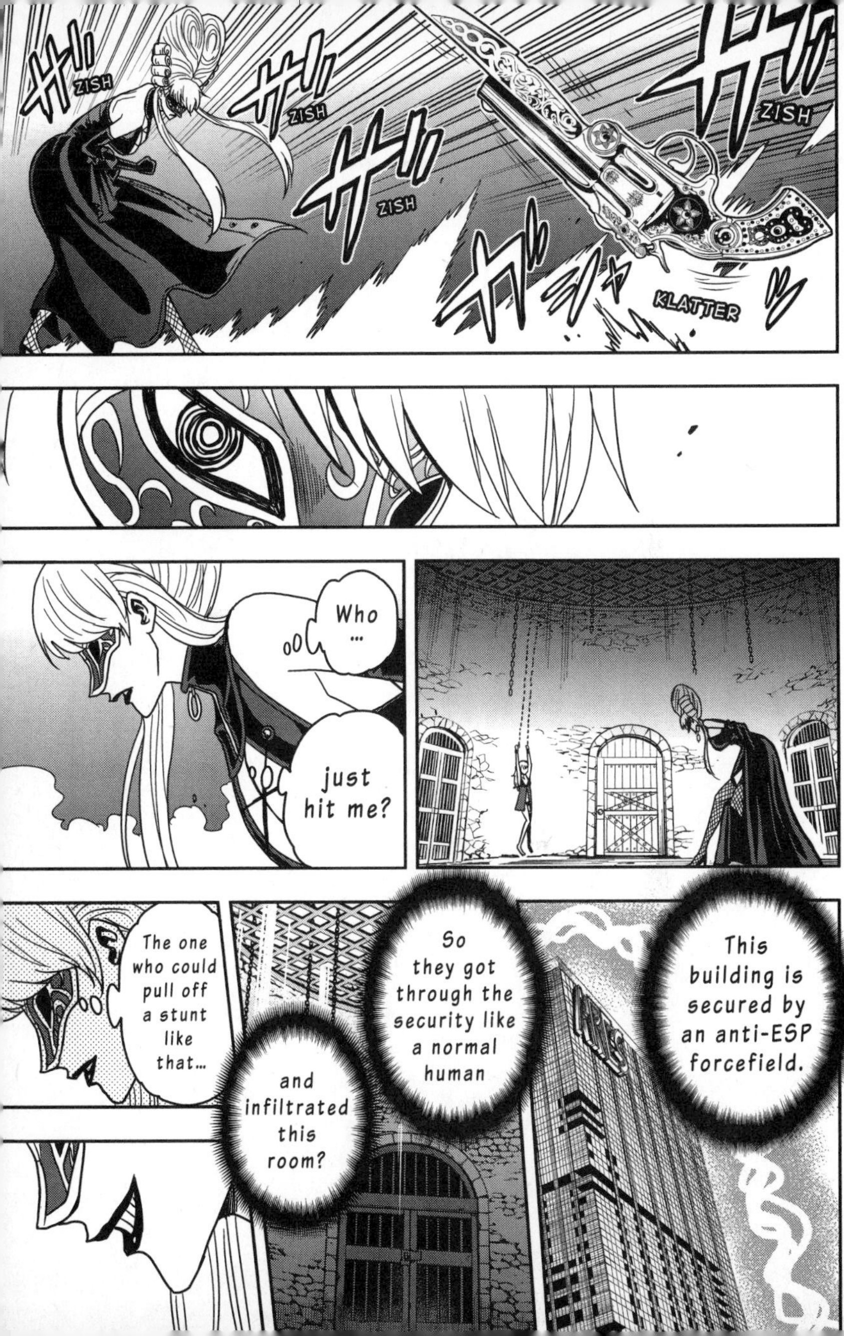
ZISH
ZISH
ZISH
KLATTER
ZISH
Who ...
just hit me?
This building is secured by an anti-ESP forcefield.
So they got through the security like a normal human
and infiltrated this room?
The one who could pull off a stunt like that...

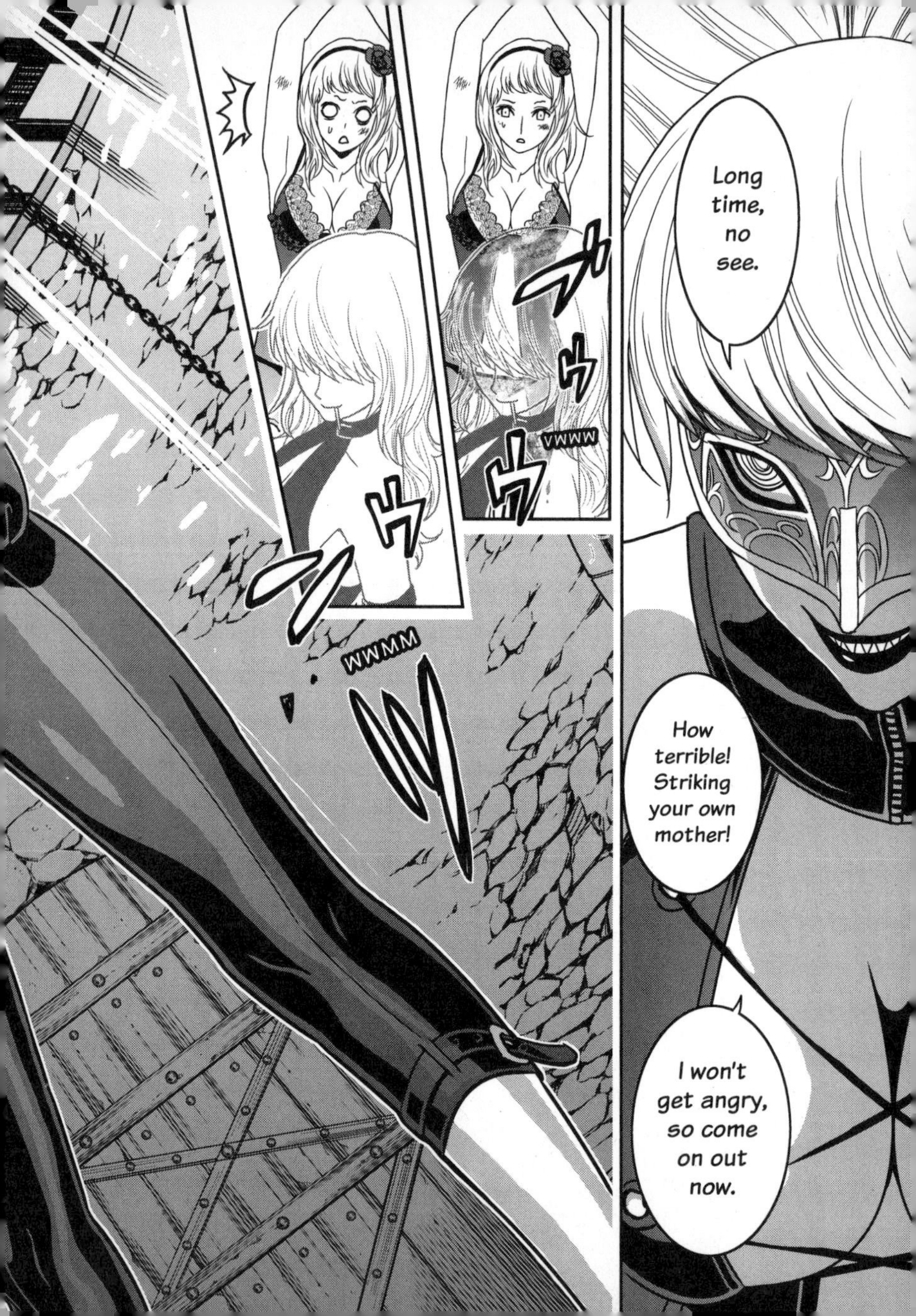
Long time, no see.
How terrible! Striking your own mother!
I won't get angry, so come on out now.
VWWW
WWMM

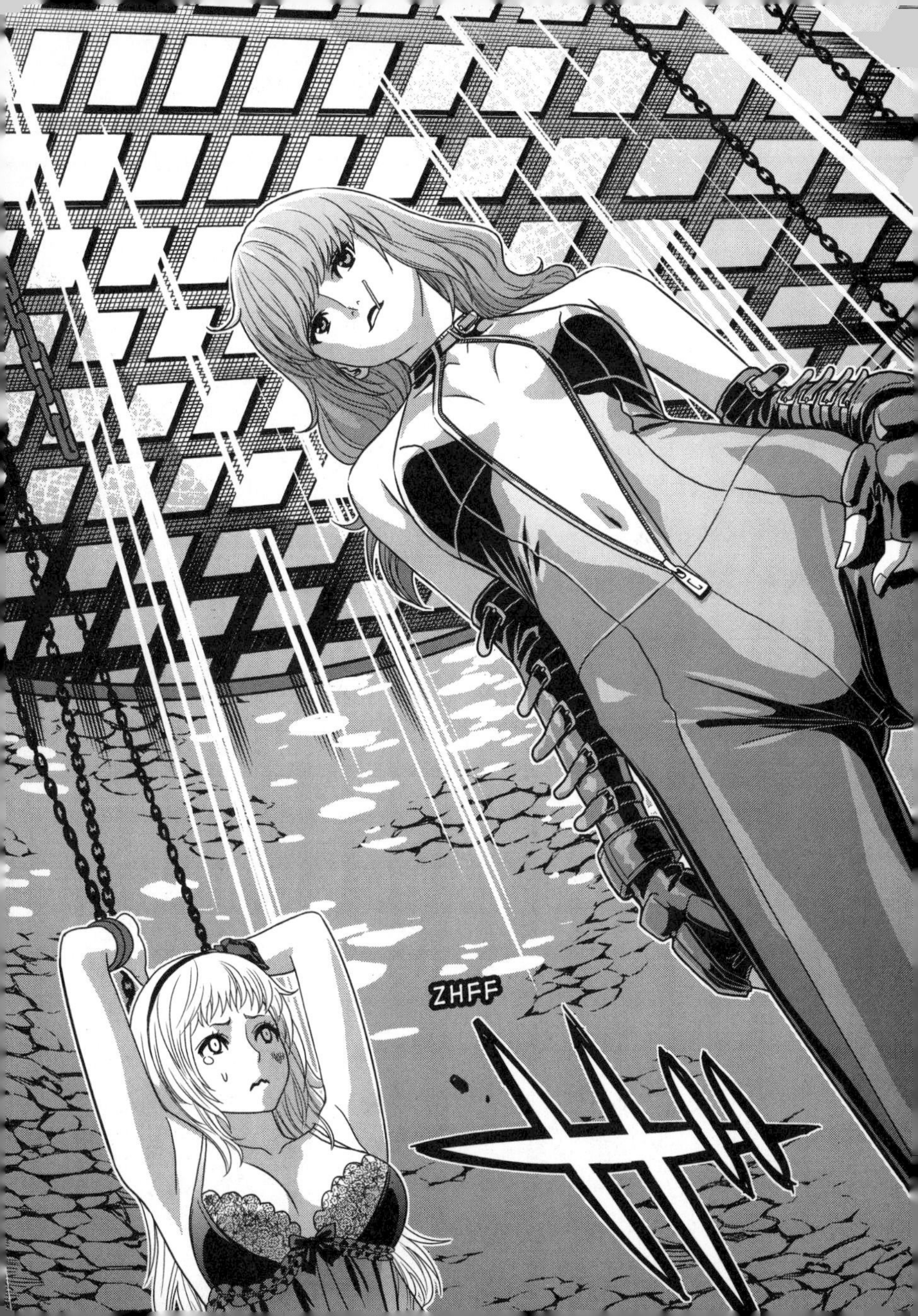
ZHFF

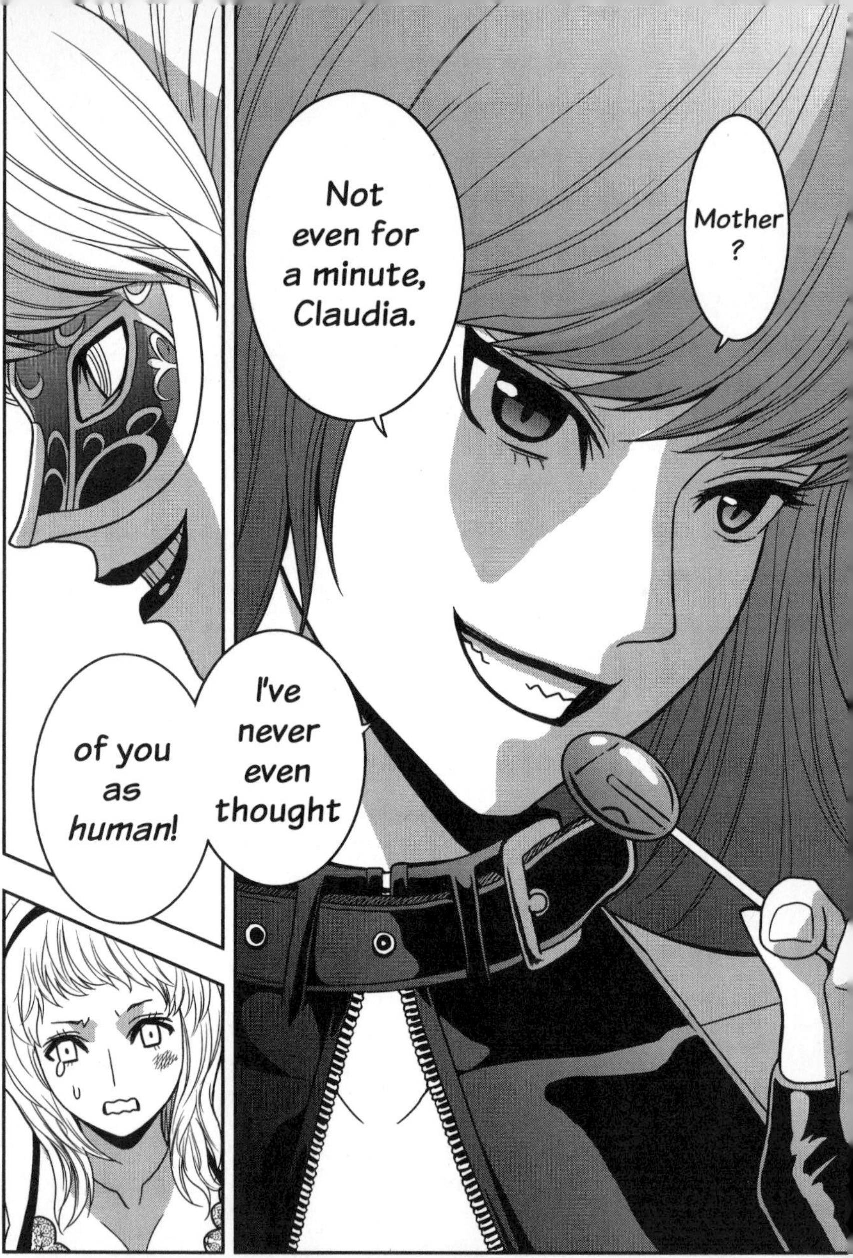
Mother?
Not even for a minute, Claudia.
I've never even thought
of you as human!

SCENE 62 /// END

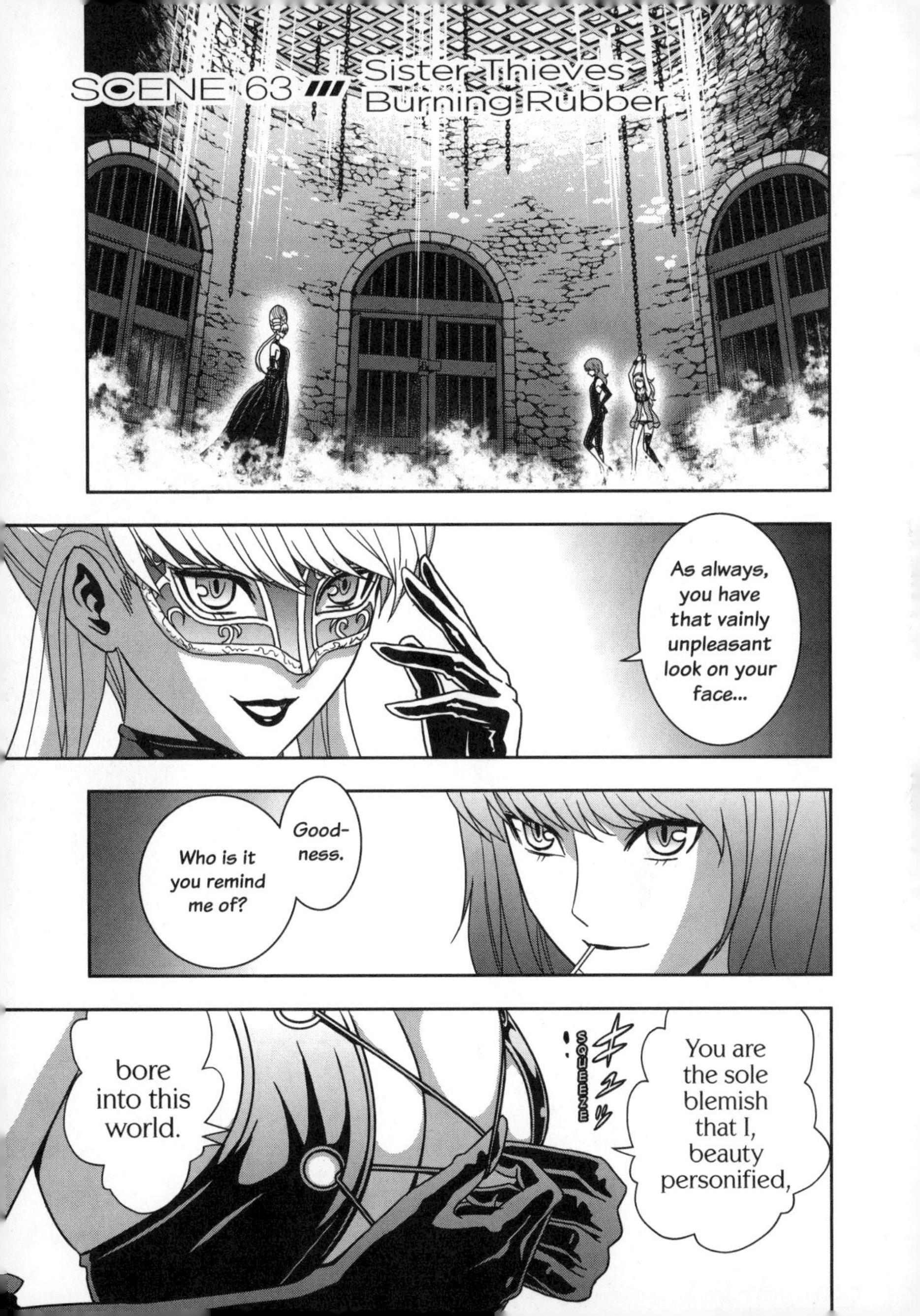
SCENE 63 /// Sister Thieves Burning Rubber
As always, you have that vainly unpleasant look on your face...
Good- ness.
Who is it you remind me of?
You are the sole blemish that I, beauty personified,
SQUEEZE
bore into this world.

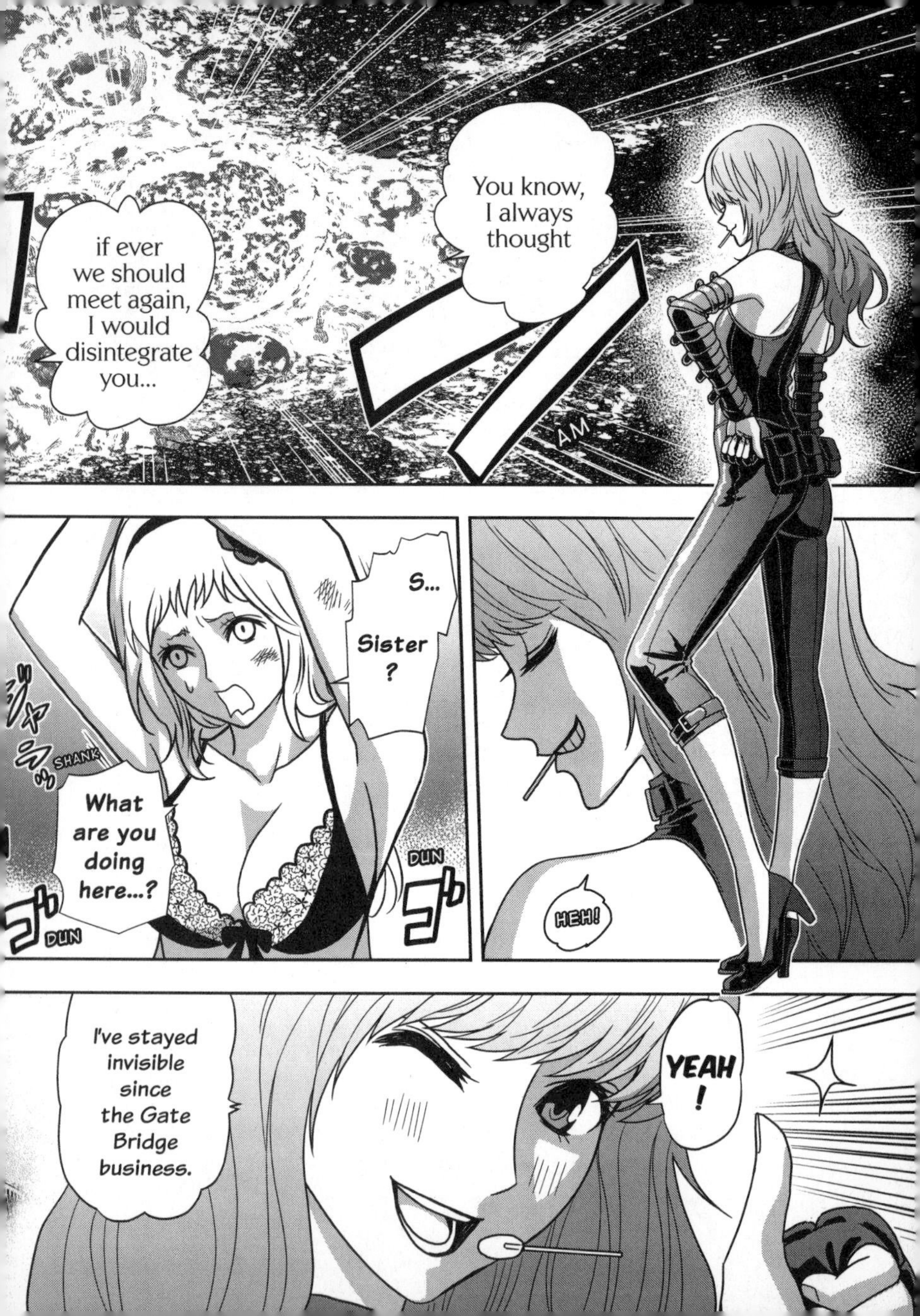
You know, I always thought
if ever we should meet again, I would disintegrate you...
AM
HEH!
S...
Sister?
SHANK
What are you doing here...?
DUN
DUN
YEAH!
I've stayed invisible since the Gate Bridge business.

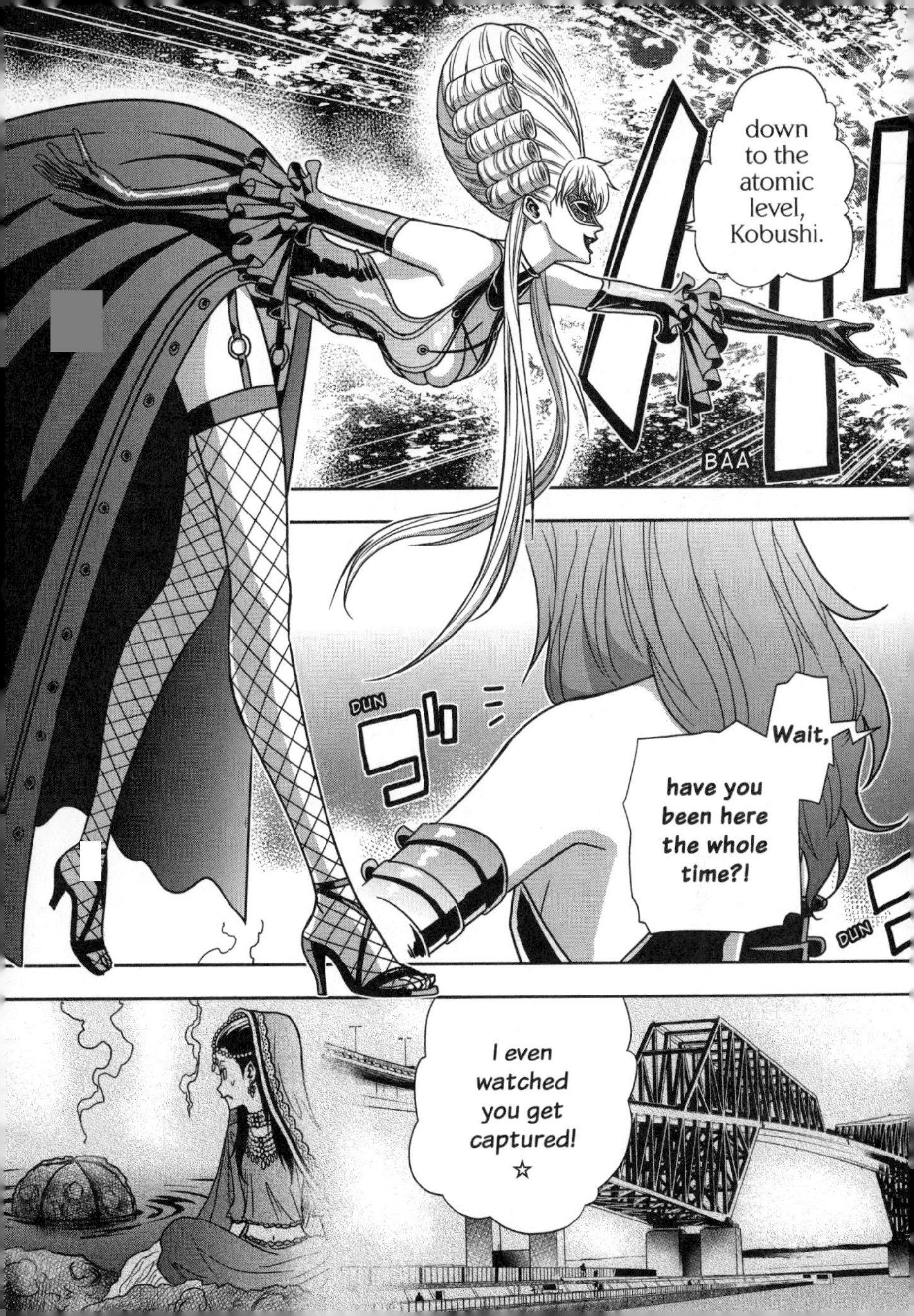
down to the atomic level, Kobushi.
BAA
Wait,
have you been here the whole time?!
DUN
DUN
I even watched you get captured! ☆

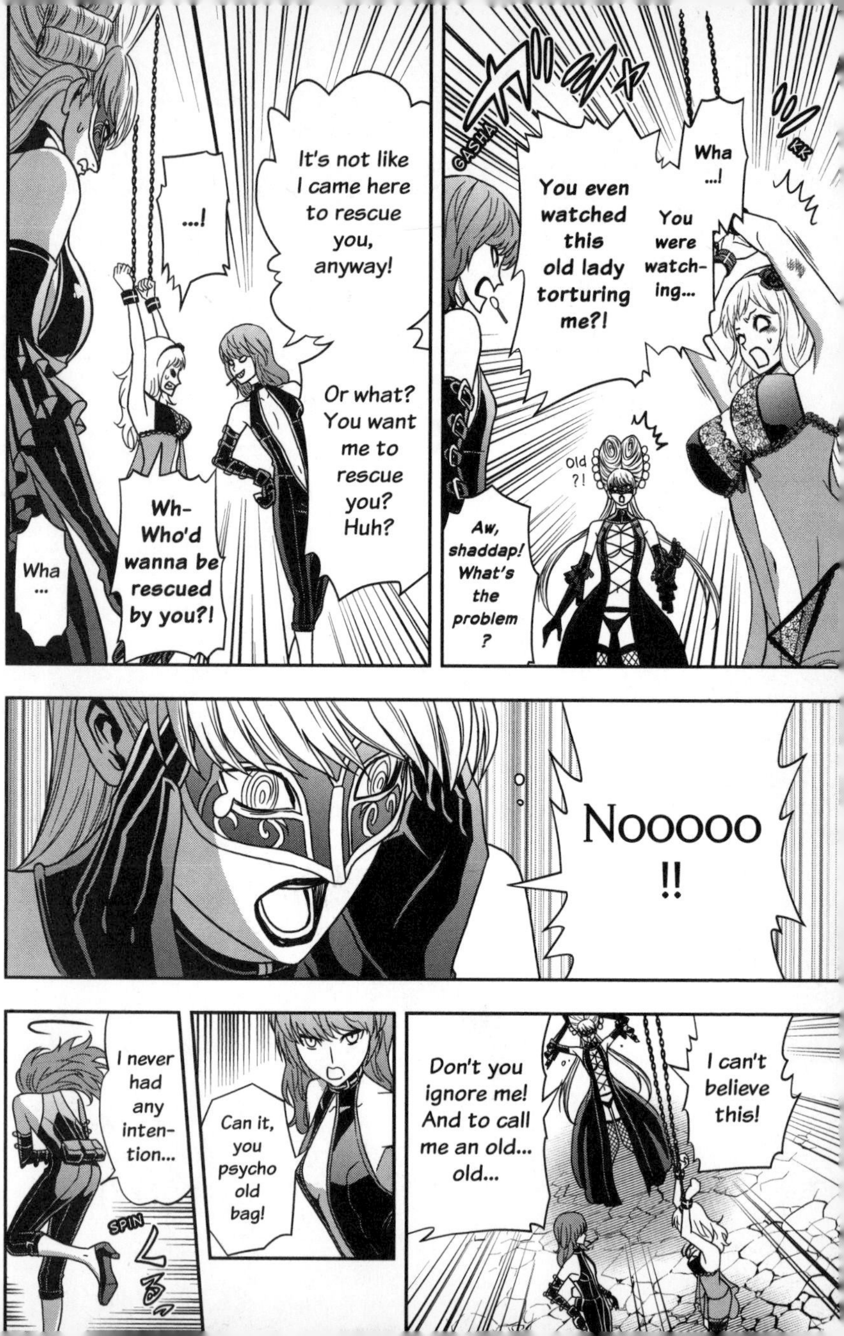
GASHA
KK
Wha ...!
You were watch- ing...
You even watched this old lady torturing me?!
Old ?!
Aw, shaddap! What's the problem ?
It's not like I came here to rescue you, anyway!
...!
Or what? You want me to rescue you? Huh?
Wh- Who'd wanna be rescued by you?!
Wha ...
Noooooo !!
I can't believe this!
Don't you ignore me! And to call me an old... old...
Can it, you psycho old bag!
I never had any inten- tion...
SPIN

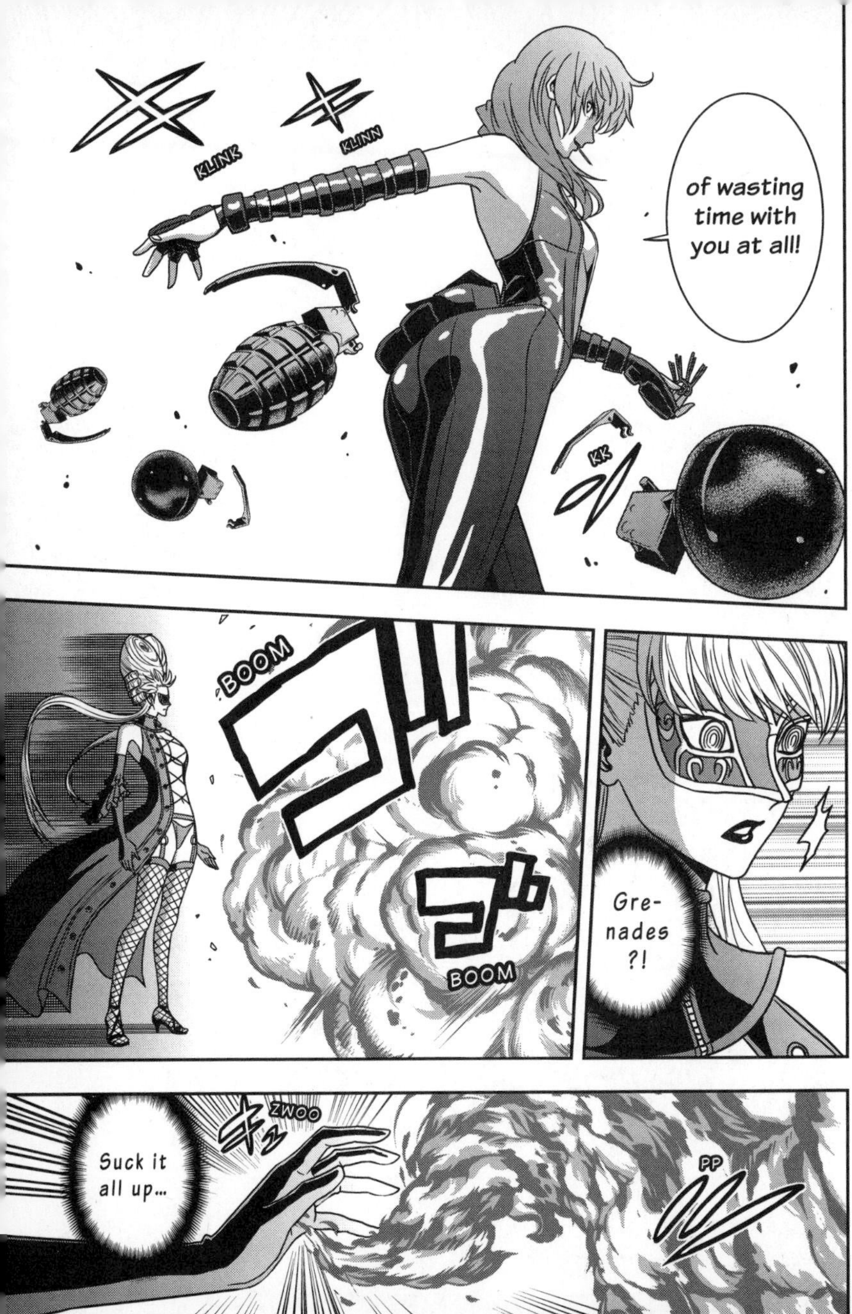
of wasting time with you at all!
KLINN
KLINK
KK
Gre-nades ?!
BOOM
BOOM
PP
ZWOO
Suck it all up...

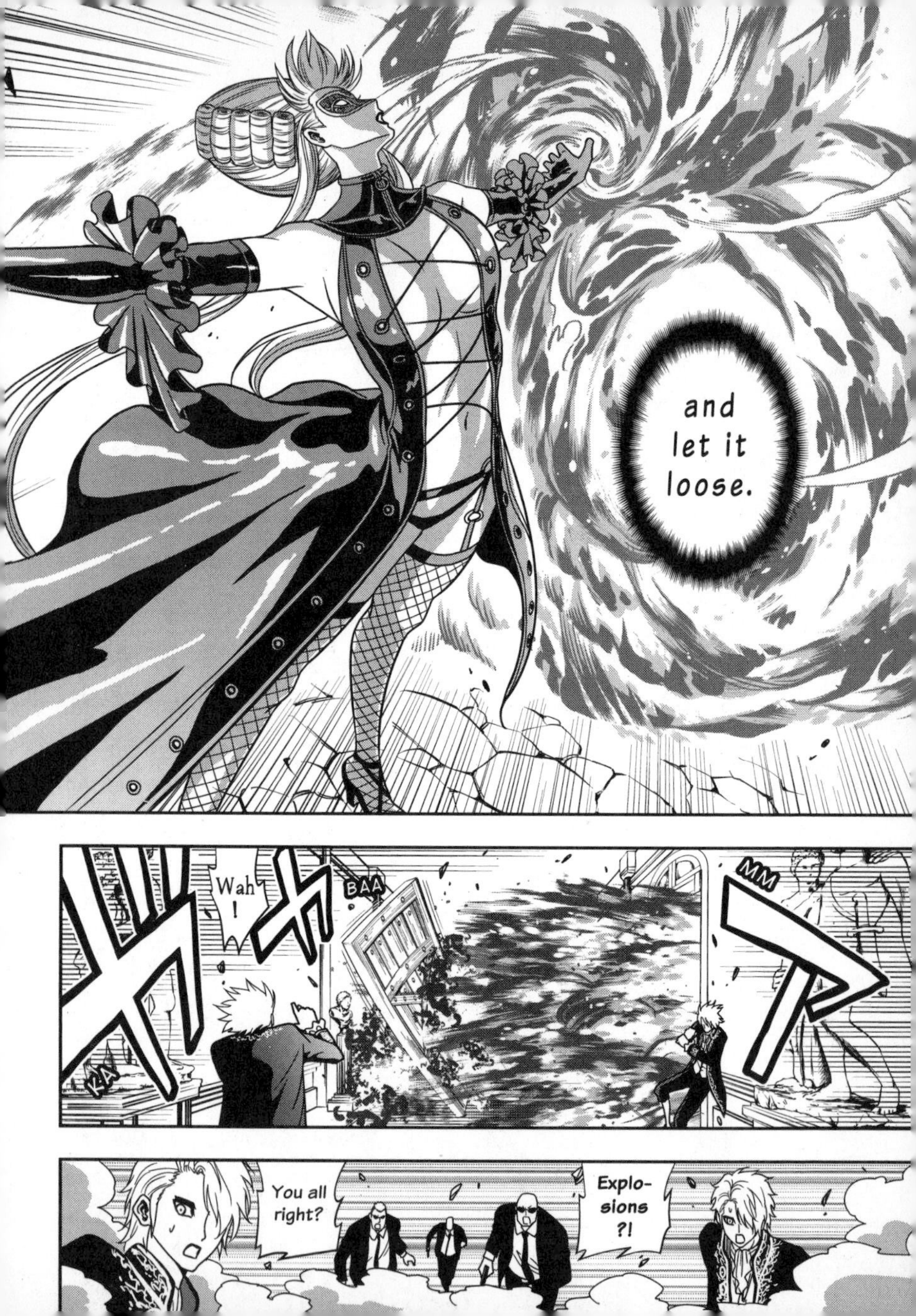
and let it loose.
MM
BAA
Wah !
KA
Explo-sions ?!
You all right?

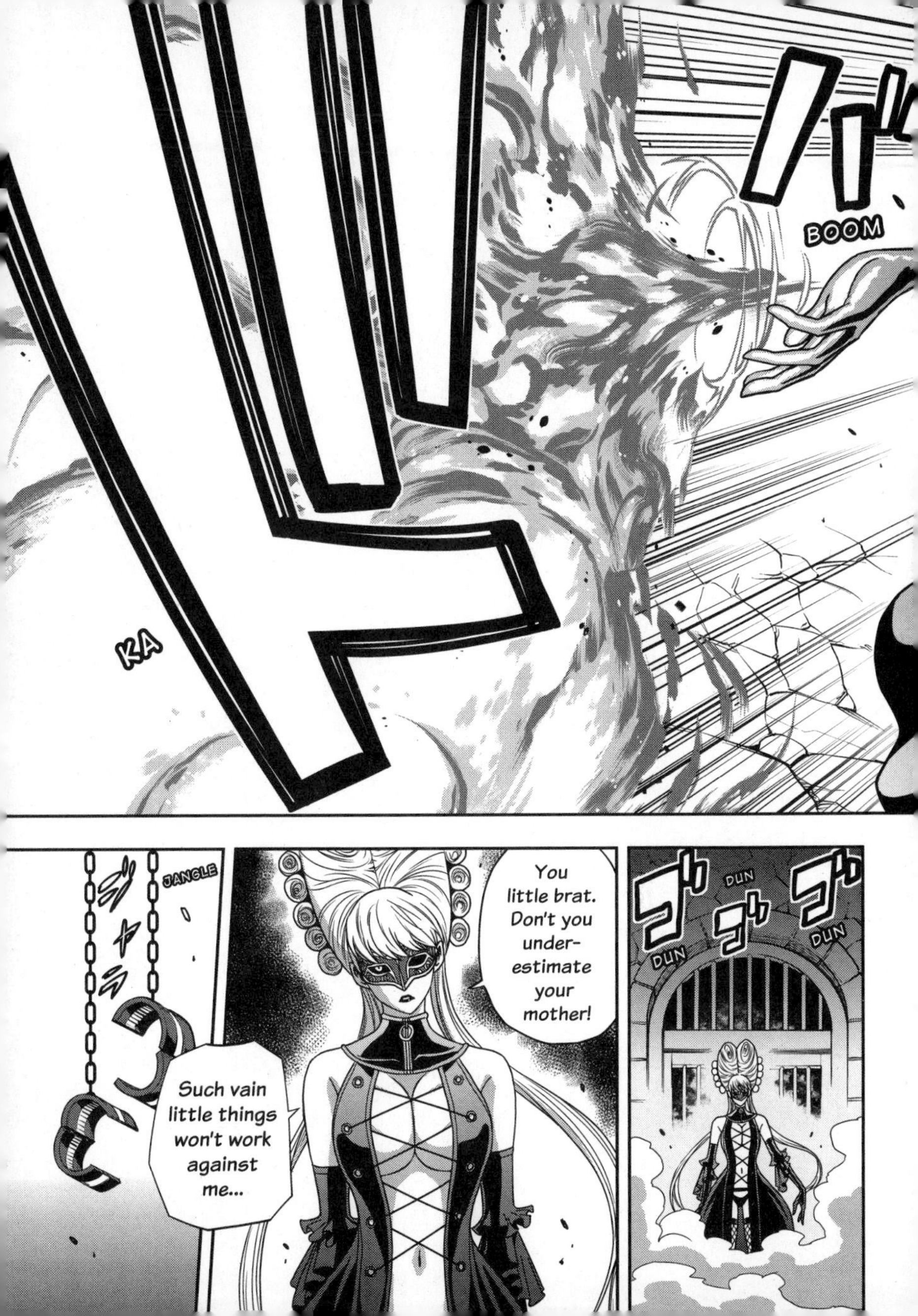
BOOM
KA
DUN
DUN
DUN
You little brat. Don't you under-estimate your mother!
Such vain little things won't work against me...
JANGLE

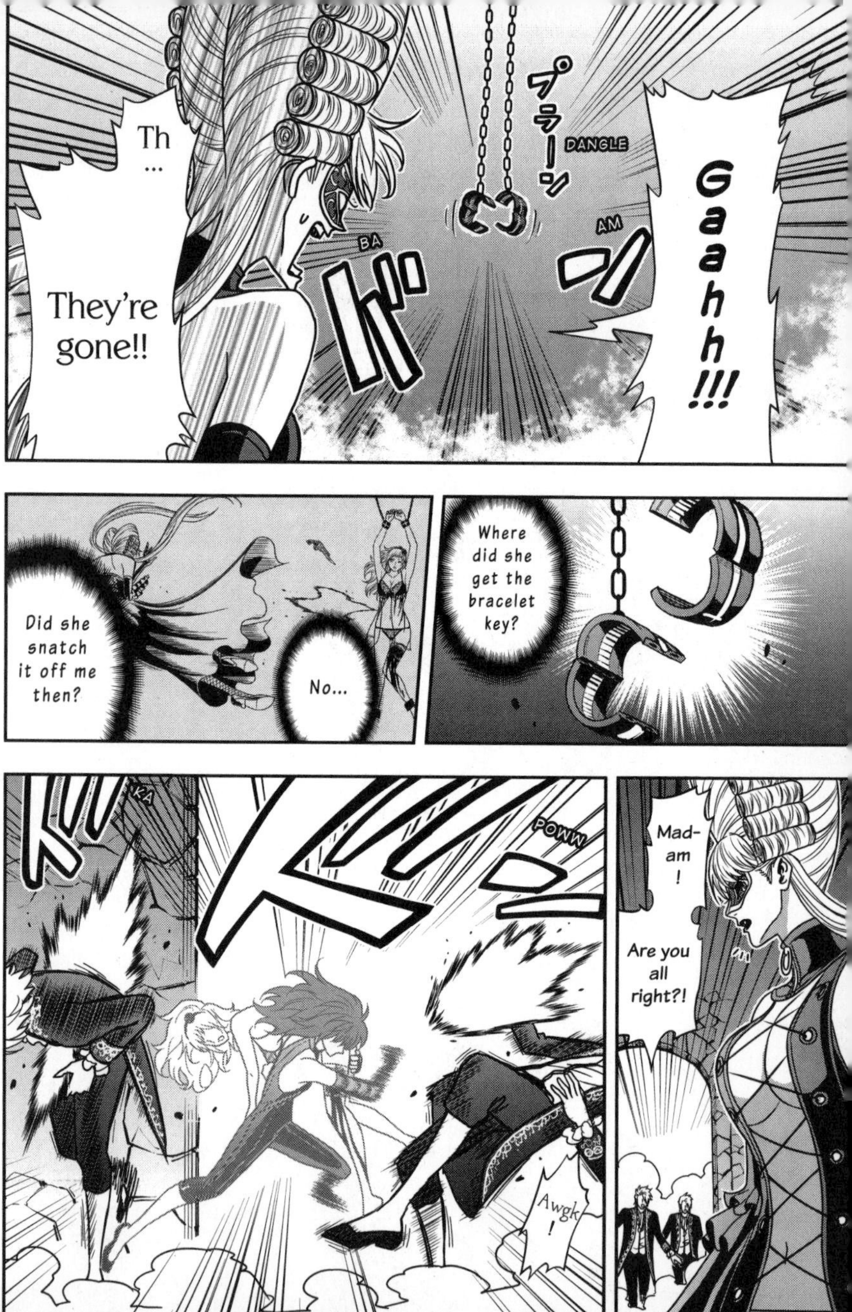
Gaahh!!!
DANGLE
AM
BA
Th...
They're gone!!
Where did she get the bracelet key?
No...
Did she snatch it off me then?
Mad-am!
Are you all right?!
POWW
KA
Awgk!

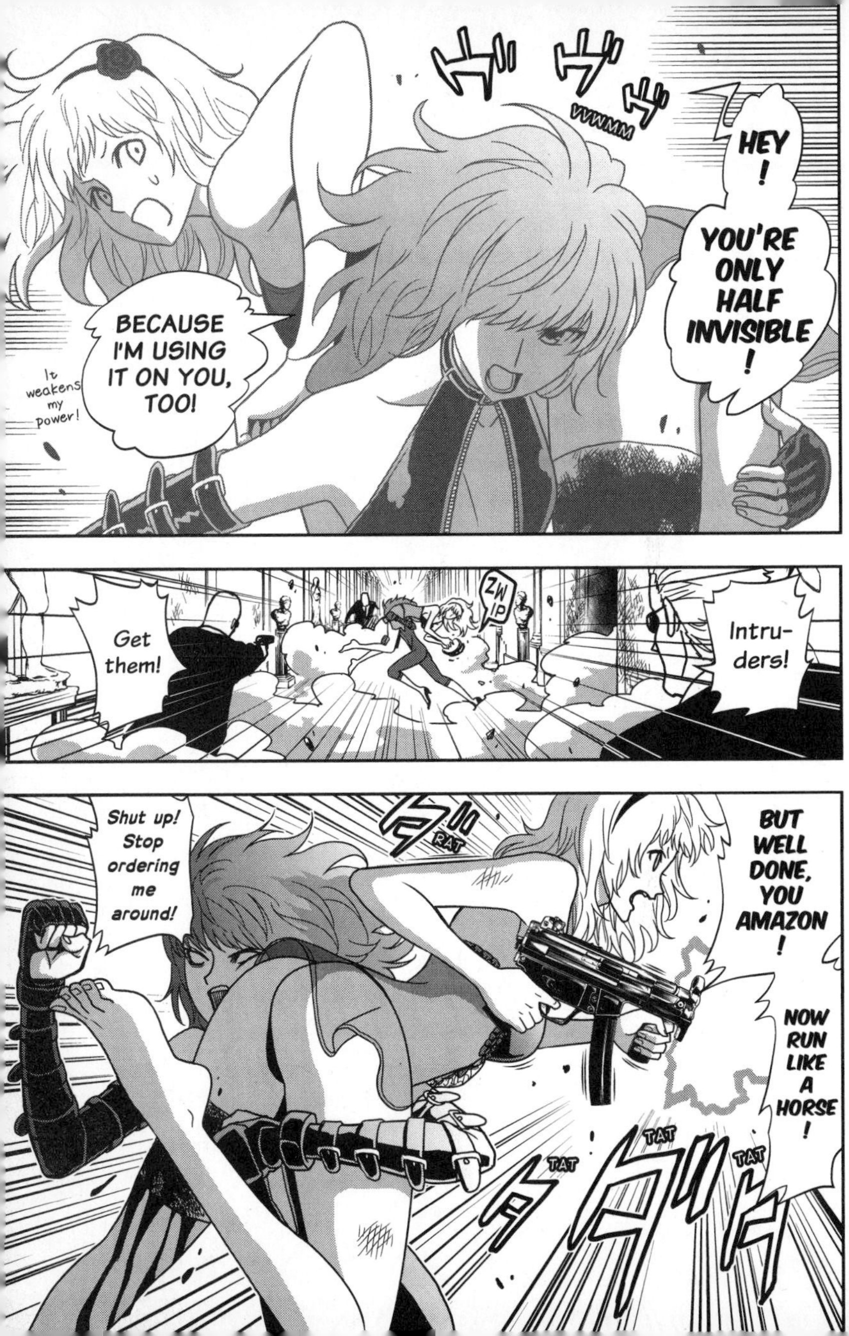
VVWMM
HEY! YOU'RE ONLY HALF INVISIBLE!
BECAUSE I'M USING IT ON YOU, TOO!
It weakens my power!
Intru-ders!
ZWIP
Get them!
BUT WELL DONE, YOU AMAZON!
NOW RUN LIKE A HORSE!
RAT
TAT
TAT
TAT
Shut up! Stop ordering me around!

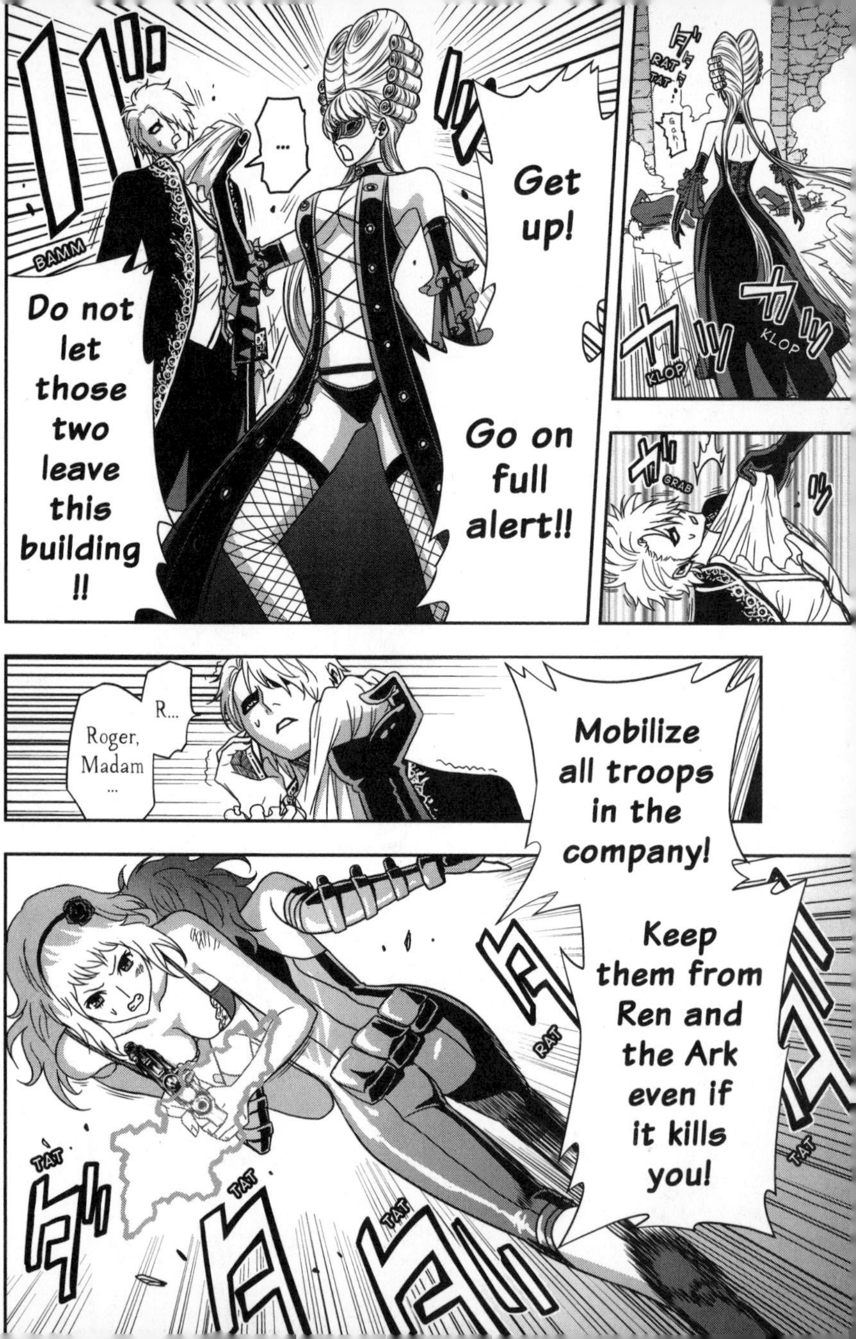
RAT
TAT
...
Gah!
KLOP
KLOP
GRAB
...
Get up!
Go on full alert!!
Do not let those two leave this building !!
BAMM
Mobilize all troops in the company!
R... Roger, Madam ...
Keep them from Ren and the Ark even if it kills you!
RAT
TAT
TAT
TAT
TAT

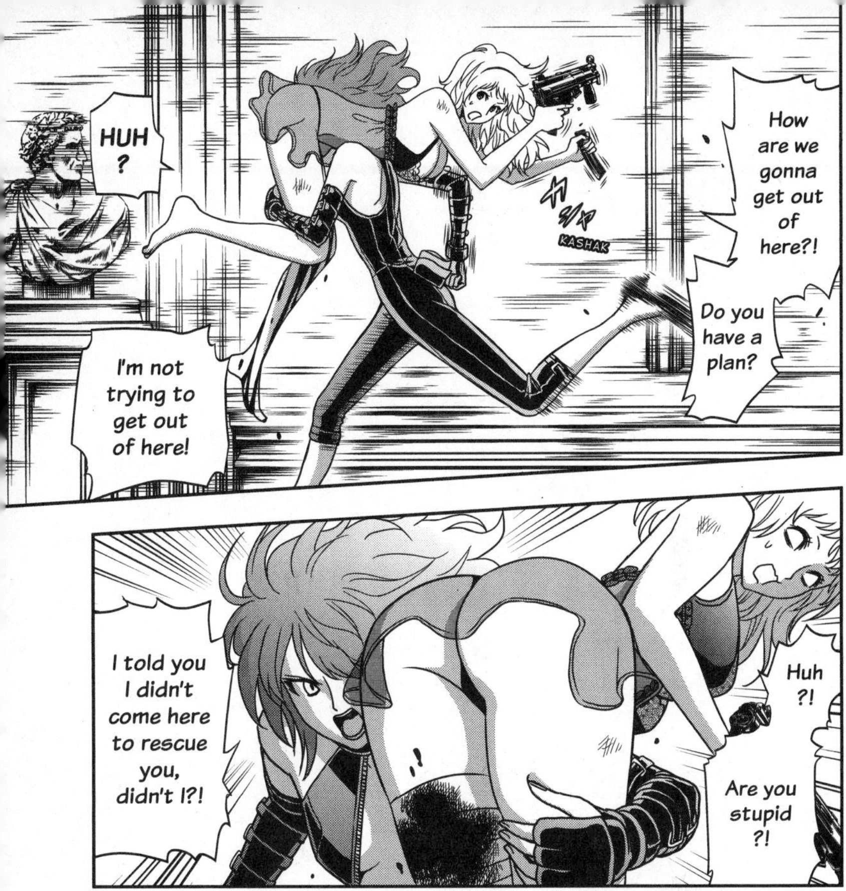
How are we gonna get out of here?!
Do you have a plan?
KASHAK
HUH ?
I'm not trying to get out of here!
Huh ?!
Are you stupid ?!
I told you I didn't come here to rescue you, didn't I?!

*Nobita often requests Doraemon to pull various objects out of his magical stomach hatch.

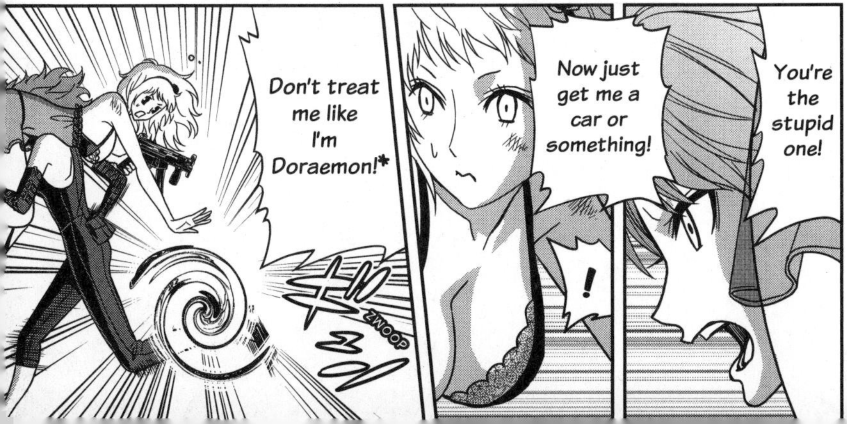
You're the stupid one!
Now just get me a car or something!
!
Don't treat me like I'm Doraemon!*
ZOOMP

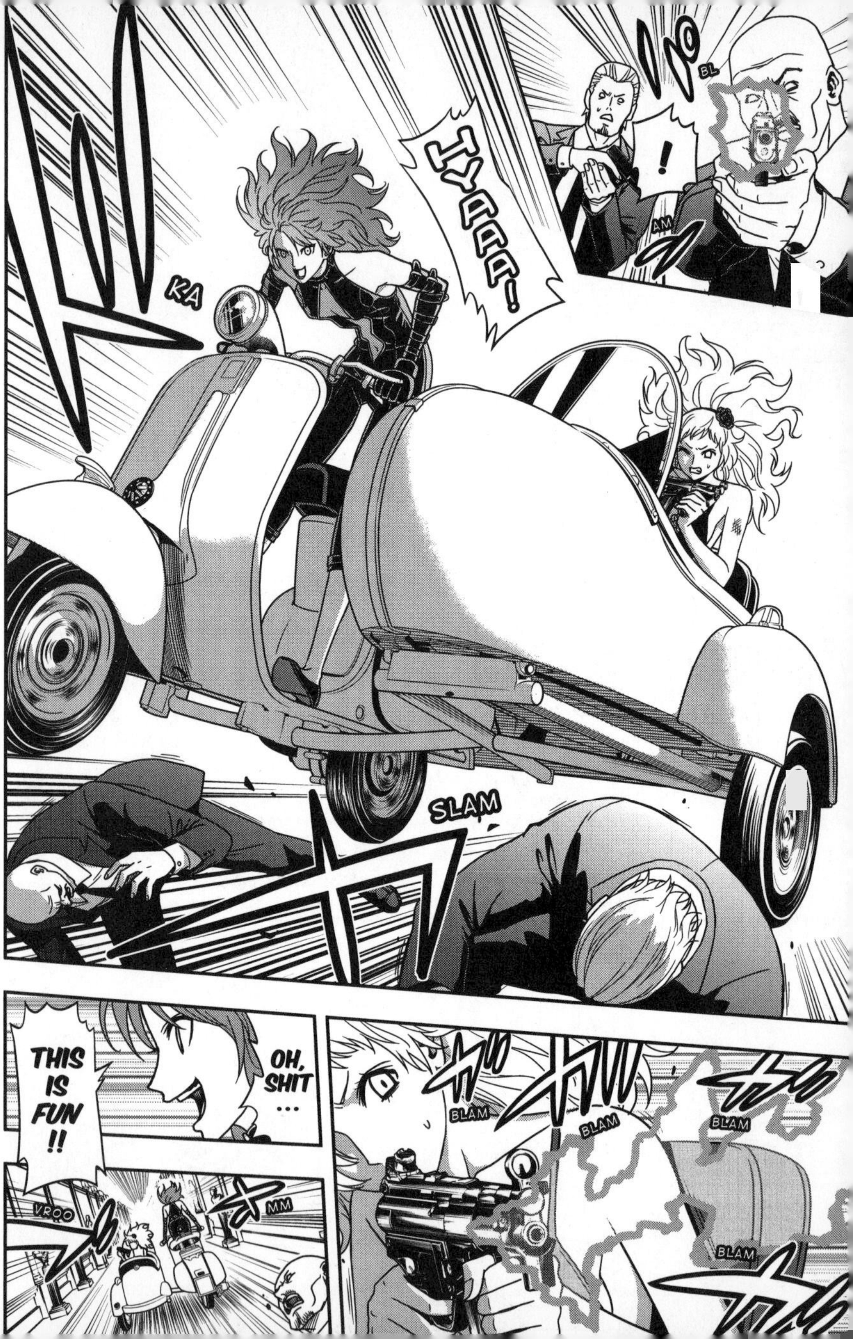
BL
AM
HYAAAA!
KA
SLAM
OH, SHIT ...
THIS IS FUN !!
BLAM
BLAM
BLAM
BLAM
VROO
MM

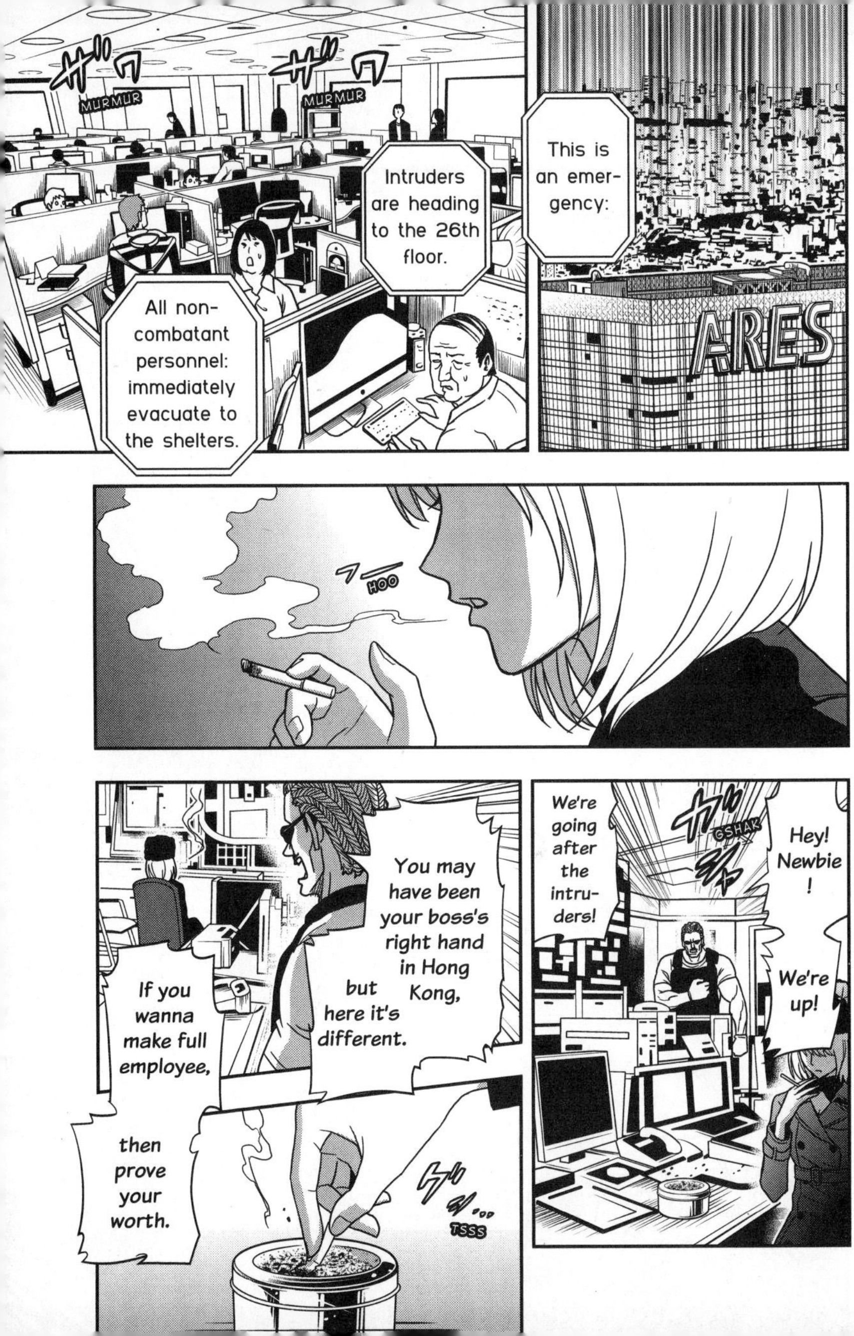
This is an emergency:
MURMUR
Intruders are heading to the 26th floor.
MURMUR
All non-combatant personnel: immediately evacuate to the shelters.
HOO
Hey! Newbie!
GSHAK
We're going after the intruders!
We're up!
You may have been your boss's right hand in Hong Kong,
but here it's different.
If you wanna make full employee,
then prove your worth.
TSSS

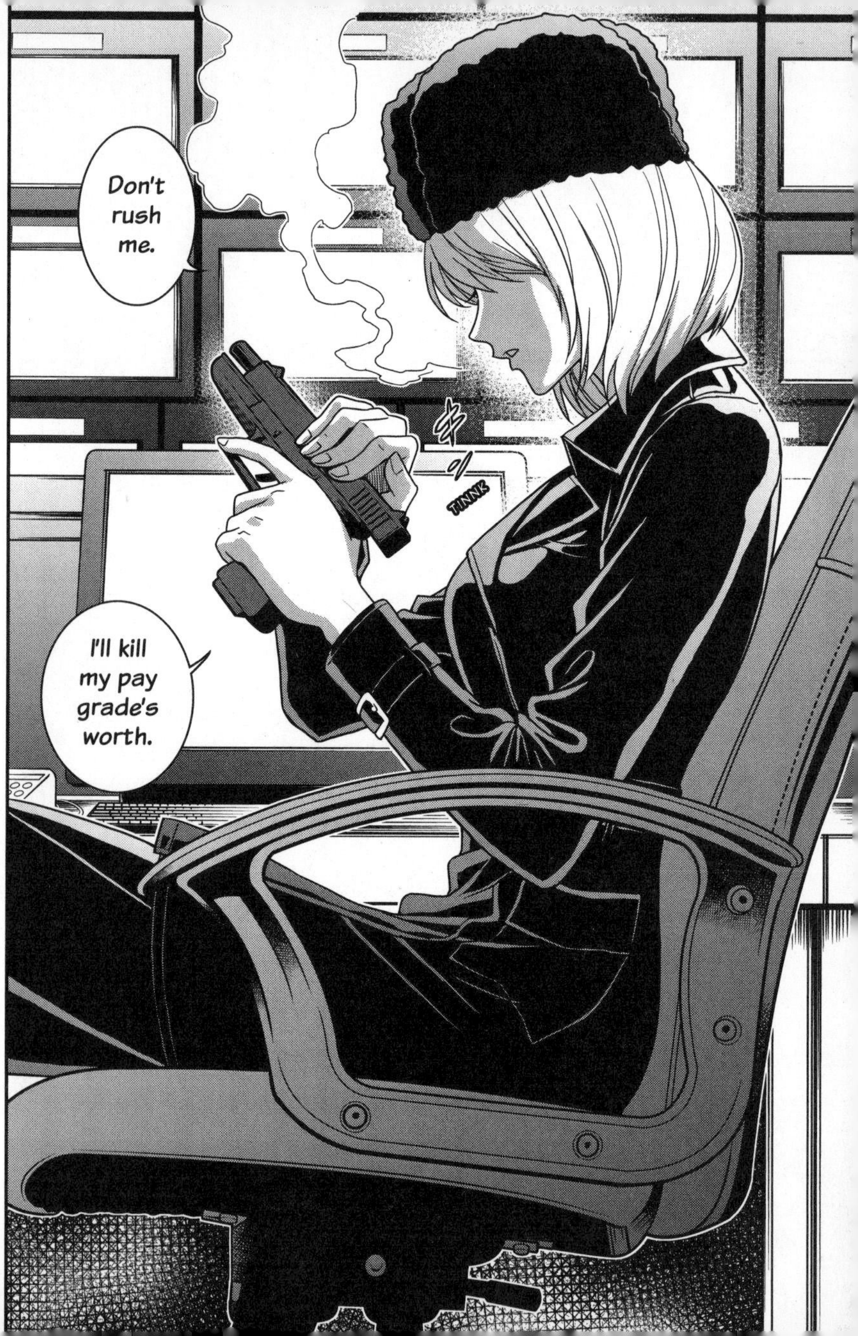
TINNK
Don't rush me.
I'll kill my pay grade's worth.

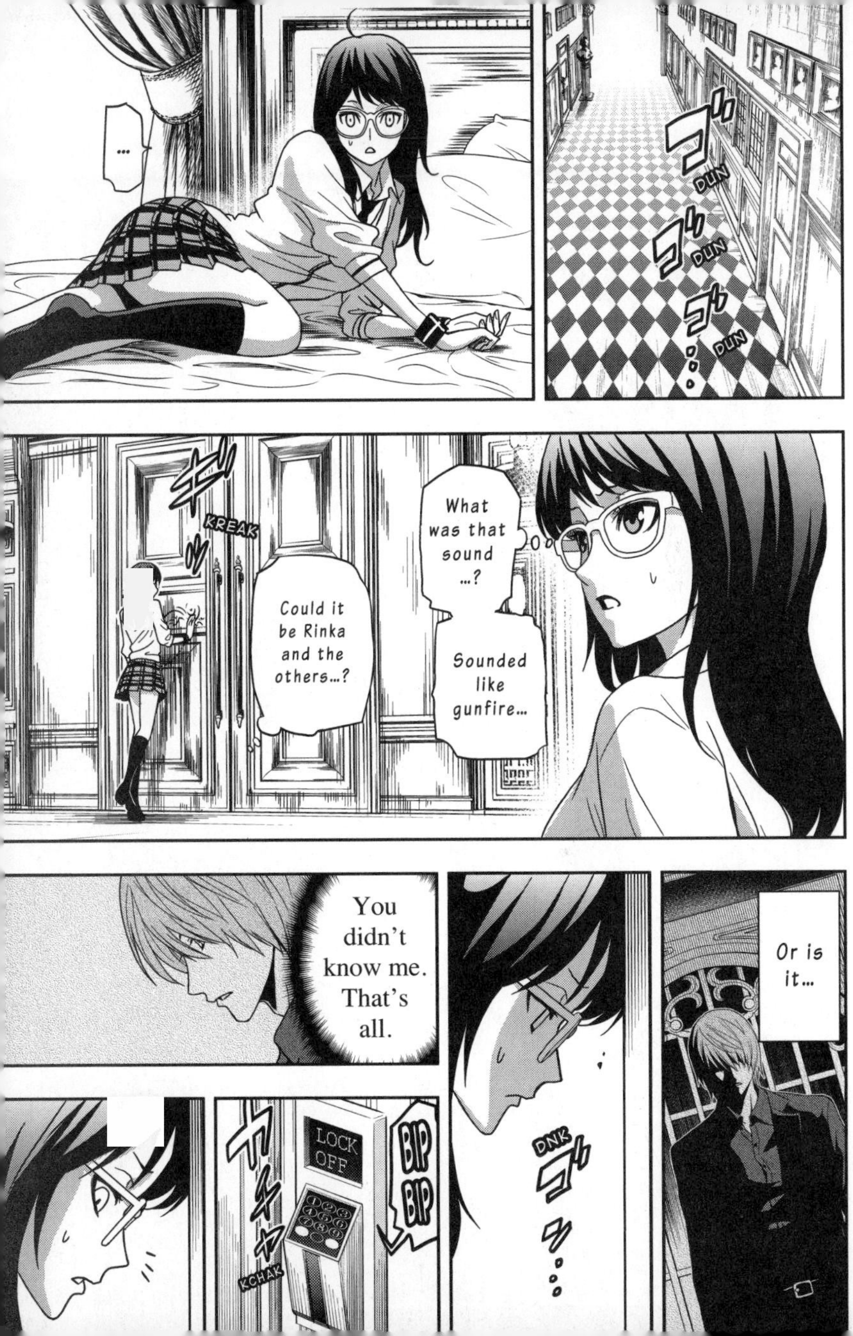
DUN
DUN
DUN
...
What was that sound ...?
Sounded like gunfire...
Could it be Rinka and the others...?
KREAK
Or is it...
DNK
You didn't know me. That's all.
BIP BIP
LOCK OFF
KCHAK

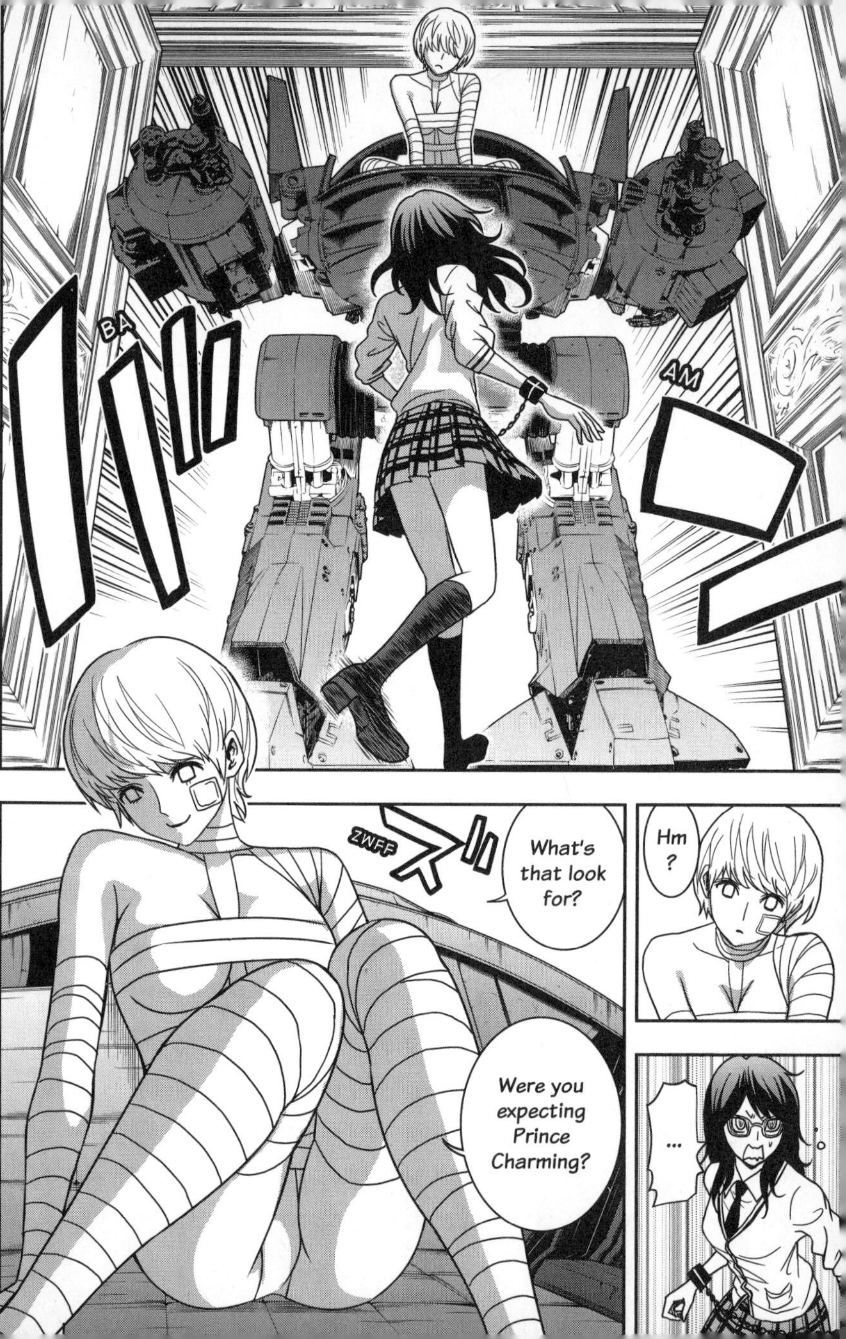
BA
AM
Hm
?
...
ZWFF
What's that look for?
Were you expecting Prince Charming?

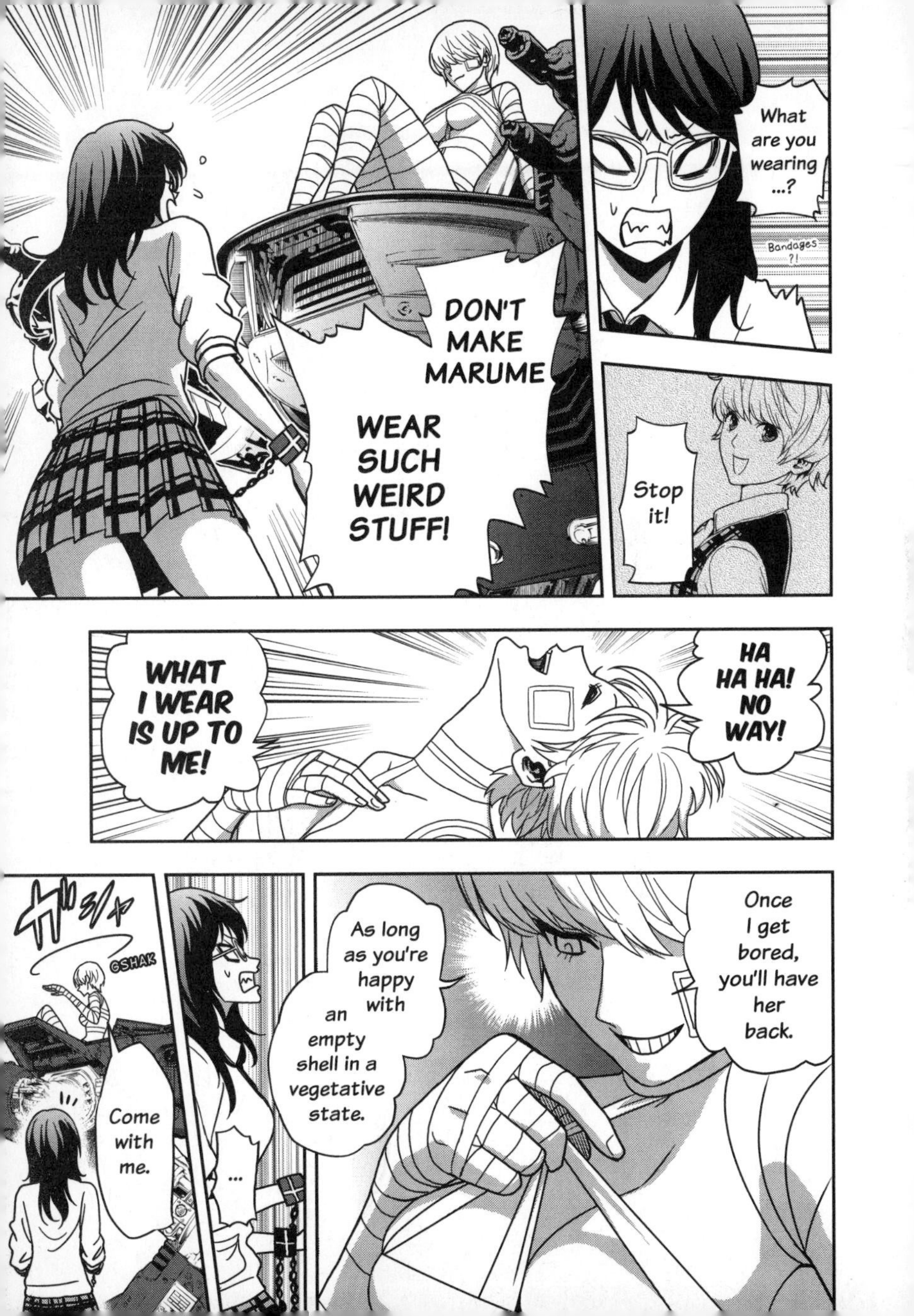
What are you wearing ...?
Bandages ?!
Stop it!
DON'T MAKE MARUME
WEAR SUCH WEIRD STUFF!
HA HA HA! NO WAY!
WHAT I WEAR IS UP TO ME!
Once I get bored, you'll have her back.
As long as you're happy with an empty shell in a vegetative state.
...
GSHAK
Come with me.

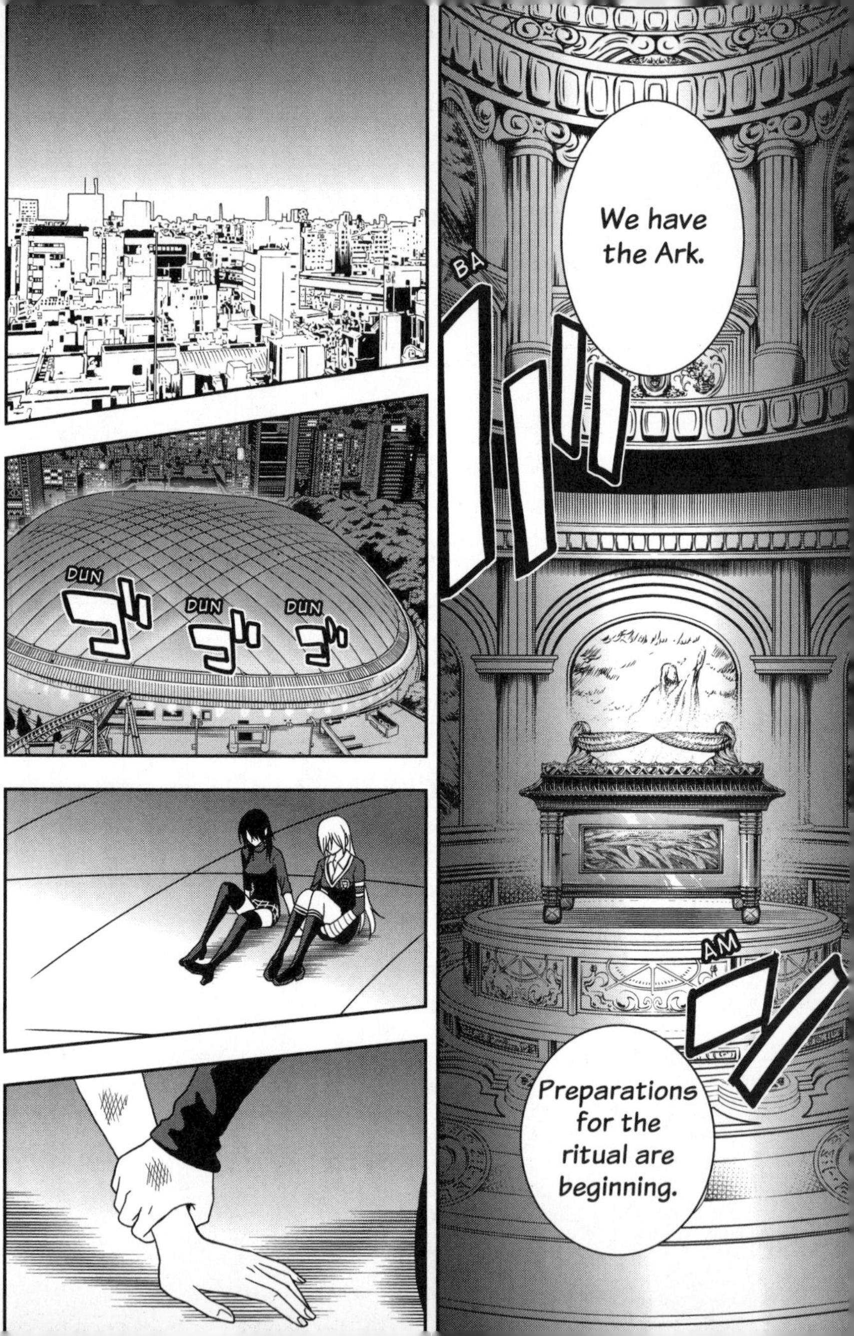
We have the Ark.
BA
AM
Preparations for the ritual are beginning.
DUN
DUN
DUN

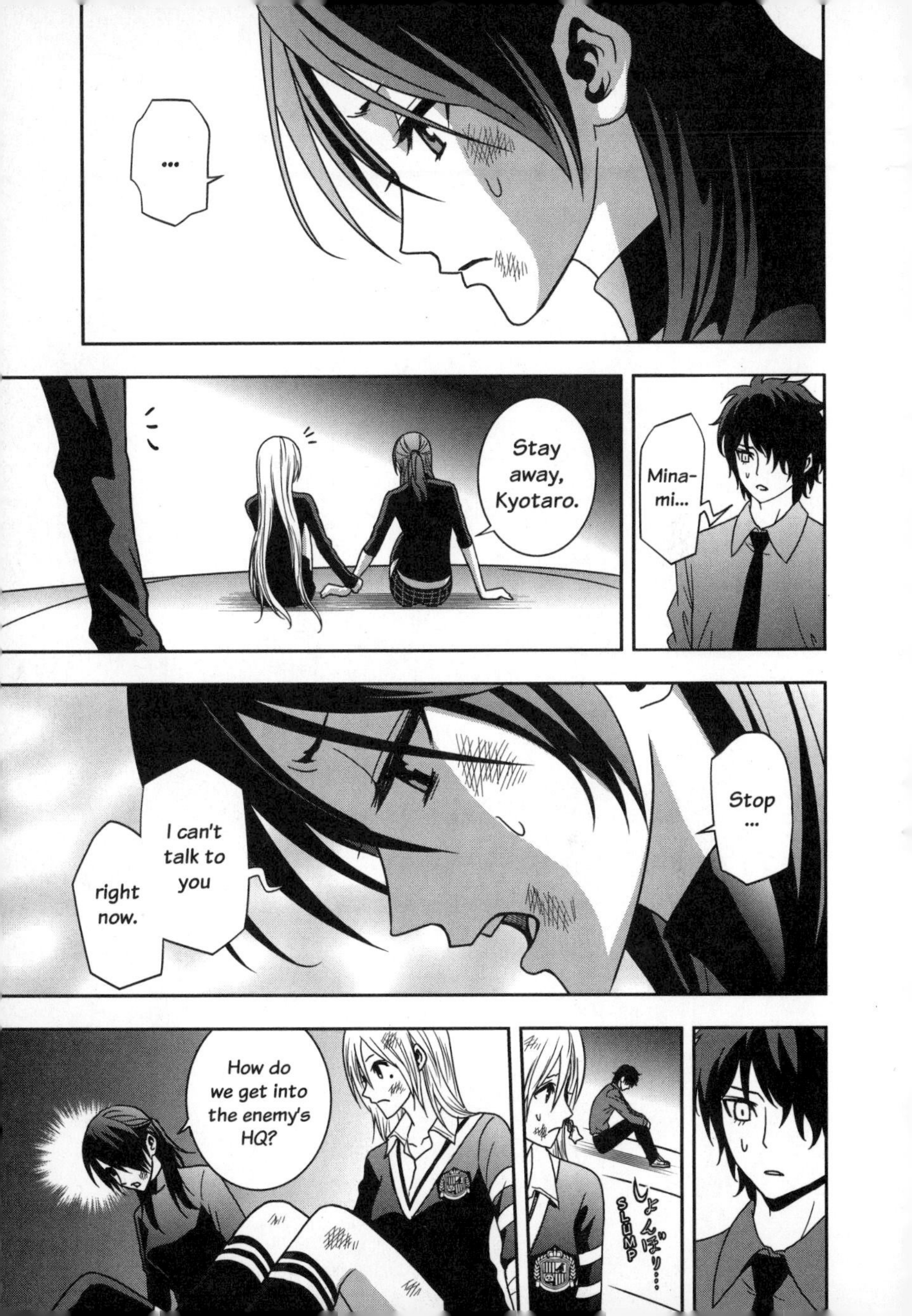
...
Mina- mi...
Stay away, Kyotaro.
Stop ...
I can't talk to you right now.
しょんぼり…
SLUMP
How do we get into the enemy's HQ?

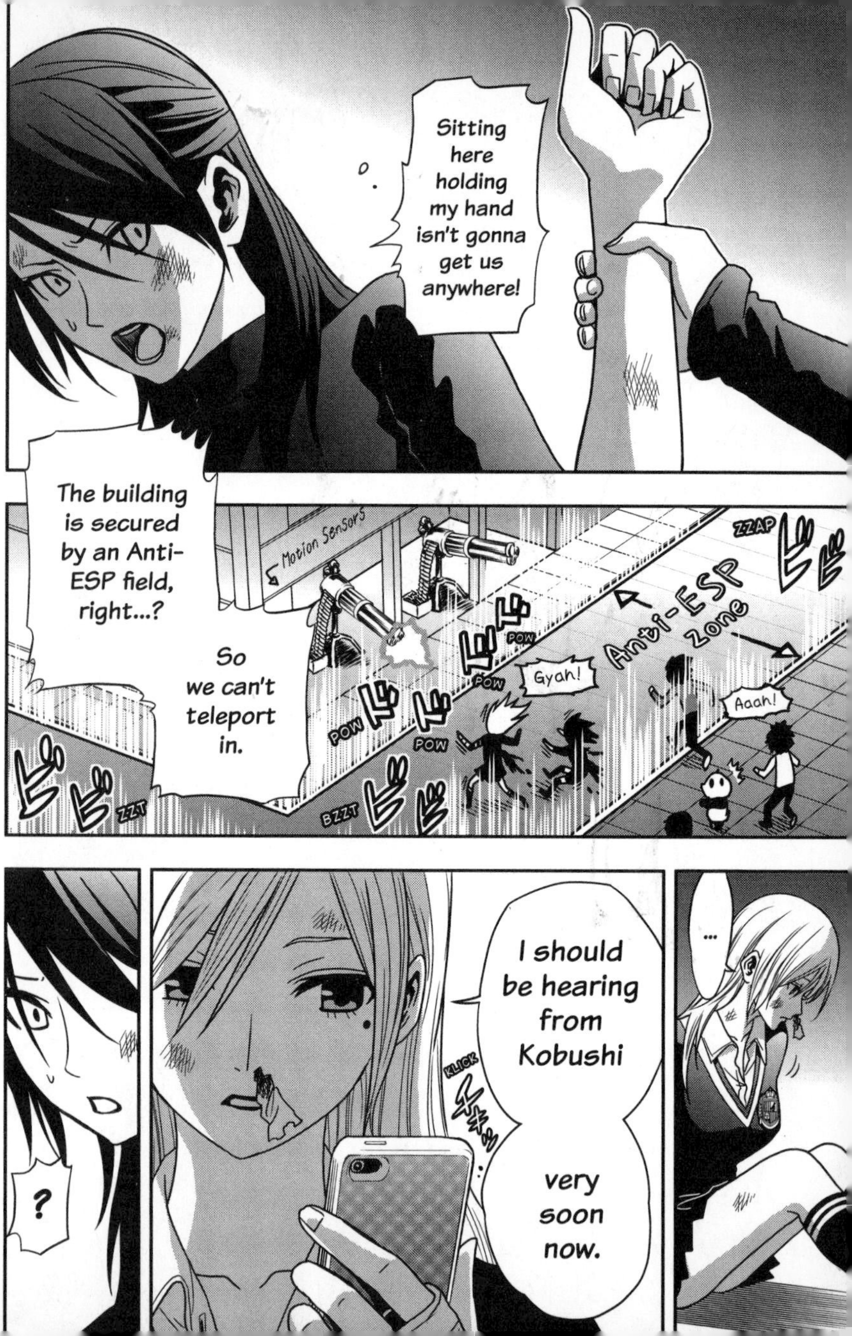
Sitting here holding my hand isn't gonna get us anywhere!
ZZAP
Motion Sensors
Anti-ESP zone
Aaah!
Gyah!
POW
POW
POW
POW
The building is secured by an Anti-ESP field, right...?
So we can't teleport in.
BZZT
ZZZT
...
I should be hearing from Kobushi
very soon now.
KLICK
?

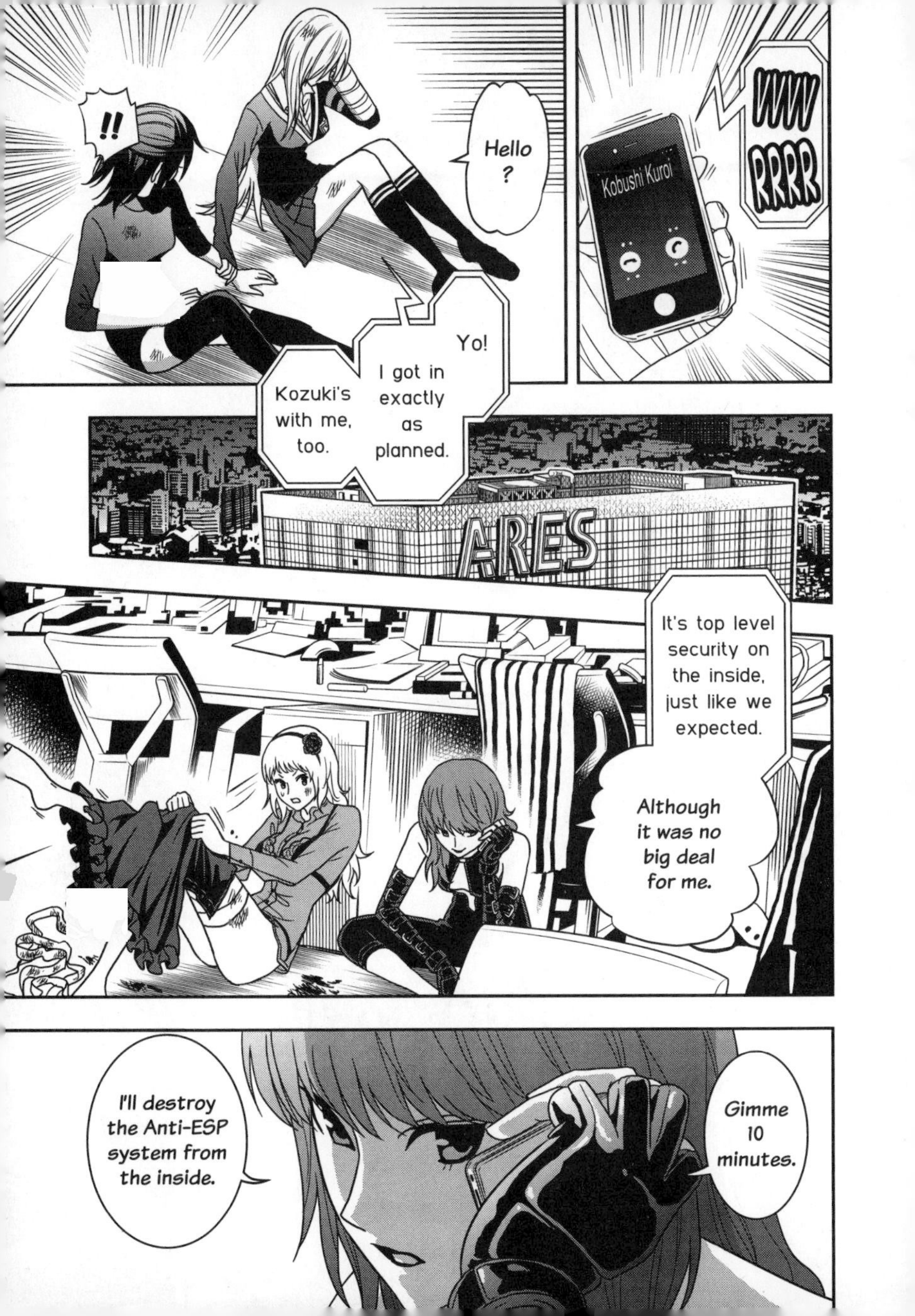
VVVV RRRR
Kobushi Kuroi
Hello ?
!!
Yo!
I got in exactly as planned.
Kozuki's with me, too.
ARES
It's top level security on the inside, just like we expected.
Although it was no big deal for me.
I'll destroy the Anti-ESP system from the inside.
Gimme 10 minutes.

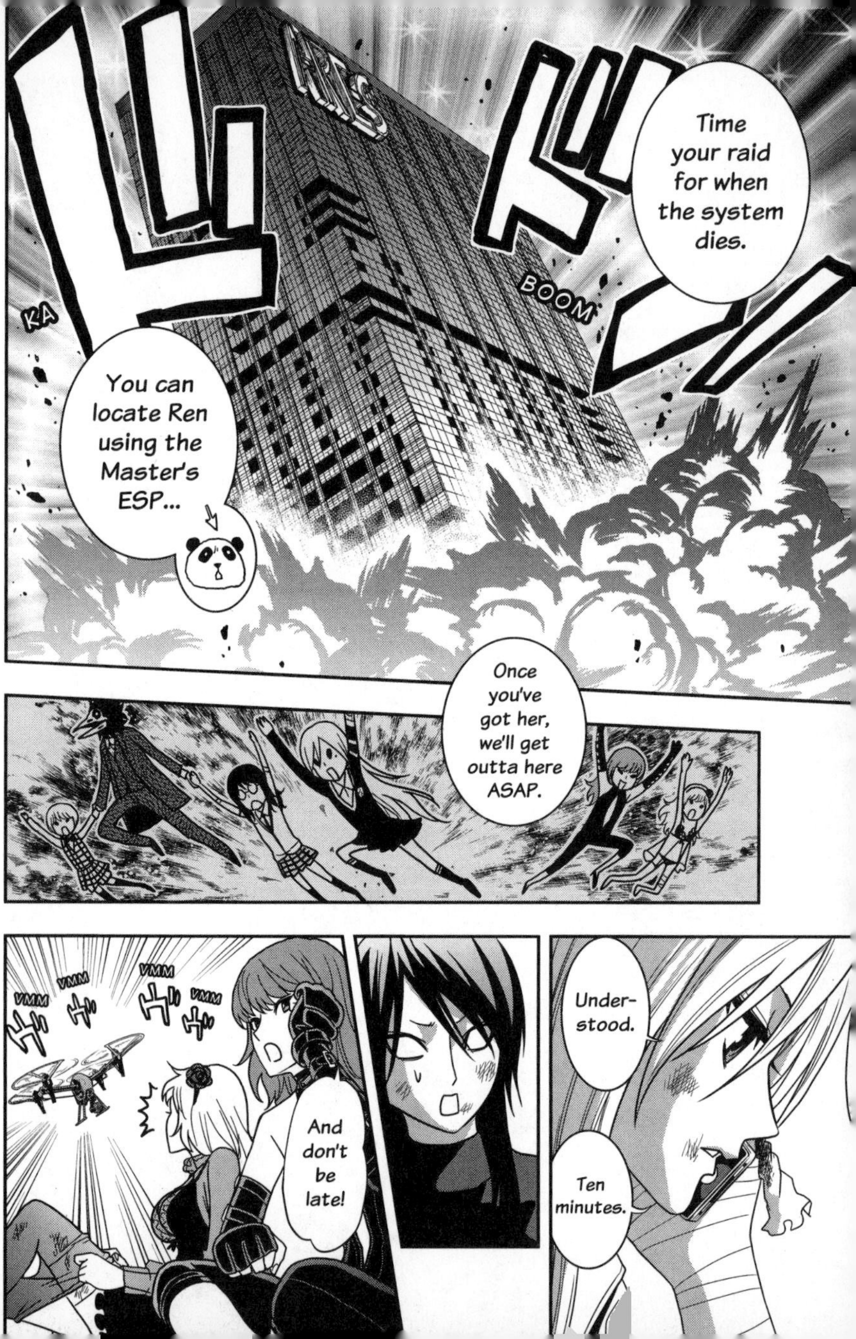
Time your raid for when the system dies.
BOOM
You can locate Ren using the Master's ESP...
KA
Once you've got her, we'll get outta here ASAP.
Under-stood.
Ten minutes.
And don't be late!
VMM
VMM
VMM
VMM

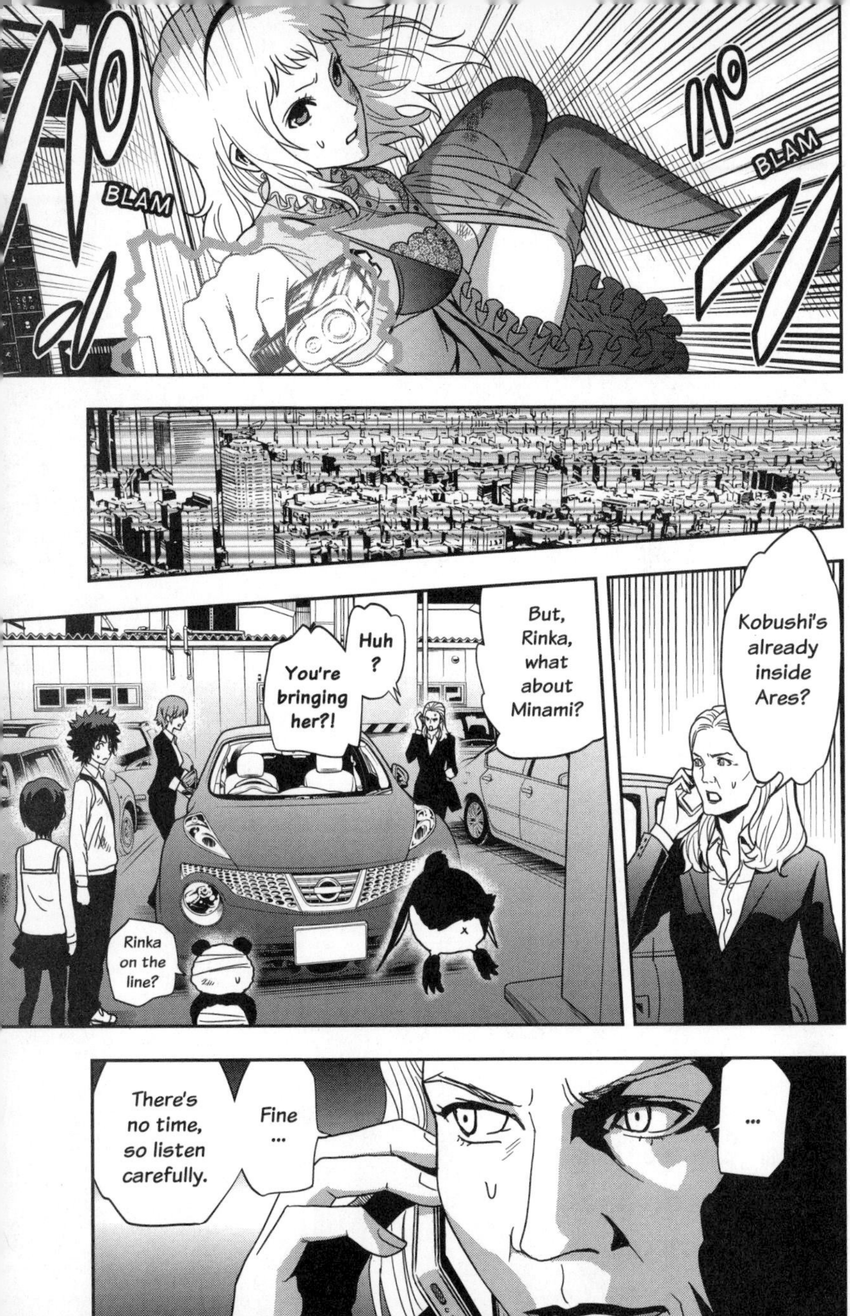
BLAM
BLAM
Kobushi's already inside Ares?
But, Rinka, what about Minami?
Huh?
You're bringing her?!
Rinka on the line?
...
Fine ...
There's no time, so listen carefully.

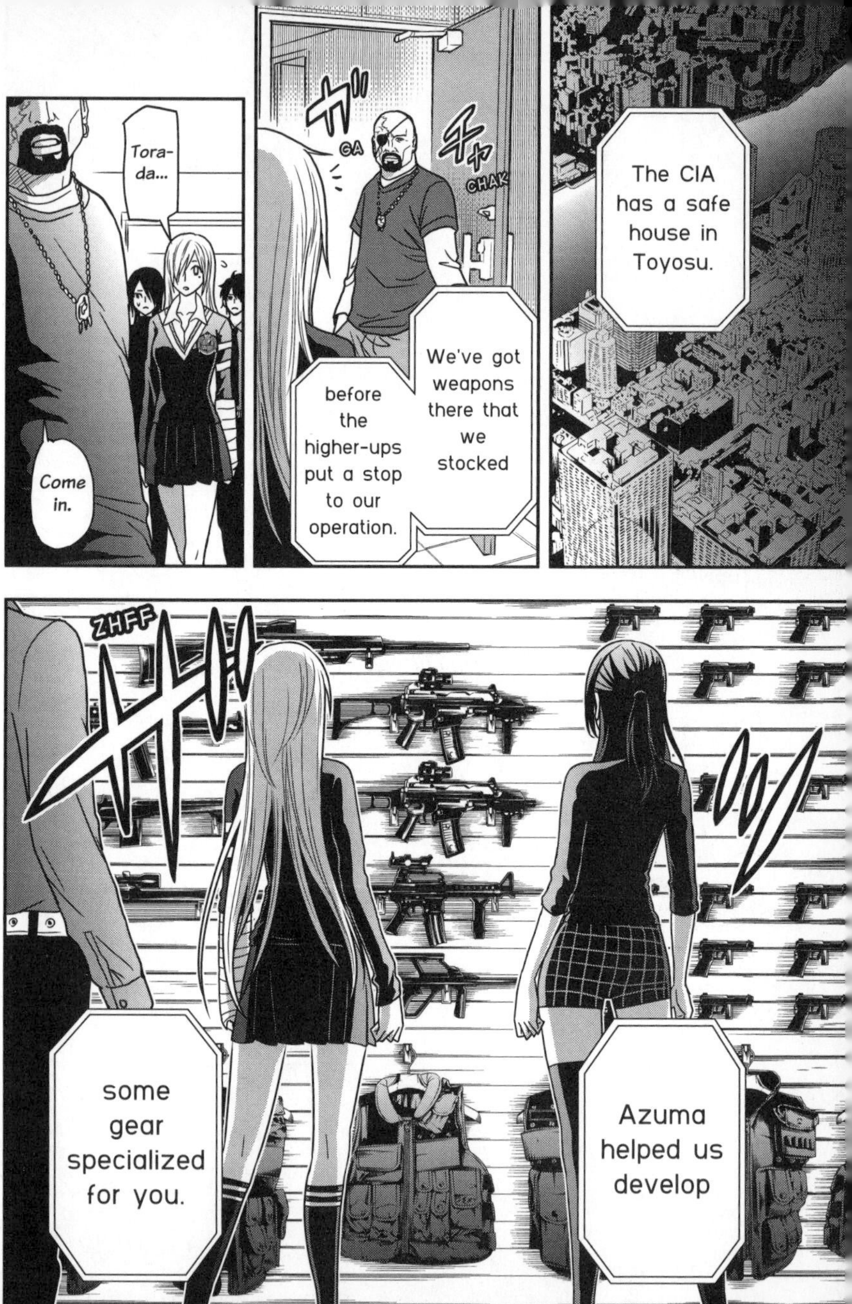
The CIA has a safe house in Toyosu.
GA
CHAK
We've got weapons there that we stocked
before the higher-ups put a stop to our operation.
Tora-da...
Come in.
ZHFF
Azuma helped us develop
some gear specialized for you.

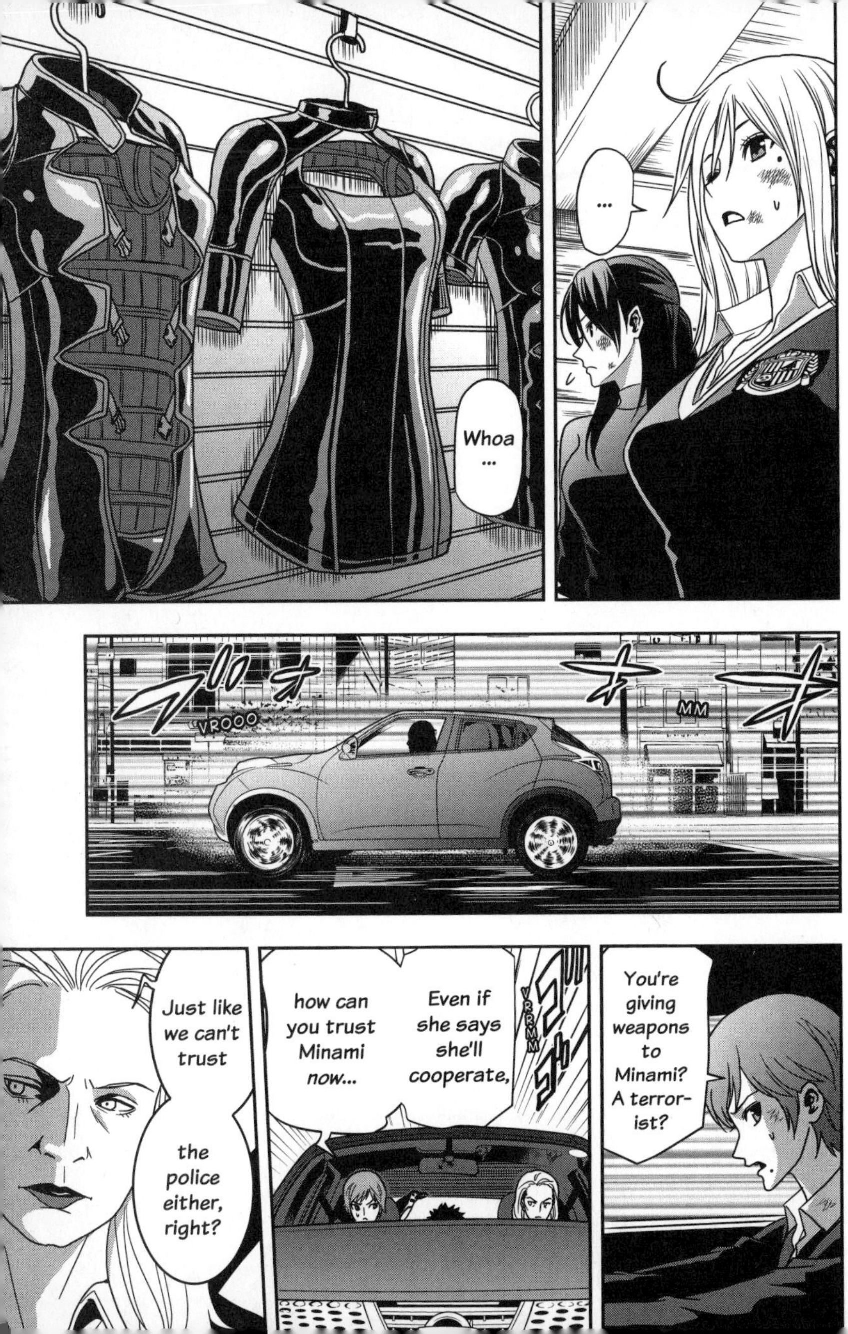
...
Whoa ...
VROOO
MM
You're giving weapons to Minami? A terrorist?
Even if she says she'll cooperate,
how can you trust Minami now...
VRRMM
Just like we can't trust
the police either, right?

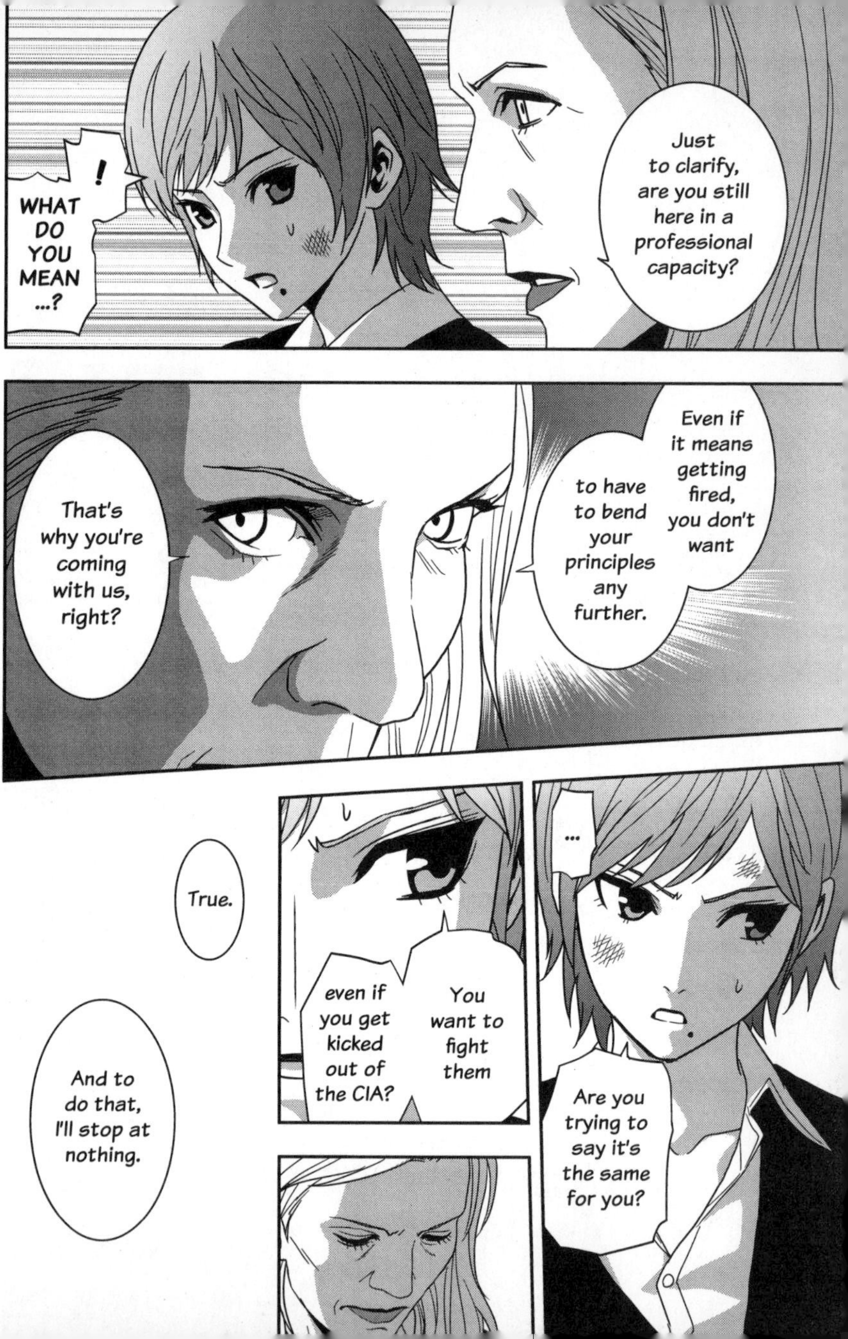
Just to clarify, are you still here in a professional capacity?
!
WHAT DO YOU MEAN ...?
Even if it means getting fired, you don't want to have to bend your principles any further.
That's why you're coming with us, right?
...
Are you trying to say it's the same for you?
You want to fight them even if you get kicked out of the CIA?
True.
And to do that, I'll stop at nothing.

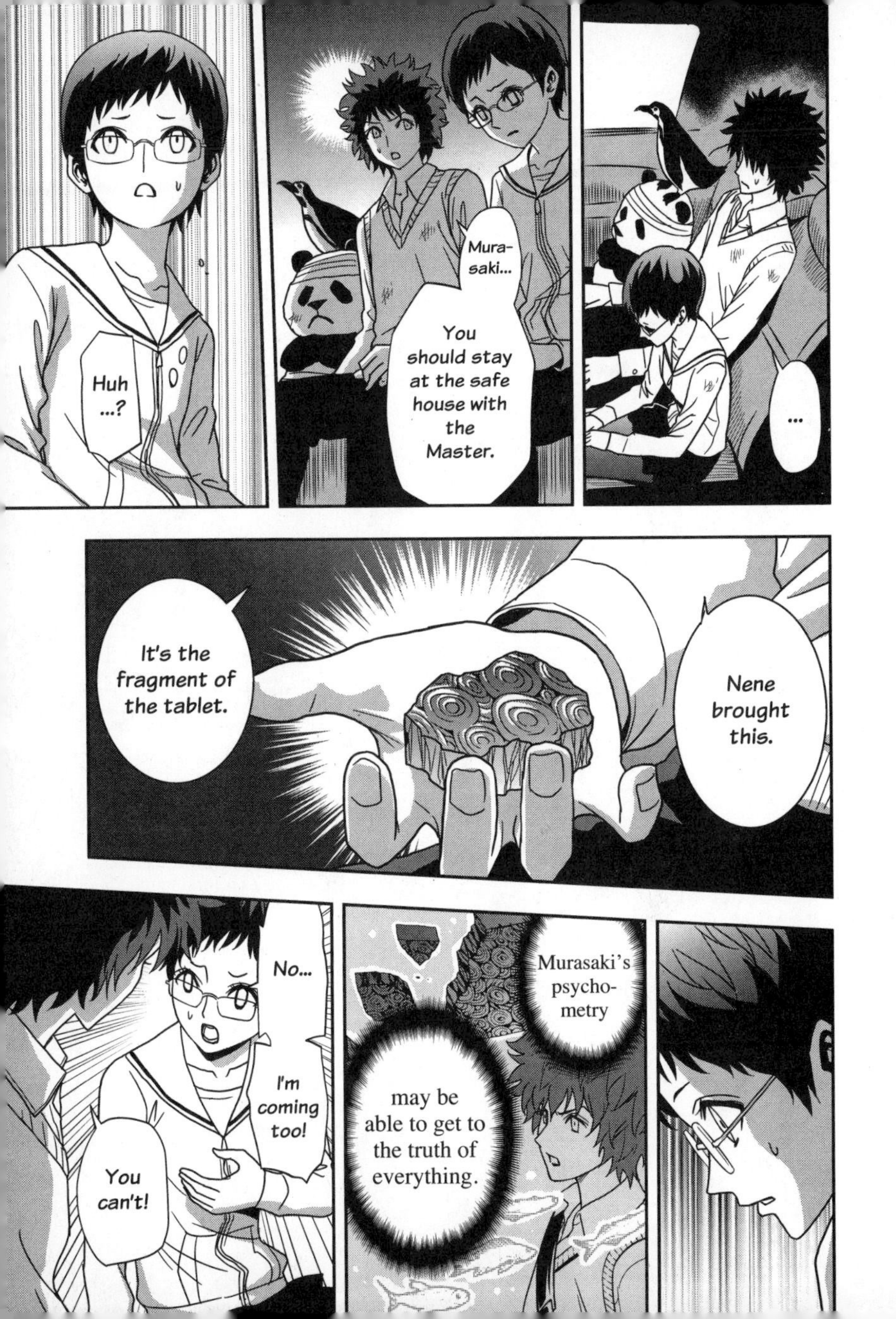
...
Murasaki...
You should stay at the safe house with the Master.
Huh ...?
Nene brought this.
It's the fragment of the tablet.
Murasaki's psychometry
may be able to get to the truth of everything.
No...
I'm coming too!
You can't!

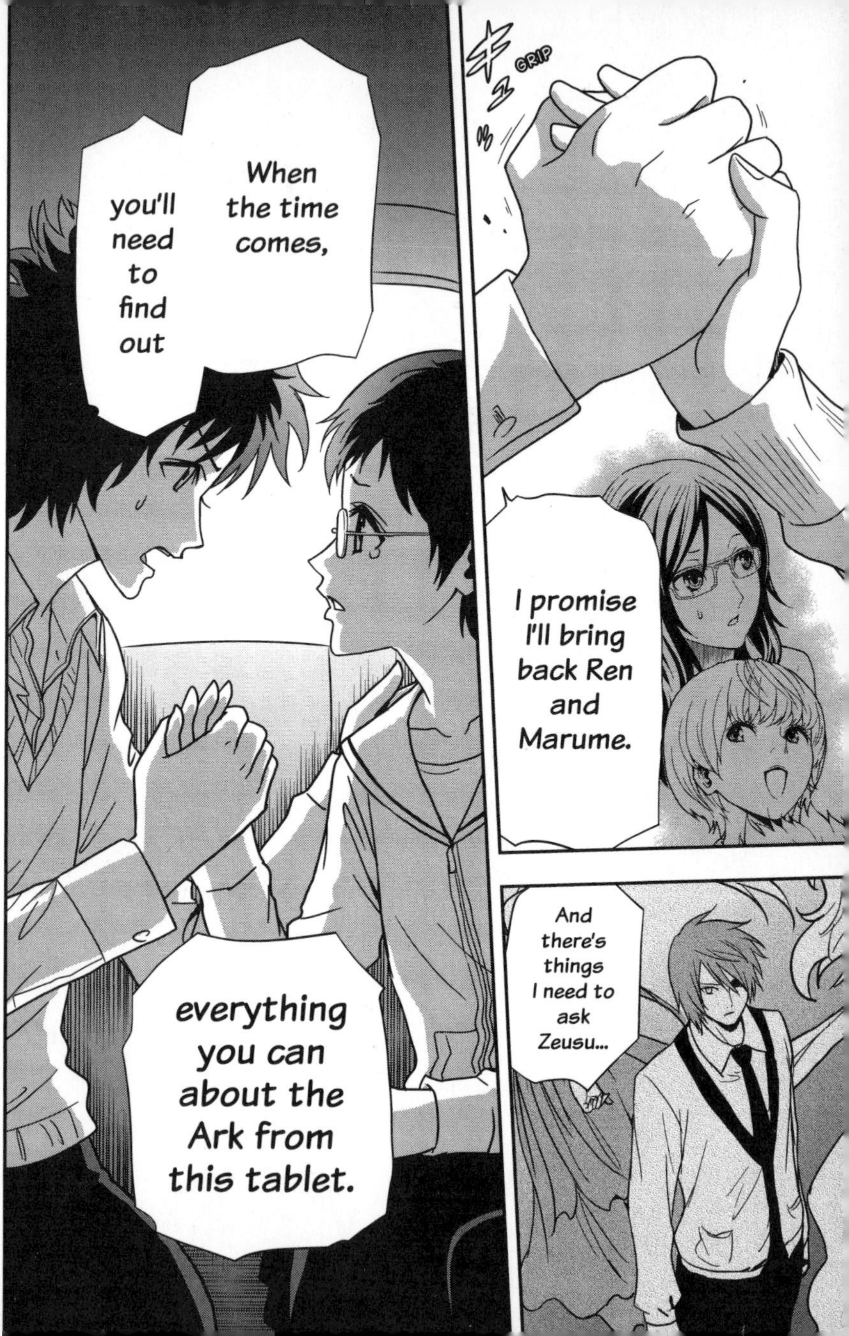
GRIP
I promise I'll bring back Ren and Marume.
And there's things I need to ask Zeusu...
When the time comes,
you'll need to find out
everything you can about the Ark from this tablet.

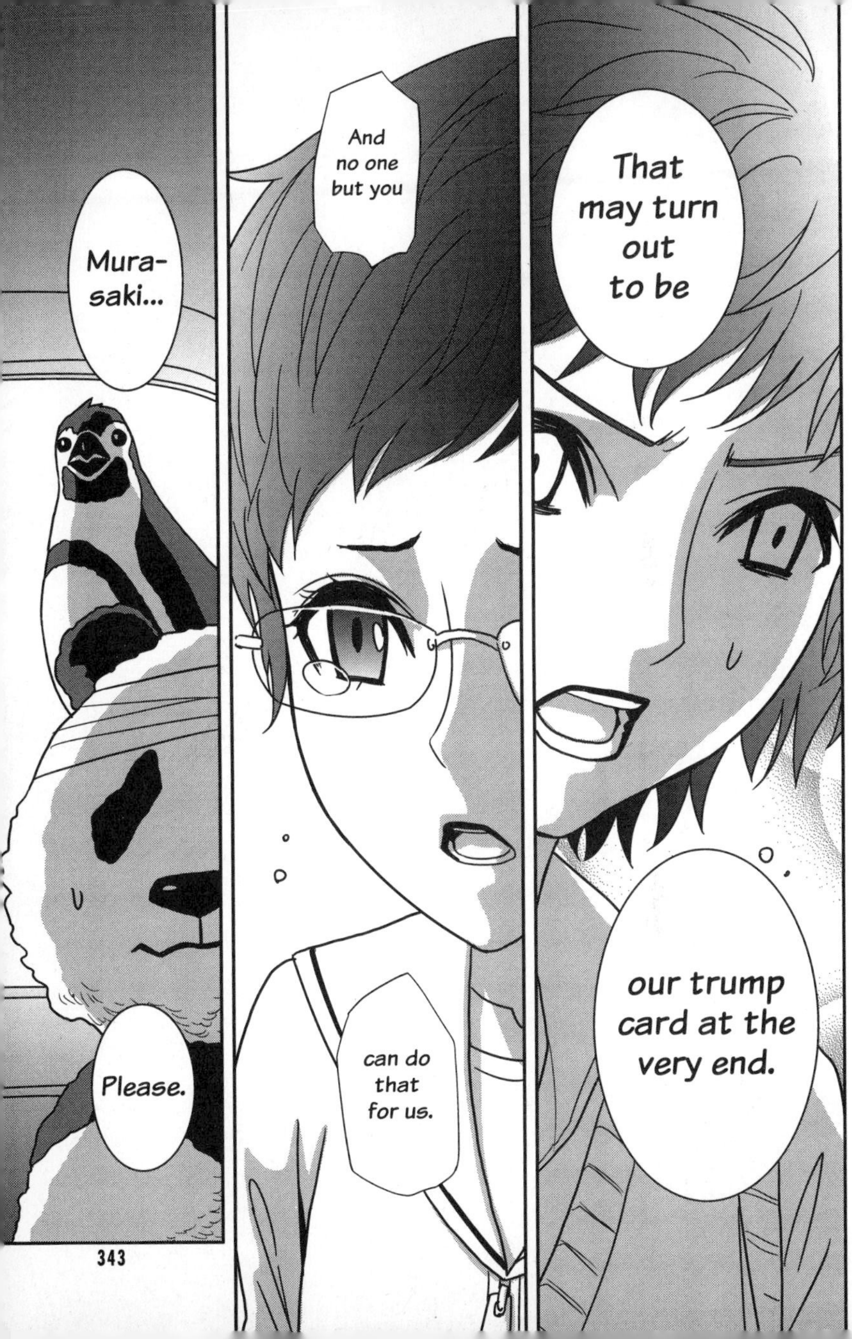
That may turn out to be
our trump card at the very end.
And no one but you
can do that for us.
Mura-saki...
Please.

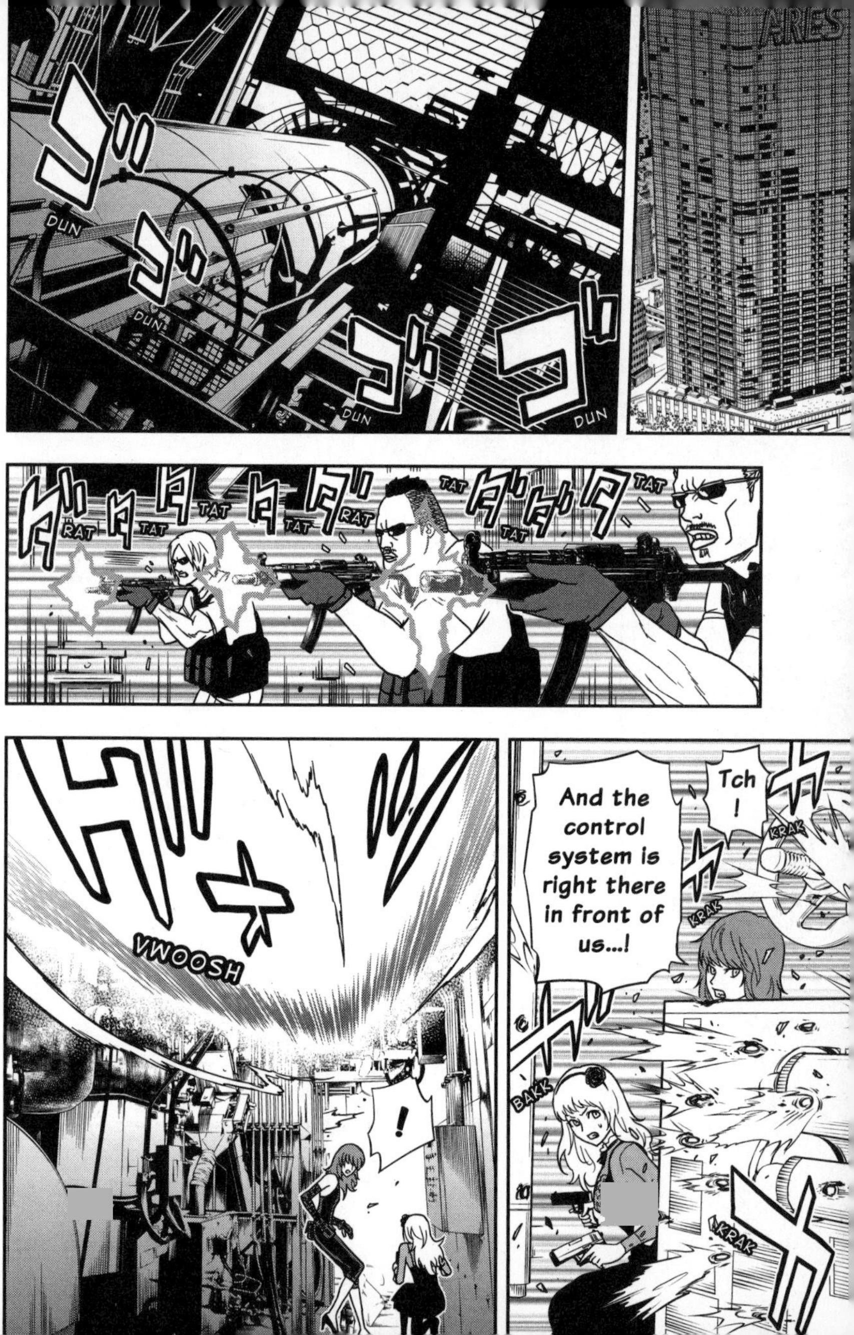
ARES
DUN
DUN
DUN
DUN
TAT
TAT
TAT
RAT
TAT
TAT
RAT
TAT
RAT
Tch!
And the control system is right there in front of us...!
KRAK
KRAK
BAKK
KRAK
VWOOSH
!

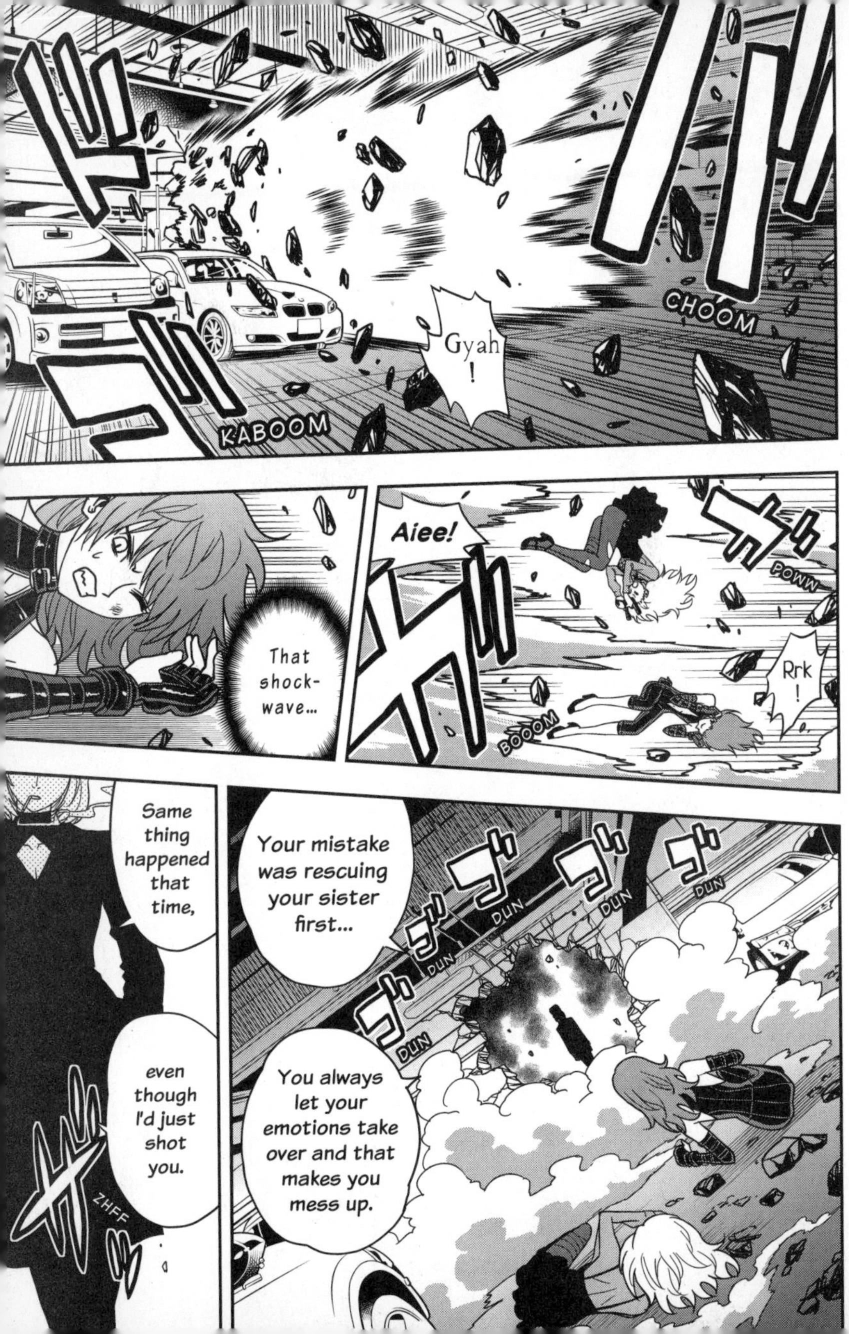
CHOOM
Gyah!
KABOOM
POWW
Aiee!
Rrk!
BOOOM
That shock-wave...
DUN
DUN
DUN
DUN
DUN
Your mistake was rescuing your sister first...
You always let your emotions take over and that makes you mess up.
Same thing happened that time,
even though I'd just shot you.
ZHFF

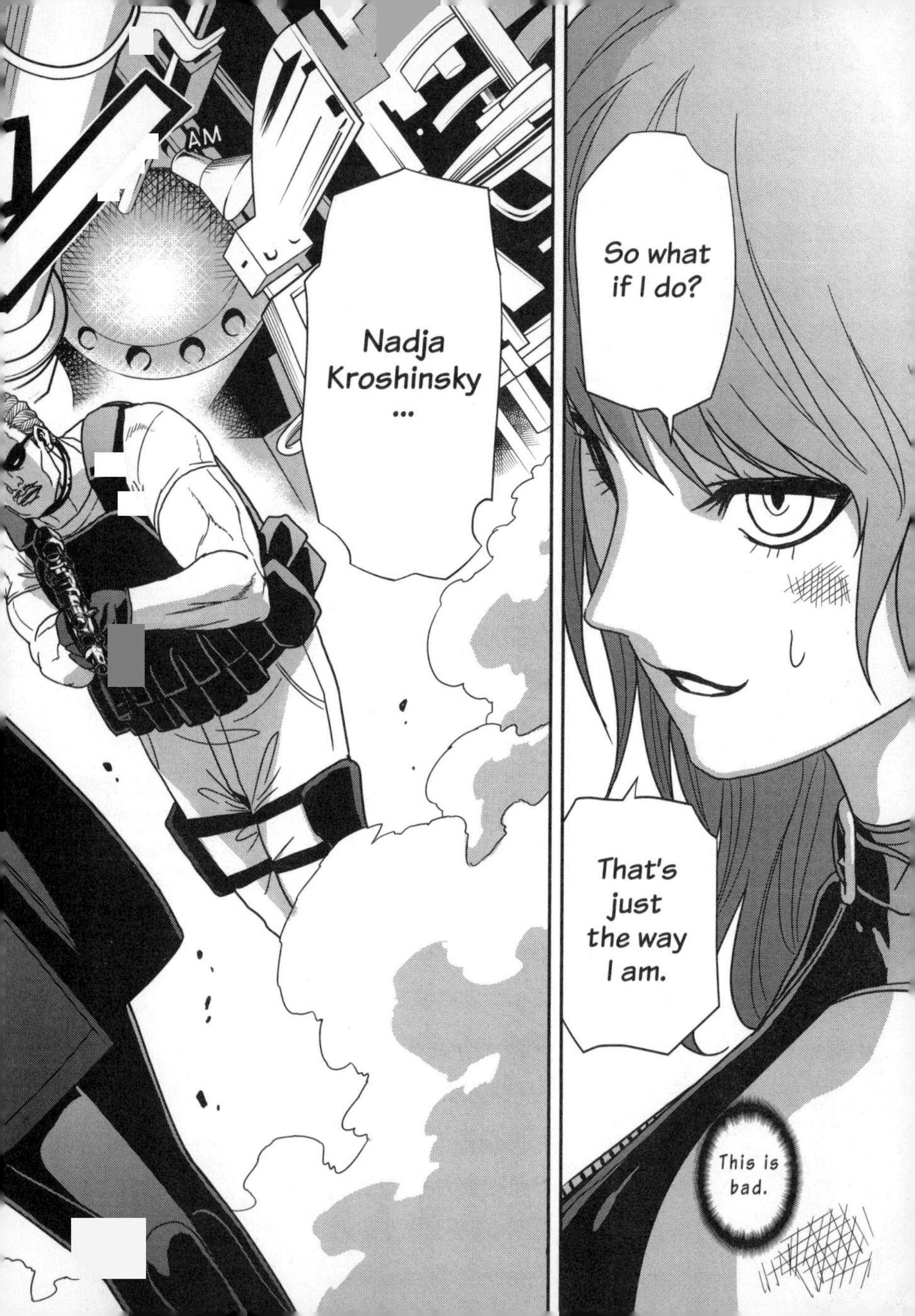
So what if I do?
That's just the way I am.
This is bad.
Nadja Kroshinsky ...

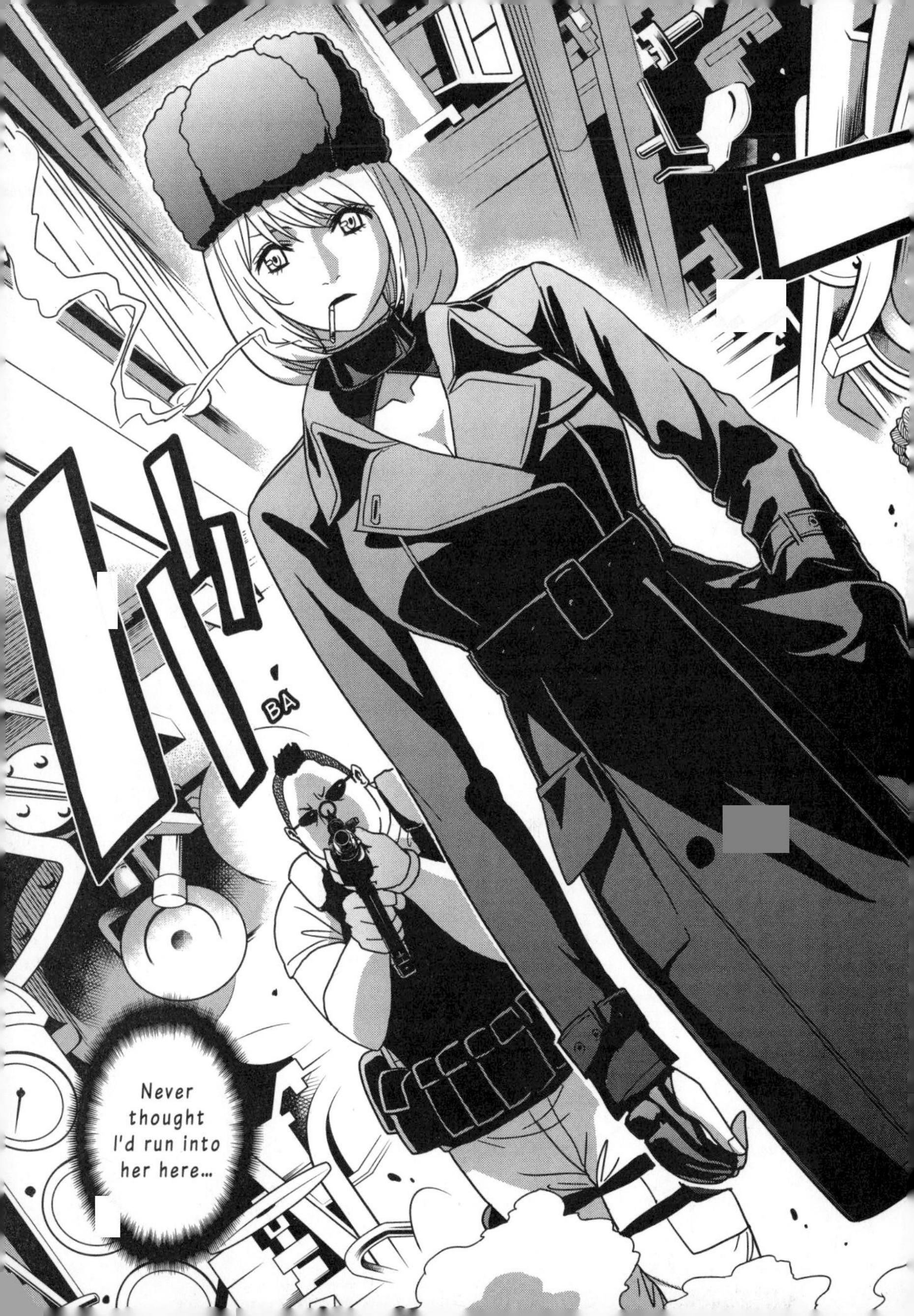
BA
Never thought I'd run into her here...

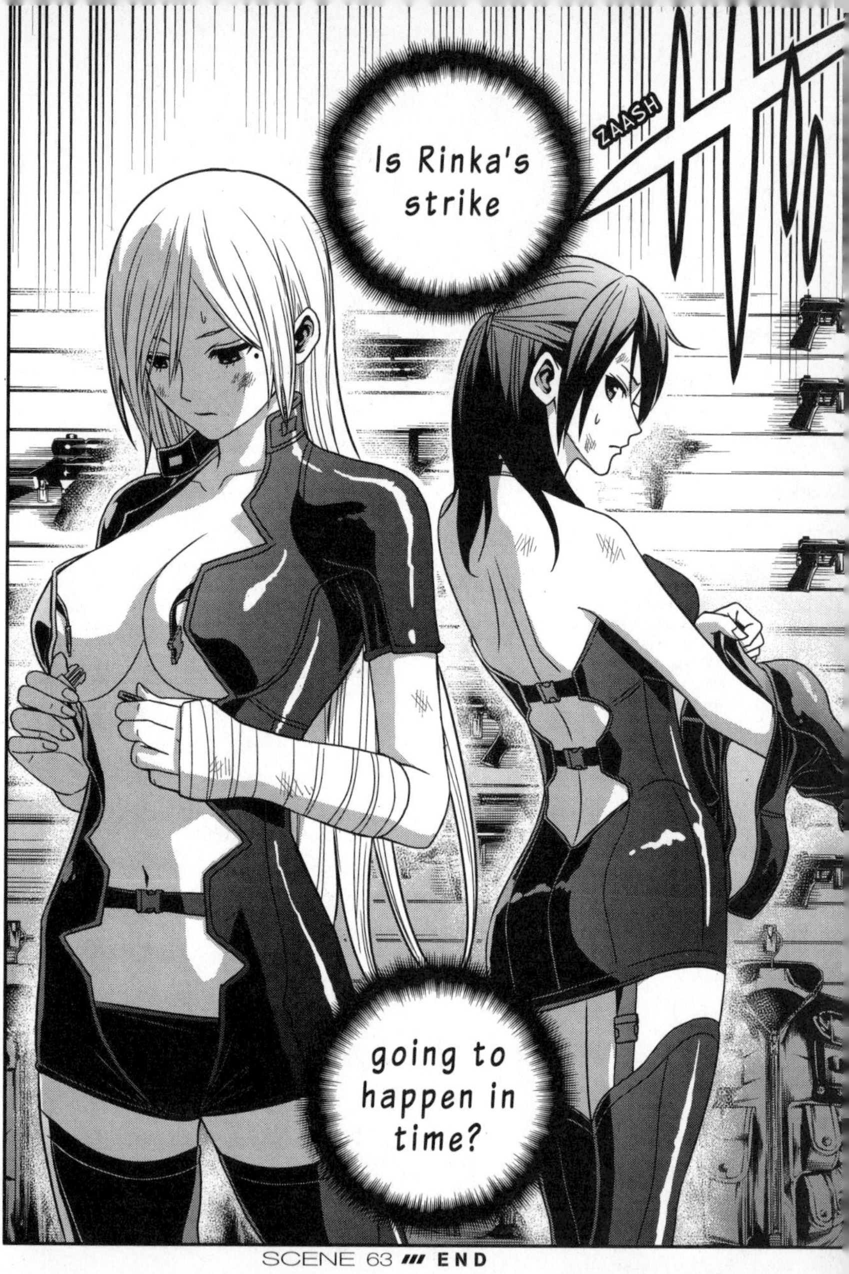
ZAASH
Is Rinka's strike
going to happen in time?

SCENE 63 /// END

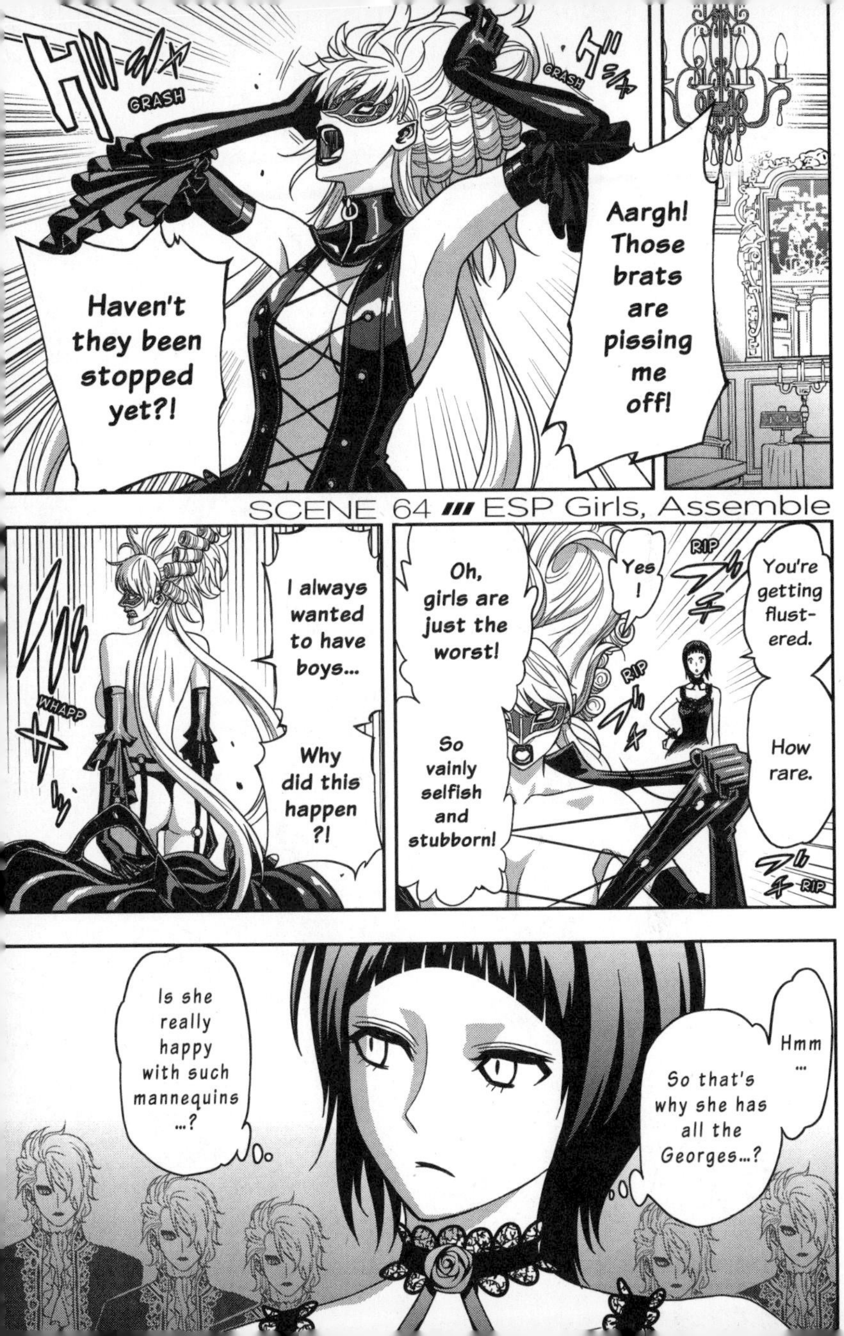
GRASH
GRASH
Aargh! Those brats are pissing me off!
Haven't they been stopped yet?!
SCENE 64 /// ESP Girls, Assemble
RIP
You're getting flustered.
How rare.
Yes!
Oh, girls are just the worst!
So vainly selfish and stubborn!
RIP
RIP
I always wanted to have boys...
Why did this happen?!
WHAPP
Hmm...
So that's why she has all the Georges...?
Is she really happy with such mannequins...?

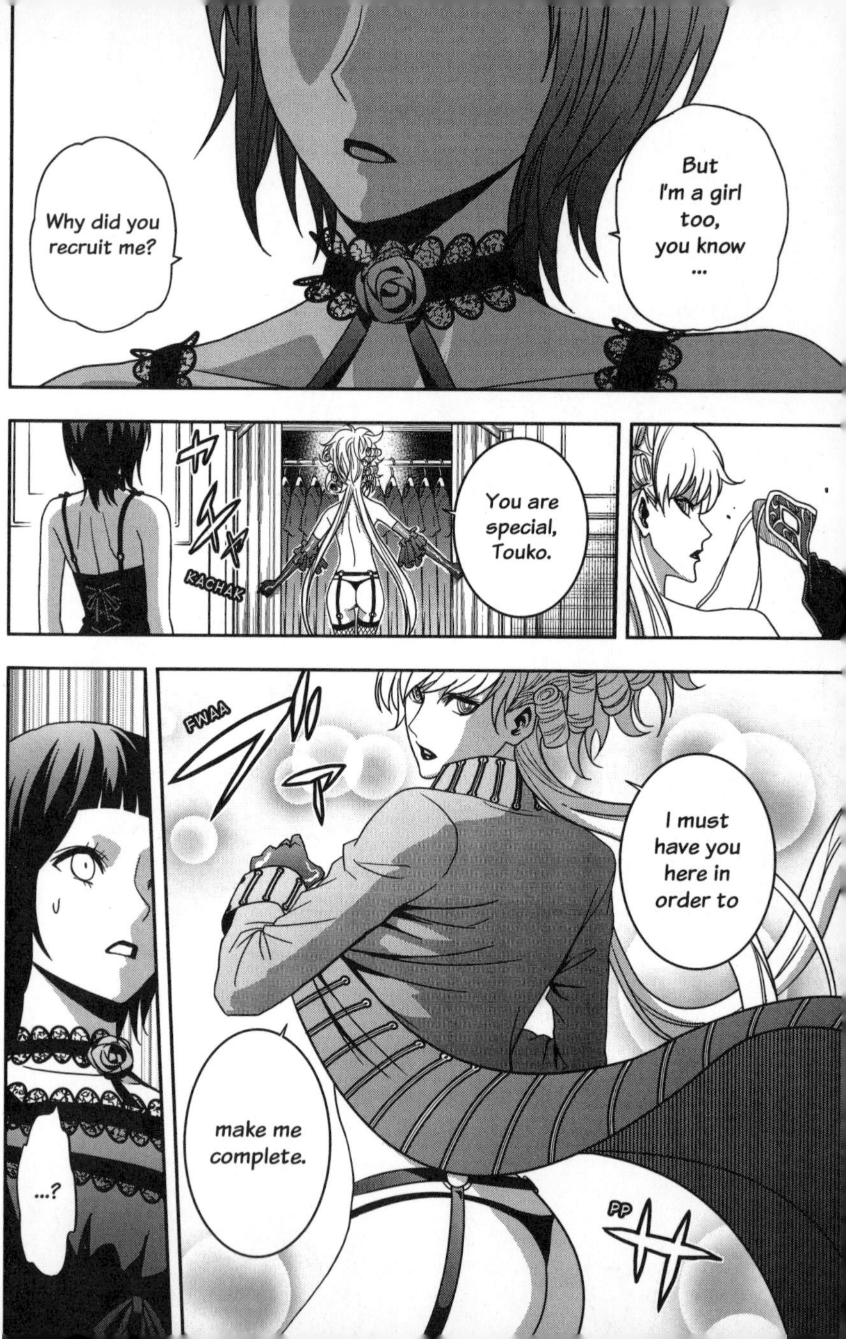
But I'm a girl too, you know ...
Why did you recruit me?
You are special, Touko.
KACHAK
FWAA
I must have you here in order to
make me complete.
PP
...?

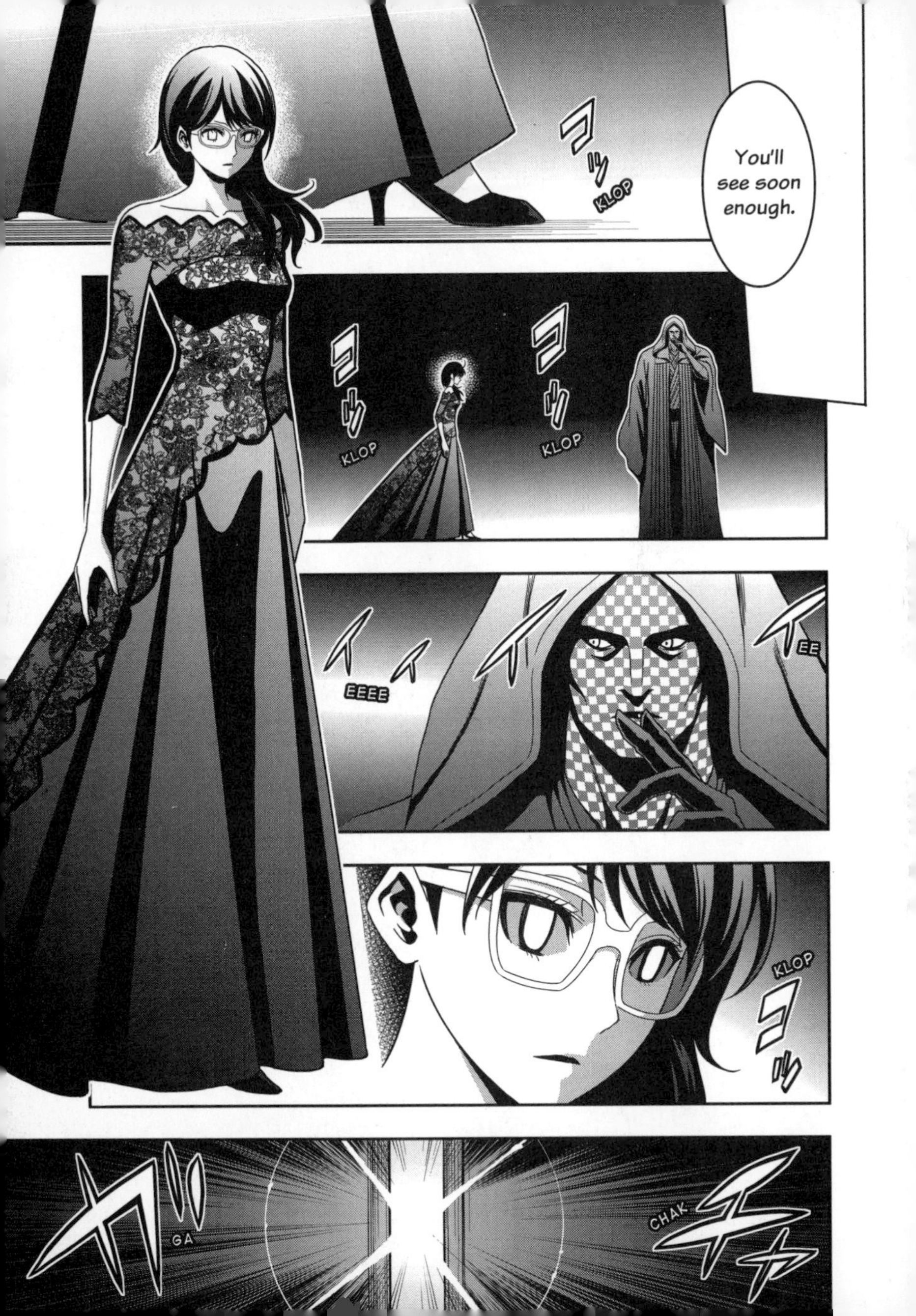

You'll see soon enough.
KLOP
KLOP
KLOP
EE
EEEE
KLOP
CHAK
GA

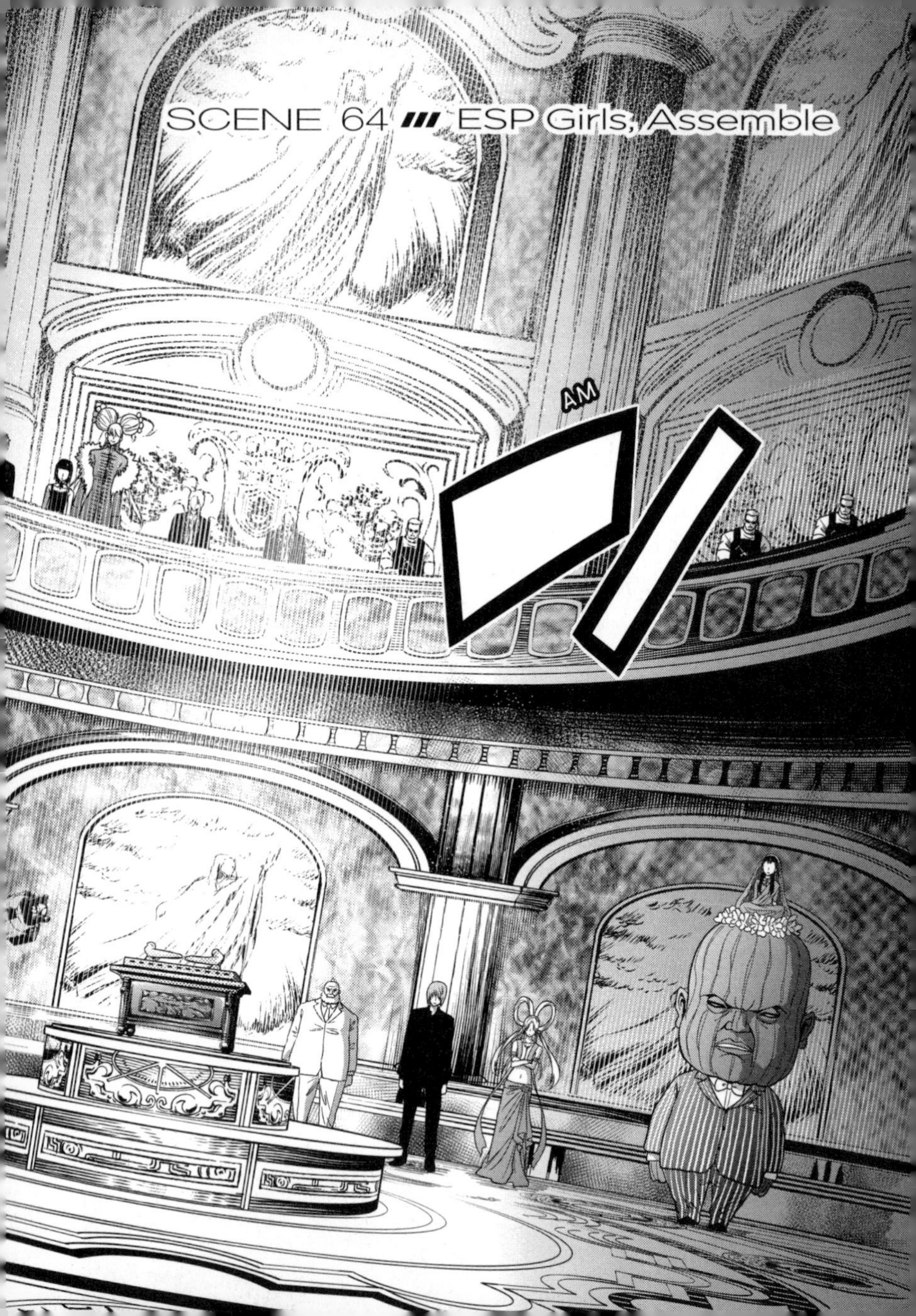
SCENE 64 /// ESP Girls, Assemble
AM

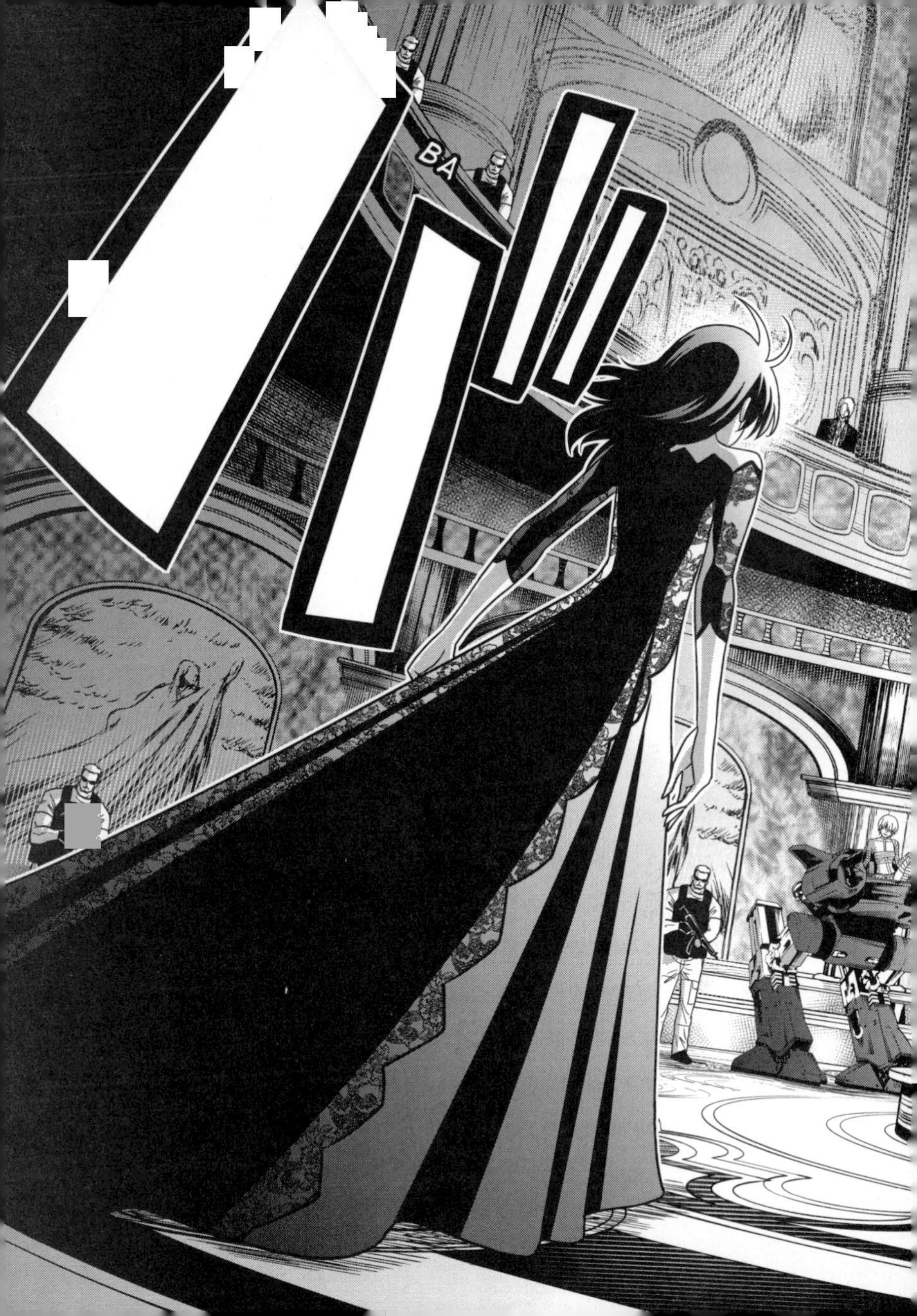
BA

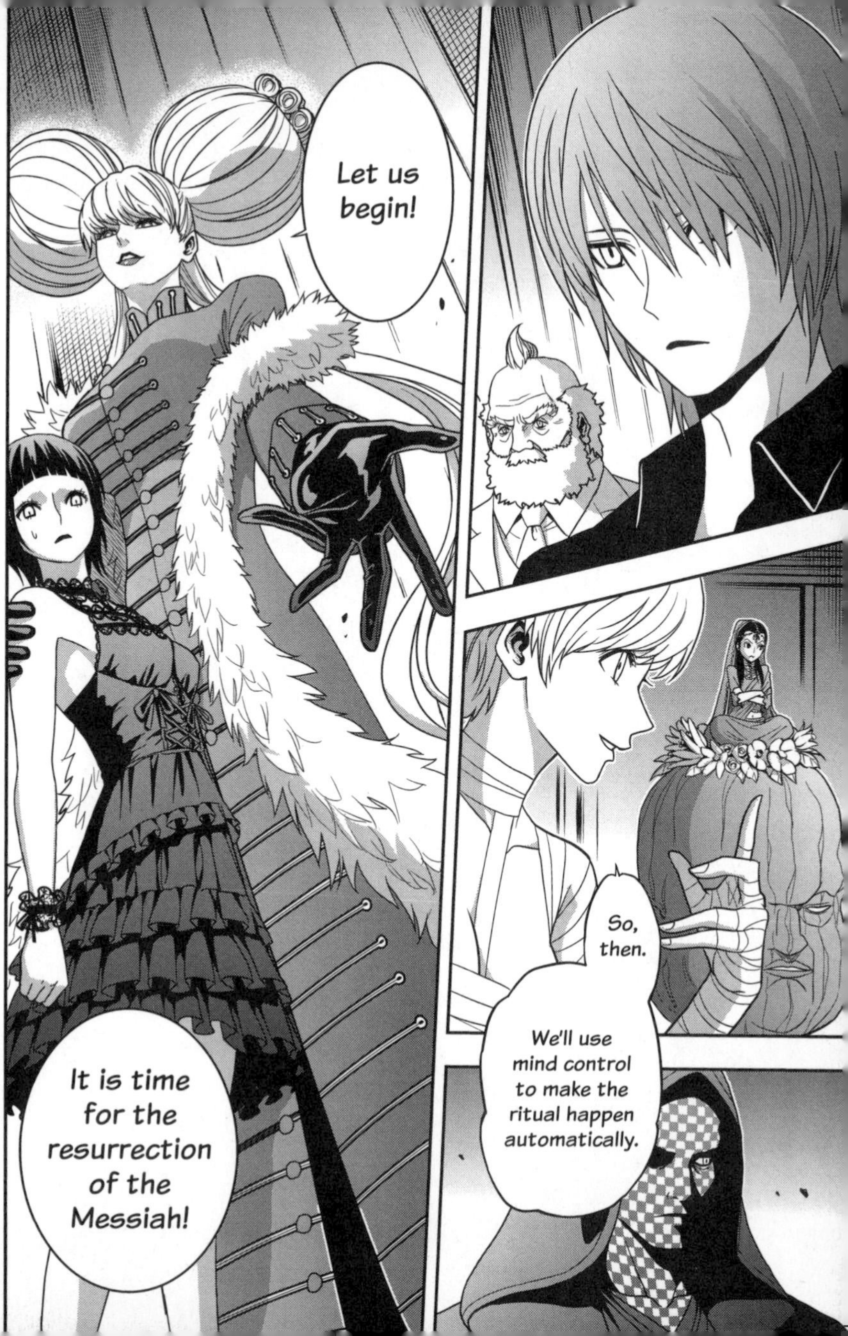
So, then.
We'll use mind control to make the ritual happen automatically.
Let us begin!
It is time for the resurrection of the Messiah!

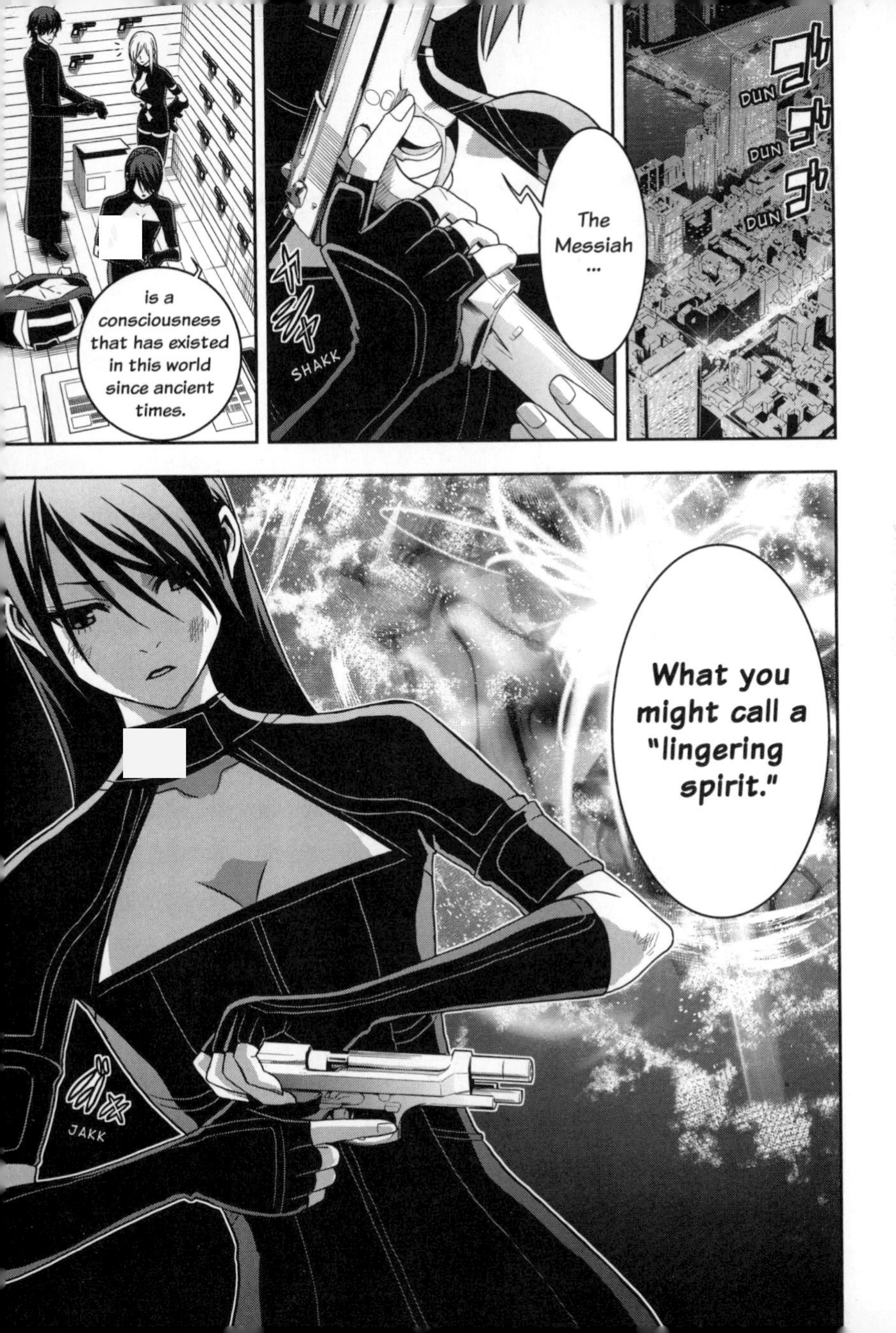
DUN
DUN
DUN
The Messiah ...
SHAKK
is a consciousness that has existed in this world since ancient times.
What you might call a "lingering spirit."
JAKK

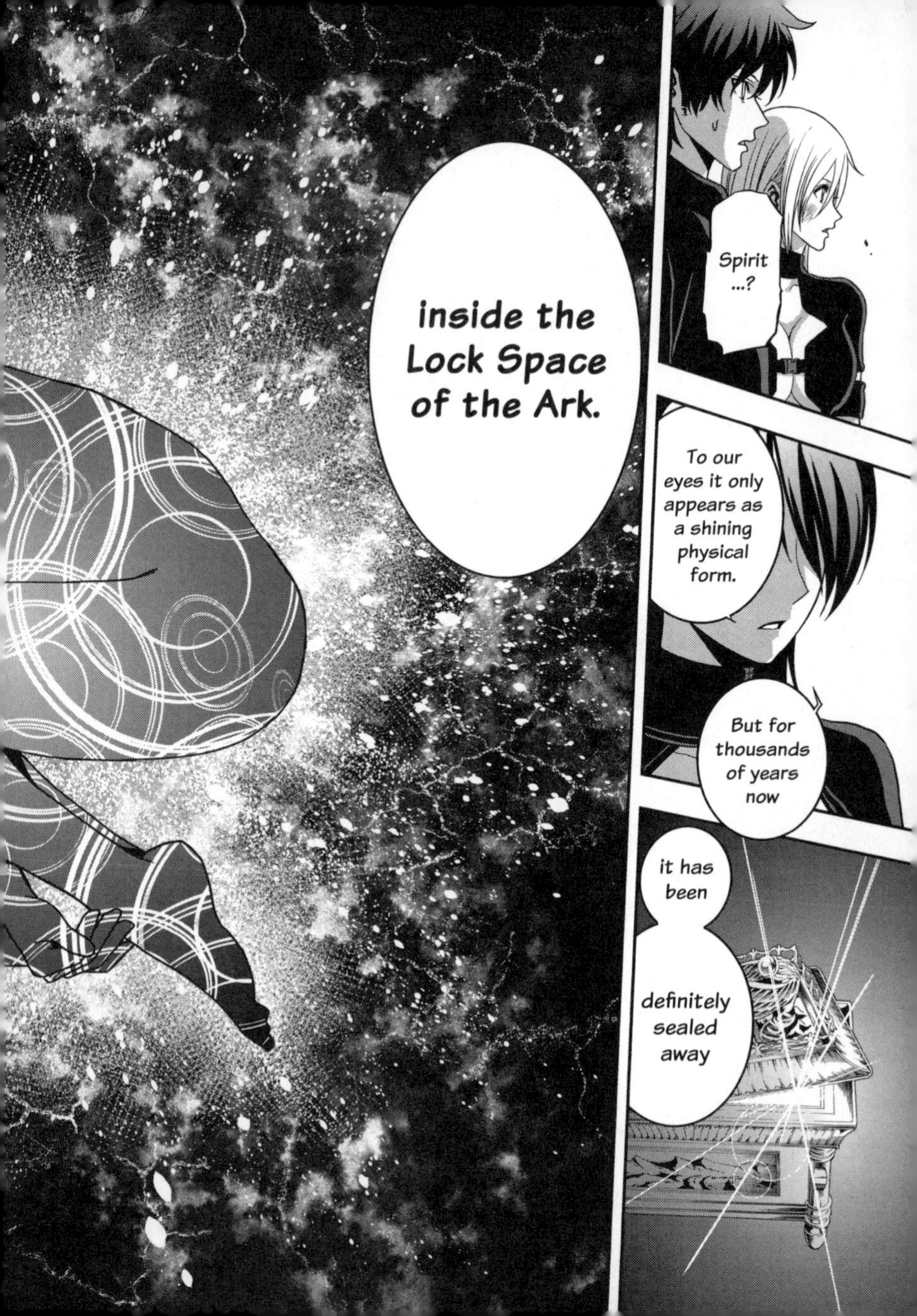
Spirit ...?
To our eyes it only appears as a shining physical form.
But for thousands of years now
it has been
definitely sealed away
inside the Lock Space of the Ark.

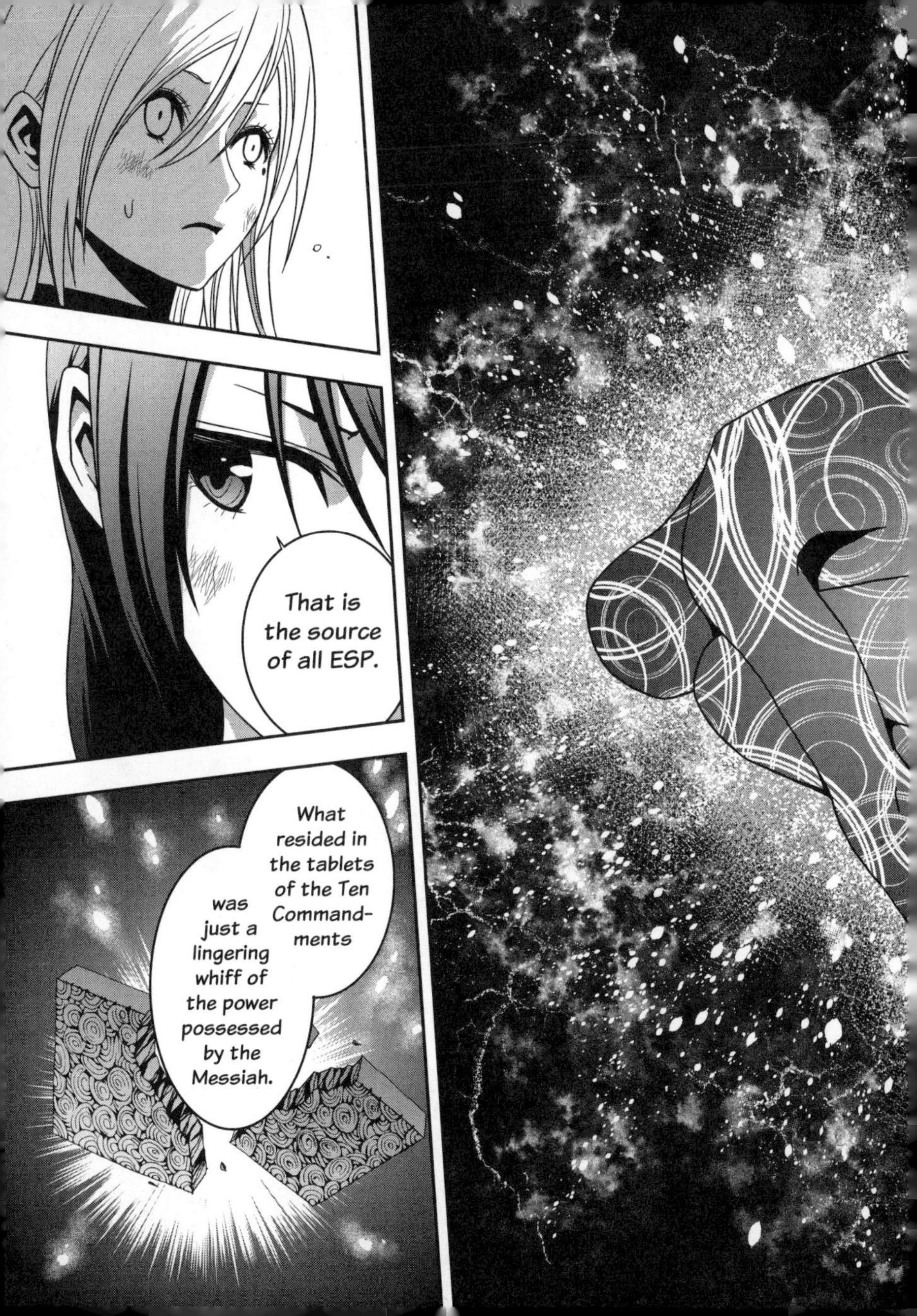

That is the source of all ESP.
What resided in the tablets of the Ten Command-ments
was just a lingering whiff of the power possessed by the Messiah.

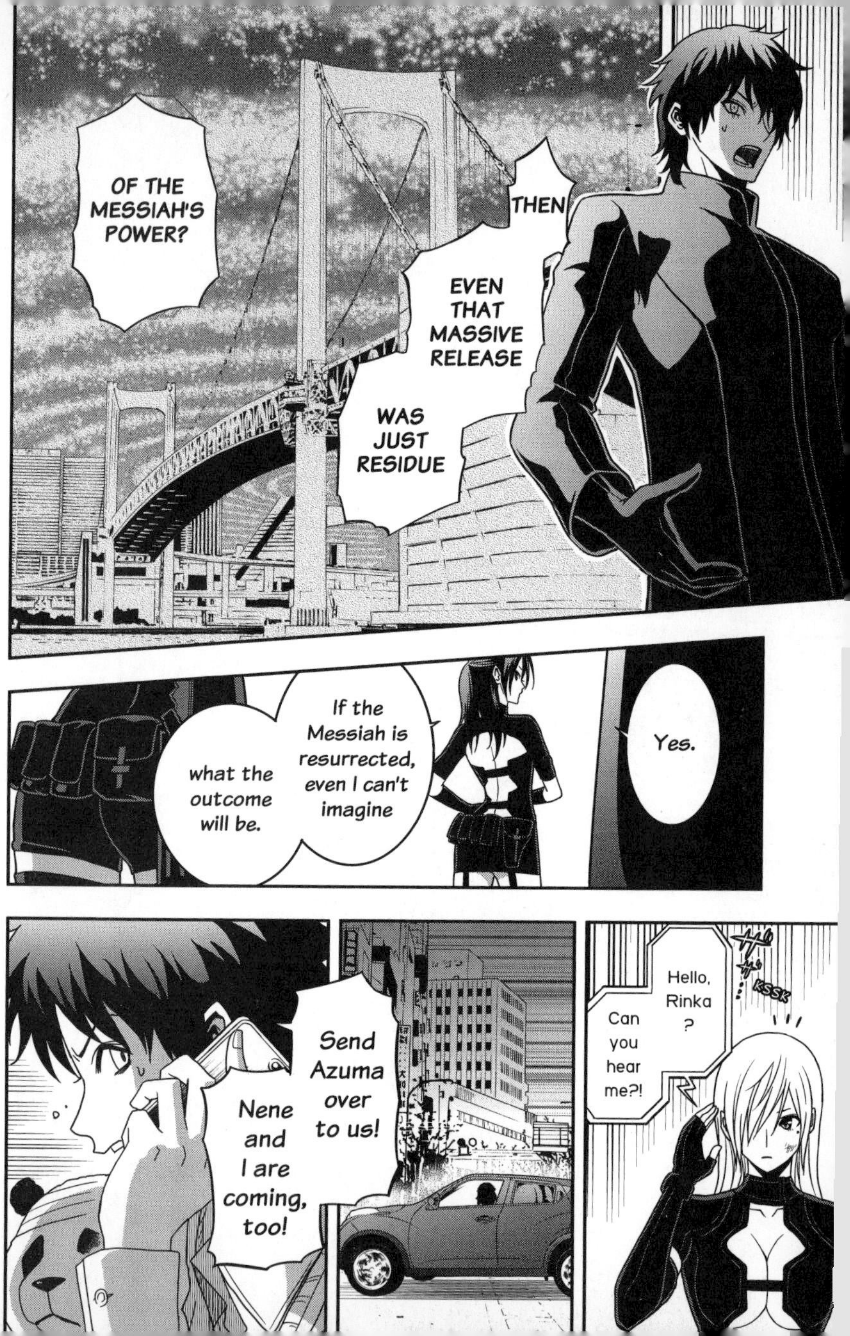
THEN
EVEN THAT MASSIVE RELEASE
WAS JUST RESIDUE
OF THE MESSIAH'S POWER?
Yes.
If the Messiah is resurrected, even I can't imagine
what the outcome will be.
KSSK
Hello, Rinka?
Can you hear me?!
Send Azuma over to us!
Nene and I are coming, too!

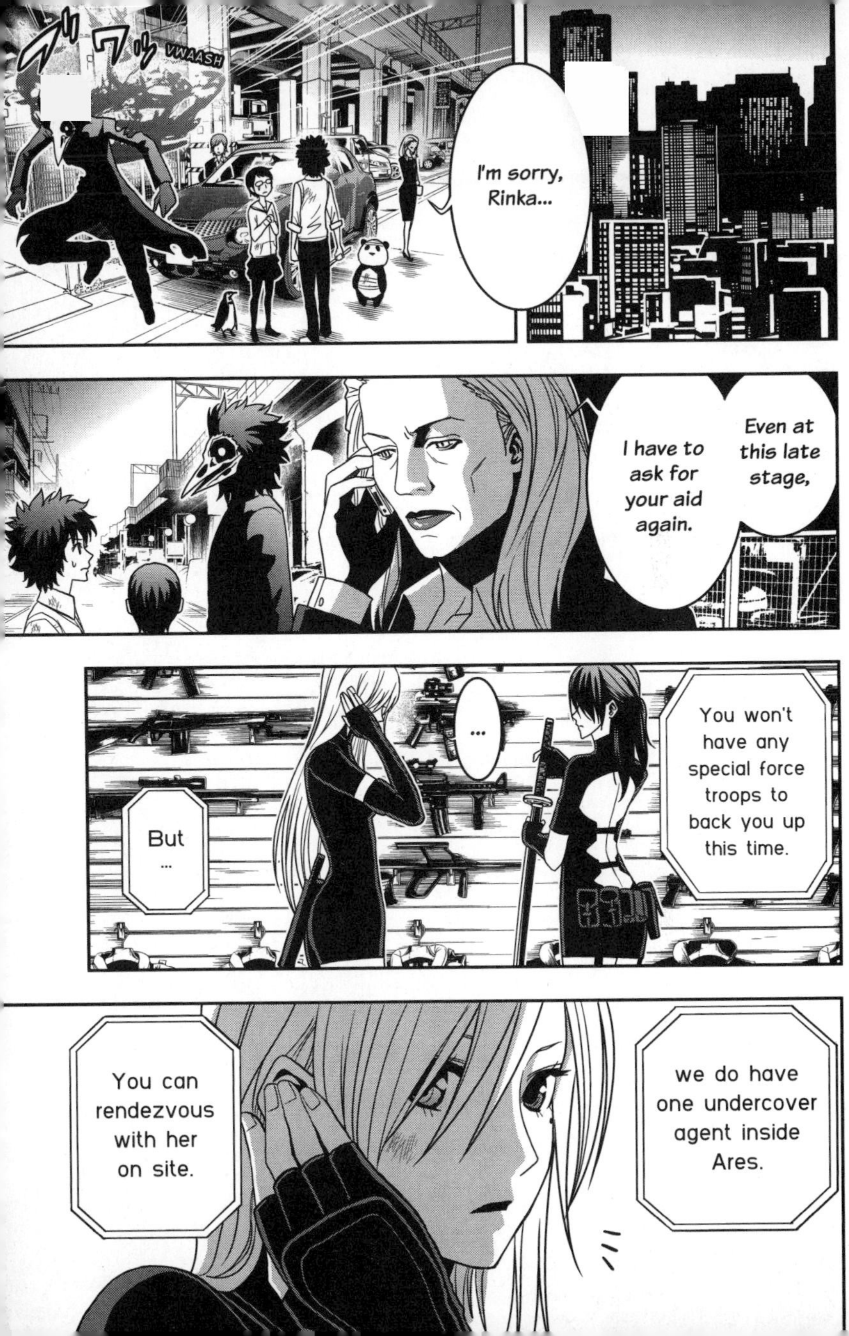
I'm sorry, Rinka...
ブワッ VWAASH
Even at this late stage,
I have to ask for your aid again.
You won't have any special force troops to back you up this time.
...
But ...
we do have one undercover agent inside Ares.
You can rendezvous with her on site.

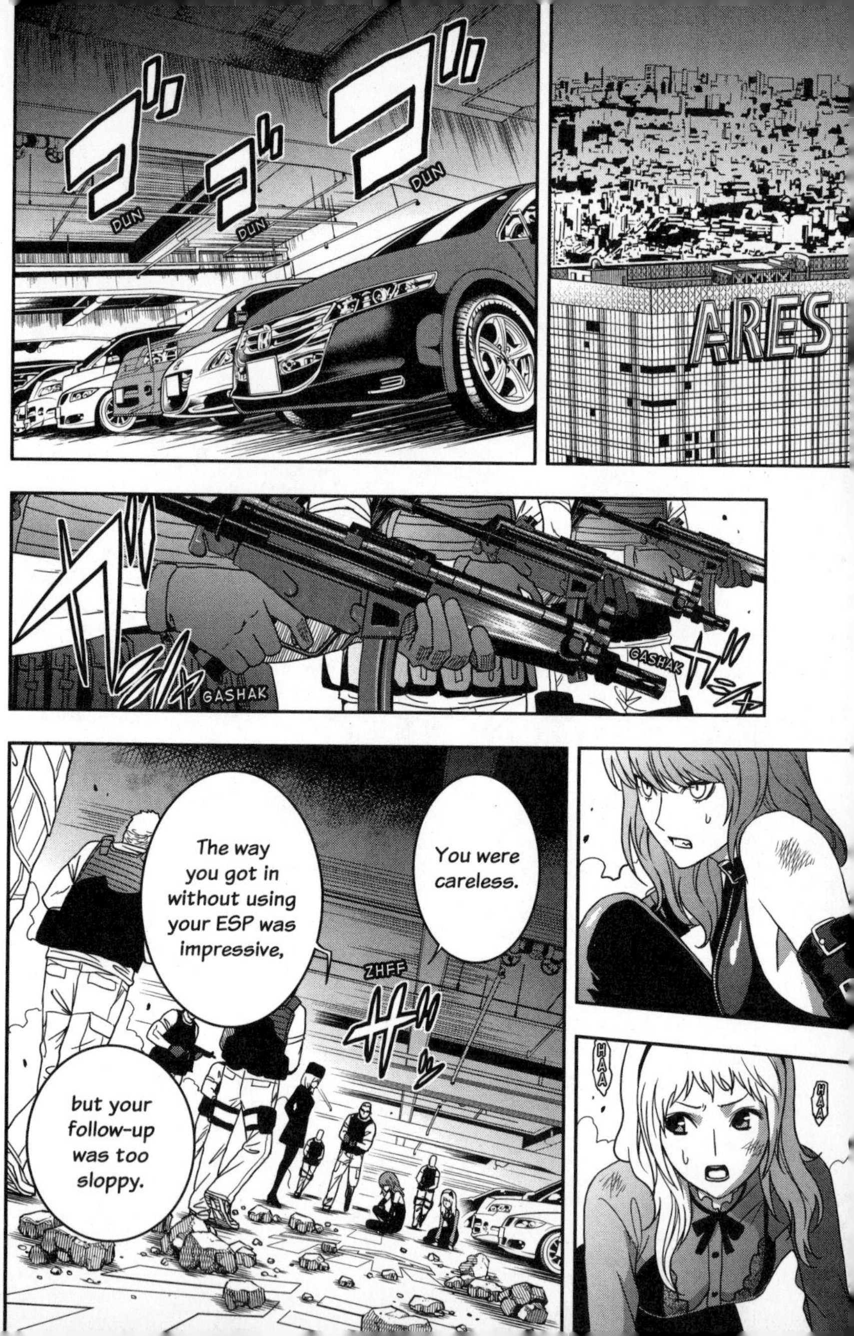
ARES
DUN
DUN
DUN
GASHAK
GASHAK
HAA
HAA
You were careless.
The way you got in without using your ESP was impressive,
ZHFF
but your follow-up was too sloppy.

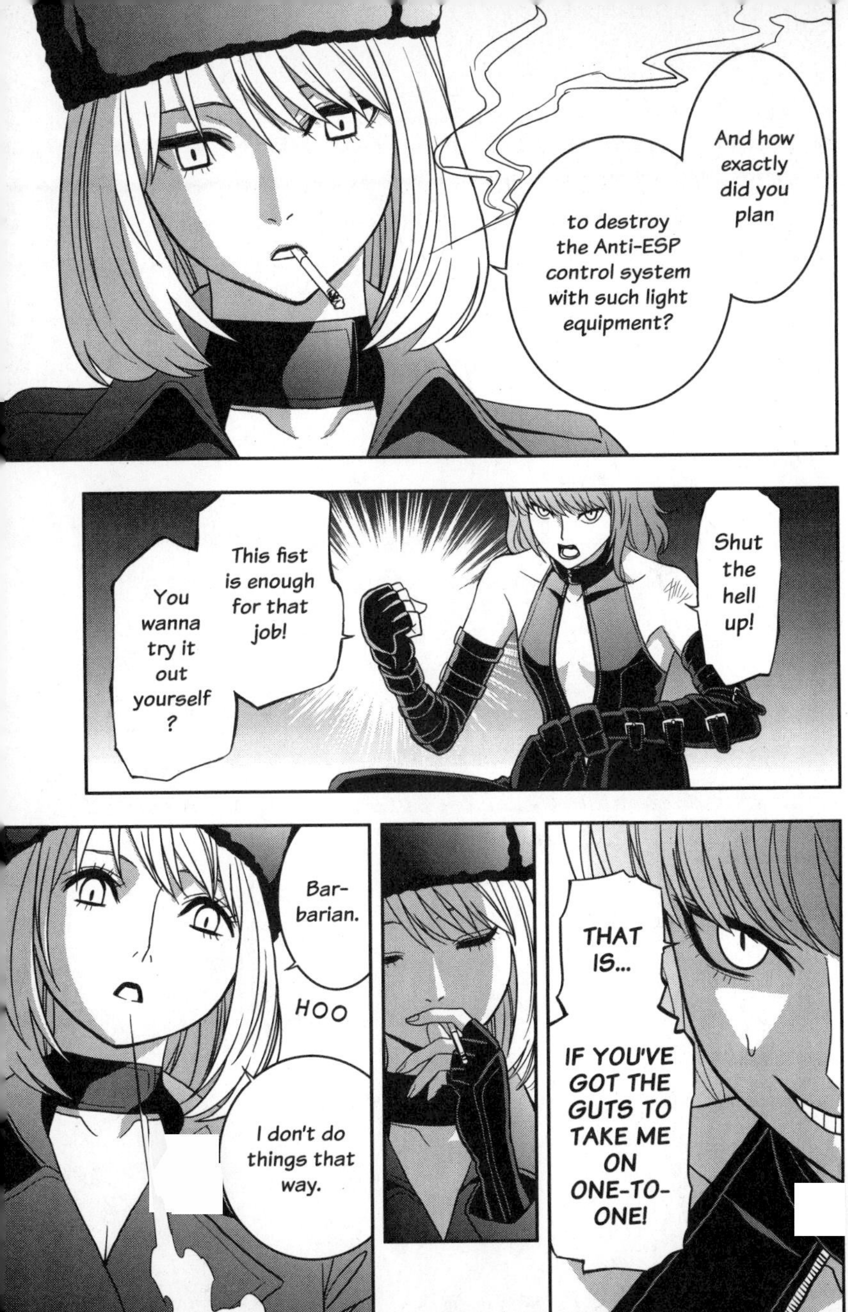
And how exactly did you plan
to destroy the Anti-ESP control system with such light equipment?
Shut the hell up!
This fist is enough for that job!
You wanna try it out yourself?
THAT IS...
IF YOU'VE GOT THE GUTS TO TAKE ME ON ONE-TO-ONE!
Bar-barian.
HOO
I don't do things that way.

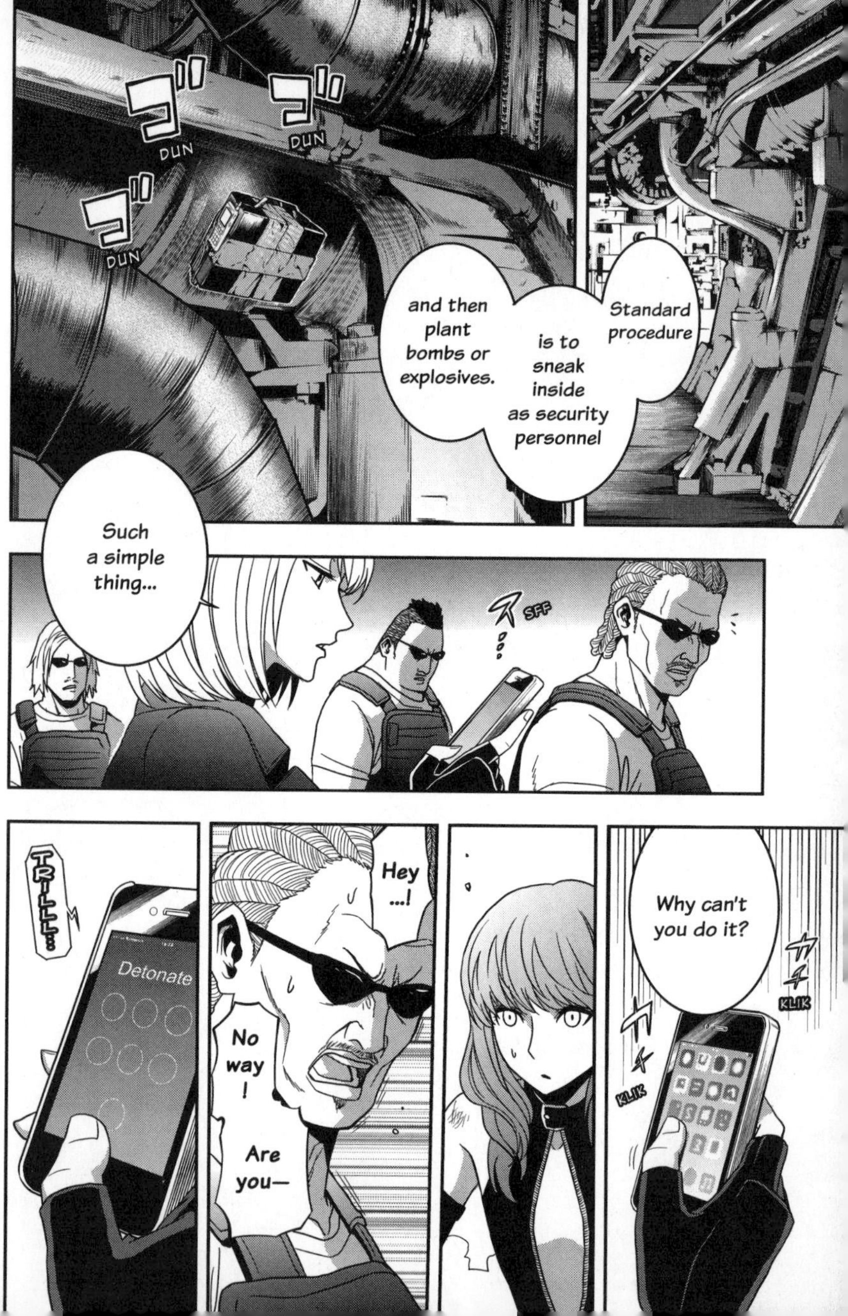

DUN
DUN
DUN
Standard procedure
is to sneak inside as security personnel
and then plant bombs or explosives.
Such a simple thing...
SFF
Why can't you do it?
KLIK
KLIK
Hey ...!
No way!
Are you—
TRILL...!!
Detonate

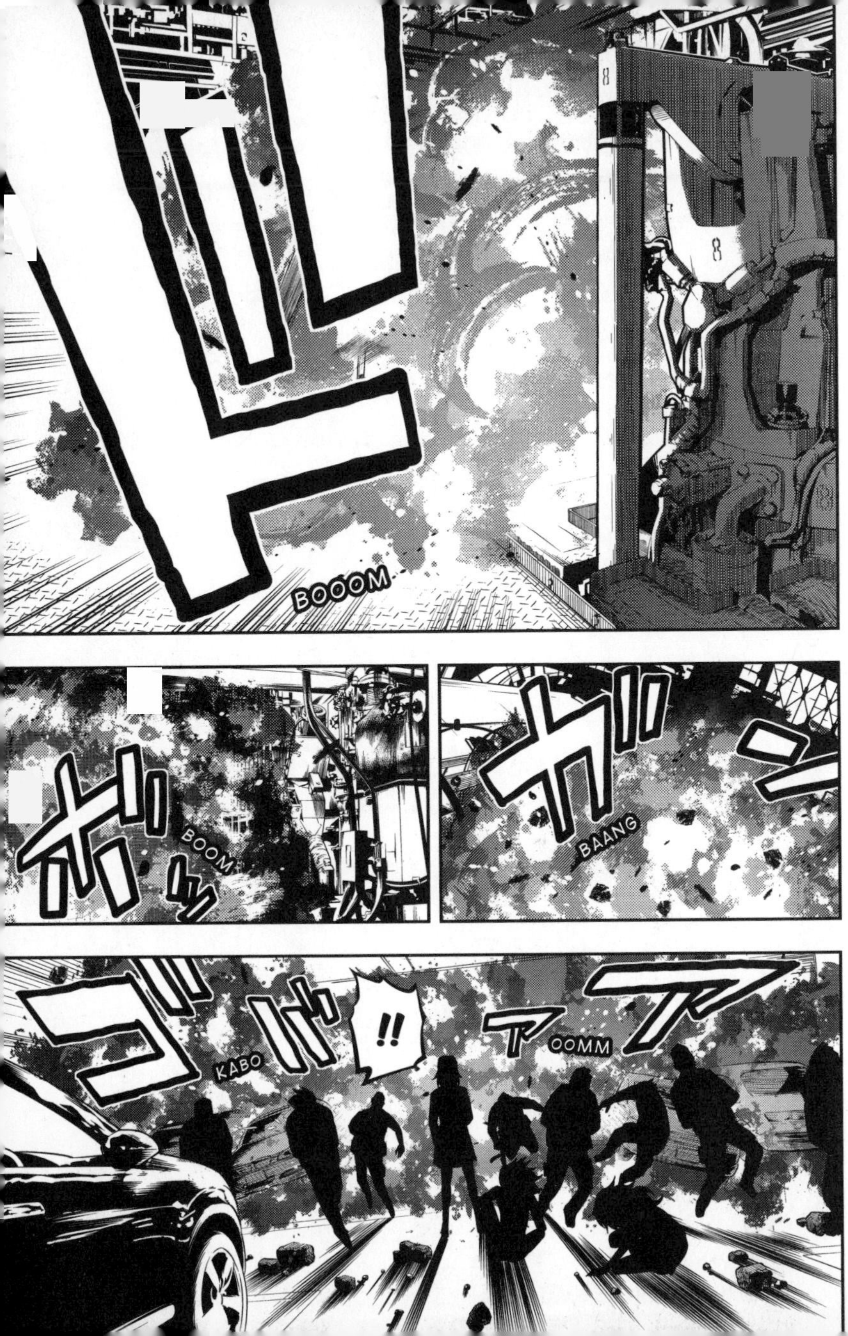
BOOOM
BAANG
BOOM
!!
KABO
OOMM

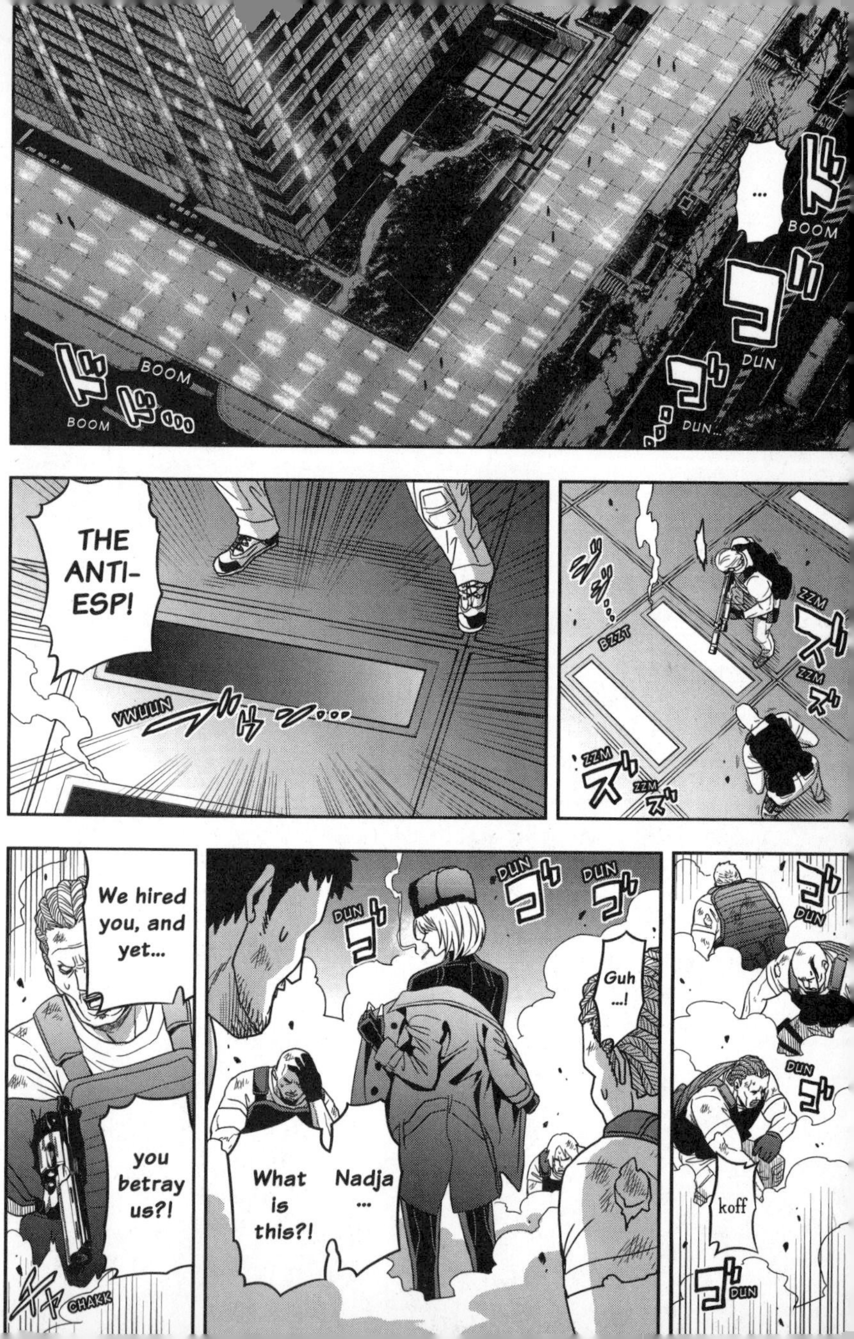
...
BOOM
DUN
DUN...
BOOM
BOOM
ZZM
ZZM
BZZT
ZZM
ZZM
THE ANTI-ESP!
VWUUN
DUN
DUN
koff
DUN
DUN
DUN
DUN
Guh ...!
Nadja ...
What is this?!
We hired you, and yet...
you betray us?!
CHAKK

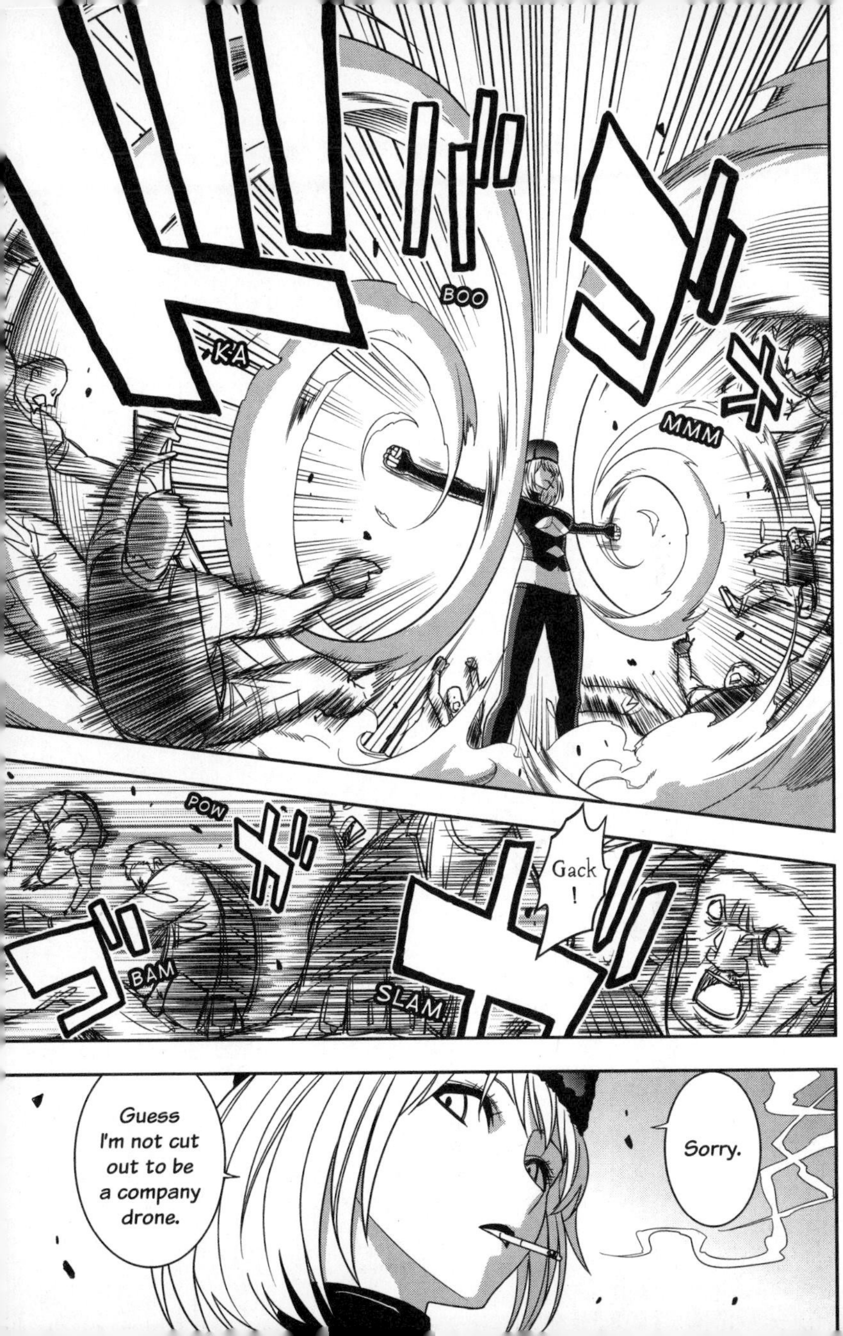
MMM
BOO
KA
Gack!
SLAM
POW
BAM
Sorry.
Guess I'm not cut out to be a company drone.

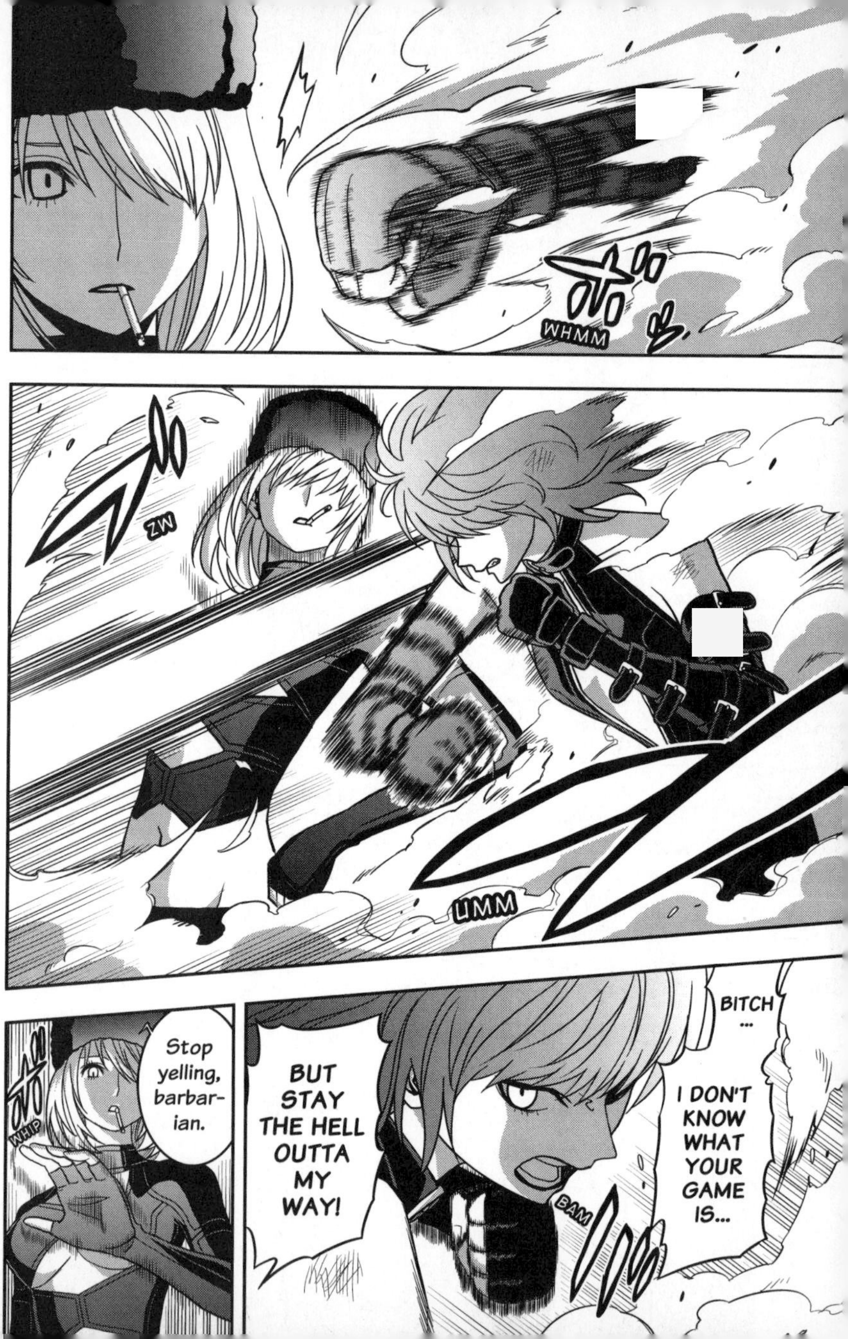
WHMM
ZW
UMM
BITCH ...
I DON'T KNOW WHAT YOUR GAME IS...
BUT STAY THE HELL OUTTA MY WAY!
BAM
Stop yelling, barbar-ian.
WHIP

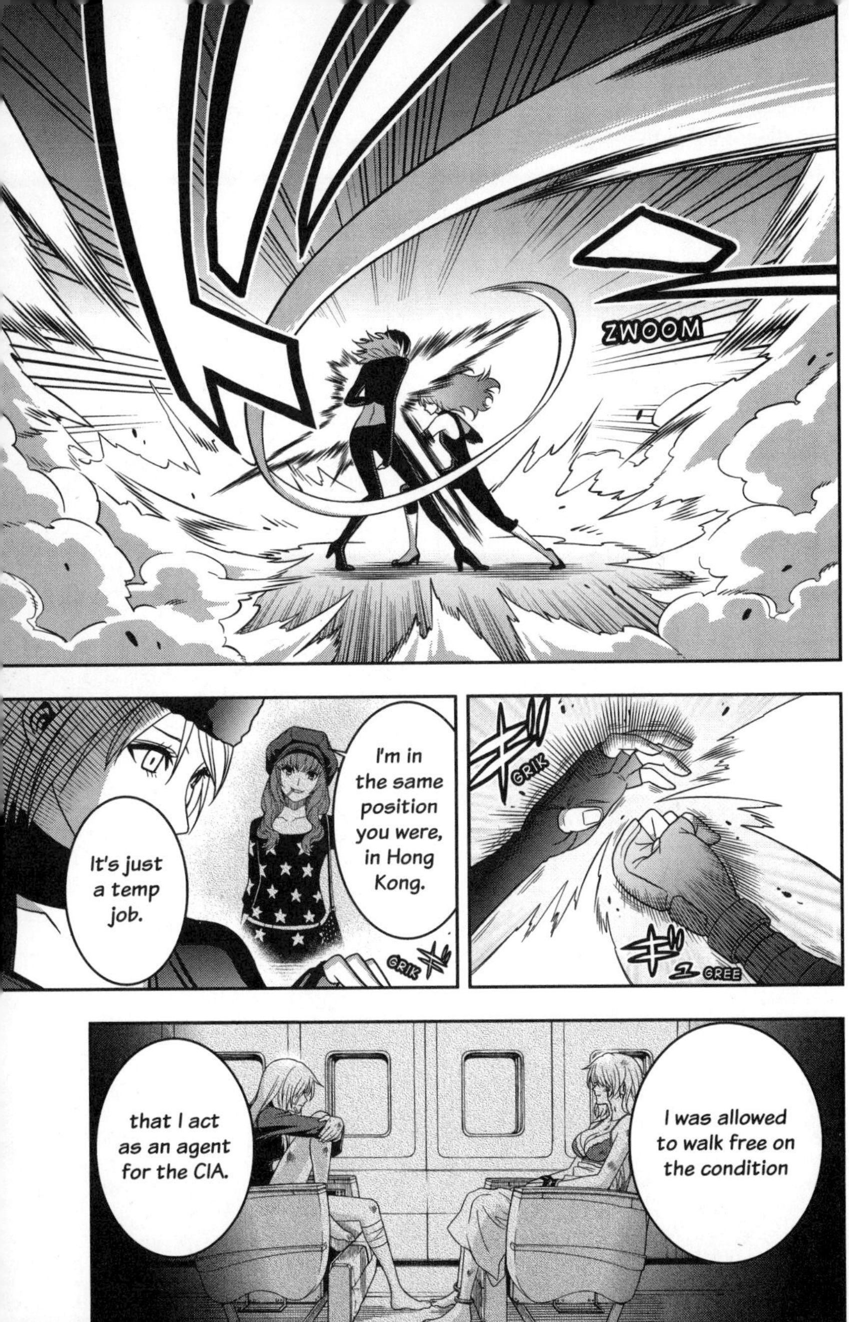
ZWOOM
GRIK
GREE
I'm in the same position you were, in Hong Kong.
It's just a temp job.
GRIK
I was allowed to walk free on the condition
that I act as an agent for the CIA.

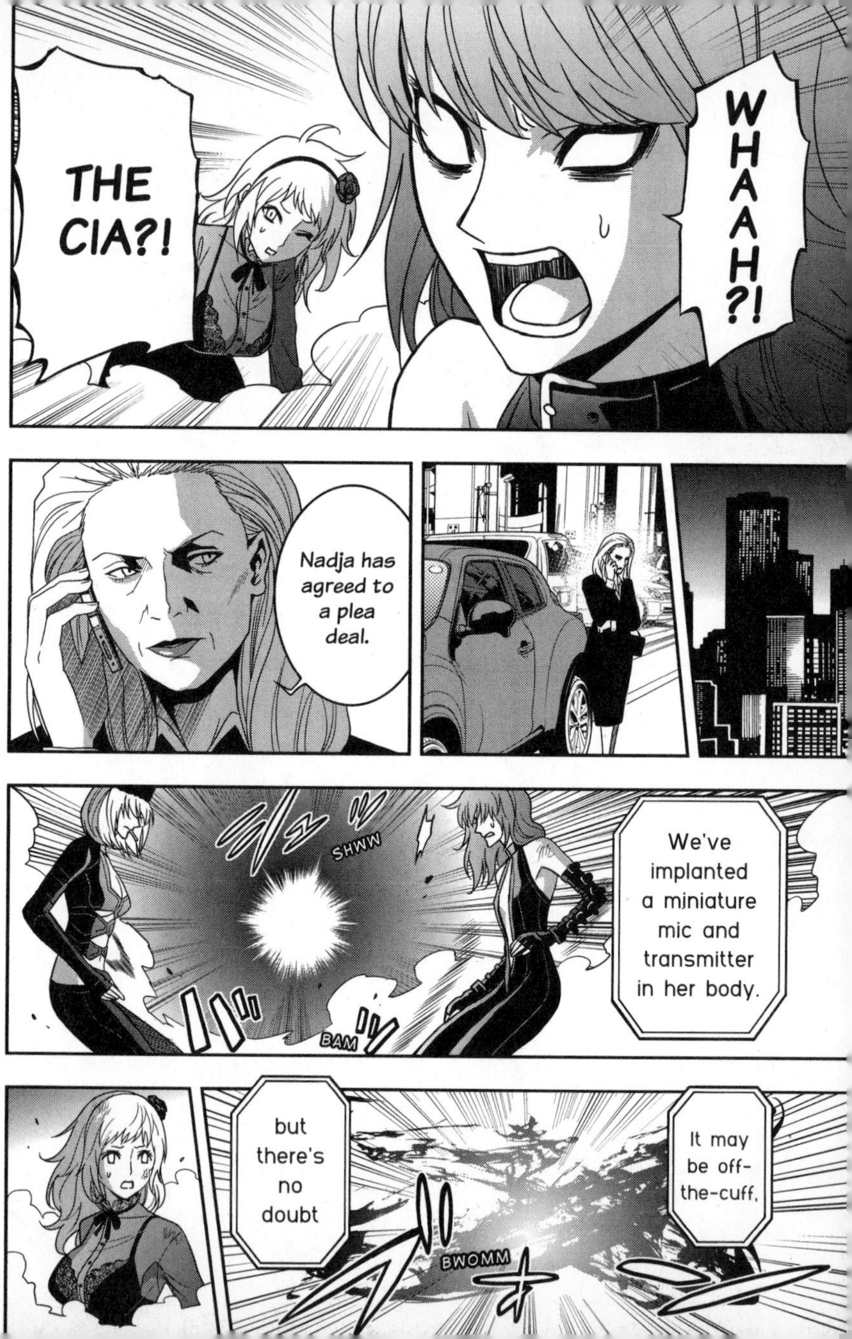
WHAAH?!
THE CIA?!
Nadja has agreed to a plea deal.
We've implanted a miniature mic and transmitter in her body.
SHWW
BAM
It may be off-the-cuff,
but there's no doubt
BWOMM

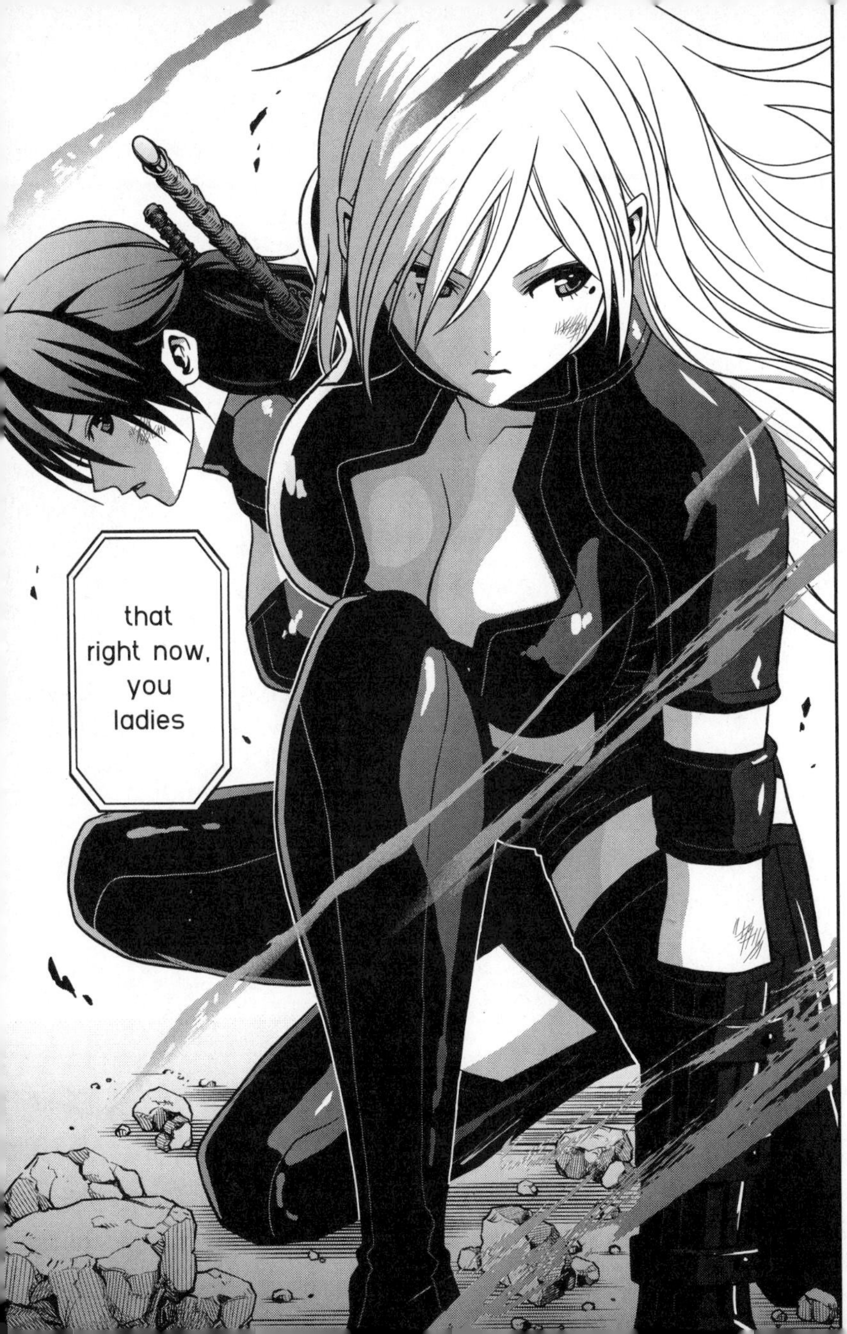
that right now, you ladies

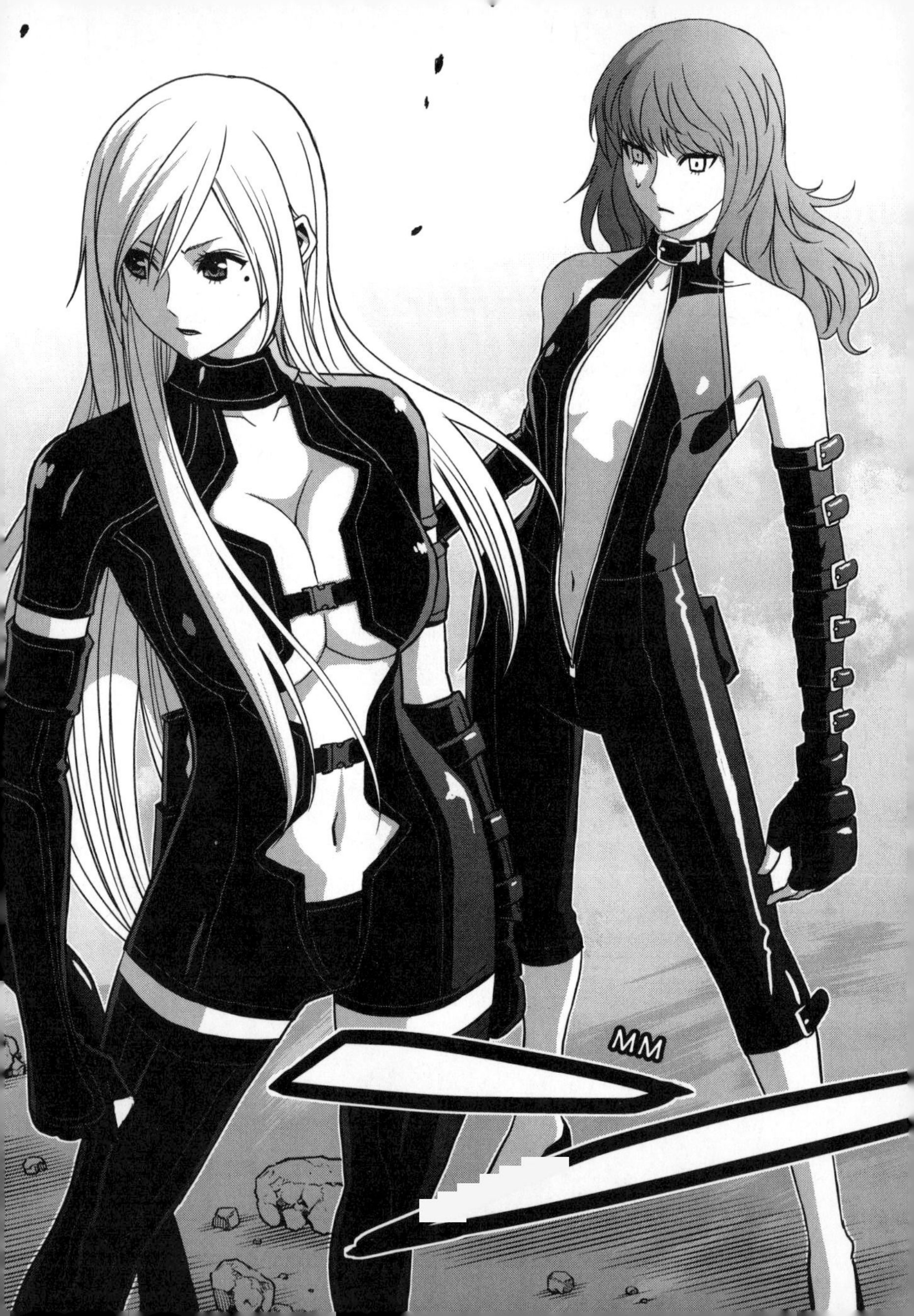
MM

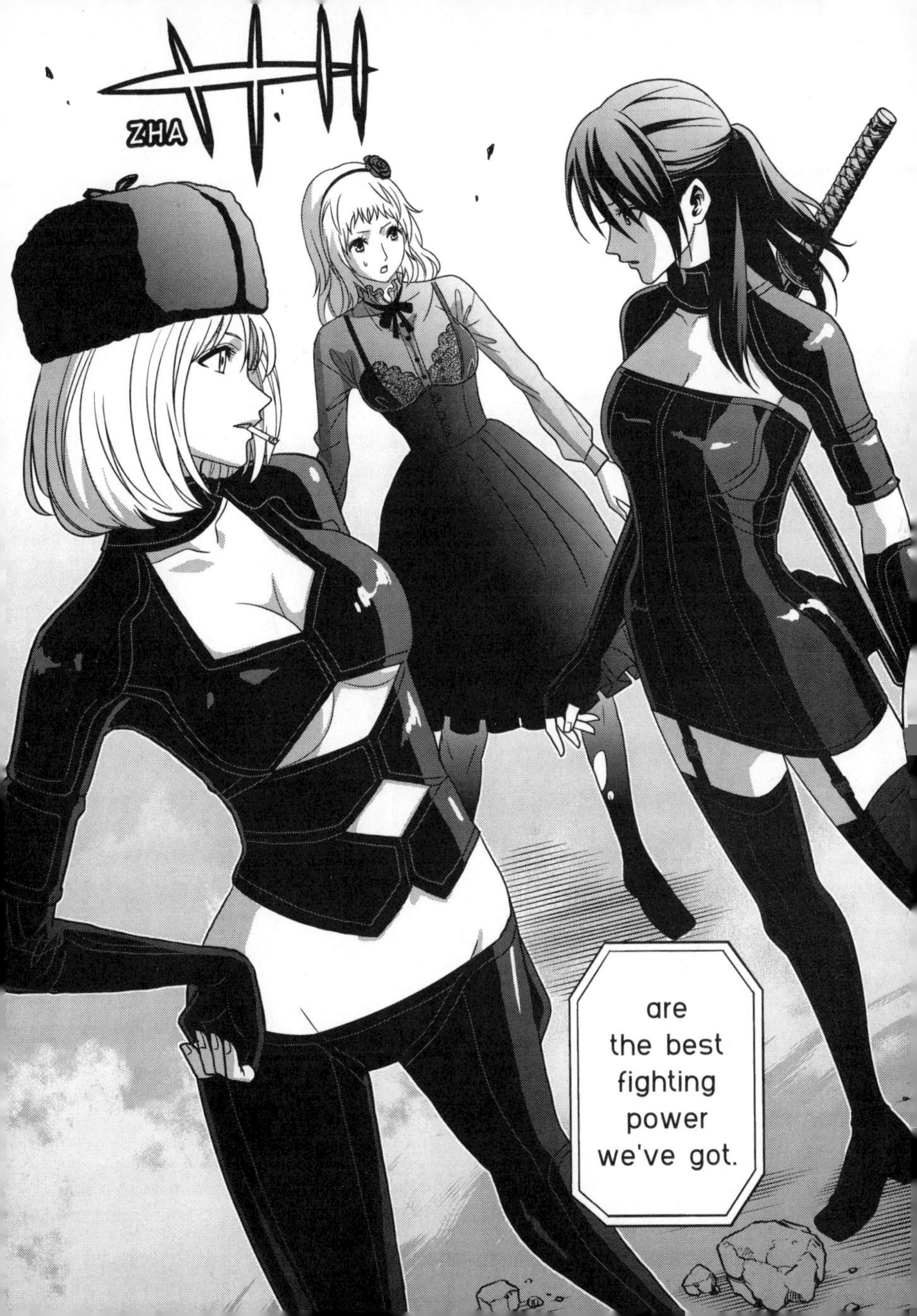
ZHA
are the best fighting power we've got.

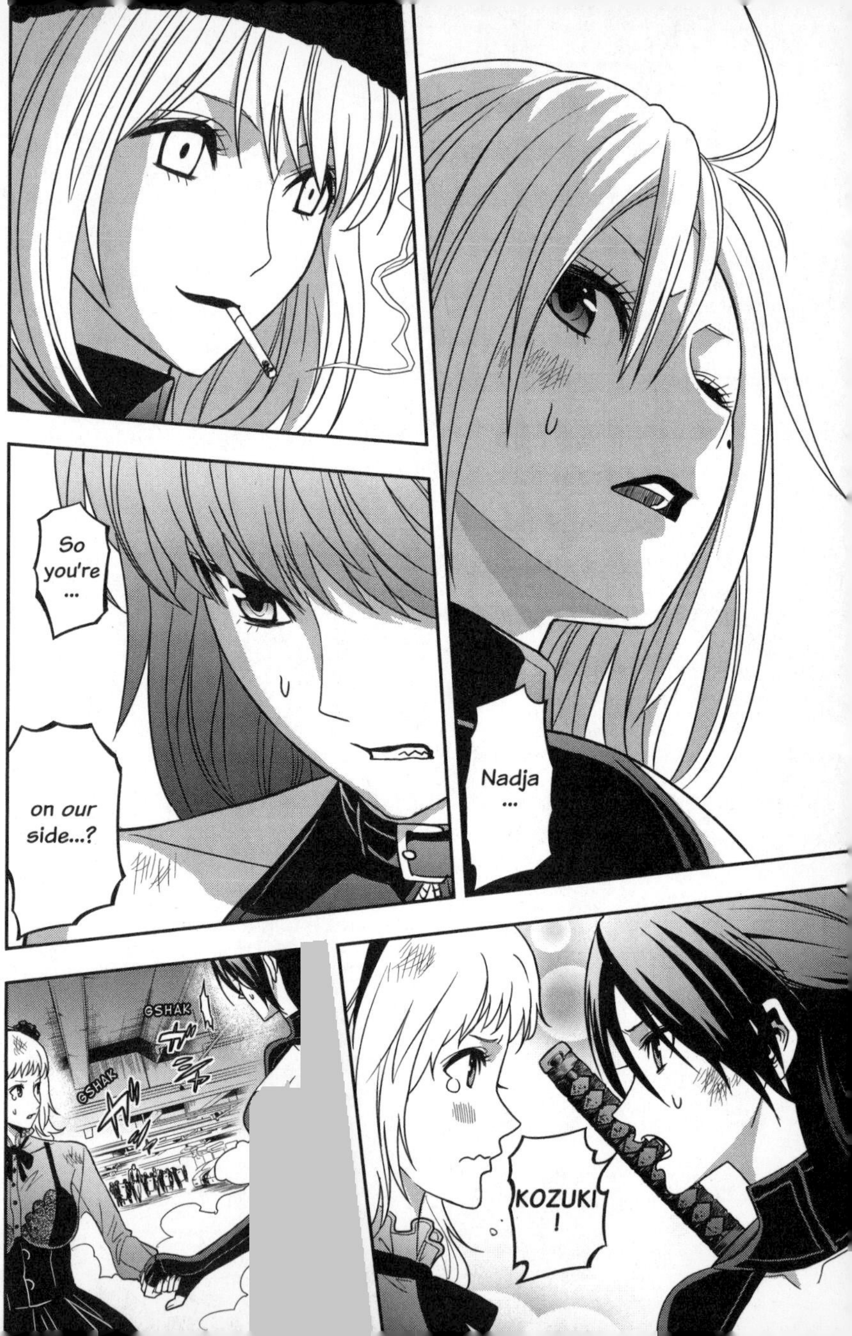
Nadja ...
So you're ...
on our side...?
KOZUKI !
GSHAK
GSHAK

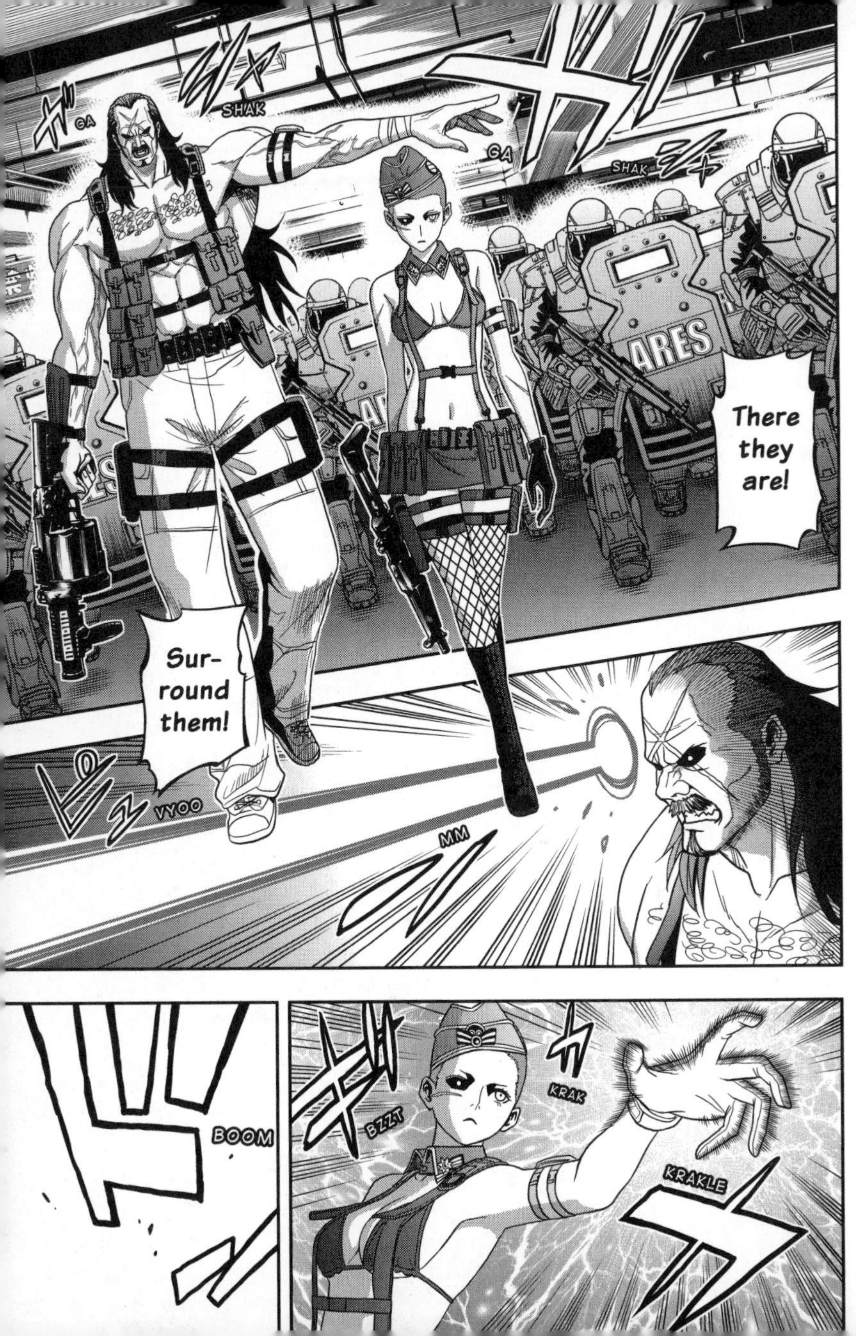
GA
SHAK
There they are!
SHAK
GA
Sur-round them!
VYOO
MM
KRAK
BZZT
KRAKLE
BOOM

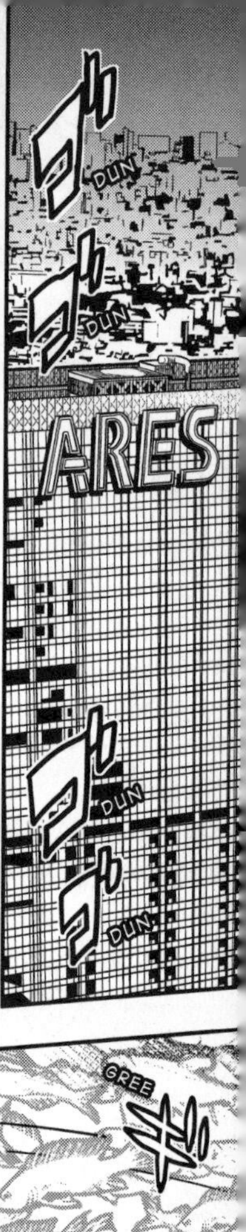
DUN
DUN
ARES
DUN
DUN
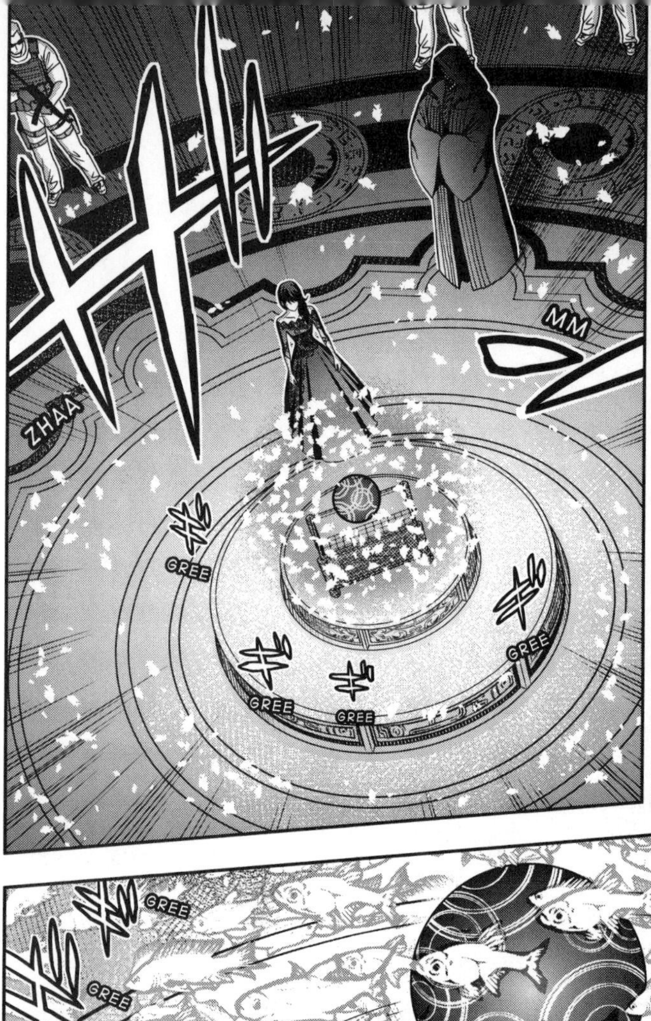
MM
ZHAA
GREE
GREE
GREE
GREE
GREE
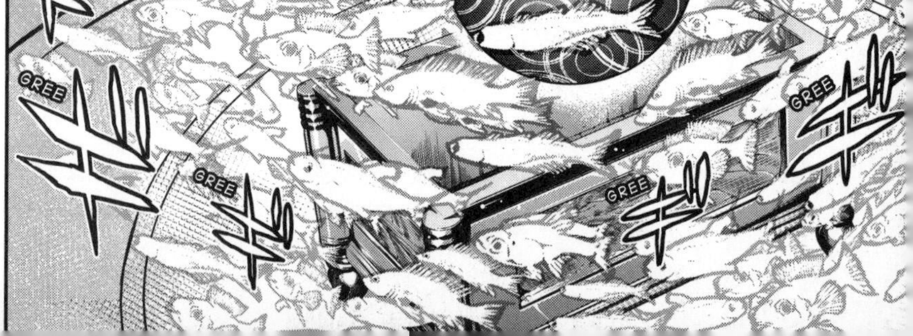
GREE
GREE
GREE
GREE
GREE
GREE
GREE

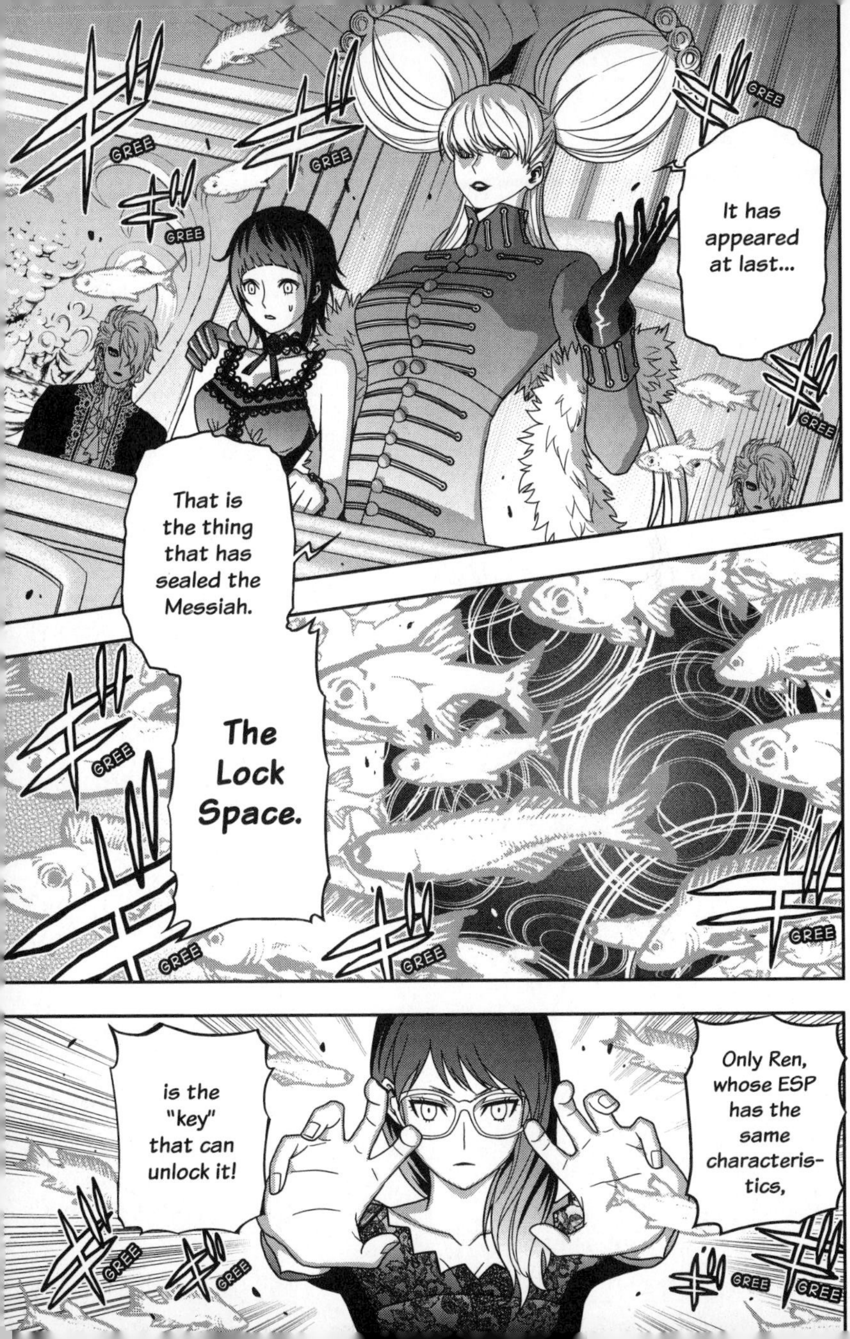
GREE
It has appeared at last...
GREE
GREE
GREE
GREE
That is the thing that has sealed the Messiah.
GREE
The Lock Space.
GREE
GREE
GREE
GREE
Only Ren, whose ESP has the same characteris-tics,
is the "key" that can unlock it!
GREE
GREE
GREE
GREE

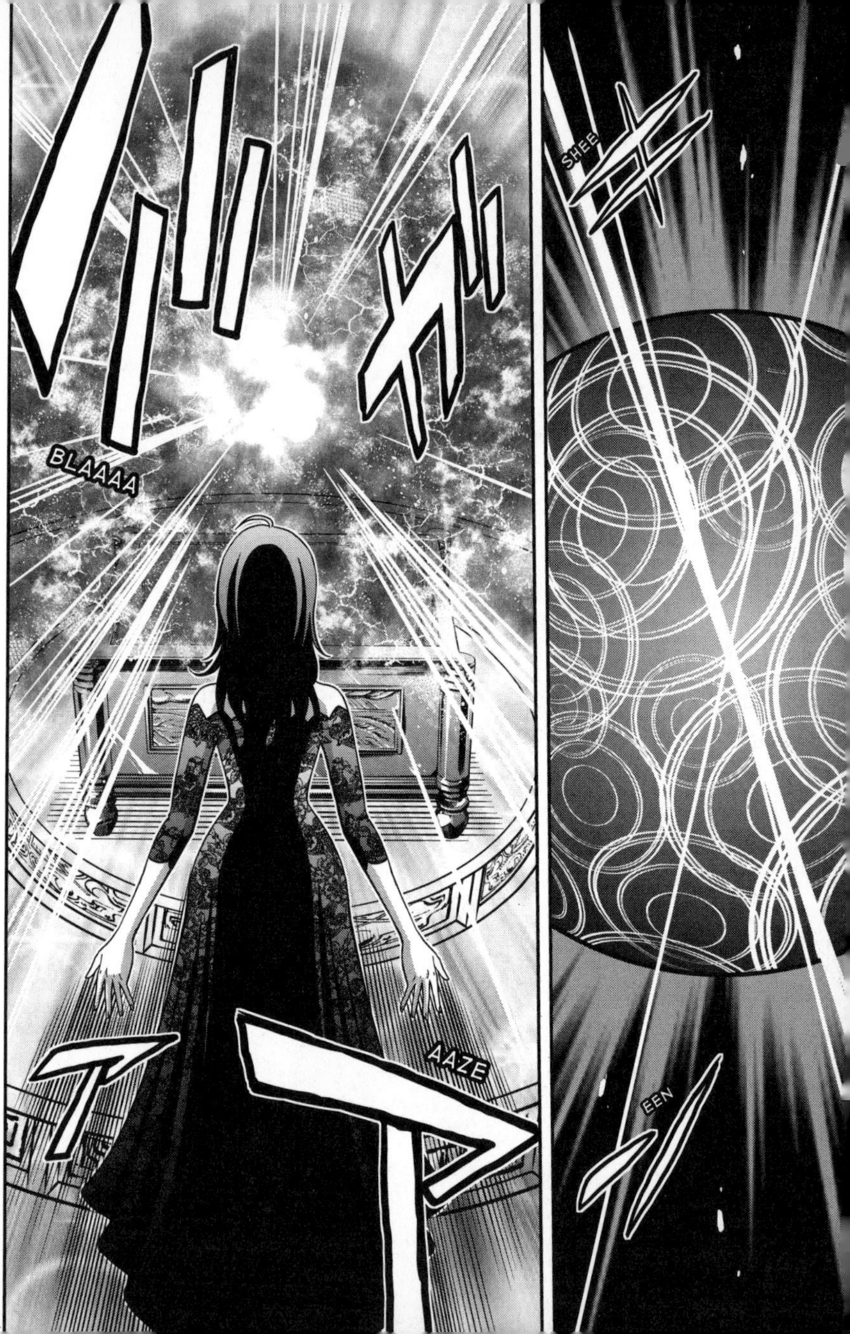
SHEE
EEN
BLAAAA
AAZE

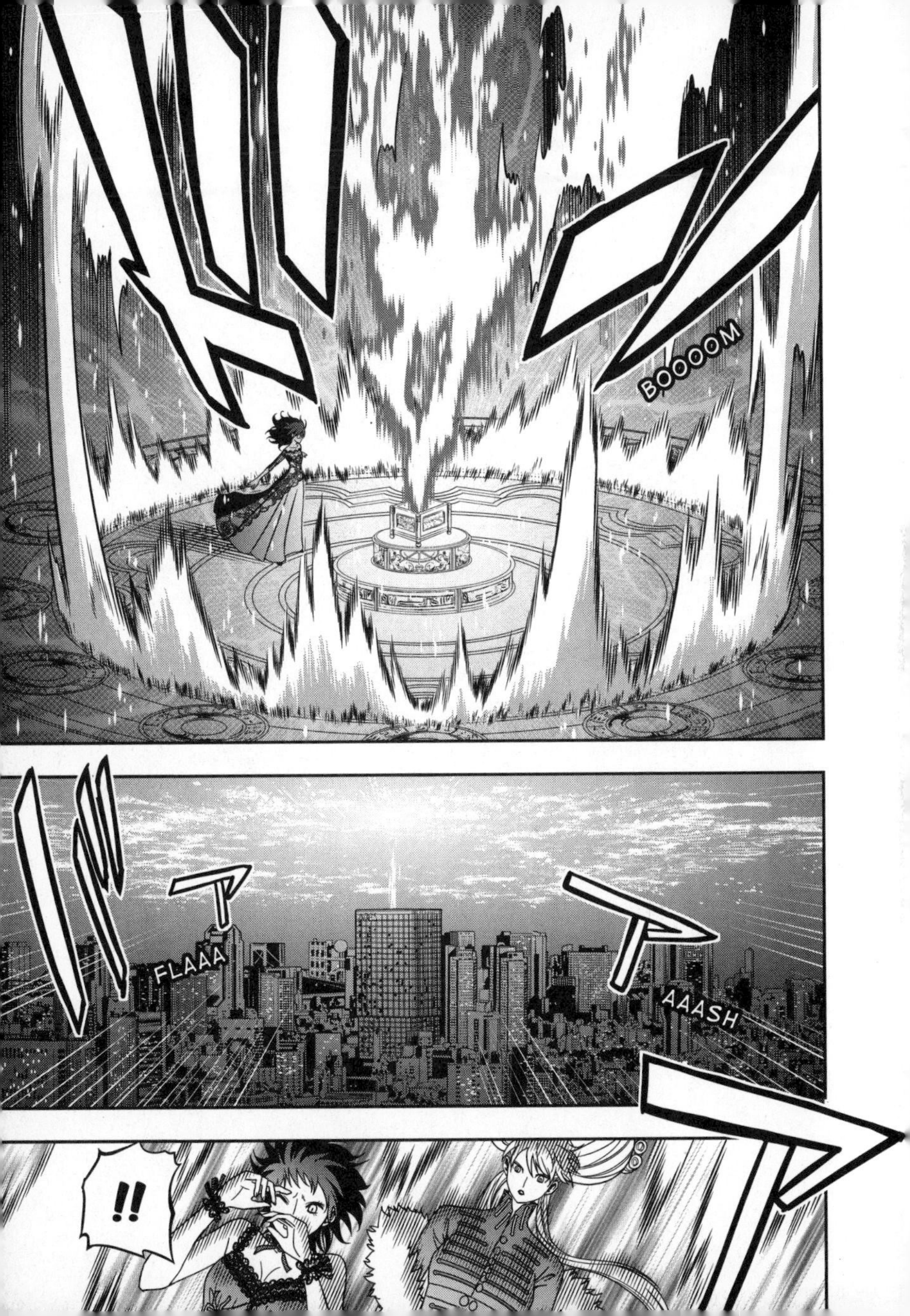
BOOOOM
FLAAA
AAASH
!!

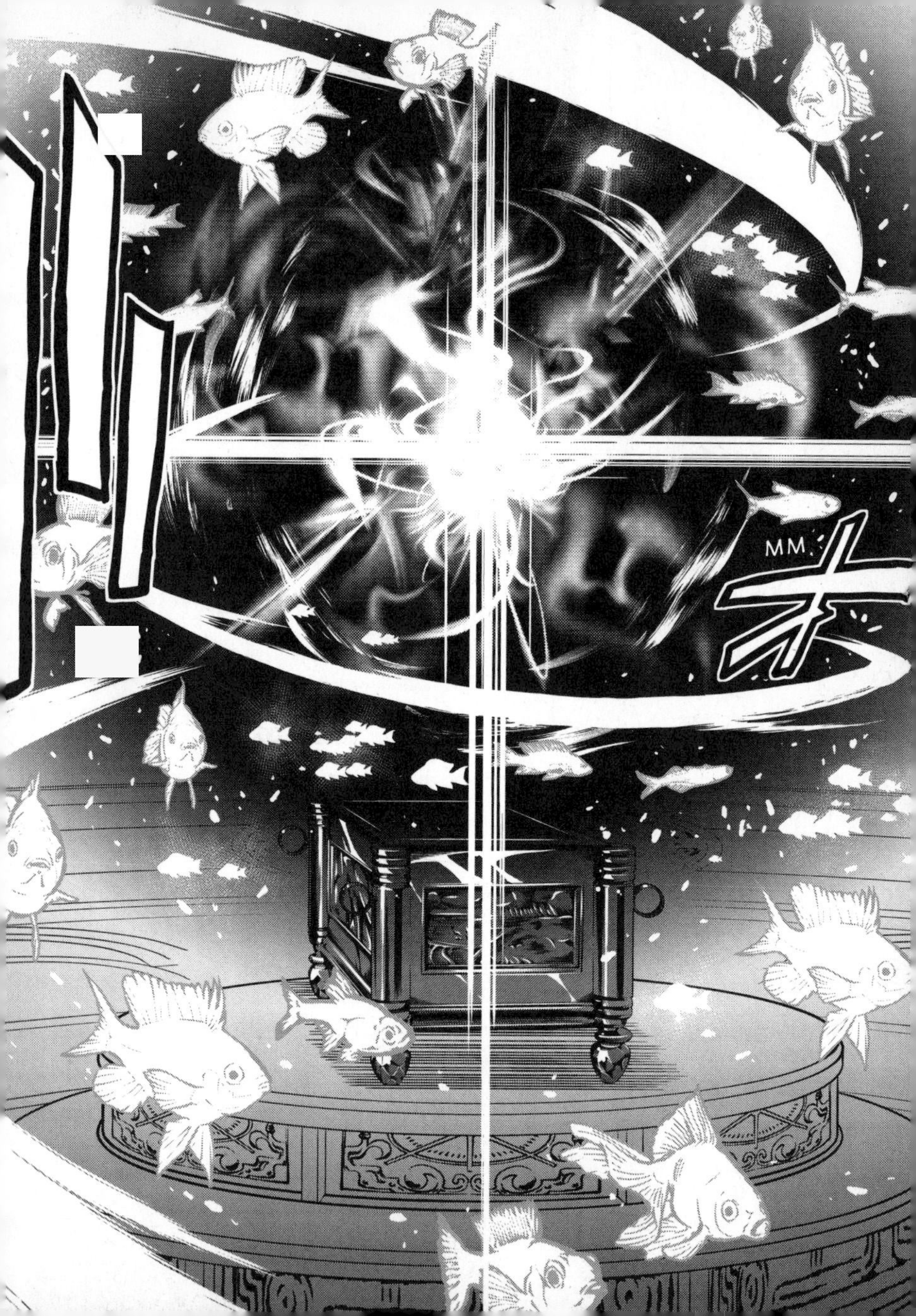
MM

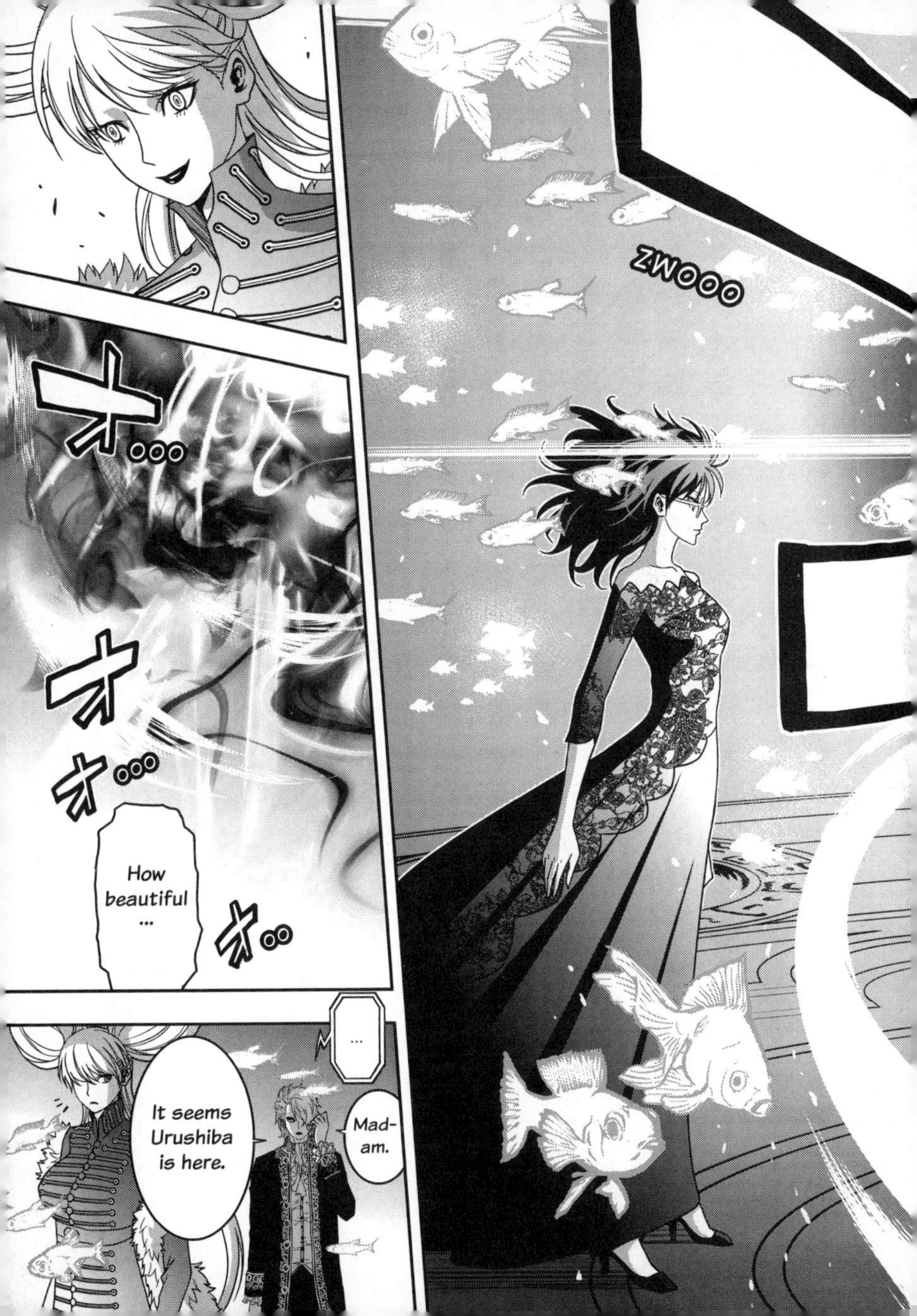
ZWOOO
オ…
オ…
How beautiful …
オ…
…
Mad-am.
It seems Urushiba is here.

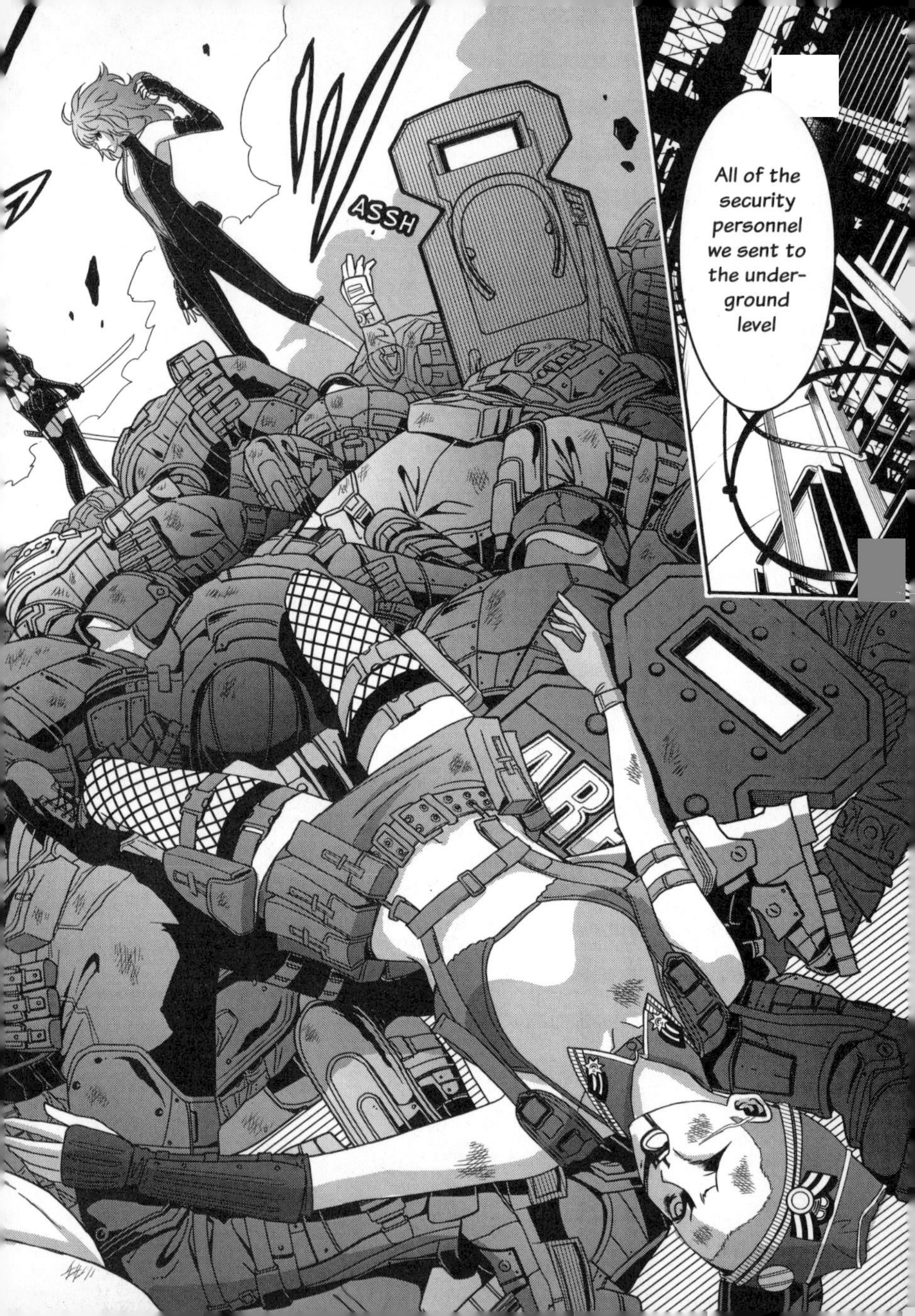
All of the security personnel we sent to the under-ground level
ASSH

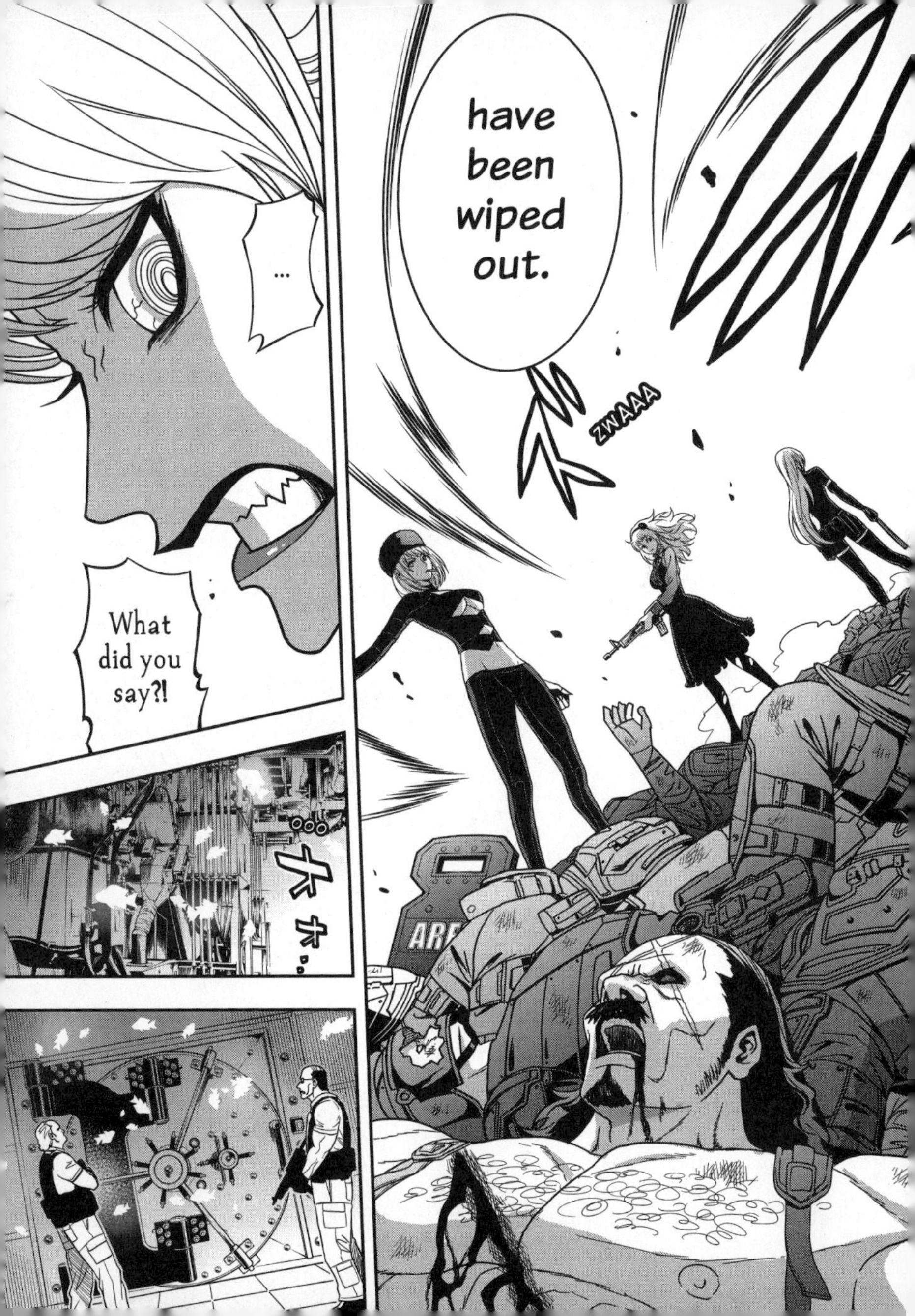
have been wiped out.
ZWAAA
...
What did you say?!
ooo
オォ..

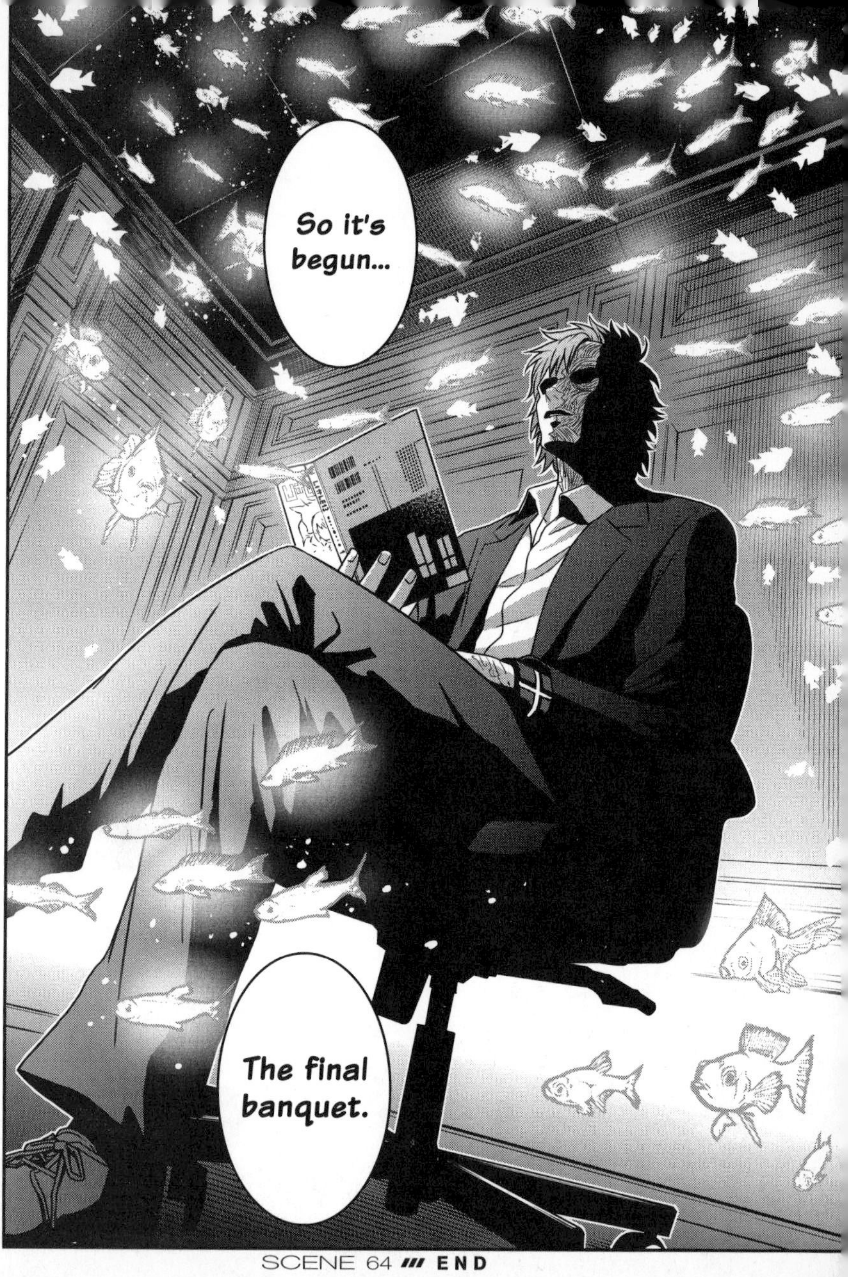
So it's begun...
The final banquet.

SCENE 64 /// END

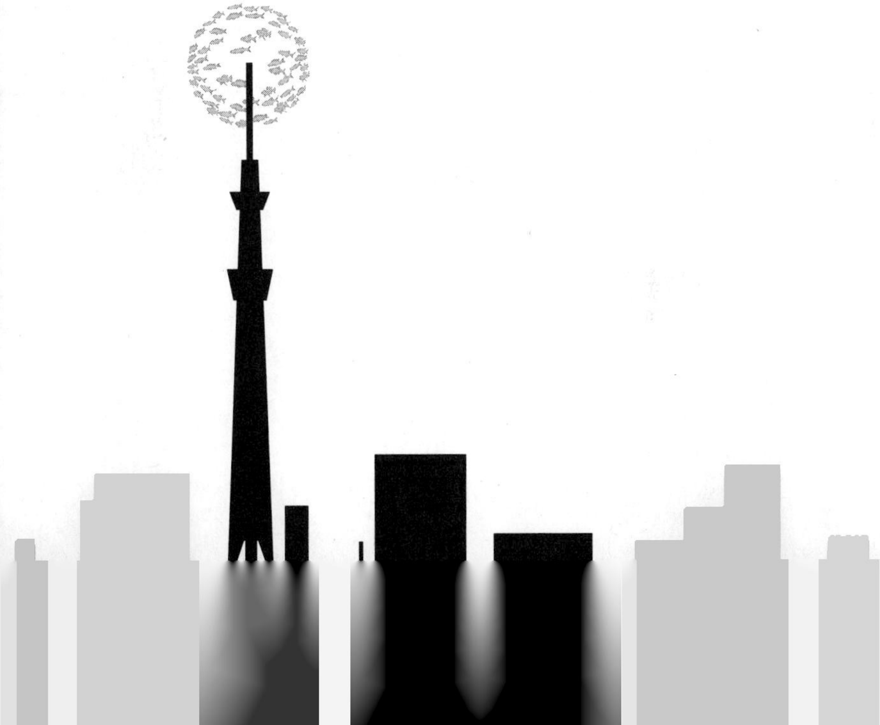

End of Book Bonus

UNUSED SCENE COLLECTION ① "THE PROFESSOR'S LIFESTYLE"

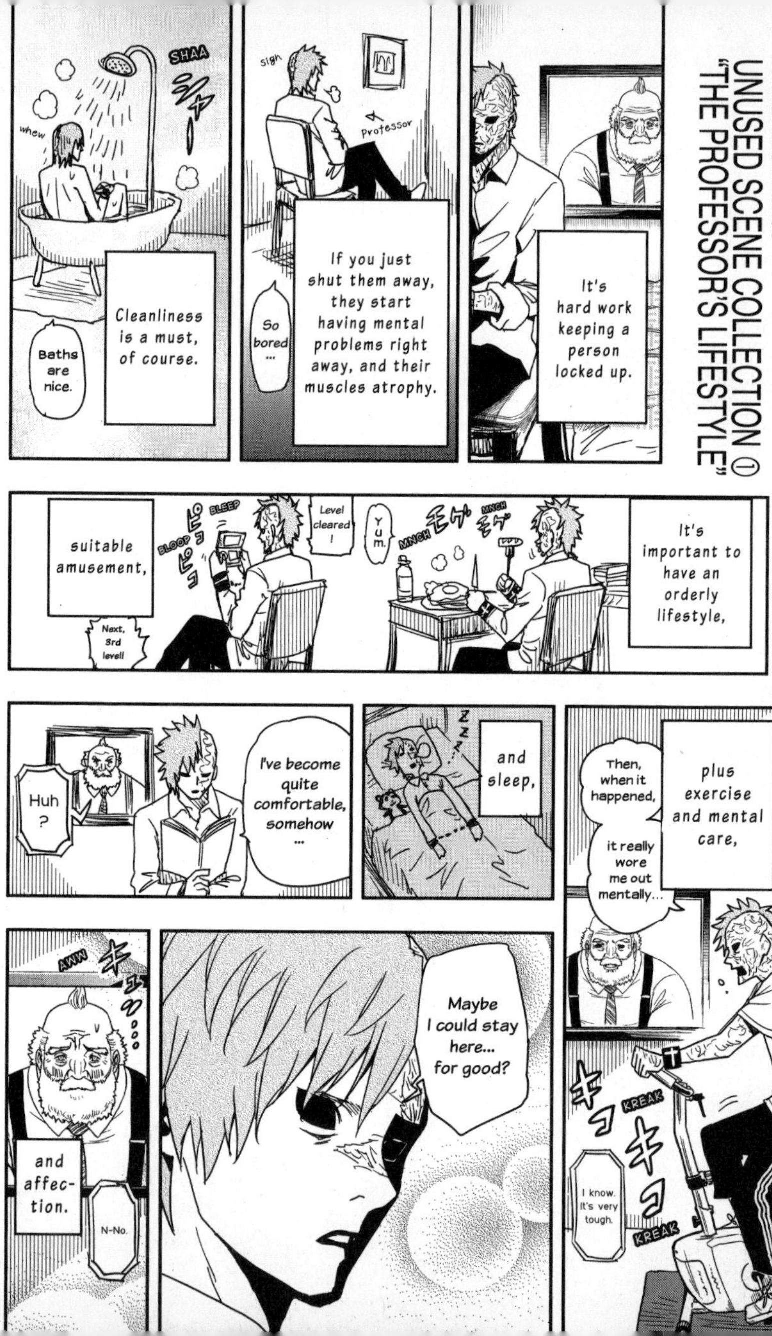
It's hard work keeping a person locked up.
Sigh
Professor
If you just shut them away, they start having mental problems right away, and their muscles atrophy.
So bored...
SHAA
whew
Cleanliness is a must, of course.
Baths are nice.
It's important to have an orderly lifestyle,
MNCH
MNCH
Yum.
Level cleared!
BLEEP
BLOOP
suitable amusement,
Next, 3rd level!
plus exercise and mental care,
HAA
HAA
Then, when it happened,
it really wore me out mentally...
KREAK
KREAK
I know. It's very tough.
and sleep,
I've become quite comfortable, somehow...
Huh?
Maybe I could stay here... for good?
AWW
and affec-tion.
N-No.

UNUSED SCENE COLLECTION ② "THE PUPPETEER AND I"

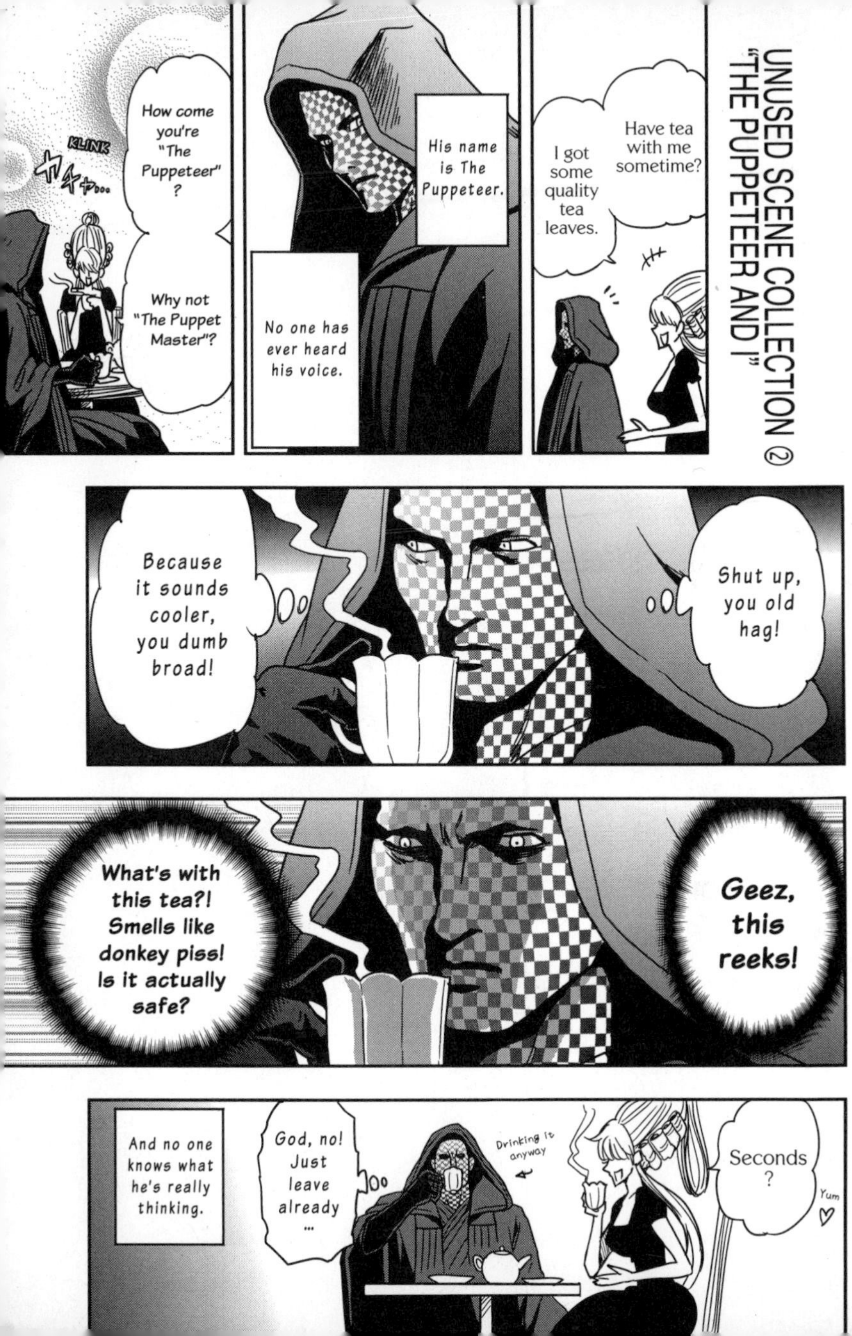
Have tea with me sometime?
I got some quality tea leaves.
His name is The Puppeteer.
No one has ever heard his voice.
KLINK
How come you're "The Puppeteer"?
Why not "The Puppet Master"?
Shut up, you old hag!
Because it sounds cooler, you dumb broad!
Geez, this reeks!
What's with this tea?! Smells like donkey piss! Is it actually safe?
Seconds?
Yum ♡
Drinking it anyway
God, no! Just leave already...
And no one knows what he's really thinking.

mRac

Tokyo ESP, volume 7

A Vertical Comics Edition

Translation: Kumar Sivasubramanian
Production: Risa Cho
        Tomoe Tsutsumi

© Hajime SEGAWA 2015
First published in Japan in 2015 by KADOKAWA CORPORATION, Tokyo.
English translation rights arranged with KADOKAWA CORPORATION, Tokyo
through TUTTLE-MORI AGENCY, INC., Tokyo.

Translation provided by Vertical Comics, 2016
Published by Vertical, Inc., New York

Originally published in Japanese as *Toukyou ESP 13* & *14* by Kadokawa Corporation, 2015
Tokyo ESP first serialized in *Gekkan Shounen Eisu*, Kadokawa Corporation, 2010-

This is a work of fiction.

ISBN: 978-1-942993-56-8

Manufactured in the United States of America

First Edition

Vertical, Inc.
451 Park Avenue South
7th Floor
New York, NY 10016
www.vertical-comics.com

Vertical books are distributed through Penguin-Random House Publisher Services.